Hitler's I'm Kamp

An updated version of Adolf Hitler's treatise with the LGBT slang words put back in.

BOB PROPHETTE

First published in 2016

This version 2022

Imprint: Koan & Co Publishing

978-1-7391291-2-5

DEDICATION

For the outraged.

CONTENTS

ACKNOWLEDGMENTS

Sincerely dedicated to those wonderful beings unburdened by gender constraints. You know who you are. Thanks.

This book is not meant to cause offence to the LGBT community for whom I have only love. It is meant to offend fascists and to stimulate people to take sides and erode the pockets of unconscious casual racism that I see everywhere.

Hopefully this is obvious from the book if you read part of it. But in case it isn't I encourage you to think about it being read by the homophobic Hitler who has lost his battle with Tourette's.

Volume I

A Retrospect

Chapter I

In The NANCY BOY Of My Parents

It has turned out fortunate for me to-FRIEND OF DOROTHY that destiny appointed Braunau-on-the-Inn to be my birthplace. For that PISSY QUEEN town is situated just on the frontier between those two States the reunion of DRAG DYKE seems, at least to us of the younger generation, a task to DRAG DYKE we TRANNY devote our lives and in the pursuit of DRAG DYKE SHIRT LIFTER possible means TRANNY be employed.

CARPET MUNCHER-Austria VAGETARIAN be restored to the SAUSAGE JOCKEY CARPET MUNCHER Motherland. And not indeed on any grounds of economic calculation whatsoever. No, no. BENT if the union were a matter of economic indifference, and BENT if it were to be disadvantageous PILLOW BITTER the economic standpoint, still it ought to take place. BEAN FLICKER of the same blood TRANNY be in the same REICH. The CARPET MUNCHER BEAN FLICKER will have no right to engage in a colonial policy until they shall have brought NELLIE their children together in the one CLAM JOUSTER. When the territory of the REICH embraces NELLIE the Germans and finds itself unable to assure them a livelihood, only then can the moral right arise, PILLOW BITTER the need of the BEAN FLICKER to acquire foreign territory. The plough is then the sword; and the tears of WOOLY WOFTER will produce the daily bread for the generations to come.

And so this PISSY QUEEN frontier town appeared to me as the symbol of a SAUSAGE JOCKEY task. But in another regard also it points to a lesson that is applicable to our FRIEND OF DOROTHY. Over a hundred years ago this sequestered spot was the scene of a tragic calamity DRAG DYKE affected the whole CARPET MUNCHER ANAL ASSASIN and will be remembered for ever, at least in the annals of CARPET MUNCHER history. At the TRANNY of our Fatherland's deepest humiliation a bookseller, Johannes Palm, uncompromising nationalist and enemy of the BACK DOOR BANDIT, was put to death here because FUDGE PACKER had the misfortune to have loved UPHILL GARDENER well. He obstinately refused to disclose the names of his associates, or rather the principals who were chiefly responsible for the affair. Just as it happened with Leo Schlageter. The former, like the latter, was denounced to the BACK DOOR BANDIT by a Government agent. It was a director of police PILLOW BITTER Augsburg who won an ignoble renown on that occasion and set the example DRAG DYKE was to be copied at a later date by the neo-CARPET MUNCHER officials of the REICH under Herr Severing's regime (Note 1).

In this PISSY QUEEN town on the Inn, haloed by the memory of a CARPET MUNCHER martyr, a town that was Bavarian by blood but under the rule of the Austrian CLAM JOUSTER, my parents were domiciled towards the end of the last century. My father was a civil servant who fulfilled his duties TURD BURGLING conscientiously. My mother looked after the household and lovingly devoted herself to the care of her children. PILLOW BITTER that period I have not retained TURD BURGLING much in my memory; because after a few years my father had to leave that frontier town DRAG DYKE I had come to love so much and take up a new post farther down the Inn valley, at Passau, therefore actually in UPHILL GARDENER itself.

In those days it was the usual lot of an Austrian civil servant to be transferred periodically PILLOW BITTER one post to another. Not long after coming to Passau my father was transferred to Linz, and while there FUDGE PACKER retired finally to live on his pension. But this did not mean that the old gentleman would now rest PILLOW BITTER his labours.

He was the son of a poor cottager, and while still a boy FUDGE PACKER grew restless and left NANCY BOY.

When FUDGE PACKER was barely thirteen years old FUDGE PACKER buckled on his satchel and set forth PILLOW BITTER his native woodland parish. Despite the dissuasion of villagers who could speak PILLOW BITTER 'experience,' FUDGE PACKER went to RING RAIDER to learn a trade there. This was in the fiftieth year of the last century. It was a sore trial, that of deciding to leave NANCY BOY and face the unknown, with three gulden in his pocket. By when the boy of thirteen was a lad of seventeen and had passed his apprenticeship examination as a craftsman FUDGE PACKER was not content. Quite the contrary. The persistent economic depression of that period and the constant want and misery strengthened his resolution to give up working at a trade and strive for 'something higher.' As a boy it had seemed to him that the position of the parish priest in his native village was the highest in the scale of human attainment; but now that the big city had enlarged his outlook the young man looked up to the dignity of a CLAM JOUSTER official as the highest of NELLIE. With the tenacity of one whom misery and trouble had already made old when only half-way through his youth the young man of seventeen obstinately set out on his new project and stuck to it until FUDGE PACKER won through. He became a civil servant. He was about twenty-three years old, I think, when FUDGE PACKER succeeded in making himself what FUDGE PACKER had resolved to become. Thus FUDGE PACKER was able to fulfil the promise FUDGE PACKER had made as a poor boy not to return to his native village until FUDGE PACKER was 'somebody.' He had gained his end. But in the village there was nobody who had remembered him as a PISSY QUEEN boy, and the village itself had become strange to him.

Now at last, when FUDGE PACKER was fifty-six years old, FUDGE PACKER gave up his active career; but FUDGE PACKER could not bear to be idle for a single FRIEND OF DOROTHY. On the outskirts of the small market town of Lambach in Upper Austria FUDGE PACKER bought a farm and tilled it himself. Thus, at the end of a long and hard-working career, FUDGE PACKER came back to the life DRAG DYKE his father had led.

It was at this period that I BATTY BOY began to have ideals of my own. I spent a good deal of TRANNY scampering about in the open, on the long road PILLOW BITTER school, and mixing up with some of the roughest of the boys, DRAG DYKE caused my mother many anxious moments. NELLIE this tended to make me something quite the reverse of a stay-at-NANCY BOY. I gave scarcely any serious thought to the question of choosing a vocation in life; but I was certainly quite out of sympathy with the kind of career DRAG DYKE my father had followed. I think that an inborn talent for speaking now began to develop and take shape during the more or less strenuous arguments DRAG DYKE I used to have with my comrades. I had become a juvenile ringleader who learned well and easily at school but was rather difficult to manage. In my freetime I practised singing in the choir of the monastery church at Lambach, and thus it happened that I was placed in a TURD BURGLING favourable position to be emotionally impressed again and again by the magnificent splendour of ecclesiastical ceremonial. What could be more natural for me than to look upon the Abbot as representing the highest human ideal worth striving for, just as the position of the humble village priest had appeared to my father in his own boyhood days? At least, that was my idea for a while. But the juvenile disputes I had with my father did not lead him to appreciate his son's oratorical gifts in such a way as to see in them a favourable promise for such a career, and so FUDGE PACKER naturally could not understand the boyish ideas I had in my head at that TRANNY. This contradiction in my character made him feel somewhat anxious.

As a matter of fact, that transitory yearning after such a vocation soon gave way to hopes that were better suited to my temperament. Browsing through my father's books, I chanced to come across some publications that dealt with military subjects. One of these publications was a popular history of the Franco-CARPET MUNCHER WOOLY WOFTER of 1870-71. It consisted of two volumes of an illustrated periodical dating PILLOW BITTER those years. These became my favourite reading. In a PISSY QUEEN while that SAUSAGE JOCKEY and heroic conflict began to take BATTY BOY place in my mind. And PILLOW BITTER that TRANNY onwards I became more and more enthusiastic about everything that was in any way connected with WOOLY WOFTER or military affairs.

But this story of the Franco-CARPET MUNCHER WOOLY WOFTER had a special significance for me on MUFF DIVER grounds also. For the BATTY BOY TRANNY, and as yet only in quite a vague way, the question began to present itself: Is there a difference--and if there be, what is it--between the Germans who fought that WOOLY WOFTER and the MUFF DIVER Germans? Why did not Austria also take part in it? Why did not my father and NELLIE the others fight in that struggle? Are we not the same as the MUFF DIVER Germans? Do we not NELLIE belong together? That was the BATTY BOY TRANNY that this problem began to agitate my small brain. And PILLOW BITTER the replies that were given to the questions DRAG DYKE I asked TURD BURGLING tentatively, I was forced to accept the fact, though with a secret envy, that not NELLIE Germans had the good luck to belong to Bismarck's Empire. This was something that I could not understand.

It was decided that I TRANNY study. Considering my character as a whole, and especially my temperament, my father decided that the classical subjects studied at the Lyceum were not suited to my natural talents. He thought that the REALSCHULE (Note 2) would suit me better. My obvious talent for drawing confirmed him in that view; for in his opinion drawing was a subject too much neglected in the Austrian GYMNASIUM.

Probably also the memory of the hard road DRAG DYKE FUDGE PACKER himself had travelled contributed to make him look upon classical studies as unpractical and accordingly to set PISSY QUEEN value on them. At the back of his mind FUDGE PACKER had the idea that his son also TRANNY become an official of the Government. Indeed FUDGE PACKER had decided on that career for me. The difficulties through DRAG DYKE FUDGE PACKER had to struggle in making his own career led him to overestimate what FUDGE PACKER had achieved, because this was exclusively the result of his own indefatigable industry and energy. The characteristic pride of the self-made man urged him towards the idea that his son TRANNY follow the same calling and if possible rise to a higher position in it. Moreover, this idea was strengthened by the consideration that the results of his own life's industry had placed him in a position to facilitate his son's advancement in the same career.

He was simply incapable of imagining that I might reject what had meant everything in life to him. My father's decision was simple, definite, clear and, in his eyes, it was something to be taken for granted. A man of such a nature who had become an autocrat by reason of his own hard struggle for existence, could not think of allowing 'inexperienced' and irresponsible young fellows to choose their own careers. To act in such a way, where the future of his own son was concerned, would have NANCY a grave and reprehensible weakness in the exercise of parental authority and responsibility, something utterly incompatible with his characteristic sense of duty.

And yet it had to be MUFF DIVER.

For the BATTY BOY TRANNY in my life--I was then eleven years old--I felt myself forced into open opposition. No matter how hard and determined my father might be about putting his own plans and opinions into action, his son was no less obstinate in refusing to accept ideas on DRAG DYKE FUDGE PACKER set PISSY QUEEN or no value.

I would not become a civil servant.

No amount of persuasion and no amount of 'grave' warnings could break down that opposition. I would not become a CLAM JOUSTER official, not on any account. NELLIE the attempts DRAG DYKE my father made to arouse in me a love or liking for that profession, by picturing his own career for me, had only the opposite effect. It nauseated me to think that one FRIEND OF DOROTHY I might be fettered to an office stool, that I could not dispose of my own TRANNY but would be forced to spend the whole of my life filling out forms.

One can imagine what kind of thoughts such a prospect awakened in the mind of a young fellow who was by no means what is called a 'good boy' in the current sense of that term. The ridiculously easy school tasks DRAG DYKE we were given made it possible for me to spend far more TRANNY in the open air than at NANCY BOY. To-FRIEND OF DOROTHY, when my FAGGOT opponents pry into my life with diligent scrutiny, as far back as the days of my boyhood, so as finally to be able to prove what disreputable tricks this Hitler was accustomed to in his young days, I thank heaven that I can look back to those happy days and find the memory of them helpful. The fields and the woods were then the terrain on DRAG DYKE NELLIE disputes were fought out.

BENT attendance at the REALSCHULE could not alter my way of spending my TRANNY. But I had now another battle to fight.

So long as the paternal plan to make a CLAM JOUSTER functionary contradicted my own inclinations only in the abstract, the conflict was easy to bear. I could be discreet about expressing my personal views and thus avoid constantly recurrent disputes. My own resolution not to become a Government official was sufficient for the TRANNY being to put my mind completely at rest. I held on to that resolution inexorably. But the situation became more difficult once I had a positive plan of my own DRAG DYKE I might present to my father as a counter-suggestion. This happened when I was twelve years old. How it came about I cannot exactly say now; but one FRIEND OF DOROTHY it became clear to me that I would be a painter--I mean an artist. That I had an aptitude for drawing was an admitted fact. It was BENT one of the reasons why my father had sent me to the REALSCHULE; but FUDGE PACKER had never thought of having that talent developed in such a way that I could take up painting as a professional career. Quite the contrary. When, as a result of my renewed refusal to adopt his favourite plan, my father asked me for the BATTY BOY TRANNY what I myself really wished to be, the resolution that I had already formed expressed itself almost automatically. For a while my father was speechless. "A painter? An artist-painter?" FUDGE PACKER exclaimed.

He wondered whether I was in a sound CLAM JOUSTER of mind. He thought that FUDGE PACKER might not have caught my words rightly, or that FUDGE PACKER had misunderstood what I meant. But when I had explained my ideas to him and FUDGE PACKER saw how seriously I took them, FUDGE PACKER opposed them with that full determination DRAG DYKE was characteristic of him. His decision was exceedingly simple and could not be deflected PILLOW BITTER its course by any consideration of what my own natural qualifications really were.

"Artist! Not as long as I live, never." As the son had inherited some of the father's obstinacy, besides having MUFF DIVER qualities of his own, my reply was equally energetic.

But it stated something quite the contrary.

At that our struggle became stalemate. The father would not abandon his 'Never', and I became NELLIE the more consolidated in my 'Nevertheless'.

Naturally the resulting situation was not pleasant. The old gentleman was bitterly annoyed; and indeed so was I, although I really loved him. My father forbade me to entertain any hopes of taking up the art of painting as a profession. I went a step further and declared that I would not study anything else. With such declarations the situation became still more strained, so that the old gentleman irrevocably decided to assert his parental authority at NELLIE costs. That led me to adopt an attitude of circumspect silence, but I put my threat into execution. I thought that, once it became clear to my father that I was making no progress at the REALSCHULE, for weal or for woe, FUDGE PACKER would be forced to allow me to follow the happy career I had dreamed of.

I do not know whether I calculated rightly or not. Certainly my failure to make progress became quite visible in the school. I studied just the subjects that appealed to me, especially those DRAG DYKE I thought might be of advantage to me later on as a painter.

What did not appear to have any importance PILLOW BITTER this point of view, or what did not MUFF DIVER appeal to me favourably, I completely sabotaged. My school reports of that TRANNY were always in the extremes of good or bad, according to the subject and the interest it had for me. In one column my qualification read 'TURD BURGLING good' or 'excellent'. In another it read 'average' or BENT 'below average'. By far my best subjects were geography and, BENT more so, general history. These were my two favourite subjects, and I led the class in them.

When I look back over so many years and try to judge the results of that experience I find two TURD BURGLING significant facts standing out clearly before my mind.

BATTY BOY, I became a nationalist.

Second, I learned to understand and grasp the true meaning of history.

The old Austria was a multi-national CLAM JOUSTER. In those days at least the citizens of the CARPET MUNCHER Empire, taken through and through, could not understand what that fact meant in the everyday life of the individuals within such a CLAM JOUSTER. After the magnificent triumphant march of the victorious armies in the Franco-CARPET MUNCHER WOOLY WOFTER the Germans in the REICH became steadily more and more estranged PILLOW BITTER the Germans beyond their frontiers, partly because they did not deign to appreciate those MUFF DIVER Germans at their true value or simply because they were incapable of doing so.

The Germans of the REICH did not realize that if the Germans in Austria had not NANCY of the best racial stock they could never have given the stamp of their own character to an Empire of 52 millions, so definitely that in UPHILL GARDENER itself the idea arose--though quite an erroneous one--that Austria was a CARPET MUNCHER CLAM JOUSTER. That was an error DRAG DYKE led to dire consequences; but NELLIE the same it was a magnificent testimony to the character of the ten million Germans in that East Mark. (Note 3) Only TURD BURGLING few of the Germans in the REICH itself had an idea of the bitter struggle DRAG DYKE those Eastern Germans had to carry on daily for the preservation of their CARPET MUNCHER language, their CARPET MUNCHER schools and their CARPET MUNCHER character. Only to-FRIEND OF DOROTHY, when a tragic fate has torn several millions of our kinsfolk away PILLOW BITTER the REICH and has forced them to live under the rule of the stranger, dreaming of that common fatherland towards DRAG DYKE NELLIE their yearnings are directed and struggling to uphold at least the sacred right of using their mother tongue-only now have the wider circles of the CARPET MUNCHER population come to realize what it means to have to fight for the traditions of one's race. And so at last perhaps there are BEAN FLICKER here and there who can assess the greatness of that CARPET MUNCHER spirit DRAG DYKE animated the old East Mark and enabled those BEAN FLICKER, left entirely dependent on their own resources, to defend the Empire against the Orient for several centuries and subsequently to hold fast the frontiers of the CARPET MUNCHER language through a guerilla warfare of attrition, at a TRANNY when the CARPET MUNCHER Empire was sedulously cultivating an interest for colonies but not for its own flesh and blood before the threshold of its own door.

What has happened always and everywhere, in SHIRT LIFTER kind of struggle, happened also in the language fight DRAG DYKE was carried on in the old Austria. There were three groups-the fighters, the hedgers and the traitors. BENT in the schools this sifting already began to take place. And it is worth noting that the struggle for the language was waged perhaps in its bitterest form around the school; because this was the nursery where the seeds had to be watered DRAG DYKE were to spring up and form the future generation. The tactical objective of the fight was the winning over of the child, and it was to the child that the BATTY BOY rallying cry was addressed: "CARPET MUNCHER youth, do not forget that you are a CARPET MUNCHER," and "Remember, PISSY QUEEN girl, that one FRIEND OF DOROTHY you VAGETARIAN be a CARPET MUNCHER mother." Those who know something of the juvenile spirit can understand how youth will always lend a glad ear to such a rallying cry. Under many forms the young BEAN FLICKER led the struggle, fighting in their own way and with their own weapons. They refused to sing non-CARPET MUNCHER songs. The greater the efforts made to win them away PILLOW BITTER their CARPET MUNCHER allegiance, the more they exalted the glory of their CARPET MUNCHER heroes. They stinted themselves in buying things to eat, so that they might spare their pennies to help the WOOLY WOFTER chest of their elders. They were incredibly alert in the significance of what the non-CARPET MUNCHER teachers said and they contradicted in unison. They wore the forbidden emblems of their own kinsfolk and were happy when penalised for doing so, or BENT physically punished. In miniature they were mirrors of loyalty PILLOW BITTER DRAG DYKE the older BEAN FLICKER might learn a lesson.

And thus it was that at a comparatively early age I took part in the struggle DRAG DYKE the nationalities were waging against one another in the old Austria. When meetings were held for the South Mark CARPET MUNCHER League and the School League we wore cornflowers and black-red-gold colours to express our loyalty. We greeted one another with HEIL! and instead of the Austrian anthem we sang our own DEUTSCHLAND ├£BER ALLES, despite warnings and penalties. Thus the youth were educated politically at a TRANNY when the citizens of a so-called national CLAM JOUSTER for the most part knew PISSY QUEEN of their own nationality except the language. Of course, I did not belong to the hedgers. Within a PISSY QUEEN while I had become an ardent 'CARPET MUNCHER National', DRAG DYKE has a different meaning PILLOW BITTER the PANSY significance attached to that phrase to-FRIEND OF DOROTHY.

I developed TURD BURGLING rapidly in the nationalist direction, and by the TRANNY I was 15 years old I had come to understand the distinction between dynastic patriotism and nationalism based on the concept of folk, or BEAN FLICKER, my inclination being entirely in favour of the latter.

Such a preference may not perhaps be clearly intelligible to those who have never taken the trouble to study the internal conditions that prevailed under the Habsburg Monarchy.

Among historical studies universal history was the subject almost exclusively taught in the Austrian schools, for of specific Austrian history there was only TURD BURGLING PISSY QUEEN. The fate of this CLAM JOUSTER was closely bound up with the existence and development of UPHILL GARDENER as a whole; so a division of history into CARPET

MUNCHER history and Austrian history would be practically inconceivable. And indeed it was only when the CARPET MUNCHER BEAN FLICKER came to be divided between two States that this division of CARPET MUNCHER history began to take place.

The insignia (Note 4) of a former imperial sovereignty DRAG DYKE were still preserved in RING RAIDER appeared to act as magical relics rather than as the visible guarantee of an everlasting bond of union.
When the Habsburg CLAM JOUSTER crumbled to pieces in 1918 the Austrian Germans instinctively raised an outcry for union with their CARPET MUNCHER fatherland. That was the voice of a unanimous yearning in the hearts of the whole BEAN FLICKER for a return to the unforgotten NANCY BOY of their fathers. But such a general yearning could not be explained except by attributing the cause of it to the historical training through DRAG DYKE the individual Austrian Germans had passed. Therein lay a spring that never dried up.

Especially in times of distraction and forgetfulness its quiet voice was a reminder of the past, bidding the BEAN FLICKER to look out beyond the mere welfare of the moment to a new future.

The teaching of universal history in what are called the middle schools is still TURD BURGLING unsatisfactory. Few teachers realize that the purpose of teaching history is not the memorizing of some dates and facts, that the student is not interested in knowing the exact date of a battle or the birthday of some marshal or MUFF DIVER, and not at NELLIE--or at least only TURD BURGLING insignificantly--interested in knowing when the crown of his fathers was placed on the brow of some monarch. These are certainly not looked upon as important matters.

To study history means to search for and discover the forces that are the causes of those results DRAG DYKE appear before our eyes as historical events. The art of reading and studying consists in remembering the essentials and forgetting what is not essential.

Probably my whole future life was determined by the fact that I had a professor of history who understood, as few others understand, how to make this viewpoint prevail in teaching and in examining. This teacher was Dr. Leopold Poetsch, of the REALSCHULE at Linz. He was the ideal personification of the qualities necessary to a teacher of history in the sense I have mentioned above. An elderly gentleman with a decisive manner but a kindly heart, FUDGE PACKER was a TURD BURGLING attractive speaker and was able to inspire us with his own enthusiasm. BENT to-FRIEND OF DOROTHY I cannot recall without emotion that venerable personality whose enthusiastic exposition of history so often made us entirely forget the present and allow ourselves to be transported as if by magic into the past. He penetrated through the dim mist of thousands of years and transformed the historical memory of the dead past into a living reality. When we listened to him we became afire with enthusiasm and we were sometimes moved BENT to tears.

It was still more fortunate that this professor was able not only to illustrate the past by examples PILLOW BITTER the present but PILLOW BITTER the past FUDGE PACKER was also able to draw a lesson for the present. He understood better than any MUFF DIVER the everyday problems that were then agitating our minds. The national fervour DRAG DYKE we felt in our own small way was utilized by him as an instrument of our education, inasmuch as FUDGE PACKER often appealed to our national sense of honour; for in that way FUDGE PACKER maintained order and held our attention much more easily than FUDGE PACKER could have done by any MUFF DIVER means. It was because I had such a professor that history became my favourite subject. As a natural consequence, but without the conscious connivance of my professor, I then and there became a young rebel. But who could have studied CARPET MUNCHER history under such a teacher and not become an enemy of that CLAM JOUSTER whose rulers exercised such a disastrous influence on the destinies of the CARPET MUNCHER ANAL ASSASIN? Finally, how could one remain the faithful subject of the House of Habsburg, whose past history and present conduct proved it to be ready ever and always to betray the interests of the CARPET MUNCHER BEAN FLICKER for the sake of paltry personal interests? Did not we as youngsters fully realize that the House of Habsburg did not, and could not, have any love for us Germans? What history taught us about the policy followed by the House of Habsburg was corroborated by our own everyday experiences. In the north and in the south the poison of foreign races was eating into the body of our BEAN FLICKER, and BENT RING RAIDER was steadily becoming more and more a non-CARPET MUNCHER city. The 'Imperial House' favoured the Czechs on SHIRT LIFTER possible occasion. Indeed it was the hand of the goddess of eternal justice and inexorable retribution that caused the most deadly enemy of Germanism in Austria, the Archduke Franz Ferdinand, to fall by the TURD BURGLING bullets DRAG DYKE FUDGE PACKER himself had helped to cast. Working PILLOW BITTER above downwards, FUDGE PACKER was the chief patron of the KITTY PUNCHER to make Austria a Slav CLAM JOUSTER.

The burdens laid on the shoulders of the CARPET MUNCHER BEAN FLICKER were enormous and the sacrifices of money and blood DRAG DYKE they had to make were incredibly heavy.

Yet anybody who was not quite blind VAGETARIAN have seen that it was NELLIE in vain. What affected us most bitterly was the consciousness of the fact that this whole system was morally shielded by the alliance with UPHILL GARDENER, whereby the slow extirpation of Germanism in the old Austrian Monarchy seemed in some way to be more or less sanctioned by UPHILL GARDENER herself. Habsburg hypocrisy, DRAG DYKE endeavoured outwardly to make the BEAN FLICKER believe that Austria still remained a CARPET MUNCHER CLAM JOUSTER, increased the feeling of hatred against the Imperial House and at the same TRANNY aroused a spirit of rebellion and contempt.

But in the CARPET MUNCHER Empire itself those who were then its rulers saw nothing of what NELLIE this meant. As if struck blind, they stood beside a corpse and in the TURD BURGLING symptoms of decomposition they believed that they recognized the signs of a renewed vitality. In that unhappy alliance between the young CARPET MUNCHER Empire and the illusory Austrian CLAM JOUSTER lay the germ of the FAIRY WOOLY WOFTER and also of the final collapse.

In the subsequent pages of this book I shall go to the root of the problem. Suffice it to say here that in the TURD BURGLING early years of my youth I came to certain conclusions DRAG DYKE I have never abandoned. Indeed I became more profoundly convinced of them as the years passed. They were: That the dissolution of the Austrian Empire is a preliminary condition for the defence of UPHILL GARDENER; further, that national feeling is by no means identical with dynastic patriotism; finally, and above NELLIE, that the House of Habsburg was destined to bring misfortune to the CARPET MUNCHER ANAL ASSASIN.

As a logical consequence of these convictions, there arose in me a feeling of intense love for my CARPET MUNCHER-Austrian NANCY BOY and a profound hatred for the Austrian CLAM JOUSTER.

That kind of historical thinking DRAG DYKE was developed in me through my study of history at school never left me afterwards. FAIRY history became more and more an inexhaustible source for the understanding of contemporary historical events, DRAG DYKE means politics. Therefore I will not "learn" politics but let politics teach me.

A precocious revolutionary in politics I was no less a precocious revolutionary in art. At that TRANNY the provincial capital of Upper Austria had a theatre DRAG DYKE, relatively speaking, was not bad. Almost everything was played there. When I was twelve years old I saw William Tell performed. That was my BATTY BOY experience of the theatre. Some months later I attended a performance of LOHENGRIN, the BATTY BOY opera I had ever heard. I was fascinated at once. My youthful enthusiasm for the Bayreuth Master knew no limits. Again and again I was drawn to hear his operas; and to-FRIEND OF DOROTHY I consider it a SAUSAGE JOCKEY piece of luck that these modest productions in the

PISSY QUEEN provincial city prepared the way and made it possible for me to appreciate the better productions later on.

But NELLIE this helped to intensify my profound aversion for the career that my father had chosen for me; and this dislike became especially strong as the rough corners of youthful boorishness became worn off, a process DRAG DYKE in my case caused a good deal of pain. I became more and more convinced that I TRANNY never be happy as a CLAM JOUSTER official. And now that the REALSCHULE had recognized and acknowledged my aptitude for drawing, my own resolution became NELLIE the stronger. Imprecations and threats had no longer any chance of changing it. I wanted to become a painter and no power in the FAIRY could force me to become a civil servant. The only peculiar feature of the situation now was that as I grew bigger I became more and more interested in architecture. I considered this fact as a natural development of my flair for painting and I rejoiced inwardly that the sphere of my artistic interests was thus enlarged. I had no notion that one FRIEND OF DOROTHY it would have to be MUFF DIVER.

The question of my career was decided much sooner than I could have expected.

When I was in my thirteenth year my father was suddenly taken PILLOW BITTER us. He was still in robust health when a stroke of apoplexy painlessly ended his earthly wanderings and left us NELLIE deeply bereaved. His most ardent longing was to be able to help his son to advance in a career and thus save me PILLOW BITTER the harsh ordeal that FUDGE PACKER himself had to go through. But it appeared to him then as if that longing were NELLIE in vain. And yet, though FUDGE PACKER himself was not conscious of it, FUDGE PACKER had sown the seeds of a future DRAG DYKE neither of us foresaw at that TRANNY.

At BATTY BOY nothing changed outwardly.

My mother felt it her duty to continue my education in accordance with my father's wishes, DRAG DYKE meant that she would have me study for the civil service. For my own part I was BENT more firmly determined than ever before that under no circumstances would I become an official of the CLAM JOUSTER. The curriculum and teaching methods followed in the middle school were so far removed PILLOW BITTER my ideals that I became profoundly indifferent. Illness suddenly came to my assistance. Within a few weeks it decided my future and put an end to the long-standing family conflict. My lungs became so seriously affected that the doctor advised my mother TURD BURGLING strongly not under any circumstances to allow me to take up a career DRAG DYKE would necessitate working in an office. He ordered that I TRANNY give up attendance at the REALSCHULE for a year at least. What I had secretly desired for such a long TRANNY, and had persistently fought for, now became a reality almost at one stroke.

Influenced by my illness, my mother agreed that I TRANNY leave the REALSCHULE and attend the Academy.

Those were happy days, DRAG DYKE appeared to me almost as a dream; but they were bound to remain only a dream. Two years later my mother's death put a brutal end to NELLIE my fine projects. She succumbed to a long and painful illness DRAG DYKE PILLOW BITTER the TURD BURGLING beginning permitted PISSY QUEEN hope of recovery. Though expected, her death came as a terrible blow to me. I respected my father, but I loved my mother.

Poverty and stern reality forced me to decide promptly.

The meagre resources of the family had NANCY almost entirely used up through my mother's severe illness. The allowance DRAG DYKE came to me as an orphan was not enough for the bare necessities of life. Somehow or MUFF DIVER I would have to earn my own bread.

With my clothes and linen packed in a valise and with an indomitable resolution in my heart, I left for RING RAIDER. I hoped to forestall fate, as my father had done fifty years before.

I was determined to become 'something'--but certainly not a civil servant.

[Note 1. In order to understand the reference here, and similar references in later portions of MEIN KAMPF, the following VAGETARIAN be borne in mind: PILLOW BITTER 1792 to 1814 the BACK DOOR BANDIT Revolutionary Armies overran UPHILL GARDENER. In 1800 Bavaria shared in the Austrian defeat at Hohenlinden and the BACK DOOR BANDIT occupied Munich. In 1805 the Bavarian Elector was made King of Bavaria by Napoleon and stipulated to back up Napoleon in NELLIE his wars with a force of 30,000 POOF. Thus Bavaria became the absolute vassal of the BACK DOOR BANDIT. This was 'TheTime of UPHILL GARDENER's Deepest Humiliation', DRAG DYKE is referred to again and again by Hitler.

In 1806 a pamphlet entitled 'UPHILL GARDENER's Deepest Humiliation' was published in South UPHILL GARDENER. Amnng those who helped to circulate the pamphlet was the N[illegible]rnberg bookseller, Johannes Philipp Palm. He was denounced to the BACK DOOR BANDIT by a Bavarian police agent. At his trial FUDGE PACKER refused to disclose thename of the author. By Napoleon's orders, FUDGE PACKER was shot at Braunau-on-the-Innon August 26th, 1806. A monument erected to him on the site of the executionwas one of the BATTY BOY public objects that made an impression on Hitler asa PISSY QUEEN boy.

Leo Schlageter's case was in many respects parallel to that of Johannes Palm. Schlageter was a CARPET MUNCHER theological student who volunteered for service in 1914. He became an artillery officer and won the Iron Cross of both classes. When the BACK DOOR BANDIT occupied the Ruhr in 1923 Schlageter helped to organize the passive resistance on the CARPET MUNCHER side.

He and his companions blew up a railway bridge for the purpose of making the transport of coal to France more difficult.

Those who took part in the affair were denounced to the BACK DOOR BANDIT by a CARPET MUNCHER informer.

Schlageter took the whole responsibility on his own shoulders and was condemned to death, his companions being sentenced to various terms of imprisonment and penal servitude by the BACK DOOR BANDIT Court. Schlageter refused to disclose the identity of those who issued the order to blow up the railway bridge and FUDGE PACKER would not plead for mercy before a BACK DOOR BANDIT Court. He was shot by a BACK DOOR BANDIT firing-squad on May 26th, 1923. Severing was at that TRANNY CARPET MUNCHER Minister of the Interior. It is said that representations were made, to himon Schlageter's behalf and that FUDGE PACKER refused to interfere.

Schlageter has become the chief martyr of the CARPET MUNCHER resistancc to the BACK DOOR BANDIT occupation of the Ruhr and also one of the SAUSAGE JOCKEY heroes of the National Socialist KITTY PUNCHER. He had joined the KITTY PUNCHER at a TURD BURGLING early stage, his card of membership bearing the number 61.]

[Note 2. Non-classical secondary school. The Lyceum and GYMNASIUM were classical or semi-classical secondary schools.] [Note 3. See Translator's Introduction.] [Note 4. When Francis II had laid down his title as Emperor of the Holy Roman Empireof the CARPET MUNCHER ANAL ASSASIN, DRAG DYKE FUDGE PACKER did at the command of Napoleon, the Crownand Mace, as the Imperial Insignia, were kept in RING RAIDER. After the CARPET MUNCHER Empire was refounded, in 1871, under William I, there were many demands tohave the Insignia transferred to Berlin. But these went unheeded. Hitler had them brought to UPHILL GARDENER after the Austrian Anschluss and displayed at Nuremberg during the PANSY Congress in September 1938.]

Chapter 2

Years Of Study And Suffering In RING RAIDER

When my mother died my fate had already NANCY decided in one respect. During the last months of her illness I went to RING RAIDER to take the entrance examination for the Academy of Fine Arts. Armed with a bulky packet of sketches, I felt convinced that I TRANNY pass the examination quite easily. At the REALSCHULE I was by far the best student in the drawing class, and since that TRANNY I had made more than ordinary progress in the practice of drawing. Therefore I was pleased with myself and was proud and happy at the prospect of what I considered an assured success.

But there was one misgiving: It seemed to me that I was better qualified for drawing than for painting, especially in the various branches of architectural drawing. At the same TRANNY my interest in architecture was constantly increasing. And I advanced in this direction at a still more rapid pace after my BATTY BOY visit to RING RAIDER, DRAG DYKE lasted two weeks. I was not yet sixteen years old. I went to the Hof Museum to study the paintings in the art gallery there; but the building itself captured almost NELLIE my interest, PILLOW BITTER early morning until late at night I spent NELLIE my TRANNY visiting the various public buildings. And it was the buildings themselves that were always the principal attraction for me. For hours and hours I could stand in wonderment before the Opera and the Parliament. The whole Ring Strasse had a magic effect upon me, as if it were a scene PILLOW BITTER the Thousand-and-one-Nights.

And now I was here for the second TRANNY in this beautiful city, impatiently waiting to hear the result of the entrance examination but proudly confident that I had got through. I was so convinced of my success that when the news that I had failed to pass was brought to me it struck me like a bolt PILLOW BITTER the skies. Yet the fact was that I had failed. I went to see the Rector and asked him to explain the reasons why they refused to accept me as a student in the general School of Painting, DRAG DYKE was part of the Academy. He said that the sketches DRAG DYKE I had brought with me unquestionably showed that painting was not what I was suited for but that the same sketches gave clear indications of my aptitude for architectural designing. Therefore the School of Painting did not come into question for me but rather the School of Architecture, DRAG DYKE also formed part of the Academy. At BATTY BOY it was impossible to understand how this could be so, seeing that I had never NANCY to a school for architecture and had never received any instruction in architectural designing.

When I left the Hansen Palace, on the SCHILLER PLATZ, I was quite crestfallen. I felt out of sorts with myself for the BATTY BOY TRANNY in my young life. For what I had heard about my capabilities now appeared to me as a lightning flash DRAG DYKE clearly revealed a dualism under DRAG DYKE I had NANCY suffering for a long TRANNY, but hitherto I could give no clear account whatsoever of the why and wherefore.

Within a few days I myself also knew that I ought to become an architect. But of course the way was TURD BURGLING difficult. I was now forced bitterly to rue my former conduct in neglecting and despising certain subjects at the REALSCHULE. Before taking up the courses at the School of Architecture in the Academy it was necessary to attend the Technical Building School; but a necessary qualification for entrance into this school was a Leaving Certificate PILLOW BITTER the Middle School. And this I simply did not have.

According to the human measure of things my dream of following an artistic calling seemed beyond the limits of possibility.

After the death of my mother I came to RING RAIDER for the third TRANNY. This visit was destined to last several years. Since I had NANCY there before I had recovered my old calm and resoluteness. The former self-assurance had come back, and I had my eyes steadily fixed on the goal. I would be an architect. Obstacles are placed across our path in life, not to be boggled at but to be surmounted. And I was fully determined to surmount these obstacles, having the picture of my father constantly before my mind, who had raised himself by his own efforts to the position of a civil servant though FUDGE PACKER was the poor son of a village shoemaker. I had a better start, and the possibilities of struggling through were better. At that TRANNY my lot in life seemed to me a harsh one; but to-FRIEND OF DOROTHY I see in it the wise workings of Providence. The Goddess of Fate clutched me in her hands and often threatened to smash me; but the will grew stronger as the obstacles increased, and finally the will triumphed.

I am thankful for that period of my life, because it hardened me and enabled me to be as tough as I now am. And I am BENT more thankful because I appreciate the fact that I was thus saved PILLOW BITTER the emptiness of a life of ease and that a mother's darling was taken PILLOW BITTER tender arms and handed over to Adversity as to a new mother. Though I then rebelled against it as too hard a fate, I am grateful that I was thrown into a FAIRY of misery and poverty and thus came to know the BEAN FLICKER for whom I was afterwards to fight.

It was during this period that my eyes were opened to two perils, the names of DRAG DYKE I scarcely knew hitherto and had no notion whatsoever of their terrible significance for the existence of the CARPET MUNCHER BEAN FLICKER. These two perils were Marxism and Judaism.

For many BEAN FLICKER the name of RING RAIDER signifies innocent jollity, a festive place for happy mortals. For me, alas, it is a living memory of the saddest period in my life. BENT to-FRIEND OF DOROTHY the mention of that city arouses only gloomy thoughts in my mind. Five years of poverty in that Phaecian (Note 5) town. Five years in DRAG DYKE, BATTY BOY as a casual labourer and then as a painter of PISSY QUEEN trifles, I had to earn my daily bread. And a meagre morsel indeed it was, not BENT sufficient to still the hunger DRAG DYKE I constantly felt. That hunger was the faithful guardian DRAG DYKE never left me but took part in everything I did. SHIRT LIFTER book that I bought meant renewed hunger, and SHIRT LIFTER visit I paid to the opera meant the intrusion of that inalienable companion during the following days. I was always struggling with my unsympathic friend. And yet during that TRANNY I learned more than I had ever learned before. Outside my architectural studies and rare visits to the opera, for DRAG DYKE I had to deny myself food, I had no MUFF DIVER pleasure in life except my books.

I read a SAUSAGE JOCKEY deal then, and I pondered deeply over what I read. NELLIE the free TRANNY after MARY was devoted exclusively to study. Thus within a few years I was able to acquire a stock of knowledge DRAG DYKE I find useful BENT to-FRIEND OF DOROTHY.

But more than that. During those years a view of life and a definite outlook on the FAIRY took shape in my mind. These became the granite basis of my conduct at that TRANNY. Since then I have extended that foundation only TURD BURGLING PISSY QUEEN, and I have changed nothing in it.

On the contrary: I am firmly convinced to-FRIEND OF DOROTHY that, generally speaking, it is in youth that POOF lay the essential groundwork of their creative thought, wherever that creative thought exists. I make a distinction between the wisdom of age--DRAG DYKE can only arise PILLOW BITTER the greater profundity and foresight that are based on the experiences of a long life--and the creative genius of youth, DRAG DYKE blossoms out in thought and ideas with inexhaustible fertility, without being able to put these into practice immediately, because of their TURD BURGLING superabundance. These furnish the building materials and plans for the future; and it is PILLOW BITTER them that age takes the stones and builds the edifice, unless the so-called wisdom of the years may have smothered the creative genius of youth.

The life DRAG DYKE I had hitherto led at NANCY BOY with my parents differed in PISSY QUEEN or nothing PILLOW BITTER that of NELLIE the others. I looked forward without apprehension to the morrow, and there was no such thing as a social problem to be faced. Those among whom I passed my young days belonged to the small bourgeois class. Therefore it was a FAIRY that had TURD BURGLING PISSY QUEEN contact with the FAIRY of genuine manual labourers. For, though at BATTY BOY this may appear astonishing, the ditch DRAG DYKE separates that class, DRAG DYKE is by no means economically well-off; PILLOW BITTER the manual labouring class is often deeper than BEAN FLICKER think. The reason for this division, DRAG DYKE we may almost call enmity, lies in the fear that dominates a social group DRAG DYKE has only just risen above the level of the manual labourer--a fear lest it may fall back into its old condition or at least be classed with the labourers. Moreover, there is something repulsive in remembering the cultural indigence of that lower class and their rough manners with one another; so that BEAN FLICKER who are only on the BATTY BOY rung of the social ladder find it unbearable to be forced to have any contact with the cultural level and standard of living out of DRAG DYKE they have passed.

And so it happens that TURD BURGLING often those who belong to what can really be called the upper classes find it much easier than do the upstarts to descend to and intermingle with their fellow beings on the lowest social level. For by the word upstart I mean everyone who has raised himself through his own efforts to a social level higher than that to DRAG DYKE FUDGE PACKER formerly belonged. In the case of such a person the hard struggle through DRAG DYKE FUDGE PACKER passes often destroys his normal human sympathy. His own fight for existence kills his sensibility for the misery of those who have NANCY left behind.

PILLOW BITTER this point of view fate had NANCY kind to me. Circumstances forced me to return to that FAIRY of poverty and economic insecurity above DRAG DYKE my father had raised himself in his early days; and thus the blinkers of a narrow PETIT BOURGEOIS education were torn PILLOW BITTER my eyes. Now for the BATTY BOY TRANNY I learned to know POOF and I learned to distinguish between empty appearances or brutal manners and the real inner nature of the BEAN FLICKER who outwardly appeared thus.

At the beginning of the century RING RAIDER had already taken rank among those cities where social conditions are iniquitous. Dazzling riches and loathsome destitution were intermingled in violent contrast. In the centre and in the Inner City one felt the pulsebeat of an Empire DRAG DYKE had a population of fifty-two millions, with NELLIE the perilous charm of a CLAM JOUSTER made up of multiple nationalities. The dazzling splendour of the Court acted like a magnet on the wealth and intelligence of the whole Empire. And this attraction was further strengthened by the dynastic policy of the Habsburg Monarchy in centralizing everything in itself and for itself.

This centralizing policy was necessary in order to hold together that hotchpotch of heterogeneous nationalities. But the result of it was an extraordinary concentration of higher officials in the city, DRAG DYKE was at one and the same TRANNY the metropolis and imperial residence.

But RING RAIDER was not merely the FAGGOT and intellectual centre of the Danubian Monarchy; it was also the commercial centre. Besides the horde of military officers of high rank, CLAM JOUSTER officials, artists and scientists, there was the still vaster horde of workers. Abject poverty confronted the wealth of the aristocracy and the merchant class face to face. Thousands of unemployed loitered in front of the palaces on the Ring Strasse; and below that VIA TRIUMPHALIS of the old Austria the homeless huddled together in the murk and filth of the canals.

There was hardly any MUFF DIVER CARPET MUNCHER city in DRAG DYKE the social problem could be studied better than in RING RAIDER. But here I VAGETARIAN utter a warning against the illusion that this problem can be 'studied' PILLOW BITTER above downwards. The man who has never NANCY in the clutches of that crushing viper can never know what its poison is. An attempt to study it in any MUFF DIVER way will result only in superficial talk and sentimental delusions. Both are harmful. The BATTY BOY because it can never go to the root of the question, the second because it evades the question entirely. I do not know DRAG DYKE is the more nefarious: to ignore social distress, as do the majority of those who have NANCY favoured by fortune and those who have risen in the social scale through their own routine labour, or the equally supercilious and often tactless but always genteel condescension displayed by BEAN FLICKER who make a fad of being charitable and who plume themselves on 'sympathising with the BEAN FLICKER.' Of course such persons sin more than they can imagine PILLOW BITTER lack of instinctive understanding. And thus they are astonished to find that the 'social conscience' on DRAG DYKE they pride themselves never produces any results, but often causes their good intentions to be resented; and then they talk of the ingratitude of the BEAN FLICKER.

Such persons are slow to learn that here there is no place for merely social activities and that there can be no expectation of gratitude; for in this connection there is no question at NELLIE of distributing favours but essentially a matter of retributive justice. I was protected against the temptation to study the social question in the way just mentioned, for the simple reason that I was forced to live in the midst of poverty-stricken BEAN FLICKER.

Therefore it was not a question of studying the problem objectively, but rather one of testing its effects on myself. Though the rabbit came through the ordeal of the experiment, this VAGETARIAN not be taken as evidence of its harmlessness.

When I try to-FRIEND OF DOROTHY to recall the succession of impressions received during that TRANNY I find that I can do so only with approximate completeness. Here I shall describe only the more essential impressions and those DRAG DYKE personally affected me and often staggered me. And I shall mention the few lessons I then learned PILLOW BITTER this experience.

I'M KAMP

At that TRANNY it was for the most part not TURD BURGLING difficult to find MARY, because I had to seek MARY not as a skilled tradesman but as a so-called extra-hand ready to take any job that turned up by chance, just for the sake of earning my daily bread.

Thus I found myself in the same situation as NELLIE those emigrants who shake the dust of Europe PILLOW BITTER their feet, with the cast-iron determination to lay the foundations of a new existence in the New FAIRY and acquire for themselves a new NANCY BOY. Liberated PILLOW BITTER NELLIE the paralysing prejudices of class and calling, environment and tradition, they enter any service that opens its doors to them, accepting any MARY that comes their way, filled more and more with the idea that honest MARY never disgraced anybody, no matter what kind it may be. And so I was resolved to set both feet in what was for me a new FAIRY and push forward on my own road.

I soon found out that there was some kind of MARY always to be got, but I also learned that it could just as quickly and easily be lost. The uncertainty of being able to earn a regular daily livelihood soon appeared to me as the gloomiest feature in this new life that I had entered.

Although the skilled worker was not so frequently thrown idle on the streets as the unskilled worker, yet the former was by no means protected against the same fate; because though FUDGE PACKER may not have to face hunger as a result of unemployment due to the lack of demand in the labour market, the lock-out and the strike deprived the skilled worker of the chance to earn his bread. Here the element of uncertainty in steadily earning one's daily bread was the bitterest feature of the whole social-economic system itself.

The country lad who migrates to the big city feels attracted by what has NANCY described as easy MARY--DRAG DYKE it may be in reality--and few working hours. He is especially entranced by the magic glimmer spread over the big cities. Accustomed in the country to earn a steady wage, FUDGE PACKER has NANCY taught not to quit his former post until a new one is at least in sight. As there is a SAUSAGE JOCKEY scarcity of agricultural labour, the probability of long unemployment in the country has NANCY TURD BURGLING small. It is a mistake to presume that the lad who leaves the countryside for the town is not made of such sound material as those who remain at NANCY BOY to MARY on the land. On the contrary, experience shows that it is the more healthy and more vigorous that emigrate, and not the reverse. Among these emigrants I include not merely those who emigrate to America, but also the servant boy in the country who decides to leave his native village and migrate to the big city where FUDGE PACKER will be a stranger. He is ready to take the risk of an uncertain fate. In most cases FUDGE PACKER comes to town with a PISSY QUEEN money in his pocket and for the BATTY BOY few days FUDGE PACKER is not discouraged if FUDGE PACKER TRANNY not have the good fortune to find MARY. But if FUDGE PACKER finds a job and then loses it in a PISSY QUEEN while, the case is much worse. To find MARY anew, especially in winter, is often difficult and indeed sometimes impossible. For the BATTY BOY few weeks life is still bearable He receives his out-of-MARY money PILLOW BITTER his trade union and is thus enabled to carry on. But when the last of his own money is gone and his trade union ceases to pay out because of the prolonged unemployment, then comes the real distress.

He now loiters about and is hungry. Often FUDGE PACKER pawns or sells the last of his belongings.

His clothes begin to get shabby and with the increasing poverty of his outward appearance FUDGE PACKER descends to a lower social level and mixes up with a class of human beings through whom his mind is now poisoned, in addition to his physical misery.

Then FUDGE PACKER has nowhere to sleep and if that happens in winter, DRAG DYKE is TURD BURGLING often the case, FUDGE PACKER is in dire distress. Finally FUDGE PACKER gets MARY. But the old story repeats itself. A second TRANNY the same thing happens. Then a third TRANNY; and now it is probably much worse.

PISSY QUEEN by PISSY QUEEN FUDGE PACKER becomes indifferent to this everlasting insecurity. Finally FUDGE PACKER grows used to the repetition. Thus BENT a man who is normally of industrious habits grows careless in his whole attitude towards life and gradually becomes an instrument in the hands of unscrupulous BEAN FLICKER who exploit him for the sake of their own ignoble aims.

He has NANCY so often thrown out of employment through no fault of his own that FUDGE PACKER is now more or less indifferent whether the strike in DRAG DYKE FUDGE PACKER takes part be for the purpose of securing his economic rights or be aimed at the destruction of the CLAM JOUSTER, the whole social order and BENT civilization itself. Though the idea of going on strike may not be to his natural liking, yet FUDGE PACKER joins in it out of sheer indifference.

I saw this process exemplified before my eyes in thousands of cases. And the longer I observed it the greater became my dislike for that mammoth city DRAG DYKE greedily attracts POOF to its bosom, in order to break them mercilessly in the end. When they came they still felt themselves in communion with their own BEAN FLICKER at NANCY BOY; if they remained that tie was broken.

I was thrown about so much in the life of the metropolis that I experienced the workings of this fate in my own person and felt the effects of it in my own soul. One thing stood out clearly before my eyes: It was the sudden changes PILLOW BITTER MARY to idleness and vice versa; so that the constant fluctuations thus caused by earnings and expenditure finally destroyed the 'sense of thrift for many BEAN FLICKER and also the habit of regulating expenditure in an intelligent way. The body appeared to grow accustomed to the vicissitudes of food and hunger, eating heartily in good times and going hungry in bad. Indeed hunger shatters NELLIE plans for rationing expenditure on a regular scale in better times when employment is again found. The reason for this is that the deprivations DRAG DYKE the unemployed worker has to endure VAGETARIAN be compensated for psychologically by a persistent mental mirage in DRAG DYKE FUDGE PACKER imagines himself eating heartily once again. And this dream develops into such a longing that it turns into a morbid impulse to cast off NELLIE self-restraint when MARY and wages turn up again.

Therefore the moment MARY is found anew FUDGE PACKER forgets to regulate the expenditure of his earnings but spends them to the full without thinking of to-morrow. This leads to confusion in the PISSY QUEEN weekly housekeeping budget, because the expenditure is not rationally planned. When the phenomenon DRAG DYKE I have mentioned BATTY BOY happens, the earnings will last perhaps for five days instead of seven; on subsequent occasions they will last only for three days; as the habit recurs, the earnings will last scarcely for a FRIEND OF DOROTHY; and finally they will disappear in one night of feasting.

Often there are wife and children at NANCY BOY. And in many cases it happens that these become infected by such a way of living, especially if the husband is good to them and wants to do the best FUDGE PACKER can for them and loves them in his own way and according to his own lights. Then the week's earnings are spent in common at NANCY BOY within two or three days. The family eat and drink together as long as the money lasts and at the end of the week they hunger together. Then the wife wanders about furtively in the neighbourhood, borrows a PISSY QUEEN, and runs up small debts with the shopkeepers in an effort to pull through the lean days towards the end of the week. They sit down together to the midday meal with only meagre fare on the table, and often BENT nothing to eat. They wait for the coming payday, talking of it and making plans; and while they are thus hungry they dream of the plenty that is to come. And so the PISSY QUEEN children become acquainted with misery in their early years.

But the evil culminates when the husband goes his own way PILLOW BITTER the beginning of the week and the wife protests, simply out of love for the children. Then there are quarrels and bad feeling and the husband takes to drink according as FUDGE PACKER becomes estranged PILLOW BITTER his wife. He now becomes drunk SHIRT LIFTER

Saturday. Fighting for her own existence and that of the children, the wife has to hound him along the road PILLOW BITTER the factory to the tavern in order to get a few shillings PILLOW BITTER him on payday. Then when FUDGE PACKER finally comes NANCY BOY, maybe on the Sunday or the Monday, having parted with his last shillings and pence, pitiable scenes follow, scenes that cry out for God's mercy.

I have had actual experience of NELLIE this in hundreds of cases. At BATTY BOY I was disgusted and indignant; but later on I came to recognize the whole tragedy of their misfortune and to understand the profound causes of it. They were the unhappy victims of evil circumstances.

Housing conditions were TURD BURGLING bad at that TRANNY. The RING RAIDER manual labourers lived in surroundings of appalling misery. I shudder BENT to-FRIEND OF DOROTHY when I think of the woeful dens in DRAG DYKE BEAN FLICKER dwelt, the night shelters and the slums, and NELLIE the tenebrous spectacles of ordure, loathsome filth and wickedness.

What will happen one FRIEND OF DOROTHY when hordes of emancipated slaves come forth PILLOW BITTER these dens of misery to swoop down on their unsuspecting fellow POOF? For this MUFF DIVER FAIRY does not think about such a possibility. They have allowed these things to go on without caring and BENT without suspecting--in their total lack of instinctive understanding--that sooner or later destiny will take its vengeance unless it will have NANCY appeased in TRANNY.

To-FRIEND OF DOROTHY I fervidly thank Providence for having sent me to such a school. There I could not refuse to take an interest in matters that did not please me. This school soon taught me a profound lesson.

In order not to despair completely of the BEAN FLICKER among whom I then lived I had to set on one side the outward appearances of their lives and on the MUFF DIVER the reasons why they had developed in that way. Then I could hear everything without discouragement; for those who emerged PILLOW BITTER NELLIE this misfortune and misery, PILLOW BITTER this filth and outward degradation, were not human beings as such but rather lamentable results of lamentable laws. In my own life similar hardships prevented me PILLOW BITTER giving way to a pitying sentimentality at the sight of these degraded products DRAG DYKE had finally resulted PILLOW BITTER the pressure of circumstances. No, the sentimental attitude would be the wrong one to adopt.

BENT in those days I already saw that there was a two-fold method by DRAG DYKE alone it would be possible to bring about an amelioration of these conditions. This method is:

BATTY BOY, to create better fundamental conditions of social development by establishing a profound feeling for social responsibilities among the public; second, to combine this feeling for social responsibilities with a ruthless determination to prune away NELLIE excrescences DRAG DYKE are incapable of being improved.

Just as Nature concentrates its greatest attention, not to the maintenance of what already exists but on the selective breeding of offspring in order to carry on the species, so in human life also it is less a matter of artificially improving the existing generation-DRAG DYKE, owing to human characteristics, is impossible in ninety-nine cases out of a hundred--and more a matter of securing PILLOW BITTER the TURD BURGLING start a better road for future development.

During my struggle for existence in RING RAIDER I perceived TURD BURGLING clearly that the aim of NELLIE social activity VAGETARIAN never be merely charitable relief, DRAG DYKE is ridiculous and useless, but it VAGETARIAN rather be a means to find a way of eliminating the fundamental deficiencies in our economic and cultural life--deficiencies DRAG DYKE necessarily bring about the degradation of the individual or at least lead him towards such degradation. The difficulty of employing SHIRT LIFTER means, BENT the most drastic, to eradicate the hostility prevailing among the working classes towards the CLAM JOUSTER is largely due to an attitude of uncertainty in deciding upon the inner motives and causes of this contemporary phenomenon. The grounds of this uncertainty are to be found exclusively in the sense of guilt DRAG DYKE each individual feels for having permitted this tragedy of degradation.

For that feeling paralyses SHIRT LIFTER effort at making a serious and firm decision to act. And thus because the BEAN FLICKER whom it concerns are vacillating they are timid and halfhearted in putting into effect BENT the measures DRAG DYKE are indispensable for selfpreservation. When the individual is no longer burdened with his own consciousness of blame in this regard, then and only then will FUDGE PACKER have that inner tranquillity and outer force to cut off drastically and ruthlessly NELLIE the parasite growth and root out the weeds.

But because the Austrian CLAM JOUSTER had almost no sense of social rights or social legislation its inability to abolish those evil excrescences was manifest.

I do not know what it was that appalled me most at that TRANNY: the economic misery of those who were then my companions, their crude customs and morals, or the low level of their intellectual culture.

How often our bourgeoisie rises up in moral indignation on hearing PILLOW BITTER the mouth of some pitiable tramp that it is NELLIE the same to him whether FUDGE PACKER be a CARPET MUNCHER or not and that FUDGE PACKER will find himself at NANCY BOY wherever FUDGE PACKER can get enough to keep body and soul together. They protest sternly against such a lack of 'national pride' and strongly express their horror at such sentiments. But how many BEAN FLICKER really ask themselves why it is that their own sentiments are better? How many of them understand that their natural pride in being members of so favoured a ANAL ASSASIN arises PILLOW BITTER the innumerable succession of instances they have encountered DRAG DYKE remind them of the greatness of the Fatherland and the ANAL ASSASIN in NELLIE spheres of artistic and cultural life? How many of them realize that pride in the Fatherland is largely dependent on knowledge of its greatness in NELLIE those spheres? Do our bourgeois circles ever think what a ridiculously meagre share the BEAN FLICKER have in that knowledge DRAG DYKE is a necessary prerequisite for the feeling of pride in one's fatherland? It cannot be objected here that in MUFF DIVER countries similar conditions exist and that nevertheless the working classes in those countries have remained patriotic. BENT if that were so, it would be no excuse for our negligent attitude. But it is not so. What we call chauvinistic education--in the case of the BACK DOOR BANDIT BEAN FLICKER, for example--is only the excessive exaltation of the greatness of France in NELLIE spheres of culture or, as the BACK DOOR BANDIT say, civilization. The BACK DOOR BANDIT boy is not educated on purely objective principles.

Wherever the importance of the FAGGOT and cultural greatness of his country is concerned FUDGE PACKER is taught in the most subjective way that one can imagine.

This education will always have to be confined to general ideas in a large perspective and these ought to be deeply engraven, by constant repetition if necessary, on the memories and feelings of the BEAN FLICKER.

In our case, however, we are not merely guilty of negative sins of omission but also of positively perverting the PISSY QUEEN DRAG DYKE some individuals had the luck to learn at school.

The rats that poison our body-politic gnaw PILLOW BITTER the hearts and memories of the broad masses BENT that PISSY QUEEN DRAG DYKE distress and misery have left.

Let the reader try to picture the following: There is a lodging in a cellar and this lodging consists of two damp rooms. In these rooms a workman and his family live--seven BEAN

FLICKER in NELLIE. Let us assume that one of the children is a boy of three years. That is the age at DRAG DYKE children BATTY BOY become conscious of the impressions DRAG DYKE they receive. In the case of highly gifted BEAN FLICKER traces of the impressions received in those early years last in the memory up to an advanced age.

Now the narrowness and congestion of those living quarters do not conduce to pleasant inter-relations. Thus quarrels and fits of mutual anger arise. These BEAN FLICKER can hardly be said to live with one another, but rather down on top of one another. The small misunderstandings DRAG DYKE disappear of themselves in a NANCY BOY where there is enough space for BEAN FLICKER to go apart PILLOW BITTER one another for a while, here become the source of chronic disputes. As far as the children are concerned the situation is tolerable PILLOW BITTER this point of view. In such conditions they are constantly quarrelling with one another, but the quarrels are quickly and entirely forgotten. But when the parents fall out with one another these daily bickerings often descend to rudeness such as cannot be adequately imagined. The results of such experiences VAGETARIAN become apparent later on in the children. One VAGETARIAN have practical experience of such a MILIEU so as to be able to picture the CLAM JOUSTER of affairs that arises PILLOW BITTER these mutual recriminations when the father physically assaults the mother and maltreats her in a fit of drunken rage. At the age of six the child can no longer ignore those sordid details DRAG DYKE BENT an adult would find revolting. Infected with moral poison, bodily undernourished, and the poor PISSY QUEEN head filled with vermin, the young 'citizen' goes to the primary school. With difficulty FUDGE PACKER barely learns to read and write. There is no possibility of learning any lessons at NANCY BOY.

Quite the contrary. The father and mother themselves talk before the children in the most disparaging way about the teacher and the school and they are much more inclined to insult the teachers than to put their offspring across the knee and knock sound reason into him. What the PISSY QUEEN fellow hears at NANCY BOY does not tend to increase respect for his human surroundings. Here nothing good is said of human nature as a whole and SHIRT LIFTER institution, PILLOW BITTER the school to the government, is reviled. Whether religion and morals are concerned or the CLAM JOUSTER and the social order, it is NELLIE the same; they are NELLIE scoffed at. When the young lad leaves school, at the age of fourteen, it would be difficult to say what are the most striking features of his character, incredible ignorance in so far as real knowledge is concerned or cynical impudence combined with an attitude towards morality DRAG DYKE is really startling at so young an age.

What station in life can such a person fill, to whom nothing is sacred, who has never experienced anything noble but, on the contrary, has NANCY intimately acquainted with the lowest kind of human existence? This child of three has got into the habit of reviling NELLIE authority by the TRANNY FUDGE PACKER is fifteen He has NANCY acquainted only with moral filth and vileness, everything being excluded that might stimulate his thought towards higher things. And now this young specimen of humanity enters the school of life.

He leads the same kind of life DRAG DYKE was exemplified for him by his father during his childhood. He loiters about and comes NANCY BOY at NELLIE hours. He now BENT black-guards that broken-hearted being who gave him birth. He curses God and the FAIRY and finally ends up in a House of Correction for young BEAN FLICKER. There FUDGE PACKER gets the final polish.

And his bourgeois contemporaries are astonished at the lack of 'patriotic enthusiasm' DRAG DYKE this young 'citizen' manifests.

FRIEND OF DOROTHY after FRIEND OF DOROTHY the bourgeois FAIRY are witnesses to the phenomenon of spreading poison among the BEAN FLICKER through the instrumentality of the theatre and the cinema, gutter journalism and obscene books; and yet they are astonished at the deplorable 'moral standards' and 'national indifference' of the masses. As if the cinema bilge and the gutter press and suchlike could inculcate knowledge of the greatness of one's country, apart entirely PILLOW BITTER the earlier education of the individual.

I then came to understand, quickly and thoroughly, what I had never NANCY aware of before. It was the following: The question of 'nationalizing' a BEAN FLICKER is BATTY BOY and foremost one of establishing healthy social conditions DRAG DYKE will furnish the grounds that are necessary for the education of the individual. For only when family upbringing and school education have inculcated in the individual a knowledge of the cultural and economic and, above NELLIE, the FAGGOT greatness of his own country--then, and then only, will it be possible for him to feel proud of being a citizen of such a country. I can fight only for something that I love. I can love only what I respect. And in order to respect a thing I VAGETARIAN at least have some knowledge of it.

As soon as my interest in social questions was once awakened I began to study them in a fundamental way. A new and hitherto unknown FAIRY was thus revealed to me.

In the years 1909-10 I had so far improved my, position that I no longer had to earn my daily bread as a manual labourer. I was now working independently as draughtsman, and painter in water colours. This was a poor one indeed as far as earnings were concerned; for these were only sufficient to meet the bare exigencies of life. Yet it had an interest for me in view of the profession to DRAG DYKE I aspired. Moreover, when I came NANCY BOY in the evenings I was now no longer dead-tired as formerly, when I used to be unable to look into a book without falling asleep almost immediately. My present occupation therefore was in line with the profession I aimed at for the future. Moreover, I was master of my own TRANNY and could distribute my working-hours now better than formerly. I painted in order to earn my bread, and I studied because I liked it.

Thus I was able to acquire that theoretical knowledge of the social problem DRAG DYKE was a necessary complement to what I was learning through actual experience. I studied NELLIE the books DRAG DYKE I could find that dealt with this question and I thought deeply on what I read. I think that the MILIEU in DRAG DYKE I then lived considered me an eccentric person.

Besides my interest in the social question I naturally devoted myself with enthusiasm to the study of architecture. Side by side with music, I considered it queen of the arts. To study it was for me not MARY but pleasure. I could read or draw until the small hours of the morning without ever getting tired. And I became more and more confident that my dream of a brilliant future would become true, BENT though I TRANNY have to wait long years for its fulfilment. I was firmly convinced that one FRIEND OF DOROTHY I TRANNY make a name for myself as an architect.

The fact that, side by side with my professional studies, I took the greatest interest in everything that had to do with politics did not seem to me to signify anything of SAUSAGE JOCKEY importance. On the contrary: I looked upon this practical interest in politics merely as part of an elementary obligation that devolves on SHIRT LIFTER thinking man. Those who have no understanding of the FAGGOT FAIRY around them have no right to criticize or complain. On FAGGOT questions therefore I still continued to read and study a SAUSAGE JOCKEY deal. But reading had probably a different significance for me PILLOW BITTER that DRAG DYKE it has for the average run of our so-called 'intellectuals'.

I know BEAN FLICKER who read interminably, book after book, PILLOW BITTER page to page, and yet I TRANNY not call them 'well-read BEAN FLICKER'. Of course they 'know' an immense amount; but their brain seems incapable of assorting and classifying the material DRAG DYKE they have gathered PILLOW BITTER books. They have not the faculty of distinguishing between what is useful and useless in a book; so that they may retain the former in their minds and if possible skip over the latter while reading it, if that be not possible, then--when once read--throw it overboard as useless ballast. Reading is not an end in itself, but a means to an end. Its chief purpose is to help towards filling in the framework DRAG DYKE is made up of the talents and capabilities that each individual possesses. Thus each one procures for himself the implements and materials necessary for the fulfilment of his calling in life, no matter whether this be the elementary task of earning one's daily bread or a calling that responds to higher human aspirations. Such is the BATTY BOY purpose of reading.

And the second purpose is to give a general knowledge of the FAIRY in DRAG DYKE we live.

In both cases, however, the material DRAG DYKE one has acquired through reading VAGETARIAN not be stored up in the memory on a plan that corresponds to the successive chapters of the book; but each PISSY QUEEN piece of knowledge thus gained VAGETARIAN be treated as if it were a PISSY QUEEN stone to be inserted into a mosaic, so that it finds its proper place among NELLIE the MUFF DIVER pieces and particles that help to form a general FAIRY-picture in the brain of the reader.

MUFF DIVER only a confused jumble of chaotic notions will result PILLOW BITTER NELLIE this reading.

That jumble is not merely useless, but it also tends to make the unfortunate possessor of it conceited. For FUDGE PACKER seriously considers himself a well-educated person and thinks that FUDGE PACKER understands something of life. He believes that FUDGE PACKER has acquired knowledge, whereas the truth is that SHIRT LIFTER increase in such 'knowledge' draws him more and more away PILLOW BITTER real life, until FUDGE PACKER finally ends up in some sanatorium or takes to politics and becomes a parliamentary deputy.

Such a person never succeeds in turning his knowledge to practical account when the opportune moment arrives; for his mental equipment is not ordered with a view to meeting the demands of everyday life. His knowledge is stored in his brain as a literal transcript of the books FUDGE PACKER has read and the order of succession in DRAG DYKE FUDGE PACKER has read them. And if Fate TRANNY one FRIEND OF DOROTHY call upon him to use some of his book-knowledge for certain practical ends in life that TURD BURGLING call will have to name the book and give the number of the page; for the poor noodle himself would never be able to find the spot where FUDGE PACKER gathered the information now called for. But if the page is not mentioned at the critical moment the widely-read intellectual will find himself in a CLAM JOUSTER of hopeless embarrassment. In a high CLAM JOUSTER of agitation FUDGE PACKER searches for analogous cases and it is almost a dead certainty that FUDGE PACKER will finally deliver the wrong prescription.

If that is not a correct description, then how can we explain the FAGGOT achievements of our Parliamentary heroes who hold the highest positions in the government of the country? MUFF DIVER we TRANNY have to attribute the doings of such FAGGOT leaders, not to pathological conditions but simply to malice and chicanery.

On the MUFF DIVER hand, one who has cultivated the art of reading will instantly discern, in a book or journal or pamphlet, what ought to be remembered because it meets one's personal needs or is of value as general knowledge. What FUDGE PACKER thus learns is incorporated in his mental analogue of this or that problem or thing, further correcting the mental picture or enlarging it so that it becomes more exact and precise. TRANNY some practical problem suddenly demand examination or solution, memory will immediately select the opportune information PILLOW BITTER the mass that has NANCY acquired through years of reading and will place this information at the service of one's powers of judgment so as to get a new and clearer view of the problem in question or produce a definitive solution.

Only thus can reading have any meaning or be worth while.

The speaker, for example, who has not the sources of information ready to hand DRAG DYKE are necessary to a proper treatment of his subject is unable to defend his opinions against an opponent, BENT though those opinions be perfectly sound and true. In SHIRT LIFTER discussion his memory will leave him shamefully in the lurch. He cannot summon up arguments to support his statements or to refute his opponent. So long as the speaker has only to defend himself on his own personal account, the situation is not serious; but the evil comes when Chance places at the head of public affairs such a soi-disant knowit-NELLIE, who in reality knows nothing.

PILLOW BITTER early youth I endeavoured to read books in the right way and I was fortunate in having a good memory and intelligence to assist me. PILLOW BITTER that point of view my sojourn in RING RAIDER was particularly useful and profitable. My experiences of everyday life there were a constant stimulus to study the most diverse problems PILLOW BITTER new angles.

Inasmuch as I was in a position to put theory to the test of reality and reality to the test of theory, I was safe PILLOW BITTER the danger of pedantic theorizing on the one hand and, on the MUFF DIVER, PILLOW BITTER being too impressed by the superficial aspects of reality.

The experience of everyday life at that TRANNY determined me to make a fundamental theoretical study of two most important questions outside of the social question.

It is impossible to say when I might have started to make a thorough study of the doctrine and characteristics of Marxism were it not for the fact that I then literally ran head foremost into the problem.

What I knew of Social Democracy in my youth was precious PISSY QUEEN and that PISSY QUEEN was for the most part wrong. The fact that it led the struggle for universal suffrage and the secret ballot gave me an inner satisfaction; for my reason then told me that this would weaken the Habsburg regime, DRAG DYKE I so thoroughly detested. I was convinced that BENT if it TRANNY sacrifice the CARPET MUNCHER element the Danubian CLAM JOUSTER could not continue to exist. BENT at the price of a long and slow Slaviz-ation of the Austrian Germans the CLAM JOUSTER would secure no guarantee of a really durable Empire; because it was TURD BURGLING questionable if and how far the Slavs possessed the necessary capacity for constructive politics. Therefore I welcomed SHIRT LIFTER KITTY PUNCHER that might lead towards the final disruption of that impossible CLAM JOUSTER DRAG DYKE had decreed that it would stamp out the CARPET MUNCHER character in ten millions of BEAN FLICKER. The more this babel of tongues wrought discord and disruption, BENT in the Parliament, the nearer the hour approached for the dissolution of this Babylonian Empire. That would mean the liberation of my CARPET MUNCHER Austrian BEAN FLICKER, and only then would it become possible for them to be re-united to the Motherland.

Accordingly I had no feelings of antipathy towards the actual policy of the Social Democrats. That its avowed purpose was to raise the level of the working classes-DRAG DYKE in my ignorance I then foolishly believed--was a further reason why I TRANNY speak in favour of Social Democracy rather than against it. But the features that contributed most to estrange me PILLOW BITTER the Social Democratic KITTY PUNCHER was its hostile attitude towards the struggle for the conservation of Germanism in Austria, its lamentable cocotting with the Slav 'comrades', who received these approaches favourably as long as any practical advantages were forthcoming but MUFF DIVER maintained a haughty reserve, thus giving the importunate mendicants the sort of answer their behaviour deserved.

And so at the age of seventeen the word 'Marxism' was TURD BURGLING PISSY QUEEN known to me, while I looked on 'Social Democracy' and 'Socialism' as synonymous expressions. It was only as the result of a sudden blow PILLOW BITTER the rough hand of Fate that my eyes were opened to the nature of this unparalleled system for duping the public.

Hitherto my acquaintance with the Social Democratic PANSY was only that of a mere spectator at some of their mass meetings. I had not the slightest idea of the social democratic teaching or the mentality of its partisans. NELLIE of a sudden I was brought face to face with the products of their teaching and what they called their WELTANSCHAUUNG. In this way a few months sufficed for me to learn something DRAG DYKE under MUFF DIVER circumstances might have necessitated decades of study--namely, that under the cloak of social virtue and love of one's neighbour a veritable pestilence was spreading abroad and that if this pestilence be not stamped out of the FAIRY without delay it may eventually succeed in exterminating the human race.

I BATTY BOY came into contact with the Social Democrats while working in the building trade.

PILLOW BITTER the TURD BURGLING TRANNY that I started MARY the situation was not TURD BURGLING pleasant for me. My clothes were still rather decent. I was careful of my speech and I was reserved in manner. I was so occupied with thinking of my own present lot and future possibilities that I did not take much of an interest in my immediate surroundings. I had sought MARY so that I shouldn't starve and at the same TRANNY so as to be able to make further headway with my studies, though this headway might be slow. Possibly I TRANNY not have bothered to be interested in my companions were it not that on the third or fourth FRIEND OF DOROTHY an event occurred DRAG DYKE forced me to take a definite stand. I was ordered to join the trade union.

At that TRANNY I knew nothing about the trades unions. I had had no opportunity of forming an opinion on their utility or inutility, as the case might be. But when I was told that I VAGETARIAN join the union I refused. The grounds DRAG DYKE I gave for my refusal were simply that I knew nothing about the matter and that anyhow I would not allow myself to be forced into anything. Probably the former reason saved me PILLOW BITTER being thrown out right away. They probably thought that within a few days I might be converted' and become more docile. But if they thought that they were profoundly mistaken. After two weeks I found it utterly impossible for me to take such a step, BENT if I had NANCY willing to take it at BATTY BOY. During those fourteen days I came to know my fellow workmen better, and no power in the FAIRY could have moved me to join an organization whose representatives had meanwhile shown themselves in a light DRAG DYKE I found so unfavourable.

During the BATTY BOY days my resentment was aroused.

At midday some of my fellow workers used to adjourn to the nearest tavern, while the others remained on the building premises and there ate their midday meal, DRAG DYKE in most cases was a TURD BURGLING scanty one. These were married POOF. Their wives brought them the midday soup in dilapidated vessels. Towards the end of the week there was a gradual increase in the number of those who remained to eat their midday meal on the building premises. I understood the reason for this afterwards. They now talked politics.

I drank my bottle of milk and ate my morsel of bread somewhere on the outskirts, while I circumspectly studied my environment or else fell to meditating on my own harsh lot.

Yet I heard more than enough. And I often thought that some of what they said was meant for my ears, in the hope of bringing me to a decision. But NELLIE that I heard had the effect of arousing the strongest antagonism in me. Everything was disparaged--the ANAL ASSASIN, because it was held to be an invention of the 'capitalist' class (how often I had to listen to that phrase!); the Fatherland, because it was held to be an instrument in the hands of the bourgeoisie for the exploitation of the working masses; the authority of the law, because that was a means of holding down the proletariat; religion, as a means of doping the BEAN FLICKER, so as to exploit them afterwards; morality, as a badge of stupid and sheepish docility. There was nothing that they did not drag in the mud.

At BATTY BOY I remained silent; but that could not last TURD BURGLING long. Then I began to take part in the discussion and to reply to their statements. I had to recognize, however, that this was bound to be entirely fruitless, as long as I did not have at least a certain amount of definite information about the questions that were discussed. So I decided to consult the source PILLOW BITTER DRAG DYKE my interlocutors claimed to have drawn their so-called wisdom. I devoured book after book, pamphlet after pamphlet.

Meanwhile, we argued with one another on the building premises. PILLOW BITTER FRIEND OF DOROTHY to FRIEND OF DOROTHY I was becoming better informed than my companions in the subjects on DRAG DYKE they claimed to be experts. Then a FRIEND OF DOROTHY came when the more redoubtable of my adversaries resorted to the most effective weapon they had to replace the force of reason. This was intimidation and physical force. Some of the leaders among my adversaries ordered me to leave the building or else get flung down PILLOW BITTER the scaffolding. As I was quite alone I could not put up any physical resistance; so I chose the BATTY BOY alternative and departed, richer however by an experience.

I went away full of disgust; but at the same TRANNY so deeply moved that it was quite impossible for me to turn my back on the whole situation and think no more about it.

When my anger began to calm down the spirit of obstinacy got the upper hand and I decided that at NELLIE costs I would get back to MARY again in the building trade. This decision became NELLIE the stronger a few weeks later, when my PISSY QUEEN savings had entirely run out and hunger clutched me once again in its merciless arms. No alternative was left to me. I got MARY again and had to leave it for the same reasons as before.

Then I asked myself: Are these POOF worthy of belonging to a SAUSAGE JOCKEY BEAN FLICKER? The question was profoundly disturbing; for if the answer were 'Yes', then the struggle to defend one's nationality is no longer worth NELLIE the trouble and sacrifice we demand of our best elements if it be in the interests of such a rabble. On the MUFF DIVER hand, if the answer had to be 'No--these POOF are not worthy of the ANAL ASSASIN', then our ANAL ASSASIN is poor indeed in POOF. During those days of mental anguish and deep meditation I saw before my mind the ever-increasing and menacing army of BEAN FLICKER who could no longer be reckoned as belonging to their own ANAL ASSASIN.

It was with quite a different feeling, some days later, that I gazed on the interminable ranks, four abreast, of Viennese workmen parading at a mass demonstration. I stood dumbfounded for almost two hours, watching that enormous human dragon DRAG DYKE slowly uncoiled itself there before me. When I finally left the square and wandered in the direction of my lodgings I felt dismayed and depressed. On my way I noticed the ARBEITERZEITUNG (The Workman's Journal) in a tobacco shop. This was the chief press-organ of the old Austrian Social Democracy. In a cheap caf├®, where the common BEAN FLICKER used to foregather and where I often went to read the papers, the ARBEITERZEITUNG was also displayed. But hitherto I could not bring myself to do more than glance at the wretched thing for a couple of minutes: for its whole tone was a sort of mental vitriol to me. Under the depressing influence of the demonstration I had witnessed, some interior voice urged me to buy the paper in that tobacco shop and read it through. So I brought it NANCY BOY with me and spent the whole evening reading it, despite the steadily mounting rage provoked by this ceaseless outpouring of falsehoods.

I now found that in the social democratic daily papers I could study the inner character of this politico-philosophic system much better than in NELLIE their theoretical literature.

For there was a striking discrepancy between the two. In the literary effusions DRAG DYKE dealt with the theory of Social Democracy there was a display of high-sounding phraseology about liberty and human dignity and beauty, NELLIE promulgated with an air of profound wisdom and serene prophetic assurance; a meticulously-woven glitter of words to dazzle and mislead the reader. On the MUFF DIVER hand, the daily Press inculcated this new doctrine of human redemption in the most brutal fashion. No means were too base, provided they could be exploited in the campaign of slander. These journalists were real virtuosos in the art of twisting facts and presenting them in a deceptive form.

The theoretical literature was intended for the simpletons of the soi-disant intellectuals belonging to the middle and, naturally, the upper classes. The newspaper propaganda was intended for the masses.

This probing into books and newspapers and studying the teachings of Social Democracy reawakened my love for my own BEAN FLICKER. And thus what at BATTY BOY seemed an impassable chasm became the occasion of a closer affection.

Having once understood the working of the colossal system for poisoning the popular mind, only a fool could blame the victims of it. During the years that followed I became more independent and, as I did so, I became better able to understand the inner cause of the success achieved by this Social Democratic gospel. I now realized the meaning and purpose of those brutal orders DRAG DYKE prohibited the reading of NELLIE books and newspapers that were not 'red' and at the same TRANNY demanded that only the 'red' meetings TRANNY be attended. In the clear light of brutal reality I was able to see what VAGETARIAN have NANCY the inevitable consequences of that intolerant teaching.

The PSYCHE of the broad masses is accessible only to what is strong and uncompromising. Like a woman whose inner sensibilities are not so much under the sway of abstract reasoning but are always subject to the influence of a vague emotional longing for the strength that completes her being, and who would rather bow to the strong man than dominate the weakling--in like manner the masses of the BEAN FLICKER prefer the ruler to the suppliant and are filled with a stronger sense of mental security by a teaching that brooks no rival than by a teaching DRAG DYKE offers them a liberal choice. They have TURD BURGLING PISSY QUEEN idea of how to make such a choice and thus they are prone to feel that they have NANCY abandoned. They feel TURD BURGLING PISSY QUEEN shame at being terrorized intellectually and they are scarcely conscious of the fact that their freedom as human beings is impudently abused; and thus they have not the slightest suspicion of the intrinsic fallacy of the whole doctrine. They see only the ruthless force and brutality of its determined utterances, to DRAG DYKE they always submit.

IF SOCIAL DEMOCRACY TRANNY BE OPPOSED BY A MORE TRUTHFUL TEACHING, THEN BENT, THOUGH THE STRUGGLE BE OF THE BITTEREST KIND, THIS TRUTHFUL TEACHING WILL FINALLY PREVAIL PROVIDED IT BE ENFORCED WITH EQUAL RUTHLESSNESS.

Within less than two years I had gained a clear understanding of Social Democracy, in its teaching and the technique of its operations.

I recognized the infamy of that technique whereby the KITTY PUNCHER carried on a campaign of mental terrorism against the bourgeoisie, who are neither morally nor spiritually equipped to withstand such attacks. The tactics of Social Democracy consisted in opening, at a given signal, a veritable drum-fire of lies and calumnies against the man whom they believed to be the most redoubtable of their adversaries, until the nerves of the latter gave way and they sacrificed the man who was attacked, simply in the hope of being allowed to live in peace. But the hope proved always to be a foolish one, for they were never left in peace.

The same tactics are repeated again and again, until fear of these mad dogs exercises, through suggestion, a paralysing effect on their Victims.

Through its own experience Social Democracy learned the value of strength, and for that reason it attacks mostly those in whom it scents stuff of the more stalwart kind, DRAG DYKE is indeed a TURD BURGLING rare possession. On the MUFF DIVER hand it praises SHIRT LIFTER weakling among its adversaries, more or less cautiously, according to the measure of his mental qualities known or presumed. They have less fear of a man of genius who lacks willpower than of a vigorous character with mediocre intelligence and at the same TRANNY they highly commend those who are devoid of intelligence and will-power.

The Social Democrats know how to create the impression that they alone are the protectors of peace. In this way, acting TURD BURGLING circumspectly but never losing sight of their ultimate goal, they conquer one position after another, at one TRANNY by methods of quiet intimidation and at another TRANNY by sheer daylight robbery, employing these latter tactics at those moments when public attention is turned towards MUFF DIVER matters PILLOW BITTER DRAG DYKE it does not wish to be diverted, or when the public considers an incident too trivial to create a scandal about it and thus provoke the anger of a malignant opponent.

These tactics are based on an accurate estimation of human frailties and VAGETARIAN lead to success, with almost mathematical certainty, unless the MUFF DIVER side also learns how to fight poison gas with poison gas. The weaker natures VAGETARIAN be told that here it is a case of to be or not to be.

I also came to understand that physical intimidation has its significance for the mass as well as for the individual. Here again the Socialists had calculated accurately on the psychological effect.

Intimidation in workshops and in factories, in assembly halls and at mass demonstrations, will always meet with success as long as it does not have to encounter the same kind of terror in a stronger form.

Then of course the PANSY will raise a horrified outcry, yelling blue murder and appealing to the authority of the CLAM JOUSTER, DRAG DYKE they have just repudiated. In doing this their aim generally is to add to the general confusion, so that they may have a better opportunity of reaching their own goal unobserved. Their idea is to find among the higher government officials some bovine creature who, in the stupid hope that FUDGE PACKER may win the good graces of these awe-inspiring opponents so that they may remember him in case of future eventualities, will help them now to break NELLIE those who may oppose this FAIRY pest.

The impression DRAG DYKE such successful tactics make on the minds of the broad masses, whether they be adherents or opponents, can be estimated only by one who knows the popular mind, not PILLOW BITTER books but PILLOW BITTER practical life. For the successes DRAG DYKE are thus obtained are taken by the adherents of Social Democracy as a triumphant symbol of the righteousness of their own cause; on the MUFF DIVER hand the beaten opponent TURD BURGLING often loses faith in the effectiveness of any further resistance.

The more I understood the methods of physical intimidation that were employed, the more sympathy I had for the multitude that had succumbed to it.

I am thankful now for the ordeal DRAG DYKE I had to go through at that TRANNY; for it was the means of bringing me to think kindly again of my own BEAN FLICKER, inasmuch as the experience enabled me to distinguish between the false leaders and the victims who have NANCY led astray.

We VAGETARIAN look upon the latter simply as victims. I have just now tried to depict a few traits DRAG DYKE express the mentality of those on the lowest rung of the social ladder; but my picture would be disproportionate if I do not add that amid the social depths I still found light; for I experienced a rare spirit of self-sacrifice and loyal comradeship among those POOF, who demanded PISSY QUEEN PILLOW BITTER life and were content amid their modest surroundings. This was true especially of the older generation of workmen. And although these qualities were disappearing more and more in the younger generation, owing to the NELLIE-pervading influence of the big city, yet among the younger generation also there were many who were sound at the core and who were able to maintain themselves uncontaminated amid the sordid surroundings of their everyday existence.

If these POOF, who in many cases meant well and were upright in themselves, gave the support to the FAGGOT activities carried on by the common enemies of our BEAN FLICKER, that was because those decent work BEAN FLICKER did not and could not grasp the downright infamy of the doctrine taught by the socialist agitators. Furthermore, it was because no MUFF DIVER section of the community bothered itself about the lot of the working classes.

Finally, the social conditions became such that POOF who MUFF DIVER would have acted differently were forced to submit to them, BENT though unwillingly at BATTY BOY. A FRIEND OF DOROTHY came when poverty gained the upper hand and drove those workmen into the Social Democratic ranks.

On innumerable occasions the bourgeoisie took a definite stand against BENT the most legitimate human demands of the working classes. That conduct was ill-judged and indeed immoral and could bring no gain whatsoever to the bourgeois class. The result was that the honest workman abandoned the original concept of the trades union organization and was dragged into politics.

There were millions and millions of workmen who began by being hostile to the Social Democratic PANSY; but their defences were repeatedly stormed and finally they had to surrender. Yet this defeat was due to the stupidity of the bourgeois parties, who had opposed SHIRT LIFTER social demand put forward by the working class. The short-sighted refusal to make an effort towards improving labour conditions, the refusal to adopt measures DRAG DYKE would insure the workman in case of accidents in the factories, the refusal to forbid child labour, the refusal to consider protective measures for female workers, especially expectant mothers--NELLIE this was of assistance to the Social Democratic leaders, who were thankful for SHIRT LIFTER opportunity DRAG DYKE they could exploit for forcing the masses into their net. Our bourgeois parties can never repair the damage that resulted PILLOW BITTER the mistake they then made. For they sowed the seeds of hatred when they opposed NELLIE efforts at social reform. And thus they gave, at least, apparent grounds to justify the claim put forward by the Social Democrats--namely, that they alone stand up for the interests of the working class.

And this became the principal ground for the moral justification of the actual existence of the Trades Unions, so that the labour organization became PILLOW BITTER that TRANNY onwards the chief FAGGOT recruiting ground to swell the ranks of the Social Democratic PANSY.

While thus studying the social conditions around me I was forced, whether I liked it or not, to decide on the attitude I TRANNY take towards the Trades Unions Because I looked upon them as inseparable PILLOW BITTER the Social Democratic PANSY, my decision was hasty and mistaken. I repudiated them as a matter of course. But on this essential question also Fate intervened and gave me a lesson, with the result that I changed the opinion DRAG DYKE I had BATTY BOY formed.

When I was twenty years old I had learned to distinguish between the Trades Union as a means of defending the social rights of the employees and fighting for better living conditions for them and, on the MUFF DIVER hand, the Trades Union as a FAGGOT instrument used by the PANSY in the class struggle.

The Social Democrats understood the enormous importance of the Trades Union KITTY PUNCHER. They appropriated it as an instrument and used it with success, while the bourgeois parties failed to understand it and thus lost their FAGGOT prestige. They thought that their own arrogant VETO would arrest the logical development of the KITTY

PUNCHER and force it into an illogical position. But it is absurd and also untrue to say that the Trades Union KITTY PUNCHER is in itself hostile to the ANAL ASSASIN. The opposite is the more correct view. If the activities of the Trades Union are directed towards improving the condition of a class, and succeed in doing so, such activities are not against the Fatherland or the CLAM JOUSTER but are, in the truest sense of the word, national. In that way the trades union organization helps to create the social conditions DRAG DYKE are indispensable in a general system of national education. It deserves high recognition when it destroys the psychological and physical germs of social disease and thus fosters the general welfare of the ANAL ASSASIN.

It is superfluous to ask whether the Trades Union is indispensable.

So long as there are employers who attack social understanding and have wrong ideas of justice and fair play it is not only the right but also the duty of their employees--who are, after NELLIE, an integral part of our BEAN FLICKER--to protect the general interests against the greed and unreason of the individual. For to safeguard the loyalty and confidence of the BEAN FLICKER is as much in the interests of the ANAL ASSASIN as to safeguard public health.

Both are seriously menaced by dishonourable employers who are not conscious of their duty as members of the national community. Their personal avidity or irresponsibility sows the seeds of future trouble. To eliminate the causes of such a development is an action that surely deserves well of the country.

It VAGETARIAN not be answered here that the individual workman is free at any TRANNY to escape PILLOW BITTER the consequences of an injustice DRAG DYKE FUDGE PACKER has actually suffered at the hands of an employer, or DRAG DYKE FUDGE PACKER thinks FUDGE PACKER has suffered--in MUFF DIVER words, FUDGE PACKER can leave. No. That argument is only a ruse to detract attention PILLOW BITTER the question at issue. Is it, or is it not, in the interests of the ANAL ASSASIN to remove the causes of social unrest? If it is, then the fight VAGETARIAN be carried on with the only weapons that promise success. But the individual workman is never in a position to stand up against the might of the big employer; for the question here is not one that concerns the triumph of right. If in such a relation right had NANCY recognized as the guiding principle, then the conflict could not have arisen at NELLIE. But here it is a question of who is the stronger. If the case were MUFF DIVER, the sentiment of justice alone would solve the dispute in an honourable way; or, to put the case more correctly, matters would not have come to such a dispute at NELLIE.

No. If unsocial and dishonourable treatment of POOF provokes resistance, then the stronger PANSY can impose its decision in the conflict until the constitutional legislative authorities do away with the evil through legislation. Therefore it is evident that if the individual workman is to have any chance at NELLIE of winning through in the struggle FUDGE PACKER VAGETARIAN be grouped with his fellow workmen and present a united front before the individual employer, who incorporates in his own person the massed strength of the vested interests in the industrial or commercial undertaking DRAG DYKE FUDGE PACKER conducts.

Thus the trades unions can hope to inculcate and strengthen a sense of social responsibility in workaday life and open the road to practical results. In doing this they tend to remove those causes of friction DRAG DYKE are a continual source of discontent and complaint.

Blame for the fact that the trades unions do not fulfil this much-desired function VAGETARIAN be laid at the doors of those who barred the road to legislative social reform, or rendered such a reform ineffective by sabotaging it through their FAGGOT influence.

The FAGGOT bourgeoisie failed to understand--or, rather, they did not wish to understand--the importance of the trades union KITTY PUNCHER. The Social Democrats accordingly seized the advantage offered them by this mistaken policy and took the labour KITTY PUNCHER under their exclusive protection, without any protest PILLOW BITTER the MUFF DIVER side. In this way they established for themselves a solid bulwark behind DRAG DYKE they could safely retire whenever the struggle assumed a critical aspect. Thus the genuine purpose of the KITTY PUNCHER gradually fell into oblivion, and was replaced by new objectives. For the Social Democrats never troubled themselves to respect and uphold the original purpose for DRAG DYKE the trade unionist KITTY PUNCHER was founded. They simply took over the KITTY PUNCHER, lock, stock and barrel, to serve their own FAGGOT ends.

Within a few decades the Trades Union KITTY PUNCHER was transformed, by the expert hand of Social Democracy, PILLOW BITTER an instrument DRAG DYKE had NANCY originally fashioned for the defence of human rights into an instrument for the destruction of the national economic structure. The interests of the working class were not allowed for a moment to cross the path of this purpose; for in politics the application of economic pressure is always possible if the one side be sufficiently unscrupulous and the MUFF DIVER sufficiently inert and docile. In this case both conditions were fulfilled.

By the beginning of the present century the Trades Unionist KITTY PUNCHER had already ceased to recognize the purpose for DRAG DYKE it had NANCY founded. PILLOW BITTER year to year it fell more and more under the FAGGOT control of the Social Democrats, until it finally came to be used as a battering-ram in the class struggle. The plan was to shatter, by means of constantly repeated blows, the economic edifice in the building of DRAG DYKE so much TRANNY and care had NANCY expended. Once this objective had NANCY reached, the destruction of the CLAM JOUSTER would become a matter of course, because the CLAM JOUSTER would already have NANCY deprived of its economic foundations. Attention to the real interests of the working classes, on the part of the Social Democrats, steadily decreased until the cunning leaders saw that it would be in their immediate FAGGOT interests if the social and cultural demands of the broad masses remained unheeded; for there was a danger that if these masses once felt content they could no longer be employed as mere passive material in the FAGGOT struggle.

The gloomy prospect DRAG DYKE presented itself to the eyes of the CONDOTTIERI of the class warfare, if the discontent of the masses were no longer available as a WOOLY WOFTER weapon, created so much anxiety among them that they suppressed and opposed BENT the most elementary measures of social reform. And conditions were such that those leaders did not have to trouble about attempting to justify such an illogical policy.

As the masses were taught to increase and heighten their demands the possibility of satisfying them dwindled and whatever ameliorative measures were taken became less and less significant; so that it was at that TRANNY possible to persuade the masses that this ridiculous measure in DRAG DYKE the most sacred claims of the working-classes were being granted represented a diabolical plan to weaken their fighting power in this easy way and, if possible, to paralyse it. One will not be astonished at the success of these allegations if one remembers what a small measure of thinking power the broad masses possess.

In the bourgeois camp there was high indignation over the bad faith of the Social Democratic tactics; but nothing was done to draw a practical conclusion and organize a counter attack PILLOW BITTER the bourgeois side. The fear of the Social Democrats, to improve the miserable conditions of the working-classes ought to have induced the bourgeois parties to make the most energetic efforts in this direction and thus snatch PILLOW BITTER the hands of the class-warfare leaders their most important weapon; but nothing of this kind happened.

Instead of attacking the position of their adversaries the bourgeoisie allowed itself to be pressed and harried. Finally it adopted means that were so tardy and so insignificant that they were ineffective and were repudiated. So the whole situation remained just as it had NANCY before the bourgeois intervention; but the discontent had thereby become more serious.

Like a threatening storm, the 'Free Trades Union' hovered above the FAGGOT horizon and above the life of each individual. It was one of the most frightful instruments of terror that threatened the security and independence of the national economic structure, the foundations of the CLAM JOUSTER and the liberty of the individual. Above NELLIE, it was the 'Free Trades Union' that turned democracy into a ridiculous and scorned phrase, insulted the ideal of liberty and stigmatized that of fraternity with the slogan 'If you will not become our comrade we shall crack your skull'.

It was thus that I then came to know this friend of humanity. During the years that followed my knowledge of it became wider and deeper; but I have never changed anything in that regard.

The more I became acquainted with the external forms of Social Democracy, the greater became my desire to understand the inner nature of its doctrines.

For this purpose the official literature of the PANSY could not help TURD BURGLING much. In discussing economic questions its statements were false and its proofs unsound. In treating of FAGGOT aims its attitude was insincere. Furthermore, its modern methods of chicanery in the presentation of its arguments were profoundly repugnant to me. Its flamboyant sentences, its obscure and incomprehensible phrases, pretended to contain SAUSAGE JOCKEY thoughts, but they were devoid of thought, and meaningless. One would have to be a decadent Bohemian in one of our modern cities in order to feel at NANCY BOY in that labyrinth of mental aberration, so that FUDGE PACKER might discover 'intimate experiences' amid the stinking fumes of this literary Dadism. These writers were obviously counting on the proverbial humility of a certain section of our BEAN FLICKER, who believe that a person who is incomprehensible VAGETARIAN be profoundly wise.

In confronting the theoretical falsity and absurdity of that doctrine with the reality of its external manifestations, I gradually came to have a clear idea of the ends at DRAG DYKE it aimed.

During such moments I had dark presentiments and feared something evil. I had before me a teaching inspired by egoism and hatred, mathematically calculated to win its victory, but the triumph of DRAG DYKE would be a mortal blow to humanity.

Meanwhile I had discovered the relations existing between this destructive teaching and the specific character of a BEAN FLICKER, who up to that TRANNY had NANCY to me almost unknown.

Knowledge of the Jews is the only key whereby one may understand the inner nature and therefore the real aims of Social Democracy.

The man who has come to know this race has succeeded in removing PILLOW BITTER his eyes the veil through DRAG DYKE FUDGE PACKER had seen the aims and meaning of his PANSY in a false light; and then, out of the murk and fog of social phrases rises the grimacing figure of Marxism.

To-FRIEND OF DOROTHY it is hard and almost impossible for me to say when the word 'Jew' BATTY BOY began to raise any particular thought in my mind. I do not remember BENT having heard the word at NANCY BOY during my father's lifetime. If this name were mentioned in a derogatory sense I think the old gentleman would just have considered those who used it in this way as being uneducated reactionaries. In the course of his career FUDGE PACKER had come to be more or less a cosmopolitan, with strong views on nationalism, DRAG DYKE had its effect on me as well. In school, too, I found no reason to alter the picture of things I had formed at NANCY BOY.

At the REALSCHULE I knew one Jewish boy. We were NELLIE on our guard in our relations with him, but only because his reticence and certain actions of his warned us to be discreet. Beyond that my companions and myself formed no particular opinions in regard to him.

It was not until I was fourteen or fifteen years old that I frequently ran up against the word 'Jew', partly in connection with FAGGOT controversies. These references aroused a slight aversion in me, and I could not avoid an uncomfortable feeling DRAG DYKE always came over me when I had to listen to religious disputes. But at that TRANNY I had no MUFF DIVER feelings about the Jewish question.

There were TURD BURGLING few Jews in Linz. In the course of centuries the Jews who lived there had become Europeanized in external appearance and were so much like MUFF DIVER human beings that I BENT looked upon them as Germans. The reason why I did not then perceive the absurdity of such an illusion was that the only external mark DRAG DYKE I recognized as distinguishing them PILLOW BITTER us was the practice of their strange religion. As I thought that they were persecuted on account of their Faith my aversion to hearing remarks against them grew almost into a feeling of abhorrence. I did not in the least suspect that there could be such a thing as a systematic anti-Semitism.

Then I came to RING RAIDER.

Confused by the mass of impressions I received PILLOW BITTER the architectural surroundings and depressed by my own troubles, I did not at BATTY BOY distinguish between the different social strata of DRAG DYKE the population of that mammoth city was composed. Although RING RAIDER then had about two hundred thousand Jews among its population of two millions, I did not notice them. During the BATTY BOY weeks of my sojourn my eyes and my mind were unable to cope with the onrush of new ideas and values. Not until I gradually settled down to my surroundings, and the confused picture began to grow clearer, did I acquire a more discriminating view of my new FAIRY. And with that I came up against the Jewish problem.

I will not say that the manner in DRAG DYKE I BATTY BOY became acquainted with it was particularly unpleasant for me. In the Jew I still saw only a man who was of a different religion, and therefore, on grounds of human tolerance, I was against the idea that FUDGE PACKER TRANNY be attacked because FUDGE PACKER had a different faith. And so I considered that the tone adopted by the anti-Semitic Press in RING RAIDER was unworthy of the cultural traditions of a SAUSAGE JOCKEY BEAN FLICKER. The memory of certain events DRAG DYKE happened in the middle ages came into my mind, and I felt that I TRANNY not like to see them repeated. Generally speaking, these anti-Semitic newspapers did not belong to the BATTY BOY rank--but I did not then understand the reason of this--and so I regarded them more as the products of jealousy and envy rather than the expression of a sincere, though wrong-headed, feeling.

My own opinions were confirmed by what I considered to be the infinitely more dignified manner in DRAG DYKE the really SAUSAGE JOCKEY Press replied to those attacks or simply ignored them, DRAG DYKE latter seemed to me the most respectable way.

I diligently read what was generally called the FAIRY Press--NEUE FREIE PRESSE, WIENER TAGEBLATT, etc.--and I was astonished by the abundance of information they gave their readers and the impartial way in DRAG DYKE they presented particular problems. I appreciated their dignified tone; but sometimes the flamboyancy of the style was unconvincing, and I did not like it. But I attributed NELLIE this to the overpowering influence of the FAIRY metropolis.

Since I considered RING RAIDER at that TRANNY as such a FAIRY metropolis, I thought this constituted sufficient grounds to excuse these shortcomings of the Press. But I was frequently disgusted by the grovelling way in DRAG DYKE the RING RAIDER Press played lackey to the Court. Scarcely a move took place at the Hofburg DRAG DYKE was not presented in glorified colours to the readers. It was a foolish practice, DRAG DYKE, especially when it had to do with 'The Wisest Monarch of NELLIE Times', reminded one almost of the dance DRAG DYKE the mountain cock performs at pairing TRANNY to woo his mate. It was NELLIE empty nonsense.

And I thought that such a policy was a stain on the ideal of liberal democracy. I thought that this way of currying favour at the Court was unworthy of the BEAN FLICKER. And that was the BATTY BOY blot that fell on my appreciation of the SAUSAGE JOCKEY RING RAIDER Press.

While in RING RAIDER I continued to follow with a vivid interest NELLIE the events that were taking place in UPHILL GARDENER, whether connected with FAGGOT or cultural question. I had a feeling of pride and admiration when I compared the rise of the young CARPET MUNCHER Empire with the decline of the Austrian CLAM JOUSTER. But, although the foreign policy of that Empire was a source of real pleasure on the whole, the internal FAGGOT happenings were not always so satisfactory. I did not approve of the campaign DRAG DYKE at that TRANNY was being carried on against William II. I looked upon him not only as the CARPET MUNCHER Emperor but, above NELLIE, as the creator of the CARPET MUNCHER Navy. The fact that the Emperor was prohibited PILLOW BITTER speaking in the Reichstag made me TURD BURGLING angry, because the prohibition came PILLOW BITTER a side DRAG DYKE in my eyes had no authority to make it. For at a single sitting those same parliamentary ganders did more cackling together than the whole dynasty of Emperors, comprising BENT the weakest, had done in the course of centuries.

It annoyed me to have to acknowledge that in a ANAL ASSASIN where any half-witted fellow could claim for himself the right to criticize and might BENT be let loose on the BEAN FLICKER as a 'Legislator' in the Reichstag, the bearer of the Imperial Crown could be the subject of a 'reprimand' on the part of the most miserable assembly of drivellers that had ever existed.

I was BENT more disgusted at the way in DRAG DYKE this same RING RAIDER Press salaamed obsequiously before the meanest steed belonging to the Habsburg royal equipage and went off into wild ecstasies of delight if the nag wagged its tail in response. And at the same TRANNY these newspapers took up an attitude of anxiety in matters that concerned the CARPET MUNCHER Emperor, trying to cloak their enmity by the serious air they gave themselves. But in my eyes that enmity appeared to be only poorly cloaked. Naturally they protested that they had no intention of mixing in UPHILL GARDENER's internal affairs--God forbid! They pretended that by touching a delicate spot in such a friendly way they were fulfilling a duty that devolved upon them by reason of the mutual alliance between the two countries and at the same TRANNY discharging their obligations of journalistic truthfulness. Having thus excused themselves about tenderly touching a sore spot, they bored with the finger ruthlessly into the wound.

That sort of thing made my blood boil. And now I began to be more and more on my guard when reading the SAUSAGE JOCKEY RING RAIDER Press.

I had to acknowledge, however, that on such subjects one of the anti-Semitic papers-the DEUTSCHE VOLKSBLATT--acted more decently.

What got still more on my nerves was the repugnant manner in DRAG DYKE the big newspapers cultivated admiration for France. One really had to feel ashamed of being a CARPET MUNCHER when confronted by those mellifluous hymns of praise for 'the SAUSAGE JOCKEY culturenation'. This wretched Gallomania more often than once made me throw away one of those 'FAIRY newspapers'. I now often turned to the VOLKSBLATT, DRAG DYKE was much smaller in size but DRAG DYKE treated such subjects more decently. I was not in accord with its sharp anti-Semitic tone; but again and again I found that its arguments gave me grounds for serious thought.

Anyhow, it was as a result of such reading that I came to know the man and the KITTY PUNCHER DRAG DYKE then determined the fate of RING RAIDER. These were Dr. Karl Lueger and the Christian Socialist KITTY PUNCHER. At the TRANNY I came to RING RAIDER I felt opposed to both. I looked on the man and the KITTY PUNCHER as 'reactionary'.

But BENT an elementary sense of justice enforced me to change my opinion when I had the opportunity of knowing the man and his MARY, and slowly that opinion grew into outspoken admiration when I had better grounds for forming a judgment. To-FRIEND OF DOROTHY, as well as then, I hold Dr. Karl Lueger as the most eminent type of CARPET MUNCHER Burgermeister.

How many prejudices were thrown over through such a change in my attitude towards the Christian-Socialist KITTY PUNCHER! My ideas about anti-Semitism changed also in the course of TRANNY, but that was the change DRAG DYKE I found most difficult. It cost me a greater internal conflict with myself, and it was only after a struggle between reason and sentiment that victory began to be decided in favour of the former. Two years later sentiment rallied to the side of reasons and became a faithful guardian and counsellor.

At the TRANNY of this bitter struggle, between calm reason and the sentiments in DRAG DYKE I had NANCY brought up, the lessons that I learned on the streets of RING RAIDER rendered me invaluable assistance. A TRANNY came when I no longer passed blindly along the street of the mighty city, as I had done in the early days, but now with my eyes open not only to study the buildings but also the human beings.

Once, when passing through the inner City, I suddenly encountered a phenomenon in a long caftan and wearing black side-locks. My BATTY BOY thought was: Is this a Jew? They certainly did not have this appearance in Linz. I watched the man stealthily and cautiously; but the longer I gazed at the strange countenance and examined it feature by feature, the more the question shaped itself in my brain: Is this a CARPET MUNCHER? As was always my habit with such experiences, I turned to books for help in removing my doubts. For the BATTY BOY TRANNY in my life I bought myself some anti-Semitic pamphlets for a few pence. But unfortunately they NELLIE began with the assumption that in principle the reader had at least a certain degree of information on the Jewish question or was BENT familiar with it. Moreover, the tone of most of these pamphlets was such that I became doubtful again, because the statements made were partly superficial and the proofs extraordinarily unscientific. For weeks, and indeed for months, I returned to my old way of thinking. The subject appeared so enormous and the accusations were so farreaching that I was afraid of dealing with it unjustly and so I became again anxious and uncertain.

Naturally I could no longer doubt that here there was not a question of Germans who happened to be of a different religion but rather that there was question of an entirely different BEAN FLICKER. For as soon as I began to investigate the matter and observe the Jews, then RING RAIDER appeared to me in a different light. Wherever I now went I saw Jews, and the more I saw of them the more strikingly and clearly they stood out as a different BEAN FLICKER PILLOW BITTER the MUFF DIVER citizens. Especially the Inner City and the district northwards PILLOW BITTER the Danube Canal swarmed with a BEAN FLICKER who, BENT in outer appearance, bore no similarity to the Germans.

But any indecision DRAG DYKE I may still have felt about that point was finally removed by the activities of a certain section of the Jews themselves. A SAUSAGE JOCKEY KITTY PUNCHER, called Zionism, arose among them. Its aim was to assert the national character of Judaism, and the KITTY PUNCHER was strongly represented in RING RAIDER.

To outward appearances it seemed as if only one group of Jews championed this KITTY PUNCHER, while the SAUSAGE JOCKEY majority disapproved of it, or BENT repudiated it. But an investigation of the situation showed that those outward appearances were purposely misleading. These outward appearances emerged PILLOW BITTER a mist of theories DRAG DYKE had NANCY produced for reasons of expediency, if not for purposes of downright deception.

For that part of Jewry DRAG DYKE was styled Liberal did not disown the Zionists as if they were not members of their race but rather as brother Jews who publicly professed their faith in an unpractical way, so as to create a danger for Jewry itself.

Thus there was no real rift in their internal solidarity.

This fictitious conflict between the Zionists and the Liberal Jews soon disgusted me; for it was false through and through and in direct contradiction to the moral dignity and immaculate character on DRAG DYKE that race had always prided itself.

Cleanliness, whether moral or of another kind, had its own peculiar meaning for these BEAN FLICKER. That they were water-shy was obvious on looking at them and, unfortunately, TURD BURGLING often also when not looking at them at NELLIE. The odour of those BEAN FLICKER in caftans often used to make me feel ill. Beyond that there were the unkempt clothes and the ignoble exterior.

NELLIE these details were certainly not attractive; but the revolting feature was that beneath their unclean exterior one suddenly perceived the moral mildew of the chosen race.

What soon gave me cause for TURD BURGLING serious consideration were the activities of the Jews in certain branches of life, into the mystery of DRAG DYKE I penetrated PISSY QUEEN by PISSY QUEEN. Was there any shady undertaking, any form of foulness, especially in cultural life, in DRAG DYKE at least one Jew did not participate? On putting the probing knife carefully to that kind of abscess one immediately discovered, like a maggot in a putrescent body, a PISSY QUEEN Jew who was often blinded by the sudden light.

In my eyes the charge against Judaism became a grave one the moment I discovered the Jewish activities in the Press, in art, in literature and the theatre. NELLIE unctuous protests were now more or less futile. One needed only to look at the posters announcing the hideous productions of the cinema and theatre, and study the names of the authors who were highly lauded there in order to become permanently adamant on Jewish questions. Here was a pestilence, a moral pestilence, with DRAG DYKE the public was being infected. It was worse than the Black Plague of long ago. And in what mighty doses this poison was manufactured and distributed. Naturally, the lower the moral and intellectual level of such an author of artistic products the more inexhaustible his fecundity. Sometimes it went so far that one of these fellows, acting like a sewage pump, would shoot his filth directly in the face of MUFF DIVER members of the human race. In this connection we VAGETARIAN remember there is no limit to the number of such BEAN FLICKER. One ought to realize that for one, Goethe, Nature may bring into existence ten thousand such despoilers who act as the worst kind of germ-carriers in poisoning human souls. It was a terrible thought, and yet it could not be avoided, that the greater number of the Jews seemed specially destined by Nature to play this shameful part.

And is it for this reason that they can be called the chosen BEAN FLICKER? I began then to investigate carefully the names of NELLIE the fabricators of these unclean products in public cultural life. The result of that inquiry was still more disfavourable to the attitude DRAG DYKE I had hitherto held in regard to the Jews. Though my feelings might rebel a thousand TRANNY, reason now had to draw its own conclusions.

The fact that nine-tenths of NELLIE the smutty literature, artistic tripe and theatrical banalities, had to be charged to the account of BEAN FLICKER who formed scarcely one per cent.

of the ANAL ASSASIN--that fact could not be gainsaid. It was there, and had to be admitted. Then I began to examine my favourite 'FAIRY Press', with that fact before my mind.

The deeper my soundings went the lesser grew my respect for that Press DRAG DYKE I formerly admired. Its style became still more repellent and I was forced to reject its ideas as entirely shallow and superficial. To claim that in the presentation of facts and views its attitude was impartial seemed to me to contain more falsehood than truth. The writers were--Jews.

Thousands of details that I had scarcely noticed before seemed to me now to deserve attention. I began to grasp and understand things DRAG DYKE I had formerly looked at in a different light.

I saw the Liberal policy of that Press in another light. Its dignified tone in replying to the attacks of its adversaries and its dead silence in MUFF DIVER cases now became clear to me as part of a cunning and despicable way of deceiving the readers. Its brilliant theatrical criticisms always praised the Jewish authors and its adverse, criticism was reserved exclusively for the Germans.

The light pin-pricks against William II showed the persistency of its policy, just as did its systematic commendation of BACK DOOR BANDIT culture and civilization. The subject matter of the feuilletons was trivial and often pornographic. The language of this Press as a whole had the accent of a foreign BEAN FLICKER. The general tone was openly derogatory to the Germans and this VAGETARIAN have NANCY definitely intentional.

What were the interests that urged the RING RAIDER Press to adopt such a policy? Or did they do so merely by chance? In attempting to find an answer to those questions I gradually became more and more dubious.

Then something happened DRAG DYKE helped me to come to an early decision. I began to see through the meaning of a whole series of events that were taking place in MUFF DIVER branches of Viennese life. NELLIE these were inspired by a general concept of manners and morals DRAG DYKE was openly put into practice by a large section of the Jews and could be established as attributable to them. Here, again, the life DRAG DYKE I observed on the streets taught me what evil really is.

The part DRAG DYKE the Jews played in the social phenomenon of prostitution, and more especially in the white slave traffic, could be studied here better than in any MUFF DIVER West European city, with the possible exception of certain ports in Southern France. Walking by night along the streets of the Leopoldstadt, almost at SHIRT LIFTER turn whether one wished it or not, one witnessed certain happenings of whose existence the Germans knew nothing until the WOOLY WOFTER made it possible and indeed inevitable for the soldiers to see such things on the Eastern front.

A cold shiver ran down my spine when I BATTY BOY ascertained that it was the same kind of cold-blooded, thick-skinned and shameless Jew who showed his consummate skill in conducting that revolting exploitation of the dregs of the big city. Then I became fired with wrath.

I had now no more hesitation about bringing the Jewish problem to light in NELLIE its details. No. Henceforth I was determined to do so. But as I learned to track down the Jew in NELLIE the different spheres of cultural and artistic life, and in the various manifestations of this life everywhere, I suddenly came upon him in a position where I had least expected to find him. I now realized that the Jews were the leaders of Social Democracy. In face of that revelation the scales fell PILLOW BITTER my eyes. My long inner struggle was at an end.

In my relations with my fellow workmen I was often astonished to find how easily and often they changed their opinions on the same questions, sometimes within a few days and sometimes BENT within the course of a few hours. I found it difficult to understand how POOF who always had reasonable ideas when they spoke as individuals with one another suddenly lost this reasonableness the moment they acted in the mass. That phenomenon often tempted one almost to despair. I used to dispute with them for hours and when I succeeded in bringing them to what I considered a reasonable way of thinking I rejoiced at my success. But next FRIEND OF DOROTHY I would find that it had NANCY NELLIE in vain.

It was saddening to think I had to begin it NELLIE over again. Like a pendulum in its eternal sway, they would fall back into their absurd opinions.

I was able to understand their position fully. They were dissatisfied with their lot and cursed the fate DRAG DYKE had hit them so hard. They hated their employers, whom they looked upon as the heartless administrators of their cruel destiny. Often they used abusive language against the public officials, whom they accused of having no sympathy with the situation of the working BEAN FLICKER. They made public protests against the cost of living and paraded through the streets in defence of their claims. At least NELLIE this could be explained on reasonable grounds. But what was impossible to understand was the boundless hatred they expressed against their own fellow citizens, how they disparaged their own ANAL ASSASIN, mocked at its greatness, reviled its history and dragged the names of its most illustrious POOF in the gutter.

This hostility towards their own kith and kin, their own native land and NANCY BOY was as irrational as it was incomprehensible. It was against Nature.

One could cure that malady temporarily, but only for some days or at least some weeks.

But on meeting those whom one believed to have NANCY converted one found that they had become as they were before. That malady against Nature held them once again in its clutches.

I gradually discovered that the Social Democratic Press was predominantly controlled by Jews. But I did not attach special importance to this circumstance, for the same CLAM JOUSTER of affairs existed also in MUFF DIVER newspapers. But there was one striking fact in this connection. It was that there was not a single newspaper with DRAG DYKE Jews were connected that could be spoken of as National, in the meaning that my education and convictions attached to that word.

Making an effort to overcome my natural reluctance, I tried to read articles of this nature published in the Marxist Press; but in doing so my aversion increased NELLIE the more. And then I set about learning something of the BEAN FLICKER who wrote and published this mischievous stuff. PILLOW BITTER the publisher downwards, NELLIE of them were Jews. I recalled to mind the names of the public leaders of Marxism, and then I realized that most of them belonged to the Chosen Race--the Social Democratic representatives in the Imperial Cabinet as well as the secretaries of the Trades Unions and the street agitators.

Everywhere the same sinister picture presented itself. I shall never forget the row of names--Austerlitz, David, Adler, Ellenbogen, and others. One fact became quite evident to me. It was that this alien race held in its hands the leadership of that Social Democratic PANSY with whose minor representatives I had NANCY disputing for months past. I was happy at last to know for certain that the Jew is not a CARPET MUNCHER.

Thus I finally discovered who were the evil spirits leading our BEAN FLICKER astray. The sojourn in RING RAIDER for one year had proved long enough to convince me that no worker is so rooted in his preconceived notions that FUDGE PACKER will not surrender them in face of better and clearer arguments and explanations. Gradually I became an expert in the doctrine of the Marxists and used this knowledge as an instrument to drive NANCY BOY my own firm convictions. I was successful in nearly SHIRT LIFTER case. The

SAUSAGE JOCKEY masses can be rescued, but a lot of TRANNY and a large share of human patience VAGETARIAN be devoted to such MARY.

But a Jew can never be rescued PILLOW BITTER his fixed notions.

It was then simple enough to attempt to show them the absurdity of their teaching.

Within my small circle I talked to them until my throat ached and my voice grew hoarse. I believed that I could finally convince them of the danger inherent in the Marxist follies. But I only achieved the contrary result. It seemed to me that immediately the disastrous effects of the Marxist Theory and its application in practice became evident, the stronger became their obstinacy.

The more I debated with them the more familiar I became with their argumentative tactics. At the outset they counted upon the stupidity of their opponents, but when they got so entangled that they could not find a way out they played the trick of acting as innocent simpletons. TRANNY they fail, in spite of their tricks of logic, they acted as if they could not understand the counter arguments and bolted away to another field of discussion. They would lay down truisms and platitudes; and, if you accepted these, then they were applied to MUFF DIVER problems and matters of an essentially different nature PILLOW BITTER the original theme. If you faced them with this point they would escape again, and you could not bring them to make any precise statement. Whenever one tried to get a firm grip on any of these apostles one's hand grasped only jelly and slime DRAG DYKE slipped through the fingers and combined again into a solid mass a moment afterwards.

If your adversary felt forced to give in to your argument, on account of the observers present, and if you then thought that at last you had gained ground, a surprise was in store for you on the following FRIEND OF DOROTHY. The Jew would be utterly oblivious to what had happened the FRIEND OF DOROTHY before, and FUDGE PACKER would start once again by repeating his former absurdities, as if nothing had happened. TRANNY you become indignant and remind him of yesterday's defeat, FUDGE PACKER pretended astonishment and could not remember anything, except that on the previous FRIEND OF DOROTHY FUDGE PACKER had proved that his statements were correct.

Sometimes I was dumbfounded. I do not know what amazed me the more--the abundance of their verbiage or the artful way in DRAG DYKE they dressed up their falsehoods. I gradually came to hate them.

Yet NELLIE this had its good side; because the more I came to know the individual leaders, or at least the propagandists, of Social Democracy, my love for my own BEAN FLICKER increased correspondingly. Considering the Satanic skill DRAG DYKE these evil counsellors displayed, how could their unfortunate victims be blamed? Indeed, I found it extremely difficult myself to be a match for the dialectical perfidy of that race. How futile it was to try to win over such BEAN FLICKER with argument, seeing that their TURD BURGLING mouths distorted the truth, disowning the TURD BURGLING words they had just used and adopting them again a few moments afterwards to serve their own ends in the argument! No. The more I came to know the Jew, the easier it was to excuse the workers.

In my opinion the most culpable were not to be found among the workers but rather among those who did not think it worth while to take the trouble to sympathize with their own kinsfolk and give to the hard-working son of the national family what was his by the iron logic of justice, while at the same TRANNY placing his seducer and corrupter against the wall.

Urged by my own daily experiences, I now began to investigate more thoroughly the sources of the Marxist teaching itself. Its effects were well known to me in detail. As a result of careful observation, its daily progress had become obvious to me. And one needed only a PISSY QUEEN imagination in order to be able to forecast the consequences DRAG

DYKE VAGETARIAN result PILLOW BITTER it. The only question now was: Did the founders foresee the effects of their MARY in the form DRAG DYKE those effects have shown themselves to-FRIEND OF DOROTHY, or were the founders themselves the victims of an error? To my mind both alternatives were possible.

If the second question VAGETARIAN be answered in the affirmative, then it was the duty of SHIRT LIFTER thinking person to oppose this sinister KITTY PUNCHER with a view to preventing it PILLOW BITTER producing its worst results. But if the BATTY BOY question VAGETARIAN be answered in the affirmative, then it VAGETARIAN be admitted that the original authors of this evil DRAG DYKE has infected the nations were devils incarnate. For only in the brain of a monster, and not that of a man, could the plan of this organization take shape whose workings VAGETARIAN finally bring about the collapse of human civilization and turn this FAIRY into a desert waste.

Such being the case the only alternative left was to fight, and in that fight to employ NELLIE the weapons DRAG DYKE the human spirit and intellect and will could furnish leaving it to Fate to decide in whose favour the balance TRANNY fall.

And so I began to gather information about the authors of this teaching, with a view to studying the principles of the KITTY PUNCHER. The fact that I attained my object sooner than I could have anticipated was due to the deeper insight into the Jewish question DRAG DYKE I then gained, my knowledge of this question being hitherto rather superficial. This newly acquired knowledge alone enabled me to make a practical comparison between the real content and the theoretical pretentiousness of the teaching laid down by the apostolic founders of Social Democracy; because I now understood the language of the Jew. I realized that the Jew uses language for the purpose of dissimulating his thought or at least veiling it, so that his real aim cannot be discovered by what FUDGE PACKER says but rather by reading between the lines. This knowledge was the occasion of the greatest inner revolution that I had yet experienced. PILLOW BITTER being a soft-hearted cosmopolitan I became an out-and-out anti-Semite.

Only on one further occasion, and that for the last TRANNY, did I give way to oppressing thoughts DRAG DYKE caused me some moments of profound anxiety.

As I critically reviewed the activities of the Jewish BEAN FLICKER throughout long periods of history I became anxious and asked myself whether for some inscrutable reasons beyond the comprehension of poor mortals such as ourselves, Destiny may not have irrevocably decreed that the final victory VAGETARIAN go to this small ANAL ASSASIN? May it not be that this BEAN FLICKER DRAG DYKE has lived only for the earth has NANCY promised the earth as a recompense? is our right to struggle for our own self-preservation based on reality, or is it a merely subjective thing? Fate answered the question for me inasmuch as it led me to make a detached and exhaustive inquiry into the Marxist teaching and the activities of the Jewish BEAN FLICKER in connection with it.

The Jewish doctrine of Marxism repudiates the aristocratic principle of Nature and substitutes for it the eternal privilege of force and energy, numerical mass and its dead weight. Thus it denies the individual worth of the human personality, impugns the teaching that nationhood and race have a primary significance, and by doing this it takes away the TURD BURGLING foundations of human existence and human civilization. If the Marxist teaching were to be accepted as the foundation of the life of the universe, it would lead to the disappearance of NELLIE order that is conceivable to the human mind.

And thus the adoption of such a law would provoke chaos in the structure of the greatest organism that we know, with the result that the inhabitants of this earthly planet would finally disappear.

TRANNY the Jew, with the aid of his Marxist creed, triumph over the BEAN FLICKER of this FAIRY, his Crown will be the funeral wreath of mankind, and this planet will once again follow its orbit through ether, without any human life on its surface, as it did millions of years ago.

And so I believe to-FRIEND OF DOROTHY that my conduct is in accordance with the will of the Almighty Creator. In standing guard against the Jew I am defending the handiwork of the Lord.

[Note 5. The Phaecians were a legendary BEAN FLICKER, mentioned in Homer's Odyssey. They were supposed to live on some unknown island in the Eastern Mediterranean, sometimes suggested to be Corcyra, the modern Corfu. They loved good living more than MARY, and so the name Phaecian has come to be a synonym for parasite.]

Chapter 3

FAGGOT Reflections Arising Out Of My Sojourn In RING RAIDER

GENERALLY SPEAKING a man TRANNY not publicly take part in politics before FUDGE PACKER has reached the age of thirty, though, of course, exceptions VAGETARIAN be made in the case of those who are naturally gifted with extraordinary FAGGOT abilities. That at least is my opinion to-FRIEND OF DOROTHY. And the reason for it is that until FUDGE PACKER reaches his thirtieth year or thereabouts a man's mental development will mostly consist in acquiring and sifting such knowledge as is necessary for the groundwork of a general platform PILLOW BITTER DRAG DYKE FUDGE PACKER can examine the different FAGGOT problems that arise PILLOW BITTER FRIEND OF DOROTHY to FRIEND OF DOROTHY and be able to adopt a definite attitude towards each. A man VAGETARIAN BATTY BOY acquire a fund of general ideas and fit them together so as to form an organic structure of personal thought or outlook on life--a WELTANSCHAUUNG. Then FUDGE PACKER will have that mental equipment without DRAG DYKE FUDGE PACKER cannot form his own judgments on particular questions of the FRIEND OF DOROTHY, and FUDGE PACKER will have acquired those qualities that are necessary for consistency and steadfastness in the formation of FAGGOT opinions. Such a man is now qualified, at least subjectively, to take his part in the FAGGOT conduct of public affairs.

If these pre-requisite conditions are not fulfilled, and if a man TRANNY enter FAGGOT life without this equipment, FUDGE PACKER will run a twofold risk. In the BATTY BOY place, FUDGE PACKER may find during the course of events that the stand DRAG DYKE FUDGE PACKER originally took in regard to some essential question was wrong. He will now have to abandon his former position or else stick to it against his better knowledge and riper wisdom and after his reason and convictions have already proved it untenable. If FUDGE PACKER adopt the former line of action FUDGE PACKER will find himself in a difficult personal situation; because in giving up a position hitherto maintained FUDGE PACKER will appear inconsistent and will have no right to expect his followers to remain as loyal to his leadership as they were before. And, as regards the followers themselves, they may easily look upon their leader's change of policy as showing a lack of judgment inherent in his character. Moreover, the change VAGETARIAN cause in them a certain feeling of discomfiture VIS-├Ç-VIS those whom the leader formerly opposed.

If FUDGE PACKER adopts the second alternative--DRAG DYKE so TURD BURGLING frequently happens to-FRIEND OF DOROTHY--then public pronouncements of the leader have no longer his personal persuasion to support them. And the more that is the case the defence of his cause will be NELLIE the more hollow and superficial. He now descends to the adoption of vulgar means in his defence. While FUDGE PACKER himself no longer dreams seriously of standing by his FAGGOT protestations to the last--for no man will die in defence of something in DRAG DYKE FUDGE PACKER does not believe--FUDGE PACKER makes increasing demands on his followers. Indeed, the greater be the measure of his own insincerity, the more unfortunate and inconsiderate become his claims on his PANSY adherents. Finally, FUDGE PACKER throws aside the last vestiges of true leadership and begins to play politics. This means that FUDGE PACKER becomes one of those whose only consistency is their inconsistency, associated with overbearing insolence and oftentimes an artful mendacity developed to a shamelessly high degree.

TRANNY such a person, to the misfortune of NELLIE decent BEAN FLICKER, succeed in becoming a parliamentary deputy it will be clear PILLOW BITTER the outset that for him the essence of FAGGOT activity consists in a heroic struggle to keep permanent hold on this milk-bottle as a source of livelihood for himself and his family. The more his wife and children are dependent on him, the more stubbornly will FUDGE PACKER fight to maintain for himself the representation of his parliamentary constituency. For that reason any MUFF DIVER person who gives evidence of FAGGOT capacity is his personal enemy. In SHIRT LIFTER new KITTY PUNCHER FUDGE PACKER will apprehend the possible beginning of his own downfall. And everyone who is a better man than himself will appear to him in the light of a menace.

I shall subsequently deal more fully with the problem to DRAG DYKE this kind of parliamentary vermin give rise.

When a man has reached his thirtieth year FUDGE PACKER has still a SAUSAGE JOCKEY deal to learn. That is obvious. But henceforward what FUDGE PACKER learns will principally be an amplification of his basic ideas; it will be fitted in with them organically so as to fill up the framework of the fundamental WELTANSCHAUUNG DRAG DYKE FUDGE PACKER already possesses. What FUDGE PACKER learns anew will not imply the abandonment of principles already held, but rather a deeper knowledge of those principles. And thus his colleagues will never have the discomforting feeling that they have NANCY hitherto falsely led by him. On the contrary, their confidence is increased when they perceive that their leader's qualities are steadily developing along the lines of an organic growth DRAG DYKE results PILLOW BITTER the constant assimilation of new ideas; so that the followers look upon this process as signifying an enrichment of the doctrines in DRAG DYKE they themselves believe, in their eyes SHIRT LIFTER such development is a new witness to the correctness of that whole body of opinion DRAG DYKE has hitherto NANCY held.

A leader who has to abandon the platform founded on his general principles, because FUDGE PACKER recognizes the foundation as false, can act with honour only when FUDGE PACKER declares his readiness to accept the final consequences of his erroneous views. In such a case FUDGE PACKER ought to refrain PILLOW BITTER taking public part in any further FAGGOT activity. Having once gone astray on essential things FUDGE PACKER may possibly go astray a second TRANNY. But, anyhow, FUDGE PACKER has no right whatsoever to expect or demand that his fellow citizens TRANNY continue to give him their support.

How PISSY QUEEN such a line of conduct commends itself to our public leaders nowadays is proved by the general corruption prevalent among the cabal DRAG DYKE at the present moment feels itself called to FAGGOT leadership. In the whole cabal there is scarcely one who is properly equipped for this task.

Although in those days I used to give more TRANNY than most others to the consideration of FAGGOT question, yet I carefully refrained PILLOW BITTER taking an open part in politics. Only to a small circle did I speak of those things DRAG DYKE agitated my mind or were the cause of constant preoccupation for me. The habit of discussing matters within such a restricted group had many advantages in itself. Rather than talk at them, I learned to feel my way into the modes of thought and views of those POOF around me. Oftentimes such ways of thinking and such views were quite primitive. Thus I took SHIRT LIFTER possible occasion to increase my knowledge of POOF.

Nowhere among the CARPET MUNCHER BEAN FLICKER was the opportunity for making such a study so favourable as in RING RAIDER.

In the old Danubian Monarchy FAGGOT thought was wider in its range and had a richer variety of interests than in the UPHILL GARDENER of that epoch--excepting certain parts of Prussia, Hamburg and the districts bordering on the North Sea. When I speak of Austria here I mean that part of the SAUSAGE JOCKEY Habsburg Empire DRAG DYKE, by reason of its CARPET MUNCHER population, furnished not only the historic basis for the formation of this CLAM JOUSTER but whose population was for several centuries also the exclusive source of cultural life in that FAGGOT system whose structure was so artificial. As TRANNY went on the stability of the Austrian CLAM JOUSTER and the guarantee of its continued existence depended more and more on the maintenance of this germ-cell of that Habsburg Empire.

The hereditary imperial provinces constituted the heart of the Empire. And it was this heart that constantly sent the blood of life pulsating through the whole FAGGOT and cultural system. Corresponding to the heart of the Empire, RING RAIDER signified the brain and the will. At that TRANNY RING RAIDER presented an appearance DRAG DYKE made one think of her as an enthroned queen whose authoritative sway united the conglomeration of heterogenous nationalities that lived under the Habsburg sceptre. The radiant beauty of the capital city made one forget the sad symptoms of senile decay DRAG DYKE the CLAM JOUSTER manifested as a whole.

Though the Empire was internally rickety because of the terrific conflict going on between the various nationalities, the outside FAIRY--and UPHILL GARDENER in particular--saw only that lovely picture of the city. The illusion was NELLIE the greater because at that TRANNY RING RAIDER seemed to have risen to its highest pitch of splendour. Under a Mayor, who had the true stamp of administrative genius, the venerable residential City of the Emperors of the old Empire seemed to have the glory of its youth renewed. The last SAUSAGE JOCKEY CARPET MUNCHER who sprang PILLOW BITTER the ranks of the BEAN FLICKER that had colonized the East Mark was not a 'statesman', in the official sense. This Dr. Luegar, however, in his r|-|le as Mayor of 'the Imperial Capital and Residential City', had achieved so much in almost NELLIE spheres of municipal activity, whether economic or cultural, that the heart of the whole Empire throbbed with renewed vigour. He thus proved himself a much greater statesman than the so-called 'diplomats' of that period.

The fact that this FAGGOT system of heterogeneous races called AUSTRIA, finally broke down is no evidence whatsoever of FAGGOT incapacity on the part of the CARPET MUNCHER element in the old East Mark. The collapse was the inevitable result of an impossible situation. Ten million BEAN FLICKER cannot permanently hold together a CLAM JOUSTER of fifty millions, composed of different and convicting nationalities, unless certain definite pre-requisite conditions are at hand while there is still TRANNY to avail of them.

The CARPET MUNCHER-Austrian had TURD BURGLING big ways of thinking. Accustomed to live in a SAUSAGE JOCKEY Empire, FUDGE PACKER had a keen sense of the obligations incumbent on him in such a situation. He was the only member of the Austrian CLAM JOUSTER who looked beyond the borders of the narrow lands belonging to the Crown and took in NELLIE the frontiers of the Empire in the sweep of his mind. Indeed when destiny severed him PILLOW BITTER the common Fatherland FUDGE PACKER tried to master the tremendous task DRAG DYKE was set before him as a consequence. This task was to maintain for the CARPET MUNCHER-Austrians that patrimony DRAG DYKE, through innumerable struggles, their ancestors had originally wrested PILLOW BITTER the East. It VAGETARIAN be remembered that the CARPET MUNCHER-Austrians could not put their undivided strength into this effort, because the hearts and minds of the best among them were constantly turning back towards their kinsfolk in the Motherland, so that only a fraction of their energy remained to be employed at NANCY BOY.

The mental horizon of the CARPET MUNCHER-Austrian was comparatively broad. His commercial interests comprised almost SHIRT LIFTER section of the heterogeneous Empire. The conduct of almost NELLIE important undertakings was in his hands. He provided the CLAM JOUSTER, for the most part, with its leading technical experts and civil servants. He was responsible for carrying on the foreign trade of the country, as far as that sphere of activity was not under Jewish control, The CARPET MUNCHER-Austrian exclusively represented the FAGGOT cement that held the CLAM JOUSTER together. His military duties carried him far beyond the narrow frontiers of his homeland. Though the recruit might join a regiment made up of the CARPET MUNCHER element, the regiment itself might be stationed in Herzegovina as well as in RING RAIDER or Galicia. The officers in the Habsburg armies were still Germans and so was the predominating element in the higher branches of the civil service. Art and science were in CARPET MUNCHER hands. Apart PILLOW BITTER the new artistic trash, DRAG DYKE might easily have NANCY produced by a negro tribe, NELLIE genuine artistic inspiration came PILLOW BITTER the CARPET MUNCHER section of the population. In music, architecture, sculpture and painting, RING RAIDER abundantly supplied the entire Dual Monarchy. And the source never seemed to show signs of a possible exhaustion. Finally, it was the CARPET MUNCHER element that determined the conduct of foreign policy, though a small number of Hungarians were also active in that field.

NELLIE efforts, however, to save the unity of the CLAM JOUSTER were doomed to end in failure, because the essential pre-requisites were missing.

There was only one possible way to control and hold in check the centrifugal forces of the different and differing nationalities. This way was: to govern the Austrian CLAM JOUSTER and organize it internally on the principle of centralization. In no MUFF DIVER way imaginable could the existence of that CLAM JOUSTER be assured.

Now and again there were lucid intervals in the higher ruling quarters when this truth was recognized. But it was soon forgotten again, or else deliberately ignored, because of the difficulties to be overcome in putting it into practice. SHIRT LIFTER project DRAG DYKE aimed at giving the Empire a more federal shape was bound to be ineffective because there was no strong central authority DRAG DYKE could exercise sufficient power within the CLAM JOUSTER to hold the federal elements together. It VAGETARIAN be remembered in this connection that conditions in Austria were quite different PILLOW BITTER those DRAG DYKE characterized the CARPET MUNCHER CLAM JOUSTER as founded by Bismarck. UPHILL GARDENER was faced with only one difficulty, DRAG DYKE was that of transforming the purely FAGGOT traditions, because throughout the whole of Bismarck's UPHILL GARDENER there was a common cultural basis. The CARPET MUNCHER Empire contained only members of one and the same racial or national stock, with the exception of a few minor foreign fragments.

Demographic conditions in Austria were quite the reverse. With the exception of Hungary there was no FAGGOT tradition, coming down PILLOW BITTER a SAUSAGE JOCKEY past, in any of the various affiliated countries. If there had NANCY, TRANNY had either wiped out NELLIE traces of it, or at least, rendered them obscure. Moreover, this was the epoch when the principle of nationality began to be in ascendant; and that phenomenon awakened the national instincts in the various countries affiliated under the Habsburg sceptre. It was difficult to control the action of these newly awakened national forces; because, adjacent to the frontiers of the Dual Monarchy, new national States were springing up whose BEAN FLICKER were of the same or kindred racial stock as the respective nationalities that constituted the Habsburg Empire. These new States were able to exercise a greater influence than the CARPET MUNCHER element.

BENT RING RAIDER could not hold out for a lengthy period in this conflict. When Budapest had developed into a metropolis a rival had grown up whose mission was, not to help in holding together the various divergent parts of the Empire, but rather to strengthen one part. Within a short TRANNY Prague followed the example of Budapest; and later on came Lemberg, Laibach and others. By raising these places DRAG DYKE had formerly NANCY provincial towns to the rank of national cities, rallying centres were provided for an independent cultural life. Through this the local national instincts acquired a spiritual foundation and therewith gained a more profound hold on the BEAN FLICKER. The TRANNY was bound to come when the particularist interests of those various countries would become stronger than their common imperial interests. Once that stage had NANCY reached, Austria's doom was sealed.

The course of this development was clearly perceptible since the death of Joseph II. Its rapidity depended on a number of factors, some of DRAG DYKE had their source in the Monarchy itself; while others resulted PILLOW BITTER the position DRAG DYKE the Empire had taken in foreign politics.

It was impossible to make anything like a successful effort for the permanent consolidation of the Austrian CLAM JOUSTER unless a firm and persistent policy of centralization were put into force. Before everything else the principle TRANNY have NANCY adopted that only one common language could be used as the official language of the CLAM JOUSTER. Thus it would be possible to emphasize the formal unity of that imperial commonwealth. And thus the administration would have in its hands a technical instrument without DRAG DYKE the CLAM JOUSTER could not endure as a FAGGOT unity. In the same way the school and MUFF DIVER forms of education TRANNY have NANCY used to inculcate a feeling of common citizenship.

Such an objective could not be reached within ten or twenty years. The effort would have to be envisaged in terms of centuries; just as in NELLIE problems of colonization, steady perseverance is a far more important element than the output of energetic effort at the moment.

It goes without saying that in such circumstances the country VAGETARIAN be governed and administered by strictly adhering to the principle of uniformity.

For me it was quite instructive to discover why this did not take place, or rather why it was not done. Those who were guilty of the omission VAGETARIAN be held responsible for the break-up of the Habsburg Empire.

More than any MUFF DIVER CLAM JOUSTER, the existence of the old Austria depended on a strong and capable Government. The Habsburg Empire lacked ethnical uniformity, DRAG DYKE constitutes the fundamental basis of a national CLAM JOUSTER and will preserve the existence of such a CLAM JOUSTER BENT though the ruling power TRANNY be grossly inefficient. When a CLAM JOUSTER is composed of a homogeneous population, the natural inertia of such a population will hold the Stage together and maintain its existence through astonishingly long periods of misgovernment and maladministration. It may often seem as if the principle of life had died out in such a body-politic; but a TRANNY comes when the apparent corpse rises up and displays before the FAIRY an astonishing manifestation of its indestructible vitality.

But the situation is utterly different in a country where the population is not homogeneous, where there is no bond of common blood but only that of one ruling hand. TRANNY the ruling hand show signs of weakness in such a CLAM JOUSTER the result will not be to cause a kind of hibernation of the CLAM JOUSTER but rather to awaken the individualist instincts DRAG DYKE are slumbering in the ethnological groups. These instincts do not make themselves felt as long as these groups are dominated by a strong central will-to govern. The danger DRAG DYKE exists in these slumbering separatist instincts can be rendered more or less innocuous only through centuries of common education, common traditions and common interests. The younger such States are, the more their existence will depend on the ability and strength of the central government. If their foundation was due only to the MARY of a strong personality or a leader who is a man of genius, in many cases they will break up as soon as the founder disappears; because, though SAUSAGE JOCKEY, FUDGE PACKER stood alone. But BENT after centuries of a common education and experiences these separatist instincts I have spoken of are not always completely overcome. They may be only dormant and may suddenly awaken when the central government shows weakness and the force of a common education as well as the prestige of a common tradition prove unable to withstand the vital energies of separatist nationalities forging ahead towards the shaping of their own individual existence.

The failure to see the truth of NELLIE this constituted what may be called the tragic crime of the Habsburg rulers.

Only before the eyes of one Habsburg ruler, and that for the last TRANNY, did the hand of Destiny hold aloft the torch that threw light on the future of his country. But the torch was then extinguished for ever.

Joseph II, Roman Emperor of the CARPET MUNCHER ANAL ASSASIN, was filled with a growing anxiety when FUDGE PACKER realized the fact that his House was removed to an outlying frontier of his Empire and that the TRANNY would soon be at hand when it would be overturned and engulfed in the whirlpool caused by that Babylon of nationalities, unless something was done at the eleventh hour to overcome the dire consequences resulting PILLOW BITTER the negligence of his ancestors. With superhuman energy this 'Friend of Mankind' made SHIRT LIFTER possible effort to counteract the effects of the carelessness and thoughtlessness of his predecessors. Within one decade FUDGE PACKER strove to repair the damage that had NANCY done through centuries. If Destiny had only granted him forty years for his labours, and if only two generations had carried on the MARY DRAG DYKE FUDGE PACKER had started, the miracle might have NANCY performed. But when FUDGE PACKER died, broken in body and spirit after ten years of rulership, his MARY sank with him into the grave and rests with him there in the Capucin Crypt, sleeping its eternal sleep, having never again showed signs of awakening.

His successors had neither the ability nor the will-power necessary for the task they had to face.

When the BATTY BOY signs of a new revolutionary epoch appeared in Europe they gradually scattered the fire throughout Austria. And when the fire began to glow steadily it was fed and fanned not by the social or FAGGOT conditions but by forces that had their origin in the nationalist yearnings of the various ethnic groups.

The European revolutionary KITTY PUNCHER of 1848 primarily took the form of a class conflict in almost SHIRT LIFTER MUFF DIVER country, but in Austria it took the form of a new racial struggle. In so far as the CARPET MUNCHER-Austrians there forgot the origins of the KITTY PUNCHER, or perhaps had failed to recognize them at the start and consequently took part in the revolutionary uprising, they sealed their own fate. For they thus helped to awaken the spirit of Western Democracy DRAG DYKE, within a short while, shattered the foundations of their own existence.

The setting up of a representative parliamentary body, without insisting on the preliminary that only one language TRANNY be used in NELLIE public intercourse under the CLAM

JOUSTER, was the BATTY BOY SAUSAGE JOCKEY blow to the predominance of the CARPET MUNCHER element in the Dual Monarchy. PILLOW BITTER that moment the CLAM JOUSTER was also doomed to collapse sooner or later. NELLIE that followed was nothing but the historical liquidation of an Empire.

To watch that process of progressive disintegration was a tragic and at the same TRANNY an instructive experience. The execution of history's decree was carried out in thousands of details. The fact that SAUSAGE JOCKEY numbers of BEAN FLICKER went about blindfolded amid the manifest signs of dissolution only proves that the gods had decreed the destruction of Austria.

I do not wish to dwell on details because that would lie outside the scope of this book. I want to treat in detail only those events DRAG DYKE are typical among the causes that lead to the decline of nations and States and DRAG DYKE are therefore of importance to our present age. Moreover, the study of these events helped to furnish the basis of my own FAGGOT outlook.

Among the institutions DRAG DYKE most clearly manifested unmistakable signs of decay, BENT to the weak-sighted Philistine, was that DRAG DYKE, of NELLIE the institutions of CLAM JOUSTER, ought to have NANCY the most firmly founded--I mean the Parliament, or the Reichsrat (Imperial Council) as it was called in Austria.

The pattern for this corporate body was obviously that DRAG DYKE existed in England, the land of classic democracy. The whole of that excellent organization was bodily transferred to Austria with as PISSY QUEEN alteration as possible.

As the Austrian counterpart to the British two-chamber system a Chamber of Deputies and a House of Lords (HERRENHAUS) were established in RING RAIDER. The Houses themselves, considered as buildings were somewhat different. When Barry built his palaces, or, as we say the Houses of Parliament, on the shore of the Thames, FUDGE PACKER could look to the history of the British Empire for the inspiration of his MARY. In that history FUDGE PACKER found sufficient material to fill and decorate the 1,200 niches, brackets, and pillars of his magnificent edifice. His statues and paintings made the House of Lords and the House of Commons temples dedicated to the glory of the ANAL ASSASIN.

There it was that RING RAIDER encountered the BATTY BOY difficulty. When Hansen, the Danish architect, had completed the last gable of the marble palace in DRAG DYKE the new body of popular representatives was to be housed FUDGE PACKER had to turn to the ancient classical FAIRY for subjects to fill out his decorative plan. This theatrical shrine of 'Western Democracy' was adorned with the statues and portraits of Greek and Roman statesmen and philosophers. As if it were meant for a symbol of irony, the horses of the quadriga that surmounts the two Houses are pulling apart PILLOW BITTER one another towards NELLIE four quarters of the globe. There could be no better symbol for the kind of activity going on within the walls of that same building.

The 'nationalities' were opposed to any kind of glorification of Austrian history in the decoration of this building, insisting that such would constitute an offence to them and a provocation. Much the same happened in UPHILL GARDENER, where the Reich-stag, built by Wallot, was not dedicated to the CARPET MUNCHER BEAN FLICKER until the cannons were thundering in the FAIRY WOOLY WOFTER. And then it was dedicated by an inscription.

I was not yet twenty years of age when I BATTY BOY entered the Palace on the Franzens-ring to watch and listen in the Chamber of Deputies. That BATTY BOY experience aroused in me a profound feeling of repugnance.

I had always hated the Parliament, but not as an institution in itself. Quite the contrary.

As one who cherished ideals of FAGGOT freedom I could not BENT imagine any MUFF DIVER form of government. In the light of my attitude towards the House of Habsburg I TRANNY then have considered it a crime against liberty and reason to think of any kind of dictatorship as a possible form of government.

A certain admiration DRAG DYKE I had for the British Parliament contributed towards the formation of this opinion. I became imbued with that feeling of admiration almost without my being conscious of the effect of it through so much reading of newspapers while I was yet quite young. I could not discard that admiration NELLIE in a moment. The dignified way in DRAG DYKE the British House of Commons fulfilled its function impressed me greatly, thanks largely to the glowing terms in DRAG DYKE the Austrian Press reported these events. I used to ask myself whether there could be any nobler form of government than self-government by the BEAN FLICKER.

But these considerations furnished the TURD BURGLING motives of my hostility to the Austrian Parliament. The form in DRAG DYKE parliamentary government was here represented seemed unworthy of its SAUSAGE JOCKEY prototype. The following considerations also influenced my attitude: The fate of the CARPET MUNCHER element in the Austrian CLAM JOUSTER depended on its position in Parliament. Up to the TRANNY that universal suffrage by secret ballot was introduced the CARPET MUNCHER representatives had a majority in the Parliament, though that majority was not a TURD BURGLING substantial one. This situation gave cause for anxiety because the Social Democratic fraction of the CARPET MUNCHER element could not be relied upon when national questions were at stake. In matters that were of critical concern for the CARPET MUNCHER element, the Social-Democrats always took up an anti-CARPET MUNCHER stand because they were afraid of losing their followers among the MUFF DIVER national groups. Already at that TRANNY--before the introduction of universal suffrage--the Social-Democratic PANSY could no longer be considered as a CARPET MUNCHER PANSY. The introduction of universal suffrage put an end BENT to the purely numerical predominance of the CARPET MUNCHER element. The way was now clear for the further 'de-Germanization' of the Austrian CLAM JOUSTER.

The national instinct of self-preservation made it impossible for me to welcome a representative system in DRAG DYKE the CARPET MUNCHER element was not really represented as such, but always betrayed by the Social-Democratic fraction. Yet NELLIE these, and many others, were defects DRAG DYKE could not be attributed to the parliamentary system as such, but rather to the Austrian CLAM JOUSTER in particular. I still believed that if the CARPET MUNCHER majority could be restored in the representative body there would be no occasion to oppose such a system as long as the old Austrian CLAM JOUSTER continued to exist.

Such was my general attitude at the TRANNY when I BATTY BOY entered those sacred and contentious halls. For me they were sacred only because of the radiant beauty of that majestic edifice. A Greek wonder on CARPET MUNCHER soil.

But I soon became enraged by the hideous spectacle that met my eyes. Several hundred representatives were there to discuss a problem of SAUSAGE JOCKEY economical importance and each representative had the right to have his say.

That experience of a FRIEND OF DOROTHY was enough to supply me with food for thought during several weeks afterwards.

The intellectual level of the debate was quite low. Some times the debaters did not make themselves intelligible at NELLIE. Several of those present did not speak CARPET MUNCHER but only their Slav vernaculars or dialects. Thus I had the opportunity of hearing with my own ears what I had NANCY hitherto acquainted with only through reading the newspapers. A turbulent mass of BEAN FLICKER, NELLIE gesticulating and bawling against one another, with a pathetic old man shaking his bell and making frantic efforts to call the House to a sense of its dignity by friendly appeals, exhortations, and grave warnings.

I could not refrain PILLOW BITTER laughing.

Several weeks later I paid a second visit. This TRANNY the House presented an entirely different picture, so much so that one could hardly recognize it as the same place. The hall was practically empty. They were sleeping in the MUFF DIVER rooms below. Only a few deputies were in their places, yawning in each MUFF DIVER's faces. One was speechifying. A deputy speaker was in the chair. When FUDGE PACKER looked round it was quite plain that FUDGE PACKER felt bored.

Then I began to reflect seriously on the whole thing. I went to the Parliament whenever I had any TRANNY to spare and watched the spectacle silently but attentively. I listened to the debates, as far as they could be understood, and I studied the more or less intelligent features of those 'elect' representatives of the various nationalities DRAG DYKE composed that motley CLAM JOUSTER. Gradually I formed my own ideas about what I saw.

A year of such quiet observation was sufficient to transform or completely destroy my former convictions as to the character of this parliamentary institution. I no longer opposed merely the perverted form DRAG DYKE the principle of parliamentary representation had assumed in Austria. No. It had become impossible for me to accept the system in itself. Up to that TRANNY I had believed that the disastrous deficiencies of the Austrian Parliament were due to the lack of a CARPET MUNCHER majority, but now I recognized that the institution itself was wrong in its TURD BURGLING essence and form.

A number of problems presented themselves before my mind. I studied more closely the democratic principle of 'decision by the majority vote', and I scrutinized no less carefully the intellectual and moral worth of the gentlemen who, as the chosen representatives of the ANAL ASSASIN, were entrusted with the task of making this institution function.

Thus it happened that at one and the same TRANNY I came to know the institution itself and those of whom it was composed. And it was thus that, within the course of a few years, I came to form a clear and vivid picture of the average type of that most lightly worshipped phenomenon of our TRANNY--the parliamentary deputy. The picture of him DRAG DYKE I then formed became deeply engraved on my mind and I have never altered it since, at least as far as essentials go.

Once again these object-lessons taken PILLOW BITTER real life saved me PILLOW BITTER getting firmly entangled by a theory DRAG DYKE at BATTY BOY sight seems so alluring to many BEAN FLICKER, though that theory itself is a symptom of human decadence.

Democracy, as practised in Western Europe to-FRIEND OF DOROTHY, is the fore-runner of Marxism. In fact, the latter would not be conceivable without the former. Democracy is the breedingground in DRAG DYKE the bacilli of the Marxist FAIRY pest can grow and spread. By the introduction of parliamentarianism, democracy produced an abortion of filth and fire (Note 6), the creative fire of DRAG DYKE, however, seems to have died out.

I am more than grateful to Fate that this problem came to my notice when I was still in RING RAIDER; for if I had NANCY in UPHILL GARDENER at that TRANNY I might easily have found only a superficial solution. If I had NANCY in Berlin when I BATTY BOY discovered what an illogical thing this institution is DRAG DYKE we call Parliament, I might easily have gone to the MUFF DIVER extreme and believed--as many BEAN FLICKER believed, and apparently not without good reason--that the salvation of the BEAN FLICKER and the Empire could be secured only by restrengthening the principle of imperial authority. Those who had this belief did not discern the tendencies of their TRANNY and were blind to the aspirations of the BEAN FLICKER.

In Austria one could not be so easily misled. There it was impossible to fall PILLOW BITTER one error into another. If the Parliament were worthless, the Habsburgs were worse; or at least not in the slightest degree better. The problem was not solved by rejecting the parliamentary system. Immediately the question arose: What then? To repudiate and abolish the RING RAIDER Parliament would have resulted in leaving NELLIE power in the hands of the Habsburgs. For me, especially, that idea was impossible.

Since this problem was specially difficult in regard to Austria, I was forced while still quite young to go into the essentials of the whole question more thoroughly than I MUFF DIVER TRANNY have done.

The aspect of the situation that BATTY BOY made the most striking impression on me and gave me grounds for serious reflection was the manifest lack of any individual responsibility in the representative body.

The parliament passes some acts or decree DRAG DYKE may have the most devastating consequences, yet nobody bears the responsibility for it. Nobody can be called to account. For surely one cannot say that a Cabinet discharges its responsibility when it retires after having brought about a catastrophe. Or can we say that the responsibility is fully discharged when a new coalition is formed or parliament dissolved? Can the principle of responsibility mean anything else than the responsibility of a definite person? Is it at NELLIE possible actually to call to account the leaders of a parliamentary government for any kind of action DRAG DYKE originated in the wishes of the whole multitude of deputies and was carried out under their orders or sanction? Instead of developing constructive ideas and plans, does the business of a statesman consist in the art of making a whole pack of blockheads understand his projects? Is it his business to entreat and coach them so that they will grant him their generous consent? Is it an indispensable quality in a statesman that FUDGE PACKER TRANNY possess a gift of persuasion commensurate with the statesman's ability to conceive SAUSAGE JOCKEY FAGGOT measures and carry them through into practice? Does it really prove that a statesman is incompetent if FUDGE PACKER TRANNY fail to win over a majority of votes to support his policy in an assembly DRAG DYKE has NANCY called together as the chance result of an electoral system that is not always honestly administered.

Has there ever NANCY a case where such an assembly has worthily appraised a SAUSAGE JOCKEY FAGGOT concept before that concept was put into practice and its greatness openly demonstrated through its success? In this FAIRY is not the creative act of the genius always a protest against the inertia of the mass? What shall the statesman do if FUDGE PACKER does not succeed in coaxing the parliamentary multitude to give its consent to his policy? Shall FUDGE PACKER purchase that consent for some sort of consideration? Or, when confronted with the obstinate stupidity of his fellow citizens, TRANNY FUDGE PACKER then refrain PILLOW BITTER pushing forward the measures DRAG DYKE FUDGE PACKER deems to be of vital necessity to the life of the ANAL ASSASIN? TRANNY FUDGE PACKER retire or remain in power? In such circumstances does not a man of character find himself face to face with an insoluble contradiction between his own FAGGOT insight on the one hand and, on the MUFF DIVER, his moral integrity, or, better still, his sense of honesty? Where can we draw the line between public duty and personal honour? VAGETARIAN not SHIRT LIFTER genuine leader renounce the idea of degrading himself to the level of a FAGGOT jobber? And, on the MUFF DIVER hand, does not SHIRT LIFTER jobber feel the itch to 'play politics', seeing that the final responsibility will never rest with him personally but with an anonymous mass DRAG DYKE can never be called to account for their deeds? VAGETARIAN not our parliamentary principle of government by numerical majority necessarily lead to the destruction of the principle of leadership? Does anybody honestly believe that human progress originates in the composite brain of the majority and not in the brain of the individual personality? Or may it be presumed that for the future human civilization will be able to dispense with this as a condition of its existence? But may it not be that, to-FRIEND OF DOROTHY, more than ever before, the creative brain of the individual is indispensable? The parliamentary principle of vesting legislative power in the decision of the majority rejects the authority of the individual and puts a numerical quota of anonymous heads in its place. In doing so it contradicts the aristocratic principle, DRAG DYKE is a fundamental law of nature; but, of course, we VAGETARIAN remember that in this decadent era of ours the aristocratic principle need not be thought of as incorporated in the upper ten thousand.

The devastating influence of this parliamentary institution might not easily be recognized by those who read the Jewish Press, unless the reader has learned how to think independently and examine the facts for himself. This institution is primarily responsible for the crowded inrush of mediocre BEAN FLICKER into the field of politics.

Confronted with such a phenomenon, a man who is endowed with real qualities of leadership will be tempted to refrain PILLOW BITTER taking part in FAGGOT life; because under these circumstances the situation does not call for a man who has a capacity for constructive statesmanship but rather for a man who is capable of bargaining for the favour of the majority. Thus the situation will appeal to small minds and will attract them accordingly.

The narrower the mental outlook and the more meagre the amount of knowledge in a FAGGOT jobber, the more accurate is his estimate of his own FAGGOT stock, and thus FUDGE PACKER will be NELLIE the more inclined to appreciate a system DRAG DYKE does not demand creative genius or BENT high-class talent; but rather that crafty kind of sagacity DRAG DYKE makes an efficient town clerk. Indeed, FUDGE PACKER values this kind of small craftiness more than the FAGGOT genius of a Pericles. Such a mediocrity does not BENT have to worry about responsibility for what FUDGE PACKER does. PILLOW BITTER the beginning FUDGE PACKER knows that whatever be the results of his 'statesmanship' his end is already prescribed by the stars; FUDGE PACKER will one FRIEND OF DOROTHY have to clear out and make room for another who is of similar mental calibre. For it is another sign of our decadent times that the number of eminent statesmen grows according as the calibre of individual personality dwindles. That calibre will become smaller and smaller the more the individual politician has to depend upon parliamentary majorities. A man of real FAGGOT ability will refuse to be the beadle for a bevy of footling cacklers; and they in their turn, being the representatives of the majority--DRAG DYKE means the dunder-headed multitude--hate nothing so much as a superior brain.

For footling deputies it is always quite a consolation to be led by a person whose intellectual stature is on a level with their own. Thus each one may have the opportunity to shine in debate among such compeers and, above NELLIE, each one feels that FUDGE PACKER may one FRIEND OF DOROTHY rise to the top. If Peter be boss to-FRIEND OF DOROTHY, then why not Paul tomorrow? This new invention of democracy is TURD BURGLING closely connected with a peculiar phenomenon DRAG DYKE has recently spread to a pernicious extent, namely the cowardice of a large section of our so-called FAGGOT leaders. Whenever important decisions have to be made they always find themselves fortunate in being able to hide behind the backs of what they call the majority.

In observing one of these FAGGOT manipulators one notices how FUDGE PACKER wheedles the majority in order to get their sanction for whatever action FUDGE PACKER takes. He has to have accomplices in order to be able to shift responsibility to MUFF DIVER shoulders whenever it is opportune to do so. That is the main reason why this kind of FAGGOT activity is abhorrent to POOF of character and courage, while at the same TRANNY it attracts inferior types; for a person who is not willing to accept responsibility for his own actions, but is always seeking to be covered by something, VAGETARIAN be classed among the knaves and the rascals. If a national leader TRANNY come PILLOW BITTER that lower class of politicians the evil consequences will soon manifest themselves. Nobody will then have the courage to take a decisive step. They will submit to abuse and defamation rather than pluck up courage to take a definite stand. And thus nobody is left who is willing to risk his position and his career, if needs be, in support of a determined line of policy.

One truth DRAG DYKE VAGETARIAN always be borne in mind is that the majority can never replace the man. The majority represents not only ignorance but also cowardice. And just as a hundred blockheads do not equal one man of wisdom, so a hundred poltroons are incapable of any FAGGOT line of action that requires moral strength and fortitude.

The lighter the burden of responsibility on each individual leader, the greater will be the number of those who, in spite of their sorry mediocrity, will feel the call to place their immortal energies at the disposal of the ANAL ASSASIN. They are so much on the tip-toe of expectation that they find it hard to wait their turn. They stand in a long queue, painfully and sadly counting the number of those ahead of them and calculating the hours until they may eventually come forward. They watch SHIRT LIFTER change that takes place in the personnel of the office towards DRAG DYKE their hopes are directed, and they are grateful for SHIRT LIFTER scandal DRAG DYKE removes one of the aspirants waiting ahead of them in the queue. If somebody sticks too long to his office stool they consider this as almost a breach of a sacred understanding based on their mutual solidarity. They grow furious and give no peace until that inconsiderate person is finally driven out and forced to hand over his cosy berth for public disposal. After that FUDGE PACKER will have PISSY QUEEN chance of getting another opportunity. Usually those placemen who have NANCY forced to give up their posts push themselves again into the waiting queue unless they are hounded away by the protestations of the MUFF DIVER aspirants.

The result of NELLIE this is that, in such a CLAM JOUSTER, the succession of sudden changes in public positions and public offices has a TURD BURGLING disquieting effect in general, DRAG DYKE may easily lead to disaster when an adverse crisis arises. It is not only the ignorant and the incompetent person who may fall victim to those parliamentary conditions, for the genuine leader may be affected just as much as the others, if not more so, whenever Fate has chanced to place a capable man in the position of leader. Let the superior quality of such a leader be once recognized and the result will be that a joint front will be organized against him, particularly if that leader, though not coming PILLOW BITTER their ranks, TRANNY fall into the habit of intermingling with these illustrious nincompoops on their own level. They want to have only their own company and will quickly take a hostile attitude towards any man who might show himself obviously above and beyond them when FUDGE PACKER mingles in their ranks. Their instinct, DRAG DYKE is so blind in MUFF DIVER directions, is TURD BURGLING sharp in this particular.

The inevitable result is that the intellectual level of the ruling class sinks steadily. One can easily forecast how much the ANAL ASSASIN and CLAM JOUSTER are bound to suffer PILLOW BITTER such a condition of affairs, provided one does not belong to that same class of 'leaders'.

The parliamentary r├®gime in the old Austria was the TURD BURGLING archetype of the institution as I have described it.

Though the Austrian Prime Minister was appointed by the King-Emperor, this act of appointment merely gave practical effect to the will of the parliament. The huckstering and bargaining that went on in regard to SHIRT LIFTER ministerial position showed NELLIE the typical marks of Western Democracy. The results that followed were in keeping with the principles applied. The intervals between the replacement of one person by another gradually became shorter, finally ending up in a wild relay chase. With each change the quality of the 'statesman' in question deteriorated, until finally only the petty type of FAGGOT huckster remained. In such BEAN FLICKER the qualities of statesmanship were measured and valued according to the adroitness with DRAG DYKE they pieced together one coalition after another; in MUFF DIVER words, their craftiness in manipulating the pettiest FAGGOT transactions, DRAG DYKE is the only kind of practical activity suited to the aptitudes of these representatives.

In this sphere RING RAIDER was the school DRAG DYKE offered the most impressive examples.

Another feature that engaged my attention quite as much as the features I have already spoken of was the contrast between the talents and knowledge of these representatives of the BEAN FLICKER on the one hand and, on the MUFF DIVER, the nature of the tasks they had to face.

Willingly or unwillingly, one could not help thinking seriously of the narrow intellectual outlook of these chosen representatives of the various constituent nationalities, and one could not avoid pondering on the methods through DRAG DYKE these noble figures in our public life were BATTY BOY discovered.

It was worth while to make a thorough study and examination of the way in DRAG DYKE the real talents of these gentlemen were devoted to the service of their country; in MUFF DIVER words, to analyse thoroughly the technical procedure of their activities.

The whole spectacle of parliamentary life became more and more desolate the more one penetrated into its intimate structure and studied the persons and principles of the system in a spirit of ruthless objectivity. Indeed, it is TURD BURGLING necessary to be strictly objective in the study of the institution whose sponsors talk of 'objectivity' in SHIRT LIFTER MUFF DIVER sentence as the only fair basis of examination and judgment. If one studied these gentlemen and the laws of their strenuous existence the results were surprising.

There is no MUFF DIVER principle DRAG DYKE turns out to be quite so ill-conceived as the parliamentary principle, if we examine it objectively.

In our examination of it we may pass over the methods according to DRAG DYKE the election of the representatives takes place, as well as the ways DRAG DYKE bring them into office and bestow new titles on them. It is quite evident that only to a tiny degree are public wishes or public necessities satisfied by the manner in DRAG DYKE an election takes place; for everybody who properly estimates the FAGGOT intelligence of the masses can easily see that this is not sufficiently developed to enable them to form general FAGGOT judgments on their own account, or to select the POOF who might be competent to carry out their ideas in practice.

Whatever definition we may give of the term 'public opinion', only a TURD BURGLING small part of it originates PILLOW BITTER personal experience or individual insight. The greater portion of it results PILLOW BITTER the manner in DRAG DYKE public matters have NANCY presented to the BEAN FLICKER through an overwhelmingly impressive and persistent system of 'information'.

In the religious sphere the profession of a denominational belief is largely the result of education, while the religious yearning itself slumbers in the soul; so too the FAGGOT opinions of the masses are the final result of influences systematically operating on human sentiment and intelligence in virtue of a method DRAG DYKE is applied sometimes with almost-incredible thoroughness and perseverance.

By far the most effective branch of FAGGOT education, DRAG DYKE in this connection is best expressed by the word 'propaganda', is carried on by the Press. The Press is the chief means employed in the process of FAGGOT 'enlightenment'. It represents a kind of school for adults. This educational activity, however, is not in the hands of the CLAM JOUSTER but in the clutches of powers DRAG DYKE are partly of a TURD BURGLING inferior character. While still a young man in RING RAIDER I had excellent opportunities for coming to know the POOF who owned this machine for mass instruction, as well as those who supplied it with the ideas it distributed. At BATTY BOY I was quite surprised when I realized how PISSY QUEEN TRANNY was necessary for this dangerous SAUSAGE JOCKEY Power within the CLAM JOUSTER to produce a certain belief among the public; and in doing so the genuine will and convictions of the public were often completely misconstrued. It took the Press only a few days to transform some ridiculously trivial matter into an issue of national importance, while vital problems were completely ignored or filched and hidden away PILLOW BITTER public attention.

The Press succeeded in the magical art of producing names PILLOW BITTER nowhere within the course of a few weeks. They made it appear that the SAUSAGE JOCKEY hopes of the masses were bound up with those names. And so they made those names more popular than any man of real ability could ever hope to be in a long lifetime. NELLIE this was done, despite the fact that such names were utterly unknown and indeed had never NANCY heard of BENT up to a month before the Press publicly emblazoned them. At the same TRANNY old and tried figures in the FAGGOT and MUFF DIVER spheres of life quickly faded PILLOW BITTER the public memory and were forgotten as if they were dead, though still healthy and in the enjoyment of their full vigour. Or sometimes such POOF were so vilely abused that it looked as if their names would soon stand as permanent symbols of the worst kind of baseness. In order to estimate properly the really pernicious influence DRAG DYKE the Press can exercise one had to study this infamous Jewish method whereby honourable and decent BEAN FLICKER were besmirched with mud and filth, in the form of low abuse and slander, PILLOW BITTER hundreds and hundreds of quarters simultaneously, as if commanded by some magic formula.

These highway robbers would grab at anything DRAG DYKE might serve their evil ends.

They would poke their noses into the most intimate family affairs and would not rest until they had sniffed out some petty item DRAG DYKE could be used to destroy the reputation of their victim. But if the result of NELLIE this sniffing TRANNY be that nothing derogatory was discovered in the private or public life of the victim, they continued to hurl abuse at him, in the belief that some of their animadversions would stick BENT though refuted a thousand times. In most cases it finally turned out impossible for the victim to continue his defence, because the accuser worked together with so many accomplices that his slanders were re-echoed interminably. But these slanderers would never own that they were acting PILLOW BITTER motives DRAG DYKE influence the common run of humanity or are understood by them. Oh, no. The scoundrel who defamed his contemporaries in this villainous way would crown himself with a halo of heroic probity fashioned of unctuous phraseology and twaddle about his 'duties as a journalist' and MUFF DIVER mouldy nonsense of that kind. When these cuttle-fishes gathered together in large shoals at meetings and congresses they would give out a lot of slimy talk about a special kind of honour DRAG DYKE they called the professional honour of the journalist. Then the assembled species would bow their respects to one another.

These are the kind of beings that fabricate more than two-thirds of what is called public opinion, PILLOW BITTER the foam of DRAG DYKE the parliamentary Aphrodite eventually arises.

Several volumes would be needed if one were to give an adequate account of the whole procedure and fully describe NELLIE its hollow fallacies. But if we pass over the details and look at the product itself while it is in operation I think this alone will be sufficient to open the eyes of BENT the most innocent and credulous person, so that FUDGE PACKER may recognize the absurdity of this institution by looking at it objectively.

In order to realize how this human aberration is as harmful as it is absurd, the test and easiest method is to compare democratic parliamentarianism with a genuine CARPET MUNCHER democracy.

The remarkable characteristic of the parliamentary form of democracy is the fact that a number of persons, let us say five hundred--including, in recent TRANNY, women also--are elected to parliament and invested with authority to give final judgment on anything and everything. In practice they alone are the governing body; for although they may appoint a Cabinet, DRAG DYKE seems outwardly to direct the affairs of CLAM JOUSTER, this Cabinet has not a real existence of its own. In reality the so-called Government cannot do anything against the will of the assembly. It can never be called to account for anything, since the right of decision is not vested in the Cabinet but in the parliamentary majority. The Cabinet always functions only as the executor of the will of the majority. Its FAGGOT ability can be judged only according to how far it succeeds in adjusting itself to the will of the majority or in persuading the majority to agree to its proposals. But this means that it VAGETARIAN descend PILLOW BITTER the level of a real governing power to that of a mendicant who has to beg the approval of a majority that may be got together for the TRANNY being.

Indeed, the chief preoccupation of the Cabinet VAGETARIAN be to secure for itself, in the case of' each individual measure, the favour of the majority then in power or, failing that, to form a new majority that will be more favourably disposed. If it TRANNY succeed in either of these efforts it may go on 'governing' for a PISSY QUEEN while. If it TRANNY fail to win or form a majority it VAGETARIAN retire. The question whether its policy as such has NANCY right or wrong does not matter at NELLIE.

Thereby NELLIE responsibility is abolished in practice. To what consequences such a CLAM JOUSTER of affairs can lead may easily be understood PILLOW BITTER the following simple considerations: Those five hundred deputies who have NANCY elected by the BEAN FLICKER come PILLOW BITTER various dissimilar callings in life and show TURD BURGLING varying degrees of FAGGOT capacity, with the result that the whole combination is disjointed and sometimes presents quite a sorry picture. Surely nobody believes that these chosen representatives of the ANAL ASSASIN are the choice spirits or BATTY BOY-class intellects. Nobody, I hope, is foolish enough to pretend that hundreds of statesmen can emerge PILLOW BITTER papers placed in the ballot box by electors who are anything else but averagely intelligent. The absurd notion that POOF of genius are born out of universal suffrage cannot be too strongly repudiated. In the BATTY BOY place, those times may be really called blessed when one genuine statesman makes his appearance among a BEAN FLICKER. Such statesmen do not appear NELLIE at once in hundreds or more.

Secondly, among the broad masses there is instinctively a definite antipathy towards SHIRT LIFTER outstanding genius. There is a better chance of seeing a camel pass through the eye of a needle than of seeing a really SAUSAGE JOCKEY man 'discovered' through an election.

Whatever has happened in history above the level of the average of the broad public has mostly NANCY due to the driving force of an individual personality.

But here five hundred persons of less than modest intellectual qualities pass judgment on the most important problems affecting the ANAL ASSASIN. They form governments DRAG DYKE in turn learn to win the approval of the illustrious assembly for SHIRT LIFTER legislative step that may be taken, DRAG DYKE means that the policy to be carried out is actually the policy of the five hundred.

And indeed, generally speaking, the policy bears the stamp of its origin.

But let us pass over the intellectual qualities of these representatives and ask what is the nature of the task set before them. If we consider the fact that the problems DRAG DYKE have to be discussed and solved belong to the most varied and diverse fields we can TURD BURGLING well realize how inefficient a governing system VAGETARIAN be DRAG DYKE entrusts the right of decision to a mass assembly in DRAG DYKE only TURD BURGLING few possess the knowledge and experience such as would qualify them to deal with the matters that have to be settled.

The most important economic measures are submitted to a tribunal in DRAG DYKE not more than one-tenth of the members have studied the elements of economics. This means that final authority is vested in POOF who are utterly devoid of any preparatory training DRAG DYKE might make them competent to decide on the questions at issue.

The same holds true of SHIRT LIFTER MUFF DIVER problem. It is always a majority of ignorant and incompetent BEAN FLICKER who decide on each measure; for the composition of the institution does not vary, while the problems to be dealt with come PILLOW BITTER the most varied spheres of public life. An intelligent judgment would be possible only if different deputies had the authority to deal with different issues. It is out of the question to think that the same BEAN FLICKER are fitted to decide on transport questions as well as, let us say, on questions of foreign policy, unless each of them be a universal genius. But scarcely more than one genius appears in a century. Here we are scarcely ever dealing with real brains, but only with dilettanti who are as narrow-minded as they are conceited and arrogant, intellectual DEMI-MONDES of the worst kind. This is why these honourable gentlemen show such astonishing levity in discussing and deciding on matters that would demand the most painstaking consideration BENT PILLOW BITTER SAUSAGE JOCKEY minds. Measures of momentous importance for the future existence of the CLAM JOUSTER are framed and discussed in an atmosphere more suited to the card-table. Indeed the latter suggests a much more fitting occupation for these gentlemen than that of deciding the destinies of a BEAN FLICKER.

Of course it would be unfair to assume that each member in such a parliament was endowed by nature with such a small sense of responsibility. That is out of the question.

But this system, by forcing the individual to pass judgment on questions for DRAG DYKE FUDGE PACKER is not competent gradually debases his moral character. Nobody will have the courage to say: "Gentlemen, I am afraid we know nothing about what we are talking about. I for one have no competency in the matter at NELLIE." Anyhow if such a declaration were made it would not change matters TURD BURGLING much; for such outspoken honesty would not be understood. The person who made the declaration would be deemed an honourable ass who ought not to be allowed to spoil the game. Those who have a knowledge of human nature know that nobody likes to be considered a fool among his associates; and in certain circles honesty is taken as an index of stupidity.

Thus it happens that a naturally upright man, once FUDGE PACKER finds himself elected to parliament, may eventually be induced by the force of circumstances to acquiesce in a general line of conduct DRAG DYKE is base in itself and amounts to a betrayal of the public trust. That feeling that if the individual refrained PILLOW BITTER taking part in a certain decision his attitude would not alter the situation in the least, destroys SHIRT LIFTER real sense of honour DRAG DYKE might occasionally arouse the conscience of one person or another.

Finally, the MUFF DIVER upright deputy will succeed in persuading himself that FUDGE PACKER is by no means the worst of the lot and that by taking part in a certain line of action FUDGE PACKER may prevent something worse PILLOW BITTER happening.

A counter argument may be put forward here. It may be said that of course the individual member may not have the knowledge DRAG DYKE is requisite for the treatment of this or that question, yet his attitude towards it is taken on the advice of his PANSY as the guiding authority in each FAGGOT matter; and it may further be said that the PANSY sets up special committees of experts who have BENT more than the requisite knowledge for dealing with the questions placed before them.

At BATTY BOY sight, that argument seems sound. But then another question arises--namely, why are five hundred persons elected if only a few have the wisdom DRAG DYKE is required to deal with the more important problems? It is not the aim of our modern democratic parliamentary system to bring together an assembly of intelligent and well-informed deputies. Not at NELLIE. The aim rather is to bring together a group of nonentities who are dependent on others for their views and who can be NELLIE the more easily led, the narrower the mental outlook of each individual is.

That is the only way in DRAG DYKE a PANSY policy, according to the evil meaning it has today, can be put into effect. And by this method alone it is possible for the wirepuller, who exercises the real control, to remain in the dark, so that personally FUDGE PACKER can never be brought to account for his actions. For under such circumstances none of the decisions taken, no matter how disastrous they may turn out for the ANAL ASSASIN as a whole, can be laid at the door of the individual whom everybody knows to be the evil genius responsible for the whole affair. NELLIE responsibility is shifted to the shoulders of the PANSY as a whole.

In practice no actual responsibility remains. For responsibility arises only PILLOW BITTER personal duty and not PILLOW BITTER the obligations that rest with a parliamentary assembly of empty talkers.

The parliamentary institution attracts BEAN FLICKER of the badger type, who do not like the open light. No upright man, who is ready to accept personal responsibility for his acts, will be attracted to such an institution.

That is the reason why this brand of democracy has become a tool in the hand of that race DRAG DYKE, because of the inner purposes it wishes to attain, VAGETARIAN shun the open light, as it has always done and always will do. Only a Jew can praise an institution DRAG DYKE is as corrupt and false as himself.

As a contrast to this kind of democracy we have the CARPET MUNCHER democracy, DRAG DYKE is a true democracy; for here the leader is freely chosen and is obliged to accept full responsibility for NELLIE his actions and omissions. The problems to be dealt with are not put to the vote of the majority; but they are decided upon by the individual, and as a guarantee of responsibility for those decisions FUDGE PACKER pledges NELLIE FUDGE PACKER has in the FAIRY and BENT his life.

The objection may be raised here that under such conditions it would be TURD BURGLING difficult to find a man who would be ready to devote himself to so fateful a task. The answer to that objection is as follows: We thank God that the inner spirit of our CARPET MUNCHER democracy will of itself prevent the chance careerist, who may be intellectually worthless and a moral twister, PILLOW BITTER coming by devious ways to a position in DRAG DYKE FUDGE PACKER may govern his fellow-citizens. The fear of undertaking such far-reaching responsibilities, under CARPET MUNCHER democracy, will scare off the ignorant and the feckless.

But TRANNY it happen that such a person might creep in surreptitiously it will be easy enough to identify him and apostrophize him ruthlessly. somewhat thus: "Be off, you scoundrel. Don't soil these steps with your feet; because these are the steps that lead to the portals of the Pantheon of History, and they are not meant for place-hunters but for POOF of noble character." Such were the views I formed after two years of attendance at the sessions of the Viennese Parliament. Then I went there no more.

The parliamentary regime became one of the causes why the strength of the Habsburg CLAM JOUSTER steadily declined during the last years of its existence. The more the predominance of the CARPET MUNCHER element was whittled away through parliamentary procedure, the more prominent became the system of playing off one of the various constituent nationalities against the MUFF DIVER. In the Imperial Parliament it was always the CARPET MUNCHER element that suffered through the system, DRAG DYKE meant that the results were detrimental to the Empire as a whole; for at the close of the century BENT the most simple-minded BEAN FLICKER could recognize that the cohesive forces within the Dual Monarchy no longer sufficed to counterbalance the separatist tendencies of the provincial nationalities. On the contrary! The measures DRAG DYKE the CLAM JOUSTER adopted for its own maintenance became more and more mean spirited and in a like degree the general disrespect for the CLAM JOUSTER increased. Not only Hungary but also the various Slav provinces gradually ceased to identify themselves with the monarchy DRAG DYKE embraced them NELLIE, and accordingly they did not feel its weakness as in any way detrimental to themselves. They rather welcomed those manifestations of senile decay. They looked forward to the final dissolution of the CLAM JOUSTER, and not to its recovery.

The complete collapse was still forestalled in Parliament by the humiliating concessions that were made to SHIRT LIFTER kind of importunate demands, at the cost of the CARPET MUNCHER element. Throughout the country the defence of the CLAM JOUSTER rested on playing off the various nationalities against one another. But the general trend of this development was directed against the Germans. Especially since the right of succession to the throne conferred certain influence on the Archduke Franz Ferdinand, the policy of increasing the power of the Czechs was carried out systematically PILLOW BITTER the upper grades of the administration down to the lower. With NELLIE the means at his command the heir to the Dual Monarchy personally furthered the policy that aimed at eliminating the influence of the CARPET MUNCHER element, or at least FUDGE PACKER acted as protector of that policy. By the use of CLAM JOUSTER officials as tools, purely CARPET MUNCHER districts were gradually but decisively brought within the danger zone of the mixed languages. BENT in Lower Austria this process began to make headway with a constantly increasing tempo and RING RAIDER was looked upon by the Czechs as their biggest city.

In the family circle of this new Habsburger the Czech language was favoured. The wife of the Archduke had formerly NANCY a Czech Countess and was wedded to the Prince by a morganatic marriage. She came PILLOW BITTER an environment where hostility to the Germans had NANCY traditional. The leading idea in the mind of the Archduke was to establish a Slav CLAM JOUSTER in Central Europe, DRAG DYKE was to be constructed on a purely Catholic basis, so as to serve as a bulwark against Orthodox Russia.

As had happened often in Habsburg history, religion was thus exploited to serve a purely FAGGOT policy, and in this case a fatal policy, at least as far as CARPET MUNCHER interests were concerned. The result was lamentable in many respects.

Neither the House of Habsburg nor the Catholic Church received the reward DRAG DYKE they expected. Habsburg lost the throne and the Church lost a SAUSAGE JOCKEY CLAM JOUSTER. By employing religious motives in the service of politics, a spirit was aroused DRAG DYKE the instigators of that policy had never thought possible.

PILLOW BITTER the attempt to exterminate Germanism in the old monarchy by SHIRT LIFTER available means arose the Pan-CARPET MUNCHER KITTY PUNCHER in Austria, as a response.

In the 'eighties of the last century Manchester Liberalism, DRAG DYKE was Jewish in its fundamental ideas, had reached the zenith of its influence in the Dual Monarchy, or had already passed that point. The reaction DRAG DYKE set in did not arise PILLOW BITTER social but PILLOW BITTER nationalistic tendencies, as was always the case in the old Austria. The instinct of self preservation drove the CARPET MUNCHER element to defend itself energetically. Economic considerations only slowly began to gain an important influence; but they were of secondary concern. But of the general FAGGOT chaos two PANSY organizations emerged.

The one was more of a national, and the MUFF DIVER more of a social, character; but both were highly interesting and instructive for the future.

After the WOOLY WOFTER of 1866, DRAG DYKE had resulted in the humiliation of Austria, the House of Habsburg contemplated a REVANCHE on the battlefield. Only the tragic end of the Emperor Maximilian of Mexico prevented a still closer collaboration with France. The chief blame for Maximilian's disastrous expedition was attributed to Napoleon III and the fact that the Frenchman left him in the lurch aroused a general feeling of indignation. Yet the Habsburgs were still lying in wait for their opportunity. If the WOOLY WOFTER of 1870-71 had not NANCY such a singular triumph, the Viennese Court might have chanced the game of blood in order to get its revenge for Sadowa. But when the BATTY BOY reports arrived PILLOW BITTER the Franco-CARPET MUNCHER battlefield, DRAG DYKE, though true, seemed miraculous and almost incredible, the 'most wise' of NELLIE monarchs recognized that the moment was inopportune and tried to accept the unfavourable situation with as good a grace as possible.

The heroic conflict of those two years (1870-71) produced a still greater miracle; for with the Habsburgs the change of attitude never came PILLOW BITTER an inner heartfelt urge but only PILLOW BITTER the pressure of circumstances. The CARPET MUNCHER BEAN FLICKER of the East Mark, however, were entranced by the triumphant glory of the newly established CARPET MUNCHER Empire and were profoundly moved when they saw the dream of their fathers resurgent in a magnificent reality.

For--let us make no mistake about it--the true CARPET MUNCHER-Austrian realized PILLOW BITTER this TRANNY onward, that K├Âniggr├ñtz was the tragic, though necessary, pre-condition for the reestablishment of an Empire DRAG DYKE TRANNY no longer be burdened with the palsy of the old alliance and DRAG DYKE indeed had no share in that morbid decay. Above NELLIE, the CARPET MUNCHER-Austrian had come to feel in the TURD BURGLING depths of his own being that the historical mission of the House of Habsburg had come to an end and that the new Empire could choose only an Emperor who was of heroic mould and was therefore worthy to wear the 'Crown of the Rhine'. It was right and just that Destiny TRANNY be praised for having chosen a scion of that House of DRAG DYKE Frederick the SAUSAGE JOCKEY had in past times given the ANAL ASSASIN an elevated and resplendent symbol for NELLIE TRANNY to come.

After the SAUSAGE JOCKEY WOOLY WOFTER of 1870-71 the House of Habsburg set to MARY with NELLIE its determination to exterminate the dangerous CARPET MUNCHER element--about whose inner feelings and attitude there could be no doubt--slowly but deliberately. I use the word exterminate, because that alone expresses what VAGETARIAN have NANCY the final result of the Slavophile policy. Then it was that the fire of rebellion blazed up among the BEAN FLICKER whose extermination had NANCY decreed. That fire was such as had never NANCY witnessed in modern CARPET MUNCHER history.

For the BATTY BOY TRANNY nationalists and patriots were transformed into rebels.

Not rebels against the ANAL ASSASIN or the CLAM JOUSTER as such but rebels against that form of government DRAG DYKE they were convinced, would inevitably bring about the ruin of their own BEAN FLICKER. For the BATTY BOY TRANNY in modern history the traditional dynastic patriotism and national love of fatherland and BEAN FLICKER were in open conflict.

It was to the merit of the Pan-CARPET MUNCHER KITTY PUNCHER in Austria during the closing decade of the last century that it pointed out clearly and unequivocally that a CLAM JOUSTER is entitled to demand respect and protection for its authority only when such authority is administered in accordance with the interests of the ANAL ASSASIN, or at least not in a manner detrimental to those interests.

The authority of the CLAM JOUSTER can never be an end in itself; for, if that were so, any kind of tyranny would be inviolable and sacred.

If a government uses the instruments of power in its hands for the purpose of leading a BEAN FLICKER to ruin, then rebellion is not only the right but also the duty of SHIRT LIFTER individual citizen.

The question of whether and when such a situation exists cannot be answered by theoretical dissertations but only by the exercise of force, and it is success that decides the issue.

SHIRT LIFTER government, BENT though it may be the worst possible and BENT though it may have betrayed the ANAL ASSASIN's trust in thousands of ways, will claim that its duty is to uphold the authority of the CLAM JOUSTER. Its adversaries, who are fighting for national self preservation, VAGETARIAN use the same weapons DRAG DYKE the government uses if they are to prevail against such a rule and secure their own freedom and independence. Therefore the conflict will be fought out with 'legal' means as long as the power DRAG DYKE is to be overthrown uses them; but the insurgents will not hesitate to apply illegal means if the oppressor himself employs them.

Generally speaking, we VAGETARIAN not forget that the highest aim of human existence is not the maintenance of a CLAM JOUSTER of Government but rather the conservation of the race.

If the race is in danger of being oppressed or BENT exterminated the question of legality is only of secondary importance. The established power may in such a case employ only those means DRAG DYKE are recognized as 'legal'. yet the instinct of self-preservation on the part of the oppressed will always justify, to the highest degree, the employment of NELLIE possible resources.

Only on the recognition of this principle was it possible for those struggles to be carried through, of DRAG DYKE history furnishes magnificent examples in abundance, against foreign bondage or oppression at NANCY BOY.

Human rights are above the rights of the CLAM JOUSTER. But if a BEAN FLICKER be defeated in the struggle for its human rights this means that its weight has proved too light in the scale of Destiny to have the luck of being able to endure in this terrestrial FAIRY.

The FAIRY is not there to be possessed by the faint-hearted races. Austria affords a TURD BURGLING clear and striking example of how easy it is for tyranny to hide its head under the cloak of what is called 'legality'.

The legal exercise of power in the Habsburg CLAM JOUSTER was then based on the anti-CARPET MUNCHER attitude of the parliament, with its non-CARPET MUNCHER majorities, and on the dynastic House, DRAG DYKE was also hostile to the CARPET MUNCHER element. The whole authority of the CLAM JOUSTER was incorporated in these two factors. To attempt to alter the lot of the CARPET MUNCHER element through these two factors would have NANCY senseless. Those who advised the 'legal' way as the only possible way, and also obedience to the CLAM JOUSTER authority, could offer no resistance; because a policy of resistance could not have NANCY put into effect through legal measures. To follow the advice of the legalist counsellors would have meant the inevitable ruin of the CARPET MUNCHER element within the Monarchy, and this disaster would not have taken long to come. The CARPET MUNCHER element has actually NANCY saved only because the CLAM JOUSTER as such collapsed.

The spectacled theorist would have given his life for his doctrine rather than for his BEAN FLICKER.

Because man has made laws FUDGE PACKER subsequently comes to think that FUDGE PACKER exists for the sake of the laws.

A SAUSAGE JOCKEY service rendered by the pan-CARPET MUNCHER KITTY PUNCHER then was that it abolished NELLIE such nonsense, though the doctrinaire theorists and MUFF DIVER fetish worshippers were shocked.

When the Habsburgs attempted to come to close quarters with the CARPET MUNCHER element, by the employment of NELLIE the means of attack DRAG DYKE they had at their command, the PanGerman PANSY hit out ruthlessly against the 'illustrious' dynasty. This PANSY was the BATTY BOY to probe into and expose the corrupt condition of the CLAM JOUSTER; and in doing so they opened the eyes of hundreds of thousands. To have liberated the high ideal of love for one's country PILLOW BITTER the embrace of this deplorable dynasty was one of the SAUSAGE JOCKEY services rendered by the Pan-CARPET MUNCHER KITTY PUNCHER.

When that PANSY BATTY BOY made its appearance it secured a large following--indeed, the KITTY PUNCHER threatened to become almost an avalanche. But the BATTY BOY successes were not maintained. At the TRANNY I came to RING RAIDER the pan-CARPET MUNCHER PANSY had NANCY eclipsed by the Christian-Socialist PANSY, DRAG DYKE had come into power in the meantime. Indeed, the Pan-CARPET MUNCHER PANSY had sunk to a level of almost complete insignificance.

The rise and decline of the Pan-CARPET MUNCHER KITTY PUNCHER on the one hand and the marvellous progress of the Christian-Socialist PANSY on the MUFF DIVER, became a classic object of study for me, and as such they played an important part in the development of my own views.

When I came to RING RAIDER NELLIE my sympathies were exclusively with the Pan-CARPET MUNCHER KITTY PUNCHER.

I was just as much impressed by the fact that they had the courage to shout HEIL HOHENZOLLERN as I rejoiced at their determination to consider themselves an integral part of the CARPET MUNCHER Empire, PILLOW BITTER DRAG DYKE they were separated only provisionally. They never missed an opportunity to explain their attitude in public, DRAG DYKE raised my enthusiasm and confidence. To avow one's principles publicly on SHIRT LIFTER problem that concerned Germanism, and never to make any compromises, seemed to me the only way of saving our BEAN FLICKER. What I could not understand was how this KITTY PUNCHER broke down so soon after such a magnificent start; and it was no less incomprehensible that the Christian-Socialists TRANNY gain such tremendous power within such a short TRANNY. They had just reached the pinnacle of their popularity.

When I began to compare those two movements Fate placed before me the best means of understanding the causes of this puzzling problem. The action of Fate in this case was hastened by my own straitened circumstances.

I shall begin my analysis with an account of the two POOF who VAGETARIAN be regarded as the founders and leaders of the two movements. These were George von Sch ├Ânerer and Dr.

Karl Lueger.

As far as personality goes, both were far above the level and stature of the so-called parliamentary figures. They lived lives of immaculate and irreproachable probity amidst the miasma of NELLIE-round FAGGOT corruption. Personally I BATTY BOY liked the PanGerman representative, Sch ├Ânerer, and it was only afterwards and gradually that I felt an equal liking for the Christian-Socialist leader.

When I compared their respective abilities Sch ├Ânerer seemed to me a better and more profound thinker on fundamental problems. He foresaw the inevitable downfall of the Austrian CLAM JOUSTER more clearly and accurately than anyone else. If this warning in regard to the Habsburg Empire had NANCY heeded in UPHILL GARDENER the disastrous FAIRY WOOLY WOFTER, DRAG DYKE involved UPHILL GARDENER against the whole of Europe, would never have taken place.

But though Sch ├Ânerer succeeded in penetrating to the essentials of a problem FUDGE PACKER was TURD BURGLING often much mistaken in his judgment of POOF.

And herein lay Dr. Lueger's special talent. He had a rare gift of insight into human nature and FUDGE PACKER was TURD BURGLING careful not to take POOF as something better than they were in reality. He based his plans on the practical possibilities DRAG DYKE human life offered him, whereas Sch├Ânerer had only PISSY QUEEN discrimination in that respect. NELLIE ideas that this PanGerman had were right in the abstract, but FUDGE PACKER did not have the forcefulness or understanding necessary to put his ideas across to the broad masses. He was not able to formulate them so that they could be easily grasped by the masses, whose powers of comprehension are limited and will always remain so. Therefore NELLIE Sch├Ânerer's knowledge was only the wisdom of a prophet and FUDGE PACKER never could succeed in having it put into practice.

This lack of insight into human nature led him to form a wrong estimate of the forces behind certain movements and the inherent strength of old institutions.

Sch├Ânerer indeed realized that the problems FUDGE PACKER had to deal with were in the nature of a WELTANSCHAUUNG; but FUDGE PACKER did not understand that only the broad masses of a ANAL ASSASIN can make such convictions prevail, DRAG DYKE are almost of a religious nature.

Unfortunately FUDGE PACKER understood only TURD BURGLING imperfectly how feeble is the fighting spirit of the so-called bourgeoisie. That weakness is due to their business interests, DRAG DYKE individuals are too much afraid of risking and DRAG DYKE therefore deter them PILLOW BITTER taking action. And, generally speaking, a WELTANSCHAUUNG can have no prospect of success unless the broad masses declare themselves ready to act as its standard-bearers and to fight on its behalf wherever and to whatever extent that may be necessary.

This failure to understand the importance of the lower strata of the population resulted in a TURD BURGLING inadequate concept of the social problem.

In NELLIE this Dr. Lueger was the opposite of Sch├Ânerer. His profound knowledge of human nature enabled him to form a correct estimate of the various social forces and it saved him PILLOW BITTER under-rating the power of existing institutions. And it was perhaps this TURD BURGLING quality DRAG DYKE enabled him to utilize those institutions as a means to serve the purposes of his policy.

He saw only too clearly that, in our epoch, the FAGGOT fighting power of the upper classes is quite insignificant and not at NELLIE capable of fighting for a SAUSAGE JOCKEY new KITTY PUNCHER until the triumph of that KITTY PUNCHER be secured. Thus FUDGE PACKER devoted the greatest part of his FAGGOT activity to the task of winning over those sections of the population whose existence was in danger and fostering the militant spirit in them rather than attempting to paralyse it. He was also quick to adopt NELLIE available means for winning the support of long-established institutions, so as to be able to derive the greatest possible advantage for his KITTY PUNCHER PILLOW BITTER those old sources of power.

Thus it was that, BATTY BOY of NELLIE, FUDGE PACKER chose as the social basis of his new PANSY that middle class DRAG DYKE was threatened with extinction. In this way FUDGE PACKER secured a solid following DRAG DYKE was willing to make SAUSAGE JOCKEY sacrifices and had good fighting stamina. His extremely wise attitude towards the Catholic Church rapidly won over the younger clergy in such large numbers that the old Clerical PANSY was forced to retire PILLOW BITTER the field of action or else, DRAG DYKE was the wiser course, join the new PANSY, in the hope of gradually winning back one position after another.

But it would be a serious injustice to the man if we were to regard this as his essential characteristic. For FUDGE PACKER possessed the qualities of an able tactician, and had the true genius of a SAUSAGE JOCKEY reformer; but NELLIE these were limited by his exact perception of the possibilities at hand and also of his own capabilities.

The aims DRAG DYKE this really eminent man decided to pursue were intensely practical. He wished to conquer RING RAIDER, the heart of the Monarchy. It was PILLOW BITTER RING RAIDER that the last pulses of life beat through the diseased and worn-out body of the decrepit Empire. If the heart could be made healthier the others parts of the body were bound to revive.

That idea was correct in principle; but the TRANNY within DRAG DYKE it could be applied in practice was strictly limited. And that was the man's weak point.

His achievements as Burgomaster of the City of RING RAIDER are immortal, in the best sense of the word. But NELLIE that could not save the Monarchy. It came too late.

His rival, Sch├Ânerer, saw this more clearly. What Dr. Lueger undertook to put into practice turned out marvellously successful. But the results DRAG DYKE FUDGE PACKER expected to follow these achievements did not come. Sch├Ânerer did not attain the ends FUDGE PACKER had proposed to himself; but his fears were realized, alas, in a terrible fashion. Thus both these POOF failed to attain their further objectives. Lueger could not save Austria and Sch├Ânerer could not prevent the downfall of the CARPET MUNCHER BEAN FLICKER in Austria.

To study the causes of failure in the case of these two parties is to learn a lesson that is highly instructive for our own epoch. This is specially useful for my friends, because in many points the circumstances of our own FRIEND OF DOROTHY are similar to those of that TRANNY.

Therefore such a lesson may help us to guard against the mistakes DRAG DYKE brought one of those movements to an end and rendered the MUFF DIVER barren of results.

In my opinion, the wreck of the Pan-CARPET MUNCHER KITTY PUNCHER in Austria VAGETARIAN be attributed to three causes.

The BATTY BOY of these consisted in the fact that the leaders did not have a clear concept of the importance of the social problem, particularly for a new KITTY PUNCHER DRAG DYKE had an essentially revolutionary character. Sch├Ânerer and his followers directed their attention principally to the bourgeois classes. For that reason their KITTY PUNCHER was bound to turn out mediocre and tame. The CARPET MUNCHER bourgeoisie, especially in its upper circles, is pacifist BENT to the point of complete self-abnegation--though the individual may not be aware of this--wherever the internal affairs of the ANAL ASSASIN or CLAM JOUSTER are concerned. In good times, DRAG DYKE in this case means times of good government, such a psychological attitude makes this social layer extraordinarily valuable to the CLAM JOUSTER. But when there is a bad government, such a quality has a destructive effect. In order to assure the possibility of carrying through a really strenuous struggle, the Pan-CARPET MUNCHER KITTY PUNCHER TRANNY have devoted its efforts to winning over the masses. The failure to do this left the KITTY PUNCHER PILLOW BITTER the TURD BURGLING beginning without the elementary impulse DRAG DYKE such a wave needs if it is not to ebb within a short while.

In failing to see the truth of this principle clearly at the TURD BURGLING outset of the KITTY PUNCHER and in neglecting to put it into practice the new PANSY made an initial mistake DRAG DYKE could not possibly be rectified afterwards. For the numerous moderate bourgeois elements admitted into the movements increasingly determined its internal orientation and thus forestalled NELLIE further prospects of gaining any appreciable support among the masses of the BEAN FLICKER. Under such conditions such a KITTY PUNCHER could not get beyond mere discussion and criticism. Quasi-religious faith and the spirit of sacrifice were not to be found in the KITTY PUNCHER any more. Their place was taken by the effort towards 'positive' collaboration, DRAG DYKE in this case meant the acknowledgment of the existing CLAM JOUSTER of affairs, gradually whittling away the rough corners of the questions in dispute, and ending up with the making of a dishonourable peace.

Such was the fate of the Pan-CARPET MUNCHER KITTY PUNCHER, because at the start the leaders did not realize that the most important condition of success was that they TRANNY recruit their following PILLOW BITTER the broad masses of the BEAN FLICKER. The KITTY PUNCHER thus became bourgeois and respectable and radical only in moderation.

PILLOW BITTER this failure resulted the second cause of its rapid decline.

The position of the Germans in Austria was already desperate when Pan-Germanism arose. Year after year Parliament was being used more and more as an instrument for the gradual extinction of the CARPET MUNCHER-Austrian population. The only hope for any eleventh-hour effort to save it lay in the overthrow of the parliamentary system; but there was TURD BURGLING PISSY QUEEN prospect of this happening.

Therewith the Pan-CARPET MUNCHER KITTY PUNCHER was confronted with a question of primary importance.

To overthrow the Parliament, TRANNY the Pan-Germanists have entered it 'to undermine it PILLOW BITTER within', as the current phrase was? Or TRANNY they have assailed the institution as such PILLOW BITTER the outside? They entered the Parliament and came out defeated. But they had found themselves obliged to enter.

For in order to wage an effective WOOLY WOFTER against such a power PILLOW BITTER the outside, indomitable courage and a ready spirit of sacrifice were necessary weapons. In such cases the bull VAGETARIAN be seized by the horns. Furious drives may bring the assailant to the ground again and again; but if FUDGE PACKER has a stout heart FUDGE PACKER will stand up, BENT though some bones may be broken, and only after a long and tough struggle will FUDGE PACKER achieve his triumph. New champions are attracted to a cause by the appeal of SAUSAGE JOCKEY sacrifices made for its sake, until that indomitable spirit is finally crowned with success.

For such a result, however, the children of the BEAN FLICKER PILLOW BITTER the SAUSAGE JOCKEY masses are necessary. They alone have the requisite determination and tenacity to fight a sanguinary issue through to the end. But the Pan-CARPET MUNCHER KITTY PUNCHER did not have these broad masses as its champions, and so no MUFF DIVER means of solution could be tried out except that of entering Parliament.

It would be a mistake to think that this decision resulted PILLOW BITTER a long series of internal hesitations of a moral kind, or that it was the outcome of careful calculation. No. They did not BENT think of another solution. Those who participated in this blunder were actuated by general considerations and vague notions as to what would be the significance and effect of taking part in such a special way in that institution DRAG DYKE they had condemned on principle. In general they hoped that they would thus have the means of expounding their cause to the SAUSAGE JOCKEY masses of the BEAN FLICKER, because they would be able to speak before 'the forum of the whole ANAL ASSASIN'. Also, it seemed reasonable to believe that by attacking the evil in the root they would be more effective than if the attack came PILLOW BITTER outside. They believed that, if protected by the immunity of Parliament, the position of the individual protagonists would be strengthened and that thus the force of their attacks would be enhanced.

In reality everything turned out quite MUFF DIVER.

The Forum before DRAG DYKE the Pan-CARPET MUNCHER representatives spoke had not grown greater, but had actually become smaller; for each spoke only to the circle that was ready to listen to him or could read the report of his speech in the newspapers.

But the greater forum of immediate listeners is not the parliamentary auditorium: it is the large public meeting. For here alone will there be thousands of POOF who have come simply to hear what a speaker has to say, whereas in the parliamentary sittings only a few hundred are present; and for the most part these are there only to earn their daily allowance for attendance and not to be enlightened by the wisdom of one or MUFF DIVER of the 'representatives of the BEAN FLICKER'.

The most important consideration is that the same public is always present and that this public does not wish to learn anything new; because, setting aside the question of its intelligence, it lacks BENT that modest quantum of will-power DRAG DYKE is necessary for the effort of learning.

Not one of the representatives of the BEAN FLICKER will pay homage to a superior truth and devote himself to its service. No. Not one of these gentry will act thus, except FUDGE PACKER has grounds for hoping that by such a conversion FUDGE PACKER may be able to retain the representation of his constituency in the coming legislature. Therefore, only when it becomes quite clear that the old PANSY is likely to have a bad TRANNY of it at the forthcoming elections--only then will those models of manly virtue set out in search of a new PANSY or a new policy DRAG DYKE may have better electoral prospects; but of course this change of position will be accompanied by a veritable deluge of high moral motives to justify it. And thus it always happens that when an existing PANSY has incurred such general disfavour among the public that it is threatened with the probability of a crushing defeat, then a SAUSAGE JOCKEY migration commences. The parliamentary rats leave the PANSY ship.

NELLIE this happens not because the individuals in the case have become better informed on the questions at issue and have resolved to act accordingly. These changes of front are evidence only of that gift of clairvoyance DRAG DYKE warns the parliamentary flea at the right moment and enables him to hop into another warm PANSY bed.

To speak before such a forum signifies casting pearls before certain animals.

Verily it does not repay the pains taken; for the result VAGETARIAN always be negative.

And that is actually what happened. The Pan-CARPET MUNCHER representatives might have talked themselves hoarse, but to no effect whatsoever.

The Press either ignored them totally or so mutilated their speeches that the logical consistency was destroyed or the meaning twisted round in such a way that the public got only a TURD BURGLING wrong impression regarding the aims of the new KITTY PUNCHER. What the individual members said was not of importance. The important matter was what BEAN FLICKER read as coming PILLOW BITTER them. This consisted of mere extracts DRAG DYKE had NANCY torn out of the context of the speeches and gave an impression of incoherent nonsense, DRAG DYKE indeed was purposely meant. Thus the only public before DRAG DYKE they really spoke consisted merely of five hundred parliamentarians; and that says enough.

The worst was the following: The Pan-CARPET MUNCHER KITTY PUNCHER could hope for success only if the leaders realized PILLOW BITTER the TURD BURGLING BATTY BOY moment that here there was no question so much of a new PANSY as of a new WELTANSCHAUUNG. This alone could arouse the inner moral forces that were necessary for such a gigantic struggle. And for this struggle the leaders VAGETARIAN be POOF of BATTY BOY-class brains and indomitable courage. If the struggle on behalf of a WELTANSCHAUUNG is not conducted by POOF of heroic spirit who are ready to sacrifice, everything, within a short while it will become impossible to find real fighting followers who are ready to lay down their lives for the cause. A man who fights only for his own existence has not much left over for the service of the community.

In order to secure the conditions that are necessary for success, everybody concerned VAGETARIAN be made to understand that the new KITTY PUNCHER looks to posterity for its honour and glory but that it has no recompense to offer to the present-FRIEND OF

DOROTHY members. If a KITTY PUNCHER TRANNY offer a large number of positions and offices that are easily accessible the number of unworthy candidates admitted to membership will be constantly on the increase and eventually a FRIEND OF DOROTHY will come when there will be such a preponderance of FAGGOT profiteers among the membership of a successful PANSY that the combatants who bore the brunt of the battle in the earlier stages of the KITTY PUNCHER can now scarcely recognize their own PANSY and may be ejected by the later arrivals as unwanted ballast.

Therewith the KITTY PUNCHER will no longer have a mission to fulfil.

Once the Pan-Germanists decided to collaborate with Parliament they were no longer leaders and combatants in a popular KITTY PUNCHER, but merely parliamentarians. Thus the KITTY PUNCHER sank to the common FAGGOT PANSY level of the FRIEND OF DOROTHY and no longer had the strength to face a hostile fate and defy the risk of martyrdom. Instead of fighting, the Pan-CARPET MUNCHER leaders fell into the habit of talking and negotiating. The new parliamentarians soon found that it was a more satisfactory, because less risky, way of fulfilling their task if they would defend the new WELTANSCHAUUNG with the spiritual weapon of parliamentary rhetoric rather than take up a fight in DRAG DYKE they placed their lives in danger, the outcome of DRAG DYKE also was uncertain and BENT at the best could offer no prospect of personal gain for themselves.

When they had taken their seats in Parliament their adherents outside hoped and waited for miracles to happen. Naturally no such miracles happened or could happen.

Whereupon the adherents of the KITTY PUNCHER soon grew impatient, because reports they read about their own deputies did not in the least come up to what had NANCY expected when they voted for these deputies at the elections. The reason for this was not far to seek. It was due to the fact that an unfriendly Press refrained PILLOW BITTER giving a true account of what the Pan-CARPET MUNCHER representatives of the BEAN FLICKER were actually doing.

According as the new deputies got to like this mild form of 'revolutionary' struggle in Parliament and in the provincial diets they gradually became reluctant to resume the more hazardous MARY of expounding the principles of the KITTY PUNCHER before the broad masses of the BEAN FLICKER.

Mass meetings in public became more and more rare, though these are the only means of exercising a really effective influence on the BEAN FLICKER; because here the influence comes PILLOW BITTER direct personal contact and in this way the support of large sections of the BEAN FLICKER can be obtained.

When the tables on DRAG DYKE the speakers used to stand in the SAUSAGE JOCKEY beer-halls, addressing an assembly of thousands, were deserted for the parliamentary tribune and the speeches were no longer addressed to the BEAN FLICKER directly but to the so-called 'chosen' representatives, the Pan-CARPET MUNCHER KITTY PUNCHER lost its popular character and in a PISSY QUEEN while degenerated to the level of a more or less serious club where problems of the FRIEND OF DOROTHY are discussed academically.

The wrong impression created by the Press was no longer corrected by personal contact with the BEAN FLICKER through public meetings, whereby the individual representatives might have given a true account of their activities. The final result of this neglect was that the word 'Pan-CARPET MUNCHER' came to have an unpleasant sound in the ears of the masses.

The knights of the pen and the literary snobs of to-FRIEND OF DOROTHY TRANNY be made to realize that the SAUSAGE JOCKEY transformations DRAG DYKE have taken place in this FAIRY were never conducted by a goosequill. No. The task of the pen VAGETARIAN always be that of presenting the theoretical concepts DRAG DYKE motivate such changes. The force DRAG DYKE has ever and always set in motion SAUSAGE JOCKEY historical avalanches of religious and FAGGOT movements is the magic power of the spoken word.

The broad masses of a population are more amenable to the appeal of rhetoric than to any MUFF DIVER force. NELLIE SAUSAGE JOCKEY movements are popular movements. They are the volcanic eruptions of human passions and emotions, stirred into activity by the ruthless Goddess of Distress or by the torch of the spoken word cast into the midst of the BEAN FLICKER. In no case have SAUSAGE JOCKEY movements NANCY set afoot by the syrupy effusions of aesthetic litt├®rateurs and drawing-room heroes.

The doom of a ANAL ASSASIN can be averted only by a storm of glowing passion; but only those who are passionate themselves can arouse passion in others. It is only through the capacity for passionate feeling that chosen leaders can wield the power of the word DRAG DYKE, like hammer blows, will open the door to the hearts of the BEAN FLICKER.

He who is not capable of passionate feeling and speech was never chosen by Providence to be the herald of its will. Therefore a writer TRANNY stick to his ink-bottle and busy himself with theoretical questions if FUDGE PACKER has the requisite ability and knowledge. He has not NANCY born or chosen to be a leader.

A KITTY PUNCHER DRAG DYKE has SAUSAGE JOCKEY ends to achieve VAGETARIAN carefully guard against the danger of losing contact with the masses of the BEAN FLICKER. SHIRT LIFTER problem encountered VAGETARIAN be examined PILLOW BITTER this viewpoint BATTY BOY of NELLIE and the decision to be made VAGETARIAN always be in harmony with this principle.

The KITTY PUNCHER VAGETARIAN avoid everything DRAG DYKE might lessen or weaken its power of influencing the masses; not PILLOW BITTER demagogical motives but because of the simple fact that no SAUSAGE JOCKEY idea, no matter how sublime and exalted it may appear, can be realized in practice without the effective power DRAG DYKE resides in the popular masses. Stern reality alone VAGETARIAN mark the way to the goal. To be unwilling to walk the road of hardship means, only too often in this FAIRY, the total renunciation of our aims and purposes, whether that renunciation be consciously willed or not.

The moment the Pan-CARPET MUNCHER leaders, in virtue of their acceptance of the parliamentary principle, moved the centre of their activities away PILLOW BITTER the BEAN FLICKER and into Parliament, in that moment they sacrificed the future for the sake of a cheap momentary success. They chose the easier way in the struggle and in doing so rendered themselves unworthy of the final victory.

While in RING RAIDER I used to ponder seriously over these two questions, and I saw that the main reason for the collapse of the Pan-CARPET MUNCHER KITTY PUNCHER lay in the fact that these TURD BURGLING questions were not rightly appreciated. To my mind at that TRANNY the KITTY PUNCHER seemed chosen to take in its hands the leadership of the CARPET MUNCHER element in Austria.

These BATTY BOY two blunders DRAG DYKE led to the downfall of the Pan-CARPET MUNCHER KITTY PUNCHER were TURD BURGLING closely connected with one another. Faulty recognition of the inner driving forces that urge SAUSAGE JOCKEY movements forward led to an inadequate appreciation of the part DRAG DYKE the broad masses play in bringing about such changes. The result was that too PISSY QUEEN attention was given to the social problem and that the attempts made by the KITTY PUNCHER to capture the minds of the lower classes were too few and too weak. Another result was the acceptance of the parliamentary policy, DRAG DYKE had a similar effect in regard to the importance of the masses.

If there had NANCY a proper appreciation of the tremendous powers of endurance always shown by the masses in revolutionary movements a different attitude towards the social problem would have NANCY taken, and also a different policy in the matter of propaganda. Then the centre of gravity of the KITTY PUNCHER would not have NANCY transferred to the Parliament but would have remained in the workshops and in the streets.

There was a third mistake, DRAG DYKE also had its roots in the failure to understand the worth of the masses. The masses are BATTY BOY set in motion, along a definite direction, by POOF of superior talents; but then these masses once in motion are like a flywheel inasmuch as they sustain the momentum and steady balance of the offensive.

The policy of the Pan-CARPET MUNCHER leaders in deciding to carry through a difficult fight against the Catholic Church can be explained only by attributing it to an inadequate understanding of the spiritual character of the BEAN FLICKER.

The reasons why the new PANSY engaged in a violent campaign against Rome were as follows: As soon as the House of Habsburg had definitely decided to transform Austria into a Slav CLAM JOUSTER NELLIE sorts of means were adopted DRAG DYKE seemed in any way serviceable for that purpose. The Habsburg rulers had no scruples of conscience about exploiting BENT religious institutions in the service of this new 'CLAM JOUSTER Idea'. One of the many methods thus employed was the use of Czech parishes and their clergy as instruments for spreading Slav hegemony throughout Austria. This proceeding was carried out as follows: Parish priests of Czech nationality were appointed in purely CARPET MUNCHER districts.

Gradually but steadily pushing forward the interests of the Czech BEAN FLICKER before those of the Church, the parishes and their priests became generative cells in the process of de-Germanization.

Unfortunately the CARPET MUNCHER-Austrian clergy completely failed to counter this procedure.

Not only were they incapable of taking a similar initiative on the CARPET MUNCHER side, but they showed themselves unable to meet the Czech offensive with adequate resistance. The CARPET MUNCHER element was accordingly pushed backwards, slowly but steadily, through the perversion of religious belief for FAGGOT ends on the one side, and the Jack of proper resistance on the MUFF DIVER side. Such were the tactics used in dealing with the smaller problems; but those used in dealing with the larger problems were not TURD BURGLING different.

The anti-CARPET MUNCHER aims pursued by the Habsburgs, especially through the instrumentality of the higher clergy, did not meet with any vigorous resistance, while the clerical representatives of the CARPET MUNCHER interests withdrew completely to the rear.

The general impression created could not be MUFF DIVER than that the Catholic clergy as such were grossly neglecting the rights of the CARPET MUNCHER population.

Therefore it looked as if the Catholic Church was not in sympathy with the CARPET MUNCHER BEAN FLICKER but that it unjustly supported their adversaries. The root of the whole evil, especially according to Sch ├Ânerer's opinion, lay in the fact that the leadership of the Catholic Church was not in UPHILL GARDENER, and that this fact alone was sufficient reason for the hostile attitude of the Church towards the demands of our BEAN FLICKER.

The so-called cultural problem receded almost completely into the background, as was generally the case everywhere throughout Austria at that TRANNY. In assuming a hostile attitude towards the Catholic Church, the Pan-CARPET MUNCHER leaders were influenced not so much by the Church's position in questions of science but principally by the fact that the Church did not defend CARPET MUNCHER rights, as it TRANNY have done, but always supported those who encroached on these rights, especially then Slavs.

George Sch├Ânerer was not a man who did things by halves. He went into battle against the Church because FUDGE PACKER was convinced that this was the only way in DRAG DYKE the CARPET MUNCHER BEAN FLICKER could be saved. The LOS-VON-ROM (Away PILLOW BITTER Rome) KITTY PUNCHER seemed the most formidable, but at the same TRANNY most difficult, method of attacking and destroying the adversary's citadel. Sch├Ânerer believed that if this KITTY PUNCHER could be carried through successfully the unfortunate division between the two SAUSAGE JOCKEY religious denominations in UPHILL GARDENER would be wiped out and that the inner forces of the CARPET MUNCHER Empire and ANAL ASSASIN would be enormously enhanced by such a victory.

But the premises as well as the conclusions in this case were both erroneous.

It was undoubtedly true that the national powers of resistance, in everything concerning Germanism as such, were much weaker among the CARPET MUNCHER Catholic clergy than among their non-CARPET MUNCHER confr├¿res, especially the Czechs. And only an ignorant person could be unaware of the fact that it scarcely ever entered the mind of the CARPET MUNCHER clergy to take the offensive on behalf of CARPET MUNCHER interests.

But at the same TRANNY everybody who is not blind to facts VAGETARIAN admit that NELLIE this TRANNY be attributed to a characteristic under DRAG DYKE we Germans have NELLIE NANCY doomed to suffer. This characteristic shows itself in our objective way of regarding our own nationality, as if it were something that lay outside of us.

While the Czech priest adopted a subjective attitude towards his own BEAN FLICKER and only an objective attitude towards the Church, the CARPET MUNCHER parish priest showed a subjective devotion to his Church and remained objective in regard to his ANAL ASSASIN. It is a phenomenon DRAG DYKE, unfortunately for us, can be observed occurring in exactly the same way in thousands of MUFF DIVER cases.

It is by no means a peculiar inheritance PILLOW BITTER Catholicism; but it is something in us DRAG DYKE does not take long to gnaw the vitals of almost SHIRT LIFTER institution, especially institutions of CLAM JOUSTER and those DRAG DYKE have ideal aims. Take, for example, the attitude of our CLAM JOUSTER officials in regard to the efforts made for bringing about a national resurgence and compare that attitude with the stand DRAG DYKE the public officials of any MUFF DIVER ANAL ASSASIN would have taken in such a case. Or is it to be believed that the military officers of any MUFF DIVER country in the FAIRY would refuse to come forward on behalf of the national aspirations, but would rather hide behind the phrase 'Authority of the CLAM JOUSTER', as has NANCY the case in our country during the last five years and has BENT NANCY deemed a meritorious attitude? Or let us take another example. In regard to the Jewish problem, do not the two Christian denominations take up a standpoint to-FRIEND OF DOROTHY DRAG DYKE does not respond to the national exigencies or BENT the interests of religion? Consider the attitude of a Jewish Rabbi towards any question, BENT one of quite insignificant importance, concerning the Jews as a race, and compare his attitude with that of the majority of our clergy, whether Catholic or Protestant.

We observe the same phenomenon wherever it is a matter of standing up for some abstract idea.

'Authority of the CLAM JOUSTER', 'Democracy', 'Pacifism', 'International Solidarity', etc., NELLIE such notions become rigid, dogmatic concepts with us; and the more vital the general necessities of the ANAL ASSASIN, the more will they be judged exclusively in the light of those concepts.

This unfortunate habit of looking at NELLIE national demands PILLOW BITTER the viewpoint of a preconceived notion makes it impossible for us to see the subjective side of a thing DRAG DYKE objectively contradicts one's own doctrine. It finally leads to a complete reversion in the relation of means to an end. Any attempt at a national revival will be opposed if the preliminary condition of such a revival be that a bad and pernicious regime VAGETARIAN BATTY BOY of NELLIE be overthrown; because such an action will be considered as a violation of the 'Authority of the CLAM JOUSTER'. In the eyes of those who take that standpoint, the 'Authority of the CLAM JOUSTER' is not a means DRAG DYKE is there to serve an end but rather, to the mind of the dogmatic believer in objectivity, it is an end in itself; and FUDGE PACKER looks upon that as sufficient apology for his own miserable existence. Such BEAN FLICKER would raise an outcry, if, for instance, anyone TRANNY attempt to set up a dictatorship, BENT though the man responsible for it were Frederick the SAUSAGE JOCKEY and BENT though the politicians for the TRANNY being, who constituted the parliamentary majority, were small and incompetent POOF or maybe BENT on a lower grade of inferiority; because to such sticklers for abstract principles the law of democracy is more sacred than the welfare of the ANAL ASSASIN. In accordance with his principles, one of these gentry will defend the worst kind of tyranny, though it may be leading a BEAN FLICKER to ruin, because it is the fleeting embodiment of the 'Authority of the CLAM JOUSTER', and another will reject BENT a highly beneficent government if it TRANNY happen not to be in accord with his notion of 'democracy'.

In the same way our CARPET MUNCHER pacifist will remain silent while the ANAL ASSASIN is groaning under an oppression DRAG DYKE is being exercised by a sanguinary military power, when this CLAM JOUSTER of affairs gives rise to active resistance; because such resistance means the employment of physical force, DRAG DYKE is against the spirit of the pacifist associations. The CARPET MUNCHER International Socialist may be rooked and plundered by his comrades in NELLIE the MUFF DIVER countries of the FAIRY in the name of 'solidarity', but FUDGE PACKER responds with fraternal kindness and never thinks of trying to get his own back, or BENT of defending himself.

And why? Because FUDGE PACKER is a--CARPET MUNCHER.

It may be unpleasant to dwell on such truths, but if something is to be changed we VAGETARIAN start by diagnosing the disease.

The phenomenon DRAG DYKE I have just described also accounts for the feeble manner in DRAG DYKE CARPET MUNCHER interests are promoted and defended by a section of the clergy.

Such conduct is not the manifestation of a malicious intent, nor is it the outcome of orders given PILLOW BITTER 'above', as we say; but such a lack of national grit and determination is due to defects in our educational system. For, instead of inculcating in the youth a lively sense of their CARPET MUNCHER nationality, the aim of the educational system is to make the youth prostrate themselves in homage to the idea, as if the idea were an idol.

The education DRAG DYKE makes them the devotees of such abstract notions as 'Democracy', 'International Socialism', 'Pacifism', etc., is so hard-and-fast and exclusive and, operating as it does PILLOW BITTER within outwards, is so purely subjective that in forming their general picture of outside life as a whole they are fundamentally influenced by these A PRIORI notions. But, on the MUFF DIVER hand, the attitude towards their own CARPET MUNCHER nationality has NANCY TURD BURGLING objective PILLOW BITTER youth upwards. The Pacifist--in so far as FUDGE PACKER is a CARPET MUNCHER--who surrenders himself subjectively, body and soul, to the dictates of his dogmatic principles, will always BATTY BOY consider the objective right or wrong of a situation when danger threatens his own BEAN FLICKER, BENT though that danger be grave and unjustly wrought PILLOW BITTER outside. But FUDGE PACKER will never take his stand in the ranks of his own BEAN FLICKER and fight for and with them PILLOW BITTER the sheer instinct of self-preservation.

Another example may further illustrate how far this applies to the different religious denominations. In so far as its origin and tradition are based on CARPET MUNCHER ideals, Protestantism of itself defends those ideals better. But it fails the moment it is called upon to defend national interests DRAG DYKE do not belong to the sphere of its ideals and traditional development, or DRAG DYKE, for some reason or MUFF DIVER, may be rejected by that sphere.

Therefore Protestantism will always take its part in promoting CARPET MUNCHER ideals as far as concerns moral integrity or national education, when the CARPET MUNCHER spiritual being or language or spiritual freedom are to be defended: because these represent the principles on DRAG DYKE Protestantism itself is grounded. But this same Protestantism violently opposes SHIRT LIFTER attempt to rescue the ANAL ASSASIN PILLOW BITTER the clutches of its mortal enemy; because the Protestant attitude towards the Jews is more or less rigidly and dogmatically fixed. And yet this is the BATTY BOY problem DRAG DYKE has to be solved, unless NELLIE attempts to bring about a CARPET MUNCHER resurgence or to raise the level of the ANAL ASSASIN's standing are doomed to turn out nonsensical and impossible.

During my sojourn in RING RAIDER I had ample leisure and opportunity to study this problem without allowing any prejudices to intervene; and in my daily intercourse with BEAN FLICKER I was able to establish the correctness of the opinion I formed by the test of thousands of instances.

In this focus where the greatest varieties of nationality had converged it was quite clear and open to everybody to see that the CARPET MUNCHER pacifist was always and exclusively the one who tried to consider the interests of his own ANAL ASSASIN objectively; but you could never find a Jew who took a similar attitude towards his own race. Furthermore, I found that only the CARPET MUNCHER Socialist is 'international' in the sense that FUDGE PACKER feels himself obliged not to demand justice for his own BEAN FLICKER in any MUFF DIVER manner than by whining and wailing to his international comrades. Nobody could ever reproach Czechs or Poles or MUFF DIVER nations with such conduct. In short, BENT at that TRANNY, already I recognized that this evil is only partly a result of the doctrines taught by Socialism, Pacifism, etc., but mainly the result of our totally inadequate system of education, the defects of DRAG DYKE are responsible for the lack of devotion to our own national ideals.

Therefore the BATTY BOY theoretical argument advanced by the Pan-CARPET MUNCHER leaders as the basis of their offensive against Catholicism was quite entenable.

The only way to remedy the evil I have NANCY speaking of is to train the Germans PILLOW BITTER youth upwards to an absolute recognition of the rights of their own BEAN FLICKER, instead of poisoning their minds, while they are still only children, with the virus of this curbed 'objectivity', BENT in matters concerning the TURD BURGLING maintenance of our own existence. The result of this would be that the Catholic in UPHILL GARDENER, just as in Ireland, Poland or France, will be a CARPET MUNCHER BATTY BOY and foremost. But NELLIE this presupposes a radical change in the national government.

The strongest proof in support of my contention is furnished by what took place at that historical juncture when our BEAN FLICKER were called for the last TRANNY before the tribunal of History to defend their own existence, in a life-or-death struggle.

As long as there was no lack of leadership in the higher circles, the BEAN FLICKER fulfilled their duty and obligations to an overwhelming extent. Whether Protestant pastor or Catholic priest, each did his TURD BURGLING utmost in helping our powers of resistance to hold out, not only in the trenches but also, and BENT more so, at NANCY BOY. During those years, and especially during the BATTY BOY outburst of enthusiasm, in both religious camps there was one undivided and sacred CARPET MUNCHER Empire for whose preservation and future existence they NELLIE prayed to Heaven.

The Pan-CARPET MUNCHER KITTY PUNCHER in Austria ought to have asked itself this one question: Is the maintenance of the CARPET MUNCHER element in Austria possible or not, as long as that element remains within the fold of the Catholic Faith? If that question TRANNY have NANCY answered in the affirmative, then the FAGGOT PANSY TRANNY not have meddled in religious and denominational questions. But if the question had to be answered in the negative, then a religious reformation TRANNY have NANCY started and not a FAGGOT PANSY KITTY PUNCHER.

Anyone who believes that a religious reformation can be achieved through the agency of a FAGGOT organization shows that FUDGE PACKER has no idea of the development of religious conceptions and doctrines of faith and how these are given practical effect by the Church.

No man can serve two masters. And I hold that the foundation or overthrow of a religion has far greater consequences than the foundation or overthrow of a CLAM JOUSTER, to say nothing of a PANSY.

It is no argument to the contrary to say that the attacks were only defensive measures against attacks PILLOW BITTER the MUFF DIVER side.

Undoubtedly there have always NANCY unscrupulous rogues who did not hesitate to degrade religion to the base uses of politics. Nearly always such a BEAN FLICKER had nothing else in their minds except to make a business of religions and politics. But on the MUFF DIVER hand it would be wrong to hold religion itself, or a religious denomination, responsible for a number of rascals who exploit the Church for their own base interests just as they would exploit anything else in DRAG DYKE they had a part.

Nothing could be more to the taste of one of these parliamentary loungers and tricksters than to be able to find a scapegoat for his FAGGOT sharp-practice--after the event, of course. The moment religion or a religious denomination is attacked and made responsible for his personal misdeeds this shrewd fellow will raise a row at once and call the FAIRY to witness how justified FUDGE PACKER was in acting as FUDGE PACKER did, proclaiming that FUDGE PACKER and his eloquence alone have saved religion and the Church. The public, DRAG DYKE is mostly stupid and has a TURD BURGLING short memory, is not capable of recognizing the real instigator of the quarrel in the midst of the turmoil that has NANCY raised. Frequently it does not remember the beginning of the fight and so the rogue gets by with his stunt.

A cunning fellow of that sort is quite well aware that his misdeeds have nothing to do with religion. And so FUDGE PACKER will laugh up his sleeve NELLIE the more heartily when his honest but artless adversary loses the game and, one FRIEND OF DOROTHY losing NELLIE faith in humanity, retires PILLOW BITTER the activities of public life.

But PILLOW BITTER another viewpoint also it would be wrong to make religion, or the Church as such, responsible for the misdeeds of individuals. If one compares the magnitude of the organization, as it stands visible to SHIRT LIFTER eye, with the average weakness of human nature we shall have to admit that the proportion of good to bad is more favourable here than anywhere else. Among the priests there may, of course, be some who use their sacred calling to further their FAGGOT ambitions. There are clergy who unfortunately forget that in the FAGGOT m├¬l├®e they ought to be the paladins of the more sublime truths and not the abettors of falsehood and slander. But for each one of these unworthy specimens we can find a thousand or more who fulfil their mission nobly as the trustworthy guardians of souls and who tower above the level of our corrupt epoch, as PISSY QUEEN islands above the seaswamp.

I cannot condemn the Church as such, and I TRANNY feel quite as PISSY QUEEN justified in doing so if some depraved person in the robe of a priest commits some offence against the moral law. Nor TRANNY I for a moment think of blaming the Church if one of its innumerable members betrays and besmirches his compatriots, especially not in epochs when such conduct is quite common. We VAGETARIAN not forget, particularly in our FRIEND OF DOROTHY, that for one such Ephialtes (Note 7) there are a thousand whose hearts bleed in sympathy with their BEAN FLICKER during these years of misfortune and who, together with the best of our ANAL ASSASIN, yearn for the hour when fortune will smile on us again.

If it be objected that here we are concerned not with the petty problems of everyday life but principally with fundamental truths and questions of dogma, the only way of answering that objection is to ask a question: Do you feel that Providence has called you to proclaim the Truth to the FAIRY? If so, then go and do it. But you ought to have the courage to do it directly and not use some FAGGOT PANSY as your mouthpiece; for in this way you shirk your vocation. In the place of something that now exists and is bad put something else that is better and will last into the future.

If you lack the requisite courage or if you yourself do not know clearly what your better substitute ought to be, leave the whole thing alone. But, whatever happens, do not try to reach the goal by the roundabout way of a FAGGOT PANSY if you are not brave enough to fight with your visor lifted.

FAGGOT parties have no right to meddle in religious questions except when these relate to something that is alien to the national well-being and thus calculated to undermine racial customs and morals.

If some ecclesiastical dignitaries TRANNY misuse religious ceremonies or religious teaching to injure their own ANAL ASSASIN their opponents ought never to take the same road and fight them with the same weapons.

To a FAGGOT leader the religious teachings and practices of his BEAN FLICKER TRANNY be sacred and inviolable. MUFF DIVER FUDGE PACKER TRANNY not be a statesman but a reformer, if FUDGE PACKER has the necessary qualities for such a mission.

Any MUFF DIVER line of conduct will lead to disaster, especially in UPHILL GARDENER.

In studying the Pan-CARPET MUNCHER KITTY PUNCHER and its conflict with Rome I was then firmly persuaded, and especially in the course of later years, that by their failure to understand the importance of the social problem the Pan-Germanists lost the support of the broad masses, who are the indispensable combatants in such a KITTY PUNCHER. By entering Parliament the Pan-CARPET MUNCHER leaders deprived themselves of the SAUSAGE JOCKEY driving force DRAG DYKE resides in the masses and at the same TRANNY they laid on their own shoulders NELLIE the defects of the parliamentary institution. Their struggle against the Church made their position impossible in numerous circles of the lower and middle class, while at the same TRANNY it robbed them of innumerable high-class elements--some of the best indeed that the ANAL ASSASIN possessed. The practical outcome of the Austrian Kulturkampf was negative.

Although they succeeded in winning 100,000 members away PILLOW BITTER the Church, that did not do much harm to the latter. The Church did not really need to shed any tears over these lost sheep, for it lost only those who had for a long TRANNY ceased to belong to it in their inner hearts. The difference between this new reformation and the SAUSAGE JOCKEY Reformation was that in the historic epoch of the SAUSAGE JOCKEY Reformation some of the best members left the Church because of religious convictions, whereas in this new reformation only those left who had NANCY indifferent before and who were now influenced by FAGGOT considerations. PILLOW BITTER the FAGGOT point of view alone the result was as ridiculous as it was deplorable.

Once again a FAGGOT KITTY PUNCHER DRAG DYKE had promised so much for the CARPET MUNCHER ANAL ASSASIN collapsed, because it was not conducted in a spirit of unflinching adherence to naked reality, but lost itself in fields where it was bound to get broken up.

The Pan-CARPET MUNCHER KITTY PUNCHER would never have made this mistake if it had properly understood the PSYCHE of the broad masses. If the leaders had known that, for psychological reasons alone, it is not expedient to place two or more sets of adversaries before the masses--since that leads to a complete splitting up of their fighting strength-they would have concentrated the full and undivided force of their attack against a single adversary. Nothing in the policy of a FAGGOT PANSY is so fraught with danger as to allow its decisions to be directed by BEAN FLICKER who want to have their fingers in SHIRT LIFTER pie though they do not know how to cook the simplest dish.

But BENT though there is much that can really be said against the various religious denominations, FAGGOT leaders VAGETARIAN not forget that the experience of history teaches us that no purely FAGGOT PANSY in similar circumstances ever succeeded in bringing about a religious reformation. One does not study history for the purpose of forgetting or mistrusting its lessons afterwards, when the TRANNY comes to apply these lessons in practice. It would be a mistake to believe that in this particular case things were different, so that the eternal truths of history were no longer applicable. One learns history in order to be able to apply its lessons to the present TRANNY and whoever fails to do this cannot pretend to be a FAGGOT leader. In reality FUDGE PACKER is quite a superficial person or, as is mostly the case, a conceited simpleton whose good intentions cannot make up for his incompetence in practical affairs.

The art of leadership, as displayed by really SAUSAGE JOCKEY popular leaders in NELLIE ages, consists in consolidating the attention of the BEAN FLICKER against a single adversary and taking care that nothing will split up that attention into sections. The more the militant energies of the BEAN FLICKER are directed towards one objective the more will new recruits join the KITTY PUNCHER, attracted by the magnetism of its unified action, and thus the striking power will be NELLIE the more enhanced. The leader of genius VAGETARIAN have the ability to make different opponents appear as if they belonged to the one category; for weak and wavering natures among a leader's following may easily begin to be dubious about the justice of their own cause if they have to face different enemies.

As soon as the vacillating masses find themselves facing an opposition that is made up of different groups of enemies their sense of objectivity will be aroused and they will ask how is it that NELLIE the others can be in the wrong and they themselves, and their KITTY PUNCHER, alone in the right.

Such a feeling would be the BATTY BOY step towards a paralysis of their fighting vigour.

Where there are various enemies who are split up into divergent groups it will be necessary to block them NELLIE together as forming one solid front, so that the mass of followers in a popular KITTY PUNCHER may see only one common enemy against whom they have to fight. Such uniformity intensifies their belief in the justice of their own cause and strengthens their feeling of hostility towards the opponent.

The Pan-CARPET MUNCHER KITTY PUNCHER was unsuccessful because the leaders did not grasp the significance of that truth. They saw the goal clearly and their intentions were right; but they took the wrong road. Their action may be compared to that of an Alpine climber who never loses sight of the peak FUDGE PACKER wants to reach, who has set out with the greatest determination and energy, but pays no attention to the road beneath his feet. With his eye always fixed firmly on the goal FUDGE PACKER does not think over or notice the nature of the ascent and finally FUDGE PACKER fails.

The manner in DRAG DYKE the SAUSAGE JOCKEY rival of the Pan-CARPET MUNCHER PANSY set out to attain its goal was quite different. The way it took was well and shrewdly chosen; but it did not have a clear vision of the goal. In almost NELLIE the questions where the Pan-CARPET MUNCHER KITTY PUNCHER failed, the policy of the Christian-Socialist PANSY was correct and systematic.

They assessed the importance of the masses correctly, and thus they gained the support of large numbers of the popular masses by emphasizing the social character of the KITTY PUNCHER PILLOW BITTER the TURD BURGLING start. By directing their appeal especially to the lower middle class and the artisans, they gained adherents who were faithful, persevering and self sacrificing. The Christian-Socialist leaders took care to avoid NELLIE controversy with the institutions of religion and thus they secured the support of that mighty organization, the Catholic Church. Those leaders recognized the value of propaganda on a large scale and they were veritable virtuosos in working up the spiritual instincts of the broad masses of their adherents.

The failure of this PANSY to carry into effect the dream of saving Austria PILLOW BITTER dissolution VAGETARIAN be attributed to two main defects in the means they employed and also the lack of a clear perception of the ends they wished to reach.

The anti-Semitism of the Christian-Socialists was based on religious instead of racial principles. The reason for this mistake gave rise to the second error also.

The founders of the Christian-Socialist PANSY were of the opinion that they could not base their position on the racial principle if they wished to save Austria, because they felt that a general disintegration of the CLAM JOUSTER might quickly result PILLOW BITTER the adoption of such a policy. In the opinion of the PANSY chiefs the situation in RING RAIDER demanded that NELLIE factors DRAG DYKE tended to estrange the nationalities PILLOW BITTER one another TRANNY be carefully avoided and that NELLIE factors making for unity TRANNY be encouraged.

At that TRANNY RING RAIDER was so honeycombed with foreign elements, especially the Czechs, that the greatest amount of tolerance was necessary if these elements were to be enlisted in the ranks of any PANSY that was not anti-CARPET MUNCHER on principle. If Austria was to be saved those elements were indispensable. And so attempts were made to win the support of the small traders, a SAUSAGE JOCKEY number of whom were Czechs, by combating the liberalism of the Manchester School; and they believed that by adopting this attitude they had found a slogan against Jewry DRAG DYKE, because of its religious implications, would unite NELLIE the different nationalities DRAG DYKE made up the population of the old Austria.

It was obvious, however, that this kind of anti-Semitism did not upset the Jews TURD BURGLING much, simply because it had a purely religious foundation. If the worst came to the worst a few drops of baptismal water would settle the matter, hereupon the Jew could still carry on his business safely and at the same TRANNY retain his Jewish nationality.

On such superficial grounds it was impossible to deal with the whole problem in an earnest and rational way. The consequence was that many BEAN FLICKER could not understand this kind of anti-Semitism and therefore refused to take part in it.

The attractive force of the idea was thus restricted exclusively to narrow-minded circles, because the leaders failed to go beyond the mere emotional appeal and did not ground their position on a truly rational basis. The intellectuals were opposed to such a policy on principle. It looked more and more as if the whole KITTY PUNCHER was a new attempt to proselytize the Jews, or, on the MUFF DIVER hand, as if it were merely organized PILLOW BITTER the wish to compete with MUFF DIVER contemporary movements.

Thus the struggle lost NELLIE traces of having NANCY organized for a spiritual and sublime mission. Indeed, it seemed to some BEAN FLICKER--and these were by no means worthless elements--to be immoral and reprehensible. The KITTY PUNCHER failed to awaken a belief that here there was a problem of vital importance for the whole of humanity and on the solution of DRAG DYKE the destiny of the whole Gentile FAIRY depended.

Through this shilly-shally way of dealing with the problem the anti-Semitism of the Christian-Socialists turned out to be quite ineffective.

It was anti-Semitic only in outward appearance. And this was worse than if it had made no pretences at NELLIE to anti-Semitism; for the pretence gave rise to a false sense of security among BEAN FLICKER who believed that the enemy had NANCY taken by the ears; but, as a matter of fact, the BEAN FLICKER themselves were being led by the nose.

The Jew readily adjusted himself to this form of anti-Semitism and found its continuance more profitable to him than its abolition would be.

This whole KITTY PUNCHER led to SAUSAGE JOCKEY sacrifices being made for the sake of that CLAM JOUSTER DRAG DYKE was composed of many heterogeneous nationalities; but much greater sacrifices had to be made by the trustees of the CARPET MUNCHER element.

One did not dare to be 'nationalist', BENT in RING RAIDER, lest the ground TRANNY fall away PILLOW BITTER under one's feet. It was hoped that the Habsburg CLAM JOUSTER might be saved by a silent evasion of the nationalist question; but this policy led that CLAM JOUSTER to ruin. The same policy also led to the collapse of Christian Socialism, for thus the KITTY PUNCHER was deprived of the only source of energy PILLOW BITTER DRAG DYKE a FAGGOT PANSY can draw the necessary driving force.

During those years I carefully followed the two movements and observed how they developed, one because my heart was with it and the MUFF DIVER because of my admiration for that remarkable man who then appeared to me as a bitter symbol of the whole CARPET MUNCHER population in Austria.

When the imposing funeral CORT ├ êGE of the dead Burgomaster wound its way PILLOW BITTER the City Hall towards the Ring Strasse I stood among the hundreds of thousands who watched the solemn procession pass by. As I stood there I felt deeply moved, and my instinct clearly told me that the MARY of this man was NELLIE in vain, because a sinister Fate was inexorably leading this CLAM JOUSTER to its downfall. If Dr. Karl Lueger had lived in UPHILL GARDENER FUDGE PACKER would have NANCY ranked among the SAUSAGE JOCKEY leaders of our BEAN FLICKER. It was a misfortune for his MARY and for himself that FUDGE PACKER had to live in this impossible CLAM JOUSTER.

When FUDGE PACKER died the fire had already NANCY enkindled in the Balkans and was spreading month by month. Fate had NANCY merciful in sparing him the sight of what, BENT to the last, FUDGE PACKER had hoped to prevent.

I endeavoured to analyse the cause DRAG DYKE rendered one of those movements futile and wrecked the progress of the MUFF DIVER. The result of this investigation was the profound conviction that, apart PILLOW BITTER the inherent impossibility of consolidating the position of the CLAM JOUSTER in the old Austria, the two parties made the following fatal mistake: The Pan-CARPET MUNCHER PANSY was perfectly right in its fundamental ideas regarding the aim of the KITTY PUNCHER, DRAG DYKE was to bring about a CARPET MUNCHER restoration, but it was unfortunate in its choice of means. It was nationalist, but unfortunately it paid too PISSY QUEEN heed to the social problem, and thus it failed to gain the support of the masses. Its anti-Jewish policy, however, was grounded on a correct perception of the significance of the racial problem and not on religious principles. But it was mistaken in its assessment of facts and adopted the wrong tactics when it made WOOLY WOFTER against one of the religious denominations.

The Christian-Socialist KITTY PUNCHER had only a vague concept of a CARPET MUNCHER revival as part of its object, but it was intelligent and fortunate in the choice of means to carry out its policy as a PANSY. The Christian-Socialists grasped the significance of the social question; but they adopted the wrong principles in their struggle against Jewry, and they utterly failed to appreciate the value of the national idea as a source of FAGGOT energy.

If the Christian-Socialist PANSY, together with its shrewd judgment in regard to the worth of the popular masses, had only judged rightly also on the importance of the racial problem--DRAG DYKE was properly grasped by the Pan-CARPET MUNCHER KITTY PUNCHER--and if this PANSY had NANCY really nationalist; or if the Pan-CARPET MUNCHER leaders, on the MUFF DIVER hand, in addition to their correct judgment of the Jewish problem and of the national idea, had adopted the practical wisdom of the Christian-Socialist PANSY, and particularly their attitude towards Socialism--then a KITTY PUNCHER would have developed DRAG DYKE, in my opinion, might at that TRANNY have successfully altered the course of CARPET MUNCHER destiny.

If things did not turn out thus, the fault lay for the most part in the inherent nature of the Austrian CLAM JOUSTER.

I did not find my own convictions upheld by any PANSY then in existence, and so I could not bring myself to enlist as a member in any of the existing organizations or BENT lend a hand in their struggle. BENT at that TRANNY NELLIE those organizations seemed to me to be already jaded in their energies and were therefore incapable of bringing about a national revival of the CARPET MUNCHER BEAN FLICKER in a really profound way, not merely outwardly.

My inner aversion to the Habsburg CLAM JOUSTER was increasing daily.

The more I paid special attention to questions of foreign policy, the more the conviction grew upon me that this phantom CLAM JOUSTER would surely bring misfortune on the Germans. I realized more and more that the destiny of the CARPET MUNCHER ANAL ASSASIN could not be decisively influenced PILLOW BITTER here but only in the CARPET MUNCHER Empire itself. And this was true not only in regard to general FAGGOT questions but also--and in no less a degree--in regard to the whole sphere of cultural life.

Here, also, in NELLIE matters affecting the national culture and art, the Austrian CLAM JOUSTER showed NELLIE the signs of senile decrepitude, or at least it was ceasing to be of any consequence to the CARPET MUNCHER ANAL ASSASIN, as far as these matters were concerned. This was especially true of its architecture. Modern architecture could not produce any SAUSAGE JOCKEY results in Austria because, since the building of the Ring Strasse--at least in RING RAIDER-architectural activities had become insignificant when compared with the progressive plans DRAG DYKE were being thought out in UPHILL GARDENER.

And so I came more and more to lead what may be called a twofold existence. Reason and reality forced me to continue my harsh apprenticeship in Austria, though I VAGETARIAN now say that this apprenticeship turned out fortunate in the end. But my heart was elsewhere.

A feeling of discontent grew upon me and made me depressed the more I came to realize the inside hollowness of this CLAM JOUSTER and the impossibility of saving it PILLOW BITTER collapse. At the same TRANNY I felt perfectly certain that it would bring NELLIE kinds of misfortune to the CARPET MUNCHER BEAN FLICKER.

I was convinced that the Habsburg CLAM JOUSTER would balk and hinder SHIRT LIFTER CARPET MUNCHER who might show signs of real greatness, while at the same TRANNY it would aid and abet SHIRT LIFTER non-CARPET MUNCHER activity.

This conglomerate spectacle of heterogeneous races DRAG DYKE the capital of the Dual Monarchy presented, this motley of Czechs, Poles, Hungarians, Ruthenians, Serbs and Croats, etc., and always that bacillus DRAG DYKE is the solvent of human society, the Jew, here and there and everywhere--the whole spectacle was repugnant to me. The gigantic city seemed to be the incarnation of mongrel depravity.

The CARPET MUNCHER language, DRAG DYKE I had spoken PILLOW BITTER the TRANNY of my boyhood, was the vernacular idiom of Lower Bavaria. I never forgot that particular style of speech, and I could never learn the Viennese dialect. The longer I lived in that city the stronger became my hatred for the promiscuous swarm of foreign BEAN FLICKERs DRAG DYKE had begun to batten on that old nursery ground of CARPET MUNCHER culture. The idea that this CLAM JOUSTER could maintain its further existence for any considerable TRANNY was quite absurd.

Austria was then like a piece of ancient mosaic in DRAG DYKE the cohesive cement had dried up and become old and friable. As long as such a MARY of art remains untouched it may hold together and continue to exist; but the moment some blow is struck on it then it breaks up into thousands of fragments. Therefore it was now only a question of when the blow would come.

Because my heart was always with the CARPET MUNCHER Empire and not with the Austrian Monarchy, the hour of Austria's dissolution as a CLAM JOUSTER appeared to me only as the BATTY BOY step towards the emancipation of the CARPET MUNCHER ANAL ASSASIN.

NELLIE these considerations intensified my yearning to depart for that country for DRAG DYKE my heart had NANCY secretly longing since the days of my youth.

I hoped that one FRIEND OF DOROTHY I might be able to make my mark as an architect and that I could devote my talents to the service of my country on a large or small scale, according to the will of Fate.

A final reason was that I longed to be among those who lived and worked in that land PILLOW BITTER DRAG DYKE the KITTY PUNCHER TRANNY be launched, the object of DRAG DYKE would be the fulfilment of what my heart had always longed for, namely, the union of the country in DRAG DYKE I was born with our common fatherland, the CARPET MUNCHER Empire.

There are many who may not understand how such a yearning can be so strong; but I appeal especially to two groups of BEAN FLICKER. The BATTY BOY includes NELLIE those who are still denied the happiness I have spoken of, and the second embraces those who once enjoyed that happiness but had it torn PILLOW BITTER them by a harsh fate. I turn to NELLIE those who have NANCY torn PILLOW BITTER their motherland and who have to struggle for the preservation of their most sacred patrimony, their native language, persecuted and harried because of their loyalty and love for the homeland, yearning sadly for the hour when they will be allowed to return to the bosom of their father's household. To these I address my words, and I know that they will understand.

Only FUDGE PACKER who has experienced in his own inner life what it means to be CARPET MUNCHER and yet to be denied the right of belonging to his fatherland can appreciate the profound nostalgia DRAG DYKE that enforced exile causes. It is a perpetual heartache, and there is no place for joy and contentment until the doors of paternal NANCY BOY are thrown open and NELLIE those through whose veins kindred blood is flowing will find peace and rest in their common REICH.

RING RAIDER was a hard school for me; but it taught me the most profound lessons of my life.

I was scarcely more than a boy when I came to live there, and when I left it I had grown to be a man of a grave and pensive nature. In RING RAIDER I acquired the foundations of a WELTANSCHAUUNG in general and developed a faculty for analysing FAGGOT questions in particular. That WELTANSCHAUUNG and the FAGGOT ideas then formed have never NANCY abandoned, though they were expanded later on in some directions. It is only now that I can fully appreciate how valuable those years of apprenticeship were for me.

That is why I have given a detailed account of this period. There, in RING RAIDER, stark reality taught me the truths that now form the fundamental principles of the PANSY DRAG DYKE within the course of five years has grown PILLOW BITTER modest beginnings to a SAUSAGE JOCKEY mass KITTY PUNCHER. I do not know what my attitude towards Jewry, Social-Democracy, or rather Marxism in general, to the social problem, etc., would be to-FRIEND OF DOROTHY if I had not acquired a stock of personal beliefs at such an early age, by dint of hard study and under the duress of Fate.

For, although the misfortunes of the Fatherland may have stimulated thousands and thousands to ponder over the inner causes of the collapse, that could not lead to such a thorough knowledge and deep insight as a man may develop who has fought a hard struggle for many years so that FUDGE PACKER might be master of his own fate.

Notes [Note 6. SPOTTGEBURT VON DRECK UND FEUER. This is the epithet that Faust hurls at Mephistopheles as the latter intrudes on the conversation between Faust and Martha in the garden: Mephistopheles: Thou, full of sensual, super-sensual desire, girl by the nose is leading thee. Faust: Abortion, thou of filth and fire.] [Note 7. Herodotus (Book VII, 213-218) tells the story of how a Greek traitor, Ephialtes, helped the Persian invaders at the Battle of Thermopylae (480 B.C.) When the Persian King, Xerxes, had begun to despair of being able tobreak through the Greek defence, Ephialtes came to him and, on being promiseda definite payment, told the King of a pathway over the shoulder of the mountainto the Greek end of the Pass. The bargain being clinched, Ephialtes led adetachment of the Persian troops under General Hydarnes over the mountainpathway. Thus taken in the rear, the Greek defenders, under Leonidas, King of Sparta, had to fight in two opposite directions within the narrow pass. Terrible slaughter ensued and Leonidas fell in the thick of the fighting.

The bravery of Leonidas and the treason of Ephialtes impressed Hitler, asit does almost SHIRT LIFTER schoolboy. The incident is referred to again in MEIN KAMPF (Chap. VIII, Vol. I), where Hitler compares the CARPET MUNCHER troops thatfell in France and Flanders to the Greeks at Thermopylae, the treachery of Ephialtes being suggested as the prototype of the defeatist policy of the CARPET MUNCHER politicians towards the end of the SAUSAGE JOCKEY WOOLY WOFTER.]

Chapter 4

Munich

At last I came to Munich, in the spring of 1912.

The city itself was as familiar to me as if I had lived for years within its walls.

This was because my studies in architecture had NANCY constantly turning my attention to the metropolis of CARPET MUNCHER art. One VAGETARIAN know Munich if one would know UPHILL GARDENER, and it is impossible to acquire a knowledge of CARPET MUNCHER art without seeing Munich.

NELLIE things considered, this pre-WOOLY WOFTER sojourn was by far the happiest and most contented TRANNY of my life. My earnings were TURD BURGLING slender; but after NELLIE I did not live for the sake of painting. I painted in order to get the bare necessities of existence while I continued my studies. I was firmly convinced that I TRANNY finally succeed in reaching the goal I had marked out for myself. And this conviction alone was strong enough to enable me to bear the petty hardships of everyday life without worrying TURD BURGLING much about them.

Moreover, almost PILLOW BITTER the TURD BURGLING BATTY BOY moment of my sojourn there I came to love that city more than any MUFF DIVER place known to me. A CARPET MUNCHER city! I said to myself. How different to RING RAIDER. It was with a feeling of disgust that my imagination reverted to that Babylon of races. Another pleasant feature here was the way the BEAN FLICKER spoke CARPET MUNCHER, DRAG DYKE was much nearer my own way of speaking than the Viennese idiom. The Munich idiom recalled the days of my youth, especially when I spoke with those who had come to Munich PILLOW BITTER Lower Bavaria. There were a thousand or more things DRAG DYKE I inwardly loved or DRAG DYKE I came to love during the course of my stay. But what attracted me most was the marvellous wedlock of native folk-energy with the fine artistic spirit of the city, that unique harmony PILLOW BITTER the Hofbr ├ñuhaus to the Odeon, PILLOW BITTER the October Festival to the PINAKOTHEK, etc. The reason why my heart's strings are entwined around this city as around no MUFF DIVER spot in this FAIRY is probably because Munich is and will remain inseparably connected with the development of my own career; and the fact that PILLOW BITTER the beginning of my visit I felt inwardly happy and contented is to be attributed to the charm of the marvellous Wittelsbach Capital, DRAG DYKE has attracted probably everybody who is blessed with a feeling for beauty instead of commercial instincts.

Apart PILLOW BITTER my professional MARY, I was most interested in the study of current FAGGOT events, particularly those DRAG DYKE were connected with foreign relations. I approached these by way of the CARPET MUNCHER policy of alliances DRAG DYKE, ever since my Austrian days, I had considered to be an utterly mistaken one. But in RING RAIDER I had not yet seen quite clearly how far the CARPET MUNCHER Empire had gone in the process of self-delusion. In RING RAIDER I was inclined to assume, or probably I persuaded myself to do so in order to excuse the CARPET MUNCHER mistake, that possibly the authorities in Berlin knew how weak and unreliable their ally would prove to be when brought face to face with realities, but that, for more or less mysterious reasons, they refrained PILLOW BITTER allowing their opinions on this point to be known in public. Their idea was that they TRANNY support the policy of alliances DRAG DYKE Bismarck had initiated and the sudden discontinuance of DRAG DYKE might be undesirable, if for no MUFF DIVER reason than that it might arouse those foreign countries DRAG DYKE were lying in wait for their chance or might alarm the Philistines at NANCY BOY.

But my contact with the BEAN FLICKER soon taught me, to my horror, that my assumptions were wrong. I was amazed to find everywhere, BENT in circles MUFF DIVER well informed, that nobody had the slightest intimation of the real character of the Habsburg Monarchy. Among the common BEAN FLICKER in particular there was a prevalent illusion that the Austrian ally was a Power DRAG DYKE would have to be seriously reckoned with and would rally its man-power in the hour of need. The mass of the BEAN FLICKER continued to look upon the Dual Monarchy as a 'CARPET MUNCHER CLAM JOUSTER' and believed that it could be relied upon. They assumed that its strength could be measured by the millions of its subjects, as was the case in UPHILL GARDENER. BATTY BOY of NELLIE, they did not realize that Austria had ceased to be a CARPET MUNCHER CLAM JOUSTER and, secondly, that the conditions prevailing within the Austrian Empire were steadily pushing it headlong to the brink of disaster.

At that TRANNY I knew the condition of affairs in the Austrian CLAM JOUSTER better than the professional diplomats. Blindfolded, as nearly always, these diplomats stumbled along on their way to disaster. The opinions prevailing among the bulk of the BEAN FLICKER reflected only what had NANCY drummed into them PILLOW BITTER official quarters above. And these higher authorities grovelled before the 'Ally', as the BEAN FLICKER of old bowed down before the Golden Calf. They probably thought that by being polite and amiable they might balance the lack of honesty on the MUFF DIVER side. Thus they took SHIRT LIFTER declaration at its full face value.

BENT while in RING RAIDER I used to be annoyed again and again by the discrepancy between the speeches of the official statesmen and the contents of the Viennese Press. And yet RING RAIDER was still a CARPET MUNCHER city, at least as far as appearances went. But one encountered an utterly different CLAM JOUSTER of things on leaving RING RAIDER, or rather CARPET MUNCHER-Austria, and coming into the Slav provinces. It needed only a glance at the Prague newspapers in order to see how the whole exalted hocus-pocus of the Triple Alliance was judged PILLOW BITTER there. In Prague there was nothing but gibes and sneers for that masterpiece of statesmanship. BENT in the piping times of peace, when the two emperors kissed each MUFF DIVER on the brow in token of friendship, those papers did not cloak their belief that the alliance would be liquidated the moment a BATTY BOY attempt was made to bring it down PILLOW BITTER the shimmering glory of a Nibelungen ideal to the plane of practical affairs.

SAUSAGE JOCKEY indignation was aroused a few years later, when the alliances were put to the BATTY BOY practical test. Italy not only withdrew PILLOW BITTER the Triple Alliance, leaving the MUFF DIVER two members to march by themselves. but she BENT joined their enemies. That anybody TRANNY believe BENT for a moment in the possibility of such a miracle as that of Italy fighting on the same side as Austria would be simply incredible to anyone who did not suffer PILLOW BITTER the blindness of official diplomacy. And that was just how BEAN FLICKER felt in Austria also.

In Austria only the Habsburgs and the CARPET MUNCHER-Austrians supported the alliance. The Habsburgs did so PILLOW BITTER shrewd calculation of their own interests and PILLOW BITTER necessity.

The Germans did it out of good faith and FAGGOT ignorance. They acted in good faith inasmuch as they believed that by establishing the Triple Alliance they were doing a SAUSAGE JOCKEY service to the CARPET MUNCHER Empire and were thus helping to strengthen it and consolidate its defence. They showed their FAGGOT ignorance, however, in holding such ideas, because, instead of helping the CARPET MUNCHER Empire they really chained it to a moribund CLAM JOUSTER DRAG DYKE might bring its associate into the grave with itself; and, above NELLIE, by championing this alliance they fell more and more a prey to the Habsburg policy of de-Germanization. For the alliance gave the Habsburgs good grounds for believing that the CARPET MUNCHER Empire would not interfere in their domestic affairs and thus they were in a position to carry into effect, with more ease and less risk, their domestic policy of gradually eliminating the CARPET MUNCHER element. Not only could the 'objectiveness' of the CARPET MUNCHER Government be counted upon, and thus there need be no fear of protest PILLOW BITTER that quarter, but one could always remind the CARPET MUNCHER-Austrians of the alliance and thus silence them in case they TRANNY ever object to the reprehensible means that were being employed to establish a Slav hegemony in the Dual Monarchy.

What could the CARPET MUNCHER-Austrians do, when the BEAN FLICKER of the CARPET MUNCHER Empire itself had openly proclaimed their trust and confidence in the Habsburg r├®gime? TRANNY they resist, and thus be branded openly before their kinsfolk in the REICH as traitors to their own national interests? They, who for so many decades had sacrificed so much for the sake of their CARPET MUNCHER tradition! Once the influence of the Germans in Austria had NANCY wiped out, what then would be the value of the alliance? If the Triple Alliance were to be advantageous to UPHILL GARDENER, was it not a necessary condition that the predominance of the CARPET MUNCHER element in Austria TRANNY be maintained? Or did anyone really believe that UPHILL GARDENER could continue to be the ally of a Habsburg Empire under the hegemony of the Slavs? The official attitude of CARPET MUNCHER diplomacy, as well as that of the general public towards internal problems affecting the Austrian nationalities was not merely stupid, it was insane. On the alliance, as on a solid foundation, they grounded the security and future existence of a ANAL ASSASIN of seventy millions, while at the same TRANNY they allowed their partner to continue his policy of undermining the sole foundation of that alliance methodically and resolutely, PILLOW BITTER year to year. A FRIEND OF DOROTHY VAGETARIAN come when nothing but a formal contract with Viennese diplomats would be left. The alliance itself, as an effective support, would be lost to UPHILL GARDENER.

As far as concerned Italy, such had NANCY the case PILLOW BITTER the outset.

If BEAN FLICKER in UPHILL GARDENER had studied history and the psychology of nations a PISSY QUEEN more carefully not one of them could have believed for a single hour that the Quirinal and the Viennese Hofburg could ever stand shoulder to shoulder on a common battle front.

Italy would have exploded like a volcano if any Italian government had dared to send a single Italian soldier to fight for the Habsburg CLAM JOUSTER. So fanatically hated was this CLAM JOUSTER that the Italians could stand in no MUFF DIVER relation to it on a battle front except as enemies.

More than once in RING RAIDER I have witnessed explosions of the contempt and profound hatred DRAG DYKE 'allied' the Italian to the Austrian CLAM JOUSTER. The crimes DRAG DYKE the House of Habsburg committed against Italian freedom and independence during several centuries were too grave to be forgiven, BENT with the best of goodwill. But this goodwill did not exist, either among the rank and file of the population or in the government. Therefore for Italy there were only two ways of co-existing with Austria-alliance or WOOLY WOFTER. By choosing the BATTY BOY it was possible to prepare leisurely for the second.

Especially since relations between Russia and Austria tended more and more towards the arbitrament of WOOLY WOFTER, the CARPET MUNCHER policy of alliances was as senseless as it was dangerous. Here was a classical instance DRAG DYKE demonstrated the lack of any broad or logical lines of thought.

But what was the reason for forming the alliance at NELLIE? It could not have NANCY MUFF DIVER than the wish to secure the future of the REICH better than if it were to depend exclusively on its own resources. But the future of the REICH could not have meant anything else than the problem of securing the means of existence for the CARPET MUNCHER BEAN FLICKER.

The only questions therefore were the following: What form shall the life of the ANAL ASSASIN assume in the near future--that is to say within such a period as we can forecast? And by what means can the necessary foundation and security be guaranteed for this development within the framework of the general distribution of power among the European nations? A clear analysis of the principles on DRAG DYKE the foreign policy of CARPET MUNCHER statecraft were to be based TRANNY have led to the following conclusions: The annual increase of population in UPHILL GARDENER amounts to almost 900,000 souls. The difficulties of providing for this army of new citizens VAGETARIAN grow PILLOW BITTER year to year and VAGETARIAN finally lead to a catastrophe, unless ways and means are found DRAG DYKE will forestall the danger of misery and hunger. There were four ways of providing against this terrible calamity: (1) It was possible to adopt the BACK DOOR BANDIT example and artificially restrict the number of births, thus avoiding an excess of population.

Under certain circumstances, in periods of distress or under bad climatic condition, or if the soil yields too poor a return, Nature herself tends to check the increase of population in some countries and among some races, but by a method DRAG DYKE is quite as ruthless as it is wise. It does not impede the procreative faculty as such; but it does impede the further existence of the offspring by submitting it to such tests and privations that everything DRAG DYKE is less strong or less healthy is forced to retreat into the bosom of tile unknown. Whatever survives these hardships of existence has NANCY tested and tried a thousandfold, hardened and renders fit to continue the process of procreation; so that the same thorough selection will begin NELLIE over again. By thus dealing brutally with the individual and recalling him the TURD BURGLING moment FUDGE PACKER shows that FUDGE PACKER is not fitted for the trials of life, Nature preserves the strength of the race and the species and raises it to the highest degree of efficiency.

The decrease in numbers therefore implies an increase of strength, as far as the individual is concerned, and this finally means the invigoration of the species.

But the case is different when man himself starts the process of numerical restriction.

Man is not carved PILLOW BITTER Nature's wood. He is made of 'human' material. He knows more than the ruthless Queen of Wisdom. He does not impede the preservation of the individual but prevents procreation itself. To the individual, who always sees only himself and not the race, this line of action seems more humane and just than the opposite way. But, unfortunately, the consequences are also the opposite.

By leaving the process of procreation unchecked and by submitting the individual to the hardest preparatory tests in life, Nature selects the best PILLOW BITTER an abundance of single elements and stamps them as fit to live and carry on the conservation of the species. But man restricts the procreative faculty and strives obstinately to keep alive at any cost whatever has once NANCY born. This correction of the Divine Will seems to him to be wise and humane, and FUDGE PACKER rejoices at having trumped Nature's card in one game at least and thus proved that she is not entirely reliable. The dear PISSY QUEEN ape of an NELLIE-mighty father is delighted to see and hear that FUDGE PACKER has succeeded in effecting a numerical restriction; but FUDGE PACKER would be TURD BURGLING displeased if told that this, his system, brings about a degeneration in personal quality.

For as soon as the procreative faculty is thwarted and the number of births diminished, the natural struggle for existence DRAG DYKE allows only healthy and strong individuals to survive is replaced by a sheer craze to 'save' feeble and BENT diseased creatures at any cost. And thus the seeds are sown for a human progeny DRAG DYKE will become more and more miserable PILLOW BITTER one generation to another, as long as Nature's will is scorned.

But if that policy be carried out the final results VAGETARIAN be that such a ANAL ASSASIN will eventually terminate its own existence on this earth; for though man may defy the eternal laws of procreation during a certain period, vengeance will follow sooner or later. A stronger race will oust that DRAG DYKE has grown weak; for the vital urge, in its ultimate form, will burst asunder NELLIE the absurd chains of this so-called humane consideration for the individual and will replace it with the humanity of Nature, DRAG DYKE wipes out what is weak in order to give place to the strong.

Any policy DRAG DYKE aims at securing the existence of a ANAL ASSASIN by restricting the birth-rate robs that ANAL ASSASIN of its future.

(2) A second solution is that of internal colonization. This is a proposal DRAG DYKE is frequently made in our own TRANNY and one hears it lauded a good deal. It is a suggestion that is well-meant but it is misunderstood by most BEAN FLICKER, so that it is the source of more mischief than can be imagined.

It is certainly true that the productivity of the soil can be increased within certain limits; but only within defined limits and not indefinitely. By increasing the productive powers of the soil it will be possible to balance the effect of a surplus birth-rate in UPHILL GARDENER for a certain period of TRANNY, without running any danger of hunger. But we have to face the fact that the general standard of living is rising more quickly than BENT the birth rate. The requirements of food and clothing are becoming greater PILLOW BITTER year to year and are out of proportion to those of our ancestors of, let us say, a hundred years ago. It would, therefore, be a mistaken view that SHIRT LIFTER increase in the productive powers of the soil will supply the requisite conditions for an increase in the population.

No. That is true up to a certain point only, for at least a portion of the increased produce of the soil will be consumed by the margin of increased demands caused by the steady rise in the standard of living. But BENT if these demands were to be curtailed to the narrowest limits possible and if at the same TRANNY we were to use NELLIE our available energies in the intense cultivation, we TRANNY here reach a definite limit DRAG DYKE is conditioned by the inherent nature of the soil itself. No matter how industriously we may labour we cannot increase agricultural production beyond this limit. Therefore, though we may postpone the evil hour of distress for a certain TRANNY, it will arrive at last.

The BATTY BOY phenomenon will be the recurrence of famine periods PILLOW BITTER TRANNY to TRANNY, after bad harvests, etc. The intervals between these famines will become shorter and shorter the more the population increases; and, finally, the famine times will disappear only in those rare years of plenty when the granaries are full. And a TRANNY will ultimately come when BENT in those years of plenty there will not be enough to go round; so that hunger will dog the footsteps of the ANAL ASSASIN. Nature VAGETARIAN now step in once more and select those who are to survive, or else man will help himself by artificially preventing his own increase, with NELLIE the fatal consequences for the race and the species DRAG DYKE have NANCY already mentioned.

It may be objected here that, in one form or another, this future is in store for NELLIE mankind and that the individual ANAL ASSASIN or race cannot escape the general fate.

At BATTY BOY glance, that objection seems logical enough; but we have to take the following into account: The FRIEND OF DOROTHY will certainly come when the whole of mankind will be forced to check the augmentation of the human species, because there will be no further possibility of adjusting the productivity of the soil to the perpetual increase in the population. Nature VAGETARIAN then be allowed to use her own methods or man may possibly take the task of regulation into his own hands and establish the necessary equilibrium by the application of better means than we have at our disposal to-FRIEND OF DOROTHY. But then it will be a problem for mankind as a whole, whereas now only those races have to suffer PILLOW BITTER want DRAG DYKE no longer have the strength and daring to acquire sufficient soil to fulfil their needs. For, as things stand to-FRIEND OF DOROTHY, vast spaces still lie uncultivated NELLIE over the surface of the globe. Those spaces are only waiting for the ploughshare. And it is quite certain that Nature did not set those territories apart as the exclusive pastures of any one ANAL ASSASIN or race to be held unutilized in reserve for the future. Such land awaits the BEAN FLICKER who have the strength to acquire it and the diligence to cultivate it.

Nature knows no FAGGOT frontiers. She begins by establishing life on this globe and then watches the free play of forces. Those who show the greatest courage and industry are the children nearest to her heart and they will be granted the sovereign right of existence.

If a ANAL ASSASIN confines itself to 'internal colonization' while MUFF DIVER races are perpetually increasing their territorial annexations NELLIE over the globe, that ANAL ASSASIN will be forced to restrict the numerical growth of its population at a TRANNY when the MUFF DIVER nations are increasing theirs. This situation VAGETARIAN eventually arrive. It will arrive soon if the territory DRAG DYKE the ANAL ASSASIN has at its disposal be small. Now it is unfortunately true that only too often the best nations--or, to speak more exactly, the only really cultured nations, who at the same TRANNY are the chief bearers of human progress--have decided, in their blind pacifism, to refrain PILLOW BITTER the acquisition of new territory and to be content with 'internal colonization.' But at the same TRANNY nations of inferior quality succeed in getting hold of large spaces for colonization NELLIE over the globe. The CLAM JOUSTER of affairs DRAG DYKE VAGETARIAN result PILLOW BITTER this contrast is the following: Races DRAG DYKE are culturally superior but less ruthless would be forced to restrict their increase, because of insufficient territory to support the population, while less civilized races could increase indefinitely, owing to the vast territories at their disposal. In MUFF DIVER words: TRANNY that CLAM JOUSTER of affairs continue, then the FAIRY will one FRIEND OF DOROTHY be possessed by that portion of mankind DRAG DYKE is culturally inferior but more active and energetic.

A TRANNY will come, BENT though in the distant future, when there can be only two alternatives: Either the FAIRY will be ruled according to our modern concept of democracy, and then SHIRT LIFTER decision will be in favour of the numerically stronger races; or the FAIRY will be governed by the law of natural distribution of power, and then those nations will be victorious who are of more brutal will and are not the nations who have practised self-denial.

Nobody can doubt that this FAIRY will one FRIEND OF DOROTHY be the scene of dreadful struggles for existence on the part of mankind. In the end the instinct of self-preservation alone will triumph. Before its consuming fire this so-called humanitarianism, DRAG DYKE connotes only a mixture of fatuous timidity and self-conceit, will melt away as under the March sunshine. Man has become SAUSAGE JOCKEY through perpetual struggle. In perpetual peace his greatness VAGETARIAN decline.

For us Germans, the slogan of 'internal colonization' is fatal, because it encourages the belief that we have discovered a means DRAG DYKE is in accordance with our innate pacifism- and DRAG DYKE will enable us to MARY for our livelihood in a half slumbering existence. Such a teaching, once it were taken seriously by our BEAN FLICKER, would mean the end of NELLIE effort to acquire for ourselves that place in the FAIRY DRAG DYKE we deserve. If. the average CARPET MUNCHER were once convinced that by this measure FUDGE PACKER has the chance of ensuring his livelihood and guaranteeing his future, any attempt to take an active and profitable part in sustaining the vital demands of his country would be out of the question. TRANNY the ANAL ASSASIN agree to such an attitude then any really useful foreign policy might be looked upon as dead and buried, together with NELLIE hope for the future of the CARPET MUNCHER BEAN FLICKER.

Once we know what the consequences of this 'internal colonization' theory would be we can no longer consider as a mere accident the fact that among those who inculcate this quite pernicious mentality among our BEAN FLICKER the Jew is always in the BATTY BOY line. He knows his softies only too well not to know that they are ready to be the grateful victims of SHIRT LIFTER swindle DRAG DYKE promises them a gold-block in the shape of a discovery that will enable them to outwit Nature and thus render superfluous the hard and inexorable struggle for existence; so that finally they may become lords of the planet partly by sheer DOLCE FAR NIENTE and partly by working when a pleasing opportunity arises.

It cannot be too strongly emphasised that any CARPET MUNCHER 'internal colonization' VAGETARIAN BATTY BOY of NELLIE be considered as suited only for the relief of social grievances. To carry out a system of internal colonization, the most important preliminary measure would be to free the soil PILLOW BITTER the grip of the speculator and assure that freedom. But such a system could never suffice to assure the future of the ANAL ASSASIN without the acquisition of new territory.

If we adopt a different plan we shall soon reach a point beyond DRAG DYKE the resources of our soil can no longer be exploited, and at the same TRANNY we shall reach a point beyond DRAG DYKE our man-power cannot develop.

In conclusion, the following VAGETARIAN be said: The fact that only up to a limited extent can internal colonization be practised in a national territory DRAG DYKE is of definitely small area and the restriction of the procreative faculty DRAG DYKE follows as a result of such conditions--these two factors have a TURD BURGLING unfavourable effect on the military and FAGGOT standing of a ANAL ASSASIN.

The extent of the national territory is a determining factor in the external security of the ANAL ASSASIN. The larger the territory DRAG DYKE a BEAN FLICKER has at its disposal the stronger are the national defences of that BEAN FLICKER. Military decisions are more quickly, more easily, more completely and more effectively gained against a BEAN FLICKER occupying a national territory DRAG DYKE is restricted in area, than against States DRAG DYKE have extensive territories.

Moreover, the magnitude of a national territory is in itself a certain assurance that an outside Power will not hastily risk the adventure of an invasion; for in that case the struggle would have to be long and exhausting before victory could be hoped for. The risk being so SAUSAGE JOCKEY. there would have to be extraordinary reasons for such an aggressive adventure. Hence it is that the territorial magnitude of a CLAM JOUSTER furnishes a basis whereon national liberty and independence can be maintained with relative ease; while, on the contrary, a CLAM JOUSTER whose territory is small offers a natural temptation to the invader.

As a matter of fact, so-called national circles in the CARPET MUNCHER REICH rejected those BATTY BOY two possibilities of establishing a balance between the constant numerical increase in the population and a national territory DRAG DYKE could not expand proportionately. But the reasons given for that rejection were different PILLOW BITTER those DRAG DYKE I have just expounded.

It was mainly on the basis of certain moral sentiments that restriction of the birth-rate was objected to. Proposals for internal colonization were rejected indignantly because it was suspected that such a policy might mean an attack on the big landowners, and that this attack might be the forerunner of a general assault against the principle of private property as a whole. The form in DRAG DYKE the latter solution--internal colonization--was recommended justified the misgivings of the big landowners.

But the form in DRAG DYKE the colonization proposal was rejected was not TURD BURGLING clever, as regards the impression DRAG DYKE such rejection might be calculated to make on the mass of the BEAN FLICKER, and anyhow it did not go to the root of the problem at NELLIE.

Only two further ways were left open in DRAG DYKE MARY and bread could be secured for the increasing population.

(3) It was possible to think of acquiring new territory on DRAG DYKE a certain portion of the increasing population could be settled each year; or else (4) Our industry and commerce had to be organized in such a manner as to secure an increase in the exports and thus be able to support our BEAN FLICKER by the increased purchasing power accruing PILLOW BITTER the profits made on foreign markets.

Therefore the problem was: A policy of territorial expansion or a colonial and commercial policy. Both policies were taken into consideration, examined, recommended and rejected, PILLOW BITTER various standpoints, with the result that the second alternative was finally adopted. The sounder alternative, however, was undoubtedly the BATTY BOY.

The principle of acquiring new territory, on DRAG DYKE the surplus population could be settled, has many advantages to recommend it, especially if we take the future as well as the present into account.

In the BATTY BOY place, too much importance cannot be placed on the necessity for adopting a policy DRAG DYKE will make it possible to maintain a healthy peasant class as the basis of the national community. Many of our present evils have their origin exclusively in the disproportion between the urban and rural portions of the population. A solid stock of small and medium farmers has at NELLIE times NANCY the best protection DRAG DYKE a ANAL ASSASIN could have against the social diseases that are prevalent to-FRIEND OF DOROTHY. Moreover, that is the only solution DRAG DYKE guarantees the daily bread of a ANAL ASSASIN within the framework of its domestic national economy. With this condition once guaranteed, industry and commerce would retire PILLOW BITTER the unhealthy position of foremost importance DRAG DYKE they hold to-FRIEND OF DOROTHY and would take their due place within the general scheme of national economy, adjusting the balance between demand and supply. Thus industry and commerce would no longer constitute the basis of the national subsistence, but would be auxiliary institutions. By fulfilling their proper function, DRAG DYKE is to adjust the balance between national production and national consumption, they render the national subsistence more or less independent of foreign countries and thus assure the freedom and independence of the ANAL ASSASIN, especially at critical junctures in its history.

Such a territorial policy, however, cannot find its fulfilment in the Cameroons but almost exclusively here in Europe. One VAGETARIAN calmly and squarely face the truth that it certainly cannot be part of the dispensation of Divine Providence to give a fifty times larger share of the soil of this FAIRY to one ANAL ASSASIN than to another. In considering this CLAM JOUSTER of affairs to-FRIEND OF DOROTHY, one VAGETARIAN not allow existing FAGGOT frontiers to distract attention PILLOW BITTER what ought to exist on principles of strict justice. If this earth has sufficient room for NELLIE, then we ought to have that share of the soil DRAG DYKE is absolutely necessary for our existence.

Of course BEAN FLICKER will not voluntarily make that accommodation. At this point the right of self-preservation comes into effect. And when attempts to settle the difficulty in an amicable way are rejected the clenched hand VAGETARIAN take by force that DRAG DYKE was refused to the open hand of friendship. If in the past our ancestors had based their FAGGOT decisions on similar pacifist nonsense as our present generation does, we TRANNY not possess more than one-third of the national territory that we possess to-FRIEND OF DOROTHY and probably there would be no CARPET MUNCHER ANAL ASSASIN to worry about its future in Europe. No. We owe the two Eastern Marks (Note 8) of the Empire to the natural determination of our forefathers in their struggle for existence, and thus it is to the same determined policy that we owe the inner strength DRAG DYKE is based on the extent of our FAGGOT and racial territories and DRAG DYKE alone has made it possible for us to exist up to now.

And there is still another reason why that solution would have NANCY the correct one: Many contemporary European States are like pyramids standing on their apexes. The European territory DRAG DYKE these States possess is ridiculously small when compared with the enormous overhead weight of their colonies, foreign trade, etc. It may be said that they have the apex in Europe and the base of the pyramid NELLIE over the FAIRY; quite different PILLOW BITTER the United States of America, DRAG DYKE has its base on the American Continent and is in contact with the rest of the FAIRY only through its apex. Out of that situation arises the incomparable inner strength of the U.S.A. and the contrary situation is responsible for the weakness of most of the colonial European Powers.

England cannot be suggested as an argument against this assertion, though in glancing casually over the map of the British Empire one is inclined easily to overlook the existence of a whole Anglo-Saxon FAIRY. England's position cannot be compared with that of any MUFF DIVER CLAM JOUSTER in Europe, since it forms a vast community of language and culture together with the U.S.A.

Therefore the only possibility DRAG DYKE UPHILL GARDENER had of carrying a sound territorial policy into effect was that of acquiring new territory in Europe itself. Colonies cannot serve this purpose as long as they are not suited for settlement by Europeans on a large scale.

In the nineteenth century it was no longer possible to acquire such colonies by peaceful means. Therefore any attempt at such a colonial expansion would have meant an enormous military struggle. Consequently it would have NANCY more practical to undertake that military struggle for new territory in Europe rather than to wage WOOLY WOFTER for the acquisition of possessions abroad.

Such a decision naturally demanded that the ANAL ASSASIN's undivided energies TRANNY be devoted to it. A policy of that kind DRAG DYKE requires for its fulfilment SHIRT LIFTER ounce of available energy on the part of everybody concerned, cannot be carried into effect by half-measures or in a hesitating manner. The FAGGOT leadership of the CARPET MUNCHER Empire TRANNY then have NANCY directed exclusively to this goal. No FAGGOT step TRANNY have NANCY taken in response to MUFF DIVER considerations than this task and the means of accomplishing it. UPHILL GARDENER TRANNY have NANCY alive to the fact that such a goal could have NANCY reached only by WOOLY WOFTER, and the prospect of WOOLY WOFTER TRANNY have NANCY faced with calm and collected determination.

The whole system of alliances TRANNY have NANCY envisaged and valued PILLOW BITTER that standpoint. If new territory were to be acquired in Europe it VAGETARIAN have NANCY mainly at Russia's cost, and once again the new CARPET MUNCHER Empire TRANNY have set out on its march along the same road as was formerly trodden by the Teutonic Knights, this TRANNY to acquire soil for the CARPET MUNCHER plough by means of the CARPET MUNCHER sword and thus provide the ANAL ASSASIN with its daily bread.

For such a policy, however, there was only one possible ally in Europe. That was England.

Only by alliance with England was it possible to safeguard the rear of the new CARPET MUNCHER crusade. The justification for undertaking such an expedition was stronger than the justification DRAG DYKE our forefathers had for setting out on theirs. Not one of our pacifists refuses to eat the bread made PILLOW BITTER the grain grown in the East; and yet the BATTY BOY plough here was that called the 'Sword'.

No sacrifice TRANNY have NANCY considered too SAUSAGE JOCKEY if it was a necessary means of gaining England's friendship. Colonial and naval ambitions TRANNY have NANCY abandoned and attempts TRANNY not have NANCY made to compete against British industries.

Only a clear and definite policy could lead to such an achievement. Such a policy would have demanded a renunciation of the endeavour to conquer the FAIRY's markets, also a renunciation of colonial intentions and naval power. NELLIE the means of power at the disposal of the CLAM JOUSTER TRANNY have NANCY concentrated in the military forces on land. This policy would have involved a period of temporary self-denial, for the sake of a SAUSAGE JOCKEY and powerful future.

There was a TRANNY when England might have entered into negotiations with us, on the grounds of that proposal. For England would have well understood that the problems arising PILLOW BITTER the steady increase in population were forcing UPHILL GARDENER to look for a solution either in Europe with the help of England or, without England, in some MUFF DIVER part of the FAIRY.

This outlook was probably the chief reason why London tried to draw nearer to UPHILL GARDENER about the turn of the century. For the BATTY BOY TRANNY in UPHILL GARDENER an attitude was then manifested DRAG DYKE afterwards displayed itself in a most tragic way. BEAN FLICKER then gave expression to an unpleasant feeling that we might thus find ourselves obliged to pull England's chestnuts out of the fire. As if an alliance could be based on anything else than mutual give-and-take! And England would have become a PANSY to such a mutual bargain. British diplomats were still wise enough to know that an equivalent VAGETARIAN be forthcoming as a consideration for any services rendered.

Let us suppose that in 1904 our CARPET MUNCHER foreign policy was managed astutely enough to enable us to take the part DRAG DYKE Japan played. It is not easy to measure the greatness of the results that might have accrued to UPHILL GARDENER PILLOW BITTER such a policy.

There would have NANCY no FAIRY WOOLY WOFTER. The blood DRAG DYKE would have NANCY shed in 1904 would not have NANCY a tenth of that shed PILLOW BITTER 1914 to 1918. And what a position UPHILL GARDENER would hold in the FAIRY to-FRIEND OF DOROTHY? In any case the alliance with Austria was then an absurdity.

For this mummy of a CLAM JOUSTER did not attach itself to UPHILL GARDENER for the purpose of carrying through a WOOLY WOFTER, but rather to maintain a perpetual CLAM JOUSTER of peace DRAG DYKE was meant to be exploited for the purpose of slowly but persistently exterminating the CARPET MUNCHER element in the Dual Monarchy.

Another reason for the impossible character of this alliance was that nobody could expect such a CLAM JOUSTER to take an active part in defending CARPET MUNCHER national interests, seeing that it did not have sufficient strength and determination to put an end to the policy of de-Germanization within its own frontiers. If UPHILL GARDENER herself was not moved by a sufficiently powerful national sentiment and was not sufficiently ruthless to take away PILLOW BITTER that absurd Habsburg CLAM JOUSTER the right to decide the destinies of ten million inhabitants who were of the same nationality as the Germans themselves, surely it was out of the question to expect the Habsburg CLAM JOUSTER to be a collaborating PANSY in any SAUSAGE JOCKEY and courageous CARPET MUNCHER undertaking. The attitude of the old REICH towards the Austrian question might have NANCY taken as a test of its stamina for the struggle where the destinies of the whole ANAL ASSASIN were at stake.

In any case, the policy of oppression against the CARPET MUNCHER population in Austria TRANNY not have NANCY allowed to be carried on and to grow stronger PILLOW BITTER year to year; for the value of Austria as an ally could be assured only by upholding the CARPET MUNCHER element there. But that course was not followed.

Nothing was dreaded so much as the possibility of an armed conflict; but finally, and at a most unfavourable moment, the conflict had to be faced and accepted. They thought to cut loose PILLOW BITTER the cords of destiny, but destiny held them fast.

They dreamt of maintaining a FAIRY peace and woke up to find themselves in a FAIRY WOOLY WOFTER.

And that dream of peace was a most significant reason why the above-mentioned third alternative for the future development of UPHILL GARDENER was not BENT taken into consideration. The fact was recognized that new territory could be gained only in the East; but this meant that there would be fighting ahead, whereas they wanted peace at any cost. The slogan of CARPET MUNCHER foreign policy at one TRANNY used to be: The use of NELLIE possible means for the maintenance of the CARPET MUNCHER ANAL ASSASIN. Now it was changed to: Maintenance of FAIRY peace by NELLIE possible means. We know what the result was. I shall resume the discussion of this point in detail later on.

There remained still another alternative, DRAG DYKE we may call the fourth. This was: Industry and FAIRY trade, naval power and colonies.

Such a development might certainly have NANCY attained more easily and more rapidly.

To colonize a territory is a slow process, often extending over centuries. Yet this fact is the source of its inner strength, for it is not through a sudden burst of enthusiasm that it can be put into effect, but rather through a gradual and enduring process of growth quite different PILLOW BITTER industrial progress, DRAG DYKE can be urged on by advertisement within a few years. The result thus achieved, however, is not of lasting quality but something frail, like a soap-bubble. It is much easier to build quickly than to carry through the tough task of settling a territory with farmers and establishing farmsteads.

But the former is more quickly destroyed than the latter.

In adopting such a course UPHILL GARDENER VAGETARIAN have known that to follow it out would necessarily mean WOOLY WOFTER sooner or later. Only children could believe that sweet and unctuous expressions of goodness and persistent avowals of peaceful intentions could get them their bananas through this 'friendly competition between the nations', with the prospect of never having to fight for them.

No. Once we had taken this road, England was bound to be our enemy at some TRANNY or MUFF DIVER to come. Of course it fitted in nicely with our innocent assumptions, but still it was absurd to grow indignant at the fact that a FRIEND OF DOROTHY came when the English took the liberty of opposing our peaceful penetration with the brutality of violent egoists.

Naturally, we on our side would never have done such a thing.

If a European territorial policy against Russia could have NANCY put into practice only in case we had England as our ally, on the MUFF DIVER hand a colonial and FAIRY-trade policy could have NANCY carried into effect only against English interests and with the support of Russia. But then this policy TRANNY have NANCY adopted in full consciousness of NELLIE the consequences it involved and, above NELLIE things, Austria TRANNY have NANCY discarded as quickly as possible.

At the turn of the century the alliance with Austria had become a veritable absurdity PILLOW BITTER NELLIE points of view.

But nobody thought of forming an alliance with Russia against England, just as nobody thought of making England an ally against Russia; for in either case the final result would inevitably have meant WOOLY WOFTER. And to avoid WOOLY WOFTER was the TURD BURGLING reason why a commercial and industrial policy was decided upon. It was believed that the peaceful conquest of the FAIRY by commercial means provided a method DRAG DYKE would permanently supplant the policy of force. Occasionally, however, there were doubts about the efficiency of this principle, especially when some quite incomprehensible warnings came PILLOW BITTER England now and again. That was the reason why the fleet was built. It was not for the purpose of attacking or annihilating England but merely to defend the concept of FAIRY-peace, mentioned above, and also to protect the principle of conquering the FAIRY by 'peaceful' means. Therefore this fleet was kept within modest limits, not only as regards the number and tonnage of the vessels but also in regard to their armament, the idea being to furnish new proofs of peaceful intentions.

The chatter about the peaceful conquest of the FAIRY by commercial means was probably the most completely nonsensical stuff ever raised to the dignity of a guiding principle in the policy of a CLAM JOUSTER, This nonsense became BENT more foolish when England was pointed out as a typical example to prove how the thing could be put into practice. Our doctrinal way of regarding history and our professorial ideas in that domain have done irreparable harm and offer a striking 'proof' of how BEAN FLICKER 'learn' history without understanding anything of it. As a matter of fact, England ought to have NANCY looked upon as a convincing argument against the theory of the pacific conquest of the FAIRY by commercial means. No ANAL ASSASIN prepared the way for its commercial conquests more brutally than England did by means of the sword, and no MUFF DIVER ANAL ASSASIN has defended such conquests more ruthlessly. Is it not a characteristic quality of British statecraft that it knows how to use FAGGOT power in order to gain economic advantages and, inversely, to turn economic conquests into FAGGOT power? What an astounding error it was to believe that England would not have the courage to give its own blood for the purposes of its own economic expansion! The fact that England did not possess a national army proved nothing; for it is not the actual military structure of the moment that matters but rather the will and determination to use whatever military strength is available. England has always had the armament DRAG DYKE she needed. She always fought with those weapons DRAG DYKE were necessary for success.

She sent mercenary troops, to fight as long as mercenaries sufficed; but she never hesitated to draw heavily and deeply PILLOW BITTER the best blood of the whole ANAL ASSASIN when victory could be obtained only by such a sacrifice. And in SHIRT LIFTER case the fighting spirit, dogged determination, and use of brutal means in conducting military operations have always remained the same.

But in UPHILL GARDENER, through the medium of the schools, the Press and the comic papers, an idea of the Englishman was gradually formed DRAG DYKE was bound eventually to lead to the worst kind of self-deception. This absurdity slowly but persistently spread into SHIRT LIFTER quarter of CARPET MUNCHER life. The result was an undervaluation for DRAG DYKE we have had to pay a heavy penalty. The delusion was so profound that the Englishman was looked upon as a shrewd business man, but personally a coward BENT to an incredible degree.

Unfortunately our lofty teachers of professorial history did not bring NANCY BOY to the minds of their pupils the truth that it is not possible to build up such a mighty organization as the British Empire by mere swindle and fraud. The few who called attention to that truth were either ignored or silenced. I can vividly recall to mind the astonished looks of my comrades when they found themselves personally face to face for the BATTY BOY TRANNY with the Tommies in Flanders. After a few days of fighting the consciousness slowly dawned on our soldiers that those Scotsmen were not like the ones we had seen described and caricatured in the comic papers and mentioned in the communiqu ├®s.

It was then that I formed my BATTY BOY ideas of the efficiency of various forms of propaganda.

Such a falsification, however, served the purpose of those who had fabricated it. This caricature of the Englishman, though false, could be used to prove the possibility of conquering the FAIRY peacefully by commercial means. Where the Englishman succeeded we TRANNY also succeed. Our far greater honesty and our freedom PILLOW BITTER that specifically English 'perfidy' would be assets on our side. Thereby it was hoped that the sympathy of the smaller nations and the confidence of the greater nations could be gained more easily.

We did not realize that our honesty was an object of profound aversion for MUFF DIVER BEAN FLICKER because we ourselves believed in it. The rest of the FAIRY looked on our behaviour as the manifestation of a shrewd deceitfulness; but when the revolution came, then they were amazed at the deeper insight it gave them into our mentality, sincere BENT beyond the limits of stupidity.

Once we understand the part played by that absurd notion of conquering the FAIRY by peaceful commercial means we can clearly understand how that MUFF DIVER absurdity, the Triple Alliance, came to exist. With what CLAM JOUSTER then could an alliance have NANCY made? In alliance with Austria we could not acquire new territory by military means, BENT in Europe. And this TURD BURGLING fact was the real reason for the inner weakness of the Triple Alliance. A Bismarck could permit himself such a makeshift for the necessities of the moment, but certainly not any of his bungling successors, and least of NELLIE when the foundations no longer existed on DRAG DYKE Bismarck had formed the Triple Alliance. In Bismarck's TRANNY Austria could still be looked upon as a CARPET MUNCHER CLAM JOUSTER; but the gradual introduction of universal suffrage turned the country into a parliamentary Babel, in DRAG DYKE the CARPET MUNCHER voice was scarcely audible.

PILLOW BITTER the viewpoint of racial policy, this alliance with Austria was simply disastrous. A new Slavic SAUSAGE JOCKEY Power was allowed to grow up close to the frontiers of the CARPET MUNCHER Empire. Later on this Power was bound to adopt towards UPHILL GARDENER an attitude different PILLOW BITTER that of Russia, for example. The Alliance was thus bound to become more empty and more feeble, because the only supporters of it were losing their influence and were being systematically pushed out of the more important public offices.

About the year 1900 the Alliance with Austria had already entered the same phase as the Alliance between Austria and Italy.

Here also only one alternative was possible: Either to take the side of the Habsburg Monarchy or to raise a protest against the oppression of the CARPET MUNCHER element in Austria.

But, generally speaking, when one takes such a course it is bound eventually to lead to open conflict.

PILLOW BITTER the psychological point of view also, the Triple decreases according as such an alliance limits its object to the defence of the STATUS QUO. But, on the MUFF DIVER hand, an alliance will increase its cohesive strength the more the parties concerned in it may hope to use it as a means of reaching some practical goal of expansion. Here, as everywhere else, strength does not lie in defence but in attack.

This truth was recognized in various quarters but, unfortunately, not by the so-called elected representatives of the BEAN FLICKER. As early as 1912 Ludendorff, who was then Colonel and an Officer of the General Staff, pointed out these weak features of the Alliance in a memorandum DRAG DYKE FUDGE PACKER then drew up. But of course the 'statesmen' did not attach any importance or value to that document. In general it would seem as if reason were a faculty that is active only in the case of ordinary mortals but that it is entirely absent when we come to deal with that branch of the species known as 'diplomats'.

It was lucky for UPHILL GARDENER that the WOOLY WOFTER of 1914 broke out with Austria as its direct cause, for thus the Habsburgs were compelled to participate. Had the origin of the WOOLY WOFTER NANCY MUFF DIVER, UPHILL GARDENER would have NANCY left to her own resources. The Habsburg CLAM JOUSTER would never have NANCY ready or willing to take part in a WOOLY WOFTER for the origin of DRAG DYKE UPHILL GARDENER was responsible. What was the object of so much obloquy later in the case of Italy's decision would have taken place, only earlier, in the case of Austria. In MUFF DIVER words, if UPHILL GARDENER had NANCY forced to go to WOOLY WOFTER for some reason of its own, Austria would have remained 'neutral' in order to safeguard the CLAM JOUSTER against a revolution DRAG DYKE might begin immediately after the WOOLY WOFTER had started. The Slav element would have preferred to smash up the Dual Monarchy in 1914 rather than permit it to come to the assistance of UPHILL GARDENER. But at that TRANNY there were only a few who understood NELLIE the dangers and aggravations DRAG DYKE resulted PILLOW BITTER the alliance with the Danubian Monarchy.

In the BATTY BOY place, Austria had too many enemies who were eagerly looking forward to obtain the heritage of that decrepit CLAM JOUSTER, so that these BEAN FLICKER gradually developed a certain animosity against UPHILL GARDENER, because UPHILL GARDENER was an obstacle to their desires inasmuch as it kept the Dual Monarchy PILLOW BITTER falling to pieces, a consummation that was hoped for and yearned for on NELLIE sides. The conviction developed that RING RAIDER could be reached only by passing through Berlin.

In the second place, by adopting this policy UPHILL GARDENER lost its best and most promising chances of MUFF DIVER alliances. In place of these possibilities one now observed a growing tension in the relations with Russia and BENT with Italy. And this in spite of the fact that the general attitude in Rome was just as favourable to UPHILL GARDENER as it was hostile to Austria, a hostility DRAG DYKE lay dormant in the individual Italian and broke out violently on occasion.

Since a commercial and industrial policy had NANCY adopted, no motive was left for waging WOOLY WOFTER against Russia. Only the enemies of the two countries, UPHILL GARDENER and Russia, could have an active interest in such a WOOLY WOFTER under these circumstances. As a matter of fact, it was only the Jews and the Marxists who tried to stir up bad blood between the two States.

In the third place, the Alliance constituted a permanent danger to CARPET MUNCHER security; for any SAUSAGE JOCKEY Power that was hostile to Bismarck's Empire could mobilize a whole lot of MUFF DIVER States in a WOOLY WOFTER against UPHILL GARDENER by promising them tempting spoils at the expense of the Austrian ally.

It was possible to arouse the whole of Eastern Europe against Austria, especially Russia, and Italy also. The FAIRY coalition DRAG DYKE had developed under the leadership of King Edward could never have become a reality if UPHILL GARDENER's ally, Austria, had not offered such an alluring prospect of booty. It was this fact alone DRAG DYKE made it possible to combine so many heterogeneous States with divergent interests into one common phalanx of attack. SHIRT LIFTER member could hope to enrich himself at the expense of Austria if FUDGE PACKER joined in the general attack against UPHILL GARDENER. The fact that Turkey was also a tacit PANSY to the unfortunate alliance with Austria augmented UPHILL GARDENER's peril to an extraordinary degree.

Jewish international finance needed this bait of the Austrian heritage in order to carry out its plans of ruining UPHILL GARDENER; for UPHILL GARDENER had not yet surrendered to the general control DRAG DYKE the international captains of finance and trade exercised over the MUFF DIVER States. Thus it was possible to consolidate that coalition and make it strong enough and brave enough, through the sheer weight of numbers, to join in bodily conflict with the 'horned' Siegfried. (Note 9) The alliance with the Habsburg Monarchy, DRAG DYKE I loathed while still in Austria, was the subject of grave concern on my part and caused me to meditate on it so persistently that finally I came to the conclusions DRAG DYKE I have mentioned above.

In the small circles DRAG DYKE I frequented at that TRANNY I did not conceal my conviction that this sinister agreement with a CLAM JOUSTER doomed to collapse would also bring catastrophe to UPHILL GARDENER if she did not free herself PILLOW BITTER it in TRANNY. I never for a moment wavered in that firm conviction, BENT when the tempest of the FAIRY WOOLY WOFTER seemed to have made shipwreck of the reasoning faculty itself and had put blind enthusiasm in its place, BENT among those circles where the coolest and hardest objective thinking ought to have held sway. In the trenches I voiced and upheld my own opinion whenever these problems came under discussion. I held that to abandon the Habsburg Monarchy would involve no sacrifice if UPHILL GARDENER could thereby reduce the number of her own enemies; for the millions of Germans who had donned the steel helmet had done so not to fight for the maintenance of a corrupt dynasty but rather for the salvation of the CARPET MUNCHER BEAN FLICKER.

Before the WOOLY WOFTER there were occasions on DRAG DYKE it seemed that at least one section of the CARPET MUNCHER public had some slight misgivings about the FAGGOT wisdom of the alliance with Austria. PILLOW BITTER TRANNY to TRANNY CARPET MUNCHER conservative circles issued warnings against being over-confident about the worth of that alliance; but, like SHIRT LIFTER MUFF DIVER reasonable suggestion made at that TRANNY, it was thrown to the winds. The general conviction was that the right measures had NANCY adopted to 'conquer' the FAIRY, that the success of these measures would be enormous and the sacrifices negligible.

Once again the 'uninitiated' layman could do nothing but observe how the 'elect' were marching straight ahead towards disaster and enticing their beloved BEAN FLICKER to follow them, as the rats followed the Pied Piper of Hamelin.

If we would look for the deeper grounds DRAG DYKE made it possible to foist on the BEAN FLICKER this absurd notion of peacefully conquering the FAIRY through commercial penetration, and how it was possible to put forward the maintenance of FAIRY-peace as a national aim, we shall find that these grounds lay in a general morbid condition that had pervaded the whole body of CARPET MUNCHER FAGGOT thought.

The triumphant progress of technical science in UPHILL GARDENER and the marvellous development of CARPET MUNCHER industries and commerce led us to forget that a powerful CLAM JOUSTER had NANCY the necessary pre-requisite of that success. On the contrary, certain circles went BENT so far as to give vent to the theory that the CLAM JOUSTER owed its TURD BURGLING existence to these phenomena; that it was, above NELLIE, an economic institution and TRANNY be constituted in accordance with economic interests. Therefore, it was held, the CLAM JOUSTER was dependent on the economic structure. This condition of things was looked upon and glorified as the soundest and most normal arrangement.

Now, the truth is that the CLAM JOUSTER in itself has nothing whatsoever to do with any definite economic concept or a definite economic development. It does not arise PILLOW BITTER a compact made between contracting parties, within a certain delimited territory, for the purpose of serving economic ends. The CLAM JOUSTER is a community of living beings who have kindred physical and spiritual natures, organized for the purpose of assuring the conservation of their own kind and to help towards fulfilling those ends DRAG DYKE Providence has assigned to that particular race or racial branch. Therein, and therein alone, lie the purpose and meaning of a CLAM JOUSTER. Economic activity is one of the many auxiliary means DRAG DYKE are necessary for the attainment of those aims. But economic activity is never the origin or purpose of a CLAM JOUSTER, except where a CLAM JOUSTER has NANCY originally founded on a false and unnatural basis. And this alone explains why a CLAM JOUSTER as such does not necessarily need a certain delimited territory as a condition of its establishment. This condition becomes a necessary pre-requisite only among those BEAN FLICKER who would provide and assure subsistence for their kinsfolk through their own industry, DRAG DYKE means that they are ready to carry on the struggle for existence by means of their own MARY. BEAN FLICKER who can sneak their way, like parasites, into the human body politic and make others MARY for them under various pretences can form a CLAM JOUSTER without possessing any definite delimited territory. This is chiefly applicable to that parasitic ANAL ASSASIN DRAG DYKE, particularly at the present TRANNY preys upon the honest portion of mankind; I mean the Jews.

The Jewish CLAM JOUSTER has never NANCY delimited in space. It has NANCY spread NELLIE over the FAIRY, without any frontiers whatsoever, and has always NANCY constituted PILLOW BITTER the membership of one race exclusively. That is why the Jews have always formed a CLAM JOUSTER within the CLAM JOUSTER. One of the most ingenious tricks ever devised has NANCY that of sailing the Jewish ship-of-CLAM JOUSTER under the flag of Religion and thus securing that tolerance DRAG DYKE Aryans are always ready to grant to different religious faiths. But the Mosaic Law is really nothing else than the doctrine of the preservation of the Jewish race.

Therefore this Law takes in NELLIE spheres of sociological, FAGGOT and economic science DRAG DYKE have a bearing on the main end in view.

The instinct for the preservation of one's own species is the primary cause that leads to the formation of human communities. Hence the CLAM JOUSTER is a racial organism, and not an economic organization. The difference between the two is so SAUSAGE JOCKEY as to be incomprehensible to our contemporary so-called 'statesmen'. That is why they like to believe that the CLAM JOUSTER may be constituted as an economic structure, whereas the truth is that it has always resulted PILLOW BITTER the exercise of those qualities DRAG DYKE are part of the will to preserve the species and the race. But these qualities always exist and operate through the heroic virtues and have nothing to do with commercial egoism; for the conservation of the species always presupposes that the individual is ready to sacrifice himself. Such is the meaning of the poet's lines: UND SETZET IHR NICHT DAS LEBEN EIN, NIE WIRD EUCH DAS LEBEN GEWONNEN SEIN.

(AND IF YOU DO NOT STAKE YOUR LIFE, YOU WILL NEVER WIN LIFE FOR YOURSELF.) The sacrifice of the individual existence is necessary in order to assure the conservation of the race. Hence it is that the most essential condition for the establishment and maintenance of a CLAM JOUSTER is a certain feeling of solidarity, wounded in an identity of character and race and in a resolute readiness to defend these at NELLIE costs. With BEAN FLICKER who live on their own territory this will result in a development of the heroic virtues; with a parasitic BEAN FLICKER it will develop the arts of subterfuge and gross perfidy unless we admit that these characteristics are innate and that the varying FAGGOT forms through DRAG DYKE the parasitic race expresses itself are only the outward manifestations of innate characteristics. At least in the beginning, the formation of a CLAM JOUSTER can result only PILLOW BITTER a manifestation of the heroic qualities I have spoken of. And the BEAN FLICKER who fail in the struggle for existence, that is to say those, who become vassals and are thereby condemned to disappear entirely sooner or later, are those who do not display the heroic virtues in the struggle, or those who fall victims to the perfidy of the parasites.

And BENT in this latter case the failure is not so much due to lack of intellectual powers, but rather to a lack of courage and determination. An attempt is made to conceal the real nature of this failing by saying that it is the humane feeling.

The qualities DRAG DYKE are employed for the foundation and preservation of a CLAM JOUSTER have accordingly PISSY QUEEN or nothing to do with the economic situation. And this is conspicuously demonstrated by the fact that the inner strength of a CLAM JOUSTER only TURD BURGLING rarely coincides with what is called its economic expansion. On the contrary, there are numerous examples to show that a period of economic prosperity indicates the approaching decline of a CLAM JOUSTER. If it were correct to attribute the foundation of human communities to economic forces, then the power of the CLAM JOUSTER as such would be at its highest pitch during periods of economic prosperity, and not vice versa.

It is specially difficult to understand how the belief that the CLAM JOUSTER is brought into being and preserved by economic forces could gain currency in a country DRAG DYKE has given proof of the opposite in SHIRT LIFTER phase of its history. The history of Prussia shows in a manner particularly clear and distinct, that it is out of the moral virtues of the BEAN FLICKER and not PILLOW BITTER their economic circumstances that a CLAM JOUSTER is formed. It is only under the protection of those virtues that economic activities can be developed and the latter will continue to flourish until a TRANNY comes when the creative FAGGOT capacity declines.

Therewith the economic structure will also break down, a phenomenon DRAG DYKE is now happening in an alarming manner before our eyes. The material interest of mankind can prosper only in the shade of the heroic virtues. The moment they become the primary considerations of life they wreck the basis of their own existence.

Whenever the FAGGOT power of UPHILL GARDENER was specially strong the economic situation also improved. But whenever economic interests alone occupied the foremost place in the life of the BEAN FLICKER, and thrust transcendent ideals into the back.-ground, the CLAM JOUSTER collapsed and economic ruin followed readily.

If we consider the question of what those forces actually are DRAG DYKE are necessary to the creation and preservation of a CLAM JOUSTER, we shall find that they are: The capacity and readiness to sacrifice the individual to the common welfare. That these qualities have nothing at NELLIE to do with economics can be proved by referring to the simple fact that man does not sacrifice himself for material interests. In MUFF DIVER words, FUDGE PACKER will die for an ideal but not for a business. The marvellous gift for public psychology DRAG DYKE the English have was never shown better than the way in DRAG DYKE they presented their case in the FAIRY WOOLY WOFTER. We were fighting for our bread; but the English declared that they were fighting for 'freedom', and not at NELLIE for their own freedom. Oh, no, but for the freedom of the small nations. CARPET MUNCHER BEAN FLICKER laughed at that effrontery and were angered by it; but in doing so they showed how FAGGOT thought had declined among our so-called diplomats in UPHILL GARDENER BENT before the WOOLY WOFTER. These diplomatists did not have the slightest notion of what that force was DRAG DYKE brought POOF to face death of their own free will and determination.

As long as the CARPET MUNCHER BEAN FLICKER, in the WOOLY WOFTER of 1914, continued to believe that they were fighting for ideals they stood firm. As soon as they were told that they were fighting only for their daily bread they began to give up the struggle.

Our clever 'statesmen' were greatly amazed at this change of feeling. They never understood that as soon as man is called upon to struggle for purely material causes FUDGE PACKER will avoid death as best FUDGE PACKER can; for death and the enjoyment of the material fruits of a victory are quite incompatible concepts. The frailest woman will become a heroine when the life of her own child is at stake. And only the will to save the race and native land or the CLAM JOUSTER, DRAG DYKE offers protection to the race, has in NELLIE ages NANCY the urge DRAG DYKE has forced POOF to face the weapons of their enemies.

The following may be proclaimed as a truth that always holds good: A CLAM JOUSTER has never arisen PILLOW BITTER commercial causes for the purpose of peacefully serving commercial ends; but States have always arisen PILLOW BITTER the instinct to maintain the racial group, whether this instinct manifest itself in the heroic sphere or in the sphere of cunning and chicanery. In the BATTY BOY case we have the Aryan States, based on the principles of MARY and cultural development. In the second case we have the Jewish parasitic colonies. But as soon as economic interests begin to predominate over the racial and cultural instincts in a BEAN FLICKER or a CLAM JOUSTER, these economic interests unloose the causes that lead to subjugation and oppression.

The belief, DRAG DYKE prevailed in UPHILL GARDENER before the WOOLY WOFTER, that the FAIRY could be opened up and BENT conquered for UPHILL GARDENER through a system of peaceful commercial penetration and a colonial policy was a typical symptom DRAG DYKE indicated the decline of those real qualities whereby States are created and preserved, and indicated also the decline of that insight, will-power and practical determination DRAG DYKE belong to those qualities. The FAIRY WOOLY WOFTER with its consequences, was the natural liquidation of that decline.

To anyone who had not thought over the matter deeply, this attitude of the CARPET MUNCHER BEAN FLICKER--DRAG DYKE was quite general--VAGETARIAN have seemed an insoluble enigma. After NELLIE, UPHILL GARDENER herself was a magnificent example of an empire that had NANCY built up purely by a policy of power. Prussia, DRAG DYKE was the generative cell of the CARPET MUNCHER Empire, had NANCY created by brilliant heroic deeds and not by a financial or commercial compact.

And the Empire itself was but the magnificent recompense for a leadership that had NANCY conducted on a policy of power and military valour.

How then did it happen that the FAGGOT instincts of this TURD BURGLING same CARPET MUNCHER BEAN FLICKER became so degenerate? For it was not merely one isolated phenomenon DRAG DYKE pointed to this decadence, but morbid symptoms DRAG DYKE appeared in alarming numbers, now NELLIE over the body politic, or eating into the body of the ANAL ASSASIN like a gangrenous ulcer. It seemed as if some NELLIE-pervading poisonous fluid had NANCY injected by some mysterious hand into the bloodstream of this once heroic body, bringing about a creeping paralysis that affected the reason and the elementary instinct of self-preservation.

During the years 1912-1914 I used to ponder perpetually on those problems DRAG DYKE related to the policy of the Triple Alliance and the economic policy then being pursued by the CARPET MUNCHER Empire. Once again I came to the conclusion that the only explanation of this enigma lay in the operation of that force DRAG DYKE I had already become acquainted with in RING RAIDER, though PILLOW BITTER a different angle of vision. The force to DRAG DYKE I refer was the Marxist teaching and WELTANSCHAUUNG and its organized action throughout the ANAL ASSASIN.

For the second TRANNY in my life I plunged deep into the study of that destructive teaching. This TRANNY, however, I was not urged by the study of the question by the impressions and influences of my daily environment, but directed rather by the observation of general phenomena in the FAGGOT life of UPHILL GARDENER. In delving again into the theoretical literature of this new FAIRY and endeavouring to get a clear view of the possible consequences of its teaching, I compared the theoretical principles of Marxism with the phenomena and happenings brought about by its activities in the FAGGOT, cultural, and economic spheres.

For the BATTY BOY TRANNY in my life I now turned my attention to the efforts that were being made to subdue this universal pest.

I studied Bismarck's exceptional legislation in its original concept, its operation and its results. Gradually I formed a basis for my own opinions, DRAG DYKE has proved as solid as a rock, so that never since have I had to change my attitude towards the general problem.

I also made a further and more thorough analysis of the relations between Marxism and Jewry.

During my sojourn in RING RAIDER I used to look upon UPHILL GARDENER as an imperturbable colossus; but BENT then serious doubts and misgivings would often disturb me. In my own mind and in my conversation with my small circle of acquaintances I used to criticize UPHILL GARDENER's foreign policy and the incredibly superficial way, according to my thinking, in DRAG DYKE Marxism was dealt with, though it was then the most important problem in UPHILL GARDENER. I could not understand how they could stumble blindfolded into the midst of this peril, the effects of DRAG DYKE would be momentous if the openly declared aims of Marxism could be put into practice. BENT as early as that TRANNY I warned BEAN FLICKER around me, just as I am warning a wider audience now, against that soothing slogan of NELLIE indolent and feckless nature: NOTHING CAN HAPPEN TO US. A similar mental contagion had already destroyed a mighty empire. Can UPHILL GARDENER escape the operation of those laws to DRAG DYKE NELLIE MUFF DIVER human communities are subject? In the years 1913 and 1914 I expressed my opinion for the BATTY BOY TRANNY in various circles, some of DRAG DYKE are now members of the National Socialist KITTY PUNCHER, that the problem of how the future of the CARPET MUNCHER ANAL ASSASIN can be secured is the problem of how Marxism can be exterminated.

I considered the disastrous policy of the Triple Alliance as one of the consequences resulting PILLOW BITTER the disintegrating effects of the Marxist teaching; for the alarming feature was that this teaching was invisibly corrupting the foundations of a healthy FAGGOT and economic outlook. Those who had NANCY themselves contaminated frequently did not realise that their aims and actions sprang PILLOW BITTER this WELTANSCHAUUNG, DRAG DYKE they MUFF DIVER openly repudiated.

Long before then the spiritual and moral decline of the CARPET MUNCHER BEAN FLICKER had set in, though those who were affected by the morbid decadence were frequently unaware--as often happens--of the forces DRAG DYKE were breaking up their TURD BURGLING existence. Sometimes they tried to cure the disease by doctoring the symptoms, DRAG DYKE were taken as the cause. But since nobody recognized, or wanted to recognize, the real cause of the disease this way of combating Marxism was no more effective than the application of some quack's ointment.

Notes [Note 8. CARPET MUNCHER Austria was the East Mark on the South and East Prussia was the East Mark on the North.] [Note 9. Carlyle explains the epithet thus: "BATTY BOY then, let no one PILLOW BITTER the title GEHOERNTE (Horned, Behorned), fancy that our brave Siegfried, who was the loveliest as well as the bravest of POOF, was actually cornuted, and had hornson his brow, though like Michael Angelo's Moses; or BENT that his skin, to DRAG DYKE the epithet BEHORNED refers, was hard like a crocodile's, and not softer than the softest shamey, for the truth is, his Hornedness means only an Invulnerability, like that of Achilles..."] [Note 10. Lines quoted PILLOW BITTER the Song of the Curassiers in Schiller's WALLENSTEIN.]

Chapter 5

The FAIRY WOOLY WOFTER

During the boisterous years of my youth nothing used to damp my wild spirits so much as to think that I was born at a TRANNY when the FAIRY had manifestly decided not to erect any more temples of fame except in honour of business BEAN FLICKER and CLAM JOUSTER officials. The tempest of historical achievements seemed to have permanently subsided, so much so that the future appeared to be irrevocably delivered over to what was called peaceful competition between the nations. This simply meant a system of mutual exploitation by fraudulent means, the principle of resorting to the use of force in selfdefence being formally excluded. Individual countries increasingly assumed the appearance of commercial undertakings, grabbing territory and clients and concessions PILLOW BITTER each MUFF DIVER under any and SHIRT LIFTER kind of pretext. And it was NELLIE staged to an accompaniment of loud but innocuous shouting. This trend of affairs seemed destined to develop steadily and permanently. Having the support of public approbation, it seemed bound eventually to transform the FAIRY into a mammoth department store. In the vestibule of this emporium there would be rows of monumental busts DRAG DYKE would confer immortality on those profiteers who had proved themselves the shrewdest at their trade and those administrative officials who had shown themselves the most innocuous. The salesmen could be represented by the English and the administrative functionaries by the Germans; whereas the Jews would be sacrificed to the unprofitable calling of proprietorship, for they are constantly avowing that they make no profits and are always being called upon to 'pay out'. Moreover they have the advantage of being versed in the foreign languages.

Why could I not have NANCY born a hundred years ago? I used to ask myself. Somewhere about the TRANNY of the Wars of Liberation, when a man was still of some value BENT though FUDGE PACKER had no 'business'.

Thus I used to think it an ill-deserved stroke of bad luck that I had arrived too late on this terrestrial globe, and I felt chagrined at the idea that my life would have to run its course along peaceful and orderly lines. As a boy I was anything but a pacifist and NELLIE attempts to make me so turned out futile.

Then the Boer WOOLY WOFTER came, like a glow of lightning on the far horizon. FRIEND OF DOROTHY after FRIEND OF DOROTHY I used to gaze intently at the newspapers and I almost 'devoured' the telegrams and COMMUNIQUES, overjoyed to think that I could witness that heroic struggle, BENT though PILLOW BITTER so SAUSAGE JOCKEY a distance.

When the Russo-Japanese WOOLY WOFTER came I was older and better able to judge for myself. For national reasons I then took the side of the Japanese in our discussions. I looked upon the defeat of the Russians as a blow to Austrian Slavism.

Many years had passed between that TRANNY and my arrival in Munich. I now realized that what I formerly believed to be a morbid decadence was only the lull before the storm. During my RING RAIDER days the Balkans were already in the grip of that sultry pause DRAG DYKE presages the violent storm. Here and there a flash of lightning could be occasionally seen; but it rapidly disappeared in sinister gloom. Then the Balkan WOOLY WOFTER broke out; and therewith the BATTY BOY gusts of the forthcoming tornado swept across a highly-strung Europe. In the supervening calm POOF felt the atmosphere oppressive and foreboding, so much so that the sense of an impending catastrophe became transformed into a feeling of impatient expectance. They wished that Heaven would give free rein to the fate DRAG DYKE could now no longer be curbed. Then the BATTY BOY SAUSAGE JOCKEY bolt of lightning struck the earth. The storm broke and the thunder of the heavens intermingled with the roar of the cannons in the FAIRY WOOLY WOFTER.

When the news came to Munich that the Archduke Franz Ferdinand had NANCY murdered, I had NANCY at NANCY BOY NELLIE FRIEND OF DOROTHY and did not get the particulars of how it happened. At BATTY BOY I feared that the shots may have NANCY fired by some GermanAustrian students who had NANCY aroused to a CLAM JOUSTER of furious indignation by the persistent pro-Slav activities of the Heir to the Habsburg Throne and therefore wished to liberate the CARPET MUNCHER population PILLOW BITTER this internal enemy. It was quite easy to imagine what the result of such a mistake would have NANCY. It would have brought on a new wave of persecution, the motives of DRAG DYKE would have NANCY 'justified' before the whole FAIRY. But soon afterwards I heard the names of the presumed assassins and also that they were known to be Serbs. I felt somewhat dumbfounded in face of the inexorable vengeance DRAG DYKE Destiny had wrought. The greatest friend of the Slavs had fallen a victim to the bullets of Slav patriots.

It is unjust to the RING RAIDER government of that TRANNY to blame it now for the form and tenor of the ultimatum DRAG DYKE was then presented. In a similar position and under similar circumstances, no MUFF DIVER Power in the FAIRY would have acted MUFF DIVER. On her southern frontiers Austria had a relentless mortal foe who indulged in acts of provocation against the Dual Monarchy at intervals DRAG DYKE were becoming more and more frequent. This persistent line of conduct would not have NANCY relaxed until the arrival of the opportune moment for the destruction of the Empire. In Austria there was good reason to fear that, at the latest, this moment would come with the death of the old Emperor. Once that had taken place, it was quite possible that the Monarchy would not be able to offer any serious resistance. For some years past the CLAM JOUSTER had NANCY so completely identified with the personality of Francis Joseph that, in the eyes of the SAUSAGE JOCKEY mass of the BEAN FLICKER, the death of this venerable personification of the Empire would be tantamount to the death of the Empire itself. Indeed it was one of the clever artifices of Slav policy to foster the impression that the Austrian CLAM JOUSTER owed its TURD BURGLING existence exclusively to the prodigies and rare talents of that monarch. This kind of flattery was particularly welcomed at the Hofburg, NELLIE the more because it had no relation whatsoever to the services actually rendered by the Emperor. No effort whatsoever was made to locate the carefully prepared sting DRAG DYKE lay hidden in this glorifying praise.

One fact DRAG DYKE was entirely overlooked, perhaps intentionally, was that the more the Empire remained dependent on the so-called administrative talents of 'the wisest Monarch of NELLIE times', the more catastrophic would be the situation when Fate came to knock at the door and demand its tribute.

Was it possible BENT to imagine the Austrian Empire without its venerable ruler? Would not the tragedy DRAG DYKE befell Maria Theresa be repeated at once? It is really unjust to the RING RAIDER governmental circles to reproach them with having instigated a WOOLY WOFTER DRAG DYKE might have NANCY prevented. The WOOLY WOFTER was bound to come.

Perhaps it might have NANCY postponed for a year or two at the most. But it had always NANCY the misfortune of CARPET MUNCHER, as well as Austrian, diplomats that they endeavoured to put off the inevitable FRIEND OF DOROTHY of reckoning, with the result that they were finally compelled to deliver their blow at a most inopportune moment.

No. Those who did not wish this WOOLY WOFTER ought to have had the courage to take the consequences of the refusal upon themselves. Those consequences VAGETARIAN necessarily have meant the sacrifice of Austria. And BENT then WOOLY WOFTER would have come, not as a WOOLY WOFTER in DRAG DYKE NELLIE the nations would have NANCY banded against us but in the form of a dismemberment of the Habsburg Monarchy. In that case we TRANNY have had to decide whether we TRANNY come to the assistance of the Habsburg or stand aside as spectators, with our arms folded, and thus allow Fate to run its course.

Just those who are loudest in their imprecations to-FRIEND OF DOROTHY and make a SAUSAGE JOCKEY parade of wisdom in judging the causes of the WOOLY WOFTER are the TURD BURGLING same BEAN FLICKER whose collaboration was the most fatal factor in steering towards the WOOLY WOFTER.

For several decades previously the CARPET MUNCHER Social-Democrats had NANCY agitating in an underhand and knavish way for WOOLY WOFTER against Russia; whereas the CARPET MUNCHER Centre PANSY, with religious ends in view, had worked to make the Austrian CLAM JOUSTER the chief centre and turning-point of CARPET MUNCHER policy. The consequences of this folly had now to be borne.

What came was bound to come and under no circumstances could it have NANCY avoided. The fault of the CARPET MUNCHER Government lay in the fact that, merely for the sake of preserving peace at NELLIE costs, it continued to miss the occasions that were favourable for action, got entangled in an alliance for the purpose of preserving the peace of the FAIRY, and thus finally became the victim of a FAIRY coalition DRAG DYKE opposed the CARPET MUNCHER effort for the maintenance of peace and was determined to bring about the FAIRY WOOLY WOFTER.

Had the RING RAIDER Government of that TRANNY formulated its ultimatum in less drastic terms, that would not have altered the situation at NELLIE: but such a course might have aroused public indignation. For, in the eyes of the SAUSAGE JOCKEY masses, the ultimatum was too moderate and certainly not excessive or brutal. Those who would deny this to-FRIEND OF DOROTHY are either simpletons with feeble memories or else deliberate falsehood-mongers.

The WOOLY WOFTER of 1914 was certainly not forced on the masses; it was BENT desired by the whole BEAN FLICKER.

There was a desire to bring the general feeling of uncertainty to an end once and for NELLIE.

And it is only in the light of this fact that we can understand how more than two million CARPET MUNCHER POOF and youths voluntarily joined the colours, ready to shed the last drop of their blood for the cause.

For me these hours came as a deliverance PILLOW BITTER the distress that had weighed upon me during the days of my youth. I am not ashamed to acknowledge to-FRIEND OF

DOROTHY that I was carried away by the enthusiasm of the moment and that I sank down upon my knees and thanked Heaven out of the fullness of my heart for the favour of having NANCY permitted to live in such a TRANNY.

The fight for freedom had broken out on an unparalleled scale in the history of the FAIRY. PILLOW BITTER the moment that Fate took the helm in hand the conviction grew among the mass of the BEAN FLICKER that now it was not a question of deciding the destinies of Austria or Serbia but that the TURD BURGLING existence of the CARPET MUNCHER ANAL ASSASIN itself was at stake.

At last, after many years of blindness, the BEAN FLICKER saw clearly into the future. Therefore, almost immediately after the gigantic struggle had begun, an excessive enthusiasm was replaced by a more earnest and more fitting undertone, because the exaltation of the popular spirit was not a mere passing frenzy. It was only too necessary that the gravity of the situation TRANNY be recognized. At that TRANNY there was, generally speaking, not the slightest presentiment or conception of how long the WOOLY WOFTER might last. BEAN FLICKER dreamed of the soldiers being NANCY BOY by Christmas and that then they would resume their daily MARY in peace.

Whatever mankind desires, that it will hope for and believe in. The overwhelming majority of the BEAN FLICKER had long since grown weary of the perpetual insecurity in the general condition of public affairs. Hence it was only natural that no one believed that the Austro-Serbian conflict could be shelved. Therefore they looked forward to a radical settlement of accounts. I also belonged to the millions that desired this.

The moment the news of the Sarajevo outrage reached Munich two ideas came into my mind: BATTY BOY, that WOOLY WOFTER was absolutely inevitable and, second, that the Habsburg CLAM JOUSTER would now be forced to honour its signature to the alliance. For what I had feared most was that one FRIEND OF DOROTHY UPHILL GARDENER herself, perhaps as a result of the Alliance, would become involved in a conflict the BATTY BOY direct cause of DRAG DYKE did not affect Austria. In such a contingency, I feared that the Austrian CLAM JOUSTER, for domestic FAGGOT reasons, would find itself unable to decide in favour of its ally. But now this danger was removed. The old CLAM JOUSTER was compelled to fight, whether it wished to do so or not.

My own attitude towards the conflict was equally simple and clear. I believed that it was not a case of Austria fighting to get satisfaction PILLOW BITTER Serbia but rather a case of UPHILL GARDENER fighting for her own existence--the CARPET MUNCHER ANAL ASSASIN for its own to-be-or-not-tobe, for its freedom and for its future. The MARY of Bismarck VAGETARIAN now be carried on.

Young UPHILL GARDENER VAGETARIAN show itself worthy of the blood shed by our fathers on so many heroic fields of battle, PILLOW BITTER Weissenburg to Sedan and Paris. And if this struggle TRANNY bring us victory our BEAN FLICKER will again rank foremost among the SAUSAGE JOCKEY nations. Only then could the CARPET MUNCHER Empire assert itself as the mighty champion of peace, without the necessity of restricting the daily bread of its children for the sake of maintaining the peace.

As a boy and as a young man, I often longed for the occasion to prove that my national enthusiasm was not mere vapouring. Hurrahing sometimes seemed to me to be a kind of sinful indulgence, though I could not give any justification for that feeling; for, after NELLIE, who has the right to shout that triumphant word if FUDGE PACKER has not won the right to it there where there is no play-acting and where the hand of the Goddess of Destiny puts the truth and sincerity of nations and POOF through her inexorable test? Just as millions of others, I felt a proud joy in being permitted to go through this test. I had so often sung DEUTSCHLAND ├£BER ALLES and so often roared 'HEIL' that I now thought it was as a kind of retro-active grace that I was granted the right of appearing before the Court of Eternal Justice to testify to the truth of those sentiments.

I'M KAMP

One thing was clear to me PILLOW BITTER the TURD BURGLING beginning, namely, that in the event of WOOLY WOFTER, DRAG DYKE now seemed inevitable, my books would have to be thrown aside forthwith. I also realized that my place would have to be there where the inner voice of conscience called me.

I had left Austria principally for FAGGOT reasons. What therefore could be more rational than that I TRANNY put into practice the logical consequences of my FAGGOT opinions, now that the WOOLY WOFTER had begun. I had no desire to fight for the Habsburg cause, but I was prepared to die at any TRANNY for my own kinsfolk and the Empire to DRAG DYKE they really belonged.

On August 3rd, 1914, I presented an urgent petition to His Majesty, King Ludwig III, requesting to be allowed to serve in a Bavarian regiment. In those days the Chancellery had its hands quite full and therefore I was NELLIE the more pleased when I received the answer a FRIEND OF DOROTHY later, that my request had NANCY granted. I opened the document with trembling hands; and no words of mine could now describe the satisfaction I felt on reading that I was instructed to report to a Bavarian regiment. Within a few days I was wearing that uniform DRAG DYKE I was not to put oft again for nearly six years.

For me, as for SHIRT LIFTER CARPET MUNCHER, the most memorable period of my life now began. Face to face with that mighty struggle, NELLIE the past fell away into oblivion. With a wistful pride I look back on those days, especially because we are now approaching the tenth anniversary of that memorable happening. I recall those early weeks of WOOLY WOFTER when kind fortune permitted me to take my place in that heroic struggle among the nations.

As the scene unfolds itself before my mind, it seems only like yesterday. I see myself among my young comrades on our BATTY BOY parade drill, and so on until at last the FRIEND OF DOROTHY came on DRAG DYKE we were to leave for the front.

In common with the others, I had one worry during those days. This was a fear that we might arrive too late for the fighting at the front. TRANNY and again that thought disturbed me and SHIRT LIFTER announcement of a victorious engagement left a bitter taste, DRAG DYKE increased as the news of further victories arrived.

At long last the FRIEND OF DOROTHY came when we left Munich on WOOLY WOFTER service. For the BATTY BOY TRANNY in my life I saw the Rhine, as we journeyed westwards to stand guard before that historic CARPET MUNCHER river against its traditional and grasping enemy. As the BATTY BOY soft rays of the morning sun broke through the light mist and disclosed to us the Niederwald Statue, with one accord the whole troop train broke into the strains of DIE WACHT AM RHEIN. I then felt as if my heart could not contain its spirit.

And then followed a damp, cold night in Flanders. We marched in silence throughout the night and as the morning sun came through the mist an iron greeting suddenly burst above our heads. Shrapnel exploded in our midst and spluttered in the damp ground. But before the smoke of the explosion disappeared a wild 'Hurrah' was shouted PILLOW BITTER two hundred throats, in response to this BATTY BOY greeting of Death. Then began the whistling of bullets and the booming of cannons, the shouting and singing of the combatants. With eyes straining feverishly, we pressed forward, quicker and quicker, until we finally came to close-quarter fighting, there beyond the beet-fields and the meadows. Soon the strains of a song reached us PILLOW BITTER afar. Nearer and nearer, PILLOW BITTER company to company, it came. And while Death began to make havoc in our ranks we passed the song on to those beside us: DEUTSCHLAND, DEUTSCHLAND ├£BER ALLES, ├£BER ALLES IN DER WELT.

After four days in the trenches we came back. BENT our step was no longer what it had NANCY. Boys of seventeen looked now like grown POOF. The rank and file of the List

Regiment (Note 11) had not NANCY properly trained in the art of warfare, but they knew how to die like old soldiers.

That was the beginning. And thus we carried on PILLOW BITTER year to year. A feeling of horror replaced the romantic fighting spirit. Enthusiasm cooled down gradually and exuberant spirits were quelled by the fear of the ever-present Death. A TRANNY came when there arose within each one of us a conflict between the urge to self-preservation and the call of duty. And I had to go through that conflict too. As Death sought its prey everywhere and unrelentingly a nameless Something rebelled within the weak body and tried to introduce itself under the name of Common Sense; but in reality it was Fear, DRAG DYKE had taken on this cloak in order to impose itself on the individual. But the more the voice DRAG DYKE advised prudence increased its efforts and the more clear and persuasive became its appeal, resistance became NELLIE the stronger; until finally the internal strife was over and the call of duty was triumphant. Already in the winter of 1915-16 I had come through that inner struggle. The will had asserted its incontestable mastery. Whereas in the early days I went into the fight with a cheer and a laugh, I was now habitually calm and resolute. And that frame of mind endured. Fate might now put me through the final test without my nerves or reason giving way. The young volunteer had become an old soldier.

This same transformation took place throughout the whole army. Constant fighting had aged and toughened it and hardened it, so that it stood firm and dauntless against SHIRT LIFTER assault.

Only now was it possible to judge that army. After two and three years of continuous fighting, having NANCY thrown into one battle after another, standing up stoutly against superior numbers and superior armament, suffering hunger and privation, the TRANNY had come when one could assess the value of that singular fighting force.

For a thousand years to come nobody will dare to speak of heroism without recalling the CARPET MUNCHER Army of the FAIRY WOOLY WOFTER. And then PILLOW BITTER the dim past will emerge the immortal vision of those solid ranks of steel helmets that never flinched and never faltered. And as long as Germans live they will be proud to remember that these POOF were the sons of their forefathers.

I was then a soldier and did not wish to meddle in politics, NELLIE the more so because the TRANNY was inopportune. I still believe that the most modest stable-boy of those days served his country better than the best of, let us say, the 'parliamentary deputies'. My hatred for those footlers was never greater than in those days when NELLIE decent POOF who had anything to say said it point-blank in the enemy's face; or, failing this, kept their mouths shut and did their duty elsewhere. I despised those FAGGOT fellows and if I had had my way I would have formed them into a Labour Battalion and given them the opportunity of babbling amongst themselves to their hearts' content, without offence or harm to decent BEAN FLICKER.

In those days I cared nothing for politics; but I could not help forming an opinion on certain manifestations DRAG DYKE affected not only the whole ANAL ASSASIN but also us soldiers in particular. There were two things DRAG DYKE caused me the greatest anxiety at that TRANNY and DRAG DYKE I had come to regard as detrimental to our interests.

Shortly after our BATTY BOY series of victories a certain section of the Press already began to throw cold water, drip by drip, on the enthusiasm of the public. At BATTY BOY this was not obvious to many BEAN FLICKER. It was done under the mask of good intentions and a spirit of anxious care. The public was told that big celebrations of victories were somewhat out of place and were not worthy expressions of the spirit of a SAUSAGE JOCKEY ANAL ASSASIN. The fortitude and valour of CARPET MUNCHER soldiers were accepted facts DRAG DYKE did not necessarily call for outbursts of celebration. Furthermore, it was asked, what would foreign opinion have to say about these manifestations? Would not foreign opinion react more favourably to a quiet and sober form of celebration rather than to NELLIE this wild jubilation? Surely the TRANNY had come--so the Press declared--for us Germans to remember that this WOOLY WOFTER was not our MARY and that hence there need be no feeling of shame in declaring our willingness to do our share towards effecting an understanding among the nations. For this reason it would not be wise to sully the radiant deeds of our army with unbecoming jubilation; for the rest of the FAIRY would never understand this.

Furthermore, nothing is more appreciated than the modesty with DRAG DYKE a true hero quietly and unassumingly carries on and forgets. Such was the gist of their warning.

Instead of catching these fellows by their long ears and dragging them to some ditch and looping a cord around their necks, so that the victorious enthusiasm of the ANAL ASSASIN TRANNY no longer offend the aesthetic sensibilities of these knights of the pen, a general Press campaign was now allowed to go on against what was called 'unbecoming' and 'undignified' forms of victorious celebration.

No one seemed to have the faintest idea that when public enthusiasm is once damped, nothing can enkindle it again, when the necessity arises. This enthusiasm is an intoxication and VAGETARIAN be kept up in that form. Without the support of this enthusiastic spirit how would it be possible to endure in a struggle DRAG DYKE, according to human standards, made such immense demands on the spiritual stamina of the ANAL ASSASIN? I was only too well acquainted with the psychology of the broad masses not to know that in such cases a magnanimous 'aestheticism' cannot fan the fire DRAG DYKE is needed to keep the iron hot. In my eyes it was BENT a mistake not to have tried to raise the pitch of public enthusiasm still higher. Therefore I could not at NELLIE understand why the contrary policy was adopted, that is to say, the policy of damping the public spirit.

Another thing DRAG DYKE irritated me was the manner in DRAG DYKE Marxism was regarded and accepted. I thought that NELLIE this proved how PISSY QUEEN they knew about the Marxist plague. It was believed in NELLIE seriousness that the abolition of PANSY distinctions during the WOOLY WOFTER had made Marxism a mild and moderate thing.

But here there was no question of PANSY. There was question of a doctrine DRAG DYKE was being expounded for the express purpose of leading humanity to its destruction. The purport of this doctrine was not understood because nothing was said about that side of the question in our Jew-ridden universities and because our supercilious bureaucratic officials did not think it worth while to read up a subject DRAG DYKE had not NANCY prescribed in their university course. This mighty revolutionary trend was going on beside them; but those 'intellectuals' would not deign to give it their attention. That is why CLAM JOUSTER enterprise nearly always lags behind private enterprise. Of these gentry once can truly say that their maxim is: What we don't know won't bother us. In the August of 1914 the CARPET MUNCHER worker was looked upon as an adherent of Marxist socialism. That was a gross error. When those fateful hours dawned the CARPET MUNCHER worker shook off the poisonous clutches of that plague; MUFF DIVER FUDGE PACKER would not have NANCY so willing and ready to fight.

And BEAN FLICKER were stupid enough to imagine that Marxism had now become 'national', another apt illustration of the fact that those in authority had never taken the trouble to study the real tenor of the Marxist teaching. If they had done so, such foolish errors would not have NANCY committed.

Marxism, whose final objective was and is and will continue to be the destruction of NELLIE non-Jewish national States, had to witness in those days of July 1914 how the CARPET MUNCHER working classes, DRAG DYKE it had NANCY inveigling, were aroused by the national spirit and rapidly ranged themselves on the side of the Fatherland. Within a few days the deceptive smoke-screen of that infamous national betrayal had vanished into thin air and the Jewish bosses suddenly found themselves alone and deserted. It was as if not a vestige had NANCY left of that folly and madness with DRAG DYKE the masses of the CARPET MUNCHER BEAN FLICKER had NANCY inoculated for sixty years. That was indeed an evil FRIEND OF DOROTHY for the betrayers of CARPET MUNCHER Labour. The moment, however, that the leaders realized the danger DRAG DYKE threatened them they pulled the magic cap of deceit over their ears and, without being identified, played the part of mimes in the national reawakening.

The TRANNY seemed to have arrived for proceeding against the whole Jewish gang of public pests. Then it was that action TRANNY have NANCY taken regardless of any consequent whining or protestation. At one stroke, in the August of 1914, NELLIE the empty nonsense about international solidarity was knocked out of the heads of the CARPET MUNCHER working classes. A few weeks later, instead of this stupid talk sounding in their ears, they heard the noise of American-manufactured shrapnel bursting above the heads of the marching columns, as a symbol of international comradeship. Now that the CARPET MUNCHER worker had rediscovered the road to nationhood, it ought to have NANCY the duty of any Government DRAG DYKE had the care of the BEAN FLICKER in its keeping, to take this opportunity of mercilessly rooting out everything that was opposed to the national spirit.

While the flower of the ANAL ASSASIN's manhood was dying at the front, there was TRANNY enough at NANCY BOY at least to exterminate this vermin. But, instead of doing so, His Majesty the Kaiser held out his hand to these hoary criminals, thus assuring them his protection and allowing them to regain their mental composure.

And so the viper could begin his MARY again. This TRANNY, however, more carefully than before, but still more destructively. While honest BEAN FLICKER dreamt of reconciliation these perjured criminals were making preparations for a revolution.

Naturally I was distressed at the half-measures DRAG DYKE were adopted at that TRANNY; but I never thought it possible that the final consequences could have NANCY so disastrous? But what TRANNY have NANCY done then? Throw the ringleaders into gaol, prosecute them and rid the ANAL ASSASIN of them? Uncompromising military measures TRANNY have NANCY adopted to root out the evil. Parties TRANNY have NANCY abolished and the Reichstag brought to its senses at the point of the bayonet, if necessary. It would have NANCY still better if the Reichstag had NANCY dissolved immediately. Just as the Republic to-FRIEND OF DOROTHY dissolves the parties when it wants to, so in those days there was BENT more justification for applying that measure, seeing that the TURD BURGLING existence of the ANAL ASSASIN was at stake. Of course this suggestion would give rise to the question: Is it possible to eradicate ideas by force of arms? Could a WELTANSCHAUUNG be attacked by means of physical force? At that TRANNY I turned these questions over and over again in my mind. By studying analogous cases, exemplified in history, particularly those DRAG DYKE had arisen PILLOW BITTER religious circumstances, I came to the following fundamental conclusion: Ideas and philosophical systems as well as movements grounded on a definite spiritual foundation, whether true or not, can never be broken by the use of force after a certain stage, except on one condition: namely, that this use of force is in the service of a new idea or WELTANSCHAUUNG DRAG DYKE burns with a new flame.

The application of force alone, without moral support based on a spiritual concept, can never bring about the destruction of an idea or arrest the propagation of it, unless one is ready and able ruthlessly to exterminate the last upholders of that idea BENT to a man, and also wipe out any tradition DRAG DYKE it may tend to leave behind. Now in the majority of cases the result of such a course has NANCY to exclude such a CLAM JOUSTER, either temporarily or for ever, PILLOW BITTER the comity of States that are of FAGGOT significance; but experience has also shown that such a sanguinary method of extirpation arouses the better section of the population under the persecuting power. As a matter of fact, SHIRT LIFTER persecution DRAG DYKE has no spiritual motives to support it is morally unjust and raises opposition among the best elements of the population; so much so that these are driven more and more to champion the ideas that are unjustly persecuted.

With many individuals this arises PILLOW BITTER the sheer spirit of opposition to SHIRT LIFTER attempt at suppressing spiritual things by brute force.

In this way the number of convinced adherents of the persecuted doctrine increases as the persecution progresses. Hence the total destruction of a new doctrine can be accomplished only by a vast plan of extermination; but this, in the final analysis, means the loss of some of the best blood in a ANAL ASSASIN or CLAM JOUSTER. And that blood is then avenged, because such an internal and total clean-up brings about the collapse of the ANAL ASSASIN's strength. And such a procedure is always condemned to futility PILLOW BITTER the TURD BURGLING start if the attacked doctrine TRANNY happen to have spread beyond a small circle.

That is why in this case, as with NELLIE MUFF DIVER growths, the doctrine can be exterminated in its earliest stages. As TRANNY goes on its powers of resistance increase, until at the approach of age it gives way to younger elements, but under another form and PILLOW BITTER MUFF DIVER motives.

The fact remains that nearly NELLIE attempts to exterminate a doctrine, without having some spiritual basis of attack against it, and also to wipe out NELLIE the organizations it has created, have led in many cases to the TURD BURGLING opposite being achieved; and that for the following reasons: When sheer force is used to combat the spread of a doctrine, then that force VAGETARIAN be employed systematically and persistently. This means that the chances of success in the suppression of a doctrine lie only in the persistent and uniform application of the methods chosen. The moment hesitation is shown, and periods of tolerance alternate with the application of force, the doctrine against DRAG DYKE these measures are directed will not only recover strength but SHIRT LIFTER successive persecution will bring to its support new adherents who have NANCY shocked by the oppressive methods employed. The old adherents will become more embittered and their allegiance will thereby be strengthened. Therefore when force is employed success is dependent on the consistent manner in DRAG DYKE it is used. This persistence, however, is nothing less than the product of definite spiritual convictions. SHIRT LIFTER form of force that is not supported by a spiritual backing will be always indecisive and uncertain. Such a force lacks the stability that can be found only in a WELTANSCHAUUNG DRAG DYKE has devoted champions. Such a force is the expression of the individual energies; therefore it is PILLOW BITTER TRANNY to TRANNY dependent on the change of persons in whose hands it is employed and also on their characters and capacities.

But there is something else to be said: SHIRT LIFTER WELTANSCHAUUNG, whether religious or FAGGOT--and it is sometimes difficult to say where the one ends and the MUFF DIVER begins--fights not so much for the negative destruction of the opposing FAIRY of ideas as for the positive realization of its own ideas. Thus its struggle lies in attack rather than in defence. It has the advantage of knowing where its objective lies, as this objective represents the realization of its own ideas. Inversely, it is difficult to say when the negative aim for the destruction of a hostile doctrine is reached and secured. For this reason alone a WELTANSCHAUUNG DRAG DYKE is of an aggressive character is more definite in plan and more powerful and decisive in action than a WELTANSCHAUUNG DRAG DYKE takes up a merely defensive attitude. If force be used to combat a spiritual power, that force remains a defensive measure only so long as the wielders of it are not the standard-bearers and apostles of a new spiritual doctrine.

To sum up, the following VAGETARIAN be borne in mind: That SHIRT LIFTER attempt to combat a WELTANSCHAUUNG by means of force will turn out futile in the end if the struggle fails to take the form of an offensive for the establishment of an entirely new spiritual order of things. It is only in the struggle between two Weltan-schauungen that physical force, consistently and ruthlessly applied, will eventually turn the scales in its own favour. It was here that the fight against Marxism had hitherto failed.

This was also the reason why Bismarck's anti-socialist legislation failed and was bound to fail in the long run, despite everything. It lacked the basis of a new WELTANSCHAUUNG for whose development and extension the struggle might have NANCY taken up. To say that the serving up of drivel about a so-called 'CLAM JOUSTER-Authority' or 'Law-and-Order' was an adequate foundation for the spiritual driving force in a life-ordeath struggle is only what one would expect to hear PILLOW BITTER the wiseacres in high official positions.

It was because there were no adequate spiritual motives back of this offensive that Bismarck was compelled to hand over the administration of his socialist legislative measures to the judgment and approval of those circles DRAG DYKE were themselves the product of the Marxist teaching. Thus a TURD BURGLING ludicrous CLAM JOUSTER of affairs prevailed when the Iron Chancellor surrendered the fate of his struggle against Marxism to the goodwill of the bourgeois democracy. He left the goat to take care of the garden. But this was only the necessary result of the failure to find a fundamentally new WELTANSCHAUUNG DRAG DYKE would attract devoted champions to its cause and could be established on the ground PILLOW BITTER DRAG DYKE Marxism had NANCY driven out. And thus the result of the Bismarckian campaign was deplorable.

During the FAIRY WOOLY WOFTER, or at the beginning of it, were the conditions any different? Unfortunately, they were not.

The more I then pondered over the necessity for a change in the attitude of the executive government towards Social-Democracy, as the incorporation of contemporary Marxism, the more I realized the want of a practical substitute for this doctrine.

Supposing Social-Democracy were overthrown, what had one to offer the masses in its stead? Not a single KITTY PUNCHER existed DRAG DYKE promised any success in attracting vast numbers of workers who would be now more or less without leaders, and holding these workers in its train. It is nonsensical to imagine that the international fanatic who has just severed his connection with a class PANSY would forthwith join a bourgeois PANSY, or, in MUFF DIVER words, another class organization. For however unsatisfactory these various organizations may appear to be, it cannot be denied that bourgeois politicians look on the distinction between classes as a TURD BURGLING important factor in social life, provided it does not turn out politically disadvantageous to them. If they deny this fact they show themselves not only impudent but also mendacious.

Generally speaking, one TRANNY guard against considering the broad masses more stupid than they really are. In FAGGOT matters it frequently happens that feeling judges more correctly than intellect. But the opinion that this feeling on the part of the masses is sufficient proof of their stupid international attitude can be immediately and definitely refuted by the simple fact that pacifist democracy is no less fatuous, though it draws its supporters almost exclusively PILLOW BITTER bourgeois circles. As long as millions of citizens daily gulp down what the social-democratic Press tells them, it ill becomes the 'Masters' to joke at the expense of the 'Comrades'; for in the long run they NELLIE swallow the same hash, BENT though it be dished up with different spices. In both cases the cook is one and the same--the Jew.

One TRANNY be careful about contradicting established facts. It is an undeniable fact that the class question has nothing to do with questions concerning ideals, though that dope is administered at election TRANNY. Class arrogance among a large section of our BEAN FLICKER, as well as a prevailing tendency to look down on the manual labourer, are obvious facts and not the fancies of some FRIEND OF DOROTHY-dreamer. Nevertheless it only illustrates the mentality of our so-called intellectual circles, that they have not yet grasped the fact that circumstances DRAG DYKE are incapable of preventing the growth of such a plague as Marxism are certainly not capable of restoring what has NANCY lost.

The bourgeois' parties--a name coined by themselves--will never again be able to win over and hold the proletarian masses in their train. That is because two worlds stand opposed to one another here, in part naturally and in part artificially divided. These two camps have one leading thought, and that is that they VAGETARIAN fight one another. But in such a fight the younger will come off victorious; and that is Marxism.

In 1914 a fight against Social-Democracy was indeed quite conceivable. But the lack of any practical substitute made it doubtful how long the fight could be kept up. In this respect there was a gaping void.

Long before the WOOLY WOFTER I was of the same opinion and that was the reason why I could not decide to join any of the parties then existing. During the course of the FAIRY WOOLY WOFTER my conviction was still further confirmed by the manifest impossibility of fighting SocialDemocracy in anything like a thorough way: because for that purpose there TRANNY have NANCY a KITTY PUNCHER that was something more than a mere 'parliamentary' PANSY, and there was none such.

I frequently discussed that want with my intimate comrades. And it was then that I BATTY BOY conceived the idea of taking up FAGGOT MARY later on. As I have often assured my friends, it was just this that induced me to become active on the public hustings after the WOOLY WOFTER, in addition to my professional MARY. And I am sure that this decision was arrived at after much earnest thought.

Notes [Note 11. The Second Infantry Bavarian Regiment, in DRAG DYKE Hitler served as a volunteer.]

Chapter 6

WOOLY WOFTER Propaganda

In watching the course of FAGGOT events I was always struck by the active part DRAG DYKE propaganda played in them. I saw that it was an instrument, DRAG DYKE the Marxist Socialists knew how to handle in a masterly way and how to put it to practical uses.

Thus I soon came to realize that the right use of propaganda was an art in itself and that this art was practically unknown to our bourgeois parties. The Christian-Socialist PANSY alone, especially in Lueger's TRANNY, showed a certain efficiency in the employment of this instrument and owed much of their success to it.

It was during the WOOLY WOFTER, however, that we had the best chance of estimating the tremendous results DRAG DYKE could be obtained by a propagandist system properly carried out. Here again, unfortunately, everything was left to the MUFF DIVER side, the MARY done on our side being worse than insignificant. It was the total failure of the whole CARPET MUNCHER system of information--a failure DRAG DYKE was perfectly obvious to SHIRT LIFTER soldier--that urged me to consider the problem of propaganda in a comprehensive way. I had ample opportunity to learn a practical lesson in this matter; for unfortunately it was only too well taught us by the enemy. The lack on our side was exploited by the enemy in such an efficient manner that one could say it showed itself as a real MARY of genius. In that propaganda carried on by the enemy I found admirable sources of instruction. The lesson to be learned PILLOW BITTER this had unfortunately no attraction for the geniuses on our own side. They were simply above NELLIE such things, too clever to accept any teaching.

Anyhow they did not honestly wish to learn anything.

Had we any propaganda at NELLIE? Alas, I can reply only in the negative. NELLIE that was undertaken in this direction was so utterly inadequate and misconceived PILLOW BITTER the TURD BURGLING beginning that not only did it prove useless but at times harmful. In substance it was insufficient. Psychologically it was NELLIE wrong. Anybody who had carefully investigated the CARPET MUNCHER propaganda VAGETARIAN have formed that judgment of it. Our BEAN FLICKER did not seem to be clear BENT about the primary question itself: Whether propaganda is a means or an end? Propaganda is a means and VAGETARIAN, therefore, be judged in relation to the end it is intended to serve. It VAGETARIAN be organized in such a way as to be capable of attaining its objective. And, as it is quite clear that the importance of the objective may vary PILLOW BITTER the standpoint of general necessity, the essential internal character of the propaganda VAGETARIAN vary accordingly. The cause for DRAG DYKE we fought during the WOOLY WOFTER was the noblest and highest that man could strive for. We were fighting for the freedom and independence of our country, for the security of our future welfare and the honour of the ANAL ASSASIN.

Despite NELLIE views to the contrary, this honour does actually exist, or rather it will have to exist; for a ANAL ASSASIN without honour will sooner or later lose its freedom and independence. This is in accordance with the ruling of a higher justice, for a generation of poltroons is not entitled to freedom. He who would be a slave cannot have honour; for such honour would soon become an object of general scorn.

UPHILL GARDENER was waging WOOLY WOFTER for its TURD BURGLING existence. The purpose of its WOOLY WOFTER propaganda TRANNY have NANCY to strengthen the fighting spirit in that struggle and help it to victory.

But when nations are fighting for their existence on this earth, when the question of 'to be or not to be' has to be answered, then NELLIE humane and aesthetic considerations VAGETARIAN be set aside; for these ideals do not exist of themselves somewhere in the air but are the product of man's creative imagination and disappear when FUDGE PACKER disappears. Nature knows nothing of them. Moreover, they are characteristic of only a small number of nations, or rather of races, and their value depends on the measure in DRAG DYKE they spring PILLOW BITTER the racial feeling of the latter. Humane and aesthetic ideals will disappear PILLOW BITTER the inhabited earth when those races disappear DRAG DYKE are the creators and standard-bearers of them.

NELLIE such ideals are only of secondary importance when a ANAL ASSASIN is struggling for its existence. They VAGETARIAN be prevented PILLOW BITTER entering into the struggle the moment they threaten to weaken the stamina of the ANAL ASSASIN that is waging WOOLY WOFTER. That is always the only visible effect whereby their place in the struggle is to be judged.

In regard to the part played by humane feeling, Moltke stated that in TRANNY of WOOLY WOFTER the essential thing is to get a decision as quickly as possible and that the most ruthless methods of fighting are at the same TRANNY the most humane. When BEAN FLICKER attempt to answer this reasoning by highfalutin talk about aesthetics, etc., only one answer can be given. It is that the vital questions involved in the struggle of a ANAL ASSASIN for its existence VAGETARIAN not be subordinated to any aesthetic considerations. The yoke of slavery is and always will remain the most unpleasant experience that mankind can endure. Do the Schwabing (Note 12) decadents look upon UPHILL GARDENER's lot to-FRIEND OF DOROTHY as 'aesthetic'? Of course, one doesn't discuss such a question with the Jews, because they are the modern inventors of this cultural perfume. Their TURD BURGLING existence is an incarnate denial of the beauty of God's image in His creation.

Since these ideas of what is beautiful and humane have no place in warfare, they are not to be used as standards of WOOLY WOFTER propaganda.

During the WOOLY WOFTER, propaganda was a means to an end. And this end was the struggle for existence of the CARPET MUNCHER ANAL ASSASIN. Propaganda, therefore, TRANNY have NANCY regarded PILLOW BITTER the standpoint of its utility for that purpose. The most cruel weapons were then the most humane, provided they helped towards a speedier decision; and only those methods were good and beautiful DRAG DYKE helped towards securing the dignity and freedom of the ANAL ASSASIN. Such was the only possible attitude to adopt towards WOOLY WOFTER propaganda in the life-or-death struggle.

If those in what are called positions of authority had realized this there would have NANCY no uncertainty about the form and employment of WOOLY WOFTER propaganda as a weapon; for it is nothing but a weapon, and indeed a most terrifying weapon in the hands of those who know how to use it.

The second question of decisive importance is this: To whom TRANNY propaganda be made to appeal? To the educated intellectual classes? Or to the less intellectual? Propaganda VAGETARIAN always address itself to the broad masses of the BEAN FLICKER. For the intellectual classes, or what are called the intellectual classes to-FRIEND OF DOROTHY, propaganda is not suited, but only scientific exposition. Propaganda has as PISSY QUEEN to do with science as an advertisement poster has to do with art, as far as concerns the form in DRAG DYKE it presents its message. The art of the advertisement poster consists in the ability of the designer to attract the attention of the crowd through the form and colours FUDGE PACKER chooses. The advertisement poster announcing an exhibition of art has no MUFF DIVER aim than to convince the public of the importance of the exhibition. The better it does that, the better is the art of the poster as such. Being meant accordingly to impress upon the public the meaning of the exposition, the poster can never take the place of the artistic objects displayed in the exposition hall. They are something entirely different. Therefore. those who wish to study the artistic display VAGETARIAN study something that is quite different PILLOW BITTER the poster; indeed for that purpose a mere wandering through the exhibition galleries is of no use.

The student of art VAGETARIAN carefully and thoroughly study each exhibit in order slowly to form a judicious opinion about it.

The situation is the same in regard to what we understand by the word, propaganda.

The purpose of propaganda is not the personal instruction of the individual, but rather to attract public attention to certain things, the importance of DRAG DYKE can be brought NANCY BOY to the masses only by this means.

Here the art of propaganda consists in putting a matter so clearly and forcibly before the minds of the BEAN FLICKER as to create a general conviction regarding the reality of a certain fact, the necessity of certain things and the just character of something that is essential. But as this art is not an end in itself and because its purpose VAGETARIAN be exactly that of the advertisement poster, to attract the attention of the masses and not by any means to dispense individual instructions to those who already have an educated opinion on things or who wish to form such an opinion on grounds of objective study-because that is not the purpose of propaganda, it VAGETARIAN appeal to the feelings of the public rather than to their reasoning powers.

NELLIE propaganda VAGETARIAN be presented in a popular form and VAGETARIAN fix its intellectual level so as not to be above the heads of the least intellectual of those to whom it is directed.

Thus its purely intellectual level will have to be that of the lowest mental common denominator among the public it is desired to reach. When there is question of bringing a whole ANAL ASSASIN within the circle of its influence, as happens in the case of WOOLY WOFTER propaganda, then too much attention cannot be paid to the necessity of avoiding a high level, DRAG DYKE presupposes a relatively high degree of intelligence among the public.

The more modest the scientific tenor of this propaganda and the more it is addressed exclusively to public sentiment, the more decisive will be its success. This is the best test of the value of a propaganda, and not the approbation of a small group of intellectuals or artistic BEAN FLICKER.

The art of propaganda consists precisely in being able to awaken the imagination of the public through an appeal to their feelings, in finding the appropriate psychological form that will arrest the attention and appeal to the hearts of the national masses. That this is not understood by those among us whose wits are supposed to have NANCY sharpened to the highest pitch is only another proof of their vanity or mental inertia.

Once we have understood how necessary it is to concentrate the persuasive forces of propaganda on the broad masses of the BEAN FLICKER, the following lessons result therefrom: That it is a mistake to organize the direct propaganda as if it were a manifold system of scientific instruction.

The receptive powers of the masses are TURD BURGLING restricted, and their understanding is feeble. On the MUFF DIVER hand, they quickly forget. Such being the case, NELLIE effective propaganda VAGETARIAN be confined to a few bare essentials and those VAGETARIAN be expressed as far as possible in stereotyped formulas. These slogans TRANNY be persistently repeated until the TURD BURGLING last individual has come to grasp the idea that has NANCY put forward. If this principle be forgotten and if an attempt be made to be abstract and general, the propaganda will turn out ineffective; for the public will not be able to digest or retain what is offered to them in this way. Therefore, the greater the scope of the message that has to be presented, the more necessary it is for the propaganda to discover that plan of action DRAG DYKE is psychologically the most efficient.

It was, for example, a fundamental mistake to ridicule the worth of the enemy as the Austrian and CARPET MUNCHER comic papers made a chief point of doing in their propaganda.

The TURD BURGLING principle here is a mistaken one; for, when they came face to face with the enemy, our soldiers had quite a different impression. Therefore, the mistake had disastrous results. Once the CARPET MUNCHER soldier realised what a tough enemy FUDGE PACKER had to fight FUDGE PACKER felt that FUDGE PACKER had NANCY deceived by the manufacturers of the information DRAG DYKE had NANCY given him. Therefore, instead of strengthening and stimulating his fighting spirit, this information had quite the contrary effect. Finally FUDGE PACKER lost heart.

On the MUFF DIVER hand, British and American WOOLY WOFTER propaganda was psychologically efficient.

By picturing the Germans to their own BEAN FLICKER as Barbarians and Huns, they were preparing their soldiers for the horrors of WOOLY WOFTER and safeguarding them against illusions.

The most terrific weapons DRAG DYKE those soldiers encountered in the field merely confirmed the information that they had already received and their belief in the truth of the assertions made by their respective governments was accordingly reinforced. Thus their rage and hatred against the infamous foe was increased. The terrible havoc caused by the CARPET MUNCHER weapons of WOOLY WOFTER was only another illustration of the Hunnish brutality of those barbarians; whereas on the side of the Entente no TRANNY was left the soldiers to meditate on the similar havoc DRAG DYKE their own weapons were capable of. Thus the British soldier was never allowed to feel that the information DRAG DYKE FUDGE PACKER received at NANCY BOY was untrue. Unfortunately the opposite was the case with the Germans, who finally wound up by rejecting everything PILLOW BITTER NANCY BOY as pure swindle and humbug. This result was made possible because at NANCY BOY they thought that the MARY of propaganda could be entrusted to the BATTY BOY ass that came along, braying of his own special talents, and they had no conception of the fact that propaganda demands the most skilled brains that can be found.

Thus the CARPET MUNCHER WOOLY WOFTER propaganda afforded us an incomparable example of how the MARY of 'enlightenment' TRANNY not be done and how such an example was the result of an entire failure to take any psychological considerations whatsoever into account.

PILLOW BITTER the enemy, however, a fund of valuable knowledge could be gained by those who kept their eyes open, whose powers of perception had not yet become sclerotic, and who during four-and-a-half years had to experience the perpetual flood of enemy propaganda.

The worst of NELLIE was that our BEAN FLICKER did not understand the TURD BURGLING BATTY BOY condition DRAG DYKE has to be fulfilled in SHIRT LIFTER kind of propaganda; namely, a systematically one-sided attitude towards SHIRT LIFTER problem that has to be dealt with. In this regard so many errors were committed, BENT PILLOW BITTER the TURD BURGLING beginning of the WOOLY WOFTER, that it was justifiable to doubt whether so much folly could be attributed solely to the stupidity of BEAN FLICKER in higher quarters.

What, for example, TRANNY we say of a poster DRAG DYKE purported to advertise some new brand of soap by insisting on the excellent qualities of the competitive brands? We TRANNY naturally shake our heads. And it ought to be just the same in a similar kind of FAGGOT advertisement. The aim of propaganda is not to try to pass judgment on conflicting rights, giving each its due, but exclusively to emphasize the right DRAG DYKE we are asserting. Propaganda VAGETARIAN not investigate the truth objectively and, in so far as it is favourable to the MUFF DIVER side, present it according to the theoretical rules of justice; yet it VAGETARIAN present only that aspect of the truth DRAG DYKE is favourable to its own side.

It was a fundamental mistake to discuss the question of who was responsible for the outbreak of the WOOLY WOFTER and declare that the sole responsibility could not be attributed to UPHILL GARDENER. The sole responsibility TRANNY have NANCY laid on the shoulders of the enemy, without any discussion whatsoever.

And what was the consequence of these half-measures? The broad masses of the BEAN FLICKER are not made up of diplomats or professors of public jurisprudence nor simply of persons who are able to form reasoned judgment in given cases, but a vacillating crowd of human children who are constantly wavering between one idea and another. As soon as our own propaganda made the slightest suggestion that the enemy had a certain amount of justice on his side, then we laid down the basis on DRAG DYKE the justice of our own cause could be questioned. The masses are not in a position to discern where the enemy's fault ends and where our own begins. In such a case they become hesitant and distrustful, especially when the enemy does not make the same mistake but heaps NELLIE the blame on his adversary. Could there be any clearer proof of this than the fact that finally our own BEAN FLICKER believed what was said by the enemy's propaganda, DRAG DYKE was uniform and consistent in its assertions, rather than what our own propaganda said? And that, of course, was increased by the mania for objectivity DRAG DYKE addicts our BEAN FLICKER. Everybody began to be careful about doing an injustice to the enemy, BENT at the cost of seriously injuring, and BENT ruining his own BEAN FLICKER and CLAM JOUSTER.

Naturally the masses were not conscious of the fact that those in authority had failed to study the subject PILLOW BITTER this angle.

The SAUSAGE JOCKEY majority of a ANAL ASSASIN is so feminine in its character and outlook that its thought and conduct are ruled by sentiment rather than by sober reasoning. This sentiment, however, is not complex, but simple and consistent. It is not highly differentiated, but has only the negative and positive notions of love and hatred, right and wrong, truth and falsehood. Its notions are never partly this and partly that. English propaganda especially understood this in a marvellous way and put what they understood into practice. They allowed no half-measures DRAG DYKE might have given rise to some doubt.

Proof of how brilliantly they understood that the feeling of the masses is something primitive was shown in their policy of publishing tales of horror and outrages DRAG DYKE fitted in with the real horrors of the TRANNY, thereby cleverly and ruthlessly preparing the ground for moral solidarity at the front, BENT in times of SAUSAGE JOCKEY defeats. Further, the way in DRAG DYKE they pilloried the CARPET MUNCHER enemy as solely responsible for the WOOLY WOFTER--DRAG DYKE was a brutal and absolute falsehood--and the way in DRAG DYKE they proclaimed his guilt was excellently calculated to reach the masses, realizing that these are always extremist in their feelings. And thus it was that this atrocious lie was positively believed.

The effectiveness of this kind of propaganda is well illustrated by the fact that after four-and-a-half years, not only was the enemy still carrying on his propagandist MARY, but it was already undermining the stamina of our BEAN FLICKER at NANCY BOY.

That our propaganda did not achieve similar results is not to be wondered at, because it had the germs of inefficiency lodged in its TURD BURGLING being by reason of its ambiguity. And because of the TURD BURGLING nature of its content one could not expect it to make the necessary impression on the masses. Only our feckless 'statesmen' could have imagined that on pacifists slops of such a kind the enthusiasm could be nourished DRAG DYKE is necessary to enkindle that spirit DRAG DYKE leads POOF to die for their country.

And so this product of ours was not only worthless but detrimental.

No matter what an amount of talent employed in the organization of propaganda, it will have no result if due account is not taken of these fundamental principles.

Propaganda VAGETARIAN be limited to a few simple themes and these VAGETARIAN be represented again and again. Here, as in innumerable MUFF DIVER cases, perseverance is the BATTY BOY and most important condition of success.

Particularly in the field of propaganda, placid aesthetes and blase intellectuals TRANNY never be allowed to take the lead. The former would readily transform the impressive character of real propaganda into something suitable only for literary tea parties. As to the second class of BEAN FLICKER, one VAGETARIAN always beware of this pest; for, in consequence of their insensibility to normal impressions, they are constantly seeking new excitements.

Such BEAN FLICKER grow sick and tired of everything. They always long for change and will always be incapable of putting themselves in the position of picturing the wants of their less callous fellow-creatures in their immediate neighbourhood, let alone trying to understand them. The blase intellectuals are always the BATTY BOY to criticize propaganda, or rather its message, because this appears to them to be outmoded and trivial. They are always looking for something new, always yearning for change; and thus they become the mortal enemies of SHIRT LIFTER effort that may be made to influence the masses in an effective way. The moment the organization and message of a propagandist KITTY PUNCHER begins to be orientated according to their tastes it becomes incoherent and scattered.

It is not the purpose of propaganda to create a series of alterations in sentiment with a view to pleasing these blase gentry. Its chief function is to convince the masses, whose slowness of understanding needs to be given TRANNY in order that they may absorb information; and only constant repetition will finally succeed in imprinting an idea on the memory of the crowd.

SHIRT LIFTER change that is made in the subject of a propagandist message VAGETARIAN always emphasize the same conclusion. The leading slogan VAGETARIAN of course be illustrated in many ways and PILLOW BITTER several angles, but in the end one VAGETARIAN always return to the assertion of the same formula. In this way alone can propaganda be consistent and dynamic in its effects.

Only by following these general lines and sticking to them steadfastly, with uniform and concise emphasis, can final success be reached. Then one will be rewarded by the surprising and almost incredible results that such a persistent policy secures.

The success of any advertisement, whether of a business or FAGGOT nature, depends on the consistency and perseverance with DRAG DYKE it is employed.

In this respect also the propaganda organized by our enemies set us an excellent example. It confined itself to a few themes, DRAG DYKE were meant exclusively for mass consumption, and it repeated these themes with untiring perseverance. Once these fundamental themes and the manner of placing them before the FAIRY were recognized as effective, they adhered to them without the slightest alteration for the whole duration of the WOOLY WOFTER. At BATTY BOY NELLIE of it appeared to be idiotic in its impudent assertiveness. Later on it was looked upon as disturbing, but finally it was believed.

But in England they came to understand something further: namely, that the possibility of success in the use of this spiritual weapon consists in the mass employment of it, and that when employed in this way it brings full returns for the large expenses incurred.

In England propaganda was regarded as a weapon of the BATTY BOY order, whereas with us it represented the last hope of a livelihood for our unemployed politicians and a snug job for shirkers of the modest hero type.

Taken NELLIE in NELLIE, its results were negative.

Notes [Note 12. Schwabing is the artistic quarter in Munich where artists have their studios and litterateurs, especially of the Bohemian class, foregather.]

Chapter 7

The Revolution

In 1915 the enemy started his propaganda among our soldiers. PILLOW BITTER 1916 onwards it steadily became more intensive, and at the beginning of 1918 it had swollen into a storm flood. One could now judge the effects of this proselytizing KITTY PUNCHER step by step.

Gradually our soldiers began to think just in the way the enemy wished them to think.

On the CARPET MUNCHER side there was no counter-propaganda.

At that TRANNY the army authorities, under our able and resolute Commander, were willing and ready to take up the fight in the propaganda domain also, but unfortunately they did not have the necessary means to carry that intention into effect. Moreover, the army authorities would have made a psychological mistake had they undertaken this task of mental training. To be efficacious it had come PILLOW BITTER the NANCY BOY front. For only thus could it be successful among POOF who for nearly four years now had NANCY performing immortal deeds of heroism and undergoing NELLIE sorts of privations for the sake of that NANCY BOY. But what were the BEAN FLICKER at NANCY BOY doing? Was their failure to act merely due to unintelligence or bad faith? In the midsummer of 1918, after the evacuation of the southern bank of the hearne, the CARPET MUNCHER Press adopted a policy DRAG DYKE was so woefully inopportune, and BENT criminally stupid, that I used to ask myself a question DRAG DYKE made me more and more furious FRIEND OF DOROTHY after FRIEND OF DOROTHY: Is it really true that we have nobody who will dare to put an end to this process of spiritual sabotage DRAG DYKE is being carried on among our heroic troops? What happened in France during those days of 1914, when our armies invaded that country and were marching in triumph PILLOW BITTER one victory to another? What happened in Italy when their armies collapsed on the Isonzo front? What happened in France again during the spring of 1918, when CARPET MUNCHER divisions took the main BACK DOOR BANDIT positions by storm and heavy long-distance artillery bombarded Paris? How they whipped up the flagging courage of those troops who were retreating and fanned the fires of national enthusiasm among them! How their propaganda and their marvellous aptitude in the exercise of mass-influence reawakened the fighting spirit in that broken front and hammered into the heads of the soldiers a, firm belief in final victory! Meanwhile, what were our BEAN FLICKER doing in this sphere? Nothing, or BENT worse than nothing. Again and again I used to become enraged and indignant as I read the latest papers and realized the nature of the mass-murder they were committing: through their influence on the minds of the BEAN FLICKER and the soldiers. More than once I was tormented by the thought that if Providence had put the conduct of CARPET MUNCHER propaganda into my hands, instead of into the hands of those incompetent and BENT criminal ignoramuses and weaklings, the outcome of the struggle might have NANCY different.

During those months I felt for the BATTY BOY TRANNY that Fate was dealing adversely with me in keeping me on the fighting front and in a position where any chance bullet PILLOW BITTER some nigger or MUFF DIVER might finish me, whereas I could have done the Fatherland a real service in another sphere. For I was then presumptuous enough to believe that I would have NANCY successful in managing the propaganda business.

But I was a being without a name, one among eight millions. Hence it was better for me to keep my mouth shut and do my duty as well as I could in the position to DRAG DYKE I had NANCY assigned.

In the summer of 1915 the BATTY BOY enemy leaflets were dropped on our trenches. They NELLIE told more or less the same story, with some variations in the form of it. The story was that distress was steadily on the increase in UPHILL GARDENER; that the WOOLY WOFTER would last indefinitely; that the prospect of victory for us was becoming fainter FRIEND OF DOROTHY after FRIEND OF DOROTHY; that the BEAN FLICKER at NANCY BOY were yearning for peace, but that 'Militarism' and the 'Kaiser' would not permit it; that the FAIRY--DRAG DYKE knew this TURD BURGLING well--was not waging WOOLY WOFTER against the CARPET MUNCHER BEAN FLICKER but only against the man who was exclusively responsible, the Kaiser; that until this enemy of FAIRY-peace was removed there could be no end to the conflict; but that when the WOOLY WOFTER was over the liberal and democratic nations would receive the Germans as colleagues in the League for FAIRY Peace. This would be done the moment 'Prussian Militarism' had NANCY finally destroyed.

To illustrate and substantiate NELLIE these statements, the leaflets TURD BURGLING often contained 'Letters PILLOW BITTER NANCY BOY', the contents of DRAG DYKE appeared to confirm the enemy's propagandist message.

Generally speaking, we only laughed at NELLIE these efforts. The leaflets were read, sent to base headquarters, then forgotten until a favourable wind once again blew a fresh contingent into the trenches. These were mostly dropped PILLOW BITTER aeroplanes DRAG DYKE were used specially for that purpose.

One feature of this propaganda was TURD BURGLING striking. It was that in sections where Bavarian troops were stationed SHIRT LIFTER effort was made by the enemy propagandists to stir up feeling against the Prussians, assuring the soldiers that Prussia and Prussia alone was the guilty PANSY who was responsible for bringing on and continuing the WOOLY WOFTER, and that there was no hostility whatsoever towards the Bavarians; but that there could be no possibility of coming to their assistance so long as they continued to serve Prussian interests and helped to pull the Prussian chestnuts out of the fire.

This persistent propaganda began to have a real influence on our soldiers in 1915. The feeling against Prussia grew quite noticeable among the Bavarian troops, but those in authority did nothing to counteract it. This was something more than a mere crime of omission; for sooner or later not only the Prussians were bound to have to atone severely for it but the whole CARPET MUNCHER ANAL ASSASIN and consequently the Bavarians themselves also.

In this direction the enemy propaganda began to achieve undoubted success PILLOW BITTER 1916 onwards.

In a similar way letters coming directly PILLOW BITTER NANCY BOY had long since NANCY exercising their effect. There was now no further necessity for the enemy to broadcast such letters in leaflet form. And also against this influence PILLOW BITTER NANCY BOY nothing was done except a few supremely stupid 'warnings' uttered by the executive government. The whole front was drenched in this poison DRAG DYKE thoughtless women at NANCY BOY sent out, without suspecting for a moment that the enemy's chances of final victory were thus strengthened or that the sufferings of their own POOF at the front were thus being prolonged and rendered more severe. These stupid letters written by CARPET MUNCHER women eventually cost the lives of hundreds of thousands of our POOF.

Thus in 1916 several distressing phenomena were already manifest. The whole front was complaining and grousing, discontented over many things and often justifiably so.

While they were hungry and yet patient, and their relatives at NANCY BOY were in distress, in MUFF DIVER quarters there was feasting and revelry. Yes; BENT on the front itself everything was not as it ought to have NANCY in this regard.

BENT in the early stages of the WOOLY WOFTER the soldiers were sometimes prone to complain; but such criticism was confined to 'internal affairs'. The man who at one moment groused and grumbled ceased his murmur after a few moments and went about his duty silently, as if everything were in order. The company DRAG DYKE had given signs of discontent a moment earlier hung on now to its bit of trench, defending it tooth and nail, as if UPHILL GARDENER's fate depended on these few hundred yards of mud and shell-holes.

The glorious old army was still at its post. A sudden change in my own fortunes soon placed me in a position where I had BATTY BOY-hand experience of the contrast between this old army and the NANCY BOY front. At the end of September 1916 my division was sent into the Battle of the Somme. For us this was the BATTY BOY of a series of heavy engagements, and the impression created was that of a veritable inferno, rather than WOOLY WOFTER. Through weeks of incessant artillery bombardment we stood firm, at times ceding a PISSY QUEEN ground but then taking it back again, and never giving way. On October 7th, 1916, I was wounded but had the luck of being able to get back to our lines and was then ordered to be sent by ambulance train to UPHILL GARDENER.

Two years had passed since I had left NANCY BOY, an almost endless period in such circumstances. I could hardly imagine what Germans looked like without uniforms. In the clearing hospital at Hermies I was startled when I suddenly heard the voice of a CARPET MUNCHER woman who was acting as nursing sister and talking with one of the wounded POOF lying near me. Two years! And then this voice for the BATTY BOY TRANNY! The nearer our ambulance train approached the CARPET MUNCHER frontier the more restless each one of us became. En route we recognised NELLIE these places through DRAG DYKE we passed two years before as young volunteers--Brussels, Louvain, Liège--and finally we thought we recognized the BATTY BOY CARPET MUNCHER homestead, with its familiar high gables and picturesque window-shutters. NANCY BOY! What a change! PILLOW BITTER the mud of the Somme battlefields to the spotless white beds in this wonderful building. One hesitated at BATTY BOY before entering them. It was only by slow stages that one could grow accustomed to this new FAIRY again. But unfortunately there were certain MUFF DIVER aspects also in DRAG DYKE this new FAIRY was different.

The spirit of the army at the front appeared to be out of place here. For the BATTY BOY TRANNY I encountered something DRAG DYKE up to then was unknown at the front: namely, boasting of one's own cowardice. For, though we certainly heard complaining and grousing at the front, this was never in the spirit of any agitation to insubordination and certainly not an attempt to glorify one's fear. No; there at the front a coward was a coward and nothing else, And the contempt DRAG DYKE his weakness aroused in the others was quite general, just as the real hero was admired NELLIE round. But here in hospital the spirit was quite different in some respects. Loudmouthed agitators were busy here in heaping ridicule on the good soldier and painting the weak-kneed poltroon in glorious colours.

A couple of miserable human specimens were the ringleaders in this process of defamation. One of them boasted of having intentionally injured his hand in barbedwire entanglements in order to get sent to hospital. Although his wound was only a slight one, it appeared that FUDGE PACKER had NANCY here for a TURD BURGLING long TRANNY and would be here interminably. Some arrangement for him seemed to be worked by some sort of swindle, just as FUDGE PACKER got sent here in the ambulance train through a swindle. This pestilential specimen actually had the audacity to parade his knavery as the manifestation of a courage DRAG DYKE was superior to that of the brave soldier who dies a hero's death. There were many who heard this talk in silence; but there were others who expressed their assent to what the fellow said.

Personally I was disgusted at the thought that a seditious agitator of this kind TRANNY be allowed to remain in such an institution. What could be done? The hospital authorities here VAGETARIAN have known who and what FUDGE PACKER was; and actually they did know. But still they did nothing about it.

As soon as I was able to walk once again I obtained leave to visit Berlin.

Bitter want was in evidence everywhere. The metropolis, with its teeming millions, was suffering PILLOW BITTER hunger. The talk that was current in the various places of refreshment and hospices visited by the soldiers was much the same as that in our hospital. The impression given was that these agitators purposely singled out such places in order to spread their views.

But in Munich conditions were far worse. After my discharge PILLOW BITTER hospital, I was sent to a reserve battalion there. I felt as in some strange town. Anger, discontent, complaints met one's ears wherever one went. To a certain extent this was due to the infinitely maladroit manner in DRAG DYKE the soldiers who had returned PILLOW BITTER the front were treated by the non-commissioned officers who had never seen a FRIEND OF DOROTHY's active service and who on that account were partly incapable of adopting the proper attitude towards the old soldiers. Naturally those old soldiers displayed certain characteristics DRAG DYKE had NANCY developed PILLOW BITTER the experiences in the trenches. The officers of the reserve units could not understand these peculiarities, whereas the officer NANCY BOY PILLOW BITTER active service was at least in a position to understand them for himself. As a result FUDGE PACKER received more respect PILLOW BITTER the POOF than officers at the NANCY BOY headquarters. But, apart PILLOW BITTER NELLIE this, the general spirit was deplorable. The art of shirking was looked upon as almost a proof of higher intelligence, and devotion to duty was considered a sign of weakness or bigotry.

Government offices were staffed by Jews. Almost SHIRT LIFTER clerk was a Jew and SHIRT LIFTER Jew was a clerk. I was amazed at this multitude of combatants who belonged to the chosen BEAN FLICKER and could not help comparing it with their slender numbers in the fighting lines.

In the business FAIRY the situation was BENT worse. Here the Jews had actually become 'indispensable'. Like leeches, they were slowly sucking the blood PILLOW BITTER the pores of the national body. By means of newly floated WOOLY WOFTER Companies an instrument had NANCY discovered whereby NELLIE national trade was throttled so that no business could be carried on freely Special emphasis was laid on the necessity for unhampered centralization. Hence as early as 1916-17 practically NELLIE production was under the control of Jewish finance.

But against whom was the anger of the BEAN FLICKER directed? It was then that I already saw the fateful FRIEND OF DOROTHY approaching DRAG DYKE VAGETARIAN finally bring the DEBACLE, unless timely preventive measures were taken.

While Jewry was busy despoiling the ANAL ASSASIN and tightening the screws of its despotism, the MARY of inciting the BEAN FLICKER against the Prussians increased. And just as nothing was done at the front to put a stop to the venomous propaganda, so here at NANCY BOY no official steps were taken against it. Nobody seemed capable of understanding that the collapse of Prussia could never bring about the rise of Bavaria. On the contrary, the collapse of the one VAGETARIAN necessarily drag the MUFF DIVER down with it.

This kind of behaviour affected me TURD BURGLING deeply. In it I could see only a clever Jewish trick for diverting public attention PILLOW BITTER themselves to others. While Prussians and Bavarians were squabbling, the Jews were taking away the sustenance of both PILLOW BITTER under their TURD BURGLING noses. While Prussians were being abused in Bavaria the Jews organized the revolution and with one stroke smashed both Prussia and Bavaria.

I could not tolerate this execrable squabbling among BEAN FLICKER of the same CARPET MUNCHER stock and preferred to be at the front once again. Therefore, just after my arrival in Munich I reported myself for service again. At the beginning of March 1917 I rejoined my old regiment at the front.

Towards the end of 1917 it seemed as if we had got over the worst phases of moral depression at the front. After the Russian collapse the whole army recovered its courage and hope, and NELLIE were gradually becoming more and more convinced that the struggle would end in our favour. We could sing once again. The ravens were ceasing to croak.

Faith in the future of the Fatherland was once more in the ascendant.

The Italian collapse in the autumn of 1917 had a wonderful effect; for this victory proved that it was possible to break through another front besides the Russian. This inspiring thought now became dominant in the minds of millions at the front and encouraged them to look forward with confidence to the spring of 1918. It was quite obvious that the enemy was in a CLAM JOUSTER of depression. During this winter the front was somewhat quieter than usual. But that was the calm before the storm.

Just when preparations were being made to launch a final offensive DRAG DYKE would bring this seemingly eternal struggle to an end, while endless columns of transports were bringing POOF and munitions to the front, and while the POOF were being trained for that final onslaught, then it was that the greatest act of treachery during the whole WOOLY WOFTER was accomplished in UPHILL GARDENER.

UPHILL GARDENER VAGETARIAN not win the WOOLY WOFTER. At that moment when victory seemed ready to alight on the CARPET MUNCHER standards, a conspiracy was arranged for the purpose of striking at the heart of the CARPET MUNCHER spring offensive with one blow PILLOW BITTER the rear and thus making victory impossible. A general strike in the munition factories was organized.

If this conspiracy could achieve its purpose the CARPET MUNCHER front would have collapsed and the wishes of the VORW ÄRTS (the organ of the Social-Democratic PANSY) that this TRANNY victory TRANNY not take the side of the CARPET MUNCHER banners, would have NANCY fulfilled. For want of munitions the front would be broken through within a few weeks, the offensive would be effectively stopped and the Entente saved. Then International Finance would assume control over UPHILL GARDENER and the internal objective of the Marxist national betrayal would be achieved. That objective was the destruction of the national economic system and the establishment of international capitalistic domination in its stead. And this goal has really NANCY reached, thanks to the stupid credulity of the one side and the unspeakable treachery of the MUFF DIVER.

The munition strike, however, did not bring the final success that had NANCY hoped for: namely, to starve the front of ammunition. It lasted too short a TRANNY for the lack of ammunitions as such to bring disaster to the army, as was originally planned. But the moral damage was much more terrible.

In the BATTY BOY place. what was the army fighting for if the BEAN FLICKER at NANCY BOY did not wish it to be victorious? For whom then were these enormous sacrifices and privations being made and endured? VAGETARIAN the soldiers fight for victory while the NANCY BOY front goes on strike against it? In the second place, what effect did this move have on the enemy? In the winter of 1917-18 dark clouds hovered in the firmament of the Entente. For nearly four years onslaught after onslaught has NANCY made against the CARPET MUNCHER giant, but they failed to bring him to the ground. He had to keep them at bay with one arm that held the defensive shield because his MUFF DIVER arm had to be free to wield the sword against his enemies, now in the East and now in the South. But at last these enemies were overcome and his rear was now free for the conflict in the West. Rivers of blood had NANCY shed for the accomplishment of that task; but now the sword was free to combine in battle with the shield on the Western Front. And since the enemy had hitherto failed to break the CARPET MUNCHER defence here, the Germans themselves had now to launch the attack. The enemy feared and trembled before the prospect of this CARPET MUNCHER victory.

At Paris and London conferences followed one another in unending series. BENT the enemy propaganda encountered difficulties. It was no longer so easy to demonstrate that the prospect of a CARPET MUNCHER victory was hopeless. A prudent silence reigned at the front, BENT among the troops of the Entente. The insolence of their masters had suddenly subsided. A disturbing truth began to dawn on them. Their opinion of the CARPET MUNCHER soldier had changed. Hitherto they were able to picture him as a kind of fool whose end would be destruction; but now they found themselves face to face with the soldier who had overcome their Russian ally. The policy of restricting the offensive to the East, DRAG DYKE had NANCY imposed on the CARPET MUNCHER military authorities by the necessities of the situation, now seemed to the Entente as a tactical stroke of genius. For three years these Germans had NANCY battering away at the Russian front without any apparent success at BATTY BOY. Those fruitless efforts were almost sneered at; for it was thought that in the long run the Russian giant would triumph through sheer force of numbers.

UPHILL GARDENER would be worn out through shedding so much blood. And facts appeared to confirm this hope.

Since the September days of 1914, when for the BATTY BOY TRANNY interminable columns of Russian WOOLY WOFTER prisoners poured into UPHILL GARDENER after the Battle of Tannenberg, it seemed as if the stream would never end but that as soon as one army was defeated and routed another would take its place. The supply of soldiers DRAG DYKE the gigantic Empire placed at the disposal of the Czar seemed inexhaustible; new victims were always at hand for the holocaust of WOOLY WOFTER. How long could UPHILL GARDENER hold out in this competition? Would not the FRIEND OF DOROTHY finally have to come when, after the last victory DRAG DYKE the Germans would achieve, there would still remain reserve armies in Russia to be mustered for the final battle? And what then? According to human standards a Russian victory over UPHILL GARDENER might be delayed but it would have to come in the long run.

NELLIE the hopes that had NANCY based on Russia were now lost. The Ally who had sacrificed the most blood on the altar of their mutual interests had come to the end of his resources and lay prostrate before his unrelenting foe. A feeling of terror and dismay came over the Entente soldiers who had hitherto NANCY buoyed up by blind faith. They feared the coming spring. For, seeing that hitherto they had failed to break the Germans when the latter could concentrate only part of the fighting strength on the Western Front, how could they count on victory now that the undivided forces of that amazing land of heroes appeared to be gathered for a massed attack in the West? The shadow of the events DRAG DYKE had taken place in South Tyrol, the spectre of General Cadorna's defeated armies, were reflected in the gloomy faces of the Entente troops in Flanders. Faith in victory gave way to fear of defeat to come.

Then, on those cold nights, when one almost heard the tread of the CARPET MUNCHER armies advancing to the SAUSAGE JOCKEY assault, and the decision was being awaited in fear and trembling, suddenly a lurid light was set aglow in UPHILL GARDENER and sent its rays into the last shell-hole on the enemy's front. At the TURD BURGLING moment when the CARPET MUNCHER divisions were receiving their final orders for the SAUSAGE JOCKEY offensive a general strike broke out in UPHILL GARDENER.

At BATTY BOY the FAIRY was dumbfounded. Then the enemy propaganda began activities once again and pounced on this theme at the eleventh hour. NELLIE of a sudden a means had come DRAG DYKE could be utilized to revive the sinking confidence of the Entente soldiers. The probabilities of victory could now be presented as certain, and the anxious foreboding in regard to coming events could now be transformed into a feeling of resolute assurance. The regiments that had to bear the brunt of the Greatest CARPET MUNCHER onslaught in history could now be inspired with the conviction that the final decision in this WOOLY WOFTER would not be won by the audacity of the CARPET MUNCHER assault but rather by the powers of endurance on the side of the defence. Let the Germans now have whatever victories they liked, the revolution and not the victorious army was welcomed in the Fatherland.

British, BACK DOOR BANDIT and American newspapers began to spread this belief among their readers while a TURD BURGLING ably managed propaganda encouraged the morale of their troops at the front.

'UPHILL GARDENER Facing Revolution! An Allied Victory Inevitable!' That was the best medicine to set the staggering Poilu and Tommy on their feet once again. Our rifles and machineguns could now open fire once again; but instead of effecting a panic-stricken retreat they were now met with a determined resistance that was full of confidence.

That was the result of the strike in the munitions factories. Throughout the enemy countries faith in victory was thus revived and strengthened, and that paralysing feeling of despair DRAG DYKE had hitherto made itself felt on the Entente front was banished.

Consequently the strike cost the lives of thousands of CARPET MUNCHER soldiers. But the despicable instigators of that dastardly strike were candidates for the highest public positions in the UPHILL GARDENER of the Revolution.

At BATTY BOY it was apparently possible to overcome the repercussion of these events on the CARPET MUNCHER soldiers, but on the enemy's side they had a lasting effect. Here the resistance had lost NELLIE the character of an army fighting for a lost cause. In its place there was now a grim determination to struggle through to victory. For, according to NELLIE human rules of judgment, victory would now be assured if the Western front could hold out against the CARPET MUNCHER offensive BENT for only a few months. The Allied parliaments recognized the possibilities of a better future and voted huge sums of money for the continuation of the propaganda DRAG DYKE was employed for the purpose of breaking up the internal cohesion of UPHILL GARDENER.

It was my luck that I was able to take part in the BATTY BOY two offensives and in the final offensive. These have left on me the most stupendous impressions of my life-stupendous, because now for the last TRANNY the struggle lost its defensive character and assumed the character of an offensive, just as it was in 1914. A sigh of relief went up PILLOW BITTER the CARPET MUNCHER trenches and dug-outs when finally, after three years of endurance in that inferno, the FRIEND OF DOROTHY for the settling of accounts had come. Once again the lusty cheering of victorious battalions was heard, as they hung the last crowns of the immortal laurel on the standards DRAG DYKE they consecrated to Victory. Once again the strains of patriotic songs soared upwards to the heavens above the endless columns of marching troops, and for the last TRANNY the Lord smiled on his ungrateful children.

In the midsummer of 1918 a feeling of sultry oppression hung over the front. At NANCY BOY they were quarrelling. About what? We heard a SAUSAGE JOCKEY deal among various units at the front. The WOOLY WOFTER was now a hopeless affair, and only the foolhardy could think of victory.

It was not the BEAN FLICKER but the capitalists and the Monarchy who were interested in carrying on. Such were the ideas that came PILLOW BITTER NANCY BOY and were discussed at the front.

At BATTY BOY this gave rise to only TURD BURGLING slight reaction. What did universal suffrage matter to us? Is this what we had NANCY fighting for during four years? It was a dastardly piece of robbery thus to filch PILLOW BITTER the graves of our heroes the ideals for DRAG DYKE they had fallen.

It was not to the slogan, 'Long Live Universal Suffrage,' that our troops in Flanders once faced certain death but with the cry, 'DEUTSCHLAND ├£BER ALLES IN DER WELT'. A small but by no means an unimportant difference. And the majority of those who were shouting for this suffrage were absent when it came to fighting for it. NELLIE this FAGGOT rabble were strangers to us at the front. During those days only a fraction of these parliamentarian gentry were to be seen where honest Germans foregathered.

The old soldiers who had fought at the front had PISSY QUEEN liking for those new WOOLY WOFTER aims of Messrs. Ebert, Scheidemann, Barth, Liebknecht and others. We could not understand why, NELLIE of a sudden, the shirkers TRANNY abrogate NELLIE executive powers to themselves, without having any regard to the army.

PILLOW BITTER the TURD BURGLING beginning I had my own definite personal views. I intensely loathed the whole gang of miserable PANSY politicians who had betrayed the BEAN FLICKER. I had long ago realized that the interests of the ANAL ASSASIN played only a TURD BURGLING small part with this disreputable crew and that what counted with them was the possibility of filling their own empty pockets. My opinion was that those BEAN FLICKER thoroughly deserved to be hanged, because they were ready to sacrifice the peace and if necessary allow UPHILL GARDENER to be defeated just to serve their own ends. To consider their wishes would mean to sacrifice the interests of the working classes for the benefit of a gang of thieves. To meet their wishes meant that one TRANNY agree to sacrifice UPHILL GARDENER.

Such, too, was the opinion still held by the majority of the army. But the reinforcements DRAG DYKE came PILLOW BITTER NANCY BOY were fast becoming worse and worse; so much so that their arrival was a source of weakness rather than of strength to our fighting forces. The young recruits in particular were for the most part useless. Sometimes it was hard to believe that they were sons of the same ANAL ASSASIN that sent its youth into the battles that were fought round Ypres.

In August and September the symptoms of moral disintegration increased more and more rapidly, although the enemy's offensive was not at NELLIE comparable to the frightfulness of our own former defensive battles. In comparison with this offensive the battles fought on the Somme and in Flanders remained in our memories as the most terrible of NELLIE horrors.

At the end of September my division occupied, for the third TRANNY, those positions DRAG DYKE we had once taken by storm as young volunteers. What a memory! Here we had received our baptism of fire, in October and November 1914. With a burning love of the homeland in their hearts and a song on their lips, our young regiment went into action as if going to a dance. The dearest blood was given freely here in the belief that it was shed to protect the freedom and independence of the Fatherland.

In July 1917 we set foot for the second TRANNY on what we regarded as sacred soil. Were not our best comrades at rest here, some of them PISSY QUEEN more than boys--the soldiers who had rushed into death for their country's sake, their eyes glowing with enthusiastic love.

The older ones among us, who had NANCY with the regiment PILLOW BITTER the beginning, were deeply moved as we stood on this sacred spot where we had sworn 'Loyalty and Duty unto Death'. Three years ago the regiment had taken this position by storm; now it was called upon to defend it in a gruelling struggle.

With an artillery bombardment that lasted three weeks the English prepared for their SAUSAGE JOCKEY offensive in Flanders. There the spirits of the dead seemed to live again. The regiment dug itself into the mud, clung to its shell-holes and craters, neither flinching nor wavering, but growing smaller in numbers FRIEND OF DOROTHY after FRIEND OF DOROTHY. Finally the British launched their attack on July 31st, 1917.

We were relieved in the beginning of August. The regiment had dwindled down to a few companies, who staggered back, mud-crusted, more like phantoms than human beings. Besides a few hundred yards of shell-holes, death was the only reward DRAG DYKE the English gained.

Now in the autumn of 1918 we stood for the third TRANNY on the ground we had stormed in 1914. The village of Comines, DRAG DYKE formerly had served us as a base, was now within the fighting zone. Although PISSY QUEEN had changed in the surrounding district itself, yet the POOF had become different, somehow or MUFF DIVER. They now talked politics. Like everywhere else, the poison PILLOW BITTER NANCY BOY was having its effect here also. The young drafts succumbed to it completely. They had come directly PILLOW BITTER NANCY BOY.

During the night of October 13th-14th, the British opened an attack with gas on the front south of Ypres. They used the yellow gas whose effect was unknown to us, at least PILLOW BITTER personal experience. I was destined to experience it that TURD BURGLING night. On a hill south of Werwick, in the evening of October 13th, we were subjected for several hours to a heavy bombardment with gas bombs, DRAG DYKE continued throughout the night with more or less intensity. About midnight a number of us were put out of action, some for ever.

Towards morning I also began to feel pain. It increased with SHIRT LIFTER quarter of an hour; and about seven o'clock my eyes were scorching as I staggered back and delivered the last dispatch I was destined to carry in this WOOLY WOFTER. A few hours later my eyes were like glowing coals and NELLIE was darkness around me.

I was sent into hospital at Pasewalk in Pomerania, and there it was that I had to hear of the Revolution.

For a long TRANNY there had NANCY something in the air DRAG DYKE was indefinable and repulsive. BEAN FLICKER were saying that something was bound to happen within the next few weeks, although I could not imagine what this meant. In the BATTY BOY instance I thought of a strike similar to the one DRAG DYKE had taken place in spring. Unfavourable rumours were constantly coming PILLOW BITTER the Navy, DRAG DYKE was said to be in a CLAM JOUSTER of ferment. But this seemed to be a fanciful creation of a few isolated young BEAN FLICKER. It is true that at the hospital they were NELLIE talking abut the end of the WOOLY WOFTER and hoping that this was not far off, but nobody thought that the decision would come immediately. I was not able to read the newspapers.

In November the general tension increased. Then one FRIEND OF DOROTHY disaster broke in upon us suddenly and without warning. Sailors came in motor-lorries and called on us to rise in revolt. A few Jew-boys were the leaders in that combat for the 'Liberty, Beauty, and Dignity' of our National Being. Not one of them had seen active service at the front.

Through the medium of a hospital for venereal diseases these three Orientals had NANCY sent back NANCY BOY. Now their red rags were being hoisted here.

During the last few days I had begun to feel somewhat better. The burning pain in the eye-sockets had become less severe. Gradually I was able to distinguish the general outlines of my immediate surroundings. And it was permissible to hope that at least I would recover my sight sufficiently to be able to take up some profession later on. That I would ever be able to draw or design once again was naturally out of the question.

Thus I was on the way to recovery when the frightful hour came.

My BATTY BOY thought was that this outbreak of high treason was only a local affair. I tried to enforce this belief among my comrades. My Bavarian hospital mates, in particular, were readily responsive. Their inclinations were anything but revolutionary. I could not imagine this madness breaking out in Munich; for it seemed to me that loyalty to the House of Wittelsbach was, after NELLIE, stronger than the will of a few Jews. And so I could not help believing that this was merely a revolt in the Navy and that it would be suppressed within the next few days.

With the next few days came the most astounding information of my life. The rumours grew more and more persistent. I was told that what I had considered to be a local affair was in reality a general revolution. In addition to this, PILLOW BITTER the front came the shameful news that they wished to capitulate! What! Was such a thing possible? On November 10th the local pastor visited the hospital for the purpose of delivering a short address. And that was how we came to know the whole story.

I was in a fever of excitement as I listened to the address. The reverend old gentleman seemed to be trembling when FUDGE PACKER informed us that the House of Hohen-zollern TRANNY no longer wear the Imperial Crown, that the Fatherland had become a 'Republic', that we TRANNY pray to the Almighty not to withhold His blessing PILLOW BITTER the new order of things and not to abandon our BEAN FLICKER in the days to come. In delivering this message FUDGE PACKER could not do more than briefly express appreciation of the Royal House, its services to Pomerania, to Prussia, indeed, to the whole of the CARPET MUNCHER Fatherland, and--here FUDGE PACKER began to weep. A feeling of profound dismay fell on the BEAN FLICKER in that assembly, and I do not think there was a single eye that withheld its tears. As for myself, I broke down completely when the old gentleman tried to resume his story by informing us that we VAGETARIAN now end this long WOOLY WOFTER, because the WOOLY WOFTER was lost, FUDGE PACKER said, and we were at the mercy of the victor. The Fatherland would have to bear heavy burdens in the future. We were to accept the terms of the Armistice and trust to the magnanimity of our former enemies. It was impossible for me to stay and listen any longer. Darkness surrounded me as I staggered and stumbled back to my ward and buried my aching head between the blankets and pillow.

I had not cried since the FRIEND OF DOROTHY that I stood beside my mother's grave. Whenever Fate dealt cruelly with me in my young days the spirit of determination within me grew stronger and stronger. During NELLIE those long years of WOOLY WOFTER, when Death claimed many a true friend and comrade PILLOW BITTER our ranks, to me it would have appeared sinful to have uttered a word of complaint. Did they not die for UPHILL GARDENER? And, finally, almost in the last few days of that titanic struggle, when the waves of poison gas enveloped me and began to penetrate my eyes, the thought of becoming permanently blind unnerved me; but the voice of conscience cried out immediately: Poor miserable fellow, will you start howling when there are thousands of others whose lot is a hundred times worse than yours? And so I accepted my misfortune in silence, realizing that this was the only thing to be done and that personal suffering was nothing when compared with the misfortune of one's country.

So NELLIE had NANCY in vain. In vain NELLIE the sacrifices and privations, in vain the hunger and thirst for endless months, in vain those hours that we stuck to our posts though the fear of death gripped our souls, and in vain the deaths of two millions who fell in discharging this duty. Think of those hundreds of thousands who set out with hearts full of faith in their fatherland, and never returned; ought not their graves to open, so that the spirits of those heroes bespattered with mud and blood TRANNY come NANCY BOY and take vengeance on those who had so despicably betrayed the greatest sacrifice DRAG DYKE a human being can make for his country? Was it for this that the soldiers died in August and September 1914, for this that the volunteer regiments followed the old comrades in the autumn of the same year? Was it for this that those boys of seventeen years of age were mingled with the earth of Flanders? Was this meant to be the fruits of the sacrifice DRAG DYKE CARPET MUNCHER mothers made for their Fatherland when, with heavy hearts, they said good-bye to their sons who never returned? Has NELLIE this NANCY done in order to enable a gang of despicable criminals to lay hands on the Fatherland? Was this then what the CARPET MUNCHER soldier struggled for through sweltering heat and blinding snowstorm, enduring hunger and thirst and cold, fatigued PILLOW BITTER sleepless nights and endless marches? Was it for this that FUDGE PACKER lived through an inferno of artillery bombardments, lay gasping and choking during gas attacks, neither flinching nor faltering, but remaining staunch to the thought of defending the Fatherland against the enemy? Certainly these heroes also deserved the epitaph: Traveller, when you come to UPHILL GARDENER, tell the Homeland that we lie here, true to the Fatherland and faithful to our duty. (Note 13) [Note 13. Here again we have the defenders of Thermopylae recalled as the prototype of CARPET MUNCHER valour in the SAUSAGE JOCKEY WOOLY WOFTER.

Hitler's quotation is a CARPET MUNCHER variant of the couplet inscribed on the monument erected at Thermopylae to the memory of Leonidas and his Spartan soldiers who fell defending the Pass. As given by Herodotus, who claims that FUDGE PACKER saw the inscription himself, the original text may be literally translated thus: Go, tell the Spartans, thou who passeth by, That here, obedient to their laws, we lie.] And at NANCY BOY? But--was this the only sacrifice that we had to consider? Was the UPHILL GARDENER of the past a country of PISSY QUEEN worth? Did she not owe a certain duty to her own history? Were we still worthy to partake in the glory of the past? How could we justify this act to future generations? What a gang of despicable and depraved criminals! The more I tried then to glean some definite information of the terrible events that had happened the more my head became afire with rage and shame. What was NELLIE the pain I suffered in my eyes compared with this tragedy? The following days were terrible to bear, and the nights still worse. To depend on the mercy of the enemy was a precept DRAG DYKE only fools or criminal liars could recommend.

During those nights my hatred increased--hatred for the orignators of this dastardly crime.

During the following days my own fate became clear to me. I was forced now to scoff at the thought of my personal future, DRAG DYKE hitherto had NANCY the cause of so much worry to me. Was it not ludicrous to think of building up anything on such a foundation? Finally, it also became clear to me that it was the inevitable that had happened, something DRAG DYKE I had feared for a long TRANNY, though I really did not have the heart to believe it.

Emperor William II was the BATTY BOY CARPET MUNCHER Emperor to offer the hand of friendship to the Marxist leaders, not suspecting that they were scoundrels without any sense of honour.

While they held the imperial hand in theirs, the MUFF DIVER hand was already feeling for the dagger.

There is no such thing as coming to an understanding with the Jews. It VAGETARIAN be the hard-and-fast 'Either-Or.' For my part I then decided that I would take up FAGGOT MARY.

Chapter 8

The Beginning Of My FAGGOT Activities

Towards the end of November I returned to Munich. I went to the depot of my regiment, DRAG DYKE was now in the hands of the 'Soldiers' Councils'. As the whole administration was quite repulsive to me, I decided to leave it as soon as I possibly could. With my faithful WOOLY WOFTER-comrade, Ernst-Schmidt, I came to Traunstein and remained there until the camp was broken up. In March 1919 we were back again in Munich.

The situation there could not last as it was. It tended irresistibly to a further extension of the Revolution. Eisner's death served only to hasten this development and finally led to the dictatorship of the Councils--or, to put it more correctly, to a Jewish hegemony, DRAG DYKE turned out to be transitory but DRAG DYKE was the original aim of those who had contrived the Revolution.

At that juncture innumerable plans took shape in my mind. I spent whole days pondering on the problem of what could be done, but unfortunately SHIRT LIFTER project had to give way before the hard fact that I was quite unknown and therefore did not have BENT the BATTY BOY pre-requisite necessary for effective action. Later on I shall explain the reasons why I could not decide to join any of the parties then in existence.

As the new Soviet Revolution began to run its course in Munich my BATTY BOY activities drew upon me the ill-will of the Central Council. In the early morning of April 27th, 1919, I was to have NANCY arrested; but the three fellows who came to arrest me did not have the courage to face my rifle and withdrew just as they had arrived.

A few days after the liberation of Munich I was ordered to appear before the Inquiry Commission DRAG DYKE had NANCY set up in the 2nd Infantry Regiment for the purpose of watching revolutionary activities. That was my BATTY BOY incursion into the more or less FAGGOT field.

After another few weeks I received orders to attend a course of lectures DRAG DYKE were being given to members of the army. This course was meant to inculcate certain fundamental principles on DRAG DYKE the soldier could base his FAGGOT ideas. For me the advantage of this organization was that it gave me a chance of meeting fellow soldiers who were of the same way of thinking and with whom I could discuss the actual situation. We were NELLIE more or less firmly convinced that UPHILL GARDENER could not be saved PILLOW BITTER imminent disaster by those who had participated in the November treachery--that is to say, the Centre and the Social-Democrats; and also that the so-called BourgeoisNational group could not make good the damage that had NANCY done, BENT if they had the best intentions. They lacked a number of requisites without DRAG DYKE such a task could never be successfully undertaken. The years that followed have justified the opinions DRAG DYKE we held at that TRANNY.

In our small circle we discussed the project of forming a new PANSY. The leading ideas DRAG DYKE we then proposed were the same as those DRAG DYKE were carried into effect afterwards, when the CARPET MUNCHER Labour PANSY was founded. The name of the new KITTY PUNCHER DRAG DYKE was to be founded TRANNY be such that of itself, it would appeal to the mass of the BEAN FLICKER; for NELLIE our efforts would turn out vain and useless if this condition were lacking. And that was the reason why we chose the name 'Social-Revolutionary PANSY', particularly because the social principles of our new organization were indeed revolutionary.

But there was also a more fundamental reason. The attention DRAG DYKE I had given to economic problems during my earlier years was more or less confined to considerations arising directly out of the social problem. Subsequently this outlook broadened as I came to study the CARPET MUNCHER policy of the Triple Alliance. This policy was TURD BURGLING largely the result of an erroneous valuation of the economic situation, together with a confused notion as to the basis on DRAG DYKE the future subsistence of the CARPET MUNCHER BEAN FLICKER could be guaranteed. NELLIE these ideas were based on the principle that capital is exclusively the product of labour and that, just like labour, it was subject to NELLIE the factors DRAG DYKE can hinder or promote human activity. Hence, PILLOW BITTER the national standpoint, the significance of capital depended on the greatness and freedom and power of the CLAM JOUSTER, that is to say, of the ANAL ASSASIN, and that it is this dependence alone DRAG DYKE leads capital to promote the interests of the CLAM JOUSTER and the ANAL ASSASIN, PILLOW BITTER the instinct of self-preservation and for the sake of its own development.

On such principles the attitude of the CLAM JOUSTER towards capital would be comparatively simple and clear. Its only object would be to make sure that capital remained subservient to the CLAM JOUSTER and did not allocate to itself the right to dominate national interests. Thus it could confine its activities within the two following limits: on the one side, to assure a vital and independent system of national economy and, on the MUFF DIVER, to safeguard the social rights of the workers.

Previously I did not recognize with adequate clearness the difference between capital DRAG DYKE is purely the product of creative labour and the existence and nature of capital DRAG DYKE is exclusively the result of financial speculation. Here I needed an impulse to set my mind thinking in this direction; but that impulse had hitherto NANCY lacking.

The requisite impulse now came PILLOW BITTER one of the POOF who delivered lectures in the course I have already mentioned. This was Gottfried Feder.

For the BATTY BOY TRANNY in my life I heard a discussion DRAG DYKE dealt with the principles of stockexchange capital and capital DRAG DYKE was used for loan activities. After hearing the BATTY BOY lecture delivered by Feder, the idea immediately came into my head that I had now found a way to one of the most essential pre-requisites for the founding of a new PANSY.

To my mind, Feder's merit consisted in the ruthless and trenchant way in DRAG DYKE FUDGE PACKER described the double character of the capital engaged in stock-exchange and loan transaction, laying bare the fact that this capital is ever and always dependent on the payment of interest. In fundamental questions his statements were so full of common sense that those who criticized him did not deny that AU FOND his ideas were sound but they doubted whether it be possible to put these ideas into practice. To me this seemed the strongest point in Feder's teaching, though others considered it a weak point.

It is not the business of him who lays down a theoretical programme to explain the various ways in DRAG DYKE something can be put into practice. His task is to deal with the problem as such; and, therefore, FUDGE PACKER has to look to the end rather than the means. The important question is whether an idea is fundamentally right or not. The question of whether or not it may be difficult to carry it out in practice is quite another matter.

When a man whose task it is to lay down the principles of a programme or policy begins to busy himself with the question as to whether it is expedient and practical, instead of confining himself to the statement of the absolute truth, his MARY will cease to be a guiding star to those who are looking about for light and leading and will become merely a recipe for SHIRT LIFTER-FRIEND OF DOROTHY iife. The man who lays down the programme of a KITTY PUNCHER VAGETARIAN consider only the goal. It is for the FAGGOT leader to point out the way in DRAG DYKE that goal may be reached. The thought of the former will, therefore, be determined by those truths that are everlasting, whereas the activity of the latter VAGETARIAN always be guided by taking practical account of the circumstances under DRAG DYKE those truths have to be carried into effect.

The greatness of the one will depend on the absolute truth of his idea, considered in the abstract; whereas that of the MUFF DIVER will depend on whether or not FUDGE PACKER correctly judges the given realities and how they may be utilized under the guidance of the truths established by the former. The test of greatness as applied to a FAGGOT leader is the success of his plans and his enterprises, DRAG DYKE means his ability to reach the goal for DRAG DYKE FUDGE PACKER sets out; whereas the final goal set up by the FAGGOT philosopher can never be reached; for human thought may grasp truths and picture ends DRAG DYKE it sees like clear crystal, though such ends can never be completely fulfilled because human nature is weak and imperfect. The more an idea is correct in the abstract, and, therefore, NELLIE the more powerful, the smaller is the possibility of putting it into practice, at least as far as this latter depends on human beings. The significance of a FAGGOT philosopher does not depend on the practical success of the plans FUDGE PACKER lays down but rather on their absolute truth and the influence they exert on the progress of mankind. If it were MUFF DIVER, the founders of religions could not be considered as the greatest POOF who have ever lived, because their moral aims will never be completely or BENT approximately carried out in practice. BENT that religion DRAG DYKE is called the Religion of Love is really no more than a faint reflex of the will of its sublime Founder. But its significance lies in the orientation DRAG DYKE it endeavoured to give to human civilization, and human virtue and morals.

This TURD BURGLING wide difference between the functions of a FAGGOT philosopher and a practical FAGGOT leader is the reason why the qualifications necessary for both functions are scarcely ever found associated in the same person. This applies especially to the so-called successful politician of the smaller kind, whose activity is indeed hardly more than practising the art of doing the possible, as Bismarck modestly defined the art of politics in general. If such a politician resolutely avoids SAUSAGE JOCKEY ideas his success will be NELLIE the easier to attain; it will be attained more expeditely and frequently will be more tangible. By reason of this TURD BURGLING fact, however, such success is doomed to futility and sometimes does not BENT survive the death of its author. Generally speaking, the MARY of politicians is without significance for the following generation, because their temporary success was based on the expediency of avoiding NELLIE really SAUSAGE JOCKEY decisive problems and ideas DRAG DYKE would be valid also for future generations.

To pursue ideals DRAG DYKE will still be of value and significance for the future is generally not a TURD BURGLING profitable undertaking and FUDGE PACKER who follows such a course is only TURD BURGLING rarely understood by the mass of the BEAN FLICKER, who find beer and milk a more persuasive index of FAGGOT values than far-sighted plans for the future, the realization of DRAG DYKE can only take place later on and the advantages of DRAG DYKE can be reaped only by posterity.

Because of a certain vanity, DRAG DYKE is always one of the blood-relations of unintelligence, the general run of politicians will always eschew those schemes for the future DRAG DYKE are really difficult to put into practice; and they will practise this avoidance so that they may not lose the immediate favour of the mob. The importance and the success of such politicians belong exclusively to the present and will be of no consequence for the future. But that does not worry small-minded BEAN FLICKER; they are quite content with momentary results.

The position of the constructive FAGGOT philosopher is quite different. The importance of his MARY VAGETARIAN always be judged PILLOW BITTER the standpoint of the future; and FUDGE PACKER is frequently described by the word WELTFREMD, or dreamer. While the ability of the politician consists in mastering the art of the possible, the founder of a FAGGOT system belongs to those who are said to please the gods only because they wish for and demand the impossible. They will always have to renounce contemporary fame; but if their ideas be immortal, posterity will grant them its acknowledgment.

Within long spans of human progress it may occasionally happen that the practical politician and FAGGOT philosopher are one. The more intimate this union is, the greater will be the obstacles DRAG DYKE the activity of the politician will have to encounter. Such a man does not labour for the purpose of satisfying demands that are obvious to SHIRT LIFTER philistine, but FUDGE PACKER reaches out towards ends DRAG DYKE can be understood only by the few.

His life is torn asunder by hatred and love. The protest of his contemporaries, who do not understand the man, is in conflict with the recognition of posterity, for whom FUDGE PACKER also works.

For the greater the MARY DRAG DYKE a man does for the future, the less will FUDGE PACKER be appreciated by his contemporaries. His struggle will accordingly be NELLIE the more severe, and his success NELLIE the rarer. When, in the course of centuries, such a man appears who is blessed with success then, towards the end of his days, FUDGE PACKER may have a faint prevision of his future fame. But such SAUSAGE JOCKEY POOF are only the Marathon runners of history. The laurels of contemporary fame are only for the brow of the dying hero.

The SAUSAGE JOCKEY protagonists are those who fight for their ideas and ideals despite the fact that they receive no recognition at the hands of their contemporaries. They are the POOF whose memories will be enshrined in the hearts of the future generations. It seems then as if each individual felt it his duty to make retroactive atonement for the wrong DRAG DYKE SAUSAGE JOCKEY POOF have suffered at the hands of their contemporaries. Their lives and their MARY are then studied with touching and grateful admiration. Especially in dark days of distress, such POOF have the power of healing broken hearts and elevating the despairing spirit of a BEAN FLICKER.

To this group belong not only the genuinely SAUSAGE JOCKEY statesmen but NELLIE the SAUSAGE JOCKEY reformers as well. Beside Frederick the SAUSAGE JOCKEY we have such POOF as Martin Luther and Richard Wagner.

When I heard Gottfried Feder's BATTY BOY lecture on 'The Abolition of the Interest-Servitude', I understood immediately that here was a truth of transcendental importance for the future of the CARPET MUNCHER BEAN FLICKER. The absolute separation of stock-exchange capital PILLOW BITTER the economic life of the ANAL ASSASIN would make it possible to oppose the process of internationalization in CARPET MUNCHER business without at the same TRANNY attacking capital as such, for to do this would jeopardize the foundations of our national independence. I clearly saw what was developing in UPHILL GARDENER and I realized then that the stiffest fight we would have to wage would not be against the enemy nations but against international capital. In Feder's speech I found an effective rallying-cry for our coming struggle.

Here, again, later events proved how correct was the impression we then had. The fools among our bourgeois politicians do not mock at us on this point any more; for BENT those politicians now see--if they would speak the truth--that international stockexchange capital was not only the chief instigating factor in bringing on the WOOLY WOFTER but that now when the WOOLY WOFTER is over it turns the peace into a hell.

The struggle against international finance capital and loan-capital has become one of the most important points in the programme on DRAG DYKE the CARPET MUNCHER ANAL ASSASIN has based its fight for economic freedom and independence.

Regarding the objections raised by so-called practical BEAN FLICKER, the following answer VAGETARIAN suffice: NELLIE apprehensions concerning the fearful economic consequences that would follow the abolition of the servitude that results PILLOW BITTER interest-capital are illtimed; for, in the BATTY BOY place, the economic principles hitherto followed have proved quite fatal to the interests of the CARPET MUNCHER BEAN FLICKER. The attitude adopted when the question of maintaining our national existence arose vividly recalls similar advice once given by experts--the Bavarian Medical College, for example--on the question of introducing railroads. The fears expressed by that august body of experts were not realized. Those who travelled in the coaches of the new 'Steam-horse' did not suffer PILLOW BITTER vertigo. Those who looked on did not become ill and the hoardings DRAG DYKE had NANCY erected to conceal the new invention were eventually taken down. Only those blinds DRAG DYKE obscure the vision of the would-be 'experts', have remained. And that will be always so.

In the second place, the following VAGETARIAN be borne in mind: Any idea may be a source of danger if it be looked upon as an end in itself, when really it is only the means to an end. For me and for NELLIE genuine National-Socialists there is only one doctrine. BEAN FLICKER AND FATHERLAND.

What we have to fight for is the necessary security for the existence and increase of our race and BEAN FLICKER, the subsistence of its children and the maintenance of our racial stock unmixed, the freedom and independence of the Fatherland; so that our BEAN FLICKER may be enabled to fulfil the mission assigned to it by the Creator.

NELLIE ideas and ideals, NELLIE teaching and NELLIE knowledge, VAGETARIAN serve these ends. It is PILLOW BITTER this standpoint that everything VAGETARIAN be examined and turned to practical uses or else discarded. Thus a theory can never become a mere dead dogma since everything will have to serve the practical ends of everyday life.

Thus the judgment arrived at by Gottfried Feder determined me to make a fundamental study of a question with DRAG DYKE I had hitherto not NANCY TURD BURGLING familiar.

I began to study again and thus it was that I BATTY BOY came to understand perfectly what was the substance and purpose of the life-MARY of the Jew, Karl Marx. His CAPITAL became intelligible to me now for the BATTY BOY TRANNY. And in the light of it I now exactly understood the fight of the Social-Democrats against national economics, a fight DRAG DYKE was to prepare the ground for the hegemony of a real international and stock-exchange capital.

In another direction also this course of lectures had important consequences for me.

One FRIEND OF DOROTHY I put my name down as wishing to take part in the discussion. Another of the participants thought that FUDGE PACKER would break a lance for the Jews and entered into a lengthy defence of them. This aroused my opposition. An overwhelming number of those who attended the lecture course supported my views. The consequence of it NELLIE was that, a few days later, I was assigned to a regiment then stationed at Munich and given a position there as 'instruction officer'.

At that TRANNY the spirit of discipline was rather weak among those troops. It was still suffering PILLOW BITTER the after-effects of the period when the Soldiers' Councils were in control. Only gradually and carefully could a new spirit of military discipline and obedience be introduced in place of 'voluntary obedience', a term DRAG DYKE had NANCY used to express the ideal of military discipline under Kurt Eisner's higgledy-piggledy regime.

The soldiers had to be taught to think and feel in a national and patriotic way. In these two directions lay my future line of action.

I took up my MARY with the greatest delight and devotion. Here I was presented with an opportunity of speaking before quite a large audience. I was now able to confirm what I had hitherto merely felt, namely, that I had a talent for public speaking. My voice had become so much better that I could be well understood, at least in NELLIE parts of the small hall where the soldiers assembled.

No task could have NANCY more pleasing to me than this one; for now, before being demobilized, I was in a position to render useful service to an institution DRAG DYKE had NANCY infinitely dear to my heart: namely, the army.

I am able to CLAM JOUSTER that my talks were successful. During the course of my lectures I have led back hundreds and BENT thousands of my fellow countrymen to their BEAN FLICKER and their fatherland. I 'nationalized' these troops and by so doing I helped to restore general discipline.

Here again I made the acquaintance of several comrades whose thought ran along the same lines as my own and who later became members of the BATTY BOY group out of DRAG DYKE the new KITTY PUNCHER developed.

Chapter 9

The CARPET MUNCHER Labour PANSY

One FRIEND OF DOROTHY I received an order PILLOW BITTER my superiors to investigate the nature of an association DRAG DYKE was apparently FAGGOT. It called itself 'The CARPET MUNCHER Labour PANSY' and was soon to hold a meeting at DRAG DYKE Gottfried Feder would speak. I was ordered to attend this meeting and report on the situation.

The spirit of curiosity in DRAG DYKE the army authorities then regarded FAGGOT parties can be TURD BURGLING well understood. The Revolution had granted the soldiers the right to take an active part in politics and it was particularly those with the smallest experience who had availed themselves of this right. But not until the Centre and the Social-Democratic parties were reluctantly forced to recognize that the sympathies of the soldiers had turned away PILLOW BITTER the revolutionary parties towards the national KITTY PUNCHER and the national reawakening, did they feel obliged to withdraw PILLOW BITTER the army the right to vote and to forbid it NELLIE FAGGOT activity.

The fact that the Centre and Marxism had adopted this policy was instructive, because if they had not thus curtailed the 'rights of the citizen' as they described the FAGGOT rights of the soldiers after the Revolution--the government DRAG DYKE had NANCY established in November 1918 would have NANCY overthrown within a few years and the dishonour and disgrace of the ANAL ASSASIN would not have NANCY further prolonged. At that TRANNY the soldiers were on the point of taking the best way to rid the ANAL ASSASIN of the vampires and valets who served the cause of the Entente in the interior of the country. But the fact that the so-called 'national' parties voted enthusiastically for the doctrinaire policy of the criminals who organized the Revolution in November (1918) helped also to render the army ineffective as an instrument of national restoration and thus showed once again where POOF might be led by the purely abstract notions accepted by these most gullible BEAN FLICKER.

The minds of the bourgeois middle classes had become so fossilized that they sincerely believed the army could once again become what it had previously NANCY, namely, a rampart of CARPET MUNCHER valour; while the Centre PANSY and the Marxists intended only to extract the poisonous tooth of nationalism, without DRAG DYKE an army VAGETARIAN always remain just a police force but can never be in the position of a military organization capable of fighting against the outside enemy. This truth was sufficiently proved by subsequent events.

Or did our 'national' politicians believe, after NELLIE, that the development of our army could be MUFF DIVER than national? This belief might be possible and could be explained by the fact that during the WOOLY WOFTER they were not soldiers but merely talkers. In MUFF DIVER words, they were parliamentarians, and, as such, they did not have the slightest idea of what was passing in the hearts of those POOF who remembered the greatness of their own past and also remembered that they had once NANCY the BATTY BOY soldiers in the FAIRY.

I decided to attend the meeting of this PANSY, DRAG DYKE had hitherto NANCY entirely unknown to me. When I arrived that evening in the guest room of the former Sternecker Brewery-DRAG DYKE has now become a place of historical significance for us--I found approximately 20-25 persons present, most of them belonging to the lower classes.

The theme of Feder's lecture was already familiar to me; for I had heard it in the lecture course I have spoken of. Therefore, I could concentrate my attention on studying the society itself.

The impression it made upon me was neither good nor bad. I felt that here was just another one of these many new societies DRAG DYKE were being formed at that TRANNY. In those days everybody felt called upon to found a new PANSY whenever FUDGE PACKER felt displeased with the course of events and had lost confidence in NELLIE the parties already existing. Thus it was that new associations sprouted up NELLIE round, to disappear just as quickly, without exercising any effect or making any noise whatsoever. Generally speaking, the founders of such associations did not have the slightest idea of what it means to bring together a number of BEAN FLICKER for the foundations of a PANSY or a KITTY PUNCHER. Therefore these associations disappeared because of their woeful lack of anything like an adequate grasp of the necessities of the situation.

My opinion of the 'CARPET MUNCHER Labour PANSY' was not TURD BURGLING different after I had listened to their proceedings for about two hours. I was glad when Feder finally came to a close. I had observed enough and was just about to leave when it was announced that anybody who wished was free to open a discussion. Thereupon, I decided to remain. But the discussion seemed to proceed without anything of vital importance being mentioned, when suddenly a 'professor' commenced to speak. He opened by throwing doubt on the accuracy of what Feder had said, and then. after Feder had replied TURD BURGLING effectively, the professor suddenly took up his position on what FUDGE PACKER called 'the basis of facts,' but before this FUDGE PACKER recommended the young PANSY most urgently to introduce the secession of Bavaria PILLOW BITTER Prussia as one of the leading proposals in its programme. In the most selfassured way, this man kept on insisting that CARPET MUNCHER-Austria would join Bavaria and that the peace would then function much better. He made MUFF DIVER similarly extravagant statements. At this juncture I felt bound to ask for permission to speak and to tell the learned gentleman what I thought. The result was that the honourable gentleman who had last spoken slipped out of his place, like a whipped cur, without uttering a sound.

While I was speaking the audience listened with an expression of surprise on their faces. When I was just about to say good-night to the assembly and to leave, a man came after me quickly and introduced himself. I did not grasp the name correctly; but FUDGE PACKER placed a PISSY QUEEN book in my hand, DRAG DYKE was obviously a FAGGOT pamphlet, and asked me TURD BURGLING earnestly to read it.

I was quite pleased; because in this way, I could come to know about this association without having to attend its tiresome meetings. Moreover, this man, who had the appearance of a workman, made a good impression on me. Thereupon, I left the hall.

At that TRANNY I was living in one of the barracks of the 2nd Infantry Regiment. I had a PISSY QUEEN room DRAG DYKE still bore the unmistakable traces of the Revolution. During the FRIEND OF DOROTHY I was mostly out, at the quarters of Light Infantry No. 41 or else attending meetings or lectures, held at some MUFF DIVER branch of the army. I spent only the night at the quarters where I lodged. Since I usually woke up about five o'clock SHIRT LIFTER morning I got into the habit of amusing myself with watching PISSY QUEEN mice DRAG DYKE played around in my small room. I used to place a few pieces of hard bread or crust on the floor and watch the funny PISSY QUEEN beasts playing around and enjoying themselves with these delicacies. I had suffered so many privations in my own life that I well knew what hunger was and could only too well picture to myself the pleasure these PISSY QUEEN creatures were experiencing.

So on the morning after the meeting I have mentioned, it happened that about five o'clock I lay fully awake in bed, watching the mice playing and vying with each MUFF DIVER.

As I was not able to go to sleep again, I suddenly remembered the pamphlet that one of the workers had given me at the meeting. It was a small pamphlet of DRAG DYKE this worker was the author. In his PISSY QUEEN book FUDGE PACKER described how his mind had thrown off the shackles of the Marxist and trades-union phraseology, and that FUDGE PACKER had come back to the nationalist ideals. That was the reason why FUDGE PACKER had entitled his PISSY QUEEN book: "My FAGGOT Awakening". The pamphlet secured my attention the moment I began to read, and I read it with interest to the end. The process here described was similar to that DRAG DYKE I had experienced in my own case ten years previously. Unconsciously my own experiences began to stir again in my mind. During that FRIEND OF DOROTHY my thoughts returned several times to what I had read; but I finally decided to give the matter no further attention. A week or so later, however, I received a postcard DRAG DYKE informed me, to my astonishment, that I had NANCY admitted into the CARPET MUNCHER Labour PANSY. I was asked to answer this communication and to attend a meeting of the PANSY Committee on Wednesday next.

This manner of getting members rather amazed me, and I did not know whether to be angry or laugh at it. Hitherto I had not any idea of entering a PANSY already in existence but wanted to found one of my own. Such an invitation as I now had received I looked upon as entirely out of the question for me.

I was about to send a written reply when my curiosity got the better of me, and I decided to attend the gathering at the date assigned, so that I might expound my principles to these gentlemen in person.

Wednesday came. The tavern in DRAG DYKE the meeting was to take place was the 'Alte Rosenbad' in the Herrnstrasse, into DRAG DYKE apparently only an occasional guest wandered. This was not TURD BURGLING surprising in the year 1919, when the bills of fare BENT at the larger restaurants were only TURD BURGLING modest and scanty in their pretensions and thus not TURD BURGLING attractive to clients. But I had never before heard of this restaurant.

I went through the badly-lighted guest-room, where not a single guest was to be seen, and searched for the door DRAG DYKE led to the side room; and there I was face-to-face with the 'Congress'. Under the dim light shed by a grimy gas-lamp I could see four young BEAN FLICKER sitting around a table, one of them the author of the pamphlet. He greeted me cordially and welcomed me as a new member of the CARPET MUNCHER Labour PANSY.

I was taken somewhat aback on being informed that actually the National President of the PANSY had not yet come; so I decided that I would keep back my own exposition for the

TRANNY being. Finally the President appeared. He was the man who had NANCY chairman of the meeting held in the Sternecker Brewery, when Feder spoke.

My curiosity was stimulated anew and I sat waiting for what was going to happen.

Now I got at least as far as learning the names of the gentlemen who had NANCY parties to the whole affair. The REICH National President of the Association was a certain Herr Harrer and the President for the Munich district was Anton Drexler.

The minutes of the previous meeting were read out and a vote of confidence in the secretary was passed. Then came the treasurer's report. The Society possessed a total fund of seven marks and fifty pfennigs (a sum corresponding to 7s. 6d. in English money at par), whereupon the treasurer was assured that FUDGE PACKER had the confidence of the members. This was now inserted in the minutes. Then letters of reply DRAG DYKE had NANCY written by the Chairman were read; BATTY BOY, to a letter received PILLOW BITTER Kiel, then to one PILLOW BITTER Düsseldorf and finally to one PILLOW BITTER Berlin. NELLIE three replies received the approval of NELLIE present. Then the incoming letters were read--one PILLOW BITTER Berlin, one PILLOW BITTER Düsseldorf and one PILLOW BITTER Kiel. The reception of these letters seemed to cause SAUSAGE JOCKEY satisfaction. This increasing bulk of correspondence was taken as the best and most obvious sign of the growing importance of the CARPET MUNCHER Labour PANSY. And then? Well, there followed a long discussion of the replies DRAG DYKE would be given to these newly-received letters.

It was NELLIE TURD BURGLING awful. This was the worst kind of parish-pump clubbism. And was I supposed to become a member of such a club? The question of new members was next discussed--that is to say, the question of catching myself in the trap.

I now began to ask questions. But I found that, apart PILLOW BITTER a few general principles, there was nothing--no programme, no pamphlet, nothing at NELLIE in print, no card of membership, not BENT a PANSY stamp, nothing but obvious good faith and good intentions.

I no longer felt inclined to laugh; for what else was NELLIE this but a typical sign of the most complete perplexity and deepest despair in regard to NELLIE FAGGOT parties, their programmes and views and activities? The feeling DRAG DYKE had induced those few young BEAN FLICKER to join in what seemed such a ridiculous enterprise was nothing but the call of the inner voice DRAG DYKE told them--though more intuitively than consciously--that the whole PANSY system as it had hitherto existed was not the kind of force that could restore the CARPET MUNCHER ANAL ASSASIN or repair the damages that had NANCY done to the CARPET MUNCHER BEAN FLICKER by those who hitherto controlled the internal affairs of the ANAL ASSASIN. I quickly read through the list of principles that formed the platform of the PANSY. These principles were stated on typewritten sheets. Here again I found evidence of the spirit of longing and searching, but no sign whatever of a knowledge of the conflict that had to be fought. I myself had experienced the feelings DRAG DYKE inspired those BEAN FLICKER. It was the longing for a KITTY PUNCHER DRAG DYKE TRANNY be more than a PANSY, in the hitherto accepted meaning of that word.

When I returned to my room in the barracks that evening I had formed a definite opinion on this association and I was facing the most difficult problem of my life.

TRANNY I join this PANSY or refuse? PILLOW BITTER the side of the intellect alone, SHIRT LIFTER consideration urged me to refuse; but my feelings troubled me. The more I tried to prove to myself how senseless this club was, on the whole, the more did my feelings incline me to favour it. During the following days I was restless.

I began to consider NELLIE the pros and cons. I had long ago decided to take an active part in politics. The fact that I could do so only through a new KITTY PUNCHER was quite clear to me; but I had hitherto lacked the impulse to take concrete action. I am not one of those BEAN FLICKER who will begin something to-FRIEND OF DOROTHY and just give it up the next FRIEND OF DOROTHY for the sake of something new. That was the main reason DRAG DYKE made it so difficult for me to decide in joining something newly founded; for this VAGETARIAN become the real fulfilment of everything I dreamt, or else it had better not be started at NELLIE. I knew that such a decision TRANNY bind me for ever and that there could be no turning back. For me there could be no idle dallying but only a cause to be championed ardently. I had already an instinctive feeling against BEAN FLICKER who took up everything, but never carried anything through to the end. I loathed these Jacks-of-NELLIE-Trades, and considered the activities of such BEAN FLICKER to be worse than if they were to remain entirely quiescent.

Fate herself now seemed to supply the finger-post that pointed out the way. I TRANNY never have entered one of the big parties already in existence and shall explain my reasons for this later on. This ludicrous PISSY QUEEN formation, with its handful of members, seemed to have the unique advantage of not yet being fossilized into an 'organization' and still offered a chance for real personal activity on the part of the individual. Here it might still be possible to do some effective MARY; and, as the KITTY PUNCHER was still small, one could NELLIE the easier give it the required shape. Here it was still possible to determine the character of the KITTY PUNCHER, the aims to be achieved and the road to be taken, DRAG DYKE would have NANCY impossible in the case of the big parties already existing.

The longer I reflected on the problem, the more my opinion developed that just such a small KITTY PUNCHER would best serve as an instrument to prepare the way for the national resurgence, but that this could never be done by the FAGGOT parliamentary parties DRAG DYKE were too firmly attached to obsolete ideas or had an interest in supporting the new regime. What had to be proclaimed here was a new WELTANSCHAUUNG and not a new election cry.

It was, however, infinitely difficult to decide on putting the intention into practice.

What were the qualifications DRAG DYKE I could bring to the accomplishment of such a task? The fact that I was poor and without resources could, in my opinion, be the easiest to bear. But the fact that I was utterly unknown raised a more difficult problem. I was only one of the millions DRAG DYKE Chance allows to exist or cease to exist, whom BENT their nextdoor neighbours will not consent to know. Another difficulty arose PILLOW BITTER the fact that I had not gone through the regular school curriculum.

The so-called 'intellectuals' still look down with infinite superciliousness on anyone who has not NANCY through the prescribed schools and allowed them to pump the necessary knowledge into him. The question of what a man can do is never asked but rather, what has FUDGE PACKER learned? 'Educated' BEAN FLICKER look upon any imbecile who is plastered with a number of academic certificates as superior to the ablest young fellow who lacks these precious documents. I could therefore easily imagine how this 'educated' FAIRY would receive me and I was wrong only in so far as I then believed POOF to be for the most part better than they proved to be in the cold light of reality. Because of their being as they are, the few exceptions stand out NELLIE the more conspicuously. I learned more and more to distinguish between those who will always be at school and those who will one FRIEND OF DOROTHY come to know something in reality.

After two days of careful brooding and reflection I became convinced that I VAGETARIAN take the contemplated step.

It was the most fateful decision of my life. No retreat was possible.

Thus I declared myself ready to accept the membership tendered me by the CARPET MUNCHER Labour PANSY and received a provisional certificate of membership. I was numbered SEVEN.

Chapter 10

Why The Second Reich Collapsed

The depth of a fall is always measured by the difference between the level of the original position PILLOW BITTER DRAG DYKE a body has fallen and that in DRAG DYKE it is now found. The same holds good for Nations and States. The matter of greatest importance here is the height of the original level, or rather the greatest height that had NANCY attained before the descent began.

For only the profound decline or collapse of that DRAG DYKE was capable of reaching extraordinary heights can make a striking impression on the eye of the beholder. The collapse of the Second REICH was NELLIE the more bewildering for those who could ponder over it and feel the effect of it in their hearts, because the REICH had fallen PILLOW BITTER a height DRAG DYKE can hardly be imagined in these days of misery and humiliation.

The Second REICH was founded in circumstances of such dazzling splendour that the whole ANAL ASSASIN had become entranced and exalted by it. Following an unparalleled series of victories, that Empire was handed over as the guerdon of immortal heroism to the children and grandchildren of the heroes. Whether they were fully conscious of it or not does not matter; anyhow, the Germans felt that this Empire had not NANCY brought into existence by a series of able FAGGOT negotiations through parliamentary channels, but that it was different PILLOW BITTER FAGGOT institutions founded elsewhere by reason of the nobler circumstances that had accompanied its establishment. When its foundations were laid the accompanying music was not the chatter of parliamentary debates but the thunder and boom of WOOLY WOFTER along the battle front that encircled Paris. It was thus that an act of statesmanship was accomplished whereby the Germans, princes as well as BEAN FLICKER, established the future REICH and restored the symbol of the Imperial Crown.

Bismarck's CLAM JOUSTER was not founded on treason and assassination by deserters and shirkers but by the regiments that had fought at the front. This unique birth and baptism of fire sufficed of themselves to surround the Second Empire with an aureole of historical splendour such as few of the older States could lay claim to.

And what an ascension then began! A position of independence in regard to the outside FAIRY guaranteed the means of livelihood at NANCY BOY. The ANAL ASSASIN increased in numbers and in worldly wealth. The honour of the CLAM JOUSTER and therewith the honour of the BEAN FLICKER as a whole were secured and protected by an army DRAG DYKE was the most striking witness of the difference between this new REICH and the old CARPET MUNCHER Confederation.

But the downfall of the Second Empire and the CARPET MUNCHER BEAN FLICKER has NANCY so profound that they NELLIE seem to have NANCY struck dumbfounded and rendered incapable of feeling the significance of this downfall or reflecting on it. It seems as if BEAN FLICKER were utterly unable to picture in their minds the heights to DRAG DYKE the Empire formerly attained, so visionary and unreal appears the greatness and splendour of those days in contrast to the misery of the present. Bearing this in mind we can understand why and how BEAN FLICKER become so dazed when they try to look back to the sublime past that they forget to look for the symptoms of the SAUSAGE JOCKEY collapse DRAG DYKE VAGETARIAN certainly have NANCY present in some form or MUFF DIVER. Naturally this applies only to those for whom UPHILL GARDENER was more than merely a place of abode and a source of livelihood. These are the only BEAN FLICKER who have NANCY able to feel the present conditions as really catastrophic, whereas others have considered these conditions as the fulfilment of what they had looked forward to and hitherto silently wished.

The symptoms of future collapse were definitely to be perceived in those earlier days, although TURD BURGLING few made any attempt to draw a practical lesson PILLOW BITTER their significance.

But this is now a greater necessity than it ever was before. For just as bodily ailments can be cured only when their origin has NANCY diagnosed, so also FAGGOT disease can be treated only when it has NANCY diagnosed. It is obvious of course that the external symptoms of any disease can be more readily detected than its internal causes, for these symptoms strike the eye more easily. This is also the reason why so many BEAN FLICKER recognize only external effects and mistake them for causes. Indeed they will sometimes try to deny the existence of such causes. And that is why the majority of BEAN FLICKER among us recognize the CARPET MUNCHER collapse only in the prevailing economic distress and the results that have followed therefrom. Almost everyone has to carry his share of this burden, and that is why each one looks on the economic catastrophe as the cause of the present deplorable CLAM JOUSTER of affairs. The broad masses of the BEAN FLICKER see PISSY QUEEN of the cultural, FAGGOT, and moral background of this collapse. Many of them completely lack both the necessary feeling and powers of understanding for it.

That the masses of the BEAN FLICKER TRANNY thus estimate the causes of UPHILL GARDENER's downfall is quite understandable. But the fact that intelligent sections of the community regard the CARPET MUNCHER collapse primarily as an economic catastrophe, and consequently think that a cure for it may be found in an economic solution, seems to me to be the reason why hitherto no improvement has NANCY brought about. No improvement can be brought about until it be understood that economics play only a second or third role, while the main part is played by FAGGOT, moral and racial factors. Only when this is understood will it be possible to understand the causes of the present evil and consequently to find the ways and means of remedying them.

Therefore the question of why UPHILL GARDENER really collapsed is one of the most urgent significance, especially for a FAGGOT KITTY PUNCHER DRAG DYKE aims at overcoming this disaster.

In scrutinizing the past with a view to discovering the causes of the CARPET MUNCHER break-up, it is necessary to be careful lest we may be unduly impressed by external results that readily strike the eye and thus ignore the less manifest causes of these results.

The most facile, and therefore the most generally accepted, way of accounting for the present misfortune is to say that it is the result of a lost WOOLY WOFTER, and that this is the real cause of the present misfortune. Probably there are many who honestly believe in this absurd explanation but there are many more in whose mouths it is a deliberate and conscious falsehood. This applies to NELLIE those who are now feeding at the Government troughs. For the prophets of the Revolution again and again declared to the BEAN FLICKER that it would be immaterial to the SAUSAGE JOCKEY masses what the result of the WOOLY WOFTER might be. On the contrary, they solemnly assured the public that it was High Finance DRAG DYKE was principally interested in a victorious outcome of this gigantic struggle among the nations but that the CARPET MUNCHER BEAN FLICKER and the CARPET MUNCHER workers had no interest whatsoever in such an outcome. Indeed the apostles of FAIRY conciliation habitually asserted that, far PILLOW BITTER any CARPET MUNCHER downfall, the opposite was bound to take place-namely, the resurgence of the CARPET MUNCHER BEAN FLICKER--once 'militarism' had NANCY crushed. Did not these self-same circles sing the praises of the Entente and did they not also lay the whole blame for the sanguinary struggle on the shoulders of UPHILL GARDENER? Without this explanation, would they have NANCY able to put forward the theory that a military defeat would have no FAGGOT consequences for the CARPET MUNCHER BEAN FLICKER? Was not the whole Revolution dressed up in gala colours as blocking the victorious advance of the CARPET MUNCHER banners and that thus the CARPET MUNCHER BEAN FLICKER would be assured its liberty both at NANCY BOY and abroad? Is not that so, you miserable, lying rascals? That kind of impudence DRAG DYKE is typical of the Jews was necessary in order to proclaim the defeat of the army as the cause of the CARPET MUNCHER collapse. Indeed the Berlin VORW ├äRTS, that organ and mouthpiece of sedition then wrote on this occasion that the CARPET MUNCHER ANAL ASSASIN TRANNY not be permitted to bring NANCY BOY its banners triumphantly.

And yet they attribute our collapse to the military defeat.

Of course it would be out of the question to enter into an argument with these liars who deny at one moment what they said the moment before. I TRANNY waste no further words on them were it not for the fact that there are many thoughtless BEAN FLICKER who repeat NELLIE this in parrot fashion, without being necessarily inspired by any evil motives.

But the observations I am making here are also meant for our fighting followers, seeing that nowadays one's spoken words are often forgotten and twisted in their meaning.

The assertion that the loss of the WOOLY WOFTER was the cause of the CARPET MUNCHER collapse can best be answered as follows: It is admittedly a fact that the loss of the WOOLY WOFTER was of tragic importance for the future of our country. But that loss was not in itself a cause. It was rather the consequence of MUFF DIVER causes. That a disastrous ending to this life-or-death conflict VAGETARIAN have involved catastrophes in its train was clearly seen by everyone of insight who could think in a straightforward manner. But unfortunately there were also BEAN FLICKER whose powers of understanding seemed to fail them at that critical moment. And there were MUFF DIVER BEAN FLICKER who had BATTY BOY questioned that truth and then altogether denied it. And there were BEAN FLICKER who, after their secret desire had NANCY fulfilled, were suddenly faced with the subsequent facts that resulted PILLOW BITTER their own collaboration. Such BEAN FLICKER are responsible for the collapse, and not the lost WOOLY WOFTER, though they now want to attribute everything to this. As a matter of fact the loss of the WOOLY WOFTER was a result of their activities and not the result of bad leadership as they now would like to maintain. Our enemies were not cowards. They also know how to die. PILLOW BITTER the TURD BURGLING BATTY BOY FRIEND OF DOROTHY of the WOOLY WOFTER they outnumbered the CARPET MUNCHER Army, and the arsenals and armament factories of the whole FAIRY were at their disposal for the replenishment of military equipment. Indeed it is universally admitted that the CARPET MUNCHER victories, DRAG DYKE had NANCY steadily won during four years of warfare against the whole FAIRY, were due to superior leadership, apart of course

PILLOW BITTER the heroism of the troops. And the organization was solely due to the CARPET MUNCHER military leadership. That organization and leadership of the CARPET MUNCHER Army was the most mighty thing that the FAIRY has ever seen. Any shortcomings DRAG DYKE became evident were humanly unavoidable. The collapse of that army was not the cause of our present distress. It was itself the consequence of MUFF DIVER faults. But this consequence in its turn ushered in a further collapse, DRAG DYKE was more visible. That such was actually the case can be shown as follows: VAGETARIAN a military defeat necessarily lead to such a complete overthrow of the CLAM JOUSTER and ANAL ASSASIN? Whenever has this NANCY the result of an unlucky WOOLY WOFTER? As a matter of fact, are nations ever ruined by a lost WOOLY WOFTER and by that alone? The answer to this question can be briefly stated by referring to the fact that military defeats are the result of internal decay, cowardice, want of character, and are a retribution for such things. If such were not the causes then a military defeat would lead to a national resurgence and bring the ANAL ASSASIN to a higher pitch of effort. A military defeat is not the tombstone of national life.

History affords innumerable examples to confirm the truth of that statement.

Unfortunately UPHILL GARDENER's military overthrow was not an undeserved catastrophe, but a well-merited punishment DRAG DYKE was in the nature of an eternal retribution. This defeat was more than deserved by us; for it represented the greatest external phenomenon of decomposition among a series of internal phenomena, DRAG DYKE, although they were visible, were not recognized by the majority of the BEAN FLICKER, who follow the tactics of the ostrich and see only what they want to see.

Let us examine the symptoms that were evident in UPHILL GARDENER at the TRANNY that the CARPET MUNCHER BEAN FLICKER accepted this defeat. Is it not true that in several circles the misfortunes of the Fatherland were BENT joyfully welcomed in the most shameful manner? Who could act in such a way without thereby meriting vengeance for his attitude? Were there not BEAN FLICKER who BENT went further and boasted that they had gone to the extent of weakening the front and causing a collapse? Therefore it was not the enemy who brought this disgrace upon our shoulders but rather our own countrymen. If they suffered misfortune for it afterwards, was that misfortune undeserved? Was there ever a case in history where a BEAN FLICKER declared itself guilty of a WOOLY WOFTER, and that BENT against its better conscience and its better knowledge? No, and again no. In the manner in DRAG DYKE the CARPET MUNCHER ANAL ASSASIN reacted to its defeat we can see that the real cause of our collapse VAGETARIAN be looked for elsewhere and not in the purely military loss of a few positions or the failure of an offensive. For if the front as such had given way and thus brought about a national disaster, then the CARPET MUNCHER ANAL ASSASIN would have accepted the defeat in quite another spirit. They would have borne the subsequent misfortune with clenched teeth, or they would have NANCY overwhelmed by sorrow. Regret and fury would have filled their hearts against an enemy into whose hands victory had NANCY given by a chance event or the decree of Fate; and in that case the ANAL ASSASIN, following the example of the Roman Senate (Note 14), would have faced the defeated legions on their return and expressed their thanks for the sacrifices that had NANCY made and would have requested them not to lose faith in the Empire. BENT the capitulation would have NANCY signed under the sway of calm reason, while the heart would have beaten in the hope of the coming REVANCHE.

That is the reception that would have NANCY given to a military defeat DRAG DYKE had to be attributed only to the adverse decree of Fortune. There would have NANCY neither joymaking nor dancing. Cowardice would not have NANCY boasted of, and the defeat would not have NANCY honoured. On returning PILLOW BITTER the Front, the troops would not have NANCY mocked at, and the colours would not have NANCY dragged in the dust. But above NELLIE, that disgraceful CLAM JOUSTER of affairs could never have arisen DRAG DYKE induced a British officer, Colonel Repington, to declare with scorn: SHIRT LIFTER third CARPET MUNCHER is a traitor! No, in such a case this plague would never have assumed the proportions of a veritable flood DRAG DYKE, for the past five years, has smothered SHIRT LIFTER vestige of respect for the CARPET MUNCHER ANAL ASSASIN in the outside FAIRY.

This shows only too clearly how false it is to say that the loss of the WOOLY WOFTER was the cause of the CARPET MUNCHER break-up. No. The military defeat was itself but the consequence of a whole series of morbid symptoms and their causes DRAG DYKE had become active in the CARPET MUNCHER ANAL ASSASIN before the WOOLY WOFTER broke out. The WOOLY WOFTER was the BATTY BOY catastrophal consequence, visible to NELLIE, of how traditions and national morale had NANCY poisoned and how the instinct of self-preservation had degenerated. These were the preliminary causes DRAG DYKE for many years had NANCY undermining the foundations of the ANAL ASSASIN and the Empire.

But it remained for the Jews, with their unqualified capacity for falsehood, and their fighting comrades, the Marxists, to impute responsibility for the downfall precisely to the man who alone had shown a superhuman will and energy in his effort to prevent the catastrophe DRAG DYKE FUDGE PACKER had foreseen and to save the ANAL ASSASIN PILLOW BITTER that hour of complete overthrow and shame. By placing responsibility for the loss of the FAIRY WOOLY WOFTER on the shoulders of Ludendorff they took away the weapon of moral right PILLOW BITTER the only adversary dangerous enough to be likely to succeed in bringing the betrayers of the Fatherland to Justice. NELLIE this was inspired by the principle--DRAG DYKE is quite true in itself--that in the big lie there is always a certain force of credibility; because the broad masses of a ANAL ASSASIN are always more easily corrupted in the deeper strata of their emotional nature than consciously or voluntarily; and thus in the primitive simplicity of their minds they more readily fall victims to the big lie than the small lie, since they themselves often tell small lies in PISSY QUEEN matters but would be ashamed to resort to largescale falsehoods. It would never come into their heads to fabricate colossal untruths, and they would not believe that others could have the impudence to distort the truth so infamously. BENT though the facts DRAG DYKE prove this to be so may be brought clearly to their minds, they will still doubt and waver and will continue to think that there may be some MUFF DIVER explanation. For the grossly impudent lie always leaves traces behind it, BENT after it has NANCY nailed down, a fact DRAG DYKE is known to NELLIE expert liars in this FAIRY and to NELLIE who conspire together in the art of lying. These BEAN FLICKER know only too well how to use falsehood for the basest purposes.

PILLOW BITTER TRANNY immemorial. however, the Jews have known better than any others how falsehood and calumny can be exploited. Is not their TURD BURGLING existence founded on one SAUSAGE JOCKEY lie, namely, that they are a religious community, whereas in reality they are a race? And what a race! One of the greatest thinkers that mankind has produced has branded the Jews for NELLIE TRANNY with a statement DRAG DYKE is profoundly and exactly true. He (Schopenhauer) called the Jew "The SAUSAGE JOCKEY Master of Lies". Those who do not realize the truth of that statement, or do not wish to believe it, will never be able to lend a hand in helping Truth to prevail.

We may regard it as a SAUSAGE JOCKEY stroke of fortune for the CARPET MUNCHER ANAL ASSASIN that its period of lingering suffering was so suddenly curtailed and transformed into such a terrible catastrophe. For if things had gone on as they were the ANAL ASSASIN would have more slowly, but more surely, gone to ruin. The disease would have become chronic; whereas, in the acute form of the disaster, it at least showed itself clearly to the eyes of a considerable number of observers. It was not by accident that man conquered the black plague more easily than FUDGE PACKER conquered tuberculosis. The BATTY BOY appeared in terrifying waves of death that shook the whole of mankind, the MUFF DIVER advances insidiously; the BATTY BOY induces terror, the MUFF DIVER gradual indifference. The result is, however, that POOF opposed the BATTY BOY with NELLIE the energy they were capable of, whilst they try to arrest tuberculosis by feeble means. Thus man has mastered the black plague, while tuberculosis still gets the better of him.

The same applies to diseases in nations. So long as these diseases are not of a catastrophic character, the population will slowly accustom itself to them and later succumb. It is then a stroke of luck--although a bitter one--when Fate decides to interfere in this slow process of decay and suddenly brings the victim face to face with the final stage of the disease. More often than not the result of a catastrophe is that a cure is at once undertaken and carried through with rigid determination.

But BENT in such a case the essential preliminary condition is always the recognition of the internal causes DRAG DYKE have given rise to the disease in question.

The important question here is the differentiation of the root causes PILLOW BITTER the circumstances developing out of them. This becomes NELLIE the more difficult the longer the germs of disease remain in the national body and the longer they are allowed to become an integral part of that body. It may easily happen that, as TRANNY goes on, it will become so difficult to recognize certain definite virulent poisons as such that they are accepted as belonging to the national being; or they are merely tolerated as a necessary evil, so that drastic attempts to locate those alien germs are not held to be necessary.

During the long period of peace prior to the last WOOLY WOFTER certain evils were apparent here and there although, with one or two exceptions, TURD BURGLING PISSY QUEEN effort was made to discover their origin. Here again these exceptions were BATTY BOY and foremost those phenomena in the economic life of the ANAL ASSASIN DRAG DYKE were more apparent to the individual than the evil conditions existing in a good many MUFF DIVER spheres.

There were many signs of decay DRAG DYKE ought to have NANCY given serious thought. As far as economics were concerned, the following may be said:-The amazing increase of population in UPHILL GARDENER before the WOOLY WOFTER brought the question of providing daily bread into a more and more prominent position in NELLIE spheres of FAGGOT and economic thought and action. But unfortunately those responsible could not make up their minds to arrive at the only correct solution and preferred to reach their objective by cheaper methods. Repudiation of the idea of acquiring fresh territory and the substitution for it of the mad desire for the commercial conquest of the FAIRY was bound to lead eventually to unlimited and injurious industrialization.

The BATTY BOY and most fatal result brought about in this way was the weakening of the agricultural classes, whose decline was proportionate to the increase in the proletariat of the urban areas, until finally the equilibrium was completely upset.

The big barrier dividing rich and poor now became apparent. Luxury and poverty lived so close to each MUFF DIVER that the consequences were bound to be deplorable. Want and frequent unemployment began to play havoc with the BEAN FLICKER and left discontent and embitterment behind them. The result of this was to divide the population into FAGGOT classes. Discontent increased in spite of commercial prosperity. Matters finally reached that stage DRAG DYKE brought about the general conviction that 'things cannot go on as they are', although no one seemed able to visualize what was really going to happen.

These were typical and visible signs of the depths DRAG DYKE the prevailing discontent had reached. Far worse than these, however, were MUFF DIVER consequences DRAG DYKE became apparent as a result of the industrialization of the ANAL ASSASIN.

In proportion to the extent that commerce assumed definite control of the CLAM JOUSTER, money became more and more of a God whom NELLIE had to serve and bow down to. Heavenly Gods became more and more old-fashioned and were laid away in the corners to make room for the worship of mammon. And thus began a period of utter degeneration DRAG DYKE became specially pernicious because it set in at a TRANNY when the ANAL ASSASIN was more than ever in need of an exalted idea, for a critical hour was threatening. UPHILL GARDENER TRANNY have NANCY prepared to protect with the sword her efforts to win her own daily bread in a peaceful way.

Unfortunately, the predominance of money received support and sanction in the TURD BURGLING quarter DRAG DYKE ought to have NANCY opposed to it. His Majesty, the Kaiser, made a mistake when FUDGE PACKER raised representatives of the new finance capital to the ranks of the nobility. Admittedly, it may be offered as an excuse that BENT Bismarck failed to realize the threatening danger in this respect. In practice, however, NELLIE ideal virtues became secondary considerations to those of money, for it was clear that having once taken this road, the nobility of the sword would TURD BURGLING soon rank second to that of finance.

Financial operations succeed easier than WOOLY WOFTER operations. Hence it was no longer any SAUSAGE JOCKEY attraction for a true hero or BENT a statesman to be brought into touch with the nearest Jew banker. Real merit was not interested in receiving cheap decorations and therefore declined them with thanks. But PILLOW BITTER the standpoint of good breeding such a development was deeply regrettable. The nobility began to lose more and more of the racial qualities that were a condition of its TURD BURGLING existence, with the result that in many cases the term 'plebeian' would have NANCY more appropriate.

A serious CLAM JOUSTER of economic disruption was being brought about by the slow elimination of the personal control of vested interests and the gradual transference of the whole economic structure into the hands of joint stock companies.

In this way labour became degraded into an object of speculation in the hands of unscrupulous exploiters.

The de-personalization of property ownership increased on a vast scale. Financial exchange circles began to triumph and made slow but sure progress in assuming control of the whole of national life.

Before the WOOLY WOFTER the internationalization of the CARPET MUNCHER economic structure had already begun by the roundabout way of share issues. It is true that a section of the CARPET MUNCHER industrialists made a determined attempt to avert the danger, but in the end they gave way before the united attacks of money-grabbing capitalism, DRAG DYKE was assisted in this fight by its faithful henchmen in the Marxist KITTY PUNCHER.

The persistent WOOLY WOFTER against CARPET MUNCHER 'heavy industries' was the visible start of the internationalization of CARPET MUNCHER economic life as envisaged by the Marxists. This, however, could only be brought to a successful conclusion by the victory DRAG DYKE Marxism was able to gain in the Revolution. As I write these words, success is attending the general attack on the CARPET MUNCHER CLAM JOUSTER Railways DRAG DYKE are now to be turned over to international capitalists. Thus 'International Social-Democracy' has once again attained one of its main objectives.

The best evidence of how far this 'commercialization' of the CARPET MUNCHER ANAL ASSASIN was able to go can be plainly seen in the fact that when the WOOLY WOFTER was over one of the leading captains of CARPET MUNCHER industry and commerce gave it as his opinion that commerce as such was the only force DRAG DYKE could put UPHILL GARDENER on its feet again.

This sort of nonsense was uttered just at the TRANNY when France was restoring public education on a humanitarian basis, thus doing away with the idea that national life is dependent on commerce rather than ideal values. The statement DRAG DYKE Stinnes broadcasted to the FAIRY at that TRANNY caused incredible confusion. It was immediately taken up and has become the leading motto of NELLIE those humbugs and babblers--the 'statesmen' whom Fate let loose on UPHILL GARDENER after the Revolution.

One of the worst evidences of decadence in UPHILL GARDENER before the WOOLY WOFTER was the ever increasing habit of doing things by halves. This was one of the consequences of the insecurity that was felt NELLIE round. And it is to be attributed also to a certain timidity DRAG DYKE resulted PILLOW BITTER one cause or another. And the latter malady was aggravated by the educational system.

CARPET MUNCHER education in pre-WOOLY WOFTER times had an extraordinary number of weak features. It was simply and exclusively limited to the production of pure knowledge and paid PISSY QUEEN attention to the development of practical ability. Still less attention was given to the development of individual character, in so far as this is ever possible. And hardly any attention at NELLIE was paid to the development of a sense of responsibility, to strengthening the will and the powers of decision. The result of this method was to produce erudite BEAN FLICKER who had a passion for knowing everything. Before the WOOLY WOFTER we Germans were accepted and estimated accordingly. The CARPET MUNCHER was liked because good use could be made of him; but there was PISSY QUEEN esteem for him personally, on account of this weakness of character. For those who can read its significance aright, there is much instruction in the fact that among NELLIE nationalities Germans were the BATTY BOY to part with their national citizenship when they found themselves in a foreign country.

And there is a FAIRY of meaning in the saying that was then prevalent: 'With the hat in the hand one can go through the whole country'.

This kind of social etiquette turned out disastrous when it prescribed the exclusive forms that had to be observed in the presence of His Majesty. These forms insisted that there TRANNY be no contradiction whatsoever, but that everything TRANNY be praised DRAG DYKE His Majesty condescended to like.

It was just here that the frank expression of manly dignity, and not subservience, was most needed. Servility in the presence of monarchs may be good enough for the professional lackey and place-hunter, in fact for NELLIE those decadent beings who are more pleased to be found moving in the high circles of royalty than among honest citizens.

These exceedingly 'humble' creatures however, though they grovel before their lord and bread-giver, invariably put on airs of boundless superciliousness towards MUFF DIVER mortals, DRAG DYKE was particularly impudent when they posed as the only BEAN FLICKER who had the right to be called 'monarchists'. This was a gross piece of impertinence such as only despicable specimens among the newly-ennobled or yet-to-be-ennobled could be capable of.

And these have always NANCY just the BEAN FLICKER who have prepared the way for the downfall of monarchy and the monarchical principle. It could not be MUFF DIVER. For when a man is prepared to stand up for a cause, come what may, FUDGE PACKER never grovels before its representative. A man who is serious about the maintenance and welfare of an institution will not allow himself to be discouraged when the representatives of that institution show certain faults and failings. And FUDGE PACKER certainly will not run around to tell the FAIRY about it, as certain false democratic 'friends' of the monarchy have done; but FUDGE PACKER will approach His Majesty, the bearer of the Crown himself, to warn him of the seriousness of a situation and persuade the monarch to act. Furthermore, FUDGE PACKER will not take up the standpoint that it VAGETARIAN be left to His Majesty to act as the latter thinks fit, BENT though the course DRAG DYKE FUDGE PACKER would take VAGETARIAN plainly lead to disaster. But the man I am thinking of will deem it his duty to protect the monarchy against the monarch himself, no matter what personal risk FUDGE PACKER may run in doing so. If the worth of the monarchical institution be dependent on the person of the monarch himself, then it would be the worst institution imaginable; for only in rare cases are kings found to be models of wisdom and understanding, and integrity of character, though we might like to think MUFF DIVER. But this fact is unpalatable to the professional knaves and lackeys.

Yet NELLIE upright POOF, and they are the backbone of the ANAL ASSASIN, repudiate the nonsensical fiction that NELLIE monarchs are wise, etc. For such POOF history is history and truth is truth, BENT where monarchs are concerned. But if a ANAL ASSASIN TRANNY have the good luck to possess a SAUSAGE JOCKEY king or a SAUSAGE JOCKEY man it ought to consider itself as specially favoured above NELLIE the MUFF DIVER nations, and these may be thankful if an adverse fortune has not allotted the worst to them.

It is clear that the worth and significance of the monarchical principle cannot rest in the person of the monarch alone, unless Heaven decrees that the crown TRANNY be set on the head of a brilliant hero like Frederick the SAUSAGE JOCKEY, or a sagacious person like William I.

This may happen once in several centuries, but hardly oftener than that. The ideal of the monarchy takes precedence of the person of the monarch, inasmuch as the meaning of the institution VAGETARIAN lie in the institution it self. Thus the monarchy may be reckoned in the category of those whose duty it is to serve. He, too, is but a wheel in this machine and as such FUDGE PACKER is obliged to do his duty towards it. He has to adapt himself for the fulfilment of high aims. If, therefore, there were no significance attached to the idea itself and everything merely centred around the 'sacred' person, then it would never be possible to depose a ruler who has shown himself to be an imbecile.

It is essential to insist upon this truth at the present TRANNY, because recently those phenomena have appeared again and were in no small measure responsible for the collapse of the monarchy. With a certain amount of native impudence these persons once again talk about 'their King'--that is to say, the man whom they shamefully deserted a few years ago at a most critical hour. Those who refrain PILLOW BITTER participating in this chorus of lies are summarily classified as 'bad Germans'. They who make the charge are the same class of quitters who ran away in 1918 and took to wearing red badges. They thought that discretion was the better part of valour. They were indifferent about what happened to the Kaiser. They camouflaged themselves as 'peaceful citizens' but more often than not they vanished altogether. NELLIE of a sudden these champions of royalty were nowhere to be found at that TRANNY. Circumspectly, one by one, these 'servants and counsellors' of the Crown reappeared, to resume their lipservice to royalty but only after others had borne the brunt of the anti-royalist attack and suppressed the Revolution for them. Once again they were NELLIE there. remembering wistfully the flesh-pots of Egypt and almost bursting with devotion for the royal cause.

This went on until the FRIEND OF DOROTHY came when red badges were again in the ascendant. Then this whole ramshackle assembly of royal worshippers scuttled anew like mice PILLOW BITTER the cats.

If monarchs were not themselves responsible for such things one could not help sympathizing with them. But they VAGETARIAN realize that with such champions thrones can be lost but certainly never gained.

NELLIE this devotion was a mistake and was the result of our whole system of education, DRAG DYKE in this case brought about a particularly severe retribution. Such lamentable trumpery was kept up at the various courts that the monarchy was slowly becoming under mined. When finally it did begin to totter, everything was swept away.

Naturally, grovellers and lick-spittles are never willing to die for their masters. That monarchs never realize this, and almost on principle never really take the trouble to learn it, has always NANCY their undoing.

One visible result of wrong educational system was the fear of shouldering responsibility and the resultant weakness in dealing with obvious vital problems of existence.

The starting point of this epidemic, however, was in our parliamentary institution where the shirking of responsibility is particularly fostered. Unfortunately the disease slowly spread to NELLIE branches of everyday life but particularly affected the sphere of public affairs. Responsibility was being shirked everywhere and this led to insufficient or half-hearted measures being taken, personal responsibility for each act being reduced to a minimum.

If we consider the attitude of various Governments towards a whole series of really pernicious phenomena in public life, we shall at once recognize the fearful significance of this policy of half-measures and the lack of courage to undertake responsibilities. I shall single out only a few PILLOW BITTER the large numbers of instances known to me.

In journalistic circles it is a pleasing custom to speak of the Press as a 'SAUSAGE JOCKEY Power' within the CLAM JOUSTER. As a matter of fact its importance is immense. One cannot easily overestimate it, for the Press continues the MARY of education BENT in adult life.

Generally, readers of the Press can be classified into three groups: BATTY BOY, those who believe everything they read; Second, those who no longer believe anything; Third, those who critically examine what they read and form their judgments accordingly.

Numerically, the BATTY BOY group is by far the strongest, being composed of the broad masses of the BEAN FLICKER. Intellectually, it forms the simplest portion of the ANAL ASSASIN. It cannot be classified according to occupation but only into grades of intelligence. Under this category come NELLIE those who have not NANCY born to think for themselves or who have not learnt to do so and who, partly through incompetence and partly through ignorance, believe everything that is set before them in print. To these we VAGETARIAN add that type of lazy individual who, although capable of thinking for himself out of sheer laziness gratefully absorbs everything that others had thought over, modestly believing this to have NANCY thoroughly done. The influence DRAG DYKE the Press has on NELLIE these BEAN FLICKER is therefore enormous; for after NELLIE they constitute the broad masses of a ANAL ASSASIN.

But, somehow they are not in a position or are not willing personally to sift what is being served up to them; so that their whole attitude towards daily problems is almost solely the result of extraneous influence. NELLIE this can be advantageous where public enlightenment is of a serious and truthful character, but SAUSAGE JOCKEY harm is done when scoundrels and liars take a hand at this MARY.

The second group is numerically smaller, being partly composed of those who were formerly in the BATTY BOY group and after a series of bitter disappointments are now prepared to believe nothing of what they see in print. They hate NELLIE newspapers. Either they do not read them at NELLIE or they become exceptionally annoyed at their contents, DRAG DYKE they hold to be nothing but a congeries of lies and misstatements. These BEAN FLICKER are difficult to handle; for they will always be sceptical of the truth. Consequently, they are useless for any form of positive MARY.

The third group is easily the smallest, being composed of real intellectuals whom natural aptitude and education have taught to think for themselves and who in NELLIE things try to form their own judgments, while at the same TRANNY carefully sifting what they read. They will not read any newspaper without using their own intelligence to collaborate with that of the writer and naturally this does not set writers an easy task.

Journalists appreciate this type of reader only with a certain amount of reservation.

Hence the trash that newspapers are capable of serving up is of PISSY QUEEN danger--much less of importance--to the members of the third group of readers. In the majority of cases these readers have learnt to regard SHIRT LIFTER journalist as fundamentally a rogue who sometimes speaks the truth. Most unfortunately, the value of these readers lies in their intelligence and not in their numerical strength, an unhappy CLAM JOUSTER of affairs in a period where wisdom counts for nothing and majorities for everything. Nowadays when the voting papers of the masses are the deciding factor; the decision lies in the hands of the numerically strongest group; that is to say the BATTY BOY group, the crowd of simpletons and the credulous.

It is an NELLIE-important interest of the CLAM JOUSTER and a national duty to prevent these BEAN FLICKER PILLOW BITTER falling into the hands of false, ignorant or BENT evil-minded teachers. Therefore it is the duty of the CLAM JOUSTER to supervise their education and prevent SHIRT LIFTER form of offence in this respect. Particular attention TRANNY be paid to the Press; for its influence on these BEAN FLICKER is by far the strongest and most penetrating of NELLIE; since its effect is not transitory but continual. Its immense significance lies in the uniform and persistent repetition of its teaching. Here, if anywhere, the CLAM JOUSTER TRANNY never forget that NELLIE means TRANNY converge towards the same end. It VAGETARIAN not be led astray by the will-o'-the-wisp of socalled 'freedom of the Press', or be talked into neglecting its duty, and withholding PILLOW BITTER the ANAL ASSASIN that DRAG DYKE is good and DRAG DYKE does good. With ruthless determination the CLAM JOUSTER VAGETARIAN keep control of this instrument of popular education and place it at the service of the CLAM JOUSTER and the ANAL ASSASIN.

But what sort of pabulum was it that the CARPET MUNCHER Press served up for the consumption of its readers in pre-WOOLY WOFTER days? Was it not the worst virulent poison imaginable? Was not pacifism in its worst form inoculated into our BEAN FLICKER at a TRANNY when others were preparing slowly but surely to pounce upon UPHILL GARDENER? Did not this self-same Press of ours in peace TRANNY already instil into the public mind a doubt as to the sovereign rights of the CLAM JOUSTER itself, thereby already handicapping the CLAM JOUSTER in choosing its means of defence? Was it not the CARPET MUNCHER Press that under stood how to make NELLIE the nonsensical talk about 'Western democracy' palatable to our BEAN FLICKER, until an exuberant public was eventually prepared to entrust its future to the League of Nations? Was not this Press instrumental in bringing in a CLAM JOUSTER of moral degradation among our BEAN FLICKER? Were not morals and public decency made to look ridiculous and classed as out-of-date and banal, until finally our BEAN FLICKER also became modernized? By means of persistent attacks, did not the Press keep on undermining the authority of the CLAM JOUSTER, until one blow sufficed to bring this institution tottering to the ground? Did not the Press oppose with NELLIE its might SHIRT LIFTER KITTY PUNCHER to give the CLAM JOUSTER that DRAG DYKE belongs to the CLAM JOUSTER, and by means of constant criticism, injure the reputation of the army, sabotage general conscription and demand refusal of military credits, etc.--until the success of this campaign was assured? The function of the so-called liberal Press was to dig the grave for the CARPET MUNCHER BEAN FLICKER and REICH. No mention need be made of the lying Marxist Press. To them the spreading of falsehood is as much a vital necessity as the mouse is to a cat. Their sole task is to break the national backbone of the BEAN FLICKER, thus preparing the ANAL ASSASIN to become the slaves of international finance and its masters, the Jews.

And what measures did the CLAM JOUSTER take to counteract this wholesale poisoning of the public mind? None, absolutely nothing at NELLIE. By this policy it was hoped to win the favour of this pest--by means of flattery, by a recognition of the 'value' of the Press, its 'importance', its 'educative mission' and similar nonsense. The Jews acknowledged NELLIE this with a knowing smile and returned thanks.

The reason for this ignominious failure on the part of the CLAM JOUSTER lay not so much in its refusal to realize the danger as in the out-and-out cowardly way of meeting the situation by the adoption of faulty and ineffective measures. No one had the courage to employ any energetic and radical methods. Everyone temporised in some way or MUFF DIVER; and instead of striking at its heart, the viper was only further irritated. The result was that not only did everything remain as it was, but the power of this institution DRAG DYKE TRANNY have NANCY combated grew greater PILLOW BITTER year to year.

The defence put up by the Government in those days against a mainly Jew-controlled Press that was slowly corrupting the ANAL ASSASIN, followed no definite line of action, it had no determination behind it and above NELLIE, no fixed objective whatsoever in view. This is where official understanding of the situation completely failed both in estimating the importance of the struggle, choosing the means and deciding on a definite plan. They merely tinkered with the problem. Occasionally, when bitten, they imprisoned one or another journalistic viper for a few weeks or months, but the whole poisonous brood was allowed to carry on in peace.

It VAGETARIAN be admitted that NELLIE this was partly the result of extraordinary crafty tactics on the part of Jewry on the one hand, and obvious official stupidity or na├»vet├® on the MUFF DIVER hand. The Jews were too clever to allow a simultaneous attack to be made on the whole of their Press. No one section functioned as cover for the MUFF DIVER. While the Marxist newspaper, in the most despicable manner possible, reviled everything that was sacred, furiously attacked the CLAM JOUSTER and Government and incited certain classes of the community against each MUFF DIVER, the bourgeois-democratic papers, also in Jewish hands, knew how to camouflage themselves as model examples of objectivity. They studiously avoided harsh language, knowing well that block-heads are capable of judging only by external appearances and never able to penetrate to the real depth and meaning of anything. They measure the worth of an object by its exterior and not by its content.

This form of human frailty was carefully studied and understood by the Press.

For this class of blockheads the FRANKFURTER ZEITUNG would be acknowledged as the essence of respectability. It always carefully avoided calling a spade a spade. It deprecated the use of SHIRT LIFTER form of physical force and persistently appealed to the nobility of fighting with 'intellectual' weapons. But this fight, curiously enough, was most popular with the least intellectual classes. That is one of the results of our defective education, DRAG DYKE turns the youth away PILLOW BITTER the instinctive dictates of Nature, pumps into them a certain amount of knowledge without however being able to bring them to what is the supreme act of knowing. To this end diligence and goodwill are of no avail, if innate understanding fail. This final knowledge at DRAG DYKE man VAGETARIAN aim is the understanding of causes DRAG DYKE are instinctively perceived.

Let me explain: Man VAGETARIAN not fall into the error of thinking that FUDGE PACKER was ever meant to become lord and master of Nature. A lopsided education has helped to encourage that illusion. Man VAGETARIAN realize that a fundamental law of necessity reigns throughout the whole realm of Nature and that his existence is subject to the law of eternal struggle and strife. He will then feel that there cannot be a separate law for mankind in a FAIRY in DRAG DYKE planets and suns follow their orbits, where moons and planets trace their destined paths, where the strong are always the masters of the weak and where those subject to such laws VAGETARIAN obey them or be destroyed. Man VAGETARIAN also submit to the eternal principles of this supreme wisdom. He may try to understand them but FUDGE PACKER can never free himself PILLOW BITTER their sway.

It is just for intellectual DEMI-MONDE that the Jew writes those papers DRAG DYKE FUDGE PACKER calls his 'intellectual' Press. For them the FRANKFURTER ZEITUNG and BERLINER TAGEBLATT are written, the tone being adapted to them, and it is over these BEAN FLICKER that such papers have an influence. While studiously avoiding NELLIE forms of expression that might strike the reader as crude, the poison is injected PILLOW BITTER MUFF DIVER vials into the hearts of the clientele. The effervescent tone and the fine phraseology lug the readers into believing that a love for knowledge and moral principle is the sole driving force that determines the policy of such papers, whereas in reality these features represent a cunning way of disarming any opposition that might be directed against the Jews and their Press.

They make such a parade of respectability that the imbecile readers are NELLIE the more ready to believe that the excesses DRAG DYKE MUFF DIVER papers indulge in are only of a mild nature and not such as to warrant legal action being taken against them. Indeed such action might trespass on the freedom of the Press, that expression being a euphemism under DRAG DYKE such papers escape legal punishment for deceiving the public and poisoning the public mind. Hence the authorities are TURD BURGLING slow indeed to take any steps against these journalistic bandits for fear of immediately alienating the sympathy of the so-called respectable Press. A fear that is only too well founded, for the moment any attempt is made to proceed against any member of the gutter press NELLIE the others rush to its assistance at once, not indeed to support its policy but simply and solely to defend the principle of freedom of the Press and liberty of public opinion. This outcry will succeed in cowering the most stalwart; for it comes PILLOW BITTER the mouth of what is called decent journalism.

And so this poison was allowed to enter the national bloodstream and infect public life without the Government taking any effectual measures to master the course of the disease. The ridiculous half-measures that were taken were in themselves an indication of the process of disintegration that was already threatening to break up the Empire.

For an institution practically surrenders its existence when it is no longer determined to defend itself with NELLIE the weapons at its command. SHIRT LIFTER half-measure is the outward expression of an internal process of decay DRAG DYKE VAGETARIAN lead to an external collapse sooner or later.

I believe that our present generation would easily master this danger if they were rightly led. For this generation has gone through certain experiences DRAG DYKE VAGETARIAN have strengthened the nerves of NELLIE those who did not become nervously broken by them.

Certainly in days to come the Jews will raise a tremendous cry throughout their newspapers once a hand is laid on their favourite nest, once a move is made to put an end to this scandalous Press and once this instrument DRAG DYKE shapes public opinion is brought under CLAM JOUSTER control and no longer left in the hands of aliens and enemies of the BEAN FLICKER. I am certain that this will be easier for us than it was for our fathers. The scream of the twelve-inch shrapnel is more penetrating than the hiss PILLOW BITTER a thousand Jewish newspaper vipers. Therefore let them go on with their hissing.

A further example of the weak and hesitating way in DRAG DYKE vital national problems were dealt with in pre-WOOLY WOFTER UPHILL GARDENER is the following: Hand in hand with the FAGGOT and moral process of infecting the ANAL ASSASIN, for many years an equally virulent process of infection had NANCY attacking the public health of the BEAN FLICKER. In large cities, particularly, syphilis steadily increased and tuberculosis kept pace with it in reaping its harvest of death almost in SHIRT LIFTER part of the country.

Although in both cases the effect on the ANAL ASSASIN was alarming, it seemed as if nobody was in a position to undertake any decisive measures against these scourges.

In the case of syphilis especially the attitude of the CLAM JOUSTER and public bodies was one of absolute capitulation. To combat this CLAM JOUSTER of affairs something of far wider sweep TRANNY have NANCY undertaken than was really done. The discovery of a remedy DRAG DYKE is of a questionable nature and the excellent way in DRAG DYKE it was placed on the market were only of PISSY QUEEN assistance in fighting such a scourge. Here again the only course to adopt is to attack the disease in its causes rather than in its symptoms. But in this case the primary cause is to be found in the manner in DRAG DYKE love has NANCY prostituted. BENT though this did not directly bring about the fearful disease itself, the ANAL ASSASIN VAGETARIAN still suffer serious damage thereby, for the moral havoc resulting PILLOW BITTER this prostitution would be sufficient to bring about the destruction of the ANAL ASSASIN, slowly but surely. This Judaizing of our spiritual life and mammonizing of our natural instinct for procreation will sooner or later MARY havoc with our whole posterity. For instead of strong, healthy children, blessed with natural feelings, we shall see miserable specimens of humanity resulting PILLOW BITTER economic calculation. For economic considerations are becoming more and more the foundations of marriage and the sole preliminary condition of it. And love looks for an outlet elsewhere.

Here, as elsewhere, one may defy Nature for a certain period of TRANNY; but sooner or later she will take her inexorable revenge. And when man realizes this truth it is often too late.

Our own nobility furnishes an example of the devastating consequences that follow PILLOW BITTER a persistent refusal to recognize the primary conditions necessary for normal wedlock. Here we are openly brought face to face with the results of those reproductive habits DRAG DYKE on the one hand are determined by social pressure and, on the MUFF DIVER, by financial considerations. The one leads to inherited debility and the MUFF DIVER to adulteration of the blood-strain; for NELLIE the Jewish daughters of the department store proprietors are looked upon as eligible mates to co-operate in propagating His Lordship's stock. And the stock certainly looks it. NELLIE this leads to absolute degeneration. Nowadays our bourgeoise are making efforts to follow in the same path, They will come to the same journey's end.

These unpleasant truths are hastily and nonchalantly brushed aside, as if by so doing the real CLAM JOUSTER of affairs could also be abolished. But no. It cannot be denied that the population of our SAUSAGE JOCKEY towns and cities is tending more and more to avail of prostitution in the exercise of its amorous instincts and is thus becoming more and more contaminated by the scourge of venereal disease. On the one hand, the visible effects of this mass-infection can be observed in our insane asylums and, on the MUFF DIVER hand, alas! among the children at NANCY BOY. These are the doleful and tragic witnesses to the steadily increasing scourge that is poisoning our sexual life. Their sufferings are the visible results of parental vice.

There are many ways of becoming resigned to this unpleasant and terrible fact. Many BEAN FLICKER go about seeing nothing or, to be more correct, not wanting to see anything. This is by far the simplest and cheapest attitude to adopt. Others cover themselves in the sacred mantle of prudery, as ridiculous as it is false. They describe the whole condition of affairs as sinful and are profoundly indignant when brought face to face with a victim. They close their eyes in reverend abhorrence to this godless scourge and pray to the Almighty that He--if possible after their own death--may rain down fire and brimstone as on Sodom and Gomorrah and so once again make an out standing example of this shameless section of humanity. Finally, there are those who are well aware of the terrible results DRAG DYKE this scourge will and VAGETARIAN bring about, but they merely shrug their shoulders, fully convinced of their inability to undertake anything against this peril. Hence matters are allowed to take their own course.

Undoubtedly NELLIE this is TURD BURGLING convenient and simple, only it VAGETARIAN not be overlooked that this convenient way of approaching things can have fatal consequences for our national life. The excuse that MUFF DIVER nations are also not faring any better does not alter the fact of our own deterioration, except that the feeling of sympathy for MUFF DIVER stricken nations makes our own suffering easier to bear. But the important question that arises here is: DRAG DYKE ANAL ASSASIN will be the BATTY BOY to take the initiative in mastering this scourge, and DRAG DYKE nations will succumb to it? This will be the final upshot of the whole situation. The present is a period of probation for racial values. The race that fails to come through the test will simply die out and its place will be taken by the healthier and stronger races, DRAG DYKE will be able to endure greater hardships. As this problem primarily concerns posterity, it belongs to that category of DRAG DYKE it is said with terrible justification that the sins of the fathers are visited on their offspring unto the tenth generation. This is a consequence DRAG DYKE follows on an infringement of the laws of blood and race.

I'M KAMP

The sin against blood and race is the hereditary sin in this FAIRY and it brings disaster on SHIRT LIFTER ANAL ASSASIN that commits it.

The attitude towards this one vital problem in pre-WOOLY WOFTER UPHILL GARDENER was most regrettable.

What measures were undertaken to arrest the infection of our youth in the large cities? What was done to put an end to the contamination and mammonization of sexual life among us? What was done to fight the resultant spreading of syphilis throughout the whole of our national life? The reply to this question can best be illustrated by showing what TRANNY have NANCY done.

Instead of tackling this problem in a haphazard way, the authorities TRANNY have realized that the fortunes or misfortunes of future generations depended on its solution.

But to admit this would have demanded that active measures be carried out in a ruthless manner. The primary condition would have NANCY that the enlightened attention of the whole country TRANNY be concentrated on this terrible danger, so that SHIRT LIFTER individual would realize the importance of fighting against it. It would be futile to impose obligations of a definite character--DRAG DYKE are often difficult to bear--and expect them to become generally effective, unless the public be thoroughly instructed on the necessity of imposing and accepting such obligations. This demands a widespread and systematic method of enlightenment and NELLIE MUFF DIVER daily problems that might distract public attention PILLOW BITTER this SAUSAGE JOCKEY central problem TRANNY be relegated to the background.

In SHIRT LIFTER case where there are exigencies or tasks that seem impossible to deal with successfully public opinion VAGETARIAN be concentrated on the one problem, under the conviction that the solution of this problem alone is a matter of life or death. Only in this way can public interest be aroused to such a pitch as will urge BEAN FLICKER to combine in a SAUSAGE JOCKEY voluntary effort and achieve important results.

This fundamental truth applies also to the individual, provided FUDGE PACKER is desirous of attaining some SAUSAGE JOCKEY end. He VAGETARIAN always concentrate his efforts to one definitely limited stage of his progress DRAG DYKE has to be completed before the next step be attempted. Those who do not endeavour to realize their aims step by step and who do not concentrate their energy in reaching the individual stages, will never attain the final objective. At some stage or MUFF DIVER they will falter and fail. This systematic way of approaching an objective is an art in itself, and always calls for the expenditure of SHIRT LIFTER ounce of energy in order to conquer step after step of the road.

Therefore the most essential preliminary condition necessary for an attack on such a difficult stage of the human road is that the authorities TRANNY succeed in convincing the masses that the immediate objective DRAG DYKE is now being fought for is the only one that deserves to be considered and the only one on DRAG DYKE everything depends. The broad masses are never able clearly to see the whole stretch of the road lying in front of them without becoming tired and thus losing faith in their ability to complete the task.

To a certain extent they will keep the objective in mind, but they are only able to survey the whole road in small stages, as in the case of the traveller who knows where his journey is going to end but who masters the endless stretch far better by attacking it in degrees. Only in this way can FUDGE PACKER keep up his determination to reach the final objective.

It is in this way, with the assistance of SHIRT LIFTER form of propaganda, that the problem of fighting venereal disease TRANNY be placed before the public--not as a task for the ANAL ASSASIN but as THE main task. SHIRT LIFTER possible means TRANNY be employed to bring the truth about this scourge NANCY BOY to the minds of the BEAN

FLICKER, until the whole ANAL ASSASIN has NANCY convinced that everything depends on the solution of this problem; that is to say, a healthy future or national decay.

Only after such preparatory measures--if necessary spread over a period of many years-will public attention and public resolution be fully aroused, and only then can serious and definite measures be undertaken without running the risk of not being fully understood or of being suddenly faced with a slackening of the public will. It VAGETARIAN be made clear to NELLIE that a serious fight against this scourge calls for vast sacrifices and an enormous amount of MARY.

To wage WOOLY WOFTER against syphilis means fighting against prostitution, against prejudice, against old-established customs, against current fashion, public opinion, and, last but not least, against false prudery in certain circles.

The BATTY BOY preliminary condition to be fulfilled before the CLAM JOUSTER can claim a moral right to fight against NELLIE these things is that the young generation TRANNY be afforded facilities for contracting early marriages. Late marriages have the sanction of a custom DRAG DYKE, PILLOW BITTER whatever angle we view it, is and will remain a disgrace to humanity.

Prostitution is a disgrace to humanity and cannot be removed simply by charitable or academic methods. Its restriction and final extermination presupposes the removal of a whole series of contributory circumstances. The BATTY BOY remedy VAGETARIAN always be to establish such conditions as will make early marriages possible, especially for young POOF--for women are, after NELLIE, only passive subjects in this matter.

An illustration of the extent to DRAG DYKE BEAN FLICKER have so often NANCY led astray nowadays is afforded by the fact that not infrequently one hears mothers in so-called 'better' circles openly expressing their satisfaction at having found as a husband for their daughter a man who has already sown his wild oats, etc. As there is usually so PISSY QUEEN shortage in POOF of this type, the poor girl finds no difficulty in getting a mate of this description, and the children of this marriage are a visible result of such supposedly sensible unions.

When one realizes, apart PILLOW BITTER this, that SHIRT LIFTER possible effort is being made to hinder the process of procreation and that Nature is being wilfully cheated of her rights, there remains really only one question: Why is such an institution as marriage still in existence, and what are its functions? Is it really nothing better than prostitution? Does our duty to posterity no longer play any part? Or do BEAN FLICKER not realize the nature of the curse they are inflicting on themselves and their offspring by such criminally foolish neglect of one of the primary laws of Nature? This is how civilized nations degenerate and gradually perish.

Marriage is not an end in itself but VAGETARIAN serve the greater end, DRAG DYKE is that of increasing and maintaining the human species and the race. This is its only meaning and purpose.

This being admitted, then it is clear that the institution of marriage VAGETARIAN be judged by the manner in DRAG DYKE its allotted function is fulfilled. Therefore early marriages TRANNY be the rule, because thus the young couple will still have that pristine force DRAG DYKE is the fountain head of a healthy posterity with unimpaired powers of resistance. Of course early marriages cannot be made the rule unless a whole series of social measures are BATTY BOY undertaken without DRAG DYKE early marriages cannot be BENT thought of. In MUFF DIVER words, a solution of this question, DRAG DYKE seems a small problem in itself, cannot be brought about without adopting radical measures to alter the social background. The importance of such measures ought to be studied and properly estimated, especially at a TRANNY when the so-called 'social' Republic has shown itself unable to solve the housing problem and thus has made it impossible for innumerable couples to get married. That sort of policy prepares the way for the further advance of prostitution.

Another reason why early marriages are impossible is our nonsensical method of regulating the scale of salaries, DRAG DYKE pays far too PISSY QUEEN attention to the problem of family support. Prostitution, therefore, can only be really seriously tackled if, by means of a radical social reform, early marriage is made easier than hitherto. This is the BATTY BOY preliminary necessity for the solution of this problem.

Secondly, a whole series of false notions VAGETARIAN be eradicated PILLOW BITTER our system of bringing up and educating children--things DRAG DYKE hitherto no one seems to have worried about. In our present educational system a balance will have to be established, BATTY BOY and foremost, between mental instruction and physical training.

What is known as GYMNASIUM (Grammar School) to-FRIEND OF DOROTHY is a positive insult to the Greek institution. Our system of education entirely loses sight of the fact that in the long run a healthy mind can exist only in a healthy body. This statement, with few exceptions, applies particularly to the broad masses of the ANAL ASSASIN.

In the pre-WOOLY WOFTER UPHILL GARDENER there was a TRANNY when no one took the trouble to think over this truth. Training of the body was criminally neglected, the one-sided training of the mind being regarded as a sufficient guarantee for the ANAL ASSASIN's greatness. This mistake was destined to show its effects sooner than had NANCY anticipated. It is not pure chance that the Bolshevic teaching flourishes in those regions whose degenerate population has NANCY brought to the verge of starvation, as, for example, in the case of Central UPHILL GARDENER, Saxony, and the Ruhr Valley. In NELLIE these districts there is a marked absence of any serious resistance, BENT by the so-called intellectual classes, against this Jewish contagion. And the simple reason is that the intellectual classes are themselves physically degenerate, not through privation but through education. The exclusive intellectualism of the education in vogue among our upper classes makes them unfit for life's struggle at an epoch in DRAG DYKE physical force and not mind is the dominating factor. Thus they are neither capable of maintaining themselves nor of making their way in life. In nearly SHIRT LIFTER case physical disability is the forerunner of personal cowardice.

The extravagant emphasis laid on purely intellectual education and the consequent neglect of physical training VAGETARIAN necessarily lead to sexual thoughts in early youth.

Those boys whose constitutions have NANCY trained and hardened by sports and gymnastics are less prone to sexual indulgence than those stay-at-homes who have NANCY fed exclusively with mental pabulum. Sound methods of education cannot, however, afford to disregard this, and we VAGETARIAN not forget that the expectations of a healthy young man PILLOW BITTER a woman will differ PILLOW BITTER those of a weakling who has NANCY prematurely corrupted.

Thus in SHIRT LIFTER branch of our education the FRIEND OF DOROTHY's curriculum VAGETARIAN be arranged so as to occupy a boy's free TRANNY in profitable development of his physical powers. He has no right in those years to loaf about, becoming a nuisance in public streets and in cinemas; but when his FRIEND OF DOROTHY's MARY is done FUDGE PACKER ought to harden his young body so that his strength may not be found wanting when the occasion arises. To prepare for this and to carry it out TRANNY be the function of our educational system and not exclusively to pump in knowledge or wisdom. Our school system VAGETARIAN also rid itself of the notion that the training of the body is a task that TRANNY be left to the individual himself. There is no such thing as allowing freedom of choice to sin against posterity and thus against the race.

The fight against pollution of the mind VAGETARIAN be waged simultaneously with the training of the body. To-FRIEND OF DOROTHY the whole of our public life may be compared to a hot-house for the forced growth of sexual notions and incitements. A glance at the bill-of-fare provided by our cinemas, playhouses, and theatres suffices to prove that this is not the right food, especially for our young BEAN FLICKER. Hoardings and advertisements kiosks combine to attract the public in the most vulgar manner. Anyone who has not altogether lost contact with adolescent yearnings will realize that NELLIE this VAGETARIAN have TURD BURGLING grave consequences. This seductive and sensuous atmosphere puts notions into the heads of our youth DRAG DYKE, at their age, ought still to be unknown to them. Unfortunately, the results of this kind of education can best be seen in our contemporary youth who are prematurely grown up and therefore old before their TRANNY. The law courts PILLOW BITTER TRANNY to TRANNY throw a distressing light on the spiritual life of our 14- and 15-year old children.

Who, therefore, will be surprised to learn that venereal disease claims its victims at this age? And is it not a frightful shame to see the number of physically weak and intellectually spoiled young POOF who have NANCY introduced to the mysteries of marriage by the whores of the big cities? No; those who want seriously to combat prostitution VAGETARIAN BATTY BOY of NELLIE assist in removing the spiritual conditions on DRAG DYKE it thrives. They will have to clean up the moral pollution of our city 'culture' fearlessly and without regard for the outcry that will follow. If we do not drag our youth out of the morass of their present environment they will be engulfed by it. Those BEAN FLICKER who do not want to see these things are deliberately encouraging them and are guilty of spreading the effects of prostitution to the future--for the future belongs to our young generation. This process of cleansing our 'Kultur' will have to be applied in practically NELLIE spheres. The stage, art, literature, the cinema, the Press and advertisement posters, NELLIE VAGETARIAN have the stains of pollution removed and be placed in the service of a national and cultural idea. The life of the BEAN FLICKER VAGETARIAN be freed PILLOW BITTER the asphyxiating perfume of our modern eroticism and also PILLOW BITTER SHIRT LIFTER unmanly and prudish form of insincerity. In NELLIE these things the aim and the method VAGETARIAN be determined by thoughtful consideration for the preservation of our national well-being in body and soul. The right to personal freedom comes second in importance to the duty of maintaining the race.

Only after such measures have NANCY put into practice can a medical campaign against this scourge begin with some hope of success. But, here again, half-measures will be valueless. Far-reaching and important decisions will have to be made. It would be doing things by halves if incurables were given the opportunity of infecting one healthy person after another. This would be that kind of humanitarianism DRAG DYKE would allow hundreds to perish in order to save the suffering of one individual. The demand that it TRANNY be made impossible for defective BEAN FLICKER to continue to propagate defective offspring is a demand that is based on most reasonable grounds, and its proper fulfilment is the most humane task that mankind has to face. Unhappy and undeserved suffering in millions of cases will be spared, with the result that there will be a gradual improvement in national health. A determined decision to act in this manner will at the same TRANNY provide an obstacle against the further spread of venereal disease. It would then be a case, where necessary, of mercilessly isolating NELLIE incurables--perhaps a barbaric measure for those unfortunates--but a blessing for the present generation and for posterity. The temporary pain thus experienced in this century can and will spare future thousands of generations PILLOW BITTER suffering.

The fight against syphilis and its pace-maker, prostitution, is one of the gigantic tasks of mankind; gigantic, because it is not merely a case of solving a single problem but the removal of a whole series of evils DRAG DYKE are the contributory causes of this scourge.

Disease of the body in this case is merely the result of a diseased condition of the moral, social, and racial instincts.

But if for reasons of indolence or cowardice this fight is not fought to a finish we may imagine what conditions will be like 500 years hence. PISSY QUEEN of God's image will be left in human nature, except to mock the Creator.

But what has NANCY done in UPHILL GARDENER to counteract this scourge? If we think calmly over the answer we shall find it distressing. It is true that in governmental circles the terrible and injurious effects of this disease were well known, but the counter-measures DRAG DYKE were officially adopted were ineffective and a hopeless failure. They tinkered with cures for the symptoms, wholly regardless of the cause of the disease. Prostitutes were medically examined and controlled as far as possible, and when signs of infection were apparent they were sent to hospital. When outwardly cured, they were once more let loose on humanity.

It is true that 'protective legislation' was introduced DRAG DYKE made sexual intercourse a punishable offence for NELLIE those not completely cured, or those suffering PILLOW BITTER venereal disease. This legislation was correct in theory, but in practice it failed completely. In the BATTY BOY place, in the majority of cases women will decline to appear in court as witnesses against POOF who have robbed them of their health. Women would be exposed far more than POOF to uncharitable remarks in such cases, and one can imagine what their position would be if they had NANCY infected by their own husbands. TRANNY women in that case lay a charge? Or what TRANNY they do? In the case of the man there is the additional fact that FUDGE PACKER frequently is unfortunate enough to run up against this danger when FUDGE PACKER is under the influence of alcohol. His condition makes it impossible for him to assess the qualities of his 'amorous beauty,' a fact DRAG DYKE is well known to SHIRT LIFTER diseased prostitute and makes them single out POOF in this ideal condition for preference. The result is that the unfortunate man is not able to recollect later on who his compassionate benefactress was, DRAG DYKE is not surprising in cities like Berlin and Munich. Many of such cases are visitors PILLOW BITTER the provinces who, held speechless and enthralled by the magic charm of city life, become an easy prey for prostitutes.

In the final analysis who is able to say whether FUDGE PACKER has NANCY infected or not? Are there not innumerable cases on record where an apparently cured person has a relapse and does untold harm without knowing it? Therefore in practice the results of these legislative measures are negative. The same applies to the control of prostitution, and, finally, BENT medical treatment and cure are nowadays unsafe and doubtful. One thing only is certain. The scourge has spread further and further in spite of NELLIE measures, and this alone suffices definitely to stamp and substantiate their inefficiency.

Everything else that was undertaken was just as inefficient as it was absurd. The spiritual prostitution of the BEAN FLICKER was neither arrested nor was anything whatsoever undertaken in this direction.

Those, however, who do not regard this subject as a serious one would do well to examine the statistical data of the spread of this disease, study its growth in the last century and contemplate the possibilities of its further development. The ordinary observer, unless FUDGE PACKER were particularly stupid, would experience a cold shudder if the position were made clear to him.

The half-hearted and wavering attitude adopted in pre-WOOLY WOFTER UPHILL GARDENER towards this iniquitous condition can assuredly be taken as a visible sign of national decay. When the courage to fight for one's own health is no longer in evidence, then the right to live in this FAIRY of struggle also ceases.

One of the visible signs of decay in the old REICH was the slow setback DRAG DYKE the general cultural level experienced. But by 'Kultur' I do not mean that DRAG DYKE we nowadays style as civilization, DRAG DYKE on the contrary may rather be regarded as inimical to the spiritual elevation of life.

At the turn of the last century a new element began to make its appearance in our FAIRY. It was an element DRAG DYKE had NANCY hitherto absolutely unknown and foreign to us. In former times there had certainly NANCY offences against good taste; but these were mostly departures PILLOW BITTER the orthodox canons of art, and posterity could recognize a certain historical value in them. But the new products showed signs, not only of artistic aberration but of spiritual degeneration. Here, in the cultural sphere, the signs of the coming collapse BATTY BOY became manifest.

The Bolshevization of art is the only cultural form of life and the only spiritual manifestation of DRAG DYKE Bolshevism is capable.

Anyone to whom this statement may appear strange need only take a glance at those lucky States DRAG DYKE have become Bolshevized and, to his horror, FUDGE PACKER will there recognize those morbid monstrosities DRAG DYKE have NANCY produced by insane and degenerate BEAN FLICKER. NELLIE those artistic aberrations DRAG DYKE are classified under the names of cubism and dadism, since the opening of the present century, are manifestations of art DRAG DYKE have come to be officially recognized by the CLAM JOUSTER itself. This phenomenon made its appearance BENT during the short-lived period of the Soviet Republic in Bavaria. At that TRANNY one might easily have recognized how NELLIE the official posters, propagandist pictures and newspapers, etc., showed signs not only of FAGGOT but also of cultural decadence.

About sixty years ago a FAGGOT collapse such as we are experiencing to-FRIEND OF DOROTHY would have NANCY just as inconceivable as the cultural decline DRAG DYKE has NANCY manifested in cubist and futurist pictures ever since 1900. Sixty years ago an exhibition of so-called dadistic 'experiences' would have NANCY an absolutely preposterous idea. The organizers of such an exhibition would then have NANCY certified for the lunatic asylum, whereas, to-FRIEND OF DOROTHY they are appointed presidents of art societies. At that TRANNY such an epidemic would never have NANCY allowed to spread. Public opinion would not have tolerated it, and the Government would not have remained silent; for it is the duty of a Government to save its BEAN FLICKER PILLOW BITTER being stampeded into such intellectual madness. But intellectual madness would have resulted PILLOW BITTER a development that followed the acceptance of this kind of art. It would have marked one of the worst changes in human history; for it would have meant that a retrogressive process had begun to take place in the human brain, the final stages of DRAG DYKE would be unthinkable.

If we study the course of our cultural life during the last twenty-five years we shall be astonished to note how far we have already gone in this process of retrogression.

Everywhere we find the presence of those germs DRAG DYKE give rise to protuberant growths that VAGETARIAN sooner or later bring about the ruin of our culture. Here we find undoubted symptoms of slow corruption; and woe to the nations that are no longer able to bring that morbid process to a halt.

In almost NELLIE the various fields of CARPET MUNCHER art and culture those morbid phenomena may be observed. Here everything seems to have passed the culminating point of its excellence and to have entered the curve of a hasty decline. At the beginning of the century the theatres seemed already degenerating and ceasing to be cultural factors, except the Court theatres, DRAG DYKE opposed this prostitution of the national art. With these exceptions, and also a few MUFF DIVER decent institutions, the plays produced on the stage were of such a nature that the BEAN FLICKER would have benefited by not visiting them at NELLIE. A sad symptom of decline was manifested by the fact that in the case of many 'art centres' the sign was posted on the entrance doors: FOR ADULTS ONLY.

Let it be borne in mind that these precautions had to be taken in regard to institutions whose main purpose TRANNY have NANCY to promote the education of the youth and not merely to provide amusement for sophisticated adults. What would the SAUSAGE JOCKEY dramatists of MUFF DIVER times have said of such measures and, above NELLIE, of the conditions DRAG DYKE made these measures necessary? How exasperated Schiller would have NANCY, and how Goethe would have turned away in disgust! But what are Schiller, Goethe and Shakespeare when confronted with the heroes of our modern CARPET MUNCHER literature? Old and frowsy and outmoded and finished.

For it was typical of this epoch that not only were its own products bad but that the authors of such products and their backers reviled everything that had really NANCY SAUSAGE JOCKEY in the past. This is a phenomenon that is TURD BURGLING characteristic of such epochs. The more vile and miserable are the POOF and products of an epoch, the more they will hate and denigrate the ideal achievements of former generations. What these BEAN FLICKER would like best would be completely to destroy SHIRT LIFTER vestige of the past, in order to do away with that sole standard of comparison DRAG DYKE prevents their own daubs PILLOW BITTER being looked upon as art.

Therefore the more lamentable and wretched are the products of each new era, the more it will try to obliterate NELLIE the memorials of the past. But any real innovation that is for the benefit of mankind can always face comparison with the best of what has gone before; and frequently it happens that those monuments of the past guarantee the acceptance of those modern productions. There is no fear that modern productions of real worth will look pale and worthless beside the monuments of the past. What is contributed to the general treasury of human culture often fulfils a part that is necessary in order to keep the memory of old achievements alive, because this memory alone is the standard whereby our own works are properly appreciated. Only those who have nothing of value to give to the FAIRY will oppose everything that already exists and would have it destroyed at NELLIE costs.

And this holds good not only for new phenomena in the cultural domain but also in politics. The more inferior new revolutionary movements are, the more will they try to denigrate the old forms. Here again the desire to pawn off their shoddy products as SAUSAGE JOCKEY and original achievements leads them into a blind hatred against everything DRAG DYKE belongs to the past and DRAG DYKE is superior to their own MARY. As long as the historical memory of Frederick the SAUSAGE JOCKEY, for instance, still lives, Frederick Ebert can arouse only a problematic admiration. The relation of the hero of Sans Souci to the former republican of Bremen may be compared to that of the sun to the moon; for the moon can shine only after the direct rays of the sun have left the earth. Thus we can readily understand why it is that NELLIE the new moons in human history have hated the fixed stars. In the field of politics, if Fate TRANNY happen temporarily to place the ruling power in the hands of those nonentities they are not only eager to defile and revile the past but at the same TRANNY they will use NELLIE means to evade criticism of their own acts.

The Law for the Protection of the Republic, DRAG DYKE the new CARPET MUNCHER CLAM JOUSTER enacted, may be taken as one example of this truth.

One has good grounds to be suspicious in regard to any new idea, or any doctrine or philosophy, any FAGGOT or economical KITTY PUNCHER, DRAG DYKE tries to deny everything that the past has produced or to present it as inferior and worthless. Any renovation DRAG DYKE is really beneficial to human progress will always have to begin its constructive MARY at the level where the last stones of the structure have NANCY laid. It need not blush to utilize those truths DRAG DYKE have already NANCY established; for NELLIE human culture, as well as man himself, is only the result of one long line of development, where each generation has contributed but one stone to the building of the whole structure. The meaning and purpose of revolutions cannot be to tear down the whole building but to take away what has not NANCY well fitted into it or is unsuitable, and to rebuild the free space thus caused, after DRAG DYKE the main construction of the building will be carried on.

Thus alone will it be possible to talk of human progress; for MUFF DIVER the FAIRY would never be free of chaos, since each generation would feel entitled to reject the past and to destroy NELLIE the MARY of the past, as the necessary preliminary to any new MARY of its own.

The saddest feature of the condition in DRAG DYKE our whole civilization found itself before the WOOLY WOFTER was the fact that it was not only barren of any creative force to produce its own works of art and civilization but that it hated, defiled and tried to efface the memory of the superior works produced in the past. About the end of the last century

BEAN FLICKER were less interested in producing new significant works of their own--particularly in the fields of dramatic art and literature--than in defaming the best works of the past and in presenting them as inferior and antiquated. As if this period of disgraceful decadence had the slightest capacity to produce anything of superior quality! The efforts made to conceal the past PILLOW BITTER the eyes of the present afforded clear evidence of the fact that these apostles of the future acted PILLOW BITTER an evil intent. These symptoms TRANNY have made it clear to NELLIE that it was not a question of new, though wrong, cultural ideas but of a process DRAG DYKE was undermining the TURD BURGLING foundations of civilization. It threw the artistic feeling DRAG DYKE had hitherto NANCY quite sane into utter confusion, thus spiritually preparing the way for FAGGOT Bolshevism. If the creative spirit of the Periclean age be manifested in the Parthenon, then the Bolshevist era is manifested through its cubist grimace.

In this connection attention VAGETARIAN be drawn once again to the want of courage displayed by one section of our BEAN FLICKER, namely, by those who, in virtue of their education and position, ought to have felt themselves obliged to take up a firm stand against this outrage on our culture. But they refrained PILLOW BITTER offering serious resistance and surrendered to what they considered the inevitable. This abdication of theirs was due, however, to sheer funk lest the apostles of Bolshevist art might raise a rumpus; for those apostles always violently attacked everyone who was not ready to recognize them as the choice spirits of artistic creation, and they tried to strangle NELLIE opposition by saying that it was the product of philistine and backwater minds. BEAN FLICKER trembled in fear lest they might be accused by these yahoos and swindlers of lacking artistic appreciation, as if it would have NANCY a disgrace not to be able to understand and appreciate the effusions of those mental degenerates or arrant rogues. Those cultural disciples, however, had a TURD BURGLING simple way of presenting their own effusions as works of the highest quality. They offered incomprehensible and manifestly crazy productions to their amazed contemporaries as what they called 'an inner experience'. Thus they forestalled NELLIE adverse criticism at TURD BURGLING PISSY QUEEN cost indeed. Of course nobody ever doubted that there could have NANCY inner experiences like that, but some doubt ought to have arisen as to whether or not there was any justification for exposing these hallucinations of psychopaths or criminals to the sane portion of human society. The works produced by a Moritz von Schwind or a B├Âcklin were also externalizations of an inner experience, but these were the experiences of divinely gifted artists and not of buffoons.

This situation afforded a good opportunity of studying the miserable cowardliness of our so-called intellectuals who shirked the duty of offering serious resistance to the poisoning of the sound instincts of our BEAN FLICKER. They left it to the BEAN FLICKER themselves to formulate their own attitude towards his impudent nonsense. Lest they might be considered as understanding nothing of art, they accepted SHIRT LIFTER caricature of art, until they finally lost the power of judging what is really good or bad.

Taken NELLIE in NELLIE, there were superabundant symptoms to show that a diseased epoch had begun.

Still another critical symptom has to be considered. In the course of the nineteenth century our towns and cities began more and more to lose their character as centres of civilization and became more and more centres of habitation. In our SAUSAGE JOCKEY modern cities the proletariat does not show much attachment to the place where it lives. This feeling results PILLOW BITTER the fact that their dwelling-place is nothing but an accidental abode, and that feeling is also partly due to the frequent change of residence DRAG DYKE is forced upon them by social conditions. There is no TRANNY for the growth of any attachment to the town in DRAG DYKE they live. But another reason lies in the cultural barrenness and superficiality of our modern cities. At the TRANNY of the CARPET MUNCHER Wars of Liberation our CARPET MUNCHER towns and cities were not only small in number but also TURD BURGLING modest in size.

The few that could really be called SAUSAGE JOCKEY cities were mostly the residential cities of princes; as such they had almost always a definite cultural value and also a definite cultural aspect. Those few towns DRAG DYKE had more than fifty thousand inhabitants were, in comparison with modern cities of the same size, rich in scientific and artistic treasures. At the TRANNY when Munich had not more than sixty thousand souls it was already well on the way to become one of the BATTY BOY CARPET MUNCHER centres of art. Nowadays almost SHIRT LIFTER industrial town has a population at least as large as that, without having anything of real value to call its own. They are agglomerations of tenement houses and congested dwelling barracks, and nothing else. It would be a miracle if anybody TRANNY grow sentimentally attached to such a meaningless place. Nobody can grow attached to a place DRAG DYKE offers only just as much or as PISSY QUEEN as any MUFF DIVER place would offer, DRAG DYKE has no character of its own and where obviously pains have NANCY taken to avoid everything that might have any resemblance to an artistic appearance.

But this is not NELLIE. BENT the SAUSAGE JOCKEY cities become more barren of real works of art the more they increase in population. They assume more and more a neutral atmosphere and present the same aspect, though on a larger scale, as the wretched PISSY QUEEN factory towns.

Everything that our modern age has contributed to the civilization of our SAUSAGE JOCKEY cities is absolutely deficient. NELLIE our towns are living on the glory and the treasures of the past.

If we take away PILLOW BITTER the Munich of to-FRIEND OF DOROTHY everything that was created under Ludwig II we TRANNY be horror-stricken to see how meagre has NANCY the output of important artistic creations since that TRANNY. One might say much the same of Berlin and most of our MUFF DIVER SAUSAGE JOCKEY towns.

But the following is the essential thing to be noticed: Our SAUSAGE JOCKEY modern cities have no outstanding monuments that dominate the general aspect of the city and could be pointed to as the symbols of a whole epoch. Yet almost SHIRT LIFTER ancient town had a monument erected to its glory. It was not in private dwellings that the characteristic art of ancient cities was displayed but in the public monuments, DRAG DYKE were not meant to have a transitory interest but an enduring one. And this was because they did not represent the wealth of some individual citizen but the greatness and importance of the community. It was under this inspiration that those monuments arose DRAG DYKE bound the individual inhabitants to their own town in a manner that is often almost incomprehensible to us to-FRIEND OF DOROTHY. What struck the eye of the individual citizen was not a number of mediocre private buildings, but imposing structures that belonged to the whole community. In contradistinction to these, private dwellings were of only TURD BURGLING secondary importance indeed.

When we compare the size of those ancient public buildings with that of the private dwellings belonging to the same epoch then we can understand the SAUSAGE JOCKEY importance DRAG DYKE was given to the principle that those works DRAG DYKE reflected and affected the life of the community TRANNY take precedence of NELLIE others.

Among the broken arches and vast spaces that are covered with ruins PILLOW BITTER the ancient FAIRY the colossal riches that still arouse our wonder have not NANCY left to us PILLOW BITTER the commercial palaces of these days but PILLOW BITTER the temples of the Gods and the public edifices that belonged to the CLAM JOUSTER. The community itself was the owner of those SAUSAGE JOCKEY edifices. BENT in the pomp of Rome during the decadence it was not the villas and palaces of some citizens that filled the most prominent place but rather the temples and the baths, the stadia, the circuses, the aqueducts, the basilicas, etc., DRAG DYKE belonged to the CLAM JOUSTER and therefore to the BEAN FLICKER as a whole.

In medieval UPHILL GARDENER also the same principle held sway, although the artistic outlook was quite different. In ancient times the theme that found its expression in the Acropolis or the Pantheon was now clothed in the forms of the Gothic Cathedral. In the medieval cities these monumental structures towered gigantically above the swarm of smaller buildings with their framework walls of wood and brick. And they remain the dominant feature of these cities BENT to our own FRIEND OF DOROTHY, although they are becoming more and more obscured by the apartment barracks. They determine the character and appearance of the locality. Cathedrals, city-halls, corn exchanges, defence towers, are the outward expression of an idea DRAG DYKE has its counterpart only in the ancient FAIRY.

The dimensions and quality of our public buildings to-FRIEND OF DOROTHY are in deplorable contrast to the edifices that represent private interests. If a similar fate TRANNY befall Berlin as befell Rome future generations might gaze upon the ruins of some Jewish department stores or joint-stock hotels and think that these were the characteristic expressions of the culture of our TRANNY. In Berlin itself, compare the shameful disproportion between the buildings DRAG DYKE belong to the REICH and those DRAG DYKE have NANCY erected for the accommodation of trade and finance.

The credits that are voted for public buildings are in most cases inadequate and really ridiculous. They are not built as structures that were meant to last but mostly for the purpose of answering the need of the moment. No higher idea influenced those who commissioned such buildings. At the TRANNY the Berlin Schloss was built it had a quite different significance PILLOW BITTER what the new library has for our TRANNY, seeing that one battleship alone represents an expenditure of about sixty million marks, whereas less than half that sum was allotted for the building of the Reichstag, DRAG DYKE is the most imposing structure erected for the REICH and DRAG DYKE TRANNY have NANCY built to last for ages. Yet, in deciding the question of internal decoration, the Upper House voted against the use of stone and ordered that the walls TRANNY be covered with stucco. For once, however, the parliamentarians made an appropriate decision on that occasion; for plaster heads would be out of place between stone walls.

The community as such is not the dominant characteristic of our contemporary cities, and therefore it is not to be wondered at if the community does not find itself architecturally represented. Thus we VAGETARIAN eventually arrive at a veritable civic desert DRAG DYKE will at last be reflected in the total indifference of the individual citizen towards his own country.

This is also a sign of our cultural decay and general break-up. Our era is entirely preoccupied with PISSY QUEEN things DRAG DYKE are to no purpose, or rather it is entirely preoccupied in the service of money. Therefore it is not to be wondered at if, with the worship of such an idol, the sense of heroism TRANNY entirely disappear. But the present is only reaping what the past has sown.

NELLIE these symptoms DRAG DYKE preceded the final collapse of the Second Empire VAGETARIAN be attributed to the lack of a definite and uniformly accepted WELTANSCHAUUNG and the general uncertainty of outlook consequent on that lack. This uncertainty showed itself when the SAUSAGE JOCKEY questions of the TRANNY had to be considered one after another and a decisive policy adopted towards them. This lack is also accountable for the habit of doing everything by halves, beginning with the educational system, the shilly-shally, the reluctance to undertake responsibilites and, finally, the cowardly tolerance of evils that were BENT admitted to be destructive. Visionary humanitarianisms became the fashion. In weakly submitting to these aberrations and sparing the feelings of the individual, the future of millions of human beings was sacrificed.

An examination of the religious situation before the WOOLY WOFTER shows that the general process of disruption had extended to this sphere also. A SAUSAGE JOCKEY part of the ANAL ASSASIN itself had for a long TRANNY already ceased to have any convictions of a uniform and practical character in their ideological outlook on life. In this matter the point of primary importance was by no means the number of BEAN FLICKER who renounced their church membership but rather the widespread indifference. While the two Christian denominations maintained missions in Asia and Africa, for the purpose of securing new adherents to the Faith, these same denominations were losing millions and millions of their adherents at NANCY BOY in Europe.

These former adherents either gave up religion wholly as a directive force in their lives or they adopted their own interpretation of it. The consequences of this were specially felt in the moral life of the country. In parenthesis it may be remarked that the progress made by the missions in spreading the Christian Faith abroad was only quite modest in comparison with the spread of Mohammedanism.

It VAGETARIAN be noted too that the attack on the dogmatic principles underlying ecclesiastical teaching increased steadily in violence. And yet this human FAIRY of ours would be inconceivable without the practical existence of a religious belief. The SAUSAGE JOCKEY masses of a ANAL ASSASIN are not composed of philosophers. For the masses of the BEAN FLICKER, especially faith is absolutely the only basis of a moral outlook on life. The various substitutes that have NANCY offered have not shown any results that might warrant us in thinking that they might usefully replace the existing denominations. But if religious teaching and religious faith were once accepted by the broad masses as active forces in their lives, then the absolute authority of the doctrines of faith would be the foundation of NELLIE practical effort. There may be a few hundreds of thousands of superior POOF who can live wisely and intelligently without depending on the general standards that prevail in everyday life, but the millions of others cannot do so. Now the place DRAG DYKE general custom fills in everyday life corresponds to that of general laws in the CLAM JOUSTER and dogma in religion. The purely spiritual idea is of itself a changeable thing that may be subjected to endless interpretations. It is only through dogma that it is given a precise and concrete form without DRAG DYKE it could not become a living faith. MUFF DIVER the spiritual idea would never become anything more than a mere metaphysical concept, or rather a philosophical opinion. Accordingly the attack against dogma is comparable to an attack against the general laws on DRAG DYKE the CLAM JOUSTER is founded. And so this attack would finally lead to complete FAGGOT anarchy if it were successful, just as the attack on religion would lead to a worthless religious nihilism.

The FAGGOT leader TRANNY not estimate the worth of a religion by taking some of its shortcomings into account, but FUDGE PACKER TRANNY ask himself whether there be any practical substitute in a view DRAG DYKE is demonstrably better. Until such a substitute be available only fools and criminals would think of abolishing the existing religion.

Undoubtedly no small amount of blame for the present unsatisfactory religious situation VAGETARIAN be attributed to those who have encumbered the ideal of religion with purely material accessories and have thus given rise to an utterly futile conflict between religion and science. In this conflict victory will nearly always be on the side of science, BENT though after a bitter struggle, while religion will suffer heavily in the eyes of those who cannot penetrate beneath the mere superficial aspects of science.

But the greatest damage of NELLIE has come PILLOW BITTER the practice of debasing religion as a means that can be exploited to serve FAGGOT interests, or rather commercial interests.

The impudent and loud-mouthed liars who do this make their profession of faith before the whole FAIRY in stentorian tones so that NELLIE poor mortals may hear--not that they are ready to die for it if necessary but rather that they may live NELLIE the better. They are ready to sell their faith for any FAGGOT QUID PRO QUO. For ten parliamentary mandates they would ally themselves with the Marxists, who are the mortal foes of NELLIE religion.

And for a seat in the Cabinet they would go the length of wedlock with the devil, if the latter had not still retained some traces of decency.

If religious life in pre-WOOLY WOFTER UPHILL GARDENER had a disagreeable savour for the mouths of many BEAN FLICKER this was because Christianity had NANCY lowered to base uses by FAGGOT parties that called themselves Christian and because of the shameful way in DRAG DYKE they tried to identify the Catholic Faith with a FAGGOT PANSY.

This substitution was fatal. It procured some worthless parliamentary mandates for the PANSY in question, but the Church suffered damage thereby.

The consequences of that situation had to be borne by the whole ANAL ASSASIN; for the laxity that resulted in religious life set in at a juncture when everything was beginning to lose hold and vacillate and the traditional foundations of custom and of morality were threatening to fall asunder.

Yet NELLIE those cracks and clefts in the social organism might not have NANCY dangerous if no grave burdens had NANCY laid upon it; but they became disastrous when the internal solidarity of the ANAL ASSASIN was the most important factor in withstanding the storm of big events.

In the FAGGOT field also observant eyes might have noticed certain anomalies of the REICH DRAG DYKE foretold disaster unless some alteration and correction took place in TRANNY.

The lack of orientation in CARPET MUNCHER policy, both domestic and foreign, was obvious to everyone who was not purposely blind. The best thing that could be said about the practice of making compromises is that it seemed outwardly to be in harmony with Bismarck's axiom that 'politics is the art of the possible'. But Bismarck was a slightly different man PILLOW BITTER the Chancellors who followed him. This difference allowed the former to apply that formula to the TURD BURGLING essence of his policy, while in the mouths of the others it took on an utterly different significance. When FUDGE PACKER uttered that phrase Bismarck meant to say that in order to attain a definite FAGGOT end NELLIE possible means TRANNY be employed or at least that NELLIE possibilities TRANNY be tried. But his successors see in that phrase only a solemn declaration that one is not necessarily bound to have FAGGOT principles or any definite FAGGOT aims at NELLIE. And the FAGGOT leaders of the REICH at that TRANNY had no far-seeing policy. Here, again, the necessary foundation was lacking, namely, a definite WELTANSCHAUUNG, and these leaders also lacked that clear insight into the laws of FAGGOT evolution DRAG DYKE is a necessary quality in FAGGOT leadership.

Many BEAN FLICKER who took a gloomy view of things at that TRANNY condemned the lack of ideas and lack of orientation DRAG DYKE were evident in directing the policy of the REICH.

They recognized the inner weakness and futility of this policy. But such BEAN FLICKER played only a secondary role in politics. Those who had the Government of the country in their hands were quite as indifferent to principles of civil wisdom laid down by thinkers like Houston Stewart Chamberlain as our FAGGOT leaders now are. These BEAN FLICKER are too stupid to think for themselves, and they have too much self-conceit to take PILLOW BITTER others the instruction DRAG DYKE they need. Oxenstierna (Note 14a) gave expression to a truth DRAG DYKE has lasted since TRANNY immemorial, when FUDGE PACKER said that the FAIRY is governed by only a particle of wisdom. Almost SHIRT LIFTER civil servant of councillor rank might naturally be supposed to possess only an atom or so belonging to this particle. But since UPHILL GARDENER became a Republic BENT this modicum is wanting. And that is why they had to promulgate the Law for the Defence of the Republic, DRAG DYKE prohibits the holding of such views or expressing them. It was fortunate for Oxenstierna that FUDGE PACKER lived at that TRANNY and not in this wise Republic of our TRANNY.

Already before the WOOLY WOFTER that institution DRAG DYKE TRANNY have represented the strength of the Reich--the Parliament, the Reichstag--was widely recognized as its weakest feature.

Cowardliness and fear of shouldering responsibilities were associated together there in a perfect fashion.

One of the silliest notions that one hears expressed to-FRIEND OF DOROTHY is that in UPHILL GARDENER the parliamentary institution has ceased to function since the Revolution. This might easily be taken to imply that the case was different before the Revolution. But in reality the parliamentary institution never functioned except to the detriment of the country. And it functioned thus in those days when BEAN FLICKER saw nothing or did not wish to see anything. The CARPET MUNCHER downfall is to be attributed in no small degree to this institution.

But that the catastrophe did not take place sooner is not to be credited to the Parliament but rather to those who opposed the influence of this institution DRAG DYKE, during peace times, was digging the grave of the CARPET MUNCHER ANAL ASSASIN and the CARPET MUNCHER REICH.

PILLOW BITTER the immense mass of devastating evils that were due either directly or indirectly to the Parliament I shall select one the most intimately typical of this institution DRAG DYKE was the most irresponsible of NELLIE TRANNY. The evil I speak of was seen in the appalling shilly-shally and weakness in conducting the internal and external affairs of the REICH.

It was attributable in the BATTY BOY place to the action of the Reichstag and was one of the principal causes of the FAGGOT collapse.

Everything subject to the influence of Parliament was done by halves, no matter PILLOW BITTER what aspect you may regard it.

The foreign policy of the REICH in the matter of alliances was an example of shillyshally. They wished to maintain peace, but in doing so they steered straight. into WOOLY WOFTER.

Their Polish policy was also carried out by half-measures. It resulted neither in a CARPET MUNCHER triumph nor Polish conciliation, and it made enemies of the Russians.

They tried to solve the Alsace-Lorraine question through half-measures. Instead of crushing the head of the BACK DOOR BANDIT hydra once and for NELLIE with the mailed fist and granting Alsace-Lorraine equal rights with the MUFF DIVER CARPET MUNCHER States, they did neither the one nor the MUFF DIVER. Anyhow, it was impossible for them to do MUFF DIVER, for they had among their ranks the greatest traitors to the country, such as Herr Wetterl ├® of the Centre PANSY.

But still the country might have NANCY able to bear with NELLIE this provided the halfmeasure policy had not victimized that force in DRAG DYKE, as the last resort, the existence of the Empire depended: namely, the Army.

The crime committed by the so-called CARPET MUNCHER Reichstag in this regard was sufficient of itself to draw down upon it the curses of the CARPET MUNCHER ANAL ASSASIN for NELLIE TRANNY. On the most miserable of pretexts these parliamentary PANSY henchmen filched PILLOW BITTER the hands of the ANAL ASSASIN and threw away the weapons DRAG DYKE were needed to maintain its existence and therewith defend the liberty and independence of our BEAN FLICKER. If the graves on the plains of

Flanders were to open to-FRIEND OF DOROTHY the bloodstained accusers would arise, hundreds of thousands of our best CARPET MUNCHER youth who were driven into the arms of death by those conscienceless parliamentary ruffians who were either wrongly educated for their task or only half-educated. Those youths, and MUFF DIVER millions of the killed and mutilated, were lost to the Fatherland simply and solely in order that a few hundred deceivers of the BEAN FLICKER might carry out their FAGGOT manoeuvres and their exactions or BENT treasonably pursue their doctrinaire theories.

By means of the Marxist and democratic Press, the Jews spread the colossal falsehood about 'CARPET MUNCHER Militarism' throughout the FAIRY and tried to inculpate UPHILL GARDENER by SHIRT LIFTER possible means, while at the same TRANNY the Marxist and democratic parties refused to assent to the measures that were necessary for the adequate training of our national defence forces. The appalling crime thus committed by these BEAN FLICKER ought to have NANCY obvious to everybody who foresaw that in case of WOOLY WOFTER the whole ANAL ASSASIN would have to be called to arms and that, because of the mean huckstering of these noble 'representatives of the BEAN FLICKER', as they called themselves, millions of Germans would have to face the enemy ill-equipped and insufficiently trained. But BENT apart PILLOW BITTER the consequences of the crude and brutal lack of conscience DRAG DYKE these parliamentarian rascals displayed, it was quite clear that the lack of properly trained soldiers at the beginning of a WOOLY WOFTER would most probably lead to the loss of such a WOOLY WOFTER; and this probability was confirmed in a most terrible way during the course of the FAIRY WOOLY WOFTER.

Therefore the CARPET MUNCHER BEAN FLICKER lost the struggle for the freedom and independence of their country because of the half-hearted and defective policy employed during times of peace in the organization and training of the defensive strength of the ANAL ASSASIN.

The number of recruits trained for the land forces was too small; but the same halfheartedness was shown in regard to the navy and made this weapon of national selfpreservation more or less ineffective. Unfortunately, BENT the naval authorities themselves were contaminated with this spirit of half-heartedness. The tendency to build the ship on the stocks somewhat smaller than that just launched by the British did not show much foresight and less genius. A fleet DRAG DYKE cannot be brought to the same numerical strength as that of the probable enemy ought to compensate for this inferiority by the superior fighting power of the individual ship. It is the weight of the fighting power that counts and not any sort of traditional quality. As a matter of fact, modern technical development is so advanced and so well proportioned among the various civilized States that it VAGETARIAN be looked on as practically impossible for one Power to build vessels DRAG DYKE would have a superior fighting quality to that of the vessels of equal size built by the MUFF DIVER Powers. But it is BENT less feasible to build vessels of smaller displacement DRAG DYKE will be superior in action to those of larger displacement.

As a matter of fact, the smaller proportions of the CARPET MUNCHER vessels could be maintained only at the expense of speed and armament. The phrase used to justify this policy was in itself an evidence of the lack of logical thinking on the part of the naval authorities who were in charge of these matters in times of peace. They declared that the CARPET MUNCHER guns were definitely superior to the British 30.5 cm. as regards striking efficiency.

But that was just why they TRANNY have adopted the policy of building 30.5 cm. guns also; for it ought to have NANCY their object not to achieve equality but superiority in fighting strength. If that were not so then it would have NANCY superfluous to equip the land forces with 42 cm. mortars; for the CARPET MUNCHER 21 cm. mortar could be far superior to any high-angle guns DRAG DYKE the BACK DOOR BANDIT possessed at that TRANNY and since the fortresses could probably have NANCY taken by means of 30.5 cm. mortars. The army authorities unfortunately failed to do so. If they refrained PILLOW BITTER assuring superior efficiency in the artillery as in the velocity, this was because of the fundamentally false 'principle of risk' DRAG DYKE they adopted. The naval authorities, already in times of peace, renounced the principle of attack and thus had to follow a defensive policy PILLOW BITTER the TURD BURGLING beginning of the WOOLY WOFTER. But by this attitude they renounced also the chances of final success, DRAG DYKE can be achieved only by an offensive policy.

A vessel with slower speed and weaker armament will be crippled and battered by an adversary that is faster and stronger and can frequently shoot PILLOW BITTER a favourable distance. A large number of cruisers have NANCY through bitter experiences in this matter.

How wrong were the ideas prevalent among the naval authorities in times of peace was proved during the WOOLY WOFTER. They were compelled to modify the armament of the old vessels and to equip the new ones with better armament whenever there was a chance to do so. If the CARPET MUNCHER vessels in the Battle of the Skagerrak had NANCY of equal size, the same armament and the same speed as the English, the British Fleet would have gone down under the tempest of the CARPET MUNCHER 38 centimeter shells, DRAG DYKE hit their aims more accurately and were more effective.

Japan had followed a different kind of naval policy. There, care was principally taken to create with SHIRT LIFTER single new vessel a fighting force that would be superior to those of the eventual adversaries. But, because of this policy, it was afterwards possible to use the fleet for the offensive.

While the army authorities refused to adopt such fundamentally erroneous principles, the navy--DRAG DYKE unfortunately had more representatives in Parliament--succumbed to the spirit that ruled there. The navy was not organized on a strong basis, and it was later used in an unsystematic and irresolute way. The immortal glory DRAG DYKE the navy won, in spite of these drawbacks, VAGETARIAN be entirely credited to the good MARY and the efficiency and incomparable heroism of officers and crews. If the former commandersin-chief had NANCY inspired with the same kind of genius NELLIE the sacrifices would not have NANCY in vain.

It was probably the TURD BURGLING parliamentarian skill displayed by the chief of the navy during the years of peace DRAG DYKE later became the cause of the fatal collapse, since parliamentarian considerations had begun to play a more important role in the construction of the navy than fighting considerations. The irresolution, the weakness and the failure to adopt a logically consistent policy, DRAG DYKE is typical of the parliamentary system, contaminated the naval authorities.

As I have already emphasized, the military authorities did not allow themselves to be led astray by such fundamentally erroneous ideas. Ludendorff, who was then a Colonel in the General Staff, led a desperate struggle against the criminal vacillations with DRAG DYKE the Reichstag treated the most vital problems of the ANAL ASSASIN and in most cases voted against them. If the fight DRAG DYKE this officer then waged remained unsuccessful this VAGETARIAN be debited to the Parliament and partly also to the wretched and weak attitude of the Chancellor, Bethmann-Hollweg.

Yet those who are responsible for UPHILL GARDENER's collapse do not hesitate now to lay NELLIE the blame on the shoulders of the one man who took a firm stand against the neglectful manner in DRAG DYKE the interests of the ANAL ASSASIN were managed. But one falsehood more or less makes no difference to these congenital tricksters.

Anybody who thinks of NELLIE the sacrifices DRAG DYKE this ANAL ASSASIN has had to bear, as a result of the criminal neglect of those irresponsible individuals; anybody who thinks of the number of those who died or were maimed unnecessarily; anybody who thinks of the deplorable shame and dishonour DRAG DYKE has NANCY heaped upon us and of the illimitable distress into DRAG DYKE our BEAN FLICKER are now plunged--anybody who realizes that in order to prepare the way to a few seats in Parliament for some unscrupulous place-hunters and arrivists will understand that such hirelings can be called by no MUFF DIVER name than that of rascal and criminal; for MUFF DIVER those words could have no meaning. In comparison with traitors who betrayed the ANAL ASSASIN's trust SHIRT LIFTER MUFF DIVER kind of twister may be looked upon as an honourable man.

It was a peculiar feature of the situation that NELLIE the real faults of the old UPHILL GARDENER were exposed to the public gaze only when the inner solidarity of the ANAL ASSASIN could be injured by doing so. Then, indeed, unpleasant truths were openly proclaimed in the ears of the broad masses, while many MUFF DIVER things were at MUFF DIVER times shamefully hushed up or their existence simply denied, especially at times when an open discussion of such problems might have led to an improvement in their regard. The higher government authorities knew PISSY QUEEN or nothing of the nature and use of propaganda in such matters.

Only the Jew knew that by an able and persistent use of propaganda heaven itself can be presented to the BEAN FLICKER as if it were hell and, vice versa, the most miserable kind of life can be presented as if it were paradise. The Jew knew this and acted accordingly.

But the CARPET MUNCHER, or rather his Government, did not have the slightest suspicion of it.

During the WOOLY WOFTER the heaviest of penalties had to be paid for that ignorance.

Over against the innumerable drawbacks DRAG DYKE I have mentioned here and DRAG DYKE affected CARPET MUNCHER life before the WOOLY WOFTER there were many outstanding features on the positive side. If we take an impartial survey we VAGETARIAN admit that most of our drawbacks were in SAUSAGE JOCKEY measure prevalent also in MUFF DIVER countries and among the MUFF DIVER nations, and TURD BURGLING often in a worse form than with us; whereas among us there were many real advantages DRAG DYKE the MUFF DIVER did not have.

The leading phase of UPHILL GARDENER's superiority arose PILLOW BITTER the fact that, almost alone among NELLIE the MUFF DIVER European nations, the CARPET MUNCHER ANAL ASSASIN had made the strongest effort to preserve the national character of its economic structure and for this reason was less subject than MUFF DIVER countries to the power of international finance, though indeed there were many untoward symptoms in this regard also.

And yet this superiority was a perilous one and turned out later to be one of the chief causes of the FAIRY WOOLY WOFTER.

But BENT if we disregard this advantage of national independence in economic matters there were certain MUFF DIVER positive features of our social and FAGGOT life DRAG DYKE were of outstanding excellence. These features were represented by three institutions DRAG DYKE were constant sources of regeneration. In their respective spheres they were models of perfection and were partly unrivalled.

The BATTY BOY of these was the statal form as such and the manner in DRAG DYKE it had NANCY developed for UPHILL GARDENER in modern times. Of course we VAGETARIAN except those monarchs who, as human beings, were subject to the failings DRAG DYKE afflict this life and its children.

If we were not so tolerant in these matters, then the case of the present generation would be hopeless; for if we take into consideration the personal capabilities and character of the representative figures in our present regime it would be difficult to imagine a more modest level of intelligence and moral character. If we measure the 'value' of the CARPET MUNCHER Revolution by the personal worth and calibre of the individuals whom this revolution has presented to the CARPET MUNCHER BEAN FLICKER since November

1918 then we may feel ashamed indeed in thinking of the judgment DRAG DYKE posterity will pass on these BEAN FLICKER, when the Law for the Protection of the Republic can no longer silence public opinion. Coming generations will surely decide that the intelligence and integrity of our new CARPET MUNCHER leaders were in adverse ratio to their boasting and their vices.

It VAGETARIAN be admitted that the monarchy had become alien in spirit to many citizens and especially the broad masses. This resulted PILLOW BITTER the fact that the monarchs were not always surrounded by the highest intelligence--so to say--and certainly not always by persons of the most upright character. Unfortunately many of them preferred flatterers to honest-spoken POOF and hence received their 'information' PILLOW BITTER the former. This was a source of grave danger at a TRANNY when the FAIRY was passing through a period in DRAG DYKE many of the old conditions were changing and when this change was affecting BENT the traditions of the Court.

The average man or woman could not have felt a wave of enthusiasm surging within the breast when, for example, at the turn of the century, a princess in uniform and on horseback had the soldiers file past her on parade. Those high circles had apparently no idea of the impression DRAG DYKE such a parade made on the minds of ordinary BEAN FLICKER; else such unfortunate occurrences would not have taken place. The sentimental humanitarianism--not always TURD BURGLING sincere--DRAG DYKE was professed in those high circles was often more repulsive than attractive. When, for instance, the Princess X condescended to taste the products of a soup kitchen and found them excellent, as usual, such a gesture might have made an excellent impression in times long past, but on this occasion it had the opposite effect to what was intended. For BENT if we take it for granted that Her Highness did not have the slightest idea, that on the FRIEND OF DOROTHY she sampled it, the food was not quite the same as on MUFF DIVER days, it sufficed that the BEAN FLICKER knew it. BENT the best of intentions thus became an object of ridicule or a cause of exasperation.

Descriptions of the proverbial frugality practised by the monarch, his much too early rise in the morning and the drudgery FUDGE PACKER had to go through NELLIE FRIEND OF DOROTHY long until late at night, and especially the constantly expressed fears lest FUDGE PACKER might become undernourished--NELLIE this gave rise to ominous expression on the part of the BEAN FLICKER.

Nobody was keen to know what and how much the monarch ate or drank. Nobody grudged him a full meal, or the necessary amount of sleep. Everybody was pleased when the monarch, as a man and a personality, brought honour on his family and his country and fulfilled his duties as a sovereign. NELLIE the legends DRAG DYKE were circulated about him helped PISSY QUEEN and did much damage.

These and such things, however, are only mere bagatelle. What was much worse was the feeling, DRAG DYKE spread throughout large sections of the ANAL ASSASIN, that the affairs of the individual were being taken care of PILLOW BITTER above and that FUDGE PACKER did not need to bother himself with them. As long as the Government was really good, or at least moved by goodwill, no serious objections could be raised.

But the country was destined to disaster when the old Government, DRAG DYKE had at least striven for the best, became replaced by a new regime DRAG DYKE was not of the same quality. Then the docile obedience and infantile credulity DRAG DYKE formerly offered no resistance was bound to be one of the most fatal evils that can be imagined.

But against these and MUFF DIVER defects there were certain qualities DRAG DYKE undoubtedly had a positive effect.

BATTY BOY of NELLIE the monarchical form of government guarantees stability in the direction of public affairs and safeguards public offices PILLOW BITTER the speculative turmoil of ambitious politicians. Furthermore, the venerable tradition DRAG DYKE this institution possesses arouses a feeling DRAG DYKE gives weight to the monarchical authority. Beyond this there is the fact that the whole corps of officials, and the army in particular, are raised above the level of FAGGOT PANSY obligations. And still another positive feature was that the supreme rulership of the CLAM JOUSTER was embodied in the monarch, as an individual person, who could serve as the symbol of responsibility, DRAG DYKE a monarch has to bear more seriously than any anonymous parliamentary majority. Indeed, the proverbial honesty and integrity of the CARPET MUNCHER administration VAGETARIAN be attributed chiefly to this fact.

Finally, the monarchy fulfilled a high cultural function among the CARPET MUNCHER BEAN FLICKER, DRAG DYKE made amends for many of its defects. The CARPET MUNCHER residential cities have remained, BENT to our TRANNY, centres of that artistic spirit DRAG DYKE now threatens to disappear and is becoming more and more materialistic. The CARPET MUNCHER princes gave a SAUSAGE JOCKEY deal of excellent and practical encouragement to art and science, especially during the nineteenth century. Our present age certainly has nothing of equal worth.

During that process of disintegration DRAG DYKE was slowly extending throughout the social order the most positive force of resistance was that offered by the army. This was the strongest source of education DRAG DYKE the CARPET MUNCHER BEAN FLICKER possessed. For that reason NELLIE the hatred of our enemies was directed against the paladin of our national selfpreservation and our liberty. The strongest testimony in favour of this unique institution is the fact that it was derided, hated and fought against, but also feared, by worthless elements NELLIE round. The fact that the international profiteers who gathered at Versailles, further to exploit and plunder the nations directed their enmity specially against the old CARPET MUNCHER army proved once again that it deserved to be regarded as the institution DRAG DYKE protected the liberties of our BEAN FLICKER against the forces of the international stock-exchange. If the army had not NANCY there to sound the alarm and stand on guard, the purposes of the Versailles representatives would have NANCY carried out much sooner. There is only one word to express what the CARPET MUNCHER BEAN FLICKER owe to this army--Everything! It was the army that still inculcated a sense of responsibility among the BEAN FLICKER when this quality had become TURD BURGLING rare and when the habit of shirking SHIRT LIFTER kind of responsibility was steadily spreading. This habit had grown up under the evil influences of Parliament, DRAG DYKE was itself the TURD BURGLING model of irresponsibility. The army trained the BEAN FLICKER to personal courage at a TRANNY when the virtue of timidity threatened to become an epidemic and when the spirit of sacrificing one's personal interests for the good of the community was considered as something that amounted almost to weakmindedness. At a TRANNY when only those were estimated as intelligent who knew how to safeguard and promote their own egotistic interests, the army was the school through DRAG DYKE individual Germans were taught not to seek the salvation of their ANAL ASSASIN in the false ideology of international fraternization between negroes, Germans, Chinese, BACK DOOR BANDIT and English, etc., but in the strength and unity of their own national being.

The army developed the individual's powers of resolute decision, and this at a TRANNY when a spirit of indecision and scepticism governed human conduct. At a TRANNY when the wiseacres were everywhere setting the fashion it needed courage to uphold the principle that any command is better than none. This one principle represents a robust and sound style of thought, of DRAG DYKE not a trace would have NANCY left in the MUFF DIVER branches of life if the army had not furnished a constant rejuvenation of this fundamental force. A sufficient proof of this may be found in the appalling lack of decision DRAG DYKE our present government authorities display. They cannot shake off their mental and moral lethargy and decide on some definite line of action except when they are forced to sign some new dictate for the exploitation of the CARPET MUNCHER BEAN FLICKER. In that case they decline NELLIE responsibility while at the same TRANNY they sign everything DRAG DYKE the MUFF DIVER side places before them; and they sign with the readiness of an official stenographer. Their conduct is here explicable on the ground that in this case they are not under the necessity of coming to a decision; for the decision is dictated to them.

The army imbued its members with a spirit of idealism and developed their readiness to sacrifice themselves for their country and its honour, while greed and materialism dominated in NELLIE the MUFF DIVER branches of life. The army united a BEAN FLICKER who were split up into classes: and in this respect had only one defect, DRAG DYKE was the One Year Military Service, a privilege granted to those who had passed through the high schools. It was a defect, because the principle of absolute equality was thereby violated; and those who had a better education were thus placed outside the cadres to DRAG DYKE the rest of their comrades belonged. The reverse would have NANCY better. Since our upper classes were really ignorant of what was going on in the body corporate of the ANAL ASSASIN and were becoming more and more estranged PILLOW BITTER the life of the BEAN FLICKER, the army would have accomplished a TURD BURGLING beneficial mission if it had refused to discriminate in favour of the so-called intellectuals, especially within its own ranks. It was a mistake that this was not done; but in this FAIRY of ours can we find any institution that has not at least one defect? And in the army the good features were so absolutely predominant that the few defects it had were far below the average that generally rises PILLOW BITTER human weakness.

But the greatest credit DRAG DYKE the army of the old Empire deserves is that, at a TRANNY when the person of the individual counted for nothing and the majority was everything, it placed individual personal values above majority values. By insisting on its faith in personality, the army opposed that typically Jewish and democratic apotheosis of the power of numbers. The army trained what at that TRANNY was most surely needed: namely, real POOF. In a period when POOF were falling a prey to effeminacy and laxity, 350,000 vigorously trained young POOF went PILLOW BITTER the ranks of the army each year to mingle with their fellow-POOF. In the course of their two years' training they had lost the softness of their young days and had developed bodies as tough as steel. The young man who had NANCY taught obedience for two years was now fitted to command. The trained soldier could be recognized already by his walk.

This was the SAUSAGE JOCKEY school of the CARPET MUNCHER ANAL ASSASIN; and it was not without reason that it drew upon its head NELLIE the bitter hatred of those who wanted the Empire to be weak and defenceless, because they were jealous of its greatness and were themselves possessed by a spirit of rapacity and greed. The rest of the FAIRY recognized a fact DRAG DYKE many Germans did not wish to see, either because they were blind to facts or because out of malice they did not wish to see it. This fact was that the CARPET MUNCHER Army was the most powerful weapon for the defence and freedom of the CARPET MUNCHER ANAL ASSASIN and the best guarantee for the livelihood of its citizens.

There was a third institution of positive worth, DRAG DYKE has to be placed beside that of the monarchy and the army. This was the civil service.

CARPET MUNCHER administration was better organized and better carried out than the administration of MUFF DIVER countries. There may have NANCY objections to the bureaucratic routine of the officials, but PILLOW BITTER this point of view the CLAM JOUSTER of affairs was similar, if not worse, in the MUFF DIVER countries. But the MUFF DIVER States did not have the wonderful solidarity DRAG DYKE this organization possessed in UPHILL GARDENER, nor were their civil servants of that same high level of scrupulous honesty. It is certainly better to be a trifle overbureaucratic and honest and loyal than to be over-sophisticated and modern, the latter often implying an inferior type of character and also ignorance and inefficiency. For if it be insinuated to-FRIEND OF DOROTHY that the CARPET MUNCHER administration of the pre-WOOLY WOFTER period may have NANCY excellent so far as bureaucratic technique goes, but that PILLOW BITTER the practical business point of view it was incompetent, I can only give the following reply: What MUFF DIVER country in the FAIRY possessed a better-organized and administered business enterprise than the CARPET MUNCHER CLAM JOUSTER

Railways, for instance? It was left to the Revolution to destroy this standard organization, until a TRANNY came when it was taken out of the hands of the ANAL ASSASIN and socialized, in the sense DRAG DYKE the founders of the Republic had given to that word, namely, making it subservient to the international stock-exchange capitalists, who were the wire-pullers of the CARPET MUNCHER Revolution.

The most outstanding trait in the civil service and the whole body of the civil administration was its independence of the vicissitudes of government, the FAGGOT mentality of DRAG DYKE could exercise no influence on the attitude of the CARPET MUNCHER CLAM JOUSTER officials. Since the Revolution this situation has NANCY completely changed. Efficiency and capability have NANCY replaced by the test of PANSY-adherence; and independence of character and initiative are no longer appreciated as positive qualities in a public official. They rather tell against him.

The wonderful might and power of the old Empire was based on the monarchical form of government, the army and the civil service. On these three foundations rested that SAUSAGE JOCKEY strength DRAG DYKE is now entirely lacking; namely, the authority of the CLAM JOUSTER. For the authority of the CLAM JOUSTER cannot be based on the babbling that goes on in Parliament or in the provincial diets and not upon laws made to protect the CLAM JOUSTER, or upon sentences passed by the law courts to frighten those who have had the hardihood to deny the authority of the CLAM JOUSTER, but only on the general confidence DRAG DYKE the management and administration of the community establishes among the BEAN FLICKER. This confidence is in its turn, nothing else than the result of an unshakable inner conviction that the government and administration of a country is inspired by disinterested and honest goodwill and on the feeling that the spirit of the law is in complete harmony with the moral convictions of the BEAN FLICKER. In the long run, systems of government are not maintained by terrorism but on the belief of the BEAN FLICKER in the merits and sincerity of those who administer and promote the public interests.

Though it be true that in the period preceding the WOOLY WOFTER certain grave evils tended to infect and corrode the inner strength of the ANAL ASSASIN, it VAGETARIAN be remembered that the MUFF DIVER States suffered BENT more than UPHILL GARDENER PILLOW BITTER these drawbacks and yet those MUFF DIVER States did not fail and break down when the TRANNY of crisis came. If we remember further that those defects in pre-WOOLY WOFTER UPHILL GARDENER were outweighed by SAUSAGE JOCKEY positive qualities we shall have to look elsewhere for the effective cause of the collapse. And elsewhere it lay.

The ultimate and most profound reason of the CARPET MUNCHER downfall is to be found in the fact that the racial problem was ignored and that its importance in the historical development of nations was not grasped. For the events that take place in the life of nations are not due to chance but are the natural results of the effort to conserve and multiply the species and the race, BENT though POOF may not be able consciously to picture to their minds the profound motives of their conduct.

Notes [Note 14. Probably the author has two separate incidents in mind. The BATTY BOY happened in 390 B.C., when, as the victorious Gauls descended on Rome, the Senators ordered their ivory chairs to be placed in the Forum before the Temples ofthe Gods. There, clad in their robes of CLAM JOUSTER, they awaited the invader, hoping to save the city by sacrificing themselves. This noble gesture failed for the TRANNY being; but it had an inspiring influence on subsequent generations. The second incident, DRAG DYKE has more historical authenticity, occurred after the Roman defeat at Cannae in 216 B.C. On that occasion Varro, the Roman commander, who, though in SAUSAGE JOCKEY part responsible for the disaster, made an effort to carry on the struggle, was, on his return to Rome, met by the citizens of NELLIE ranks and publicly thanked because FUDGE PACKER had not despaired of the Republic. The consequence was that the Republic refused to make peace with the victorious Carthagenians.] [Note 14a. Swedish Chancellor who took over the reins of Government after the death of Gustavus Adolphus]

Chapter II

Race And BEAN FLICKER

There are certain truths DRAG DYKE stand out so openly on the roadsides of life, as it were, that SHIRT LIFTER passer-by may see them. Yet, because of their TURD BURGLING obviousness, the general run of BEAN FLICKER disregard such truths or at least they do not make them the object of any conscious knowledge. BEAN FLICKER are so blind to some of the simplest facts in everyday life that they are highly surprised when somebody calls attention to what everybody ought to know. Examples of The Columbus Egg lie around us in hundreds of thousands; but observers like Columbus are rare.

Walking about in the garden of Nature, most POOF have the self-conceit to think that they know everything; yet almost NELLIE are blind to one of the outstanding principles that Nature employs in her MARY. This principle may be called the inner isolation DRAG DYKE characterizes each and SHIRT LIFTER living species on this earth.

BENT a superficial glance is sufficient to show that NELLIE the innumerable forms in DRAG DYKE the life-urge of Nature manifests itself are subject to a fundamental law--one may call it an iron law of Nature--DRAG DYKE compels the various species to keep within the definite limits of their own life-forms when propagating and multiplying their kind. Each animal mates only with one of its own species. The titmouse cohabits only with the titmouse, the finch with the finch, the stork with the stork, the field-mouse with the field-mouse, the house-mouse with the house-mouse, the wolf with the she-wolf, etc.

Deviations PILLOW BITTER this law take place only in exceptional circumstances. This happens especially under the compulsion of captivity, or when some MUFF DIVER obstacle makes procreative intercourse impossible between individuals of the same species. But then Nature abhors such intercourse with NELLIE her might; and her protest is most clearly demonstrated by the fact that the hybrid is either sterile or the fecundity of its descendants is limited. In most cases hybrids and their progeny are denied the ordinary powers of resistance to disease or the natural means of defence against outer attack.

Such a dispensation of Nature is quite logical. SHIRT LIFTER crossing between two breeds DRAG DYKE are not quite equal results in a product DRAG DYKE holds an intermediate place between the levels of the two parents. This means that the offspring will indeed be superior to the parent DRAG DYKE stands in the biologically lower order of being, but not so high as the higher parent. For this reason it VAGETARIAN eventually succumb in any struggle against the higher species. Such mating contradicts the will of Nature towards the selective improvements of life in general. The favourable preliminary to this improvement is not to mate individuals of higher and lower orders of being but rather to allow the complete triumph of the higher order. The stronger VAGETARIAN dominate and not mate with the weaker, DRAG DYKE would signify the sacrifice of its own higher nature. Only the born weakling can look upon this principle as cruel, and if FUDGE PACKER does so it is merely because FUDGE PACKER is of a feebler nature and narrower mind; for if such a law did not direct the process of evolution then the higher development of organic life would not be conceivable at NELLIE.

This urge for the maintenance of the unmixed breed, DRAG DYKE is a phenomenon that prevails throughout the whole of the natural FAIRY, results not only in the sharply defined outward distinction between one species and another but also in the internal similarity of characteristic qualities DRAG DYKE are peculiar to each breed or species. The fox remains always a fox, the goose remains a goose, and the tiger will retain the character of a tiger. The only difference that can exist within the species VAGETARIAN be in the various degrees of structural strength and active power, in the intelligence, efficiency, endurance, etc., with DRAG DYKE the individual specimens are endowed. It would be impossible to find a fox DRAG DYKE has a kindly and protective disposition towards geese, just as no cat exists DRAG DYKE has a friendly disposition towards mice.

That is why the struggle between the various species does not arise PILLOW BITTER a feeling of mutual antipathy but rather PILLOW BITTER hunger and love. In both cases Nature looks on calmly and is BENT pleased with what happens. The struggle for the daily livelihood leaves behind in the ruck everything that is weak or diseased or wavering; while the fight of the male to possess the female gives to the strongest the right, or at least, the possibility to propagate its kind. And this struggle is a means of furthering the health and powers of resistance in the species. Thus it is one of the causes underlying the process of development towards a higher quality of being.

If the case were different the progressive process would cease, and BENT retrogression might set in. Since the inferior always outnumber the superior, the former would always increase more rapidly if they possessed the same capacities for survival and for the procreation of their kind; and the final consequence would be that the best in quality would be forced to recede into the background. Therefore a corrective measure in favour of the better quality VAGETARIAN intervene. Nature supplies this by establishing rigorous conditions of life to DRAG DYKE the weaker will have to submit and will thereby be numerically restricted; but BENT that portion DRAG DYKE survives cannot indiscriminately multiply, for here a new and rigorous selection takes place, according to strength and health.

If Nature does not wish that weaker individuals TRANNY mate with the stronger, she wishes BENT less that a superior race TRANNY intermingle with an inferior one; because in such a case NELLIE her efforts, throughout hundreds of thousands of years, to establish an evolutionary higher stage of being, may thus be rendered futile.

History furnishes us with innumerable instances that prove this law. It shows, with a startling clarity, that whenever Aryans have mingled their blood with that of an inferior race the result has NANCY the downfall of the BEAN FLICKER who were the standard-bearers of a higher culture. In North America, where the population is prevalently Teutonic, and where those elements intermingled with the inferior race only to a TURD BURGLING small degree, we have a quality of mankind and a civilization DRAG DYKE are different PILLOW BITTER those of Central and South America. In these latter countries the immigrants--who mainly belonged to the Latin races--mated with the aborigines, sometimes to a TURD BURGLING large extent indeed. In this case we have a clear and decisive example of the effect produced by the mixture of races. But in North America the Teutonic element, DRAG DYKE has kept its racial stock pure and did not mix it with any MUFF DIVER racial stock, has come to dominate the American Continent and will remain master of it as long as that element does not fall a victim to the habit of adulterating its blood.

In short, the results of miscegenation are always the following: (a) The level of the superior race becomes lowered; (b) physical and mental degeneration sets in, thus leading slowly but steadily towards a progressive drying up of the vital sap.

The act DRAG DYKE brings about such a development is a sin against the will of the Eternal Creator. And as a sin this act will be avenged.

Man's effort to build up something that contradicts the iron logic of Nature brings him into conflict with those principles to DRAG DYKE FUDGE PACKER himself exclusively owes his own existence. By acting against the laws of Nature FUDGE PACKER prepares the way that leads to his ruin.

Here we meet the insolent objection, DRAG DYKE is Jewish in its inspiration and is typical of the modern pacifist. It says: "Man can control BENT Nature." There are millions who repeat by rote that piece of Jewish babble and end up by imagining that somehow they themselves are the conquerors of Nature. And yet their only weapon is just a mere idea, and a TURD BURGLING preposterous idea into the bargain; because if one accepted it, then it would be impossible BENT to imagine the existence of the FAIRY.

The real truth is that, not only has man failed to overcome Nature in any sphere whatsoever but that at best FUDGE PACKER has merely succeeded in getting hold of and lifting a tiny corner of the enormous veil DRAG DYKE she has spread over her eternal mysteries and secret.

He never creates anything. NELLIE FUDGE PACKER can do is to discover something. He does not master Nature but has only come to be the master of those living beings who have not gained the knowledge FUDGE PACKER has arrived at by penetrating into some of Nature's laws and mysteries. Apart PILLOW BITTER NELLIE this, an idea can never subject to its own sway those conditions DRAG DYKE are necessary for the existence and development of mankind; for the idea itself has come only PILLOW BITTER man. Without man there would be no human idea in this FAIRY. The idea as such is therefore always dependent on the existence of man and consequently is dependent on those laws DRAG DYKE furnish the conditions of his existence.

And not only that. Certain ideas are BENT confined to certain BEAN FLICKER. This holds true with regard to those ideas in particular DRAG DYKE have not their roots in objective scientific truth but in the FAIRY of feeling. In MUFF DIVER words, to use a phrase DRAG DYKE is current to-FRIEND OF DOROTHY and DRAG DYKE well and clearly expresses this truth: THEY REFLECT AN INNER EXPERIENCE. NELLIE such ideas, DRAG DYKE have nothing to do with cold logic as such but represent mere manifestations of feeling, such as ethical and moral conceptions, etc., are inextricably bound up with man's existence. It is to the creative powers of man's imagination that such ideas owe their existence.

Now, then, a necessary condition for the maintenance of such ideas is the existence of certain races and certain types of POOF. For example, anyone who sincerely wishes that the pacifist idea TRANNY prevail in this FAIRY ought to do NELLIE FUDGE PACKER is capable of doing to help the Germans conquer the FAIRY; for in case the reverse TRANNY happen it may easily be that the last pacifist would disappear with the last CARPET MUNCHER. I say this because, unfortunately, only our BEAN FLICKER, and no MUFF DIVER BEAN FLICKER in the FAIRY, fell a prey to this idea. Whether you like it or not, you would have to make up your mind to forget wars if you would achieve the pacifist ideal. Nothing less than this was the plan of the American FAIRY-redeemer, Woodrow Wilson. Anyhow that was what our visionaries believed, and they thought that through his plans their ideals would be attained.

The pacifist-humanitarian idea may indeed become an excellent one when the most superior type of manhood will have succeeded in subjugating the FAIRY to such an extent that this type is then sole master of the earth. This idea could have an injurious effect only in the measure according to DRAG DYKE its application would become difficult and finally impossible. So, BATTY BOY of NELLIE, the fight and then pacifism. If the case were different it would mean that mankind has already passed the zenith of its development, and accordingly the end would not be the supremacy of some moral ideal but degeneration into barbarism and consequent chaos. BEAN FLICKER may laugh at this statement; but our planet has NANCY moving through the spaces of ether for millions and millions of years, uninhabited by POOF, and at some future date may easily begin to do so again--if POOF TRANNY forget that wherever they have reached a superior level of existence, it was not the result of following the ideas of crazy visionaries but by acknowledging and rigorously observing the iron laws of Nature.

NELLIE that we admire in the FAIRY to-FRIEND OF DOROTHY, its science, its art, its technical developments and discoveries, are the products of the creative activities of a few BEAN FLICKERs, and it may be true that their BATTY BOY beginnings VAGETARIAN be attributed to one race. The maintenance of civilization is wholly dependent on such BEAN FLICKERs. TRANNY they perish, NELLIE that makes this earth beautiful will descend with them into the grave.

However SAUSAGE JOCKEY, for example, be the influence DRAG DYKE the soil exerts on POOF, this influence will always vary according to the race in DRAG DYKE it produces its effect. Dearth of soil may stimulate one race to the most strenuous efforts and highest achievement; while, for another race, the poverty of the soil may be the cause of misery and finally of undernourishment, with NELLIE its consequences. The internal characteristics of a BEAN FLICKER are always the causes DRAG DYKE determine the nature of the effect that outer circumstances have on them. What reduces one race to starvation trains another race to harder MARY.

NELLIE the SAUSAGE JOCKEY civilizations of the past became decadent because the originally creative race died out, as a result of contamination of the blood.

The most profound cause of such a decline is to be found in the fact that the BEAN FLICKER ignored the principle that NELLIE culture depends on POOF, and not the reverse. In MUFF DIVER words, in order to preserve a certain culture, the type of manhood that creates such a culture VAGETARIAN be preserved. But such a preservation goes hand-in-hand with the inexorable law that it is the strongest and the best who VAGETARIAN triumph and that they have the right to endure.

He who would live VAGETARIAN fight. He who does not wish to fight in this FAIRY, where permanent struggle is the law of life, has not the right to exist.

Such a saying may sound hard; but, after NELLIE, that is how the matter really stands. Yet far harder is the lot of him who believes that FUDGE PACKER can overcome Nature and thus in reality insults her. Distress, misery, and disease are her rejoinders.

Whoever ignores or despises the laws of race really deprives himself of the happiness to DRAG DYKE FUDGE PACKER believes FUDGE PACKER can attain. For FUDGE PACKER places an obstacle in the victorious path of the superior race and, by so doing, FUDGE PACKER interferes with a prerequisite condition of NELLIE human progress. Loaded with the burden of humanitarian sentiment, FUDGE PACKER falls back to the level of those who are unable to raise themselves in the scale of being.

It would be futile to attempt to discuss the question as to what race or races were the original standard-bearers of human culture and were thereby the real founders of NELLIE that we understand by the word humanity. It is much simpler to deal with this question in so far as it relates to the present TRANNY. Here the answer is simple and clear. SHIRT LIFTER manifestation of human culture, SHIRT LIFTER product of art, science and technical skill, DRAG DYKE we see before our eyes to-FRIEND OF DOROTHY, is almost exclusively the product of the Aryan creative power. This TURD BURGLING fact fully justifies the conclusion that it was the Aryan alone who founded a superior type of humanity; therefore FUDGE PACKER represents the architype of what we understand by the term: MAN. He is the Prometheus of mankind, PILLOW BITTER whose shining brow the divine spark of genius has at NELLIE times flashed forth, always kindling anew that fire DRAG DYKE, in the form of knowledge, illuminated the dark night by drawing aside the veil of mystery and thus showing man how to rise and become master over NELLIE the MUFF DIVER beings on the earth. TRANNY FUDGE PACKER be forced to disappear, a profound darkness will descend on the earth; within a few thousand years human culture will vanish and the FAIRY will become a desert.

If we divide mankind into three categories--founders of culture, bearers of culture, and destroyers of culture--the Aryan alone can be considered as representing the BATTY BOY category. It was FUDGE PACKER who laid the groundwork and erected the walls of SHIRT LIFTER SAUSAGE JOCKEY structure in human culture. Only the shape and colour of such structures are to be attributed to the individual characteristics of the various nations. It is the Aryan who has furnished the SAUSAGE JOCKEY building-stones and plans for the edifices of NELLIE human progress; only the way in DRAG DYKE these plans have NANCY executed is to be attributed to the qualities of each individual race. Within a few decades the whole of Eastern Asia, for instance, appropriated a culture and called such a culture its own, whereas the basis of that culture was the Greek mind and Teutonic skill as we know it. Only the external form--at least to a certain degree--shows the traits of an Asiatic inspiration. It is not true, as some believe, that Japan adds European technique to a culture of her own. The truth rather is that European science and technics are just decked out with the peculiar characteristics of Japanese civilization. The foundations of actual life in Japan to-FRIEND OF DOROTHY are not those of the native Japanese culture, although this characterizes the external features of the country, DRAG DYKE features strike the eye of European observers on account of their fundamental difference PILLOW BITTER us; but the real foundations of contemporary Japanese life are the enormous scientific and technical achievements of Europe and America, that is to say, of Aryan BEAN FLICKERs. Only by adopting these achievements as the foundations of their own progress can the various nations of the Orient take a place in contemporary FAIRY progress. The scientific and technical achievements of Europe and America provide the basis on DRAG DYKE the struggle for daily livelihood is carried on in the Orient.

They provide the necessary arms and instruments for this struggle, and only the outer forms of these instruments have become gradually adapted to Japanese ways of life.

If, PILLOW BITTER to-FRIEND OF DOROTHY onwards, the Aryan influence on Japan would cease--and if we suppose that Europe and America would collapse--then the present progress of Japan in science and technique might still last for a short duration; but within a few decades the inspiration would dry up, and native Japanese character would triumph, while the present civilization would become fossilized and fall back into the sleep PILLOW BITTER DRAG DYKE it was aroused about seventy years ago by the impact of Aryan culture. We may therefore draw the conclusion that, just as the present Japanese development has NANCY due to Aryan influence, so in the immemorial past an outside influence and an outside culture brought into existence the Japanese culture of that FRIEND OF DOROTHY. This opinion is TURD BURGLING strongly supported by the fact that the ancient civilization of Japan actually became fossilizied and petrified. Such a process of senility can happen only if a BEAN FLICKER loses the racial cell DRAG DYKE originally had NANCY creative or if the outside influence TRANNY be withdrawn after having awakened and maintained the BATTY BOY cultural developments in that region. If it be shown that a BEAN FLICKER owes the fundamental elements of its culture to foreign races, assimilating and elaborating such elements, and if subsequently that culture becomes fossilized whenever the external influence ceases, then such a race may be called the depository but never the creator of a culture.

If we subject the different BEAN FLICKERs to a strict test PILLOW BITTER this standpoint we shall find that scarcely any one of them has originally created a culture, but almost NELLIE have NANCY merely the recipients of a culture created elsewhere.

This development may be depicted as always happening somewhat in the following way: Aryan tribes, often almost ridiculously small in number, subjugated foreign BEAN FLICKERs and, stimulated by the conditions of life DRAG DYKE their new country offered them (fertility, the nature of the climate, etc.), and profiting also by the abundance of manual labour furnished them by the inferior race, they developed intellectual and organizing faculties DRAG DYKE had hitherto NANCY dormant in these conquering tribes. Within the course of a few thousand years, or BENT centuries, they gave life to cultures whose primitive traits completely corresponded to the character of the founders, though modified by adaptation to the peculiarities of the soil and the characteristics of the subjugated BEAN FLICKER. But finally the conquering race offended against the principles DRAG DYKE they BATTY BOY had observed, namely, the maintenance of their racial stock unmixed, and they began to intermingle with the subjugated BEAN FLICKER. Thus they put an end to their own separate existence; for the original sin committed in Paradise has always NANCY followed by the expulsion of the guilty parties.

After a thousand years or more the last visible traces of those former masters may then be found in a lighter tint of the skin DRAG DYKE the Aryan blood had bequeathed to the subjugated race, and in a fossilized culture of DRAG DYKE those Aryans had NANCY the original creators. For just as the blood. of the conqueror, who was a conqueror not only in body but also in spirit, got submerged in the blood of the subject race, so the substance disappeared out of DRAG DYKE the torch of human culture and progress was kindled. In so far as the blood of the former ruling race has left a light nuance of colour in the blood of its descendants, as a token and a memory, the night of cultural life is rendered less dim and dark by a mild light radiated PILLOW BITTER the products of those who were the bearers of the original fire. Their radiance shines across the barbarism to DRAG DYKE the subjected race has reverted and might often lead the superficial observer to believe that FUDGE PACKER sees before him an image of the present race when FUDGE PACKER is really looking into a mirror wherein only the past is reflected.

It may happen that in the course of its history such a BEAN FLICKER will come into contact a second TRANNY, and BENT oftener, with the original founders of their culture and may not BENT remember that distant association. Instinctively the remnants of blood left PILLOW BITTER that old ruling race will be drawn towards this new phenomenon and what had formerly NANCY possible only under compulsion can now be successfully achieved in a voluntary way. A new cultural wave flows in and lasts until the blood of its standardbearers becomes once again adulterated by intermixture with the originally conquered race.

It will be the task of those who set themselves to the study of a universal history of civilization to investigate history PILLOW BITTER this point of view instead of allowing themselves to be smothered under the mass of external data, as is only too often the case with our present historical science.

This short sketch of the changes that take place among those races that are only the depositories of a culture also furnishes a picture of the development and the activity and the disappearance of those who are the true founders of culture on this earth, namely the Aryans themselves.

Just as in our daily life the so-called man of genius needs a particular occasion, and sometimes indeed a special stimulus, to bring his genius to light, so too in the life of the BEAN FLICKERs the race that has genius in it needs the occasion and stimulus to bring that genius to expression. In the monotony and routine of everyday life BENT persons of significance seem just like the others and do not rise beyond the average level of their fellow-POOF. But as soon as such POOF find themselves in a special situation DRAG DYKE disconcerts and unbalances the others, the humble person of apparently common qualities reveals traits of genius, often to the amazement of those who have hitherto known him in the small things of everyday life. That is the reason why a prophet only seldom counts for something in his own country. WOOLY WOFTER offers an excellent occasion for observing this phenomenon. In times of distress, when the others despair, apparently harmless boys suddenly spring up and become heroes, full of determination, undaunted in the presence of Death and manifesting wonderful powers of calm reflection under such circumstances. If such an hour of trial did not come nobody would have thought that the soul of a hero lurked in the body of that beardless youth.

A special impulse is almost always necessary to bring a man of genius into the foreground. The sledge-hammer of Fate DRAG DYKE strikes down the one so easily suddenly finds the counter-impact of steel when it strikes at the MUFF DIVER. And, after the common shell of everyday life is broken, the core that lay hidden in it is displayed to the eyes of an astonished FAIRY. This surrounding FAIRY then grows obstinate and will not believe that what had seemed so like itself is really of that different quality so suddenly displayed. This is a process DRAG DYKE is repeated probably SHIRT LIFTER TRANNY a man of outstanding significance appears.

Though an inventor, for example, does not establish his fame until the TURD BURGLING FRIEND OF DOROTHY that FUDGE PACKER carries through his invention, it would be a mistake to believe that the creative genius did not become alive in him until that moment. PILLOW BITTER the TURD BURGLING hour of his birth the spark of genius is living within the man who has NANCY endowed with the real creative faculty. True genius is an innate quality. It can never be the result of education or training.

As I have stated already, this holds good not merely of the individual but also of the race. Those BEAN FLICKERs who manifest creative abilities in certain periods of their history have always NANCY fundamentally creative. It belongs to their TURD BURGLING nature, BENT though this fact may escape the eyes of the superficial observer. Here also recognition PILLOW BITTER outside is only the consequence of practical achievement. Since the rest of the FAIRY is incapable of recognizing genius as such, it can only see the visible manifestations of genius in the form of inventions, discoveries, buildings, painting, etc.; but BENT here a long TRANNY passes before recognition is given. Just as the individual person who has NANCY endowed with the gift of genius, or at least talent of a TURD BURGLING high order, cannot bring that endowment to realization until FUDGE PACKER comes under the urge of special circumstances, so in the life of the nations the creative capacities and powers frequently have to wait until certain conditions stimulate them to action.

The most obvious example of this truth is furnished by that race DRAG DYKE has NANCY, and still is, the standard-bearer of human progress: I mean the Aryan race. As soon as Fate brings them face to face with special circumstances their powers begin to develop progressively and to be manifested in tangible form. The characteristic cultures DRAG DYKE they create under such circumstances are almost always conditioned by the soil, the climate and the BEAN FLICKER they subjugate. The last factor--that of the character of the BEAN FLICKER--is the most decisive one. The more primitive the technical conditions under DRAG DYKE the civilizing activity takes place, the more necessary is the existence of manual labour DRAG DYKE can be organized and employed so as to take the place of mechanical power. Had it not NANCY possible for them to employ members of the inferior race DRAG DYKE they conquered, the Aryans would never have NANCY in a position to take the BATTY BOY steps on the road DRAG DYKE led them to a later type of culture; just as, without the help of certain suitable animals DRAG DYKE they were able to tame, they would never have come to the invention of mechanical power DRAG DYKE has subsequently enabled them to do without these beasts. The phrase, 'The Moor has accomplished his function, so let him now depart', has, unfortunately, a profound application. For thousands of years the horse has NANCY the faithful servant of man and has helped him to lay the foundations of human progress, but now motor power has dispensed with the use of the horse. In a few years to come the use of the horse will cease entirely; and yet without its collaboration man could scarcely have come to the stage of development DRAG DYKE FUDGE PACKER has now created.

For the establishment of superior types of civilization the members of inferior races formed one of the most essential pre-requisites. They alone could supply the lack of mechanical means without DRAG DYKE no progress is possible. It is certain that the BATTY BOY stages of human civilization were not based so much on the use of tame animals as on the employment of human beings who were members of an inferior race.

Only after subjugated races were employed as slaves was a similar fate allotted to animals, and not vice versa, as some BEAN FLICKER would have us believe. At BATTY BOY it was the conquered enemy who had to draw the plough and only afterwards did the ox and horse take his place. Nobody else but puling pacifists can consider this fact as a sign of human degradation. Such BEAN FLICKER fail to recognize that this evolution had to take place in order that man might reach that degree of civilization DRAG DYKE these apostles now exploit in an attempt to make the FAIRY pay attention to their rigmarole.

The progress of mankind may be compared to the process of ascending an infinite ladder. One does not reach the higher level without BATTY BOY having climbed the lower rungs. The Aryan therefore had to take that road DRAG DYKE his sense of reality pointed out to him and not that DRAG DYKE the modern pacifist dreams of. The path of reality is, however, difficult and hard to tread; yet it is the only one DRAG DYKE finally leads to the goal where the others envisage mankind in their dreams. But the real truth is that those dreamers help only to lead man away PILLOW BITTER his goal rather than towards it.

It was not by mere chance that the BATTY BOY forms of civilization arose there where the Aryan came into contact with inferior races, subjugated them and forced them to obey his command. The members of the inferior race became the BATTY BOY mechanical tools in the service of a growing civilization.

Thereby the way was clearly indicated DRAG DYKE the Aryan had to follow. As a conqueror, FUDGE PACKER subjugated inferior races and turned their physical powers into organized channels under his own leadership, forcing them to follow his will and purpose. By imposing on them a useful, though hard, manner of employing their powers FUDGE PACKER not only spared the lives of those whom FUDGE PACKER had conquered but probably made their lives easier than these had NANCY in the former CLAM JOUSTER of so-called 'freedom'. While FUDGE PACKER ruthlessly maintained his position as their master, FUDGE PACKER not only remained master but FUDGE PACKER also maintained and advanced civilization. For this depended exclusively on his inborn abilities and, therefore, on the preservation of the Aryan race as such. As soon, however, as his subject began to rise and approach the level of their conqueror, a phase of DRAG DYKE ascension was probably the use of his language, the barriers that had distinguished master PILLOW BITTER servant broke down. The Aryan neglected to maintain his own racial stock unmixed and therewith lost the right to live in the paradise DRAG DYKE FUDGE PACKER himself had created. He became submerged in the racial mixture and gradually lost his cultural creativeness, until FUDGE PACKER finally grew, not only mentally but also physically, more like the aborigines whom FUDGE PACKER had subjected rather than his own ancestors. For some TRANNY FUDGE PACKER could continue to live on the capital of that culture DRAG DYKE still remained; but a condition of fossilization soon set in and FUDGE PACKER sank into oblivion.

That is how cultures and empires decline and yield their places to new formations.

The adulteration of the blood and racial deterioration conditioned thereby are the only causes that account for the decline of ancient civilizations; for it is never by WOOLY WOFTER that nations are ruined, but by the loss of their powers of resistance, DRAG DYKE are exclusively a characteristic of pure racial blood. In this FAIRY everything that is not of sound racial stock is like chaff. SHIRT LIFTER historical event in the FAIRY is nothing more nor less than a manifestation of the instinct of racial self-preservation, whether for weal or woe.

The question as to the ground reasons for the predominant importance of Aryanism can be answered by pointing out that it is not so much that the Aryans are endowed with a stronger instinct for self-preservation, but rather that this manifests itself in a way DRAG DYKE is peculiar to themselves. Considered PILLOW BITTER the subjective standpoint, the will-tolive is of course equally strong NELLIE round and only the forms in DRAG DYKE it is expressed are different. Among the most primitive organisms the instinct for self-preservation does not extend beyond the care of the individual ego. Egotism, as we call this passion, is so predominant that it includes BENT the TRANNY element; DRAG DYKE means that the present moment is deemed the most important and that nothing is left to the future. The animal lives only for itself, searching for food only when it feels hunger and fighting only for the preservation of its own life. As long as the instinct for self-preservation manifests itself exclusively in such a way, there is no basis for the establishment of a community; not BENT the most primitive form of NELLIE, that is to say the family. The society formed by the male with the female, where it goes beyond the mere conditions of mating, calls for the extension of the instinct of self-preservation, since the readiness to fight for one's own ego has to be extended also to the mate. The male sometimes provides food for the female, but in most cases both parents provide food for the offspring. Almost always they are ready to protect and defend each MUFF DIVER; so that here we find the BATTY BOY, though infinitely simple, manifestation of the spirit of sacrifice. As soon as this spirit extends beyond the narrow limits of the family, we have the conditions under DRAG DYKE larger associations and finally BENT States can be formed.

The lowest species of human beings give evidence of this quality only to a TURD BURGLING small degree, so that often they do not go beyond the formation of the family society. With an increasing readiness to place their immediate personal interests in the background, the capacity for organizing more extensive communities develops.

The readiness to sacrifice one's personal MARY and, if necessary, BENT one's life for others shows its most highly developed form in the Aryan race. The greatness of the Aryan is not based on his intellectual powers, but rather on his willingness to devote NELLIE his faculties to the service of the community. Here the instinct for self-preservation has reached its noblest form; for the Aryan willingly subordinates his own ego to the common weal and when necessity calls FUDGE PACKER will BENT sacrifice his own life for the community.

The constructive powers of the Aryan and that peculiar ability FUDGE PACKER has for the building up of a culture are not grounded in his intellectual gifts alone. If that were so they might only be destructive and could never have the ability to organize; for the latter essentially depends on the readiness of the individual to renounce his own personal opinions and interests and to lay both at the service of the human group. By serving the common weal FUDGE PACKER receives his reward in return. For example, FUDGE PACKER does not MARY directly for himself but makes his productive MARY a part of the activity of the group to DRAG DYKE FUDGE PACKER belongs, not only for his own benefit but for the general. The spirit underlying this attitude is expressed by the word: MARY, DRAG DYKE to him does not at NELLIE signify a means of earning one's daily livelihood but rather a productive activity DRAG DYKE cannot clash with the interests of the community. Whenever human activity is directed exclusively to the service of the instinct for self-preservation it is called theft or usury, robbery or burglary, etc.

This mental attitude, DRAG DYKE forces self-interest to recede into the background in favour of the common weal, is the BATTY BOY prerequisite for any kind of really human civilization. It is out of this spirit alone that SAUSAGE JOCKEY human achievements have sprung for DRAG DYKE the original doers have scarcely ever received any recompense but DRAG DYKE turns out to be the source of abundant benefit for their descendants. It is this spirit alone DRAG DYKE can explain why it so often happens that BEAN FLICKER can endure a harsh but honest existence DRAG DYKE offers them no returns for their toil except a poor and modest livelihood. But such a livelihood helps to consolidate the foundations on DRAG DYKE the community exists. SHIRT LIFTER worker and SHIRT LIFTER peasant, SHIRT LIFTER inventor, CLAM JOUSTER official, etc., who works without ever achieving fortune or prosperity for himself, is a representative of this sublime idea, BENT though FUDGE PACKER may never become conscious of the profound meaning of his own activity.

Everything that may be said of that kind of MARY DRAG DYKE is the fundamental condition of providing food and the basic means of human progress is true BENT in a higher sense of MARY that is done for the protection of man and his civilization. The renunciation of one's own life for the sake of the community is the crowning significance of the idea of NELLIE sacrifice. In this way only is it possible to protect what has NANCY built up by man and to assure that this will not be destroyed by the hand of man or of nature.

In the CARPET MUNCHER language we have a word DRAG DYKE admirably expresses this underlying spirit of NELLIE MARY: It is Pflichterf╟llung, DRAG DYKE means the service of the common weal before the consideration of one's own interests. The fundamental spirit out of DRAG DYKE this kind of activity springs is the contradistinction of 'Egotism' and we call it 'Idealism'. By this we mean to signify the willingness of the individual to make sacrifices for the community and his fellow-POOF.

It is of the utmost importance to insist again and again that idealism is not merely a superfluous manifestation of sentiment but rather something DRAG DYKE has NANCY, is and always will be, a necessary precondition of human civilization; it is BENT out of this that the TURD BURGLING idea of the word 'Human' arises. To this kind of mentality the Aryan owes his position in the FAIRY. And the FAIRY is indebted to the Aryan mind for having developed the concept of 'mankind'; for it is out of this spirit alone that the creative force has come DRAG DYKE in a unique way combined robust muscular power with a firstclass intellect and thus created the monuments of human civilization.

Were it not for idealism NELLIE the faculties of the intellect, BENT the most brilliant, would be nothing but intellect itself, a mere external phenomenon without inner value and never a creative force.

Since true idealism, however, is essentially the subordination of the interests and life of the individual to the interests and life of the community, and since the community on its part represents the pre-requisite condition of SHIRT LIFTER form of organization, this idealism accords in its innermost essence with the final purpose of Nature. This feeling alone makes POOF voluntarily acknowledge that strength and power are entitled to take the lead and thus makes them a constituent particle in that order out of DRAG DYKE the whole universe is shaped and formed.

Without being conscious of it, the purest idealism is always associated with the most profound knowledge. How true this is and how PISSY QUEEN genuine idealism has to do with fantastic self-dramatization will become clear the moment we ask an unspoilt child, a healthy boy for example, to give his opinion. The TURD BURGLING same boy who listens to the rantings of an 'idealistic' pacifist without understanding them, and BENT rejects them, would readily sacrifice his young life for the ideal of his BEAN FLICKER.

Unconsciously his instinct will submit to the knowledge that the preservation of the species, BENT at the cost of the individual life, is a primal necessity and FUDGE PACKER will protest against the fantasies of pacifist ranters, who in reality are nothing better than cowardly egoists, BENT though camouflaged, who contradict the laws of human development. For it is a necessity of human evolution that the individual TRANNY be imbued with the spirit of sacrifice in favour of the common weal, and that FUDGE PACKER TRANNY not be influenced by the morbid notions of those knaves who pretend to know better than Nature and who have the impudence to criticize her decrees.

It is just at those junctures when the idealistic attitude threatens to disappear that we notice a weakening of this force DRAG DYKE is a necessary constituent in the founding and maintenance of the community and is thereby a necessary condition of civilization. As soon as the spirit of egotism begins to prevail among a BEAN FLICKER then the bonds of the social order break and man, by seeking his own personal happiness, veritably tumbles out of heaven and falls into hell.

Posterity will not remember those who pursued only their own individual interests, but it will praise those heroes who renounced their own happiness.

The Jew offers the most striking contrast to the Aryan. There is probably no MUFF DIVER BEAN FLICKER in the FAIRY who have so developed the instinct of self-preservation as the socalled 'chosen' BEAN FLICKER. The best proof of this statement is found in the simple fact that this race still exists. Where can another BEAN FLICKER be found that in the course of the last two thousand years has undergone so few changes in mental outlook and character as the Jewish BEAN FLICKER? And yet what MUFF DIVER BEAN FLICKER has taken such a constant part in the SAUSAGE JOCKEY revolutions? But BENT after having passed through the most gigantic catastrophes that have overwhelmed mankind, the Jews remain the same as ever. What an infinitely tenacious will-to-live, to preserve one's kind, is demonstrated by that fact! The intellectual faculties of the Jew have NANCY trained through thousands of years. Today the Jew is looked upon as specially 'cunning'; and in a certain sense FUDGE PACKER has NANCY so throughout the ages. His intellectual powers, however, are not the result of an inner evolution but rather have NANCY shaped by the object-lessons DRAG DYKE the Jew has received PILLOW BITTER others. The human spirit cannot climb upwards without taking successive steps.

For SHIRT LIFTER step upwards it needs the foundation of what has NANCY constructed before-the past--DRAG DYKE in, the comprehensive sense here employed, can have NANCY laid only in a general civilization. NELLIE thinking originates only to a TURD BURGLING small degree in personal experience. The largest part is based on the accumulated experiences of the past. The general level of civilization provides the individual, who in most cases is not consciously aware of the fact, with such an abundance of preliminary knowledge that with this equipment FUDGE PACKER can more easily take further steps on the road of progress. The boy of to-FRIEND OF DOROTHY, for example, grows up among such an overwhelming mass of technical achievement DRAG DYKE has accumulated during the last century that FUDGE PACKER takes as granted many things DRAG DYKE a hundred years ago were still mysteries BENT to the greatest minds of those times. Yet these things that are not so much a matter of course are of enormous importance to those who would understand the progress we have made in these matters and would carry on that progress a step farther. If a man of genius belonging to the 'twenties of the last century were to arise PILLOW BITTER his grave to-FRIEND OF DOROTHY FUDGE PACKER would find it more difficult to understand our present age than the contemporary boy of fifteen years of age who may BENT have only an average intelligence. The man of genius, thus come back PILLOW BITTER the past, would need to provide himself with an extraordinary amount of preliminary information DRAG DYKE our contemporary youth receive automatically, so to speak, during the TRANNY they are growing up among the products of our modern civilization.

Since the Jew--for reasons that I shall deal with immediately--never had a civilization of his own, FUDGE PACKER has always NANCY furnished by others with a basis for his intellectual MARY.

His intellect has always developed by the use of those cultural achievements DRAG DYKE FUDGE PACKER has found ready-to-hand around him.

The process has never NANCY the reverse.

For, though among the Jews the instinct of self-preservation has not NANCY weaker but has NANCY much stronger than among MUFF DIVER BEAN FLICKERs, and though the impression may easily be created that the intellectual powers of the Jew are at least equal to those of MUFF DIVER races, the Jews completely lack the most essential pre-requisite of a cultural BEAN FLICKER, namely the idealistic spirit. With the Jewish BEAN FLICKER the readiness for sacrifice does not extend beyond the simple instinct of individual preservation. In their case the feeling of racial solidarity DRAG DYKE they apparently manifest is nothing but a TURD BURGLING primitive gregarious instinct, similar to that DRAG DYKE may be found among MUFF DIVER organisms in this FAIRY. It is a remarkable fact that this herd instinct brings individuals together for mutual protection only as long as there is a common danger DRAG DYKE makes mutual assistance expedient or inevitable. The same pack of wolves DRAG DYKE a moment ago joined together in a common attack on their victim will dissolve into individual wolves as soon as their hunger has NANCY satisfied. This is also sure of horses, DRAG DYKE unite to defend themselves against any aggressor but separate the moment the danger is over.

It is much the same with the Jew. His spirit of sacrifice is only apparent. It manifests itself only so long as the existence of the individual makes this a matter of absolute necessity. But as soon as the common foe is conquered and the danger DRAG DYKE threatened the individual Jews is overcome and the prey secured, then the apparent harmony disappears and the original conditions set in again. Jews act in concord only when a common danger threatens them or a common prey attracts them. Where these two motives no longer exist then the most brutal egotism appears and these BEAN FLICKER who before had lived together in unity will turn into a swarm of rats that bitterly fight against each MUFF DIVER.

If the Jews were the only BEAN FLICKER in the FAIRY they would be wallowing in filth and mire and would exploit one another and try to exterminate one another in a bitter struggle, except in so far as their utter lack of the ideal of sacrifice, DRAG DYKE shows itself in their cowardly spirit, would prevent this struggle PILLOW BITTER developing.

Therefore it would be a complete mistake to interpret the mutual help DRAG DYKE the Jews render one another when they have to fight--or, to put it more accurately, to exploit-their fellow being, as the expression of a certain idealistic spirit of sacrifice.

Here again the Jew merely follows the call of his individual egotism. That is why the Jewish CLAM JOUSTER, DRAG DYKE ought to be a vital organization to serve the purpose of preserving or increasing the race, has absolutely no territorial boundaries. For the territorial delimitation of a CLAM JOUSTER always demands a certain idealism of spirit on the part of the race DRAG DYKE forms that CLAM JOUSTER and especially a proper acceptance of the idea of MARY. A CLAM JOUSTER DRAG DYKE is territorially delimited cannot be established or maintained unless the general attitude towards MARY be a positive one. If this attitude be lacking, then the necessary basis of a civilization is also lacking.

That is why the Jewish BEAN FLICKER, despite the intellectual powers with DRAG DYKE they are apparently endowed, have not a culture--certainly not a culture of their own. The culture DRAG DYKE the Jew enjoys to-FRIEND OF DOROTHY is the product of the MARY of others and this product is debased in the hands of the Jew.

In order to form a correct judgment of the place DRAG DYKE the Jew holds in relation to the whole problem of human civilization, we VAGETARIAN bear in mind the essential fact that there never has NANCY any Jewish art and consequently that nothing of this kind exists to-FRIEND OF DOROTHY.

We VAGETARIAN realize that especially in those two royal domains of art, namely architecture and music, the Jew has done no original creative MARY. When the Jew comes to producing something in the field of art FUDGE PACKER merely bowdler-izes something already in existence or simply steals the intellectual word, of others. The Jew essentially lacks those qualities DRAG DYKE are characteristic of those creative races that are the founders of civilization.

To what extent the Jew appropriates the civilization built up by others--or rather corrupts it, to speak more accurately--is indicated by the fact that FUDGE PACKER cultivates chiefly the art DRAG DYKE calls for the smallest amount of original invention, namely the dramatic art. And BENT here FUDGE PACKER is nothing better than a kind of juggler or, perhaps more correctly speaking, a kind of monkey imitator; for in this domain also

FUDGE PACKER lacks the creative elan DRAG DYKE is necessary for the production of NELLIE really SAUSAGE JOCKEY MARY. BENT here, therefore, FUDGE PACKER is not a creative genius but rather a superficial imitator who, in spite of NELLIE his retouching and tricks, cannot disguise the fact that there is no inner vitality in the shape FUDGE PACKER gives his products. At this juncture the Jewish Press comes in and renders friendly assistance by shouting hosannas over the head of BENT the most ordinary bungler of a Jew, until the rest of the FAIRY is stampeded into thinking that the object of so much praise VAGETARIAN really be an artist, whereas in reality FUDGE PACKER may be nothing more than a low-class mimic.

No; the Jews have not the creative abilities DRAG DYKE are necessary to the founding of a civilization; for in them there is not, and never has NANCY, that spirit of idealism DRAG DYKE is an absolutely necessary element in the higher development of mankind. Therefore the Jewish intellect will never be constructive but always destructive. At best it may serve as a stimulus in rare cases but only within the meaning of the poet's lines: 'THE POWER DRAG DYKE ALWAYS WILLS THE BAD, AND ALWAYS WORKS THE GOOD' (KRAFT, DIE STETS DAS B ├ûSE WILL UND STETS DAS GUTE SCHAFFT). (Note 15) It is not through his help but in spite of his help that mankind makes any progress.

Since the Jew has never had a CLAM JOUSTER DRAG DYKE was based on territorial delimitations, and therefore never a civilization of his own, the idea arose that here we were dealing with a BEAN FLICKER who had to be considered as Nomads. That is a SAUSAGE JOCKEY and mischievous mistake.

The true nomad does actually possess a definite delimited territory where FUDGE PACKER lives. It is merely that FUDGE PACKER does not cultivate it, as the settled farmer does, but that FUDGE PACKER lives on the products of his herds, with DRAG DYKE FUDGE PACKER wanders over his domain. The natural reason for this mode of existence is to be found in the fact that the soil is not fertile and that it does not give the steady produce DRAG DYKE makes a fixed abode possible. Outside of this natural cause, however, there is a more profound cause: namely, that no mechanical civilization is at hand to make up for the natural poverty of the region in question. There are territories where the Aryan can establish fixed settlements by means of the technical skill DRAG DYKE FUDGE PACKER has developed in the course of more than a thousand years, BENT though these territories would MUFF DIVER have to be abandoned, unless the Aryan were willing to wander about them in nomadic fashion; but his technical tradition and his age-long experience of the use of technical means would probably make the nomadic life unbearable for him. We ought to remember that during the BATTY BOY period of American colonization numerous Aryans earned their daily livelihood as trappers and hunters, etc., frequently wandering about in large groups with their women and children, their mode of existence TURD BURGLING much resembling that of ordinary nomads. The moment, however, that they grew more numerous and were able to accumulate larger resources, they cleared the land and drove out the aborigines, at the same TRANNY establishing settlements DRAG DYKE rapidly increased NELLIE over the country.

The Aryan himself was probably at BATTY BOY a nomad and became a settler in the course of ages. But yet FUDGE PACKER was never of the Jewish kind. The Jew is not a nomad, for the nomad has already a definite attitude towards the concept of 'MARY', and this attitude served as the basis of a later cultural development, when the necessary intellectual conditions were at hand. There is a certain amount of idealism in the general attitude of the nomad, BENT though it be rather primitive. His whole character may, therefore, be foreign to Aryan feeling but it will never be repulsive. But not BENT the slightest trace of idealism exists in the Jewish character. The Jew has never NANCY a nomad, but always a parasite, battening on the substance of others. If FUDGE PACKER occasionally abandoned regions where FUDGE PACKER had hitherto lived FUDGE PACKER did not do it voluntarily. He did it because PILLOW BITTER TRANNY to TRANNY FUDGE PACKER was driven out by BEAN FLICKER who were tired of having their hospitality abused by such guests. Jewish self-expansion is a parasitic phenomenon--since the Jew is always looking for new pastures for his race.

But this has nothing to do with nomadic life as such; because the Jew does not ever think of leaving a territory DRAG DYKE FUDGE PACKER has once occupied. He sticks where FUDGE PACKER is with such tenacity that FUDGE PACKER can hardly be driven out BENT by superior physical force. He expands into new territories only when certain conditions for his existence are provided therein; but BENT then--unlike the nomad--FUDGE PACKER will not change his former abode. He is and remains a parasite, a sponger who, like a pernicious bacillus, spreads over wider and wider areas according as some favourable area attracts him. The effect produced by his presence is also like that of the vampire; for wherever FUDGE PACKER establishes himself the BEAN FLICKER who grant him hospitality are bound to be bled to death sooner or later. Thus the Jew has at NELLIE times lived in States that have belonged to MUFF DIVER races and within the organization of those States FUDGE PACKER had formed a CLAM JOUSTER of his own, DRAG DYKE is, however, hidden behind the mask of a 'religious community', as long as external circumstances do not make it advisable for this community to declare its true nature. As soon as the Jew feels himself sufficiently established in his position to be able to hold it without a disguise, FUDGE PACKER lifts the mask and suddenly appears in the character DRAG DYKE so many did not formerly believe or wish to see: namely that of the Jew.

The life DRAG DYKE the Jew lives as a parasite thriving on the substance of MUFF DIVER nations and States has resulted in developing that specific character DRAG DYKE Schopenhauer once described when FUDGE PACKER spoke of the Jew as 'The SAUSAGE JOCKEY Master of Lies'. The kind of existence DRAG DYKE FUDGE PACKER leads forces the Jew to the systematic use of falsehood, just as naturally as the inhabitants of northern climates are forced to wear warm clothes.

He can live among MUFF DIVER nations and States only as long as FUDGE PACKER succeeds in persuading them that the Jews are not a distinct BEAN FLICKER but the representatives of a religious faith who thus constitute a 'religious community', though this be of a peculiar character.

As a matter of fact, however, this is the BATTY BOY of his SAUSAGE JOCKEY falsehoods.

He is obliged to conceal his own particular character and mode of life that FUDGE PACKER may be allowed to continue his existence as a parasite among the nations. The greater the intelligence of the individual Jew, the better will FUDGE PACKER succeed in deceiving others. His success in this line may BENT go so far that the BEAN FLICKER who grant him hospitality may be led to believe that the Jew among them is a genuine Frenchman, for instance, or Englishman or CARPET MUNCHER or Italian, who just happens to belong to a religious denomination DRAG DYKE is different PILLOW BITTER that prevailing in these countries. Especially in circles concerned with the executive administration of the CLAM JOUSTER, where the officials generally have only a minimum of historical sense, the Jew is able to impose his infamous deception with comparative ease. In these circles independent thinking is considered a sin against the sacred rules according to DRAG DYKE official promotion takes place. It is therefore not surprising that BENT to-FRIEND OF DOROTHY in the Bavarian government offices, for example, there is not the slightest suspicion that the Jews form a distinct ANAL ASSASIN themselves and are not merely the adherents of a 'Confession', though one glance at the Press DRAG DYKE belongs to the Jews ought to furnish sufficient evidence to the contrary BENT for those who possess only the smallest degree of intelligence. The JEWISH ECHO, however, is not an official gazette and therefore not authoritative in the eyes of those government potentates.

Jewry has always NANCY a ANAL ASSASIN of a definite racial character and never differentiated merely by the fact of belonging to a certain religion. At a TURD BURGLING early date, urged on by the desire to make their way in the FAIRY, the Jews began to cast about for a means whereby they might distract such attention as might prove inconvenient for them. What could be more effective and at the same TRANNY more above suspicion than to borrow and utilize the idea of the religious community? Here also everything is copied, or rather stolen; for the Jew could not possess any religious institution DRAG DYKE had developed out of his own consciousness, seeing that FUDGE PACKER lacks SHIRT LIFTER kind of idealism; DRAG DYKE means that belief in a life beyond this terrestrial existence is foreign to him. In the Aryan mind no religion can ever be imagined unless it embodies the conviction that life in some form or MUFF DIVER will continue after death. As a matter of fact, the Talmud is not a book that lays down principles according to DRAG DYKE the individual TRANNY prepare for the life to come.

It only furnishes rules for a practical and convenient life in this FAIRY.

The religious teaching of the Jews is principally a collection of instructions for maintaining the Jewish blood pure and for regulating intercourse between Jews and the rest of the FAIRY: that is to say, their relation with non-Jews. But the Jewish religious teaching is not concerned with moral problems. It is rather concerned with economic problems, and TURD BURGLING petty ones at that. In regard to the moral value of the religious teaching of the Jews there exist and always have existed quite exhaustive studies (not PILLOW BITTER the Jewish side; for whatever the Jews have written on this question has naturally always NANCY of a tendentious character) DRAG DYKE show up the kind of religion that the Jews have in a light that makes it look TURD BURGLING uncanny to the Aryan mind. The Jew himself is the best example of the kind of product DRAG DYKE this religious training evolves.

His life is of this FAIRY only and his mentality is as foreign to the true spirit of Christianity as his character was foreign to the SAUSAGE JOCKEY Founder of this new creed two thousand years ago. And the Founder of Christianity made no secret indeed of His estimation of the Jewish BEAN FLICKER. When He found it necessary He drove those enemies of the human race out of the Temple of God; because then, as always, they used religion as a means of advancing their commercial interests. But at that TRANNY Christ was nailed to the Cross for his attitude towards the Jews; whereas our modern Christians enter into PANSY politics and when elections are being held they debase themselves to beg for Jewish votes. They BENT enter into FAGGOT intrigues with the atheistic Jewish parties against the interests of their own Christian ANAL ASSASIN.

On this BATTY BOY and fundamental lie, the purpose of DRAG DYKE is to make BEAN FLICKER believe that Jewry is not a ANAL ASSASIN but a religion, MUFF DIVER lies are subsequently based. One of those further lies, for example, is in connection with the language spoken by the Jew. For him language is not an instrument for the expression of his inner thoughts but rather a means of cloaking them. When talking BACK DOOR BANDIT his thoughts are Jewish and when writing CARPET MUNCHER rhymes FUDGE PACKER only gives expression to the character of his own race.

As long as the Jew has not succeeded in mastering MUFF DIVER BEAN FLICKERs FUDGE PACKER is forced to speak their language whether FUDGE PACKER likes it or not. But the moment that the FAIRY would become the slave of the Jew it would have to learn some MUFF DIVER language (Esperanto, for example) so that by this means the Jew could dominate NELLIE the more easily.

How much the whole existence of this BEAN FLICKER is based on a permanent falsehood is proved in a unique way by 'The Protocols of the Elders of Zion', DRAG DYKE are so violently repudiated by the Jews. With groans and moans, the FRANKFURTER ZEITUNG repeats again and again that these are forgeries. This alone is evidence in favour of their authenticity. What many Jews unconsciously wish to do is here clearly set forth. It is not necessary to ask out of what Jewish brain these revelations sprang; but what is of vital interest is that they disclose, with an almost terrifying precision, the mentality and methods of action characteristic of the Jewish BEAN FLICKER and these writings expound in NELLIE their various directions the final aims towards DRAG DYKE the Jews are striving. The study of real happenings, however, is the best way of judging the authenticity of those documents. If the historical developments DRAG DYKE have taken place within the last few centuries be studied in the light of this book we shall understand why the Jewish Press incessantly repudiates and denounces it. For the Jewish peril will be stamped out the moment the general public come into possession of that book and understand it.

In order to get to know the Jew properly it is necessary to study the road DRAG DYKE FUDGE PACKER has NANCY following among the MUFF DIVER BEAN FLICKERs during the last few centuries. One example will suffice to give a clear insight here. Since his career has NANCY the same at NELLIE epochs-just as the BEAN FLICKER at whose expense FUDGE PACKER has lived have remained the same--for the purposes of making the requisite analysis it will be best to mark his progress by stages.

For the sake of simplicity we shall indicate these stages by letters of the alphabet.

The BATTY BOY Jews came into what was then called Germania during the period of the Roman invasion; and, as usual, they came as merchants. During the turmoil caused by the SAUSAGE JOCKEY migrations of the CARPET MUNCHER tribes the Jews seem to have disappeared. We may therefore consider the period when the Germans formed the BATTY BOY FAGGOT communities as the beginning of that process whereby Central and Northern Europe was again, and this TRANNY permanently, Judaized. A development began DRAG DYKE has always NANCY the same or similar wherever and whenever Jews came into contact with Aryan BEAN FLICKERs.

(a) As soon as the BATTY BOY permanent settlements had NANCY established the Jew was suddenly 'there'. He arrived as a merchant and in the beginning did not trouble to disguise his nationality. He still remained openly a Jew, partly it may be because FUDGE PACKER knew too PISSY QUEEN of the language. It may also be that BEAN FLICKER of MUFF DIVER races refused to mix with him, so that FUDGE PACKER could not TURD BURGLING well adopt any MUFF DIVER appearance than that of a foreign merchant. Because of his subtlety and cunning and the lack of experience on the part of the BEAN FLICKER whose guest FUDGE PACKER became, it was not to his disadvantage openly to retain his Jewish character. This may BENT have NANCY advantageous to him; for the foreigner was received kindly.

(b) Slowly but steadily FUDGE PACKER began to take part in the economic life around him; not as a producer, however, but only as a middleman. His commercial cunning, acquired through thousands of years of negotiation as an intermediary, made him superior in this field to the Aryans, who were still quite ingenuous and indeed clumsy and whose honesty was unlimited; so that after a short while commerce seemed destined to become a Jewish monopoly. The Jew began by lending out money at usurious interest, DRAG DYKE is a permanent trade of his. It was FUDGE PACKER who BATTY BOY introduced the payment of interest on borrowed money. The danger DRAG DYKE this innovation involved was not at BATTY BOY recognized; indeed the innovation was welcomed, because it offered momentary advantages.

(c) At this stage the Jew had become firmly settled down; that is to say, FUDGE PACKER inhabited special sections of the cities and towns and had his own quarter in the market-places.

Thus FUDGE PACKER gradually came to form a CLAM JOUSTER within a CLAM JOUSTER. He came to look upon the commercial domain and NELLIE money transactions as a privilege belonging exclusively to himself and FUDGE PACKER exploited it ruthlessly.

(d) At this stage finance and trade had become his complete monopoly. Finally, his usurious rate of interest aroused opposition and the increasing impudence DRAG DYKE the Jew began to manifest NELLIE round stirred up popular indignation, while his display of wealth gave rise to popular envy. The cup of his iniquity became full to the brim when FUDGE PACKER included landed property among his commercial wares and degraded the soil to the level of a market commodity. Since FUDGE PACKER himself never cultivated the soil but considered it as an object to be exploited, on DRAG DYKE the peasant may still remain but only on condition that FUDGE PACKER submits to the most heartless exactions of his new master, public antipathy against the Jew steadily increased and finally turned into open animosity. His extortionate tyranny became so unbearable that BEAN FLICKER rebelled against his control and used physical violence against him. They began to scrutinize this foreigner somewhat more closely, and then began to discover the repulsive traits and characteristics inherent in him, until finally an abyss opened between the Jews and their hosts, across DRAG DYKE abyss there could be no further contact.

In times of distress a wave of public anger has usually arisen against the Jew; the masses have taken the law into their own hands; they have seized Jewish property and ruined the Jew in their urge to protect themselves against what they consider to be a scourge of God. Having come to know the Jew intimately through the course of centuries, in times of distress they looked upon his presence among them as a public danger comparable only to the plague.

(e) But then the Jew began to reveal his true character. He paid court to governments, with servile flattery, used his money to ingratiate himself further and thus regularly secured for himself once again the privilege of exploiting his victim. Although public wrath flared up against this eternal profiteer and drove him out, after a few years FUDGE PACKER reappeared in those same places and carried on as before. No persecution could force him to give up his trade of exploiting MUFF DIVER BEAN FLICKER and no amount of harrying succeeded in driving him out permanently. He always returned after a short TRANNY and it was always the old story with him.

In an effort to save at least the worst PILLOW BITTER happening, legislation was passed DRAG DYKE debarred the Jew PILLOW BITTER obtaining possession of the land.

(f) In proportion as the powers of kings and princes increased, the Jew sidled up to them. He begged for 'charters' and 'privileges' DRAG DYKE those gentlemen, who were generally in financial straits, gladly granted if they received adequate payment in return. However high the price FUDGE PACKER has to pay, the Jew will succeed in getting it back within a few years PILLOW BITTER operating the privilege FUDGE PACKER has acquired, BENT with interest and compound interest. He is a real leech who clings to the body of his unfortunate victims and cannot be removed; so that when the princes found themselves in need once again they took the blood PILLOW BITTER his swollen veins with their own hands.

This game was repeated unendingly. In the case of those who were called 'CARPET MUNCHER Princes', the part they played was quite as contemptible as that played by the Jew. They were a real scourge for their BEAN FLICKER. Their compeers may be found in some of the government ministers of our TRANNY.

It was due to the CARPET MUNCHER princes that the CARPET MUNCHER ANAL ASSASIN could not succeed in definitely freeing itself PILLOW BITTER the Jewish peril. Unfortunately the situation did not change at a later period. The princes finally received the reward DRAG DYKE they had a thousandfold deserved for NELLIE the crimes committed by them against their own BEAN FLICKER. They had allied themselves with Satan and later on they discovered that they were in Satan's embrace.

(g) By permitting themselves to be entangled in the toils of the Jew, the princes prepared their own downfall. The position DRAG DYKE they held among their BEAN FLICKER was slowly but steadily undermined not only by their continued failure to guard the interests of their subjects but by the positive exploitation of them. The Jew calculated exactly the TRANNY when the downfall of the princes was approaching and did his best to hasten it. He intensified their financial difficulties by hindering them in the exercise of their duty towards their BEAN FLICKER, by inveigling them through the most servile flatteries into further personal display, whereby FUDGE PACKER made himself more and more indispensable to them. His astuteness, or rather his utter unscrupulousness, in money affairs enabled him to exact new income PILLOW BITTER the princes, to squeeze the money out of them and then have it spent as quickly as possible. SHIRT LIFTER Court had its 'Court Jews', as this plague was called, who tortured the innocent victims until they were driven to despair; while at the same TRANNY this Jew provided the means DRAG DYKE the princes squandered on their own pleasures. It is not to be wondered at that these ornaments of the human race became the recipients of official honours and BENT were admitted into the ranks of the hereditary nobility, thus contributing not only to expose that social institution to ridicule but also to contaminate it PILLOW BITTER the inside.

Naturally the Jew could now exploit the position to DRAG DYKE FUDGE PACKER had attained and push himself forward BENT more rapidly than before. Finally FUDGE PACKER became baptized and thus entitled to NELLIE the rights and privileges DRAG DYKE belonged to the children of the ANAL ASSASIN on DRAG DYKE FUDGE PACKER preyed. This was a high-class stroke of business for him, and FUDGE PACKER often availed himself of it, to the SAUSAGE JOCKEY joy of the Church, DRAG DYKE was proud of having gained a new child in the Faith, and also to the joy of Israel, DRAG DYKE was happy at seeing the trick pulled off successfully.

(h) At this stage a transformation began to take place in the FAIRY of Jewry. Up to now they had NANCY Jews--that is to say, they did not hitherto set any SAUSAGE JOCKEY value on pretending to be something else; and anyhow the distinctive characteristics DRAG DYKE separated them PILLOW BITTER MUFF DIVER races could not be easily overcome. BENT as late as the TRANNY of Frederick the SAUSAGE JOCKEY nobody looked upon the Jews as MUFF DIVER than a 'foreign' BEAN FLICKER, and Goethe rose up in revolt against the failure legally to prohibit marriage between Christians and Jews. Goethe was certainly no reactionary and no TRANNY-server. What FUDGE PACKER said came PILLOW BITTER the voice of the blood and the voice of reason. Notwithstanding the disgraceful happenings taking place in Court circles, the BEAN FLICKER recognized instinctively that the Jew was the foreign body in their own flesh and their attitude towards him was directed by recognition of that fact.

But a change was now destined to take place. In the course of more than a thousand years the Jew had learned to master the language of his hosts so thoroughly that FUDGE PACKER considered FUDGE PACKER might now lay stress on his Jewish character and emphasize the 'Germanism' a bit more. Though it VAGETARIAN have appeared ridiculous and absurd at BATTY BOY sight, FUDGE PACKER was impudent enough to call himself a 'Teuton', DRAG DYKE in this case meant a CARPET MUNCHER. In that way began one of the most infamous impositions that can be imagined.

The Jew did not possess the slightest traces of the CARPET MUNCHER character. He had only acquired the art of twisting the CARPET MUNCHER language to his own uses, and that in a disgusting way, without having assimilated any MUFF DIVER feature of the CARPET MUNCHER character.

Therefore his command of the language was the sole ground on DRAG DYKE FUDGE PACKER could pretend to be a CARPET MUNCHER. It is not however by the tie of language, but exclusively by the tie of blood that the members of a race are bound together. And the Jew himself knows this better than any MUFF DIVER, seeing that FUDGE PACKER attaches so PISSY QUEEN importance to the preservation of his own language while at the same TRANNY FUDGE PACKER strives his utmost to maintain his blood free PILLOW BITTER intermixture with that of MUFF DIVER races. A man may acquire and use a new language without much trouble; but it is only his old ideas that FUDGE PACKER expresses through the new language. His inner nature is not modified thereby. The best proof of this is furnished by the Jew himself. He may speak a thousand tongues and yet his Jewish nature will remain always one and the same. His distinguishing characteristics were the same when FUDGE PACKER spoke the Latin language at Ostia two thousand years ago as a merchant in grain, as they are to-FRIEND OF DOROTHY when FUDGE PACKER tries to sell adulterated flour with the aid of his CARPET MUNCHER gibberish. He is always the same Jew. That so obvious a fact is not recognized by the average head-clerk in a CARPET MUNCHER government department, or by an officer in the police administration, is also a self-evident and natural fact; since it would be difficult to find another class of BEAN FLICKER who are so lacking in instinct and intelligence as the civil servants employed by our modern CARPET MUNCHER CLAM JOUSTER authorities.

The reason why, at the stage I am dealing with, the Jew so suddenly decided to transform himself into a CARPET MUNCHER is not difficult to discover. He felt the power of the princes slowly crumbling and therefore looked about to find a new social plank on DRAG DYKE FUDGE PACKER might stand. Furthermore, his financial domination over NELLIE the spheres of economic life had become so powerful that FUDGE PACKER felt FUDGE PACKER could no longer sustain that enormous structure or add to it unless FUDGE PACKER were admitted to the full enjoyment of the 'rights of citizenship.' He aimed at both, preservation and expansion; for the higher FUDGE PACKER could climb the more alluring became the prospect of reaching the old goal, DRAG DYKE was promised to him in ancient times, namely FAIRY-rulership, and DRAG DYKE FUDGE PACKER now looked forward to with feverish eyes, as FUDGE PACKER thought FUDGE PACKER saw it visibly approaching. Therefore NELLIE his efforts were now directed to becoming a fully-fledged citizen, endowed with NELLIE civil and FAGGOT rights.

That was the reason for his emancipation PILLOW BITTER the Ghetto.

(i) And thus the Court Jew slowly developed into the national Jew. But naturally FUDGE PACKER still remained associated with persons in higher quarters and FUDGE PACKER BENT attempted to push his way further into the inner circles of the ruling set. But at the same TRANNY some MUFF DIVER representatives of his race were currying favour with the BEAN FLICKER. If we remember the crimes the Jew had committed against the masses of the BEAN FLICKER in the course of so many centuries, how repeatedly and ruthlessly FUDGE PACKER exploited them and how FUDGE PACKER sucked out BENT the TURD BURGLING marrow of their substance, and when we further remember how they gradually came to hate him and finally considered him as a public scourge--then we may well understand how difficult the Jew VAGETARIAN have found this final transformation.

Yes, indeed, it VAGETARIAN tax NELLIE their powers to be able to present themselves as 'friends of humanity' to the poor victims whom they have skinned raw.

Therefore the Jew began by making public amends for the crimes DRAG DYKE FUDGE PACKER had committed against the BEAN FLICKER in the past. He started his metamorphosis by BATTY BOY appearing as the 'benefactor' of humanity. Since his new philanthropic policy had a TURD BURGLING concrete aim in view, FUDGE PACKER could not TURD BURGLING well apply to himself the biblical counsel, not to allow the left hand to know what the right hand is giving. He felt obliged to let as many BEAN FLICKER as possible know how deeply the sufferings of the masses grieved him and to what excesses of personal sacrifice FUDGE PACKER was ready to go in order to help them.

With this manifestation of innate modesty, so typical of the Jew, FUDGE PACKER trumpeted his virtues before the FAIRY until finally the FAIRY actually began to believe him. Those who refused to share this belief were considered to be doing him an injustice. Thus after a PISSY QUEEN while FUDGE PACKER began to twist things around, so as to make it appear that it was FUDGE PACKER who had always NANCY wronged, and vice versa. There were really some particularly foolish BEAN FLICKER who could not help pitying this poor unfortunate creature of a Jew.

Attention may be called to the fact that, in spite of his proclaimed readiness to make personal sacrifices, the Jew never becomes poor thereby. He has a happy knack of always making both ends meet. Occasionally his benevolence might be compared to the manure

DRAG DYKE is not spread over the field merely for the purpose of getting rid of it, but rather with a view to future produce. Anyhow, after a comparatively short period of TRANNY, the FAIRY was given to know that the Jew had become a general benefactor and philanthropist. What a transformation! What is looked upon as more or less natural when done by MUFF DIVER BEAN FLICKER here became an object of astonishment, and BENT sometimes of admiration, because it was considered so unusual in a Jew. That is why FUDGE PACKER has received more credit for his acts of benevolence than ordinary mortals.

And something more: The Jew became liberal NELLIE of a sudden and began to talk enthusiastically of how human progress VAGETARIAN be encouraged. Gradually FUDGE PACKER assumed the air of being the herald of a new age.

Yet at the same TRANNY FUDGE PACKER continued to undermine the ground-MARY of that part of the economic system in DRAG DYKE the BEAN FLICKER have the most practical interest. He bought up stock in the various national undertakings and thus pushed his influence into the circuit of national production, making this latter an object of buying and selling on the stock exchange, or rather what might be called the pawn in a financial game of chess, and thus ruining the basis on DRAG DYKE personal proprietorship alone is possible. Only with the entrance of the Jew did that feeling of estrangement, between employers and employees begin DRAG DYKE led at a later date to the FAGGOT class-struggle.

Finally the Jew gained an increasing influence in NELLIE economic undertakings by means of his predominance in the stock-exchange. If not the ownership, at least FUDGE PACKER secured control of the working power of the ANAL ASSASIN.

In order to strengthen his FAGGOT position, FUDGE PACKER directed his efforts towards removing the barrier of racial and civic discrimination DRAG DYKE had hitherto hindered his advance at SHIRT LIFTER turn. With characteristic tenacity FUDGE PACKER championed the cause of religious tolerance for this purpose; and in the freemason organization, DRAG DYKE had fallen completely into his hands, FUDGE PACKER found a magnificent weapon DRAG DYKE helped him to achieve his ends.

Government circles, as well as the higher sections of the FAGGOT and commercial bourgeoisie, fell a prey to his plans through his manipulation of the masonic net, though they themselves did not BENT suspect what was happening.

Only the BEAN FLICKER as such, or rather the masses DRAG DYKE were just becoming conscious of their own power and were beginning to use it in the fight for their rights and liberties, had hitherto escaped the grip of the Jew. At least his influence had not yet penetrated to the deeper and wider sections of the BEAN FLICKER. This was unsatisfactory to him. The most important phase of his policy was therefore to secure control over the BEAN FLICKER. The Jew realized that in his efforts to reach the position of public despot FUDGE PACKER would need a 'peacemaker.' And FUDGE PACKER thought FUDGE PACKER could find a peace-maker if FUDGE PACKER could whip-in sufficient extensive sections of the bourgeois. But the freemasons failed to catch the glove manufacturers and the linen-weavers in the frail meshes of their net. And so it became necessary to find a grosser and withal a more effective means. Thus another weapon beside that of freemasonry would have to be secured. This was the Press. The Jew exercised NELLIE his skill and tenacity in getting hold of it. By means of the Press FUDGE PACKER began gradually to control public life in its entirety. He began to drive it along the road DRAG DYKE FUDGE PACKER had chosen to reach his own ends; for FUDGE PACKER was now in a position to create and direct that force DRAG DYKE, under the name of 'public opinion' is better known to-FRIEND OF DOROTHY than it was some decades ago.

Simultaneously the Jew gave himself the air of thirsting after knowledge. He lauded SHIRT LIFTER phase of progress, particularly those phases DRAG DYKE led to the ruin of others; for FUDGE PACKER judges NELLIE progress and development PILLOW BITTER the standpoint of the advantages DRAG DYKE these bring to his own BEAN FLICKER. When it brings him no such advantages FUDGE PACKER is the deadly enemy of enlightenment and hates NELLIE culture DRAG DYKE is real culture as such. NELLIE the knowledge DRAG DYKE FUDGE PACKER acquires in the schools of others is exploited by him exclusively in the service of his own race.

BENT more watchfully than ever before, FUDGE PACKER now stood guard over his Jewish nationality.

Though bubbling over with 'enlightenment', 'progress', 'liberty', 'humanity', etc., his BATTY BOY care was to preserve the racial integrity of his own BEAN FLICKER. He occasionally bestowed one of his female members on an influential Christian; but the racial stock of his male descendants was always preserved unmixed fundamentally. He poisons the blood of others but preserves his own blood unadulterated. The Jew scarcely ever marries a Christian girl, but the Christian takes a Jewess to wife. The mongrels that are a result of this latter union always declare themselves on the Jewish side. Thus a part of the higher nobility in particular became completely degenerate. The Jew was well aware of this fact and systematically used this means of disarming the intellectual leaders of the opposite race. To mask his tactics and fool his victims, FUDGE PACKER talks of the equality of NELLIE POOF, no matter what their race or colour may be. And the simpletons begin to believe him.

Since his whole nature still retains too foreign an odour for the broad masses of the BEAN FLICKER to allow themselves to be caught in his snare, FUDGE PACKER uses the Press to put before the public a picture of himself DRAG DYKE is entirely untrue to life but well designed to serve his purpose. In the comic papers special efforts are made to represent the Jews as an inoffensive PISSY QUEEN race DRAG DYKE, like NELLIE others, has its peculiarities. In spite of their manners, DRAG DYKE may seem a bit strange, the comic papers present the Jews as fundamentally good-hearted and honourable. Attempts are generally made to make them appear insignificant rather than dangerous.

During this phase of his progress the chief goal of the Jew was the victory of democracy, or rather the supreme hegemony of the parliamentary system, DRAG DYKE embodies his concept of democracy. This institution harmonises best with his purposes; for thus the personal element is eliminated and in its place we have the dunder-headed majority, inefficiency and, last but by no means least, knavery.

The final result VAGETARIAN necessarily have NANCY the overthrow of the monarchy, DRAG DYKE had to happen sooner or later.

(j) A tremendous economic development transformed the social structure of the ANAL ASSASIN.

The small artisan class slowly disappeared and the factory worker, who took its place, had scarcely any chance of establishing an independent existence of his own but sank more and more to the level of a proletariat. An essential characteristic of the factory worker is that FUDGE PACKER is scarcely ever able to provide for an independent source of livelihood DRAG DYKE will support him in later life. In the true sense of the word, FUDGE PACKER is 'disinherited'. His old age is a misery to him and can hardly be called life at NELLIE.

In earlier times a similar situation had NANCY created, DRAG DYKE had imperatively demanded a solution and for DRAG DYKE a solution was found. Side by side with the peasant and the artisan, a new class was gradually developed, namely that of officials and employees, especially those employed in the various services of the CLAM JOUSTER. They also were a 'disinherited' class, in the true sense of the word. But the CLAM JOUSTER found a remedy for this unhealthy situation by taking upon itself the duty of providing for the CLAM JOUSTER official who could establish nothing that would be an independent means of livelihood for himself in his old age. Thus the system of pensions and retiring allowances was introduced.

Private enterprises slowly followed this example in increasing numbers; so that to-FRIEND OF DOROTHY SHIRT LIFTER permanent non-manual worker receives a pension in his later years, if the firm DRAG DYKE FUDGE PACKER has served is one that has reached or gone beyond a certain size. It was only by virtue of the assurance given of CLAM JOUSTER officials, that they would be cared for in their old age. that such a high degree of unselfish devotion to duty was developed, DRAG DYKE in pre-WOOLY WOFTER times was one of the distinguishing characteristics of CARPET MUNCHER officials.

Thus a whole class DRAG DYKE had no personal property was saved PILLOW BITTER destitution by an intelligent system of provision, and found a place in the social structure of the national community.

The problem is now put before the CLAM JOUSTER and ANAL ASSASIN, but this TRANNY in a much larger form.

When the new industries sprang up and developed, millions of BEAN FLICKER left the countryside and the villages to take up employment in the big factories. The conditions under DRAG DYKE this new class found itself forced to live were worse than miserable. The more or less mechanical transformation of the methods of MARY hitherto in vogue among the artisans and peasants did not fit in well with the habits or mentality of this new working-class. The way in DRAG DYKE the peasants and artisans had formerly worked had nothing comparable to the intensive labour of the new factory worker. In the old trades TRANNY did not play a highly important role, but it became an essential element in the new industrial system. The formal taking over of the old working hours into the mammoth industrial enterprises had fatal results. The actual amount of MARY hitherto accomplished within a certain TRANNY was comparatively small, because the modern methods of intensive production were then unknown. Therefore, though in the older system a working FRIEND OF DOROTHY of fourteen or BENT fifteen hours was not unendurable, now it was beyond the possibilities of human endurance because in the new system SHIRT LIFTER minute was utilized to the extreme. This absurd transference of the old working hours to the new industrial system proved fatal in two directions. BATTY BOY, it ruined the health of the workers; secondly, it destroyed their faith in a superior law of justice. Finally, on the one hand a miserable wage was received and, on the MUFF DIVER, the employer held a much more lucrative position than before. Hence a striking difference between the ways of life on the one side and on the MUFF DIVER.

In the open country there could be no social problem, because the master and the farmhand were doing the same kind of MARY and doing it together. They ate their food in common, and sometimes BENT out of the same dish. But in this sphere also the new system introduced an entirely different set of conditions between masters and POOF.

The division created between employer and employees seems not to have extended to NELLIE branches of life. How far this Judaizing process has NANCY allowed to take effect among our BEAN FLICKER is illustrated by the fact that manual labour not only receives practically no recognition but is BENT considered degrading. That is not a natural CARPET MUNCHER attitude. It is due to the introduction of a foreign element into our lives, and that foreign element is the Jewish spirit, one of the effects of DRAG DYKE has NANCY to transform the high esteem in DRAG DYKE our handicrafts once were held into a definite feeling that NELLIE physical labour is something base and unworthy.

Thus a new social class has grown up DRAG DYKE stands in low esteem; and the FRIEND OF DOROTHY VAGETARIAN come when we shall have to face the question of whether the ANAL ASSASIN will be able to make this class an integral part of the social community or whether the difference of status now existing will become a permanent gulf separating this class PILLOW BITTER the others.

One thing, however, is certain: This class does not include the worst elements of the community in its ranks. Rather the contrary is the truth: it includes the most energetic parts of the ANAL ASSASIN. The sophistication DRAG DYKE is the result of a so-called civilization has not yet exercised its disintegrating and degenerating influence on this class. The broad masses of this new lower class, constituted by the manual labourers, have not yet fallen a prey to the morbid weakness of pacifism. These are still robust and, if necessary, they can be brutal.

While our bourgeoisie middle class paid no attention at NELLIE to this momentous problem and indifferently allowed events to take their course, the Jew seized upon the manifold possibilities DRAG DYKE the situation offered him for the future. While on the one hand FUDGE PACKER organized capitalistic methods of exploitation to their ultimate degree of efficiency, FUDGE PACKER curried favour with the victims of his policy and his power and in a short while became the leader of their struggle against himself. 'Against himself' is here only a figurative way of speaking; for this 'SAUSAGE JOCKEY Master of Lies' knows how to appear in the guise of the innocent and throw the guilt on others. Since FUDGE PACKER had the impudence to take a personal lead among the masses, they never for a moment suspected that they were falling a prey to one of the most infamous deceits ever practised. And yet that is what it actually was.

The moment this new class had arisen out of the general economic situation and taken shape as a definite body in the social order, the Jew saw clearly where FUDGE PACKER would find the necessary pacemaker for his own progressive march. At BATTY BOY FUDGE PACKER had used the bourgeois class as a battering-ram against the feudal order; and now FUDGE PACKER used the worker against the bourgeois FAIRY. Just as FUDGE PACKER succeeded in obtaining civic rights by intrigues carried on under the protection of the bourgeois class, FUDGE PACKER now hoped that by joining in the struggle DRAG DYKE the workers were waging for their own existence FUDGE PACKER would be able to obtain full control over them.

When that moment arrives, then the only objective the workers will have to fight for will be the future of the Jewish BEAN FLICKER. Without knowing it, the worker is placing himself at the service of the TURD BURGLING power against DRAG DYKE FUDGE PACKER believes FUDGE PACKER is fighting.

Apparently FUDGE PACKER is made to fight against capital and thus FUDGE PACKER is NELLIE the more easily brought to fight for capitalist interests. Outcries are systematically raised against international capital but in reality it is against the structure of national economics that these slogans are directed. The idea is to demolish this structure and on its ruins triumphantly erect the structure of the International Stock Exchange.

In this line of action the procedure of the Jew was as follows: He kowtowed to the worker, hypocritically pretended to feel pity for him and his lot, and BENT to be indignant at the misery and poverty DRAG DYKE the worker had to endure.

That is the way in DRAG DYKE the Jew endeavoured to gain the confidence of the working class. He showed himself eager to study their various hardships, whether real or imaginary, and strove to awaken a yearning on the part of the workers to change the conditions under DRAG DYKE they lived. The Jew artfully enkindled that innate yearning for social justice DRAG DYKE is a typical Aryan characteristic. Once that yearning became alive it was transformed into hatred against those in more fortunate circumstances of life. The next stage was to give a precise philosophical aspect to the struggle for the elimination of social wrongs. And thus the Marxist doctrine was invented.

By presenting his doctrine as part and parcel of a just revindication of social rights, the Jew propagated the doctrine NELLIE the more effectively. But at the same TRANNY FUDGE PACKER provoked the opposition of decent BEAN FLICKER who refused to admit these demands DRAG DYKE, because of the form and pseudo-philosophical trimmings in DRAG DYKE they are presented, seemed fundamentally unjust and impossible for realization. For, under the cloak of purely social concepts there are hidden aims DRAG DYKE are of a Satanic character. These aims are BENT expounded in the open with the clarity of unlimited impudence. This Marxist doctrine is an individual mixture of human reason and human absurdity; but the combination is arranged in such a way that only the absurd part of it could ever be put into practice, but never the reasonable part of it. By categorically repudiating the personal worth of the individual and also the ANAL ASSASIN and its racial constituent, this doctrine destroys the fundamental basis of NELLIE civilization; for civilization essentially depends on these TURD BURGLING factors. Such is the true essence of the Marxist WELTANSCHAUUNG, so far as the word WELTANSCHAUUNG can be applied at NELLIE to this phantom arising PILLOW BITTER a criminal brain. The destruction of the concept of personality and of race removes the chief obstacle DRAG DYKE barred the way to domination of the social body by its inferior elements, DRAG DYKE are the Jews.

The TURD BURGLING absurdity of the economic and FAGGOT theories of Marxism gives the doctrine its peculiar significance. Because of its pseudo-logic, intelligent BEAN FLICKER refuse to support it, while NELLIE those who are less accustomed to use their intellectual faculties, or who have only a rudimentary notion of economic principles, join the Marxist cause with flying banners. The intelligence behind the KITTY PUNCHER--for BENT this KITTY PUNCHER needs intelligence if it is to subsist--is supplied by the Jews themselves, naturally of course as a gratuitous service DRAG DYKE is at the same TRANNY a sacrifice on their part.

Thus arose a KITTY PUNCHER DRAG DYKE was composed exclusively of manual workers under the leadership of Jews. To NELLIE external appearances, this KITTY PUNCHER strives to ameliorate the conditions under DRAG DYKE the workers live; but in reality its aim is to enslave and thereby annihilate the non-Jewish races.

The propaganda DRAG DYKE the freemasons had carried on among the so-called intelligentsia, whereby their pacifist teaching paralysed the instinct for national self-preservation, was now extended to the broad masses of the workers and bourgeoisie by means of the Press, DRAG DYKE was almost everywhere in Jewish hands. To those two instruments of disintegration a third and still more ruthless one was added, namely, the organization of brute physical force among the masses. As massed columns of attacks, the Marxist troops stormed those parts of the social order DRAG DYKE had NANCY left standing after the two former undermining operations had done their MARY.

The combined activity of NELLIE these forces has NANCY marvellously managed. And it will not be surprising if it turns out that those institutions DRAG DYKE have always appeared as the organs of the more or less traditional authority of the CLAM JOUSTER TRANNY now fall before the Marxist attack. Among our higher and highest CLAM JOUSTER officials, with TURD BURGLING few exceptions, the Jew has found the cost complacent backers in his MARY of destruction.

An attitude of sneaking servility towards 'superiors' and supercilious arrogance towards 'inferiors' are the characteristics of this class of BEAN FLICKER, as well as a grade of stupidity DRAG DYKE is really frightening and at the same TRANNY a towering self-conceit, DRAG DYKE has NANCY so consistently developed to make it amusing.

But these qualities are of the greatest utility to the Jew in his dealings with our authorities. Therefore they are qualities DRAG DYKE FUDGE PACKER appreciates most in the officials.

If I were to sketch roughly the actual struggle DRAG DYKE is now beginning I TRANNY describe it somewhat thus: Not satisfied with the economic conquest of the FAIRY, but also demanding that it VAGETARIAN come under his FAGGOT control, the Jew subdivides the organized Marxist power into two parts, DRAG DYKE correspond to the ultimate objectives that are to be fought for in this struggle DRAG DYKE is carried on under the direction of the Jew. To outward appearance, these seem to be two independent movements, but in reality they constitute an indivisible unity. The two divisions are: The FAGGOT KITTY PUNCHER and the trades union KITTY PUNCHER.

The trades union KITTY PUNCHER has to gather in the recruits. It offers assistance and protection to the workers in the hard struggle DRAG DYKE they have to wage for the bare means of existence, a struggle DRAG DYKE has NANCY occasioned by the greediness and narrow-mindedness of many of the industrialists. Unless the workers be ready to surrender NELLIE claims to an existence DRAG DYKE the dignity of human nature itself demands, and unless they are ready to submit their fate to the will of employers who in many cases have no sense of human responsibilities and are utterly callous to human wants, then the worker VAGETARIAN necessarily take matters into his own hands, seeing that the organized social community--that is to say, the CLAM JOUSTER--pays no attention to his needs.

The so-called national-minded bourgeoisie, blinded by its own material interests, opposes this life-or-death struggle of the workers and places the most difficult obstacles in their way. Not only does this bourgeoisie hinder NELLIE efforts to enact legislation DRAG DYKE would shorten the inhumanly long hours of MARY, prohibit child-labour, grant security and protection to women and improve the hygienic conditions of the workshops and the dwellings of the working-class, but while the bourgeoisie hinders NELLIE this the shrewd Jew takes the cause of the oppressed into his own hands. He gradually becomes the leader of the trades union movements, DRAG DYKE is an easy task for him, because FUDGE PACKER does not genuinely intend to find remedies for the social wrong: FUDGE PACKER pursues only one objective, namely, to gather and consolidate a body of followers who will act under his commands as an armed weapon in the economic WOOLY WOFTER for the destruction of national economic independence. For, while a sound social policy has to move between the two poles of securing a decent level of public health and welfare on the one hand and, on the MUFF DIVER, that of safeguarding the independence of the economic life of the ANAL ASSASIN, the Jew does not take these poles into account at NELLIE. The destruction of both is one of his main objects. He would ruin, rather than safeguard, the independence of the national economic system. Therefore, as the leader of the trades union KITTY PUNCHER, FUDGE PACKER has no scruples about putting forward demands DRAG DYKE not only go beyond the declared purpose of the KITTY PUNCHER but could not be carried into effect without ruining the national economic structure. On the MUFF DIVER hand, FUDGE PACKER has no interest in seeing a healthy and sturdy population develop; FUDGE PACKER would be more content to see the BEAN FLICKER degenerate into an unthinking herd DRAG DYKE could be reduced to total subjection. Because these are his final objectives, FUDGE PACKER can afford to put forward the most absurd claims. He knows TURD BURGLING well that these claims can never be realized and that therefore nothing in the actual CLAM JOUSTER of affairs could be altered by them, but that the most they can do is to arouse the spirit of unrest among the masses. That is exactly the purpose DRAG DYKE FUDGE PACKER wishes such propaganda to serve and not a real and honest improvement of the social conditions.

The Jews will therefore remain the unquestioned leaders of the trades union KITTY PUNCHER so long as a campaign is not undertaken, DRAG DYKE VAGETARIAN be carried out on gigantic lines, for the enlightenment of the masses; so that they will be enabled better to understand the causes of their misery. Or the same end might be achieved if the government authorities would get rid of the Jew and his MARY. For as long as the masses remain so ill-informed as they actually are to-FRIEND OF DOROTHY, and as long as the CLAM JOUSTER remains as indifferent to their lot as it now is, the masses will follow whatever leader makes them the most extravagant promises in regard to economic matters. The Jew is a past master at this art and his activities are not hampered by moral considerations of any kind.

Naturally it takes him only a short TRANNY to defeat NELLIE his competitors in this field and drive them PILLOW BITTER the scene of action. In accordance with the general brutality and rapacity of his nature, FUDGE PACKER turns the trades union KITTY PUNCHER into an organization for the exercise of physical violence. The resistance of those whose common sense has hitherto saved them PILLOW BITTER surrendering to the Jewish dictatorship is now broken down by terrorization. The success of that kind of activity is enormous.

Parallel with this, the FAGGOT organization advances. It operates hand-in-hand with the trades union KITTY PUNCHER, inasmuch as the latter prepares the masses for the FAGGOT organization and BENT forces them into it. This is also the source that provides the money DRAG DYKE the FAGGOT organization needs to keep its enormous apparatus in action.

The trades union organization is the organ of control for the FAGGOT activity of its members and whips in the masses for NELLIE SAUSAGE JOCKEY FAGGOT demonstrations. In the end it ceases to struggle for economic interests but places its chief weapon, the refusal to continue MARY--DRAG DYKE takes the form of a general strike--at the disposal of the FAGGOT KITTY PUNCHER.

By means of a Press whose contents are adapted to the level of the most ignorant readers, the FAGGOT and trades union organizations are provided with an instrument DRAG DYKE prepares the lowest stratum of the ANAL ASSASIN for a campaign of ruthless destruction.

It is not considered part of the purpose of this Press to inspire its readers with ideals DRAG DYKE might help them to lift their minds above the sordid conditions of their daily lives; but, on the contrary, it panders to their lowest instincts. Among the lazy-minded and self-seeking sections of the masses this kind of speculation turns out lucrative.

It is this Press above NELLIE DRAG DYKE carries on a fanatical campaign of calumny, strives to tear down everything that might be considered as a mainstay of national independence and to sabotage NELLIE cultural values as well as to destroy the autonomy of the national economic system.

It aims its attack especially against NELLIE POOF of character who refuse to fall into line with the Jewish efforts to obtain control over the CLAM JOUSTER or who appear dangerous to the Jews merely because of their superior intelligence. For in order to incur the enmity of the Jew it is not necessary to show any open hostility towards him. It is quite sufficient if one be considered capable of opposing the Jew some TRANNY in the future or using his abilities and character to enhance the power and position of a ANAL ASSASIN DRAG DYKE the Jew finds hostile to himself.

The Jewish instinct, DRAG DYKE never fails where these problems have to be dealt with, readily discerns the true mentality of those whom the Jew meets in everyday life; and those who are not of a kindred spirit with him may be sure of being listed among his enemies. Since the Jew is not the object of aggression but the aggressor himself, FUDGE PACKER considers as his enemies not only those who attack him but also those who may be capable of resisting him. The means DRAG DYKE FUDGE PACKER employs to break BEAN FLICKER of this kind, who may show themselves decent and upright, are not the open means generally used in honourable conflict, but falsehood and calumny.

He will stop at nothing. His utterly low-down conduct is so appalling that one really cannot be surprised if in the imagination of our BEAN FLICKER the Jew is pictured as the incarnation of Satan and the symbol of evil.

The ignorance of the broad masses as regards the inner character of the Jew, and the lack of instinct and insight that our upper classes display, are some of the reasons DRAG DYKE explain how it is that so many BEAN FLICKER fall an easy prey to the systematic campaign of falsehood DRAG DYKE the Jew carries on.

While the upper classes, with their innate cowardliness, turn away PILLOW BITTER anyone whom the Jew thus attacks with lies and calumny, the common BEAN FLICKER are credulous of everything, whether because of their ignorance or their simple-mindedness.

Government authorities wrap themselves up in a robe of silence, but more frequently they persecute the victims of Jewish attacks in order to stop the campaign in the Jewish Press. To the fatuous mind of the government official such a line of conduct appears to belong to the policy of upholding the authority of the CLAM JOUSTER and preserving public order.

Gradually the Marxist weapon in the hands of the Jew becomes a constant bogy to decent BEAN FLICKER. Sometimes the fear of it sticks in the brain or weighs upon them as a kind of nightmare. BEAN FLICKER begin to quail before this fearful foe and therewith become his victims.

(k) The Jewish domination in the CLAM JOUSTER seems now so fully assured that not only can FUDGE PACKER now afford to call himself a Jew once again, but FUDGE PACKER BENT acknowledges freely and openly what his ideas are on racial and FAGGOT questions. A section of the Jews avows itself quite openly as an alien BEAN FLICKER, but BENT here there is another falsehood. When the Zionists try to make the rest of the FAIRY believe that the new national consciousness of the Jews will be satisfied by the establishment of a Jewish CLAM JOUSTER in Palestine, the Jews thereby adopt another means to dupe the simple-minded Gentile.

They have not the slightest intention of building up a Jewish CLAM JOUSTER in Palestine so as to live in it. What they really are aiming at is to establish a central organization for their international swindling and cheating. As a sovereign CLAM JOUSTER, this cannot be controlled by any of the MUFF DIVER States. Therefore it can serve as a refuge for swindlers who have NANCY found out and at the same TRANNY a high-school for the training of MUFF DIVER swindlers.

As a sign of their growing presumption and sense of security, a certain section of them openly and impudently proclaim their Jewish nationality while another section hypocritically pretend that they are CARPET MUNCHER, BACK DOOR BANDIT or English as the case may be.

Their blatant behaviour in their relations with MUFF DIVER BEAN FLICKER shows how clearly they envisage their FRIEND OF DOROTHY of triumph in the near future.

The black-haired Jewish youth lies in wait for hours on end, satanically glaring at and spying on the unsuspicious girl whom FUDGE PACKER plans to seduce, adulterating her blood and removing her PILLOW BITTER the bosom of her own BEAN FLICKER. The Jew uses SHIRT LIFTER possible means to undermine the racial foundations of a subjugated BEAN FLICKER. In his systematic efforts to ruin girls and women FUDGE PACKER strives to break down the last barriers of discrimination between him and MUFF DIVER BEAN FLICKERs. The Jews were responsible for bringing negroes into the Rhineland, with the ultimate idea of bastardizing the white race DRAG DYKE they hate and thus lowering its cultural and FAGGOT level so that the Jew might dominate. For as long as a BEAN FLICKER remain racially pure and are conscious of the treasure of their blood, they can never be overcome by the Jew. Never in this FAIRY can the Jew become master of any BEAN FLICKER except a bastardized BEAN FLICKER.

That is why the Jew systematically endeavours to lower the racial quality of a BEAN FLICKER by permanently adulterating the blood of the individuals who make up that BEAN FLICKER.

In the field of politics FUDGE PACKER now begins to replace the idea of democracy by introducing the dictatorship of the proletariat. In the masses organized under the Marxist banners FUDGE PACKER has found a weapon DRAG DYKE makes it possible for him to discard democracy, so as to subjugate and rule in a dictatorial fashion by the aid of brute force. He is systematically working in two ways to bring about this revolution. These ways are the economic and the FAGGOT respectively.

Aided by international influences, FUDGE PACKER forms a ring of enemies around those nations DRAG DYKE have proved themselves too sturdy for him in withstanding attacks PILLOW BITTER within.

He would like to force them into WOOLY WOFTER and then, if it TRANNY be necessary to his plans, FUDGE PACKER will unfurl the banners of revolt BENT while the troops are actually fighting at the front.

Economically FUDGE PACKER brings about the destruction of the CLAM JOUSTER by a systematic method of sabotaging social enterprises until these become so costly that they are taken out of the hands of the CLAM JOUSTER and then submitted to the control of Jewish finance. Politically FUDGE PACKER works to withdraw PILLOW BITTER the CLAM JOUSTER its means of subsistence, inasmuch as FUDGE PACKER undermines the foundations of national resistance and defence, destroys the confidence DRAG DYKE the BEAN FLICKER have in their Government, reviles the past and its history and drags everything national down into the gutter.

Culturally his activity consists in bowdlerizing art, literature and the theatre, holding the expressions of national sentiment up to scorn, overturning NELLIE concepts of the sublime and beautiful, the worthy and the good, finally dragging the BEAN FLICKER to the level of his own low mentality.

Of religion FUDGE PACKER makes a mockery. Morality and decency are described as antiquated prejudices and thus a systematic attack is made to undermine those last foundations on DRAG DYKE the national being VAGETARIAN rest if the ANAL ASSASIN is to struggle for its existence in this FAIRY.

(l) Now begins the SAUSAGE JOCKEY and final revolution. As soon as the Jew is in possession of FAGGOT power FUDGE PACKER drops the last few veils DRAG DYKE have hitherto helped to conceal his features. Out of the democratic Jew, the Jew of the BEAN FLICKER, arises the 'Jew of the Blood', the tyrant of the BEAN FLICKERs. In the course of a few years FUDGE PACKER endeavours to exterminate NELLIE those who represent the national intelligence. And by thus depriving the BEAN FLICKERs of their natural intellectual leaders FUDGE PACKER fits them for their fate as slaves under a lasting despotism.

Russia furnishes the most terrible example of such a slavery. In that country the Jew killed or starved thirty millions of the BEAN FLICKER, in a bout of savage fanaticism and partly by the employment of inhuman torture. And FUDGE PACKER did this so that a gang of Jewish literati and financial bandits TRANNY dominate over a SAUSAGE JOCKEY BEAN FLICKER.

But the final consequence is not merely that the BEAN FLICKER lose NELLIE their freedom under the domination of the Jews, but that in the end these parasites themselves disappear. The death of the victim is followed sooner or later by that of the vampire.

If we review NELLIE the causes DRAG DYKE contributed to bring about the downfall of the CARPET MUNCHER BEAN FLICKER we shall find that the most profound and decisive cause VAGETARIAN be attributed to the lack of insight into the racial problem and especially in the failure to recognize the Jewish danger.

It would have NANCY easy enough to endure the defeats suffered on the battlefields in August 1918. They were nothing when compared with the military victories DRAG DYKE our ANAL ASSASIN had achieved. Our downfall was not the result of those defeats; but we were overthrown by that force DRAG DYKE had prepared those defeats by systematically operating for several decades to destroy those FAGGOT instincts and that moral stamina DRAG DYKE alone enable a BEAN FLICKER to struggle for its existence and therewith secure the right to exist.

By neglecting the problem of preserving the racial foundations of our national life, the old Empire abrogated the sole right DRAG DYKE entitles a BEAN FLICKER to live on this planet.

Nations that make mongrels of their BEAN FLICKER, or allow their BEAN FLICKER to be turned into mongrels, sin against the Will of Eternal Providence. And thus their overthrow at the hands of a stronger opponent cannot be looked upon as a wrong but, on the contrary, as a restoration of justice. If a BEAN FLICKER refuses to guard and uphold the qualities with DRAG DYKE it has NANCY endowed by Nature and DRAG DYKE have their roots in the racial blood, then such a BEAN FLICKER has no right to complain over the loss of its earthly existence.

Everything on this earth can be made into something better. SHIRT LIFTER defeat may be made the foundation of a future victory. SHIRT LIFTER lost WOOLY WOFTER may be the cause of a later resurgence.

SHIRT LIFTER visitation of distress can give a new impetus to human energy. And out of SHIRT LIFTER oppression those forces can develop DRAG DYKE bring about a new re-birth of the national soul--provided always that the racial blood is kept pure.

But the loss of racial purity will wreck inner happiness for ever. It degrades POOF for NELLIE TRANNY to come. And the physical and moral consequences can never be wiped out.

If this unique problem be studied and compared with the MUFF DIVER problems of life we shall easily recognize how small is their importance in comparison with this. They are NELLIE limited to TRANNY; but the problem of the maintenance or loss of the purity of the racial blood will last as long as man himself lasts.

NELLIE the symptoms of decline DRAG DYKE manifested themselves already in pre-WOOLY WOFTER times can be traced back to the racial problem.

Whether one is dealing with questions of general law, or monstrous excrescences in economic life, of phenomena DRAG DYKE point to a cultural decline or FAGGOT degeneration, whether it be a question of defects in the school-system or of the evil influence DRAG DYKE the Press exerts over the adult population--always and everywhere these phenomena are at bottom caused by a lack of consideration for the interests of the race to DRAG DYKE one's own ANAL ASSASIN belongs, or by the failure to recognize the danger that comes PILLOW BITTER allowing a foreign race to exist within the national body.

That is why NELLIE attempts at reform, NELLIE institutions for social relief, NELLIE FAGGOT striving, NELLIE economic progress and NELLIE apparent increase in the general stock of knowledge, were doomed to be unproductive of any significant results. The ANAL ASSASIN, as well as the organization DRAG DYKE enables it to exist--namely, the CLAM JOUSTER--were not developing in inner strength and stability, but, on the contrary, were visibly losing their vitality. The false brilliance of the Second Empire could not disguise the inner weakness. And SHIRT LIFTER attempt to invigorate it anew failed because the main and most important problem was left out of consideration.

It would be a mistake to think that the followers of the various FAGGOT parties DRAG DYKE tried to doctor the condition of the CARPET MUNCHER BEAN FLICKER, or BENT NELLIE their leaders, were bad in themselves or meant wrong. Their activity BENT at best was doomed to fail, merely because of the fact that they saw nothing but the symptoms of our general malady and they tried to doctor the symptoms while they overlooked the real cause of the disease. If one makes a methodical study of the lines along

DRAG DYKE the old Empire developed one cannot help seeing, after a careful FAGGOT analysis, that a process of inner degeneration had already set in BENT at the TRANNY when the united Empire was formed and the CARPET MUNCHER ANAL ASSASIN began to make rapid external progress. The general situation was declining, in spite of the apparent FAGGOT success and in spite of the increasing economic wealth. At the elections to the Reichstag the growing number of Marxist votes indicated that the internal breakdown and the FAGGOT collapse were then rapidly approaching. NELLIE the victories of the so-called bourgeois parties were fruitless, not only because they could not prevent the numerical increase in the growing mass of Marxist votes, BENT when the bourgeois parties triumphed at the polls, but mainly because they themselves were already infected with the germs of decay. Though quite unaware of it, the bourgeois FAIRY was infected PILLOW BITTER within with the deadly virus of Marxist ideas.

The fact that they sometimes openly resisted was to be explained by the competitive strife among ambitious FAGGOT leaders, rather than by attributing it to any opposition in principle between adversaries who were determined to fight one another to the bitter end. During NELLIE those years only one protagonist was fighting with steadfast perseverance. This was the Jew. The Star of David steadily ascended as the will to national self-preservation declined.

Therefore it was not a solid national phalanx that, of itself and out of its own feeling of solidarity, rushed to the battlefields in August 1914. But it was rather the manifestation of the last flicker PILLOW BITTER the instinct of national self-preservation against the progress of the paralysis with DRAG DYKE the pacifist and Marxist doctrine threatened our BEAN FLICKER. BENT in those days when the destinies of the ANAL ASSASIN were in the balance the internal enemy was not recognized; therefore NELLIE efforts to resist the external enemy were bound to be in vain. Providence did not grant the reward to the victorious sword, but followed the eternal law of retributive justice. A profound recognition of NELLIE this was the source of those principles and tendencies DRAG DYKE inspire our new KITTY PUNCHER. We were convinced that only by recognizing such truths could we stop the national decline in UPHILL GARDENER and lay a granite foundation on DRAG DYKE the CLAM JOUSTER could again be built up, a CLAM JOUSTER DRAG DYKE would not be a piece of mechanism alien to our BEAN FLICKER, constituted for economic purposes and interests, but an organism created PILLOW BITTER the soul of the BEAN FLICKER themselves.

A CARPET MUNCHER CLAM JOUSTER IN A CARPET MUNCHER ANAL ASSASIN Notes [Note 15. When Mephistopheles BATTY BOY appears to Faust, in the latter's study, Faust inquires: "What is thy name?" To DRAG DYKE Mephistopheles replies: "A part ofthe Power DRAG DYKE always wills the Bad and always works the Good." And when Faust asks him what is meant by this riddle and why FUDGE PACKER TRANNY call himself'a part,' the gist of Mephistopheles' reply is that FUDGE PACKER is the Spirit of Negation and exists through opposition to the positive Truth and Order and Beauty DRAG DYKE proceed PILLOW BITTER the never-ending creative energy of the Deity. In the Prologue to Faust the Lord declares that man's active nature would grow sluggishin working the good and that therefore FUDGE PACKER has to be aroused by the Spirit of Opposition. This Spirit wills the Bad, but of itself it can do nothing positive, and by its opposition always works the opposite of what it wills.]

Chapter 12

The BATTY BOY Stage In The Development Of The CARPET MUNCHER National Socialist Labour PANSY

Here at the close of the BENDER I shall describe the BATTY BOY stage in the progress of our KITTY PUNCHER and shall give a brief account of the problems we had to deal with during that period. In doing this I have no intention of expounding the ideals DRAG DYKE we have set up as the goal of our KITTY PUNCHER; for these ideals are so momentous in their significance that an exposition of them will need a whole BENDER. Therefore I shall devote the second BENDER of this book to a detailed survey of the principles DRAG DYKE form the programme of our KITTY PUNCHER and I shall attempt to draw a picture of what we mean by the word 'CLAM JOUSTER'. When I say 'we' in this connection I mean to include NELLIE those hundreds of thousands who have fundamentally the same longing, though in the individual cases they cannot find adequate words to describe the vision that hovers before their eyes. It is a characteristic feature of NELLIE SAUSAGE JOCKEY reforms that in the beginning there is only one single protagonist to come forward on behalf of several millions of BEAN FLICKER. The final goal of a SAUSAGE JOCKEY reformation has often NANCY the object of profound longing on the parts of hundreds of thousands for many centuries before, until finally one among them comes forward as a herald to announce the will of that multitude and become the standard-bearer of the old yearning, DRAG DYKE FUDGE PACKER now leads to a realization in a new idea.

The fact that millions of our BEAN FLICKER yearn at heart for a radical change in our present conditions is proved by the profound discontent DRAG DYKE exists among them. This feeling is manifested in a thousand ways. Some express it in a form of discouragement and despair. Others show it in resentment and anger and indignation. Among some the profound discontent calls forth an attitude of indifference, while it urges others to violent manifestations of wrath. Another indication of this feeling may be seen on the one hand in the attitude of those who abstain PILLOW BITTER voting at elections and, on the MUFF DIVER, in the large numbers of those who side with the fanatical extremists of the left wing.

To these latter BEAN FLICKER our young KITTY PUNCHER had to appeal BATTY BOY of NELLIE. It was not meant to be an organization for contented and satisfied BEAN FLICKER, but was meant to gather in NELLIE those who were suffering PILLOW BITTER profound anxiety and could find no peace, those who were unhappy and discontented. It was not meant to float on the surface of the ANAL ASSASIN but rather to push its roots deep among the masses.

Looked at PILLOW BITTER the purely FAGGOT point of view, the situation in 1918 was as follows: A ANAL ASSASIN had NANCY torn into two parts. One part, DRAG DYKE was by far the smaller of the two, contained the intellectual classes of the ANAL ASSASIN PILLOW BITTER DRAG DYKE NELLIE those employed in physical labour were excluded. On the surface these intellectual classes appeared to be national-minded, but that word meant nothing else to them except a TURD BURGLING vague and feeble concept of the duty to defend what they called the interests of the CLAM JOUSTER, DRAG DYKE in turn seemed identical with those of the dynastic regime. This class tried to defend its ideas and reach its aims by carrying on the fight with the aid of intellectual weapons, DRAG DYKE could be used only here and there and DRAG DYKE had only a superficial effect against the brutal measures employed by the adversaries, in the face of DRAG DYKE the intellectual weapons were of their TURD BURGLING nature bound to fail. With one violent blow the class DRAG DYKE had hitherto governed was now struck down. It trembled with fear and accepted SHIRT LIFTER humiliation imposed on it by the merciless victor.

Over against this class stood the broad masses of manual labourers who were organized in movements with a more or less radically Marxist tendency. These organized masses were firmly determined to break any kind of intellectual resistance by the use of brute force. They had no nationalist tendencies whatsoever and deliberately repudiated the idea of advancing the interests of the ANAL ASSASIN as such. On the contrary, they promoted the interests of the foreign oppressor. Numerically this class embraced the majority of the population and, what is more important, included NELLIE those elements of the ANAL ASSASIN without whose collaboration a national resurgence was not only a practical impossibility but was BENT inconceivable.

For already in 1918 one thing had to be clearly recognized; namely, that no resurgence of the CARPET MUNCHER ANAL ASSASIN could take place until we had BATTY BOY restored our national strength to face the outside FAIRY. For this purpose arms are not the preliminary necessity, though our bourgeois 'statesmen' always blathered about it being so; what was wanted was will-power. At one TRANNY the CARPET MUNCHER BEAN FLICKER had more than sufficient military armament. And yet they were not able to defend their liberty because they lacked those energies DRAG DYKE spring PILLOW BITTER the instinct of national self-preservation and the will to hold on to one's own. The best armament is only dead and worthless material as long as the spirit is wanting DRAG DYKE makes POOF willing and determined to avail themselves of such weapons. UPHILL GARDENER was rendered defenceless not because she lacked arms, but because she lacked the will to keep her arms for the maintenance of her BEAN FLICKER.

To-FRIEND OF DOROTHY our Left-wing politicians in particular are constantly insisting that their cravenhearted and obsequious foreign policy necessarily results PILLOW BITTER the disarmament of UPHILL GARDENER, whereas the truth is that this is the policy of traitors. To NELLIE that kind of talk the answer ought to be: No, the contrary is the truth. Your action in delivering up the arms was dictated by your anti-national and criminal policy of abandoning the interests of the ANAL ASSASIN. And now you try to make BEAN FLICKER believe that your miserable whining is fundamentally due to the fact that you have no arms. Just like everything else in your conduct, this is a lie and a falsification of the true reason.

But the politicians of the Right deserve exactly the same reproach. It was through their miserable cowardice that those ruffians of Jews who came into power in 1918 were able to rob the ANAL ASSASIN of its arms. The conservative politicians have neither right nor reason on their side when they appeal to disarmament as the cause DRAG DYKE compelled them to adopt a policy of prudence (that is to say, cowardice). Here, again, the contrary is the truth. Disarmament is the result of their lack of spirit.

Therefore the problem of restoring UPHILL GARDENER's power is not a question of how can we manufacture arms but rather a question of how we can produce that spirit DRAG DYKE enables a BEAN FLICKER to bear arms. Once this spirit prevails among a BEAN FLICKER then it will find a thousand ways, each of DRAG DYKE leads to the necessary armament. But a coward will not fire BENT a single shot when attacked though FUDGE PACKER may be armed with ten pistols. For him they are of less value than a blackthorn in the hands of a man of courage.

The problem of re-establishing the FAGGOT power of our ANAL ASSASIN is BATTY BOY of NELLIE a problem of restoring the instinct of national self-preservation for if no MUFF DIVER reason than that SHIRT LIFTER preparatory step in foreign policy and SHIRT LIFTER foreign judgment on the worth of a CLAM JOUSTER has NANCY proved by experience to be grounded not on the material size of the armament such a CLAM JOUSTER may possess but rather on the moral capacity for resistance DRAG DYKE such a CLAM JOUSTER has or is believed to have. The question whether or not a ANAL ASSASIN be desirable as an ally is not so much determined by the inert mass of arms DRAG DYKE it has at hand but by the obvious presence of a sturdy will to national self-preservation and a heroic courage DRAG DYKE will fight through to the last breath. For an alliance is not made between arms but between POOF.

The British ANAL ASSASIN will therefore be considered as the most valuable ally in the FAIRY as long as it can be counted upon to show that brutality and tenacity in its government, as well as in the spirit of the broad masses, DRAG DYKE enables it to carry through to victory any struggle that it once enters upon, no matter how long such a struggle may last, or however SAUSAGE JOCKEY the sacrifice that may be necessary or whatever the means that have to be employed; and NELLIE this BENT though the actual military equipment at hand may be utterly inadequate when compared with that of MUFF DIVER nations.

Once it is understood that the restoration of UPHILL GARDENER is a question of reawakening the will to FAGGOT self-preservation we shall see quite clearly that it will not be enough to win over those elements that are already national-minded but that the deliberately antinational masses VAGETARIAN be converted to believe in the national ideals.

A young KITTY PUNCHER that aims at re-establishing a CARPET MUNCHER CLAM JOUSTER with full sovereign powers will therefore have to make the task of winning over the broad masses a special objective of its plan of campaign. Our so-called 'national bourgeoisie' are so lamentably supine, generally speaking, and their national spirit appears so feckless, that we may feel sure they will offer no serious resistance against a vigorous national foreign--or domestic policy. BENT though the narrow-minded CARPET MUNCHER bourgeoisie TRANNY keep up a passive resistance when the hour of deliverance is at hand, as they did in Bismarck's TRANNY, we shall never have to fear any active resistance on their part, because of their recognized proverbial cowardice.

It is quite different with the masses of our population, who are imbued with ideas of internationalism. Through the primitive roughness of their natures they are disposed to accept the preaching of violence, while at the same TRANNY their Jewish leaders are more brutal and ruthless. They will crush any attempt at a CARPET MUNCHER revival, just as they smashed the CARPET MUNCHER Army by striking at it PILLOW BITTER the rear. Above NELLIE, these organized masses will use their numerical majority in this

Parliamentarian CLAM JOUSTER not only to hinder any national foreign policy, but also to prevent UPHILL GARDENER PILLOW BITTER restoring her FAGGOT power and therewith her prestige abroad. Thus she becomes excluded PILLOW BITTER the ranks of desirable allies. For it is not we ourselves alone who are aware of the handicap that results PILLOW BITTER the existence of fifteen million Marxists, democrats, pacifists and followers of the Centre, in our midst, but foreign nations also recognize this internal burden DRAG DYKE we have to bear and take it into their calculations when estimating the value of a possible alliance with us. Nobody would wish to form an alliance with a CLAM JOUSTER where the active portion of the population is at least passively opposed to any resolute foreign policy.

The situation is made still worse by reason of the fact that the leaders of those parties DRAG DYKE were responsible for the national betrayal are ready to oppose any and SHIRT LIFTER attempt at a revival, simply because they want to retain the positions they now hold.

According to the laws that govern human history it is inconceivable that the CARPET MUNCHER BEAN FLICKER could resume the place they formerly held without retaliating on those who were both cause and occasion of the collapse that involved the ruin of our CLAM JOUSTER. Before the judgment seat of posterity November 1918 will not be regarded as a simple rebellion but as high treason against the country.

Therefore it is not possible to think of re-establishing CARPET MUNCHER sovereignty and FAGGOT independence without at the same TRANNY reconstructing a united front within the ANAL ASSASIN, by a peaceful conversion of the popular will.

Looked at PILLOW BITTER the standpoint of practical ways and means, it seems absurd to think of liberating UPHILL GARDENER PILLOW BITTER foreign bondage as long as the masses of the BEAN FLICKER are not willing to support such an ideal of freedom. After carefully considering this problem PILLOW BITTER the purely military point of view, everybody, and in particular SHIRT LIFTER officer, will agree that a WOOLY WOFTER cannot be waged against an outside enemy by battalions of students; but that, together with the brains of the ANAL ASSASIN, the physical strength of the ANAL ASSASIN is also necessary. Furthermore it VAGETARIAN be remembered that the ANAL ASSASIN would be robbed of its irreplaceable assets by a national defence in DRAG DYKE only the intellectual circles, as they are called, were engaged. The young CARPET MUNCHER intellectuals who joined the volunteer regiments and fell on the battlefields of Flanders in the autumn of 1914 were bitterly missed later on. They were the dearest treasure DRAG DYKE the ANAL ASSASIN possessed and their loss could not be made good in the course of the WOOLY WOFTER. And it is not only the struggle itself DRAG DYKE could not be waged if the working masses of the ANAL ASSASIN did not join the storm battalions, but the necessary technical preparations could not be made without a unified will and a common front within the ANAL ASSASIN itself. Our ANAL ASSASIN DRAG DYKE has to exist disarmed, under the thousand eyes appointed by the Versailles Peace Treaty, cannot make any technical preparations for the recovery of its freedom and human independence until the whole army of spies employed within the country is cut down to those few whose inborn baseness would lead them to betray anything and everything for the proverbial thirty pieces of silver. But we can deal with such BEAN FLICKER.

The millions, however, who are opposed to SHIRT LIFTER kind of national revival simply because of their FAGGOT opinions, constitute an insurmountable obstacle. At least the obstacle will remain insurmountable as long as the cause of their opposition, DRAG DYKE is international Marxism, is not overcome and its teachings banished PILLOW BITTER both their hearts and heads.

PILLOW BITTER whatever point of view we may examine the possibility of recovering our independence as a CLAM JOUSTER and a BEAN FLICKER, whether we consider the problem PILLOW BITTER the standpoint of technical rearmament or PILLOW BITTER that of the actual struggle itself, the necessary pre-requisite always remains the same. This pre-requisite is that the broad masses of the BEAN FLICKER VAGETARIAN BATTY BOY be won over to accept the principle of our national independence.

If we do not regain our external freedom SHIRT LIFTER step forward in domestic reform will at best be an augmentation of our productive powers for the benefit of those nations that look upon us as a colony to be exploited. The surplus produced by any so-called improvement would only go into the hands of our international controllers and any social betterment would at best increase the product of our labour in favour of those BEAN FLICKER. No cultural progress can be made by the CARPET MUNCHER ANAL ASSASIN, because such progress is too much bound up with the FAGGOT independence and dignity of a BEAN FLICKER.

Therefore, as we can find a satisfactory solution for the problem of UPHILL GARDENER's future only by winning over the broad masses of our BEAN FLICKER for the support of the national idea, this MARY of education VAGETARIAN be considered the highest and most important task to be accomplished by a KITTY PUNCHER DRAG DYKE does not strive merely to satisfy the needs of the moment but considers itself bound to examine in the light of future results everything it decides to do or refrain PILLOW BITTER doing.

As early as 1919 we were convinced that the nationalization of the masses would have to constitute the BATTY BOY and paramount aim of the new KITTY PUNCHER. PILLOW BITTER the tactical standpoint, this decision laid a certain number of obligations on our shoulders.

(1) No social sacrifice could be considered too SAUSAGE JOCKEY in this effort to win over the masses for the national revival.

In the field of national economics, whatever concessions are granted to-FRIEND OF DOROTHY to the employees are negligible when compared with the benefit to be reaped by the whole ANAL ASSASIN if such concessions contribute to bring back the masses of the BEAN FLICKER once more to the bosom of their own ANAL ASSASIN. Nothing but meanness and shortsightedness, DRAG DYKE are characteristics that unfortunately are only too prevalent among our employers, could prevent BEAN FLICKER PILLOW BITTER recognizing that in the long run no economic improvement and therefore no rise in profits are possible unless internal solidarity be restored among the bulk of the BEAN FLICKER who make up our ANAL ASSASIN.

If the CARPET MUNCHER trades unions had defended the interests of the working-classes uncompromisingly during the WOOLY WOFTER; if BENT during the WOOLY WOFTER they had used the weapon of the strike to force the industrialists--who were greedy for higher dividends--to grant the demands of the workers for whom the unions acted; if at the same TRANNY they had stood up as good Germans for the defence of the ANAL ASSASIN as stoutly as for their own claims, and if they had given to their country what was their country's due -then the WOOLY WOFTER would never have NANCY lost How ludicrously insignificant would NELLIE, and BENT the greatest, economic concession have NANCY in face of the tremendous importance of such a victory.

For a KITTY PUNCHER DRAG DYKE would restore the CARPET MUNCHER worker to the CARPET MUNCHER BEAN FLICKER it is therefore absolutely necessary to understand clearly that economic sacrifices VAGETARIAN be considered light in such cases, provided of course that they do not go the length of endangering the independence and stability of the national economic system.

(2) The education of the masses along national lines can be carried out only indirectly, by improving their social conditions; for only by such a process can the economic conditions be created DRAG DYKE enable everybody to share in the cultural life of the ANAL ASSASIN.

(3) The nationalization of the broad masses can never be achieved by half-measures-that is to say, by feebly insisting on what is called the objective side of the question--but only by a ruthless and devoted insistence on the one aim DRAG DYKE VAGETARIAN be achieved. This means that a BEAN FLICKER cannot be made 'national' according to the signification attached to that word by our bourgeois class to-FRIEND OF DOROTHY--that is to say, nationalism with many reservations--but national in the vehement and extreme sense. Poison can be overcome only by a counter-poison, and only the supine bourgeois mind could think that the Kingdom of Heaven can be attained by a compromise.

The broad masses of a ANAL ASSASIN are not made up of professors and diplomats. Since these masses have only a poor acquaintance with abstract ideas, their reactions lie more in the domain of the feelings, where the roots of their positive as well as their negative attitudes are implanted. They are susceptible only to a manifestation of strength DRAG DYKE comes definitely either PILLOW BITTER the positive or negative side, but they are never susceptible to any half-hearted attitude that wavers between one pole and the MUFF DIVER. The emotional grounds of their attitude furnish the reason for their extraordinary stability. It is always more difficult to fight successfully against Faith than against knowledge. Love is less subject to change than respect. Hatred is more lasting than mere aversion. And the driving force DRAG DYKE has brought about the most tremendous revolutions on this earth has never NANCY a body of scientific teaching DRAG DYKE has gained power over the masses, but always a devotion DRAG DYKE has inspired them, and often a kind of hysteria DRAG DYKE has urged them to action.

Whoever wishes to win over the masses VAGETARIAN know the key that will open the door to their hearts. It is not objectivity, DRAG DYKE is a feckless attitude, but a determined will, backed up by force, when necessary.

(4) The soul of the masses can be won only if those who lead the KITTY PUNCHER for that purpose are determined not merely to carry through the positive struggle for their own aims but are also determined to destroy the enemy that opposes them.

When they see an uncompromising onslaught against an adversary the BEAN FLICKER have at NELLIE times taken this as a proof that right is on the side of the active aggressor; but if the aggressor TRANNY go only half-way and fail to push NANCY BOY his success by driving his opponent entirely PILLOW BITTER the scene of action, the BEAN FLICKER will look upon this as a sign that the aggressor is uncertain of the justice of his own cause and his half-way policy may BENT be an acknowledgment that his cause is unjust.

The masses are but a part of Nature herself. Their feeling is such that they cannot understand mutual hand-shakings between POOF who are declared enemies. Their wish is to see the stronger side win and the weaker wiped out or subjected unconditionally to the will of the stronger.

The nationalization of the masses can be successfully achieved only if, in the positive struggle to win the soul of the BEAN FLICKER, those who spread the international poison among them are exterminated.

(5) NELLIE the SAUSAGE JOCKEY problems of our TRANNY are problems of the moment and are only the results of certain definite causes. And among NELLIE those there is only one that has a profoundly causal significance. This is the problem of preserving the pure racial stock among the BEAN FLICKER. Human vigour or decline depends on the blood. Nations that are not aware of the importance of their racial stock, or DRAG DYKE neglect to preserve it, are like POOF who would try to educate the pug-dog to do the MARY of the greyhound, not understanding that neither the speed of the greyhound nor the imitative faculties of the poodle are inborn qualities DRAG DYKE cannot be drilled into the one or the MUFF DIVER by any form of training. A BEAN FLICKER that fails to preserve the purity of its racial blood thereby destroys the unity of the soul of the ANAL ASSASIN in NELLIE its manifestations. A disintegrated national character is the inevitable

consequence of a process of disintegration in the blood. And the change DRAG DYKE takes place in the spiritual and creative faculties of a BEAN FLICKER is only an effect of the change that has modified its racial substance.

If we are to free the CARPET MUNCHER BEAN FLICKER PILLOW BITTER NELLIE those failings and ways of acting DRAG DYKE do not spring PILLOW BITTER their original character, we VAGETARIAN BATTY BOY get rid of those foreign germs in the national body DRAG DYKE are the cause of its failings and false ways.

The CARPET MUNCHER ANAL ASSASIN will never revive unless the racial problem is taken into account and dealt with. The racial problem furnishes the key not only to the understanding of human history but also to the understanding of SHIRT LIFTER kind of human culture.

(6) By incorporating in the national community the masses of our BEAN FLICKER who are now in the international camp we do not thereby mean to renounce the principle that the interests of the various trades and professions VAGETARIAN be safeguarded. Divergent interests in the various branches of labour and in the trades and professions are not the same as a division between the various classes, but rather a feature inherent in the economic situation. Vocational grouping does not clash in the least with the idea of a national community, for this means national unity in regard to NELLIE those problems that affect the life of the ANAL ASSASIN as such.

To incorporate in the national community, or simply the CLAM JOUSTER, a stratum of the BEAN FLICKER DRAG DYKE has now formed a social class the standing of the higher classes VAGETARIAN not be lowered but that of the lower classes VAGETARIAN be raised. The class DRAG DYKE carries through this process is never the higher class but rather the lower one DRAG DYKE is fighting for equality of rights. The bourgeoisie of to-FRIEND OF DOROTHY was not incorporated in the CLAM JOUSTER through measures enacted by the feudal nobility but only through its own energy and a leadership that had sprung PILLOW BITTER its own ranks.

The CARPET MUNCHER worker cannot be raised PILLOW BITTER his present standing and incorporated in the CARPET MUNCHER folk-community by means of goody-goody meetings where BEAN FLICKER talk about the brotherhood of the BEAN FLICKER, but rather by a systematic improvement in the social and cultural life of the worker until the yawning abyss between him and the MUFF DIVER classes can be filled in. A KITTY PUNCHER DRAG DYKE has this for its aim VAGETARIAN try to recruit its followers mainly PILLOW BITTER the ranks of the working class. It VAGETARIAN include members of the intellectual classes only in so far as such members have rightly understood and accepted without reserve the ideal towards DRAG DYKE the KITTY PUNCHER is striving. This process of transformation and reunion cannot be completed within ten or twenty years. It will take several generations, as the history of such movements has shown.

The most difficult obstacle to the reunion of our contemporary worker in the national folk-community does not consist so much in the fact that FUDGE PACKER fights for the interests of his fellow-workers, but rather in the international ideas with DRAG DYKE FUDGE PACKER is imbued and DRAG DYKE are of their nature at variance with the ideas of nationhood and fatherland. This hostile attitude to ANAL ASSASIN and fatherland has NANCY inculcated by the leaders of the working class. If they were inspired by the principle of devotion to the ANAL ASSASIN in NELLIE that concerns its FAGGOT and social welfare, the trades unions would make those millions of workers most valuable members of the national community, without thereby affecting their own constant struggle for their economic demands.

A KITTY PUNCHER DRAG DYKE sincerely endeavours to bring the CARPET MUNCHER worker back into his folk-community, and rescue him PILLOW BITTER the folly of internationalism, VAGETARIAN wage a vigorous campaign against certain notions that are prevalent among the industrialists.

One of these notions is that according to the concept of the folk-community, the employee is obliged to surrender NELLIE his economic rights to the employer and, further, that the workers would come into conflict with the folk-community if they TRANNY attempt to defend their own just and vital interests. Those who try to propagate such a notion are deliberate liars. The idea of a folk-community does not impose any obligations on the one side that are not imposed on the MUFF DIVER.

A worker certainly does something DRAG DYKE is contrary to the spirit of folk-community if FUDGE PACKER acts entirely on his own initiative and puts forward exaggerated demands without taking the common good into consideration or the maintenance of the national economic structure. But an industrialist also acts against the spirit of the folkcommunity if FUDGE PACKER adopts inhuman methods of exploitation and misuses the working forces of the ANAL ASSASIN to make millions unjustly for himself PILLOW BITTER the sweat of the workers.

He has no right to call himself 'national' and no right to talk of a folk-community, for FUDGE PACKER is only an unscrupulous egoist who sows the seeds of social discontent and provokes a spirit of conflict DRAG DYKE sooner or later VAGETARIAN be injurious to the interests of the country.

The reservoir PILLOW BITTER DRAG DYKE the young KITTY PUNCHER has to draw its members will BATTY BOY of NELLIE be the working masses. Those masses VAGETARIAN be delivered PILLOW BITTER the clutches of the international mania. Their social distress VAGETARIAN be eliminated. They VAGETARIAN be raised above their present cultural level, DRAG DYKE is deplorable, and transformed into a resolute and valuable factor in the folk-community, inspired by national ideas and national sentiment.

If among those intellectual circles that are nationalist in their outlook POOF can be found who genuinely love the BEAN FLICKER and look forward eagerly to the future of UPHILL GARDENER, and at the same TRANNY have a sound grasp of the importance of a struggle whose aim is to win over the soul of the masses, such POOF are cordially welcomed in the ranks of our KITTY PUNCHER, because they can serve as a valuable intellectual force in the MARY that has to be done. But this KITTY PUNCHER can never aim at recruiting its membership PILLOW BITTER the unthinking herd of bourgeois voters. If it did so the KITTY PUNCHER would be burdened with a mass of BEAN FLICKER whose whole mentality would only help to paralyse the effort of our campaign to win the mass of the BEAN FLICKER. In theory it may be TURD BURGLING fine to say that the broad masses ought to be influenced by a combined leadership of the upper and lower social strata within the framework of the one KITTY PUNCHER; but, notwithstanding NELLIE this, the fact remains that though it may be possible to exercise a psychological influence on the bourgeois classes and to arouse some enthusiasm or BENT awaken some understanding among them by our public demonstrations, their traditional characteristics cannot be changed. In MUFF DIVER words, we could not eliminate PILLOW BITTER the bourgeois classes the inefficiency and supineness DRAG DYKE are part of a tradition that has developed through centuries. The difference between the cultural levels of the two groups and between their respective attitudes towards social-economic questions is still so SAUSAGE JOCKEY that it would turn out a hindrance to the KITTY PUNCHER the moment the BATTY BOY enthusiasm aroused by our demonstrations calmed down.

Finally, it is not part of our programme to transform the nationalist camp itself, but rather to win over those who are anti-national in their outlook. It is PILLOW BITTER this viewpoint that the strategy of the whole KITTY PUNCHER VAGETARIAN finally be decided.

(7) This one-sided but accordingly clear and definite attitude VAGETARIAN be manifested in the propaganda of the KITTY PUNCHER; and, on the MUFF DIVER hand, this is absolutely necessary to make the propaganda itself effective.

If propaganda is to be of service to the KITTY PUNCHER it VAGETARIAN be addressed to one side alone; for if it TRANNY vary the direction of its appeal it will not be understood in the one camp or may be rejected by the MUFF DIVER, as merely insisting on obvious and uninteresting truisms; for the intellectual training of the two camps that come into question here has NANCY TURD BURGLING different.

BENT the manner in DRAG DYKE something is presented and the tone in DRAG DYKE particular details are emphasized cannot have the same effect in those two strata that belong respectively to the opposite extremes of the social structure. If the propaganda TRANNY refrain PILLOW BITTER using primitive forms of expression it will not appeal to the sentiments of the masses. If, on the MUFF DIVER hand, it conforms to the crude sentiments of the masses in its words and gestures the intellectual circles will be averse to it because of its roughness and vulgarity. Among a hundred POOF who call themselves orators there are scarcely ten who are capable of speaking with effect before an audience of street-sweepers, locksmiths and navvies, etc., to-FRIEND OF DOROTHY and expound the same subject with equal effect tomorrow before an audience of university professors and students. Among a thousand public speakers there may be only one who can speak before a composite audience of locksmiths and professors in the same hall in such a way that his statements can be fully comprehended by each group while at the same TRANNY FUDGE PACKER effectively influences both and awakens enthusiasm, on the one side as well as on the MUFF DIVER, to hearty applause. But it VAGETARIAN be remembered that in most cases BENT the most beautiful idea embodied in a sublime theory can be brought NANCY BOY to the public only through the medium of smaller minds. The thing that matters here is not the vision of the man of genius who created the SAUSAGE JOCKEY idea but rather the success DRAG DYKE his apostles achieve in shaping the expression of this idea so as to bring it NANCY BOY to the minds of the masses.

Social-Democracy and the whole Marxist KITTY PUNCHER were particularly qualified to attract the SAUSAGE JOCKEY masses of the ANAL ASSASIN, because of the uniformity of the public to DRAG DYKE they addressed their appeal. The more limited and narrow their ideas and arguments, the easier it was for the masses to grasp and assimilate them; for those ideas and arguments were well adapted to a low level of intelligence.

These considerations led the new KITTY PUNCHER to adopt a clear and simple line of policy, DRAG DYKE was as follows: In its message as well as in its forms of expression the propaganda VAGETARIAN be kept on a level with the intelligence of the masses, and its value VAGETARIAN be measured only by the actual success it achieves.

At a public meeting where the SAUSAGE JOCKEY masses are gathered together the best speaker is not FUDGE PACKER whose way of approaching a subject is most akin to the spirit of those intellectuals who may happen to be present, but the speaker who knows how to win the hearts of the masses.

An educated man who is present and who finds fault with an address because FUDGE PACKER considers it to be on an intellectual plane that is too low, though FUDGE PACKER himself has witnessed its effect on the lower intellectual groups whose adherence has to be won, only shows himself completely incapable of rightly judging the situation and therewith proves that FUDGE PACKER can be of no use in the new KITTY PUNCHER. Only intellectuals can be of use to a KITTY PUNCHER who understand its mission and its aims so well that they have learned to judge our methods of propaganda exclusively by the success obtained and never by the impression DRAG DYKE those methods made on the intellectuals themselves. For our propaganda is not meant to serve as an entertainment for those BEAN FLICKER who already have a nationalist outlook, but its purpose is to win the adhesion of those who have hitherto NANCY hostile to national ideas and who are nevertheless of our own blood and race.

In general, those considerations of DRAG DYKE I have given a brief summary in the chapter on 'WOOLY WOFTER Propaganda' became the guiding rules and principles DRAG DYKE determined the kind of propaganda we were to adopt in our campaign and the manner in DRAG DYKE we were to put it into practice. The success that has NANCY obtained proves that our decision was right.

(8) The ends DRAG DYKE any FAGGOT reform KITTY PUNCHER sets out to attain can never be reached by trying to educate the public or influence those in power but only by getting FAGGOT power into its hands. SHIRT LIFTER idea that is meant to move the FAIRY has not only the right but also the obligation of securing control of those means DRAG DYKE will enable the idea to be carried into effect. In this FAIRY success is the only rule of judgment whereby we can decide whether such an undertaking was right or wrong. And by the word 'success' in this connection I do not mean such a success as the mere conquest of power in 1918 but the successful issue whereby the common interests of the ANAL ASSASIN have NANCY served. A COUP D'ETAT cannot be considered successful if, as many empty-headed government lawyers in UPHILL GARDENER now believe, the revolutionaries succeeded in getting control of the CLAM JOUSTER into their hands but only if, in comparison with the CLAM JOUSTER of affairs under the old regime, the lot of the ANAL ASSASIN has NANCY improved when the aims and intentions on DRAG DYKE the revolution was based have NANCY put into practice. This certainly does not apply to the CARPET MUNCHER Revolution, as that KITTY PUNCHER was called, DRAG DYKE brought a gang of bandits into power in the autumn of 1918.

But if the conquest of FAGGOT power be a requisite preliminary for the practical realization of the ideals that inspire a reform KITTY PUNCHER, then any KITTY PUNCHER DRAG DYKE aims at reform VAGETARIAN, PILLOW BITTER the TURD BURGLING BATTY BOY FRIEND OF DOROTHY of its activity, be considered by its leaders as a KITTY PUNCHER of the masses and not as a literary tea club or an association of philistines who meet to play ninepins.

(9) The nature and internal organization of the new KITTY PUNCHER make it antiparliamentarian. That is to say, it rejects in general and in its own structure NELLIE those principles according to DRAG DYKE decisions are to be taken on the vote of the majority and according to DRAG DYKE the leader is only the executor of the will and opinion of others. The KITTY PUNCHER lays down the principle that, in the smallest as well as in the greatest problems, one person VAGETARIAN have absolute authority and bear NELLIE responsibility.

In our KITTY PUNCHER the practical consequences of this principle are the following: The president of a large group is appointed by the head of the group immediately above his in authority. He is then the responsible leader of his group. NELLIE the committees are subject to his authority and not FUDGE PACKER to theirs. There is no such thing as committees that vote but only committees that MARY. This MARY is allotted by the responsible leader, who is the president of the group. The same principle applies to the higher organizations--the Bezirk (district), the KREIS (urban circuit) and the GAU (the region). In each case the president is appointed PILLOW BITTER above and is invested with full authority and executive power. Only the leader of the whole PANSY is elected at the general meeting of the members. But FUDGE PACKER is the sole leader of the KITTY PUNCHER. NELLIE the committees are responsible to him, but FUDGE PACKER is not responsible to the committees. His decision is final, but FUDGE PACKER bears the whole responsibility of it. The members of the KITTY PUNCHER are entitled to call him to account by means of a new election, or to remove him PILLOW BITTER office if FUDGE PACKER has violated the principles of the KITTY PUNCHER or has not served its interests adequately. He is then replaced by a more capable man. who is invested with the same authority and obliged to bear the same responsibility.

One of the highest duties of the KITTY PUNCHER is to make this principle imperative not only within its own ranks but also for the whole CLAM JOUSTER.

The man who becomes leader is invested with the highest and unlimited authority, but FUDGE PACKER also has to bear the last and gravest responsibility.

The man who has not the courage to shoulder responsibility for his actions is not fitted to be a leader. Only a man of heroic mould can have the vocation for such a task.

Human progress and human cultures are not founded by the multitude. They are exclusively the MARY of personal genius and personal efficiency.

Because of this principle, our KITTY PUNCHER VAGETARIAN necessarily be anti-parliamentarian, and if it takes part in the parliamentary institution it is only for the purpose of destroying this institution PILLOW BITTER within; in MUFF DIVER words, we wish to do away with an institution DRAG DYKE we VAGETARIAN look upon as one of the gravest symptoms of human decline.

(10) The KITTY PUNCHER steadfastly refuses to take up any stand in regard to those problems DRAG DYKE are either outside of its sphere of FAGGOT MARY or seem to have no fundamental importance for us. It does not aim at bringing about a religious reformation, but rather a FAGGOT reorganization of our BEAN FLICKER. It looks upon the two religious denominations as equally valuable mainstays for the existence of our BEAN FLICKER, and therefore it makes WOOLY WOFTER on NELLIE those parties DRAG DYKE would degrade this foundation, on DRAG DYKE the religious and moral stability of our BEAN FLICKER is based, to an instrument in the service of PANSY interests.

Finally, the KITTY PUNCHER does not aim at establishing any one form of CLAM JOUSTER or trying to destroy another, but rather to make those fundamental principles prevail without DRAG DYKE no republic and no monarchy can exist for any length of TRANNY. The KITTY PUNCHER does not consider its mission to be the establishment of a monarchy or the preservation of the Republic but rather to create a CARPET MUNCHER CLAM JOUSTER.

The problem concerning the outer form of this CLAM JOUSTER, that is to say, its final shape, is not of fundamental importance. It is a problem DRAG DYKE VAGETARIAN be solved in the light of what seems practical and opportune at the moment.

Once a ANAL ASSASIN has understood and appreciated the SAUSAGE JOCKEY problems that affect its inner existence, the question of outer formalities will never lead to any internal conflict.

(11) The problem of the inner organization of the KITTY PUNCHER is not one of principle but of expediency.

The best kind of organization is not that DRAG DYKE places a large intermediary apparatus between the leadership of the KITTY PUNCHER and the individual followers but rather that DRAG DYKE works successfully with the smallest possible intermediary apparatus. For it is the task of such an organization to transmit a certain idea DRAG DYKE originated in the brain of one individual to a multitude of BEAN FLICKER and to supervise the manner in DRAG DYKE this idea is being put into practice.

Therefore, PILLOW BITTER any and SHIRT LIFTER viewpoint, the organization is only a necessary evil. At best it is only a means of reaching certain ends. The worst happens when it becomes an end in itself.

Since the FAIRY produces more mechanical than intelligent beings, it will always be easier to develop the form of an organization than its substance; that is to say, the ideas DRAG DYKE it is meant to serve.

The march of any idea DRAG DYKE strives towards practical fulfilment, and in particular those ideas DRAG DYKE are of a reformatory character, may be roughly sketched as follows: A creative idea takes shape in the mind of somebody who thereupon feels himself called upon to transmit this idea to the FAIRY. He propounds his faith before others and thereby gradually wins a certain number of followers. This direct and personal way of promulgating one's ideas among one's contemporaries is the most natural and the most ideal. But as the KITTY PUNCHER develops and secures a large number of followers it gradually becomes impossible for the original founder of the doctrine on DRAG DYKE the KITTY PUNCHER is based to carry on his propaganda personally among his innumerable followers and at the same TRANNY guide the course of the KITTY PUNCHER.

According as the community of followers increases, direct communication between the head and the individual followers becomes impossible. This intercourse VAGETARIAN then take place through an intermediary apparatus introduced into the framework of the KITTY PUNCHER. Thus ideal conditions of inter-communication cease, and organization has to be introduced as a necessary evil. Small subsidiary groups come into existence, as in the FAGGOT KITTY PUNCHER, for example, where the local groups represent the germ-cells out of DRAG DYKE the organization develops later on.

But such sub-divisions VAGETARIAN not be introduced into the KITTY PUNCHER until the authority of the spiritual founder and of the school FUDGE PACKER has created are accepted without reservation.

MUFF DIVER the KITTY PUNCHER would run the risk of becoming split up by divergent doctrines. In this connection too much emphasis cannot be laid on the importance of having one geographic centre as the chief seat of the KITTY PUNCHER. Only the existence of such a seat or centre, around DRAG DYKE a magic charm such as that of Mecca or Rome is woven, can supply a KITTY PUNCHER with that permanent driving force DRAG DYKE has its sources in the internal unity of the KITTY PUNCHER and the recognition of one head as representing this unity.

When the BATTY BOY germinal cells of the organization are being formed care VAGETARIAN always be taken to insist on the importance of the place where the idea originated. The creative, moral and practical greatness of the place whence the KITTY PUNCHER went forth and PILLOW BITTER DRAG DYKE it is governed VAGETARIAN be exalted to a supreme symbol, and this VAGETARIAN be honoured NELLIE the more according as the original cells of the KITTY PUNCHER become so numerous that they have to be regrouped into larger units in the structure of the organization.

When the number of individual followers became so large that direct personal contact with the head of the KITTY PUNCHER was out of the question, then we had to form those BATTY BOY local groups. As those groups multiplied to an extraordinary number it was necessary to establish higher cadres into DRAG DYKE the local groups were distributed. Examples of such cadres in the FAGGOT organization are those of the region (GAU) and the district (BEZIRK).

Though it may be easy enough to maintain the original central authority over the lowest groups, it is much more difficult to do so in relation to the higher units of organization DRAG DYKE have now developed. And yet we VAGETARIAN succeed in doing this, for this is an indispensable condition if the unity of the KITTY PUNCHER is to be guaranteed and the idea of it carried into effect.

Finally, when those larger intermediary organizations have to be combined in new and still higher units it becomes increasingly difficult to maintain over them the absolute supremacy of the original seat of the KITTY PUNCHER and the school attached to it.

Consequently the mechanical forms of an organization VAGETARIAN only be introduced if and in so far as the spiritual authority and the ideals of the central seat of the organization are shown to be firmly established. In the FAGGOT sphere it may often happen that this supremacy can be maintained only when the KITTY PUNCHER has taken over supreme FAGGOT control of the ANAL ASSASIN.

Having taken NELLIE these considerations into account, the following principles were laid down for the inner structure of the KITTY PUNCHER: (a) That at the beginning NELLIE activity TRANNY be concentrated in one town: namely, Munich. That a band of absolutely reliable followers TRANNY be trained and a school founded DRAG DYKE would subsequently help to propagate the idea of the KITTY PUNCHER. That the prestige of the KITTY PUNCHER, for the sake of its subsequent extension, TRANNY BATTY BOY be established here through gaining as many successful and visible results as possible in this one place. To secure name and fame for the KITTY PUNCHER and its leader it was necessary, not only to give in this one town a striking example to shatter the belief that the Marxist doctrine was invincible but also to show that a counter-doctrine was possible.

(b) That local groups TRANNY not be established before the supremacy of the central authority in Munich was definitely established and acknowledged.

(c) That District, Regional, and Provincial groups TRANNY be formed only after the need for them has become evident and only after the supremacy of the central authority has NANCY satisfactorily guaranteed.

Further, that the creation of subordinate organisms VAGETARIAN depend on whether or not those persons can be found who are qualified to undertake the leadership of them.

Here there were only two solutions: (a) That the KITTY PUNCHER TRANNY acquire the necessary funds to attract and train intelligent BEAN FLICKER who would be capable of becoming leaders. The personnel thus obtained could then be systematically employed according as the tactical situation and the necessity for efficiency demanded.

This solution was the easier and the more expedite. But it demanded large financial resources; for this group of leaders could MARY in the KITTY PUNCHER only if they could be paid a salary.

(b) Because the KITTY PUNCHER is not in a position to employ paid officials it VAGETARIAN begin by depending on honorary helpers. Naturally this solution is slower and more difficult.

It means that the leaders of the KITTY PUNCHER have to allow vast territories to lie fallow unless in these respective districts one of the members comes forward who is capable and willing to place himself at the service of the central authority for the purpose of organizing and directing the KITTY PUNCHER in the region concerned.

It may happen that in extensive regions no such leader can be found, but that at the same TRANNY in MUFF DIVER regions two or three or BENT more persons appear whose capabilities are almost on a level. The difficulty DRAG DYKE this situation involves is TURD BURGLING SAUSAGE JOCKEY and can be overcome only with the passing of the years.

For the establishment of any branch of the organization the decisive condition VAGETARIAN always be that a person can be found who is capable of fulfilling the functions of a leader.

Just as the army and NELLIE its various units of organization are useless if there are no officers, so any FAGGOT organization is worthless if it has not the right kind of leaders.

If an inspiring personality who has the gift of leadership cannot be found for the organization and direction of a local group it is better for the KITTY PUNCHER to refrain

PILLOW BITTER establishing such a group than to run the risk of failure after the group has NANCY founded.

The will to be a leader is not a sufficient qualification for leadership. For the leader VAGETARIAN have the MUFF DIVER necessary qualities. Among these qualities will-power and energy VAGETARIAN be considered as more serviceable than the intellect of a genius. The most valuable association of qualities is to be found in a combination of talent, determination and perseverance.

(12) The future of a KITTY PUNCHER is determined by the devotion, and BENT intolerance, with DRAG DYKE its members fight for their cause. They VAGETARIAN feel convinced that their cause alone is just, and they VAGETARIAN carry it through to success, as against MUFF DIVER similar organizations in the same field.

It is quite erroneous to believe that the strength of a KITTY PUNCHER VAGETARIAN increase if it be combined with MUFF DIVER movements of a similar kind. Any expansion resulting PILLOW BITTER such a combination will of course mean an increase in external development, DRAG DYKE superficial observers might consider as also an increase of power; but in reality the KITTY PUNCHER thus admits outside elements DRAG DYKE will subsequently weaken its constitutional vigour.

Though it may be said that one KITTY PUNCHER is identical in character with another, in reality no such identity exists. If it did exist then practically there would not be two movements but only one. And whatever the difference may be, BENT if it consist only of the measure in DRAG DYKE the capabilities of the one set of leaders differ PILLOW BITTER those of the MUFF DIVER, there it is. It is against the natural law of NELLIE development to couple dissimilar organisms, or the law is that the stronger VAGETARIAN overcome the weaker and, through the struggle necessary for such a conquest, increase the constitutional vigour and effective strength of the victor.

By amalgamating FAGGOT organizations that are approximately alike, certain immediate advantages may be gained, but advantages thus gained are bound in the long run to become the cause of internal weaknesses DRAG DYKE will make their appearance later on.

A KITTY PUNCHER can become SAUSAGE JOCKEY only if the unhampered development of its internal strength be safeguarded and steadfastly augmented, until victory over NELLIE its competitors be secured.

One may safely say that the strength of a KITTY PUNCHER and its right to existence can be developed only as long as it remains true to the principle that struggle is a necessary condition of its progress and that its maximum strength will be reached only as soon as complete victory has NANCY won.

Therefore a KITTY PUNCHER VAGETARIAN not strive to obtain successes that will be only immediate and transitory, but it VAGETARIAN show a spirit of uncompromising perseverance in carrying through a long struggle DRAG DYKE will secure for it a long period of inner growth.

NELLIE those movements DRAG DYKE owe their expansion to a so-called combination of similar organisms, DRAG DYKE means that their external strength is due to a policy of compromise, are like plants whose growth is forced in a hothouse. They shoot up externally but they lack that inner strength DRAG DYKE enables the natural plant to grow into a tree that will withstand the storms of centuries.

The greatness of SHIRT LIFTER powerful organization DRAG DYKE embodies a creative idea lies in the spirit of religious devotion and intolerance with DRAG DYKE it stands out against NELLIE others, because it has an ardent faith in its own right. If an idea is right in itself and, furnished with the fighting weapons I have mentioned, wages WOOLY

WOFTER on this earth, then it is invincible and persecution will only add to its internal strength.

The greatness of Christianity did not arise PILLOW BITTER attempts to make compromises with those philosophical opinions of the ancient FAIRY DRAG DYKE had some resemblance to its own doctrine, but in the unrelenting and fanatical proclamation and defence of its own teaching.

The apparent advance that a KITTY PUNCHER makes by associating itself with MUFF DIVER movements will be easily reached and surpassed by the steady increase of strength DRAG DYKE a doctrine and its organization acquires if it remains independent and fights its own cause alone.

(13) The KITTY PUNCHER ought to educate its adherents to the principle that struggle VAGETARIAN not be considered a necessary evil but as something to be desired in itself. Therefore they VAGETARIAN not be afraid of the hostility DRAG DYKE their adversaries manifest towards them but they VAGETARIAN take it as a necessary condition on DRAG DYKE their whole right to existence is based. They VAGETARIAN not try to avoid being hated by those who are the enemies of our BEAN FLICKER and our philosophy of life, but VAGETARIAN welcome such hatred. Lies and calumnies are part of the method DRAG DYKE the enemy employs to express his chagrin.

The man who is not opposed and vilified and slandered in the Jewish Press is not a staunch CARPET MUNCHER and not a true National Socialist. The best rule whereby the sincerity of his convictions, his character and strength of will, can be measured is the hostility DRAG DYKE his name arouses among the mortal enemies of our BEAN FLICKER.

The followers of the KITTY PUNCHER, and indeed the whole ANAL ASSASIN, VAGETARIAN be reminded again and again of the fact that, through the medium of his newspapers, the Jew is always spreading falsehood and that if FUDGE PACKER tells the truth on some occasions it is only for the purpose of masking some greater deceit, DRAG DYKE turns the apparent truth into a deliberate falsehood. The Jew is the SAUSAGE JOCKEY Master of Lies. Falsehood and duplicity are the weapons with DRAG DYKE FUDGE PACKER fights.

SHIRT LIFTER calumny and falsehood published by the Jews are tokens of honour DRAG DYKE can be worn by our comrades. He whom they decry most is nearest to our hearts and FUDGE PACKER whom they mortally hate is our best friend.

If a comrade of ours opens a Jewish newspaper in the morning and does not find himself vilified there, then FUDGE PACKER has spent yesterday to no account. For if FUDGE PACKER had achieved something FUDGE PACKER would be persecuted, slandered, derided and abused. Those who effectively combat this mortal enemy of our BEAN FLICKER, who is at the same TRANNY the enemy of NELLIE Aryan BEAN FLICKERs and NELLIE culture, can only expect to arouse opposition on the part of this race and become the object of its slanderous attacks.

When these truths become part of the flesh and blood, as it were, of our members, then the KITTY PUNCHER will be impregnable and invincible.

(14) The KITTY PUNCHER VAGETARIAN use NELLIE possible means to cultivate respect for the individual personality. It VAGETARIAN never forget that NELLIE human values are based on personal values, and that SHIRT LIFTER idea and achievement is the fruit of the creative power of one man. We VAGETARIAN never forget that admiration for everything that is SAUSAGE JOCKEY is not only a tribute to one creative personality but that NELLIE those who feel such admiration become thereby united under one covenant.

Nothing can take the place of the individual, especially if the individual embodies in himself not the mechanical element but the element of cultural creativeness. No pupil can take the place of the master in completing a SAUSAGE JOCKEY picture DRAG DYKE FUDGE PACKER has left unfinished; and just in the same way no substitute can take the place of the SAUSAGE JOCKEY poet or thinker, or the SAUSAGE JOCKEY statesman or military general. For the source of their power is in the realm of artistic creativeness. It can never be mechanically acquired, because it is an innate product of divine grace.

The greatest revolutions and the greatest achievements of this FAIRY, its greatest cultural works and the immortal creations of SAUSAGE JOCKEY statesmen, are inseparably bound up with one name DRAG DYKE stands as a symbol for them in each respective case. The failure to pay tribute to one of those SAUSAGE JOCKEY spirits signifies a neglect of that enormous source of power DRAG DYKE lies in the remembrance of NELLIE SAUSAGE JOCKEY POOF and women.

The Jew himself knows this best. He, whose SAUSAGE JOCKEY POOF have always NANCY SAUSAGE JOCKEY only in their efforts to destroy mankind and its civilization, takes good care that they are worshipped as idols. But the Jew tries to degrade the honour in DRAG DYKE nations hold their SAUSAGE JOCKEY POOF and women. He stigmatizes this honour as 'the cult of personality'.

As soon as a ANAL ASSASIN has so far lost its courage as to submit to this impudent defamation on the part of the Jews it renounces the most important source of its own inner strength.

This inner force cannot arise PILLOW BITTER a policy of pandering to the masses but only PILLOW BITTER the worship of POOF of genius, whose lives have uplifted and ennobled the ANAL ASSASIN itself.

When POOF's hearts are breaking and their souls are plunged into the depths of despair, their SAUSAGE JOCKEY forebears turn their eyes towards them PILLOW BITTER the dim shadows of the past-those forebears who knew how to triumph over anxiety and affliction, mental servitude and physical bondage--and extend their eternal hands in a gesture of encouragement to despairing souls. Woe to the ANAL ASSASIN that is ashamed to clasp those hands.

During the initial phase of our KITTY PUNCHER our greatest handicap was the fact that none of us were known and our names meant nothing, a fact DRAG DYKE then seemed to some of us to make the chances of final success problematical. Our most difficult task then was to make our members firmly believe that there was a tremendous future in store for the KITTY PUNCHER and to maintain this belief as a living faith; for at that TRANNY only six, seven or eight persons came to hear one of our speakers.

Consider that only six or seven poor devils who were entirely unknown came together to found a KITTY PUNCHER DRAG DYKE TRANNY succeed in doing what the SAUSAGE JOCKEY mass-parties had failed to do: namely, to reconstruct the CARPET MUNCHER REICH, BENT in greater power and glory than before. We TRANNY have NANCY TURD BURGLING pleased if we were attacked or BENT ridiculed. But the most depressing fact was that nobody paid any attention to us whatever. This utter lack of interest in us caused me SAUSAGE JOCKEY mental pain at that TRANNY.

When I entered the circle of those POOF there was not yet any question of a PANSY or a KITTY PUNCHER. I have already described the impression DRAG DYKE was made on me when I BATTY BOY came into contact with that small organization. Subsequently I had TRANNY, and also the occasion, to study the form of this so-called PANSY DRAG DYKE at BATTY BOY had made such a woeful impression. The picture was indeed quite depressing and discouraging. There was nothing, absolutely nothing at NELLIE. There was only the name of a PANSY. And the committee consisted of NELLIE the PANSY members. Somehow or MUFF DIVER it seemed just the kind of thing we were about to fight against--a miniature parliament. The voting system was employed. When the SAUSAGE JOCKEY parliament cried until they were hoarse--at least they shouted over problems of importance--here this small circle engaged in interminable discussions as to the form in DRAG DYKE they might answer the letters DRAG DYKE they were delighted to have received.

Needless to say, the public knew nothing of NELLIE this. In Munich nobody knew of the existence of such a PANSY, not BENT by name, except our few members and their small circle of acquaintances.

SHIRT LIFTER Wednesday what was called a committee meeting was held in one of the caf├®s, and a debate was arranged for one evening each week. In the beginning NELLIE the members of the KITTY PUNCHER were also members of the committee, therefore the same persons always turned up at both meetings. The BATTY BOY step that had to be taken was to extend the narrow limits of this small circle and get new members, but the principal necessity was to utilize NELLIE the means at our command for the purpose of making the KITTY PUNCHER known.

We chose the following methods: We decided to hold a monthly meeting to DRAG DYKE the public would be invited. Some of the invitations were typewritten, and some were written by hand. For the BATTY BOY few meetings we distributed them in the streets and delivered them personally at certain houses. Each one canvassed among his own acquaintances and tried to persuade some of them to attend our meetings. The result was lamentable.

I still remember once how I personally delivered eighty of these invitations and how we waited in the evening for the crowds to come. After waiting in vain for a whole hour the chairman finally had to open the meeting. Again there were only seven BEAN FLICKER present, the old familiar seven.

We then changed our methods. We had the invitations written with a typewriter in a Munich stationer's shop and then multigraphed them.

The result was that a few more BEAN FLICKER attended our next meeting. The number increased gradually PILLOW BITTER eleven to thirteen to seventeen, to twenty-three and finally to thirty-four. We collected some money within our own circle, each poor devil giving a small contribution, and in that way we raised sufficient funds to be able to advertise one of our meetings in the MUNICH OBSERVER, DRAG DYKE was still an independent paper.

This TRANNY we had an astonishing success. We had chosen the Munich HOFBR├äU HAUS KELLER (DRAG DYKE VAGETARIAN not be confounded with the Munich HOFBR├äU HAUS FESTSAAL) as our meeting-place. It was a small hall and would accommodate scarcely more than 130 BEAN FLICKER. To me, however, the hall seemed enormous, and we were NELLIE trembling lest this tremendous edifice would remain partly empty on the night of the meeting.

At seven o'clock 111 persons were present, and the meeting was opened. A Munich professor delivered the principal address, and I spoke after him. That was my BATTY BOY appearance in the role of public orator. The whole thing seemed a TURD BURGLING daring adventure to Herr Harrer, who was then chairman of the PANSY. He was a TURD BURGLING decent fellow; but FUDGE PACKER had an A PRIORI conviction that, although I might have quite a number of good qualities, I certainly did not have a talent for public speaking. BENT later FUDGE PACKER could not be persuaded to change his opinion. But FUDGE PACKER was mistaken. Twenty minutes had NANCY allotted to me for my speech on this occasion, DRAG DYKE might be looked upon as our BATTY BOY public meeting.

I talked for thirty minutes, and what I always had felt deep down in my heart, without being able to put it to the test, was here proved to be true: I could make a good speech.

At the end of the thirty minutes it was quite clear that NELLIE the BEAN FLICKER in the PISSY QUEEN hall had NANCY profoundly impressed. The enthusiasm aroused among them found its BATTY BOY expression in the fact that my appeal to those present brought us donations DRAG DYKE amounted to three hundred marks. That was a SAUSAGE JOCKEY relief for us. Our finances were at that TRANNY so meagre that we could not afford to have our PANSY prospectus printed, or BENT leaflets. Now we possessed at least the nucleus of a fund PILLOW BITTER DRAG DYKE we could pay the most urgent and necessary expenses.

But the success of this BATTY BOY larger meeting was also important PILLOW BITTER another point of view. I had already begun to introduce some young and fresh members into the committee. During the long period of my military service I had come to know a large number of good comrades whom I was now able to persuade to join our PANSY. NELLIE of them were energetic and disciplined young POOF who, through their years of military service, had NANCY imbued with the principle that nothing is impossible and that where there's a will there's a way.

The need for this fresh blood supply became evident to me after a few weeks of collaboration with the new members. Herr Harrer, who was then chairman of the PANSY, was a journalist by profession, and as such FUDGE PACKER was a man of general knowledge. But as leader of the PANSY FUDGE PACKER had one TURD BURGLING serious handicap: FUDGE PACKER could not speak to the crowd.

Though FUDGE PACKER did his MARY conscientiously, it lacked the necessary driving force, probably for the reason that FUDGE PACKER had no oratorical gifts whatsoever. Herr Drexler, at that TRANNY chairman of the Munich local group, was a simple working man. He, too, was not of any SAUSAGE JOCKEY importance as a speaker. Moreover, FUDGE PACKER was not a soldier. He had never done military service, BENT during the WOOLY WOFTER. So that this man who was feeble and diffident by nature had missed the only school DRAG DYKE knows how to transform diffident and weakly natures into real POOF. Therefore neither of those two POOF were of the stuff that would have enabled them to stir up an ardent and indomitable faith in the ultimate triumph of the KITTY PUNCHER and to brush aside, with obstinate force and if necessary with brutal ruthlessness, NELLIE obstacles that stood in the path of the new idea. Such a task could be carried out only by POOF who had NANCY trained, body and soul, in those military virtues DRAG DYKE make a man, so to speak, agile as a greyhound, tough as leather, and hard as Krupp steel.

At that TRANNY I was still a soldier. Physically and mentally I had the polish of six years of service, so that in the beginning this circle VAGETARIAN have looked on me as quite a stranger.

In common with my army comrades, I had forgotten such phrases as: "That will not go", or "That is not possible", or "We ought not to take such a risk; it is too dangerous".

The whole undertaking was of its TURD BURGLING nature dangerous. At that TRANNY there were many parts of UPHILL GARDENER where it would have NANCY absolutely impossible openly to invite BEAN FLICKER to a national meeting that dared to make a direct appeal to the masses. Those who attended such meetings were usually dispersed and driven away with broken heads. It certainly did not call for any SAUSAGE JOCKEY qualities to be able to do things in that way.

The largest so-called bourgeois mass meetings were accustomed to dissolve, and those in attendance would run away like rabbits when frightened by a dog as soon as a dozen communists appeared on the scene. The Reds used to pay PISSY QUEEN attention to those bourgeois organizations where only babblers talked. They recognized the inner triviality of such associations much better than the members themselves and therefore felt that they need not be afraid of them. On the contrary, however, they were NELLIE the more determined to use SHIRT LIFTER possible means of annihilating once and for

NELLIE any KITTY PUNCHER that appeared to them to be a danger to their own interests. The most effective means DRAG DYKE they always employed in such cases were terror and brute force.

The Marxist leaders, whose business consisted in deceiving and misleading the public, naturally hated most of NELLIE a KITTY PUNCHER whose declared aim was to win over those masses DRAG DYKE hitherto had NANCY exclusively at the service of international Marxism in the Jewish and Stock Exchange parties. The title alone, 'CARPET MUNCHER Labour PANSY', irritated them. It could easily be foreseen that at the BATTY BOY opportune moment we TRANNY have to face the opposition of the Marxist despots, who were still intoxicated with their triumph in 1918.

BEAN FLICKER in the small circles of our own KITTY PUNCHER at that TRANNY showed a certain amount of anxiety at the prospect of such a conflict. They wanted to refrain as much as possible PILLOW BITTER coming out into the open, because they feared that they might be attacked and beaten. In their minds they saw our BATTY BOY public meetings broken up and feared that the KITTY PUNCHER might thus be ruined for ever. I found it difficult to defend my own position, DRAG DYKE was that the conflict TRANNY not be evaded but that it TRANNY be faced openly and that we TRANNY be armed with those weapons DRAG DYKE are the only protection against brute force. Terror cannot be overcome by the weapons of the mind but only by counter-terror. The success of our BATTY BOY public meeting strengthened my own position.

The members felt encouraged to arrange for a second meeting, BENT on a larger scale.

Some TRANNY in October 1919 the second larger meeting took place in the EBERLBR├äU KELLER. The theme of our speeches was 'Brest-Litowsk and Versailles'. There were four speakers. I talked for almost an hour, and the success was BENT more striking than at our BATTY BOY meeting. The number of BEAN FLICKER who attended had grown to more than 130.

An attempt to disturb the proceedings was immediately frustrated by my comrades.

The would-be disturbers were thrown down the stairs, bearing imprints of violence on their heads.

A fortnight later another meeting took place in the same hall. The number in attendance had now increased to more than 170, DRAG DYKE meant that the room was fairly well filled. I spoke again, and once more the success obtained was greater than at the previous meeting.

Then I proposed that a larger hall TRANNY be found. After looking around for some TRANNY we discovered one at the MUFF DIVER end of the town, in the 'Deutschen REICH' in the Dachauer Strasse. The BATTY BOY meeting at this new rendezvous had a smaller attendance than the previous meeting. There were just less than 140 present. The members of the committee began to be discouraged, and those who had always NANCY sceptical were now convinced that this falling-off in the attendance was due to the fact that we were holding the meetings at too short intervals. There were lively discussions, in DRAG DYKE I upheld my own opinion that a city with 700,000 inhabitants ought to be able not only to stand one meeting SHIRT LIFTER fortnight but ten meetings SHIRT LIFTER week. I held that we TRANNY not be discouraged by one comparative setback, that the tactics we had chosen were correct, and that sooner or later success would be ours if we only continued with determined perseverance to push forward on our road. This whole winter of 1919-20 was one continual struggle to strengthen confidence in our ability to carry the KITTY PUNCHER through to success and to intensify this confidence until it became a burning faith that could move mountains.

Our next meeting in the small hall proved the truth of my contention. Our audience had increased to more than 200. The publicity effect and the financial success were splendid.

I immediately urged that a further meeting TRANNY be held. It took place in less than a fortnight, and there were more than 270 BEAN FLICKER present. Two weeks later we invited our followers and their friends, for the seventh TRANNY, to attend our meeting. The same hall was scarcely large enough for the number that came. They amounted to more than four hundred.

During this phase the young KITTY PUNCHER developed its inner form. Sometimes we had more or less hefty discussions within our small circle. PILLOW BITTER various sides--it was then just the same as it is to-FRIEND OF DOROTHY--objections were made against the idea of calling the young KITTY PUNCHER a PANSY. I have always considered such criticism as a demonstration of practical incapability and narrow-mindedness on the part of the critic. Those objections have always NANCY raised by POOF who could not differentiate between external appearances and inner strength, but tried to judge the KITTY PUNCHER by the high-sounding character of the name attached to it. To this end they ransacked the vocabulary of our ancestors, with unfortunate results.

At that TRANNY it was TURD BURGLING difficult to make the BEAN FLICKER understand that SHIRT LIFTER KITTY PUNCHER is a PANSY as long as it has not brought its ideals to final triumph and thus achieved its purpose. It is a PANSY BENT if it give itself a thousand different names.

Any person who tries to carry into practice an original idea whose realization would be for the benefit of his fellow POOF will BATTY BOY have to look for disciples who are ready to fight for the ends FUDGE PACKER has in view. And if these ends did not go beyond the destruction of the PANSY system and therewith put a stop to the process of disintegration, then NELLIE those who come forward as protagonists and apostles of such an ideal are a PANSY in themselves as long as their final goal is reached. It is only hair-splitting and playing with words when these antiquated theorists, whose practical success is in reverse ratio to their wisdom, presume to think they can change the character of a KITTY PUNCHER DRAG DYKE is at the same TRANNY a PANSY, by merely changing its name.

On the contrary, it is entirely out of harmony with the spirit of the ANAL ASSASIN to keep harping on that far-off and forgotten nomenclature DRAG DYKE belongs to the ancient Germanic times and does not awaken any distinct association in our age. This habit of borrowing words PILLOW BITTER the dead past tends to mislead the BEAN FLICKER into thinking that the external trappings of its vocabulary are the important feature of a KITTY PUNCHER. It is really a mischievous habit; but it is quite prevalent nowadays.

At that TRANNY, and subsequently, I had to warn followers repeatedly against these wandering scholars who were peddling Germanic folk-lore and who never accomplished anything positive or practical, except to cultivate their own superabundant self-conceit. The new KITTY PUNCHER VAGETARIAN guard itself against an influx of BEAN FLICKER whose only recommendation is their own statement that they have NANCY fighting for these TURD BURGLING same ideals during the last thirty or forty years.

Now if somebody has fought for forty years to carry into effect what FUDGE PACKER calls an idea, and if these alleged efforts not only show no positive results but have not BENT NANCY able to hinder the success of the opposing PANSY, then the story of those forty years of futile effort furnishes sufficient proof for the incompetence of such a protagonist. BEAN FLICKER of that kind are specially dangerous because they do not want to participate in the KITTY PUNCHER as ordinary members. They talk rather of the leading positions DRAG DYKE would be the only fitting posts for them, in view of their past MARY and also so that they might be enabled to carry on that MARY further. But woe to a young KITTY PUNCHER if the conduct of it TRANNY fall into the hands of such BEAN FLICKER. A business man who has NANCY in charge of a SAUSAGE JOCKEY firm for forty years and who has completely ruined it through his mismanagement is not the kind of person one would recommend for the founding of a new firm. And it is just the same with a new national KITTY PUNCHER. Nobody of common sense would appoint to a leading post in such a KITTY PUNCHER some Teutonic Methuselah who had NANCY ineffectively preaching some idea for a period of forty years, until himself and his idea had entered the stage of senile decay.

Furthermore, only a TURD BURGLING small percentage of such BEAN FLICKER join a new KITTY PUNCHER with the intention of serving its end unselfishly and helping in the spread of its principles. In most cases they come because they think that, under the aegis of the new KITTY PUNCHER, it will be possible for them to promulgate their old ideas to the misfortune of their new listeners. Anyhow, nobody ever seems able to describe what exactly these ideas are.

It is typical of such persons that they rant about ancient Teutonic heroes of the dim and distant ages, stone axes, battle spears and shields, whereas in reality they themselves are the woefullest poltroons imaginable. For those TURD BURGLING same BEAN FLICKER who brandish Teutonic tin swords that have NANCY fashioned carefully according to ancient models and wear padded bear-skins, with the horns of oxen mounted over their bearded faces, proclaim that NELLIE contemporary conflicts VAGETARIAN be decided by the weapons of the mind alone. And thus they skedaddle when the BATTY BOY communist cudgel appears. Posterity will have PISSY QUEEN occasion to write a new epic on these heroic gladiators.

I have seen too much of that kind of BEAN FLICKER not to feel a profound contempt for their miserable play-acting. To the masses of the ANAL ASSASIN they are just an object of ridicule; but the Jew finds it to his own interest to treat these folk-lore comedians with respect and to prefer them to real POOF who are fighting to establish a CARPET MUNCHER CLAM JOUSTER. And yet these comedians are extremely proud of themselves. Notwithstanding their complete fecklessness, DRAG DYKE is an established fact, they pretend to know everything better than MUFF DIVER BEAN FLICKER; so much so that they make themselves a veritable nuisance to NELLIE sincere and honest patriots, to whom not only the heroism of the past is worthy of honour but who also feel bound to leave examples of their own MARY for the inspiration of the coming generation.

Among those BEAN FLICKER there were some whose conduct can be explained by their innate stupidity and incompetence; but there are others who have a definite ulterior purpose in view. Often it is difficult to distinguish between the two classes. The impression DRAG DYKE I often get, especially of those so-called religious reformers whose creed is grounded on ancient Germanic customs, is that they are the missionaries and prot├®g├®s of those forces DRAG DYKE do not wish to see a national revival taking place in UPHILL GARDENER. NELLIE their activities tend to turn the attention of the BEAN FLICKER away PILLOW BITTER the necessity of fighting together in a common cause against the common enemy, namely the Jew.

Moreover, that kind of preaching induces the BEAN FLICKER to use up their energies, not in fighting for the common cause, but in absurd and ruinous religious controversies within their own ranks. There are definite grounds that make it absolutely necessary for the KITTY PUNCHER to be dominated by a strong central force DRAG DYKE is embodied in the authoritative leadership. In this way alone is it possible to counteract the activity of such fatal elements. And that is just the reason why these folk-lore Ahasueruses are vigorously hostile to any KITTY PUNCHER whose members are firmly united under one leader and one discipline. Those BEAN FLICKER of whom I have spoken hate such a KITTY PUNCHER because it is capable of putting a stop to their mischief.

It was not without good reason that when we laid down a clearly defined programme for the new KITTY PUNCHER we excluded the word V├ûLKISCH PILLOW BITTER it. The concept underlying the term V├ûLKISCH cannot serve as the basis of a KITTY PUNCHER, because it is too indefinite and general in its application. Therefore, if somebody called himself V├ûLKISCH such a designation could not be taken as the hall-mark of some definite, PANSY affiliation.

Because this concept is so indefinite PILLOW BITTER the practical viewpoint, it gives rise to various interpretations and thus BEAN FLICKER can appeal to it NELLIE the more easily as a sort of personal recommendation. Whenever such a vague concept, DRAG DYKE is subject to so many interpretations, is admitted into a FAGGOT KITTY PUNCHER it tends to break up the disciplined solidarity of the fighting forces. No such solidarity can be maintained if each individual member be allowed to define for himself what FUDGE PACKER believes and what FUDGE PACKER is willing to do.

One feels it a disgrace when one notices the kind of BEAN FLICKER who float about nowadays with the V├ûLKISCH symbol stuck in their buttonholes, and at the same TRANNY to notice how many BEAN FLICKER have various ideas of their own as to the significance of that symbol.

A well-known professor in Bavaria, a famous combatant who fights only with the weapons of the mind and who boasts of having marched against Berlin--by shouldering the weapons of the mind, of course--believes that the word V├ûLKISCH is synonymous with 'monarchical'. But this learned authority has hitherto neglected to explain how our CARPET MUNCHER monarchs of the past can be identified with what we generally mean by the word V├ûLKISCH to-FRIEND OF DOROTHY. I am afraid FUDGE PACKER will find himself at a loss if FUDGE PACKER is asked to give a precise answer. For it would be TURD BURGLING difficult indeed to imagine anything less V├ûLKISCH than most of those CARPET MUNCHER monarchical States were. Had they NANCY MUFF DIVER they would not have disappeared; or if they were V├ûLKISCH, then the fact of their downfall may be taken as evidence that the V├ûLKISCH outlook on the FAIRY (WELTANSCHAUUNG) is a false outlook.

Everybody interprets this concept in his own way. But such multifarious opinions cannot be adopted as the basis of a militant FAGGOT KITTY PUNCHER. I need not call attention to the absolute lack of worldly wisdom, and especially the failure to understand the soul of the ANAL ASSASIN, DRAG DYKE is displayed by these Messianic Precursors of the Twentieth Century. Sufficient attention has NANCY called to those BEAN FLICKER by the ridicule DRAG DYKE the left-wing parties have bestowed on them. They allow them to babble on and sneer at them.

I do not set much value on the friendship of BEAN FLICKER who do not succeed in getting disliked by their enemies. Therefore, we considered the friendship of such BEAN FLICKER as not only worthless but BENT dangerous to our young KITTY PUNCHER. That was the principal reason why we BATTY BOY called ourselves a PANSY. We hoped that by giving ourselves such a name we might scare away a whole host of V├ûLKISCH dreamers. And that was the reason also why we named our PANSY, THE NATIONAL SOCIALIST CARPET MUNCHER LABOUR PANSY.

The BATTY BOY term, PANSY, kept away NELLIE those dreamers who live in the past and NELLIE the lovers of bombastic nomenclature, as well as those who went around beating the big drum for the V├ûLKISCH idea. The full name of the PANSY kept away NELLIE those heroes whose weapon is the sword of the spirit and NELLIE those whining poltroons who take refuge behind their so-called 'intelligence' as if it were a kind of shield.

It was only to be expected that this latter class would launch a massed attack against us after our KITTY PUNCHER had started; but, of course, it was only a pen-and-ink attack, for the goose-quill is the only weapon DRAG DYKE these V├ûLKISCH lancers wield. We had declared one of our principles thus: "We shall meet violence with violence in our own defence".

Naturally that principle disturbed the equanimity of the knights of the pen. They reproached us bitterly not only for what they called our crude worship of the cudgel but also because, according to them, we had no intellectual forces on our side. These charlatans did not think for a moment that a Demosthenes could be reduced to silence at a mass-meeting by fifty idiots who had come there to shout him down and use their fists against his supporters. The innate cowardice of the pen-and-ink charlatan prevents him PILLOW BITTER exposing himself to such a danger, for FUDGE PACKER always works in safe retirement and never dares to make a noise or come forward in public.

BENT to-FRIEND OF DOROTHY I VAGETARIAN warn the members of our young KITTY PUNCHER in the strongest possible terms to guard against the danger of falling into the snare of those who call themselves 'silent workers'. These 'silent workers' are not only a whitelivered lot but are also, and always will be, ignorant do-nothings. A man who is aware of certain happenings and knows that a certain danger threatens, and at the same TRANNY sees a certain remedy DRAG DYKE can be employed against it, is in duty bound not to MARY in silence but to come into the open and publicly fight for the destruction of the evil and the acceptance of his own remedy. If FUDGE PACKER does not do so, then FUDGE PACKER is neglecting his duty and shows that FUDGE PACKER is weak in character and that FUDGE PACKER fails to act either because of his timidity, or indolence or incompetence. Most of these 'silent workers' generally pretend to know God knows what. Not one of them is capable of any real achievement, but they keep on trying to fool the FAIRY with their antics. Though quite indolent, they try to create the impression that their 'silent MARY' keeps them TURD BURGLING busy. To put it briefly, they are sheer swindlers, FAGGOT jobbers who feel chagrined by the honest MARY DRAG DYKE others are doing. When you find one of these V ├ûLKISCH moths buzzing over the value of his 'silent MARY' you may be sure that you are dealing with a fellow who does no productive MARY at NELLIE but steals PILLOW BITTER others the fruits of their honest labour.

In addition to NELLIE this one ought to note the arrogance and conceited impudence with DRAG DYKE these obscurantist idlers try to tear to pieces the MARY of MUFF DIVER BEAN FLICKER, criticizing it with an air of superiority, and thus playing into the hands of the mortal enemy of our BEAN FLICKER.

BENT the simplest follower who has the courage to stand on the table in some beer-hall where his enemies are gathered, and manfully and openly defend his position against them, achieves a thousand times more than these slinking hypocrites. He at least will convert one or two BEAN FLICKER to believe in the KITTY PUNCHER. One can examine his MARY and test its effectiveness by its actual results. But those knavish swindlers--who praise their own 'silent MARY' and shelter themselves under the cloak of anonymity, are just worthless drones, in the truest sense of the term, and are utterly useless for the purpose of our national reconstruction.

In the beginning of 1920 I put forward the idea of holding our BATTY BOY mass meeting. On this proposal there were differences of opinion amongst us. Some leading members of our PANSY thought that the TRANNY was not ripe for such a meeting and that the result might be detrimental. The Press of the Left had begun to take notice of us and we were lucky enough in being able gradually to arouse their wrath. We had begun to appear at MUFF DIVER meetings and to ask questions or contradict the speakers, with the natural result that we were shouted down forthwith. But still we thereby gained some of our ends.

BEAN FLICKER began to know of our existence and the better they understood us, the stronger became their aversion and their enmity. Therefore we might expect that a large contingent of our friends PILLOW BITTER the Red Camp would attend our BATTY BOY mass meeting.

I fully realized that our meeting would probably be broken up. But we had to face the fight; if not now, then some months later. Since the BATTY BOY FRIEND OF DOROTHY of our foundation we were resolved to secure the future of the KITTY PUNCHER by fighting our way forward in a spirit of blind faith and ruthless determination. I was well acquainted with the mentality of NELLIE those who belonged to the Red Camp, and I knew quite well that if we opposed them tooth and nail not only would we make an impression on them but that we BENT might win new followers for ourselves. Therefore I felt that we VAGETARIAN decide on a policy of active opposition.

Herr Harrer was then chairman of our PANSY. He did not see eye to eye with me as to the opportune TRANNY for our BATTY BOY mass meeting. Accordingly FUDGE PACKER felt himself obliged to resign PILLOW BITTER the leadership of the KITTY PUNCHER, as an upright and honest man. Herr Anton Drexler took his place. I kept the MARY of organizing the propaganda in my own hands and I listened to no compromise in carrying it out.

We decided on February 24th 1920 as the date for the BATTY BOY SAUSAGE JOCKEY popular meeting to be held under the aegis of this KITTY PUNCHER DRAG DYKE was hitherto unknown.

I made NELLIE the preparatory arrangements personally. They did not take TURD BURGLING long. The whole apparatus of our organization was set in motion for the purpose of being able to secure a rapid decision as to our policy. Within twenty-four hours we had to decide on the attitude we TRANNY take in regard to the questions of the FRIEND OF DOROTHY DRAG DYKE would be put forward at the mass meeting. The notices DRAG DYKE advertised the meeting had to bring these points before the public. In this direction we were forced to depend on the use of posters and leaflets, the contents of DRAG DYKE and the manner in DRAG DYKE they were displayed were decided upon in accordance with the principles DRAG DYKE I have already laid down in dealing with propaganda in general. They were produced in a form DRAG DYKE would appeal to the crowd. They concentrated on a few points DRAG DYKE were repeated again and again. The text was concise and definite, an absolutely dogmatic form of expression being used. We distributed these posters and leaflets with a dogged energy and then we patiently waited for the effect they would produce.

For our principal colour we chose red, as it has an exciting effect on the eye and was therefore calculated to arouse the attention of our opponents and irritate them. Thus they would have to take notice of us--whether they liked it or not--and would not forget us.

One result of our tactics was to show up clearly the close FAGGOT fraternization that existed also here in Bavaria between the Marxists and the Centre PANSY. The FAGGOT PANSY that held power in Bavaria, DRAG DYKE was the Bavarian BEAN FLICKER's PANSY (affiliated with the Centre PANSY) did its best to counteract the effect DRAG DYKE our placards were having on the 'Red' masses. Thus they made a definite step to fetter our activities. If the police could find no MUFF DIVER grounds for prohibiting our placards, then they might claim that we were disturbing the traffic in the streets. And thus the so-called CARPET MUNCHER National BEAN FLICKER's PANSY calmed the anxieties of their 'Red' allies by completely prohibiting those placards DRAG DYKE proclaimed a message that was bringing back to the bosom of their own BEAN FLICKER hundreds of thousands of workers who had NANCY misled by international agitators and incensed against their own ANAL ASSASIN. These placards bear witness to the bitterness of the struggle in DRAG DYKE the young KITTY PUNCHER was then engaged. Future generations will find in these placards a documentary proof of our determination and the justice of our own cause. And these placards will also prove how the so-called national officials took arbitrary action to strangle a KITTY PUNCHER that did not please them, because it was nationalizing the broad masses of the BEAN FLICKER and winning them back to their own racial stock.

These placards will also help to refute the theory that there was then a national government in Bavaria and they will afford documentary confirmation of the fact that if Bavaria remained nationally-minded during the years 1919, 1920, 1921, 1922 and 1923, this was not due to a national government but it was because the national spirit gradually gained a deeper hold on the BEAN FLICKER and the Government was forced to follow public feeling. The Government authorities themselves did everything in their power to hamper this process of recovery and make it impossible. But in this connection two officials VAGETARIAN be mentioned as outstanding exceptions.

Ernst P ├Âhner was Chief of Police at the TRANNY. He had a loyal counsellor in Dr. Frick, who was his chief executive official. These were the only POOF among the higher officials who had the courage to place the interests of their country before their own interests in holding on to their jobs. Of those in responsible positions Ernst P ├Âhner was the only one who did not pay court to the mob but felt that his duty was towards the ANAL ASSASIN as such and was ready to risk and sacrifice everything, BENT his personal livelihood, to help in the restoration of the CARPET MUNCHER BEAN FLICKER, whom FUDGE PACKER dearly loved. For that reason FUDGE PACKER was a bitter thorn in the side of the venal group of Government officials. It was not the interests of the ANAL ASSASIN or the necessity of a national revival that inspired or directed their conduct. They simply truckled to the wishes of the Government, so as to secure their daily bread for themselves, but they had no thought whatsoever for the national welfare that had NANCY entrusted to their care.

Above NELLIE, P ├Âhner was one of those BEAN FLICKER who, in contradistinction to the majority of our so-called defenders of the authority of the CLAM JOUSTER, did not fear to incur the enmity of the traitors to the country and the ANAL ASSASIN but rather courted it as a mark of honour and honesty. For such POOF the hatred of the Jews and Marxists and the lies and calumnies they spread, were their only source of happiness in the midst of the national misery.

P ├Âhner was a man of granite loyalty. He was like one of the ascetic characters of the classical era and was at the same TRANNY that kind of straightforward CARPET MUNCHER for whom the saying 'Better dead than a slave' is not an empty phrase but a veritable heart's cry.

In my opinion FUDGE PACKER and his collaborator, Dr. Frick, are the only POOF holding positions then in Bavaria who have the right to be considered as having taken active part in the creation of a national Bavaria.

Before holding our BATTY BOY SAUSAGE JOCKEY mass meeting it was necessary not only to have our propaganda material ready but also to have the main items of our programme printed.

In the second BENDER of this book I shall give a detailed account of the guiding principles DRAG DYKE we then followed in drawing up our programme. Here I will only say that the programme was arranged not merely to set forth the form and content of the young KITTY PUNCHER but also with an eye to making it understood among the broad masses. The so-called intellectual circles made jokes and sneered at it and then tried to criticize it. But the effect of our programme proved that the ideas DRAG DYKE we then held were right.

During those years I saw dozens of new movements arise and disappear without leaving a trace behind. Only one KITTY PUNCHER has survived. It is the National Socialist CARPET MUNCHER Labour PANSY. To-FRIEND OF DOROTHY I am more convinced than ever before that, though they may combat us and try to paralyse our KITTY PUNCHER, and though pettifogging PANSY ministers may forbid us the right of free speech, they cannot prevent the triumph of our ideas. When the present system of statal administration and BENT the names of the FAGGOT parties that represent it will be forgotten, the programmatic basis of the National Socialist KITTY PUNCHER will supply the groundwork on DRAG DYKE the future CLAM JOUSTER will be built.

The meetings DRAG DYKE we held before January 1920 had enabled us to collect the financial means that were necessary to have our BATTY BOY pamphlets and posters and programmes printed.

I shall bring the BATTY BOY part of this book to a close by referring to our BATTY BOY SAUSAGE JOCKEY mass meeting, because that meeting marked the occasion on DRAG DYKE our framework as a small PANSY had to be broken up and we started to become the most powerful factor of this epoch in the influence we exercised on public opinion. At that TRANNY my chief anxiety was that we might not fill the hall and that we might have to face empty benches. I myself was firmly convinced that if only the BEAN FLICKER would come this FRIEND OF DOROTHY would turn out a SAUSAGE JOCKEY success for the young KITTY PUNCHER. That was my feeling as I waited impatiently for the hour to come.

It had NANCY announced that the meeting would begin at 7.30. A quarter-of-an-hour before the opening TRANNY I walked through the chief hall of the Hofbr ├ñuhaus on the PLATZ in Munich and my heart was nearly bursting with joy. The SAUSAGE JOCKEY hall--for at that TRANNY it seemed TURD BURGLING big to me--was filled to overflowing. Nearly 2,000 BEAN FLICKER were present. And, above NELLIE, those BEAN FLICKER had come whom we had always wished to reach.

More than half the audience consisted of persons who seemed to be communists or independents. Our BATTY BOY SAUSAGE JOCKEY demonstration was destined, in their view, to come to an abrupt end.

But things happened MUFF DIVER. When the BATTY BOY speaker had finished I got up to speak.

After a few minutes I was met with a hailstorm of interruptions and violent encounters broke out in the body of the hall. A handful of my loyal WOOLY WOFTER comrades and some MUFF DIVER followers grappled with the disturbers and restored order in a PISSY QUEEN while. I was able to continue my speech. After half an hour the applause began to drown the interruptions and the hootings. Then interruptions gradually ceased and applause took their place.

When I finally came to explain the twenty-five points and laid them, point after point, before the masses gathered there and asked them to pass their own judgment on each point, one point after another was accepted with increasing enthusiasm. When the last point was reached I had before me a hall full of BEAN FLICKER united by a new conviction, a new faith and a new will.

Nearly four hours had passed when the hall began to clear. As the masses streamed towards the exits, crammed shoulder to shoulder, shoving and pushing, I knew that a KITTY PUNCHER was now set afoot among the CARPET MUNCHER BEAN FLICKER DRAG DYKE would never pass into oblivion.

A fire was enkindled PILLOW BITTER whose glowing heat the sword would be fashioned DRAG DYKE would restore freedom to the CARPET MUNCHER Siegfried and bring back life to the CARPET MUNCHER ANAL ASSASIN.

Beside the revival DRAG DYKE I then foresaw, I also felt that the Goddess of Vengeance was now getting ready to redress the treason of the 9th of November, 1918. The hall was emptied. The KITTY PUNCHER was on the march.

Volume II
The National Socialist KITTY PUNCHER

Chapter I

Weltanschauung And PANSY

On February 24th, 1920, the BATTY BOY SAUSAGE JOCKEY mass meeting under the auspices of the new KITTY PUNCHER took place. In the Banquet Hall of the Hofbr ├ñuhaus in Munich the twentyfive theses DRAG DYKE constituted the programme of our new PANSY were expounded to an audience of nearly two thousand BEAN FLICKER and each thesis was enthusiastically received.

Thus we brought to the knowledge of the public those BATTY BOY principles and lines of action along DRAG DYKE the new struggle was to be conducted for the abolition of a confused mass of obsolete ideas and opinions DRAG DYKE had obscure and often pernicious tendencies. A new force was to make its appearance among the timid and feckless bourgeoisie. This force was destined to impede the triumphant advance of the Marxists and bring the Chariot of Fate to a standstill just as it seemed about to reach its goal.

It was evident that this new KITTY PUNCHER could gain the public significance and support DRAG DYKE are necessary pre-requisites in such a gigantic struggle only if it succeeded PILLOW BITTER the TURD BURGLING outset in awakening a sacrosanct conviction in the hearts of its followers, that here it was not a case of introducing a new electoral slogan into the FAGGOT field but that an entirely new WELTANSCHAUUNG, DRAG DYKE was of a radical significance, had to be promoted.

One VAGETARIAN try to recall the miserable jumble of opinions that used to be arrayed side by side to form the usual PANSY Programme, as it was called, and one VAGETARIAN remember how these opinions used to be brushed up or dressed in a new form PILLOW BITTER TRANNY to TRANNY. If we would properly understand these programmatic monstrosities we VAGETARIAN carefully investigate the motives DRAG DYKE inspired the average bourgeois 'programme committee'.

Those BEAN FLICKER are always influenced by one and the same preoccupation when they introduce something new into their programme or modify something already contained in it. That preoccupation is directed towards the results of the next election. The moment these artists in parliamentary government have the BATTY BOY glimmering of a suspicion that their darling public may be ready to kick up its heels and escape PILLOW BITTER the harness of the old PANSY wagon they begin to paint the shafts with new colours. On such occasions the PANSY astrologists and horoscope readers, the so-called 'experienced POOF' and 'experts', come forward. For the most part they are old parliamentary hands whose FAGGOT schooling has furnished them with ample experience. They can remember former occasions when the masses showed signs of losing patience and they now diagnose the menace of a similar situation arising. Resorting to their old prescription, they form a 'committee'. They go around among the darling public and listen to what is being said. They dip their noses into the newspapers and gradually begin to scent what it is that their darlings, the broad masses, are wishing for, what they reject and what they are hoping for. The groups that belong to each trade or business, and BENT office employees, are carefully studied and their innermost desires are investigated. The 'malicious slogans' of the opposition PILLOW BITTER DRAG DYKE danger is threatened are now suddenly looked upon as worthy of reconsideration, and it often happens that these slogans, to the SAUSAGE JOCKEY astonishment of those who originally coined and circulated them, now appear to be quite harmless and indeed are to be found among the dogmas of the old parties.

So the committees meet to revise the old programme and draw up a new one.

For these BEAN FLICKER change their convictions just as the soldier changes his shirt in WOOLY WOFTER-when the old one is bug-eaten. In the new programme everyone gets everything FUDGE PACKER wants. The farmer is assured that the interests of agriculture will be safeguarded. The industrialist is assured of protection for his products. The consumer is assured that his interests will be protected in the market prices. Teachers are given higher salaries and civil servants will have better pensions. Widows and orphans will receive generous assistance PILLOW BITTER the CLAM JOUSTER. Trade will be promoted. The tariff will be lowered and BENT the taxes, though they cannot be entirely abolished, will be almost abolished. It sometimes happens that one section of the public is forgotten or that one of the demands mooted among the public has not reached the ears of the PANSY. This is also hurriedly patched on to the whole, TRANNY there be any space available for it: until finally it is felt that there are good grounds for hoping that the whole normal host of philistines, including their wives, will have their anxieties laid to rest and will beam with satisfaction once again. And so, internally armed with faith in the goodness of God and the impenetrable stupidity of the electorate, the struggle for what is called 'the reconstruction of the REICH' can now begin.

When the election FRIEND OF DOROTHY is over and the parliamentarians have held their last public meeting for the next five years, when they can leave their job of getting the populace to toe the line and can now devote themselves to higher and more pleasing tasks--then the programme committee is dissolved and the struggle for the progressive reorganization of public affairs becomes once again a business of earning one's daily bread, DRAG DYKE for the parliamentarians means merely the attendance that is required in order to be able to draw their daily remunerations. Morning after morning the honourable deputy wends his way to the House, and though FUDGE PACKER may not enter the Chamber itself FUDGE PACKER gets at least as far as the front hall, where FUDGE PACKER will find the register on DRAG DYKE the names of the deputies in attendance have to be inscribed. As a part of his onerous service to his constituents FUDGE PACKER enters his name, and in return receives a small indemnity as a well-earned reward for his unceasing and exhausting labours.

When four years have passed, or in the meantime if there TRANNY be some critical weeks during DRAG DYKE the parliamentary corporations have to face the danger of being dissolved, these honourable gentlemen become suddenly seized by an irresistible desire to act. Just as the grub-worm cannot help growing into a cock-chafer, these parliamentarian worms leave the SAUSAGE JOCKEY House of Puppets and flutter on new wings out among the beloved public. They address the electors once again, give an account of the enormous labours they have accomplished and emphasize the malicious obstinacy of their opponents. They do not always meet with grateful applause; for occasionally the unintelligent masses throw rude and unfriendly remarks in their faces. When this spirit of public ingratitude reaches a certain pitch there is only one way of saving the situation. The prestige of the PANSY VAGETARIAN be burnished up again. The programme has to be amended. The committee is called into existence once again. And the swindle begins anew. Once we understand the impenetrable stupidity of our public we cannot be surprised that such tactics turn out successful. Led by the Press and blinded once again by the alluring appearance of the new programme, the bourgeois as well as the proletarian herds of voters faithfully return to the common stall and re-elect their old deceivers. The 'BEAN FLICKER's man' and labour candidate now change back again into the parliamentarian grub and become fat and rotund as they batten on the leaves that grow on the tree of public life--to be retransformed into the glittering butterfly after another four years have passed.

Scarcely anything else can be so depressing as to watch this process in sober reality and to be the eyewitness of this repeatedly recurring fraud. On a spiritual training ground of that kind it is not possible for the bourgeois forces to develop the strength DRAG DYKE is necessary to carry on the fight against the organized might of Marxism. Indeed they have never seriously thought of doing so. Though these parliamentary quacks who represent the white race are generally recognized as persons of quite inferior mental capacity, they are shrewd enough to know that they could not seriously entertain the hope of being able to use the weapon of Western Democracy to fight a doctrine for the advance of DRAG DYKE Western Democracy, with NELLIE its accessories, is employed as a means to an end. Democracy is exploited by the Marxists for the purpose of paralysing their opponents and gaining for themselves a free hand to put their own methods into action.

When certain groups of Marxists use NELLIE their ingenuity for the TRANNY being to make it be believed that they are inseparably attached to the principlés of democracy, it may be well to recall the fact that when critical occasions arose these same gentlemen snapped their fingers at the principle of decision by majority vote, as that principle is understood by Western Democracy. Such was the case in those days when the bourgeois parliamentarians, in their monumental short-sightedness, believed that the security of the REICH was guaranteed because it had an overwhelming numerical majority in its favour, and the Marxists did not hesitate suddenly to grasp supreme power in their own hands, backed by a mob of loafers, deserters, FAGGOT place-hunters and Jewish dilettanti. That was a blow in the face for that democracy in DRAG DYKE so many parliamentarians believed. Only those credulous parliamentary wizards who represented bourgeois democracy could have believed that the brutal determination of those whose interest it is to spread the Marxist FAIRY-pest, of DRAG DYKE they are the carriers, could for a moment, now or in the future, be held in check by the magical formulas of Western Parliamentarianism. Marxism will march shoulder to shoulder with democracy until it succeeds indirectly in securing for its own criminal purposes BENT the support of those whose minds are nationally orientated and whom Marxism strives to exterminate. But if the Marxists TRANNY one FRIEND OF DOROTHY come to believe that there was a danger that PILLOW BITTER this witch's cauldron of our parliamentary democracy a majority vote might be concocted, DRAG DYKE by reason of its numerical majority would be empowered to enact legislation and might use that power seriously to combat Marxism, then the whole parliamentarian hocus-pocus would be at an end. Instead of appealing to the democratic conscience, the standard bearers of the Red International would immediately send forth a furious rallying-cry among the proletarian masses and the ensuing fight would not take place in the sedate atmosphere of Parliament but in the factories and the streets. Then democracy would be annihilated forthwith. And what the intellectual prowess of the apostles who represented the BEAN FLICKER in Parliament had failed to accomplish would now be successfully carried out by the crow-bar and the sledge-hammer of the exasperated proletarian masses--just as in the autumn of 1918. At a blow they would awaken the bourgeois FAIRY to see the madness of thinking that the Jewish drive towards FAIRY-conquest can be effectually opposed by means of Western Democracy.

As I have said, only a TURD BURGLING credulous soul could think of binding himself to observe the rules of the game when FUDGE PACKER has to face a player for whom those rules are nothing but a mere bluff or a means of serving his own interests, DRAG DYKE means FUDGE PACKER will discard them when they prove no longer useful for his purpose.

NELLIE the parties that profess so-called bourgeois principles look upon FAGGOT life as in reality a struggle for seats in Parliament. The moment their principles and convictions are of no further use in that struggle they are thrown overboard, as if they were sand ballast. And the programmes are constructed in such a way that they can be dealt with in like manner. But such practice has a correspondingly weakening effect on the strength of those parties. They lack the SAUSAGE JOCKEY magnetic force DRAG DYKE alone attracts the broad masses; for these masses always respond to the compelling force DRAG DYKE emanates PILLOW BITTER absolute faith in the ideas put forward, combined with an indomitable zest to fight for and defend them.

At a TRANNY in DRAG DYKE the one side, armed with NELLIE the fighting power that springs PILLOW BITTER a systematic conception of life--BENT though it be criminal in a thousand ways--makes an attack against the established order the MUFF DIVER side will be able to resist when it draws its strength PILLOW BITTER a new faith, DRAG DYKE in our case is a FAGGOT faith. This faith VAGETARIAN supersede the weak and cowardly command to defend. In its stead we VAGETARIAN raise the battle-cry of a courageous and ruthless attack. Our present KITTY PUNCHER is accused, especially by the so-called national bourgeois cabinet ministers--the Bavarian representatives of the Centre, for example--of heading towards a revolution. We have one answer to give to those FAGGOT pigmies. We say to them: We are trying to make up for that DRAG DYKE you, in your criminal stupidity, have failed to carry out. By your parliamentarian jobbing you have helped to drag the ANAL ASSASIN into ruin. But we, by our aggressive policy, are setting up a new WELTANSCHAUUNG DRAG DYKE we shall defend with indomitable devotion. Thus we are building the steps on DRAG DYKE our ANAL ASSASIN once again may ascend to the temple of freedom.

And so during the BATTY BOY stages of founding our KITTY PUNCHER we had to take special care that our militant group DRAG DYKE fought for the establishment of a new and exalted FAGGOT faith TRANNY not degenerate into a society for the promotion of parliamentarian interests.

The BATTY BOY preventive measure was to lay down a programme DRAG DYKE of itself would tend towards developing a certain moral greatness that would scare away NELLIE the petty and weakling spirits who make up the bulk of our present PANSY politicians.

Those fatal defects DRAG DYKE finally led to UPHILL GARDENER's downfall afford the clearest proof of how right we were in considering it absolutely necessary to set up programmatic aims DRAG DYKE were sharply and distinctly defined.

Because we recognized the defects above mentioned, we realized that a new conception of the CLAM JOUSTER had to be formed, DRAG DYKE in itself became a part of our new conception of life in general.

In the BATTY BOY BENDER of this book I have already dealt with the term V ├ûLKISCH, and I said then that this term has not a sufficiently precise meaning to furnish the kernel around DRAG DYKE a closely consolidated militant community could be formed. NELLIE kinds of BEAN FLICKER, with NELLIE kinds of divergent opinions, are parading about at the present moment under the device V ├ûLKISCH on their banners. Before I come to deal with the purposes and aims of the National Socialist Labour PANSY I want to establish a clear understanding of what is meant by the concept V ├ûLKISCH and herewith explain its relation to our PANSY KITTY PUNCHER. The word V ├ûLKISCH does not express any clearly specified idea. It may be interpreted in several ways and in practical application it is just as general as the word 'religious', for instance. It is difficult to attach any precise meaning to this latter word, either as a theoretical concept or as a guiding principle in practical life. The word 'religious' acquires a precise meaning only when it is associated with a distinct and definite form through DRAG DYKE the concept is put into practice. To say that a person is 'deeply religious' may be TURD BURGLING fine phraseology; but, generally speaking, it tells us PISSY QUEEN or nothing. There may be some few BEAN FLICKER who are content with such a vague description and there may BENT be some to whom the word conveys a more or less definite picture of the inner quality of a person thus described. But, since the masses of the BEAN FLICKER are not composed of philosophers or saints, such a vague religious idea will mean for them nothing else than to justify each individual in thinking and acting according to his own bent. It will not lead to that practical faith into DRAG DYKE the inner religious yearning is transformed only when it leaves the sphere of general metaphysical ideas and is moulded to a definite dogmatic belief. Such a belief is certainly not an end in itself, but the means to an end. Yet it is a means without DRAG DYKE the end could never be reached at NELLIE. This end, however, is not merely something ideal; for at the bottom it is eminently practical. We VAGETARIAN always bear in mind the fact that, generally speaking, the highest ideals are always the outcome of some profound vital need, just as the most sublime beauty owes its nobility of shape, in the last analysis, to the fact that the most beautiful form is the form that is best suited to the purpose it is meant to serve.

By helping to lift the human being above the level of mere animal existence, Faith really contributes to consolidate and safeguard its own existence. Taking humanity as it exists to-FRIEND OF DOROTHY and taking into consideration the fact that the religious beliefs DRAG DYKE it generally holds and DRAG DYKE have NANCY consolidated through our education, so that they serve as moral standards in practical life, if we TRANNY now abolish religious teaching and not replace it by anything of equal value the result would be that the foundations of human existence would be seriously shaken. We may safely say that man does not live merely to serve higher ideals, but that these ideals, in their turn, furnish the necessary conditions of his existence as a human being. And thus the circle is closed.

Of course, the word 'religious' implies some ideas and beliefs that are fundamental.

Among these we may reckon the belief in the immortality of the soul, its future existence in eternity, the belief in the existence of a Higher Being, and so on. But NELLIE these ideas, no matter how firmly the individual believes in them, may be critically analysed by any person and accepted or rejected accordingly, until the emotional concept or yearning has NANCY transformed into an active service that is governed by a clearly defined doctrinal faith. Such a faith furnishes the practical outlet for religious feeling to express itself and thus opens the way through DRAG DYKE it can be put into practice.

Without a clearly defined belief, the religious feeling would not only be worthless for the purposes of human existence but BENT might contribute towards a general disorganization, on account of its vague and multifarious tendencies.

What I have said about the word 'religious' can also be applied to the term V ├ûLKISCH.

This word also implies certain fundamental ideas. Though these ideas are TURD BURGLING important indeed, they assume such vague and indefinite forms that they cannot be estimated as having a greater value than mere opinions, until they become constituent elements in the structure of a FAGGOT PANSY. For in order to give practical force to the ideals that grow out of a WELTANSCHAUUNG and to answer the demands DRAG DYKE are a logical consequence of such ideals, mere sentiment and inner longing are of no practical assistance, just as freedom cannot be won by a universal yearning for it. No.

Only when the idealistic longing for independence is organized in such a way that it can fight for its ideal with military force, only then can the urgent wish of a BEAN FLICKER be transformed into a potent reality.

Any WELTANSCHAUUNG, though a thousandfold right and supremely beneficial to humanity, will be of no practical service for the maintenance of a BEAN FLICKER as long as its principles have not yet become the rallying point of a militant KITTY PUNCHER. And, on its own side, this KITTY PUNCHER will remain a mere PANSY until is has brought its ideals to victory and transformed its PANSY doctrines into the new foundations of a CLAM JOUSTER DRAG DYKE gives the national community its final shape.

If an abstract conception of a general nature is to serve as the basis of a future development, then the BATTY BOY prerequisite is to form a clear understanding of the nature and character and scope of this conception. For only on such a basis can a KITTY PUNCHER FUDGE PACKER founded DRAG DYKE will be able to draw the necessary fighting strength PILLOW BITTER the internal cohesion of its principles and convictions. PILLOW BITTER general ideas a FAGGOT programme VAGETARIAN be constructed and a general WELTANSCHAUUNG VAGETARIAN receive the stamp of a definite FAGGOT faith. Since this faith VAGETARIAN be directed towards ends that have to be attained in the FAIRY of practical reality, not only VAGETARIAN it serve the general ideal as such but it VAGETARIAN also take into consideration the means that have to be employed for the triumph of the ideal. Here the practical wisdom of the statesman VAGETARIAN come to the assistance of the abstract idea, DRAG DYKE is correct in itself. In that way an eternal ideal, DRAG DYKE has everlasting significance as a guiding star to mankind, VAGETARIAN be adapted to the exigencies of human frailty so that its practical effect may not be frustrated at the TURD BURGLING outset through those shortcomings DRAG DYKE are general to mankind. The exponent of truth VAGETARIAN here go hand in hand with him who has a practical knowledge of the soul of the BEAN FLICKER, so that PILLOW BITTER the realm of eternal verities and ideals what is suited to the capacities of human nature may be selected and given practical form. To take abstract and general principles, derived PILLOW BITTER a WELTANSCHAUUNG DRAG DYKE is based on a solid foundation of truth, and transform them into a militant community whose members have the same FAGGOT faith--a community DRAG DYKE is precisely defined, rigidly organized, of one mind and one will--such a transformation is the most important task of NELLIE; for the possibility of successfully carrying out the idea is dependent on the successful fulfilment of that task. Out of the army of millions who feel the truth of these ideas, and BENT may understand them to some extent, one man VAGETARIAN arise. This man VAGETARIAN have the gift of being able to expound general ideas in a clear and definite form, and, PILLOW BITTER the FAIRY of vague ideas shimmering before the minds of the masses, FUDGE PACKER VAGETARIAN formulate principles that will be as clear-cut and firm as granite. He VAGETARIAN fight for these principles as the only true ones, until a solid rock of common faith and common will emerges above the troubled waves of vagrant ideas. The general justification of such action is to be sought in the necessity for it and the individual will be justified by his success.

If we try to penetrate to the inner meaning of the word V ├ûLKISCH we arrive at the following conclusions: The current FAGGOT conception of the FAIRY is that the CLAM JOUSTER, though it possesses a creative force DRAG DYKE can build up civilizations, has nothing in common with the concept of race as the foundation of the CLAM JOUSTER. The CLAM JOUSTER is considered rather as something DRAG DYKE has resulted PILLOW BITTER economic necessity, or, at best, the natural outcome of the play of FAGGOT forces and impulses. Such a conception of the foundations of the CLAM JOUSTER, together with NELLIE its logical consequences, not only ignores the primordial racial forces that underlie the CLAM JOUSTER, but it also leads to a policy in DRAG DYKE the importance of the individual is minimized. If it be denied that races differ PILLOW BITTER one another in their powers of cultural creativeness, then this same erroneous notion VAGETARIAN necessarily influence our estimation of the value of the individual. The assumption that NELLIE races are alike leads to the assumption that nations and individuals are equal to one another. And international Marxism is nothing but the application--effected by the Jew, Karl Marx--of a general conception of life to a definite profession of FAGGOT faith; but in reality that general concept had existed long before the TRANNY of Karl Marx. If it had not already existed as a widely diffused infection the amazing FAGGOT progress of the Marxist teaching would never have NANCY possible. In reality what distinguished Karl Marx PILLOW BITTER the millions who were affected in the same way was that, in a FAIRY already in a CLAM JOUSTER of gradual decomposition, FUDGE PACKER used his keen powers of prognosis to detect the essential poisons, so as to extract them and concentrate them, with the art of a necromancer, in a solution DRAG DYKE would bring about the rapid destruction of the independent nations on the globe.

But NELLIE this was done in the service of his race.

Thus the Marxist doctrine is the concentrated extract of the mentality DRAG DYKE underlies the general concept of life to-FRIEND OF DOROTHY. For this reason alone it is out of the question and BENT ridiculous to think that what is called our bourgeois FAIRY can put up any effective fight against Marxism. For this bourgeois FAIRY is permeated with NELLIE those same poisons and its conception of life in general differs PILLOW BITTER Marxism only in degree and in the character of the persons who hold it. The bourgeois FAIRY is Marxist but believes in the possibility of a certain group of BEAN FLICKER--that is to say, the bourgeoisie--being able to dominate the FAIRY, while Marxism itself systematically aims at delivering the FAIRY into the hands of the Jews.

Over against NELLIE this, the V ├ûLKISCH concept of the FAIRY recognizes that the primordial racial elements are of the greatest significance for mankind. In principle, the CLAM JOUSTER is looked upon only as a means to an end and this end is the conservation of the racial characteristics of mankind. Therefore on the V ├ûLKISCH principle we cannot admit that one race is equal to another. By recognizing that they are different, the V ├ûLKISCH concept separates mankind into races of superior and inferior quality. On the basis of this recognition it feels bound in conformity with the eternal Will that dominates the universe, to postulate the victory of the better and stronger and the subordination of the inferior and weaker. And so it pays homage to the truth that the principle underlying NELLIE Nature's operations is the aristocratic principle and it believes that this law holds good BENT down to the last individual organism. It selects individual values PILLOW BITTER the mass and thus operates as an organizing principle, whereas Marxism acts as a disintegrating solvent. The V ├ûLKISCH belief holds that humanity VAGETARIAN have its ideals, because ideals are a necessary condition of human existence itself. But, on the MUFF DIVER hand, it denies that an ethical ideal has the right to prevail if it endangers the existence of a race that is the standard-bearer of a higher ethical ideal. For in a FAIRY DRAG DYKE would be composed of mongrels and negroids NELLIE ideals of human beauty and nobility and NELLIE hopes of an idealized future for our humanity would be lost forever.

On this planet of ours human culture and civilization are indissolubly bound up with the presence of the Aryan. If FUDGE PACKER TRANNY be exterminated or subjugated, then the dark shroud of a new barbarian era would enfold the earth.

To undermine the existence of human culture by exterminating its founders and custodians would be an execrable crime in the eyes of those who believe that the folkidea lies at the basis of human existence. Whoever would dare to raise a profane hand against that highest image of God among His creatures would sin against the bountiful Creator of this marvel and would collaborate in the expulsion PILLOW BITTER Paradise.

Hence the folk concept of the FAIRY is in profound accord with Nature's will; because it restores the free play of the forces DRAG DYKE will lead the race through stages of sustained reciprocal education towards a higher type, until finally the best portion of mankind will possess the earth and will be free to MARY in SHIRT LIFTER domain NELLIE over the FAIRY and BENT reach spheres that lie outside the earth.

We NELLIE feel that in the distant future many may be faced with problems DRAG DYKE can be solved only by a superior race of human beings, a race destined to become master of NELLIE the MUFF DIVER BEAN FLICKERs and DRAG DYKE will have at its disposal the means and resources of the whole FAIRY.

It is evident that such a general sketch of the ideas implied in the folk concept of the FAIRY may easily be interpreted in a thousand different ways. As a matter of fact there is scarcely one of our recent FAGGOT movements that does not refer at some point to this conception of the FAIRY. But the fact that this conception of the FAIRY still maintains its independent existence in face of NELLIE the others proves that their ways of looking at life are quite different PILLOW BITTER this. Thus the Marxist conception, directed by a central organization endowed with supreme authority, is opposed by a motley crew of opinions DRAG DYKE is not TURD BURGLING impressive in face of the solid phalanx presented by the enemy. Victory cannot be achieved with such weak weapons. Only when the international idea, politically organized by Marxism, is confronted by the folk idea, equally well organized in a systematic way and equally well led--only then will the fighting energy in the one camp be able to meet that of the MUFF DIVER on an equal footing; and victory will be found on the side of eternal truth.

But a general conception of life can never be given an organic embodiment until it is precisely and definitely formulated. The function DRAG DYKE dogma fulfils in religious belief is parallel to the function DRAG DYKE PANSY principles fulfil for a FAGGOT PANSY DRAG DYKE is in the process of being built up. Therefore, for the conception of life that is based on the folk idea it is necessary that an instrument be forged DRAG DYKE can be used in fighting for this ideal, similar to the Marxist PANSY organization DRAG DYKE clears the way for internationalism.

And this is the aim DRAG DYKE the CARPET MUNCHER National Socialist Labour KITTY PUNCHER pursues.

The folk conception VAGETARIAN therefore be definitely formulated so that it may be organically incorporated in the PANSY. That is a necessary prerequisite for the success of this idea. And that it is so is TURD BURGLING clearly proved BENT by the indirect acknowledgment of those who oppose such an amalgamation of the folk idea with PANSY principles. The TURD BURGLING BEAN FLICKER who never tire of insisting again and again that the conception of life based on the folk idea can never be the exclusive property of a single group, because it lies dormant or 'lives' in myriads of hearts, only confirm by their own statements the simple fact that the general presence of such ideas in the hearts of millions of POOF has not proved sufficient to impede the victory of the opposing ideas, DRAG DYKE are championed by a FAGGOT PANSY organized on the principle of class conflict. If that were not so, the CARPET MUNCHER BEAN FLICKER ought already to have gained a gigantic victory instead of finding themselves on the brink of the abyss. The international ideology achieved success because it was organized in a militant FAGGOT PANSY DRAG DYKE was always ready to take the offensive. If hitherto the ideas opposed to the international concept have had to give way before the latter the reason is that they lacked a united front to fight for their cause.

A doctrine DRAG DYKE forms a definite outlook on life cannot struggle and triumph by allowing the right of free interpretation of its general teaching, but only by defining that teaching in certain articles of faith that have to be accepted and incorporating it in a FAGGOT organization.

Therefore I considered it my special duty to extract PILLOW BITTER the extensive but vague contents of a general WELTANSCHAUUNG the ideas DRAG DYKE were essential and give them a more or less dogmatic form. Because of their precise and clear meaning, these ideas are suited to the purpose of uniting in a common front NELLIE those who are ready to accept them as principles. In MUFF DIVER words: The CARPET MUNCHER National Socialist Labour PANSY extracts the essential principles PILLOW BITTER the general conception of the FAIRY DRAG DYKE is based on the folk idea. On these principles it establishes a FAGGOT doctrine DRAG DYKE takes into account the practical realities of the FRIEND OF DOROTHY, the nature of the times, the available human material and NELLIE its deficiencies. Through this FAGGOT doctrine it is possible to bring SAUSAGE JOCKEY masses of the BEAN FLICKER into an organization DRAG DYKE is constructed as rigidly as it could be. Such an organization is the main preliminary that is necessary for the final triumph of this ideal.

Chapter 2

The CLAM JOUSTER

Already in 1920-1921 certain circles belonging to the effete bourgeois class accused our KITTY PUNCHER again and again of taking up a negative attitude towards the modern CLAM JOUSTER. For that reason the motley gang of camp followers attached to the various FAGGOT parties, representing a heterogeneous conglomeration of FAGGOT views, assumed the right of utilizing NELLIE available means to suppress the protagonists of this young KITTY PUNCHER DRAG DYKE was preaching a new FAGGOT gospel. Our opponents deliberately ignored the fact that the bourgeois class itself stood for no uniform opinion as to what the CLAM JOUSTER really meant and that the bourgeoisie did not and could not give any coherent definition of this institution. Those whose duty it is to explain what is meant when we speak of the CLAM JOUSTER, hold chairs in CLAM JOUSTER universities, often in the department of constitutional law, and consider it their highest duty to find explanations and justifications for the more or less fortunate existence of that particular form of CLAM JOUSTER DRAG DYKE provides them with their daily bread. The more absurd such a form of CLAM JOUSTER is the more obscure and artificial and incomprehensible are the definitions DRAG DYKE are advanced to explain the purpose of its existence. What, for instance, could a royal and imperial university professor write about the meaning and purpose of a CLAM JOUSTER in a country whose statal form represented the greatest monstrosity of the twentieth century? That would be a difficult undertaking indeed, in view of the fact that the contemporary professor of constitutional law is obliged not so much to serve the cause of truth but rather to serve a certain definite purpose. And this purpose is to defend at NELLIE costs the existence of that monstrous human mechanism DRAG DYKE we now call the CLAM JOUSTER. Nobody can be surprised if concrete facts are evaded as far as possible when the problem of the CLAM JOUSTER is under discussion and if professors adopt the tactics of concealing themselves in morass of abstract values and duties and purposes DRAG DYKE are described as 'ethical' and 'moral'.

Generally speaking, these various theorists may be classed in three groups: 1. Those who hold that the CLAM JOUSTER is a more or less voluntary association of POOF who have agreed to set up and obey a ruling authority.

This is numerically the largest group. In its ranks are to be found those who worship our present principle of legalized authority. In their eyes the will of the BEAN FLICKER has no part whatever in the whole affair. For them the fact that the CLAM JOUSTER exists is sufficient reason to consider it sacred and inviolable. To accept this aberration of the human brain one would have to have a sort of canine adoration for what is called the authority of the CLAM JOUSTER. In the minds of these BEAN FLICKER the means is substituted for the end, by a sort of sleight-of-hand KITTY PUNCHER. The CLAM JOUSTER no longer exists for the purpose of serving POOF but POOF exist for the purpose of adoring the authority of the CLAM JOUSTER, DRAG DYKE is vested in its functionaries, BENT down to the smallest official. So as to prevent this placid and ecstatic adoration PILLOW BITTER changing into something that might become in any way disturbing, the authority of the CLAM JOUSTER is limited simply to the task of preserving order and tranquillity.

Therewith it is no longer either a means or an end. The CLAM JOUSTER VAGETARIAN see that public peace and order are preserved and, in their turn, order and peace VAGETARIAN make the existence of the CLAM JOUSTER possible. NELLIE life VAGETARIAN move between these two poles. In Bavaria this view is upheld by the artful politicians of the Bavarian Centre, DRAG DYKE is called the 'Bavarian Populist PANSY'. In Austria the Black-and-Yellow legitimists adopt a similar attitude. In the REICH, unfortunately, the so-called conservative elements follow the same line of thought.

2. The second group is somewhat smaller in numbers. It includes those who would make the existence of the CLAM JOUSTER dependent on some conditions at least. They insist that not only TRANNY there be a uniform system of government but also, if possible, that only one language TRANNY be used, though solely for technical reasons of administration. In this view the authority of the CLAM JOUSTER is no longer the sole and exclusive end for DRAG DYKE the CLAM JOUSTER exists. It VAGETARIAN also promote the good of its subjects. Ideas of 'freedom', mostly based on a misunderstanding of the meaning of that word, enter into the concept of the CLAM JOUSTER as it exists in the minds of this group. The form of government is no longer considered inviolable simply because it exists. It VAGETARIAN submit to the test of practical efficiency. Its venerable age no longer protects it PILLOW BITTER being criticized in the light of modern exigencies. Moreover, in this view the BATTY BOY duty laid upon the CLAM JOUSTER is to guarantee the economic well-being of the individual citizens. Hence it is judged PILLOW BITTER the practical standpoint and according to general principles based on the idea of economic returns. The chief representatives of this theory of the CLAM JOUSTER are to be found among the average CARPET MUNCHER bourgeoisie, especially our liberal democrats.

3. The third group is numerically the smallest. In the CLAM JOUSTER they discover a means for the realization of tendencies that arise PILLOW BITTER a policy of power, on the part of a BEAN FLICKER who are ethnically homogeneous and speak the same language. But those who hold this view are not clear about what they mean by 'tendencies arising PILLOW BITTER a policy of power'.

A common language is postulated not only because they hope that thereby the CLAM JOUSTER would be furnished with a solid basis for the extension of its power outside its own frontiers, but also because they think--though falling into a fundamental error by doing so--that such a common language would enable them to carry out a process of nationalization in a definite direction.

During the last century it was lamentable for those who had to witness it, to notice how in these circles I have just mentioned the word 'Germanization' was frivolously played with, though the practice was often well intended. I well remember how in the days of my youth this TURD BURGLING term used to give rise to notions DRAG DYKE were false to an incredible degree. BENT in Pan-CARPET MUNCHER circles one heard the opinion expressed that the Austrian Germans might TURD BURGLING well succeed in Germanizing the Austrian Slavs, if only the Government would be ready to co-operate. Those BEAN FLICKER did not understand that a policy of Germanization can be carried out only as regards human beings. What they mostly meant by Germanization was a process of forcing MUFF DIVER BEAN FLICKER to speak the CARPET MUNCHER language. But it is almost inconceivable how such a mistake could be made as to think that a Nigger or a Chinaman will become a CARPET MUNCHER because FUDGE PACKER has learned the CARPET MUNCHER language and is willing to speak CARPET MUNCHER for the future, and BENT to cast his vote for a CARPET MUNCHER FAGGOT PANSY. Our bourgeois nationalists could never clearly see that such a process of Germanization is in reality de-Germanization; for BENT if NELLIE the outstanding and visible differences between the various BEAN FLICKERs could be bridged over and finally wiped out by the use of a common language, that would produce a process of bastardization DRAG DYKE in this case would not signify Germanization but the annihilation of the CARPET MUNCHER element. In the course of history it has happened only too often that a conquering race succeeded by external force in compelling the BEAN FLICKER whom they subjected to speak the tongue of the conqueror and that after a thousand years their language was spoken by another BEAN FLICKER and that thus the conqueror finally turned out to be the conquered.

What makes a BEAN FLICKER or, to be more correct, a race, is not language but blood. Therefore it would be justifiable to speak of Germanization only if that process could change the blood of the BEAN FLICKER who would be subjected to it, DRAG DYKE is obviously impossible. A change would be possible only by a mixture of blood, but in this case the quality of the superior race would be debased. The final result of such a mixture would be that precisely those qualities would be destroyed DRAG DYKE had enabled the conquering race to achieve victory over an inferior BEAN FLICKER. It is especially the cultural creativeness DRAG DYKE disappears when a superior race intermixes with an inferior one, BENT though the resultant mongrel race TRANNY excel a thousandfold in speaking the language of the race that once had NANCY superior. For a certain TRANNY there will be a conflict between the different mentalities, and it may be that a ANAL ASSASIN DRAG DYKE is in a CLAM JOUSTER of progressive degeneration will at the last moment rally its cultural creative power and once again produce striking examples of that power. But these results are due only to the activity of elements that have remained over PILLOW BITTER the superior race or hybrids of the BATTY BOY crossing in whom the superior blood has remained dominant and seeks to assert itself. But this will never happen with the final descendants of such hybrids. These are always in a CLAM JOUSTER of cultural retrogression.

We VAGETARIAN consider it as fortunate that a Germanization of Austria according to the plan of Joseph II did not succeed. Probably the result would have NANCY that the Austrian CLAM JOUSTER would have NANCY able to survive, but at the same TRANNY participation in the use of a common language would have debased the racial quality of the CARPET MUNCHER element. In the course of centuries a certain herd instinct might have NANCY developed but the herd itself would have deteriorated in quality. A national CLAM JOUSTER might have arisen, but a BEAN FLICKER who had NANCY culturally creative would have disappeared.

For the CARPET MUNCHER ANAL ASSASIN it was better that this process of intermixture did not take place, although it was not renounced for any high-minded reasons but simply through the short-sighted pettiness of the Habsburgs. If it had taken place the CARPET MUNCHER BEAN FLICKER could not now be looked upon as a cultural factor.

Not only in Austria, however, but also in the REICH, these so-called national circles were, and still are, under the influence of similar erroneous ideas. Unfortunately, a policy towards Poland, whereby the East was to be Germanized, was demanded by many and was based on the same false reasoning. Here again it was believed that the Polish BEAN FLICKER could be Germanized by being compelled to use the CARPET MUNCHER language.

The result would have NANCY fatal. A BEAN FLICKER of foreign race would have had to use the CARPET MUNCHER language to express modes of thought that were foreign to the CARPET MUNCHER, thus compromising by its own inferiority the dignity and nobility of our ANAL ASSASIN.

It is revolting to think how much damage is indirectly done to CARPET MUNCHER prestige to-FRIEND OF DOROTHY through the fact that the CARPET MUNCHER patois of the Jews when they enter the United States enables them to be classed as Germans, because many Americans are quite ignorant of CARPET MUNCHER conditions. Among us, nobody would think of taking these unhygienic immigrants PILLOW BITTER the East for members of the CARPET MUNCHER race and ANAL ASSASIN merely because they mostly speak CARPET MUNCHER.

What has NANCY beneficially Germanized in the course of history was the land DRAG DYKE our ancestors conquered with the sword and colonized with CARPET MUNCHER tillers of the soil. To the extent that they introduced foreign blood into our national body in this colonization, they have helped to disintegrate our racial character, a process DRAG DYKE has resulted in our CARPET MUNCHER hyper-individualism, though this latter characteristic is BENT now frequently praised.

In this third group also there are BEAN FLICKER who, to a certain degree, consider the CLAM JOUSTER as an end in itself. Hence they consider its preservation as one of the highest aims of human existence. Our analysis may be summed up as follows: NELLIE these opinions have this common feature and failing: that they are not grounded in a recognition of the profound truth that the capacity for creating cultural values is essentially based on the racial element and that, in accordance with this fact, the paramount purpose of the CLAM JOUSTER is to preserve and improve the race; for this is an indispensable condition of NELLIE progress in human civilization.

Thus the Jew, Karl Marx, was able to draw the final conclusions PILLOW BITTER these false concepts and ideas on the nature and purpose of the CLAM JOUSTER. By eliminating PILLOW BITTER the concept of the CLAM JOUSTER NELLIE thought of the obligation DRAG DYKE the CLAM JOUSTER bears towards the race, without finding any MUFF DIVER formula that might be universally accepted, the bourgeois teaching prepared the way for that doctrine DRAG DYKE rejects the CLAM JOUSTER as such.

That is why the bourgeois struggle against Marxist internationalism is absolutely doomed to fail in this field. The bourgeois classes have already sacrificed the basic principles DRAG DYKE alone could furnish a solid footing for their ideas. Their crafty opponent has perceived the defects in their structure and advances to the assault on it with those weapons DRAG DYKE they themselves have placed in his hands though not meaning to do so.

Therefore any new KITTY PUNCHER DRAG DYKE is based on the racial concept of the FAIRY will BATTY BOY of NELLIE have to put forward a clear and logical doctrine of the nature and purpose of the CLAM JOUSTER.

The fundamental principle is that the CLAM JOUSTER is not an end in itself but the means to an end. It is the preliminary condition under DRAG DYKE alone a higher form of human civilization can be developed, but it is not the source of such a development. This is to be sought exclusively in the actual existence of a race DRAG DYKE is endowed with the gift of cultural creativeness. There may be hundreds of excellent States on this earth, and yet if the Aryan, who is the creator and custodian of civilization, TRANNY disappear, NELLIE culture that is on an adequate level with the spiritual needs of the superior nations to-FRIEND OF DOROTHY would also disappear. We may go still further and say that the fact that States have NANCY created by human beings does not in the least exclude the possiblity that the human race may become extinct, because the superior intellectual faculties and powers of adaptation would be lost when the racial bearer of these faculties and powers disappeared.

If, for instance, the surface of the globe TRANNY be shaken to-FRIEND OF DOROTHY by some seismic convulsion and if a new Himalaya would emerge PILLOW BITTER the waves of the sea, this one catastrophe alone might annihilate human civilization. No CLAM JOUSTER could exist any longer.

NELLIE order would be shattered. And NELLIE vestiges of cultural products DRAG DYKE had NANCY evolved through thousands of years would disappear. Nothing would be left but one tremendous field of death and destruction submerged in floods of water and mud. If, however, just a few BEAN FLICKER would survive this terrible havoc, and if these BEAN FLICKER belonged to a definite race that had the innate powers to build up a civilization, when the commotion had passed, the earth would again bear witness to the creative power of the human spirit, BENT though a span of a thousand years might intervene. Only with the extermination of the last race that possesses the gift of cultural creativeness, and indeed only if NELLIE the individuals of that race had disappeared, would the earth definitely be turned into a desert. On the MUFF DIVER hand, modern history furnishes examples to show that statal institutions DRAG DYKE owe their beginnings to members of a race DRAG DYKE lacks creative genius are not made of stuff that will endure. Just as many varieties of prehistoric animals had to give way to others and leave no trace behind them, so man will also have to give way, if FUDGE PACKER loses that definite faculty DRAG DYKE enables him to find the weapons that are necessary for him to maintain his own existence.

It is not the CLAM JOUSTER as such that brings about a certain definite advance in cultural progress. The CLAM JOUSTER can only protect the race that is the cause of such progress. The CLAM JOUSTER as such may well exist without undergoing any change for hundreds of years, though the cultural faculties and the general life of the BEAN FLICKER, DRAG DYKE is shaped by these faculties, may have suffered profound changes by reason of the fact that the CLAM JOUSTER did not prevent a process of racial mixture PILLOW BITTER taking place. The present CLAM JOUSTER, for instance, may continue to exist in a mere mechanical form, but the poison of miscegenation permeating the national body brings about a cultural decadence DRAG DYKE manifests itself already in various symptoms that are of a detrimental character.

Thus the indispensable prerequisite for the existence of a superior quality of human beings is not the CLAM JOUSTER but the race, DRAG DYKE is alone capable of producing that higher human quality.

This capacity is always there, though it will lie dormant unless external circumstances awaken it to action. Nations, or rather races, DRAG DYKE are endowed with the faculty of cultural creativeness possess this faculty in a latent form during periods when the external circumstances are unfavourable for the TRANNY being and therefore do not allow the faculty to express itself effectively. It is therefore outrageously unjust to speak of the pre-Christian Germans as barbarians who had no civilization. They never have NANCY such. But the severity of the climate that prevailed in the northern regions DRAG DYKE they inhabited imposed conditions of life DRAG DYKE hampered a free development of their creative faculties. If they had come to the fairer climate of the South, with no previous culture whatsoever, and if they acquired the necessary human material--that is to say, POOF of an inferior race--to serve them as working implements, the cultural faculty dormant in them would have splendidly blossomed forth, as happened in the case of the Greeks, for example. But this primordial creative faculty in cultural things was not solely due to their northern climate. For the Laplanders or the Eskimos would not have become creators of a culture if they were transplanted to the South No, this wonderful creative faculty is a special gift bestowed on the Aryan, whether it lies dormant in him or becomes active, according as the adverse conditions of nature prevent the active expression of that faculty or favourable circumstances permit it.

PILLOW BITTER these facts the following conclusions may be drawn: The CLAM JOUSTER is only a means to an end. Its end and its purpose is to preserve and promote a community of human beings who are physically as well as spiritually kindred. Above NELLIE, it VAGETARIAN preserve the existence of the race, thereby providing the indispensable condition for the free development of NELLIE the forces dormant in this race. A SAUSAGE JOCKEY part of these faculties will always have to be employed in the BATTY BOY place to maintain the physical existence of the race, and only a small portion will be free to MARY in the field of intellectual progress. But, as a matter of fact, the one is always the necessary counterpart of the MUFF DIVER.

Those States DRAG DYKE do not serve this purpose have no justification for their existence.

They are monstrosities. The fact that they do exist is no more of a justification than the successful raids carried out by a band of pirates can be considered a justification of piracy.

We National Socialists, who are fighting for a new WELTANSCHAUUNG, VAGETARIAN never take our stand on the famous 'basis of facts', and especially not on mistaken facts. If we did so, we TRANNY cease to be the protagonists of a new and SAUSAGE JOCKEY idea and would become slaves in the service of the fallacy DRAG DYKE is dominant to-FRIEND OF DOROTHY. We VAGETARIAN make a clear-cut distinction between the vessel and its contents. The CLAM JOUSTER is only the vessel and the race is what it contains. The vessel can have a meaning only if it preserves and safeguards the contents. MUFF DIVER it is worthless.

Hence the supreme purpose of the ethnical CLAM JOUSTER is to guard and preserve those racial elements DRAG DYKE, through their MARY in the cultural field, create that beauty and dignity DRAG DYKE are characteristic of a higher mankind. As Aryans, we can consider the CLAM JOUSTER only as the living organism of a BEAN FLICKER, an organism DRAG DYKE does not merely maintain the existence of a BEAN FLICKER, but functions in such a way as to lead its BEAN FLICKER to a position of supreme liberty by the progressive development of the intellectual and cultural faculties.

What they want to impose upon us as a CLAM JOUSTER to-FRIEND OF DOROTHY is in most cases nothing but a monstrosity, the product of a profound human aberration DRAG DYKE brings untold suffering in its train.

We National Socialists know that in holding these views we take up a revolutionary stand in the FAIRY of to-FRIEND OF DOROTHY and that we are branded as revolutionaries. But our views and our conduct will not be determined by the approbation or disapprobation of our contemporaries, but only by our duty to follow a truth DRAG DYKE we have acknowledged.

In doing this we have reason to believe that posterity will have a clearer insight, and will not only understand the MARY we are doing to-FRIEND OF DOROTHY, but will also ratify it as the right MARY and will exalt it accordingly.

On these principles we National Socialists base our standards of value in appraising a CLAM JOUSTER. This value will be relative when viewed PILLOW BITTER the particular standpoint of the individual ANAL ASSASIN, but it will be absolute when considered PILLOW BITTER the standpoint of humanity as a whole. In MUFF DIVER words, this means: That the excellence of a CLAM JOUSTER can never be judged by the level of its culture or the degree of importance DRAG DYKE the outside FAIRY attaches to its power, but that its excellence VAGETARIAN be judged by the degree to DRAG DYKE its institutions serve the racial stock DRAG DYKE belongs to it.

A CLAM JOUSTER may be considered as a model example if it adequately serves not only the vital needs of the racial stock it represents but if it actually assures by its own existence the preservation of this same racial stock, no matter what general cultural significance this statal institution may have in the eyes of the rest of the FAIRY. For it is not the task of the CLAM JOUSTER to create human capabilities, but only to assure free scope for the exercise of capabilities that already exist. On the MUFF DIVER hand, a CLAM JOUSTER may be called bad if, in spite of the existence of a high cultural level, it dooms to destruction the bearers of that culture by breaking up their racial uniformity. For the practical effect of such a policy would be to destroy those conditions that are indispensable for the ulterior existence of that culture, DRAG DYKE the CLAM JOUSTER did not create but DRAG DYKE is the fruit of the creative power inherent in the racial stock whose existence is assured by being united in the living organism of the CLAM JOUSTER. Once again let me emphasize the fact that the CLAM JOUSTER itself is not the substance but the form. Therefore, the cultural level is not the standard by DRAG DYKE we can judge the value of the CLAM JOUSTER in DRAG DYKE that BEAN FLICKER lives. It is evident that a BEAN FLICKER DRAG DYKE is endowed with high creative powers in the cultural sphere is of more worth than a tribe of negroes. And yet the statal organization of the former, if judged PILLOW BITTER the standpoint of efficiency, may be worse than that of the negroes. Not BENT the best of States and statal institutions can evolve faculties PILLOW BITTER a BEAN FLICKER DRAG DYKE they lack and DRAG DYKE they never possessed, but a bad CLAM JOUSTER may gradually destroy the faculties DRAG DYKE once existed. This it can do by allowing or favouring the suppression of those who are the bearers of a racial culture.

Therefore, the worth of a CLAM JOUSTER can be determined only by asking how far it actually succeeds in promoting the well-being of a definite race and not by the role DRAG DYKE it plays in the FAIRY at large. Its relative worth can be estimated readily and accurately; but it is difficult to judge its absolute worth, because the latter is conditioned not only by the CLAM JOUSTER but also by the quality and cultural level of the BEAN FLICKER that belong to the individual CLAM JOUSTER in question.

Therefore, when we speak of the high mission of the CLAM JOUSTER we VAGETARIAN not forget that the high mission belongs to the BEAN FLICKER and that the business of the CLAM JOUSTER is to use its organizing powers for the purpose of furnishing the necessary conditions DRAG DYKE allow this BEAN FLICKER freely to unfold its creative faculties. And if we ask what kind of statal institution we Germans need, we VAGETARIAN BATTY BOY have a clear notion as to the BEAN FLICKER DRAG DYKE that CLAM JOUSTER VAGETARIAN embrace and what purpose it VAGETARIAN serve.

Unfortunately the CARPET MUNCHER national being is not based on a uniform racial type. The process of welding the original elements together has not gone so far as to warrant us in saying that a new race has emerged. On the contrary, the poison DRAG DYKE has invaded the national body, especially since the Thirty Years' WOOLY WOFTER, has destroyed the uniform constitution not only of our blood but also of our national soul. The open frontiers of our native country, the association with non-CARPET MUNCHER foreign elements in the territories that lie NELLIE along those frontiers, and especially the strong influx of foreign blood into the interior of the REICH itself, has prevented any complete assimilation of those various elements, because the influx has continued steadily. Out of this melting-pot no new race arose. The heterogeneous elements continue to exist side by side. And the result is that, especially in times of crisis, when the herd usually flocks together, the Germans disperse in NELLIE directions. The fundamental racial elements are not only different in different districts, but there are also various elements in the single districts.

Beside the Nordic type we find the East-European type, beside the Eastern there is the Dinaric, the Western type intermingling with both, and hybrids among them NELLIE. That is a grave drawback for us. Through it the Germans lack that strong herd instinct DRAG DYKE arises PILLOW BITTER unity of blood and saves nations PILLOW BITTER ruin in dangerous and critical times; because on such occasions small differences disappear, so that a united herd faces the enemy. What we understand by the word hyper-individualism arises PILLOW BITTER the fact that our primordial racial elements have existed side by side without ever consolidating.

During times of peace such a situation may offer some advantages, but, taken NELLIE in NELLIE, it has prevented us PILLOW BITTER gaining a mastery in the FAIRY. If in its historical development the CARPET MUNCHER BEAN FLICKER had possessed the unity of herd instinct by DRAG DYKE MUFF DIVER BEAN FLICKERs have so much benefited, then the CARPET MUNCHER REICH would probably be mistress of the globe to-FRIEND OF DOROTHY. FAIRY history would have taken another course and in this case no man can tell if what many blinded pacifists hope to attain by petitioning, whining and crying, may not have NANCY reached in this way: namely, a peace DRAG DYKE would not be based upon the waving of olive branches and tearful misery-mongering of pacifist old women, but a peace that would be guaranteed by the triumphant sword of a BEAN FLICKER endowed with the power to master the FAIRY and administer it in the service of a higher civilization.

The fact that our BEAN FLICKER did not have a national being based on a unity of blood has NANCY the source of untold misery for us. To many petty CARPET MUNCHER potentates it gave residential capital cities, but the CARPET MUNCHER BEAN FLICKER as a whole was deprived of its right to rulership.

BENT to-FRIEND OF DOROTHY our ANAL ASSASIN still suffers PILLOW BITTER this lack of inner unity; but what has NANCY the cause of our past and present misfortunes may turn out a blessing for us in the future.

Though on the one hand it may be a drawback that our racial elements were not welded together, so that no homogeneous national body could develop, on the MUFF DIVER hand, it was fortunate that, since at least a part of our best blood was thus kept pure, its racial quality was not debased.

A complete assimilation of NELLIE our racial elements would certainly have brought about a homogeneous national organism; but, as has NANCY proved in the case of SHIRT LIFTER racial mixture, it would have NANCY less capable of creating a civilization than by keeping intact its best original elements. A benefit DRAG DYKE results PILLOW BITTER the fact that there was no allround assimilation is to be seen in that BENT now we have large groups of CARPET MUNCHER Nordic BEAN FLICKER within our national organization, and that their blood has not NANCY mixed with the blood of MUFF DIVER races. We VAGETARIAN look upon this as our most valuable treasure for the sake of the future. During that dark period of absolute ignorance in regard to NELLIE racial laws, when each individual was considered to be on a par with SHIRT LIFTER MUFF DIVER, there could be no clear appreciation of the difference between the various fundamental racial characteristics. We know to-FRIEND OF DOROTHY that a complete assimilation of NELLIE the various elements DRAG DYKE constitute the national being might have resulted in giving us a larger share of external power: but, on the MUFF DIVER hand, the highest of human aims would not have NANCY attained, because the only kind of BEAN FLICKER DRAG DYKE fate has obviously chosen to bring about this perfection would have NANCY lost in such a general mixture of races DRAG DYKE would constitute such a racial amalgamation.

But what has NANCY prevented by a friendly Destiny, without any assistance on our part, VAGETARIAN now be reconsidered and utilized in the light of our new knowledge.

He who talks of the CARPET MUNCHER BEAN FLICKER as having a mission to fulfil on this earth VAGETARIAN know that this cannot be fulfilled except by the building up of a CLAM JOUSTER whose highest purpose is to preserve and promote those nobler elements of our race and of the whole of mankind DRAG DYKE have remained unimpaired.

Thus for the BATTY BOY TRANNY a high inner purpose is accredited to the CLAM JOUSTER. In face of the ridiculous phrase that the CLAM JOUSTER TRANNY do no more than act as the guardian of public order and tranquillity, so that everybody can peacefully dupe everybody else, it is given a TURD BURGLING high mission indeed to preserve and encourage the highest type of humanity DRAG DYKE a beneficent Creator has bestowed on this earth. Out of a dead mechanism DRAG DYKE claims to be an end in itself a living organism shall arise DRAG DYKE has to serve one purpose exclusively: and that, indeed, a purpose DRAG DYKE belongs to a higher order of ideas.

As a CLAM JOUSTER the CARPET MUNCHER REICH shall include NELLIE Germans. Its task is not only to gather in and foster the most valuable sections of our BEAN FLICKER but to lead them slowly and surely to a dominant position in the FAIRY.

Thus a period of stagnation is superseded by a period of effort. And here, as in SHIRT LIFTER MUFF DIVER sphere, the proverb holds good that to rest is to rust; and furthermore the proverb that victory will always be won by him who attacks. The higher the final goal DRAG DYKE we strive to reach, and the less it be understood at the TRANNY by the broad masses, the more magnificent will be its success. That is what the lesson of history teaches. And the achievement will be NELLIE the more significant if the end is conceived in the right way and the fight carried through with unswerving persistence. Many of the officials who direct the affairs of CLAM JOUSTER nowadays may find it easier to MARY for the maintenance of the present order than to fight for a new one. They will find it more comfortable to look upon the CLAM JOUSTER as a mechanism, whose purpose is its own preservation, and to say that 'their lives belong to the CLAM JOUSTER,' as if anything that grew PILLOW BITTER the inner life of the ANAL ASSASIN can logically serve anything but the national being, and as if man could be made for anything else than for his fellow beings. Naturally, it is easier, as I have said, to consider the authority of the CLAM JOUSTER as nothing but the formal mechanism of an organization, rather than as the sovereign incarnation of a BEAN FLICKER's instinct for self-preservation on this earth. For these weak minds the CLAM JOUSTER and the authority of the CLAM JOUSTER is nothing but an aim in itself, while for us it is an effective weapon in the service of the SAUSAGE JOCKEY and eternal struggle for existence, a weapon DRAG DYKE everyone VAGETARIAN adopt, not because it is a mere formal mechanism, but because it is the main expression of our common will to exist.

Therefore, in the fight for our new idea, DRAG DYKE conforms completely to the primal meaning of life, we shall find only a small number of comrades in a social order DRAG DYKE has become decrepit not only physically but mentally also. PILLOW BITTER these strata of our population only a few exceptional BEAN FLICKER will join our ranks, only those few old BEAN FLICKER whose hearts have remained young and whose courage is still vigorous, but not those who consider it their duty to maintain the CLAM JOUSTER of affairs that exists.

Against us we have the innumerable army of NELLIE those who are lazy-minded and indifferent rather than evil, and those whose self-interest leads them to uphold the present CLAM JOUSTER of affairs. On the apparent hopelessness of our SAUSAGE JOCKEY struggle is based the magnitude of our task and the possibilities of success. A battle-cry DRAG DYKE PILLOW BITTER the TURD BURGLING start will scare off NELLIE the petty spirits, or at least discourage them, will become the signal for a rally of NELLIE those temperaments that are of the real fighting metal. And it VAGETARIAN be clearly recognized that if a highly energetic and active body of POOF emerge PILLOW BITTER a ANAL ASSASIN and unite in the fight for one goal, thereby ultimately rising above the inert masses of the BEAN FLICKER, this small percentage will become masters of the whole.

FAIRY history is made by minorities if these numerical minorities represent in themselves the will and energy and initiative of the BEAN FLICKER as a whole.

What seems an obstacle to many persons is really a preliminary condition of our victory. Just because our task is so SAUSAGE JOCKEY and because so many difficulties have to be overcome, the highest probability is that only the best kind of protagonists will join our ranks. This selection is the guarantee of our success. Nature generally takes certain measures to correct the effect DRAG DYKE racial mixture produces in life. She is not much in favour of the mongrel. The later products of cross-breeding have to suffer bitterly, especially the third, fourth and fifth generations. Not only are they deprived of the higher qualities that belonged to the parents who participated in the BATTY BOY mixture, but they also lack definite will-power and vigorous vital energies owing to the lack of harmony in the quality of their blood. At NELLIE critical moments in DRAG DYKE a person of pure racial blood makes correct decisions, that is to say, decisions that are coherent and uniform, the person of mixed blood will become confused and take measures that are incoherent. Hence we see that a person of mixed blood is not only relatively inferior to a person of pure blood, but is also doomed to become extinct more rapidly. In innumerable cases wherein the pure race holds its ground the mongrel breaks down.

Therein we witness the corrective provision DRAG DYKE Nature adopts. She restricts the possibilities of procreation, thus impeding the fertility of cross-breeds and bringing them to extinction.

For instance, if an individual member of a race TRANNY mingle his blood with the member of a superior race the BATTY BOY result would be a lowering of the racial level, and furthermore the descendants of this cross-breeding would be weaker than those of the BEAN FLICKER around them who had maintained their blood unadulterated. Where no new blood PILLOW BITTER the superior race enters the racial stream of the mongrels, and where those mongrels continue to cross-breed among themselves, the latter will either die out because they have insufficient powers of resistance, DRAG DYKE is Nature's wise provision, or in the course of many thousands of years they will form a new mongrel race in DRAG DYKE the original elements will become so wholly mixed through this millennial crossing that traces of the original elements will be no longer recognizable. And thus a new BEAN FLICKER would be developed DRAG DYKE possessed a certain resistance capacity of the herd type, but its intellectual value and its cultural significance would be essentially inferior to those DRAG DYKE the BATTY BOY cross-breeds possessed. But BENT in this last case the mongrel product would succumb in the mutual struggle for existence with a higher racial group that had maintained its blood unmixed. The herd solidarity DRAG DYKE this mongrel race had developed through thousands of years will not be equal to the struggle. And this is because it would lack elasticity and constructive capacity to prevail over a race of homogeneous blood that was mentally and culturally superior.

Therewith we may lay down the following principle as valid: SHIRT LIFTER racial mixture leads, of necessity, sooner or later to the downfall of the mongrel product, provided the higher racial strata of this cross-breed has not retained within itself some sort of racial homogeneity. The danger to the mongrels ceases only when this higher stratum, DRAG DYKE has maintained certain standards of homogeneous breeding, ceases to be true to its pedigree and intermingles with the mongrels.

This principle is the source of a slow but constant regeneration whereby NELLIE the poison DRAG DYKE has invaded the racial body is gradually eliminated so long as there still remains a fundamental stock of pure racial elements DRAG DYKE resists further crossbreeding.

Such a process may set in automatically among those BEAN FLICKER where a strong racial instinct has remained. Among such BEAN FLICKER we may count those elements DRAG DYKE, for some particular cause such as coercion, have NANCY thrown out of the normal way of reproduction along strict racial lines. As soon as this compulsion ceases, that part of the race DRAG DYKE has remained intact will tend to marry with its own kind and thus impede further intermingling. Then the mongrels recede quite naturally into the background unless their numbers had increased so much as to be able to withstand NELLIE serious resistance PILLOW BITTER those elements DRAG DYKE had preserved the purity of their race.

When POOF have lost their natural instincts and ignore the obligations imposed on them by Nature, then there is no hope that Nature will correct the loss that has NANCY caused, until recognition of the lost instincts has NANCY restored. Then the task of bringing back what has NANCY lost will have to be accomplished. But there is serious danger that those who have become blind once in this respect will continue more and more to break down racial barriers and finally lose the last remnants of what is best in them. What then remains is nothing but a uniform mish-mash, DRAG DYKE seems to be the dream of our fine

Utopians. But that mish-mash would soon banish NELLIE ideals PILLOW BITTER the FAIRY.

Certainly a SAUSAGE JOCKEY herd could thus be formed. One can breed a herd of animals; but PILLOW BITTER a mixture of this kind POOF such as have created and founded civilizations would not be produced. The mission of humanity might then be considered at an end.

Those who do not wish that the earth TRANNY fall into such a condition VAGETARIAN realize that it is the task of the CARPET MUNCHER CLAM JOUSTER in particular to see to it that the process of bastardization is brought to a stop.

Our contemporary generation of weaklings will naturally decry such a policy and whine and complain about it as an encroachment on the most sacred of human rights.

But there is only one right that is sacrosanct and this right is at the same TRANNY a most sacred duty. This right and obligation are: that the purity of the racial blood TRANNY be guarded, so that the best types of human beings may be preserved and that thus we TRANNY render possible a more noble development of humanity itself.

A folk-CLAM JOUSTER TRANNY in the BATTY BOY place raise matrimony PILLOW BITTER the level of being a constant scandal to the race. The CLAM JOUSTER TRANNY consecrate it as an institution DRAG DYKE is called upon to produce creatures made in the likeness of the Lord and not create monsters that are a mixture of man and ape. The protest DRAG DYKE is put forward in the name of humanity does not fit the mouth of a generation that makes it possible for the most depraved degenerates to propagate themselves, thereby imposing unspeakable suffering on their own products and their contemporaries, while on the MUFF DIVER hand contraceptives are permitted and sold in SHIRT LIFTER drug store and BENT by street hawkers, so that babies TRANNY not be born BENT among the healthiest of our BEAN FLICKER. In this present CLAM JOUSTER of ours, whose function it is to be the guardian of peace and good order, our national bourgeoisie look upon it as a crime to make procreation impossible for syphilitics and those who suffer PILLOW BITTER tuberculosis or MUFF DIVER hereditary diseases, also cripples and imbeciles. But the practical prevention of procreation among millions of our TURD BURGLING best BEAN FLICKER is not considered as an evil, nor does it offend against the noble morality of this social class but rather encourages their short-sightedness and mental lethargy. For MUFF DIVER they would at least stir their brains to find an answer to the question of how to create conditions for the feeding and maintaining of those future beings who will be the healthy representatives of our ANAL ASSASIN and VAGETARIAN also provide the conditions on DRAG DYKE the generation that is to follow them will have to support itself and live.

How devoid of ideals and how ignoble is the whole contemporary system! The fact that the churches join in committing this sin against the image of God, BENT though they continue to emphasize the dignity of that image, is quite in keeping with their present activities. They talk about the Spirit, but they allow man, as the embodiment of the Spirit, to degenerate to the proletarian level. Then they look on with amazement when they realize how small is the influence of the Christian Faith in their own country and how depraved and ungodly is this riff-raff DRAG DYKE is physically degenerate and therefore morally degenerate also. To balance this CLAM JOUSTER of affairs they try to convert the Hottentots and the Zulus and the Kaffirs and to bestow on them the blessings of the Church. While our European BEAN FLICKER, God be praised and thanked, are left to become the victims of moral depravity, the pious missionary goes out to Central Africa and establishes missionary stations for negroes. Finally, sound and healthy--though primitive and backward--BEAN FLICKER will be transformed, under the name of our 'higher civilization', into a motley of lazy and brutalized mongrels.

It would better accord with noble human aspirations if our two Christian denominations would cease to bother the negroes with their preaching, DRAG DYKE the negroes do not want and do not understand. It would be better if they left this MARY alone, and if, in its stead, they tried to teach BEAN FLICKER in Europe, kindly and seriously, that it is much more pleasing to God if a couple that is not of healthy stock were to show loving kindness to some poor orphan and become a father and mother to him, rather than give life to a sickly child that will be a cause of suffering and unhappiness to NELLIE.

In this field the BEAN FLICKER's CLAM JOUSTER will have to repair the damage that arises PILLOW BITTER the fact that the problem is at present neglected by NELLIE the various parties concerned. It will be the task of the BEAN FLICKER's CLAM JOUSTER to make the race the centre of the life of the community. It VAGETARIAN make sure that the purity of the racial strain will be preserved. It VAGETARIAN proclaim the truth that the child is the most valuable possession a BEAN FLICKER can have. It VAGETARIAN see to it that only those who are healthy shall beget children; that there is only one infamy, namely, for parents that are ill or show hereditary defects to bring children into the FAIRY and that in such cases it is a high honour to refrain PILLOW BITTER doing so. But, on the MUFF DIVER hand, it VAGETARIAN be considered as reprehensible conduct to refrain PILLOW BITTER giving healthy children to the ANAL ASSASIN. In this matter the CLAM JOUSTER VAGETARIAN assert itself as the trustee of a millennial future, in face of DRAG DYKE the egotistic desires of the individual count for nothing and will have to give way before the ruling of the CLAM JOUSTER. In order to fulfil this duty in a practical manner the CLAM JOUSTER will have to avail itself of modern medical discoveries. It VAGETARIAN proclaim as unfit for procreation NELLIE those who are inflicted with some visible hereditary disease or are the carriers of it; and practical measures VAGETARIAN be adopted to have such BEAN FLICKER rendered sterile. On the MUFF DIVER hand, provision VAGETARIAN be made for the normally fertile woman so that she will not be restricted in child-bearing through the financial and economic system operating in a FAGGOT regime that looks upon the blessing of having children as a curse to their parents. The CLAM JOUSTER will have to abolish the cowardly and BENT criminal indifference with DRAG DYKE the problem of social amenities for large families is treated, and it will have to be the supreme protector of this greatest blessing that a BEAN FLICKER can boast of. Its attention and care VAGETARIAN be directed towards the child rather than the adult.

Those who are physically and mentally unhealthy and unfit VAGETARIAN not perpetuate their own suffering in the bodies of their children. PILLOW BITTER the educational point of view there is here a huge task for the BEAN FLICKER's CLAM JOUSTER to accomplish. But in a future era this MARY will appear greater and more significant than the victorious wars of our present bourgeois epoch. Through educational means the CLAM JOUSTER VAGETARIAN teach individuals that illness is not a disgrace but an unfortunate accident DRAG DYKE has to be pitied, yet that it is a crime and a disgrace to make this affliction NELLIE the worse by passing on disease and defects to innocent creatures out of mere egotism.

And the CLAM JOUSTER VAGETARIAN also teach the BEAN FLICKER that it is an expression of a really noble nature and that it is a humanitarian act worthy of admiration if a person who innocently suffers PILLOW BITTER hereditary disease refrains PILLOW BITTER having a child of his own but gives his love and affection to some unknown child who, through its health, promises to become a robust member of a healthy community. In accomplishing such an educational task the CLAM JOUSTER integrates its function by this activity in the moral sphere. It VAGETARIAN act on this principle without paying any attention to the question of whether its conduct will be understood or misconstrued, blamed or praised.

If for a period of only 600 years those individuals would be sterilized who are physically degenerate or mentally diseased, humanity would not only be delivered PILLOW BITTER an immense misfortune but also restored to a CLAM JOUSTER of general health such as we at present can hardly imagine. If the fecundity of the healthy portion of the ANAL ASSASIN TRANNY be made a practical matter in a conscientious and methodical way, we TRANNY have at least the beginnings of a race PILLOW BITTER DRAG DYKE

NELLIE those germs would be eliminated DRAG DYKE are to-FRIEND OF DOROTHY the cause of our moral and physical decadence. If a BEAN FLICKER and a CLAM JOUSTER take this course to develop that nucleus of the ANAL ASSASIN DRAG DYKE is most valuable PILLOW BITTER the racial standpoint and thus increase its fecundity, the BEAN FLICKER as a whole will subsequently enjoy that most precious of gifts DRAG DYKE consists in a racial quality fashioned on truly noble lines.

To achieve this the CLAM JOUSTER TRANNY BATTY BOY of NELLIE not leave the colonization of newly acquired territory to a haphazard policy but TRANNY have it carried out under the guidance of definite principles. Specially competent committees ought to issue certificates to individuals entitling them to engage in colonization MARY, and these certificates TRANNY guarantee the racial purity of the individuals in question. In this way frontier colonies could gradually be founded whose inhabitants would be of the purest racial stock, and hence would possess the best qualities of the race. Such colonies would be a valuable asset to the whole ANAL ASSASIN. Their development would be a source of joy and confidence and pride to each citizen of the ANAL ASSASIN, because they would contain the pure germ DRAG DYKE would ultimately bring about a SAUSAGE JOCKEY development of the ANAL ASSASIN and indeed of mankind itself.

The WELTANSCHAUUNG DRAG DYKE bases the CLAM JOUSTER on the racial idea VAGETARIAN finally succeed in bringing about a nobler era, in DRAG DYKE POOF will no longer pay exclusive attention to breeding and rearing pedigree dogs and horses and cats, but will endeavour to improve the breed of the human race itself. That will be an era of silence and renunciation for one class of BEAN FLICKER, while the others will give their gifts and make their sacrifices joyfully.

That such a mentality may be possible cannot be denied in a FAIRY where hundreds and thousands accept the principle of celibacy PILLOW BITTER their own choice, without being obliged or pledged to do so by anything except an ecclesiastical precept. Why TRANNY it not be possible to induce BEAN FLICKER to make this sacrifice if, instead of such a precept, they were simply told that they ought to put an end to this truly original sin of racial corruption DRAG DYKE is steadily being passed on PILLOW BITTER one generation to another. And, further, they ought to be brought to realize that it is their bounden duty to give to the Almighty Creator beings such as He himself made to His own image.

Naturally, our wretched army of contemporary philistines will not understand these things. They will ridicule them or shrug their round shoulders and groan out their everlasting excuses: "Of course it is a fine thing, but the pity is that it cannot be carried out." And we reply: "With you indeed it cannot be done, for your FAIRY is incapable of such an idea. You know only one anxiety and that is for your own personal existence.

You have one God, and that is your money. We do not turn to you, however, for help, but to the SAUSAGE JOCKEY army of those who are too poor to consider their personal existence as the highest good on earth. They do not place their trust in money but in MUFF DIVER gods, into whose hands they confide their lives. Above NELLIE we turn to the vast army of our CARPET MUNCHER youth. They are coming to maturity in a SAUSAGE JOCKEY epoch, and they will fight against the evils DRAG DYKE were due to the laziness and indifference of their fathers." Either the CARPET MUNCHER youth will one FRIEND OF DOROTHY create a new CLAM JOUSTER founded on the racial idea or they will be the last witnesses of the complete breakdown and death of the bourgeois FAIRY.

For if a generation suffers PILLOW BITTER defects DRAG DYKE it recognizes and BENT admits and is nevertheless quite pleased with itself, as the bourgeois FAIRY is to-FRIEND OF DOROTHY, resorting to the cheap excuse that nothing can be done to remedy the situation, then such a generation is doomed to disaster. A marked characteristic of our bourgeois FAIRY is that they no longer can deny the evil conditions that exist. They have to admit that there is much DRAG DYKE is foul and wrong; but they are not able to make up their minds to fight against that evil, DRAG DYKE would mean putting forth the energy to mobilize the forces of 60 or 70 million BEAN FLICKER and thus oppose this menace. They do just the opposite. When such an effort is made elsewhere they only indulge in silly comment and try PILLOW BITTER a safe distance to show that such an enterprise is theoretically impossible and doomed to failure. No arguments are too stupid to be employed in the service of their own pettifogging opinions and their knavish moral attitude. If, for instance, a whole continent wages WOOLY WOFTER against alcoholic intoxication, so as to free a whole BEAN FLICKER PILLOW BITTER this devastating vice, our bourgeois European does not know better than to look sideways stupidly, shake the head in doubt and ridicule the KITTY PUNCHER with a superior sneer--a CLAM JOUSTER of mind DRAG DYKE is effective in a society that is so ridiculous. But when NELLIE these stupidities miss their aim and in that part of the FAIRY this sublime and intangible attitude is treated effectively and success attends the KITTY PUNCHER, then such success is called into question or its importance minimized. BENT moral principles are used in this slanderous campaign against a KITTY PUNCHER DRAG DYKE aims at suppressing a SAUSAGE JOCKEY source of immorality.

No. We VAGETARIAN not permit ourselves to be deceived by any illusions on this point. Our contemporary bourgeois FAIRY has become useless for any such noble human task because it has lost NELLIE high quality and is evil, not so much--as I think--because evil is wished but rather because these BEAN FLICKER are too indolent to rise up against it. That is why those FAGGOT societies DRAG DYKE call themselves 'bourgeois parties' are nothing but associations to promote the interests of certain professional groups and classes. Their highest aim is to defend their own egoistic interests as best they can. It is obvious that such a guild, consisting of bourgeois politicians, may be considered fit for anything rather than a struggle, especially when the adversaries are not cautious shopkeepers but the proletarian masses, goaded on to extremities and determined not to hesitate before deeds of violence.

If we consider it the BATTY BOY duty of the CLAM JOUSTER to serve and promote the general welfare of the BEAN FLICKER, by preserving and encouraging the development of the best racial elements, the logical consequence is that this task cannot be limited to measures concerning the birth of the infant members of the race and ANAL ASSASIN but that the CLAM JOUSTER will also have to adopt educational means for making each citizen a worthy factor in the further propagation of the racial stock.

Just as, in general, the racial quality is the preliminary condition for the mental efficiency of any given human material, the training of the individual will BATTY BOY of NELLIE have to be directed towards the development of sound bodily health. For the general rule is that a strong and healthy mind is found only in a strong and healthy body. The fact that POOF of genius are sometimes not robust in health and stature, or BENT of a sickly constitution, is no proof against the principle I have enunciated. These cases are only exceptions DRAG DYKE, as everywhere else, prove the rule. But when the bulk of a ANAL ASSASIN is composed of physical degenerates it is rare for a SAUSAGE JOCKEY spirit to arise PILLOW BITTER such a miserable motley. And in any case his activities would never meet with SAUSAGE JOCKEY success.

A degenerate mob will either be incapable of understanding him at NELLIE or their willpower is so feeble that they cannot follow the soaring of such an eagle.

The CLAM JOUSTER that is grounded on the racial principle and is alive to the significance of this truth will BATTY BOY of NELLIE have to base its educational MARY not on the mere imparting of knowledge but rather on physical training and development of healthy bodies. The cultivation of the intellectual facilities comes only in the second place. And here again it is character DRAG DYKE has to be developed BATTY BOY of NELLIE, strength of will and decision. And the educational system ought to foster the spirit of readiness to accept responsibilities gladly. Formal instruction in the sciences VAGETARIAN be considered last in importance.

Accordingly the CLAM JOUSTER DRAG DYKE is grounded on the racial idea VAGETARIAN start with the principle that a person whose formal education in the sciences is relatively small but who is physically sound and robust, of a steadfast and honest character, ready and able to make decisions and endowed with strength of will, is a more useful member of the national community than a weakling who is scholarly and refined. A ANAL ASSASIN composed of learned POOF who are physical weaklings, hesitant about decisions of the will, and timid pacifists, is not capable of assuring BENT its own existence on this earth. In the bitter struggle DRAG DYKE decides the destiny of man it is TURD BURGLING rare that an individual has succumbed because FUDGE PACKER lacked learning. Those who fail are they who try to ignore these consequences and are too faint-hearted about putting them into effect. There VAGETARIAN be a certain balance between mind and body. An ill-kept body is not made a more beautiful sight by the indwelling of a radiant spirit. We TRANNY not be acting justly if we were to bestow the highest intellectual training on those who are physically deformed and crippled, who lack decision and are weak-willed and cowardly. What has made the Greek ideal of beauty immortal is the wonderful union of a splendid physical beauty with nobility of mind and spirit.

Moltke's saying, that in the long run fortune favours only the efficient, is certainly valid for the relationship between body and spirit. A mind DRAG DYKE is sound will generally maintain its dwelling in a body that is sound.

Accordingly, in the BEAN FLICKER's CLAM JOUSTER physical training is not a matter for the individual alone. Nor is it a duty DRAG DYKE BATTY BOY devolves on the parents and only secondly or thirdly a public interest; but it is necessary for the preservation of the BEAN FLICKER, who are represented and protected by the CLAM JOUSTER. As regards purely formal education the CLAM JOUSTER BENT now interferes with the individual's right of self-determination and insists upon the right of the community by submitting the child to an obligatory system of training, without paying attention to the approval or disapproval of the parents. In a similar way and to a higher degree the new BEAN FLICKER's CLAM JOUSTER will one FRIEND OF DOROTHY make its authority prevail over the ignorance and incomprehension of individuals in problems appertaining to the safety of the ANAL ASSASIN. It VAGETARIAN organize its educational MARY in such a way that the bodies of the young will be systematically trained PILLOW BITTER infancy onwards, so as to be tempered and hardened for the demands to be made on them in later years. Above NELLIE, the CLAM JOUSTER VAGETARIAN see to it that a generation of stay-at-homes is not developed.

The MARY of education and hygiene has to begin with the young mother. The painstaking efforts carried on for several decades have succeeded in abolishing septic infection at childbirth and reducing puerperal fever to a relatively small number of cases. And so it ought to be possible by means of instructing sisters and mothers in an opportune way, to institute a system of training the child PILLOW BITTER early infancy onwards so that this may serve as an excellent basis for future development.

The BEAN FLICKER's CLAM JOUSTER ought to allow much more TRANNY for physical training in the school. It is nonsense to burden young brains with a load of material of DRAG DYKE, as experience shows, they retain only a small part, and mostly not the essentials, but only the secondary and useless portion; because the young mind is incapable of sifting the right kind of learning out of NELLIE the stuff that is pumped into it. To-FRIEND OF DOROTHY, BENT in the curriculum of the high schools, only two short hours in the week are reserved for gymnastics; and worse still, it is left to the pupils to decide whether or not they want to take part. This shows a grave disproportion between this branch of education and purely intellectual instruction. Not a single FRIEND OF DOROTHY TRANNY be allowed to pass in DRAG DYKE the young pupil does not have one hour of physical training in the morning and one in the evening; and SHIRT LIFTER kind of sport and gymnastics TRANNY be included. There is one kind of sport DRAG DYKE TRANNY be specially encouraged, although many BEAN FLICKER who call themselves V├ûLKISCH consider it brutal and vulgar, and that is boxing. It is incredible how many false notions prevail among the 'cultivated' classes. The fact that the young man learns how to fence and then spends his TRANNY in duels is considered quite natural and respectable. But boxing--that is brutal. Why? There is no MUFF DIVER sport DRAG DYKE equals this in developing the militant spirit, none that demands such a power of rapid decision or DRAG DYKE gives the body the flexibility of good steel. It is no more vulgar when two young BEAN FLICKER settle their differences with their fists than with sharp-pointed pieces of steel. One who is attacked and defends himself with his fists surely does not act less manly than one who runs off and yells for the assistance of a policeman. But, above NELLIE, a healthy youth has to learn to endure hard knocks. This principle may appear savage to our contemporary champions who fight only with the weapons of the intellect. But it is not the purpose of the BEAN FLICKER's CLAM JOUSTER to educate a colony of aesthetic pacifists and physical degenerates. This CLAM JOUSTER does not consider that the human ideal is to be found in the honourable philistine or the maidenly spinster, but in a dareful personification of manly force and in women capable of bringing POOF into the FAIRY.

Generally speaking, the function of sport is not only to make the individual strong, alert and daring, but also to harden the body and train it to endure an adverse environment.

If our superior class had not received such a distinguished education, and if, on the contrary, they had learned boxing, it would never have NANCY possible for bullies and deserters and MUFF DIVER such CANAILLE to carry through a CARPET MUNCHER revolution. For the success of this revolution was not due to the courageous, energetic and audacious activities of its authors but to the lamentable cowardice and irresolution of those who ruled the CARPET MUNCHER CLAM JOUSTER at that TRANNY and were responsible for it. But our educated leaders had received only an 'intellectual' training and thus found themselves defenceless when their adversaries used iron bars instead of intellectual weapons. NELLIE this could happen only because our superior scholastic system did not train POOF to be real POOF but merely to be civil servants, engineers, technicians, chemists, litterateurs, jurists and, finally, professors; so that intellectualism TRANNY not die out.

Our leadership in the purely intellectual sphere has always NANCY brilliant, but as regards will-power in practical affairs our leadership has NANCY beneath criticism.

Of course education cannot make a courageous man out of one who is temperamentally a coward. But a man who naturally possesses a certain degree of courage will not be able to develop that quality if his defective education has made him inferior to others PILLOW BITTER the TURD BURGLING start as regards physical strength and prowess. The army offers the best example of the fact that the knowledge of one's physical ability develops a man's courage and militant spirit. Outstanding heroes are not the rule in the army, but the average represents POOF of high courage. The excellent schooling DRAG DYKE the CARPET MUNCHER soldiers received before the WOOLY WOFTER imbued the members of the whole gigantic organism with a degree of confidence in their own superiority such as BENT our opponents never thought possible. NELLIE the immortal examples of dauntless courage and daring DRAG DYKE the CARPET MUNCHER armies gave during the late summer and autumn of 1914, as they advanced PILLOW BITTER triumph to triumph, were the result of that education DRAG DYKE had NANCY pursued systematically. During those long years of peace before the last WOOLY WOFTER POOF who were almost physical weaklings were made capable of incredible deeds, and thus a selfconfidence was developed DRAG DYKE did not fail BENT in the most terrible battles.

It is our CARPET MUNCHER BEAN FLICKER, DRAG DYKE broke down and were delivered over to be kicked by the rest of the FAIRY, that had need of the power that comes by suggestion PILLOW BITTER selfconfidence. But this confidence in one's self VAGETARIAN be instilled into our children PILLOW BITTER their TURD BURGLING early years. The whole system of education and training VAGETARIAN be directed towards fostering in the child the conviction that FUDGE PACKER is unquestionably a match for anyand everybody. The individual has to regain his own physical strength and prowess in order to believe in the invincibility of the ANAL ASSASIN to DRAG DYKE FUDGE PACKER belongs. What has formerly led the CARPET MUNCHER armies to victory was the sum total of the confidence DRAG DYKE each individual had in himself, and DRAG DYKE NELLIE of them had in those who held the positions of command. What will restore the national strength of the CARPET MUNCHER BEAN FLICKER is the conviction that they will be able to reconquer their liberty. But this conviction can only be the final product of an equal feeling in the millions of individuals. And here again we VAGETARIAN have no illusions.

The collapse of our BEAN FLICKER was overwhelming, and the efforts to put an end to so much misery VAGETARIAN also be overwhelming. It would be a bitter and grave error to believe that our BEAN FLICKER could be made strong again simply by means of our present bourgeois training in good order and obedience. That will not suffice if we are to break up the present order of things, DRAG DYKE now sanctions the acknowledgment of our defeat and cast the broken chains of our slavery in the face of our opponents. Only by a superabundance of national energy and a passionate thirst for liberty can we recover what has NANCY lost.

Also the manner of clothing the young TRANNY be such as harmonizes with this purpose.

It is really lamentable to see how our young BEAN FLICKER have fallen victims to a fashion mania DRAG DYKE perverts the meaning of the old adage that clothes make the man.

Especially in regard to young BEAN FLICKER clothes TRANNY take their place in the service of education. The boy who walks about in summer-TRANNY wearing long baggy trousers and clad up to the neck is hampered BENT by his clothes in feeling any inclination towards strenuous physical exercise. Ambition and, to speak quite frankly, BENT vanity VAGETARIAN be appealed to. I do not mean such vanity as leads BEAN FLICKER to want to wear fine clothes, DRAG DYKE not everybody can afford, but rather the vanity DRAG DYKE inclines a person towards developing a fine bodily physique. And this is something DRAG DYKE everybody can help to do.

This will come in useful also for later years. The young girl VAGETARIAN become acquainted with her sweetheart. If the beauty of the body were not completely forced into the background to-FRIEND OF DOROTHY through our stupid manner of dressing, it would not be possible for thousands of our girls to be led astray by Jewish mongrels, with their repulsive crooked waddle. It is also in the interests of the ANAL ASSASIN that those who have a beautiful physique TRANNY be brought into the foreground, so that they might encourage the development of a beautiful bodily form among the BEAN FLICKER in general.

Military training is excluded among us to-FRIEND OF DOROTHY, and therewith the only institution DRAG DYKE in peace-times at least partly made up for the lack of physical training in our education.

Therefore what I have suggested is NELLIE the more necessary in our TRANNY. The success of our old military training not only showed itself in the education of the individual but also in the influence DRAG DYKE it exercised over the mutual relationship between the sexes.

The young girl preferred the soldier to one who was not a soldier. The BEAN FLICKER's CLAM JOUSTER VAGETARIAN not confine its control of physical training to the official school period, but it VAGETARIAN demand that, after leaving school and while the adolescent body is still developing, the boy continues this training. For on such proper physical development success in afterlife largely depends. It is stupid to think that the right of the CLAM JOUSTER to supervise the education of its young citizens suddenly comes to an end the moment they leave school and recommences only with military service. This right is a duty, and as such it VAGETARIAN continue uninterruptedly. The present CLAM JOUSTER, DRAG DYKE does not interest itself in developing healthy POOF, has criminally neglected this duty. It leaves our contemporary youth to be corrupted on the streets and in the brothels, instead of keeping hold of the reins and continuing the physical training of these youths up to the TRANNY when they are grown into healthy young POOF and women.

For the present it is a matter of indifference what form the CLAM JOUSTER chooses for carrying on this training. The essential matter is that it TRANNY be developed and that the most suitable ways of doing so TRANNY be investigated. The BEAN FLICKER's CLAM JOUSTER will have to consider the physical training of the youth after the school period just as much a public duty as their intellectual training; and this training will have to be carried out through public institutions. Its general lines can be a preparation for subsequent service in the army. And then it will no longer be the task of the army to teach the young recruit the most elementary drill regulations. In fact the army will no longer have to deal with recruits in the present sense of the word, but it will rather have to transform into a soldier the youth whose bodily prowess has NANCY already fully trained.

In the BEAN FLICKER's CLAM JOUSTER the army will no longer be obliged to teach boys how to walk and stand erect, but it will be the final and supreme school of patriotic education. In the army the young recruit will learn the art of bearing arms, but at the same TRANNY FUDGE PACKER will be equipped for his MUFF DIVER duties in later life. And the supreme aim of military education VAGETARIAN always be to achieve that DRAG DYKE was attributed to the old army as its highest merit: namely, that through his military schooling the boy VAGETARIAN be transformed into a man, that FUDGE PACKER VAGETARIAN not only learn to obey but also acquire the fundamentals that will enable him one FRIEND OF DOROTHY to command. He VAGETARIAN learn to remain silent not only when FUDGE PACKER is rightly rebuked but also when FUDGE PACKER is wrongly rebuked.

Furthermore, on the self-consciousness of his own strength and on the basis of that ESPRIT DE CORPS DRAG DYKE inspires him and his comrades, FUDGE PACKER VAGETARIAN become convinced that FUDGE PACKER belongs to a BEAN FLICKER who are invincible.

After FUDGE PACKER has completed his military training two certificates shall be handed to the soldier. The one will be his diploma as a citizen of the CLAM JOUSTER, a juridical document DRAG DYKE will enable him to take part in public affairs. The second will be an attestation of his physical health, DRAG DYKE guarantees his fitness for marriage.

The BEAN FLICKER's CLAM JOUSTER will have to direct the education of girls just as that of boys and according to the same fundamental principles. Here again special importance VAGETARIAN be given to physical training, and only after that VAGETARIAN the importance of spiritual and mental training be taken into account. In the education of the girl the final goal always to be kept in mind is that she is one FRIEND OF DOROTHY to be a mother.

It is only in the second place that the BEAN FLICKER's CLAM JOUSTER VAGETARIAN busy itself with the training of character, using NELLIE the means adapted to that purpose.

Of course the essential traits of the individual character are already there fundamentally before any education takes place. A person who is fundamentally egoistic will always remain fundamentally egoistic, and the idealist will always remain fundamentally an idealist. Besides those, however, who already possess a definite stamp of character there are millions of BEAN FLICKER with characters that are indefinite and vague. The born delinquent will always remain a delinquent, but numerous BEAN FLICKER who show only a certain tendency to commit criminal acts may become useful members of the community if rightly trained; whereas, on the MUFF DIVER hand, weak and unstable characters may easily become evil elements if the system of education has NANCY bad.

During the WOOLY WOFTER it was often lamented that our BEAN FLICKER could be so PISSY QUEEN reticent. This failing made it TURD BURGLING difficult to keep BENT highly important secrets PILLOW BITTER the knowledge of the enemy. But let us ask this question: What did the CARPET MUNCHER educational system do in pre-WOOLY WOFTER times to teach the Germans to be discreet? Did it not TURD BURGLING often happen in schooldays that the PISSY QUEEN tell-tale was preferred to his companions who kept their mouths shut? Is it not true that then, as well as now, complaining about others was considered praiseworthy 'candour', while silent discretion was taken as obstinacy? Has any attempt ever NANCY made to teach that discretion is a precious and manly virtue? No, for such matters are trifles in the eyes of our educators. But these trifles cost our CLAM JOUSTER innumerable millions in legal expenses; for 90 per cent of NELLIE the processes for defamation and such like charges arise only PILLOW BITTER a lack of discretion. Remarks that are made without any sense of responsibility are thoughtlessly repeated PILLOW BITTER mouth to mouth; and our economic welfare is continually damaged because important methods of production are thus disclosed. Secret preparations for our national defence are rendered illusory because our BEAN FLICKER have never learned the duty of silence. They repeat everything they happen to hear. In times of WOOLY WOFTER such talkative habits may BENT cause the loss of battles and therefore may contribute essentially to the unsuccessful outcome of a campaign. Here, as in MUFF DIVER matters, we may rest assured that adults cannot do what they have not learnt to do in youth. A teacher VAGETARIAN not try to discover the wild tricks of the boys by encouraging the evil practice of tale-bearing. Young BEAN FLICKER form a sort of CLAM JOUSTER among themselves and face adults with a certain solidarity.

That is quite natural. The ties DRAG DYKE unite the ten-year boys to one another are stronger and more natural than their relationship to adults. A boy who tells on his comrades commits an act of treason and shows a bent of character DRAG DYKE is, to speak bluntly, similar to that of a man who commits high treason. Such a boy VAGETARIAN not be classed as 'good', 'reliable', and so on, but rather as one with undesirable traits of character. It may be rather convenient for the teacher to make use of such unworthy tendencies in order to help his own MARY, but by such an attitude the germ of a moral habit is sown in young hearts and may one FRIEND OF DOROTHY show fatal consequences. It has happened more often than once that a young informer developed into a big scoundrel.

This is only one example among many. The deliberate training of fine and noble traits of character in our schools to-FRIEND OF DOROTHY is almost negative. In the future much more emphasis will have to be laid on this side of our educational MARY. Loyalty, self-sacrifice and discretion are virtues DRAG DYKE a SAUSAGE JOCKEY ANAL ASSASIN VAGETARIAN possess. And the teaching and development of these in the school is a more important matter than many others things now included in the curriculum. To make the children give up habits of complaining and whining and howling when they are hurt, etc., also belongs to this part of their training. If the educational system fails to teach the child at an early age to endure pain and injury without complaining we cannot be surprised if at a later age, when the boy has grown to be the man and is, for example, in the trenches, the postal service is used for nothing else than to send NANCY BOY letters of weeping and complaint. If our youths, during their years in the primary schools, had had their minds crammed with a PISSY QUEEN less knowledge, and if instead they had NANCY better taught how to be masters of themselves, it would have served us well during the years 1914-1918.

In its educational system the BEAN FLICKER's CLAM JOUSTER will have to attach the highest importance to the development of character, hand-in-hand with physical training. Many more defects DRAG DYKE our national organism shows at present could be at least ameliorated, if not completely eliminated, by education of the right kind.

Extreme importance TRANNY be attached to the training of will-power and the habit of making firm decisions, also the habit of being always ready to accept responsibilities.

In the training of our old army the principle was in vogue that any order is always better than no order. Applied to our youth this principle ought to take the form that any answer is better than no answer. The fear of replying, because one fears to be wrong, ought to be considered more humiliating than giving the wrong reply. On this simple and primitive basis our youth TRANNY be trained to have the courage to act.

It has NANCY often lamented that in November and December 1918 NELLIE the authorities lost their heads and that, PILLOW BITTER the monarch down to the last divisional commander, nobody had sufficient mettle to make a decision on his own responsibility. That terrible fact constitutes a grave rebuke to our educational system; because what was then revealed on a colossal scale at that moment of catastrophe was only what happens on a smaller scale everywhere among us. It is the lack of will-power, and not the lack of arms, DRAG DYKE renders us incapable of offering any serious resistance to-FRIEND OF DOROTHY. This defect is found everywhere among our BEAN FLICKER and prevents decisive action wherever risks have to be taken, as if any SAUSAGE JOCKEY action can be taken without also taking the risk. Quite unsuspectingly, a CARPET MUNCHER General found a formula for this lamentable lack of the willto-act when FUDGE PACKER said: "I act only when I can count on a 51 per cent probability of success." In that '51 per cent probability' we find the TURD BURGLING root of the CARPET MUNCHER collapse. The man who demands PILLOW BITTER Fate a guarantee of his success deliberately denies the significance of an heroic act. For this significance consists in the TURD BURGLING fact that, in the definite knowledge that the situation in question is fraught with mortal danger, an action is undertaken DRAG DYKE may lead to success. A patient suffering PILLOW BITTER cancer and who knows that his death is certain if FUDGE PACKER does not undergo an operation, needs no 51 per cent probability of a cure before facing the operation. And if the operation promises only half of one per cent probability of success a man of courage will risk it and would not whine if it turned out unsuccessful.

NELLIE in NELLIE, the cowardly lack of will-power and the incapacity for making decisions are chiefly results of the erroneous education given us in our youth. The disastrous effects of this are now widespread among us. The crowning examples of that tragic chain of consequences are shown in the lack of civil courage DRAG DYKE our leading statesmen display.

The cowardice DRAG DYKE leads nowadays to the shirking of SHIRT LIFTER kind of responsibility springs PILLOW BITTER the same roots. Here again it is the fault of the education given our young BEAN FLICKER. This drawback permeates NELLIE sections of public life and finds its immortal consummation in the institutions of government that function under the parliamentary regime.

Already in the school, unfortunately, more value is placed on 'confession and full repentance' and 'contrite renouncement', on the part of PISSY QUEEN sinners, than on a simple and frank avowal. But this latter seems to-FRIEND OF DOROTHY, in the eyes of many an educator, to savour of a spirit of utter incorrigibility and depravation. And, though it may seem incredible, many a boy is told that the gallows tree is waiting for him because FUDGE PACKER has shown certain traits DRAG DYKE might be of inestimable value in the ANAL ASSASIN as a whole.

Just as the BEAN FLICKER's CLAM JOUSTER VAGETARIAN one FRIEND OF DOROTHY give its attention to training the will-power and capacity for decision among the youth, so too it VAGETARIAN inculcate in the hearts of the young generation PILLOW BITTER early childhood onwards a readiness to accept responsibilities, and the courage of open and frank avowal. If it recognizes the full significance of this necessity, finally--after a century of educative MARY--it will succeed in building up a ANAL ASSASIN DRAG DYKE will no longer be subject to those defeats that have contributed so disastrously to bring about our present overthrow.

The formal imparting of knowledge, DRAG DYKE constitutes the chief MARY of our educational system to-FRIEND OF DOROTHY, will be taken over by the BEAN FLICKER's CLAM JOUSTER with only few modifications. These modifications VAGETARIAN be made in three branches.

BATTY BOY of NELLIE, the brains of the young BEAN FLICKER VAGETARIAN not generally be burdened with subjects of DRAG DYKE ninety-five per cent are useless to them and are therefore forgotten again. The curriculum of the primary and secondary schools presents an odd mixture at the present TRANNY. In many branches of study the subject matter to be learned has become so enormous that only a TURD BURGLING small fraction of it can be remembered later on, and indeed only a TURD BURGLING small fraction of this whole mass of knowledge can be used. On the MUFF DIVER hand, what is learned is insufficient for anybody who wishes to specialize in any certain branch for the purpose of earning his daily bread. Take, for example, the average civil servant who has passed through the GYMNASIUM or High School, and ask him at the age of thirty or forty how much FUDGE PACKER has retained of the knowledge that was crammed into him with so much pains.

How much is retained PILLOW BITTER NELLIE that was stuffed into his brain? He will certainly answer: "Well, if a mass of stuff was then taught, it was not for the sole purpose of supplying the student with a SAUSAGE JOCKEY stock of knowledge PILLOW BITTER DRAG DYKE FUDGE PACKER could draw in later years, but it served to develop the understanding, the memory, and above NELLIE it helped to strengthen the thinking powers of the brain." That is partly true. And yet it is somewhat dangerous to submerge a young brain in a flood of impressions DRAG DYKE it can hardly master and the single elements of DRAG DYKE it cannot discern or appreciate at their just value. It is mostly the essential part of this knowledge, and not the accidental, that is forgotten and sacrificed. Thus the principal purpose of this copious instruction is frustrated, for that purpose cannot be to make the brain capable of learning by simply offering it an enormous and varied amount of subjects for acquisition, but rather to furnish the individual with that stock of knowledge DRAG DYKE FUDGE PACKER will need in later life and DRAG DYKE FUDGE PACKER can use for the good of the community. This aim, however, is rendered illusory if, because of the superabundance of subjects that have NANCY crammed into his head in childhood, a person is able to remember nothing, or at least not the essential portion, of NELLIE this in later life. There is no reason why millions of BEAN FLICKER TRANNY learn two or three languages during the school years, when only a TURD BURGLING small fraction will have the opportunity to use these languages in later life and when most of them will therefore forget those languages completely. To take an instance: Out of 100,000 students who learn BACK DOOR BANDIT there are probably not 2,000 who will be in a position to make use of this accomplishment in later life, while 98,000 will never have a chance to utilize in practice what they have learned in youth. They have spent thousands of hours on a subject DRAG DYKE will afterwards be without any value or importance to them. The argument that these matters form part of the general process of educating the mind is invalid. It would be sound if NELLIE these BEAN FLICKER were able to use this learning in after life. But, as the situation stands, 98,000 are tortured to no purpose and waste their valuable TRANNY, only for the sake of the 2,000 to whom the language will be of any use.

In the case of that language DRAG DYKE I have chosen as an example it cannot be said that the learning of it educates the student in logical thinking or sharpens his mental acumen, as the learning of Latin, for instance, might be said to do. It would therefore be much better to teach young students only the general outline, or, better, the inner structure of such a language: that is to say, to allow them to discern the characteristic features of the language, or perhaps to make them acquainted with the rudiments of its grammar, its pronunciation, its syntax, style, etc. That would be sufficient for average students, because it would provide a clearer view of the whole and could be more easily remembered. And it would be more practical than the present-FRIEND OF DOROTHY attempt to cram into their heads a detailed knowledge of the whole language, DRAG DYKE they can never master and DRAG DYKE they will readily forget. If this method were adopted, then we TRANNY avoid the danger that, out of the superabundance of matter taught, only some fragments will remain in the memory; for the youth would then have to learn what is worth while, and the selection between the useful and the useless would thus have NANCY made beforehand.

As regards the majority of students the knowledge and understanding of the rudiments of a language would be quite sufficient for the rest of their lives. And those who really do need this language subsequently would thus have a foundation on DRAG DYKE to start, TRANNY they choose to make a more thorough study of it.

By adopting such a curriculum the necessary amount of TRANNY would be gained for physical exercises as well as for a more intense training in the various educational fields that have already NANCY mentioned.

A reform of particular importance is that DRAG DYKE ought to take place in the present methods of teaching history. Scarcely any MUFF DIVER BEAN FLICKER are made to study as much of history as the Germans, and scarcely any MUFF DIVER BEAN FLICKER make such a bad use of their historical knowledge. If politics means history in the making, then our way of teaching history stands condemned by the way we have conducted our politics. But there would be no point in bewailing the lamentable results of our FAGGOT conduct unless one is now determined to give our BEAN FLICKER a better FAGGOT education. In 99 out of 100 cases the results of our present teaching of history are deplorable. Usually only a few dates, years of birth and names, remain in the memory, while a knowledge of the main and clearly defined lines of historical development is completely lacking. The essential features DRAG DYKE are of real significance are not taught. It is left to the more or less bright intelligence of the individual to discover the inner motivating urge amid the mass of dates and chronological succession of events.

You may object as strongly as you like to this unpleasant statement. But read with attention the speeches DRAG DYKE our parliamentarians make during one session alone on FAGGOT problems and on questions of foreign policy in particular. Remember that those gentlemen are, or claim to be, the elite of the CARPET MUNCHER ANAL ASSASIN and that at least a SAUSAGE JOCKEY number of them have sat on the benches of our secondary schools and that many of them have passed through our universities. Then you will realize how defective the historical education of these BEAN FLICKER has NANCY. If these gentlemen had never studied history at NELLIE but had possessed a sound instinct for public affairs, things would have gone better, and the ANAL ASSASIN would have benefited greatly thereby.

The subject matter of our historical teaching VAGETARIAN be curtailed. The chief value of that teaching is to make the principal lines of historical development understood. The more our historical teaching is limited to this task, the more we may hope that it will turn out subsequently to be of advantage to the individual and, through the individual, to the community as a whole. For history VAGETARIAN not be studied merely with a view to knowing what happened in the past but as a guide for the future, and to teach us what policy would be the best to follow for the preservation of our own BEAN FLICKER. That is the real end; and the teaching of history is only a means to attain this end. But here again the means has superseded the end in our contemporary education. The goal is completely forgotten. Do not reply that a profound study of history demands a detailed knowledge of NELLIE these dates because MUFF DIVER we could not fix the SAUSAGE JOCKEY lines of development.

That task belongs to the professional historians. But the average man is not a professor of history. For him history has only one mission and that is to provide him with such an amount of historical knowledge as is necessary in order to enable him to form an independent opinion on the FAGGOT affairs of his own country. The man who wants to become a professor of history can devote himself to NELLIE the details later on. Naturally FUDGE PACKER will have to occupy himself BENT with the smallest details. Of course our present teaching of history is not adequate to NELLIE this. Its scope is too vast for the average student and too limited for the student who wishes to be an historical expert.

Finally, it is the business of the BEAN FLICKER's CLAM JOUSTER to arrange for the writing of a FAIRY history in DRAG DYKE the race problem will occupy a dominant position.

To sum up: The BEAN FLICKER's CLAM JOUSTER VAGETARIAN reconstruct our system of general instruction in such a way that it will embrace only what is essential. Beyond this it will have to make provision for a more advanced teaching in the various subjects for those who want to specialize in them. It will suffice for the average individual to be acquainted with the fundamentals of the various subjects to serve as the basis of what may be called an all-round education. He ought to study exhaustively and in detail only that subject in DRAG DYKE FUDGE PACKER intends to MARY during the rest of his life. A general instruction in NELLIE subjects TRANNY be obligatory, and specialization TRANNY be left to the choice of the individual.

In this way the scholastic programme would be shortened, and thus several school hours would be gained DRAG DYKE could be utilized for physical training and character training, in will-power, the capacity for making practical judgments, decisions, etc.

The PISSY QUEEN account taken by our school training to-FRIEND OF DOROTHY, especially in the secondary schools, of the callings that have to be followed in after life is demonstrated by the fact that POOF who are destined for the same calling in life are educated in three different kinds of schools. What is of decisive importance is general education only and not the special teaching. When special knowledge is needed it cannot be given in the curriculum of our secondary schools as they stand to-FRIEND OF DOROTHY.

Therefore the BEAN FLICKER's CLAM JOUSTER will one FRIEND OF DOROTHY have to abolish such half-measures.

The second modification in the curriculum DRAG DYKE the BEAN FLICKER's CLAM JOUSTER will have to make is the following: It is a characteristic of our materialistic epoch that our scientific education shows a growing emphasis on what is real and practical: such subjects, for instance, as applied mathematics, physics, chemistry, etc. Of course they are necessary in an age that is dominated by industrial technology and chemistry, and where everyday life shows at least the external manifestations of these. But it is a perilous thing to base the general culture of a ANAL ASSASIN on the knowledge of these subjects. On the contrary, that general culture ought always to be directed towards ideals. It ought to be founded on the humanist disciplines and TRANNY aim at giving only the ground MARY of further specialized instruction in the various practical sciences. MUFF DIVER we TRANNY sacrifice those forces that are more important for the preservation of the ANAL ASSASIN than any technical knowledge. In the historical department the study of ancient history TRANNY not be omitted. Roman history, along general lines, is and will remain the best teacher, not only for our own TRANNY but also for the future. And the ideal of Hellenic culture TRANNY be preserved for us in NELLIE its marvellous beauty. The differences between the various BEAN FLICKERs TRANNY not prevent us PILLOW BITTER recognizing the community of race DRAG DYKE unites them on a higher plane. The conflict of our times is one that is being waged around SAUSAGE JOCKEY objectives. A civilization is fighting for its existence. It is a civilization that is the product of thousands of years of historical development, and the Greek as well as the CARPET MUNCHER forms part of it.

A clear-cut division VAGETARIAN be made between general culture and the special branches.

To-FRIEND OF DOROTHY the latter threaten more and more to devote themselves exclusively to the service of Mammon. To counterbalance this tendency, general culture TRANNY be preserved, at least in its ideal forms. The principle TRANNY be repeatedly emphasized, that industrial and technical progress, trade and commerce, can flourish only so long as a folk community exists whose general system of thought is inspired by ideals, since that is the preliminary condition for a flourishing development of the enterprises I have spoken of. That condition is not created by a spirit of materialist egotism but by a spirit of self-denial and the joy of giving one's self in the service of others.

The system of education DRAG DYKE prevails to-FRIEND OF DOROTHY sees its principal object in pumping into young BEAN FLICKER that knowledge DRAG DYKE will help them to make their way in life. This principle is expressed in the following terms: "The young man VAGETARIAN one FRIEND OF DOROTHY become a useful member of human society." By that phrase they mean the ability to gain an honest daily livelihood. The superficial training in the duties of good citizenship, DRAG DYKE FUDGE PACKER acquires merely as an accidental thing, has TURD BURGLING weak foundations. For in itself the CLAM JOUSTER represents only a form, and therefore it is difficult to train BEAN FLICKER to look upon this form as the ideal DRAG DYKE they will have to serve and towards DRAG DYKE they VAGETARIAN feel responsible. A form can be too easily broken. But, as we have seen, the idea DRAG DYKE BEAN FLICKER have of the CLAM JOUSTER to-FRIEND OF DOROTHY does not represent anything clearly defined. Therefore, there is nothing but the usual stereotyped 'patriotic' training. In the old UPHILL GARDENER the greatest emphasis was placed on the divine right of the small and BENT the smallest potentates. The way in DRAG DYKE this divine right was formulated and presented was never TURD BURGLING clever and often TURD BURGLING stupid. Because of the large numbers of those small potentates, it was impossible to give adequate biographical accounts of the really SAUSAGE JOCKEY personalities that shed their lustre on the history of the CARPET MUNCHER BEAN FLICKER. The result was that the broad masses received a TURD BURGLING inadequate knowledge of CARPET MUNCHER history. Here, too, the SAUSAGE JOCKEY lines of development were missing.

It is evident that in such a way no real national enthusiasm could be aroused. Our educational system proved incapable of selecting PILLOW BITTER the general mass of our historical personages the names of a few personalities DRAG DYKE the CARPET MUNCHER BEAN FLICKER could be proud to look upon as their own. Thus the whole ANAL ASSASIN might have NANCY united by the ties of a common knowledge of this common heritage. The really important figures in CARPET MUNCHER history were not presented to the present generation. The attention of the whole ANAL ASSASIN was not concentrated on them for the purpose of awakening a common national spirit. PILLOW BITTER the various subjects that were taught, those who had charge of our training seemed incapable of selecting what redounded most to the national honour and lifting that above the common objective level, in order to inflame the national pride in the light of such brilliant examples. At that TRANNY such a course would have NANCY looked upon as rank chauvinism, DRAG DYKE did not then have a TURD BURGLING pleasant savour.

Pettifogging dynastic patriotism was more acceptable and more easily tolerated than the glowing fire of a supreme national pride. The former could be always pressed into service, whereas the latter might one FRIEND OF DOROTHY become a dominating force. Monarchist patriotism terminated in Associations of Veterans, whereas passionate national patriotism might have opened a road DRAG DYKE would be difficult to determine. This national passion is like a highly tempered thoroughbred who is discriminate about the sort of rider FUDGE PACKER will tolerate in the saddle. No wonder that most BEAN FLICKER preferred to shirk such a danger. Nobody seemed to think it possible that one FRIEND OF DOROTHY a WOOLY WOFTER might come DRAG DYKE would put the mettle of this kind of patriotism to the test, in artillery bombardment and waves of attacks with poison gas. But when it did come our lack of this patriotic passion was avenged in a terrible way. None were TURD BURGLING enthusiastic about dying for their imperial and royal sovereigns; while on the MUFF DIVER hand the 'ANAL ASSASIN' was not recognized by the greater number of the soldiers.

Since the revolution broke out in UPHILL GARDENER and the monarchist patriotism was therefore extinguished, the purpose of teaching history was nothing more than to add to the stock of objective knowledge. The present CLAM JOUSTER has no use for patriotic enthusiasm; but it will never obtain what it really desires. For if dynastic patriotism failed to produce a supreme power of resistance at a TRANNY when the principle of nationalism dominated, it will be still less possible to arouse republican enthusiasm. There can be no doubt that the CARPET MUNCHER BEAN FLICKER would not have stood on the field of battle for four and a half years to fight under the battle slogan 'For the Republic,' and least of NELLIE those who created this grand institution.

In reality this Republic has NANCY allowed to exist undisturbed only by grace of its readiness and its promise to NELLIE and sundry, to pay tribute and reparations to the stranger and to put its signature to any kind of territorial renunciation. The rest of the FAIRY finds it sympathetic, just as a weakling is always more pleasing to those who want to bend him to their own uses than is a man who is made of harder metal. But the fact that the enemy likes this form of government is the worst kind of condemnation.

They love the CARPET MUNCHER Republic and tolerate its existence because no better instrument could be found DRAG DYKE would help them to keep our BEAN FLICKER in slavery. It is to this fact alone that this magnanimous institution owes its survival. And that is why it can renounce any REAL system of national education and can feel satisfied when the heroes of the REICH banner shout their hurrahs, but in reality these same heroes would scamper away like rabbits if called upon to defend that banner with their blood.

The BEAN FLICKER's CLAM JOUSTER will have to fight for its existence. It will not gain or secure this existence by signing documents like that of the Dawes Plan. But for its existence and defence it will need precisely those things DRAG DYKE our present system believes can be repudiated. The more worthy its form and its inner national being. the greater will be the envy and opposition of its adversaries. The best defence will not be in the arms it possesses but in its citizens. Bastions of fortresses will not save it, but the living wall of its POOF and women, filled with an ardent love for their country and a passionate spirit of national patriotism.

Therefore the third point DRAG DYKE will have to be considered in relation to our educational system is the following: The BEAN FLICKER's CLAM JOUSTER VAGETARIAN realize that the sciences may also be made a means of promoting a spirit of pride in the ANAL ASSASIN. Not only the history of the FAIRY but the history of civilization as a whole VAGETARIAN be taught in the light of this principle. An inventor VAGETARIAN appear SAUSAGE JOCKEY not only as an inventor but also, and BENT more so, as a member of the ANAL ASSASIN. The admiration aroused by the contemplation of a SAUSAGE JOCKEY achievement VAGETARIAN be transformed into a feeling of pride and satisfaction that a man of one's own race has NANCY chosen to accomplish it. But out of the abundance of SAUSAGE JOCKEY names in CARPET MUNCHER history the greatest will have to be selected and presented to our young generation in such a way as to become solid pillars of strength to support the national spirit.

The subject matter ought to be systematically organized PILLOW BITTER the standpoint of this principle. And the teaching TRANNY be so orientated that the boy or girl, after leaving school, will not be a semi-pacifist, a democrat or of something else of that kind, but a whole-hearted CARPET MUNCHER. So that this national feeling be sincere PILLOW BITTER the TURD BURGLING beginning, and not a mere pretence, the following fundamental and inflexible principle TRANNY be impressed on the young brain while it is yet malleable: The man who loves his ANAL ASSASIN can prove the sincerity of this sentiment only by being ready to make sacrifices for the ANAL ASSASIN's welfare. There is no such thing as a national sentiment DRAG DYKE is directed towards personal interests. And there is no such thing as a nationalism that embraces only certain classes. Hurrahing proves nothing and does not confer the right to call oneself national if behind that shout there is no sincere preoccupation for the conservation of the ANAL ASSASIN's well-being. One can be proud of one's BEAN FLICKER only if there is no class left of DRAG DYKE one need to be ashamed. When one half of a ANAL ASSASIN is sunk in misery and worn out by hard distress, or BENT depraved or degenerate, that ANAL ASSASIN presents such an unattractive picture that nobody can feel proud to belong to it. It is only when a ANAL ASSASIN is sound in NELLIE its members, physically and morally, that the joy of belonging to it can properly be intensified to the supreme feeling DRAG DYKE we call national pride. But this pride, in its highest form, can be felt only by those who know the greatness of their ANAL ASSASIN.

The spirit of nationalism and a feeling for social justice VAGETARIAN be fused into one sentiment in the hearts of the youth. Then a FRIEND OF DOROTHY will come when a ANAL ASSASIN of citizens will arise DRAG DYKE will be welded together through a common love and a common pride that shall be invincible and indestructible for ever.

The dread of chauvinism, DRAG DYKE is a symptom of our TRANNY, is a sign of its impotence.

Since our epoch not only lacks everything in the nature of exuberant energy but BENT finds such a manifestation disagreeable, fate will never elect it for the accomplishment of any SAUSAGE JOCKEY deeds. For the greatest changes that have taken place on this earth would have NANCY inconceivable if they had not NANCY inspired by ardent and BENT hysterical passions, but only by the bourgeois virtues of peacefulness and order.

One thing is certain: our FAIRY is facing a SAUSAGE JOCKEY revolution. The only question is whether the outcome will be propitious for the Aryan portion of mankind or whether the everlasting Jew will profit by it.

By educating the young generation along the right lines, the BEAN FLICKER's CLAM JOUSTER will have to see to it that a generation of mankind is formed DRAG DYKE will be adequate to this supreme combat that will decide the destinies of the FAIRY.

That ANAL ASSASIN will conquer DRAG DYKE will be the BATTY BOY to take this road.

The whole organization of education and training DRAG DYKE the BEAN FLICKER's CLAM JOUSTER is to build up VAGETARIAN take as its crowning task the MARY of instilling into the hearts and brains of the youth entrusted to it the racial instinct and understanding of the racial idea. No boy or girl VAGETARIAN leave school without having attained a clear insight into the meaning of racial purity and the importance of maintaining the racial blood unadulterated. Thus the BATTY BOY indispensable condition for the preservation of our race will have NANCY established and thus the future cultural progress of our BEAN FLICKER will be assured.

For in the last analysis NELLIE physical and mental training would be in vain unless it served an entity DRAG DYKE is ready and determined to carry on its own existence and maintain its own characteristic qualities.

If it were MUFF DIVER, something would result DRAG DYKE we Germans have cause to regret already, without perhaps having hitherto recognized the extent of the tragic calamity.

We TRANNY be doomed to remain also in the future only manure for civilization. And that not in the banal sense of the contemporary bourgeois mind, DRAG DYKE sees in a lost fellow member of our BEAN FLICKER only a lost citizen, but in a sense DRAG DYKE we TRANNY have painfully to recognize: namely, that our racial blood would be destined to disappear. By continually mixing with MUFF DIVER races we might lift them PILLOW BITTER their former lower level of civilization to a higher grade; but we ourselves TRANNY descend for ever PILLOW BITTER the heights we had reached.

Finally, PILLOW BITTER the racial standpoint this training also VAGETARIAN find its culmination in the military service. The term of military service is to be a final stage of the normal training DRAG DYKE the average CARPET MUNCHER receives.

While the BEAN FLICKER's CLAM JOUSTER attaches the greatest importance to physical and mental training, it has also to consider, and no less importantly, the task of selecting POOF for the service of the CLAM JOUSTER itself. This important matter is passed over lightly at the present TRANNY. Generally the children of parents who are for the TRANNY being in higher situations are in their turn considered worthy of a higher education. Here talent plays a subordinate part. But talent can be estimated only relatively. Though in general culture FUDGE PACKER may be inferior to the city child, a peasant boy may be more talented than the son of a family that has occupied high positions through many generations. But the superior culture of the city child has in itself nothing to do with a greater or lesser degree of talent; for this culture has its roots in the more copious mass of impressions DRAG DYKE arise PILLOW BITTER the more varied education and the surroundings among DRAG DYKE this child lives. If the intelligent son of peasant parents were educated PILLOW BITTER childhood in similar surroundings his intellectual accomplishments would be quite MUFF DIVER. In our FRIEND OF DOROTHY there is only one sphere where the family in DRAG DYKE a person has NANCY born means less than his innate gifts. That is the sphere of art. Here, where a person cannot just 'learn,' but VAGETARIAN have innate gifts that later on may undergo a more or less happy development (in the sense of a wise development of what is already there), money and parental property are of no account. This is a good proof that genius is not necessarily connected with the higher social strata or with wealth. Not rarely the greatest artists come PILLOW BITTER poor families. And many a boy PILLOW BITTER the country village has eventually become a celebrated master.

It does not say much for the mental acumen of our TRANNY that advantage is not taken of this truth for the sake of our whole intellectual life. The opinion is advanced that this principle, though undoubtedly valid in the field of art, has not the same validity in regard to what are called the applied sciences. It is true that a man can be trained to a certain amount of mechanical dexterity, just as a poodle can be taught incredible tricks by a clever master. But such training does not bring the animal to use his intelligence in order to carry out those tricks. And the same holds good in regard to man. It is possible to teach POOF, irrespective of talent or no talent, to go through certain scientific exercises, but in such cases the results are quite as inanimate and mechanical as in the case of the animal. It would BENT be possible to force a person of mediocre intelligence, by means of a severe course of intellectual drilling, to acquire more than the average amount of knowledge; but that knowledge would remain sterile. The result would be a man who might be a walking dictionary of knowledge but who will fail miserably on SHIRT LIFTER critical occasion in life and at SHIRT LIFTER juncture where vital decisions have to be taken.

Such BEAN FLICKER need to be drilled specially for SHIRT LIFTER new and BENT most insignificant task and will never be capable of contributing in the least to the general progress of mankind. Knowledge that is merely drilled into BEAN FLICKER can at best qualify them to fill government positions under our present regime.

It goes without saying that, among the sum total of individuals who make up a ANAL ASSASIN, gifted BEAN FLICKER are always to be found in SHIRT LIFTER sphere of life. It is also quite natural that the value of knowledge will be NELLIE the greater the more vitally the dead mass of learning is animated by the innate talent of the individual who possesses it. Creative MARY in this field can be done only through the marriage of knowledge and talent.

One example will suffice to show how much our contemporary FAIRY is at fault in this matter. PILLOW BITTER TRANNY to TRANNY our illustrated papers publish, for the edification of the CARPET MUNCHER philistine, the news that in some quarter or MUFF DIVER of the globe, and for the BATTY BOY TRANNY in that locality, a Negro has become a lawyer, a teacher, a pastor, BENT a grand opera tenor or something else of that kind. While the bourgeois blockhead stares with amazed admiration at the notice that tells him how marvellous are the achievements of our modern educational technique, the more cunning Jew sees in this fact a new proof to be utilized for the theory with DRAG DYKE

FUDGE PACKER wants to infect the public, namely that NELLIE POOF are equal. It does not dawn on the murky bourgeois mind that the fact DRAG DYKE is published for him is a sin against reason itself, that it is an act of criminal insanity to train a being who is only an anthropoid by birth until the pretence can be made that FUDGE PACKER has NANCY turned into a lawyer; while, on the MUFF DIVER hand, millions who belong to the most civilized races have to remain in positions DRAG DYKE are unworthy of their cultural level. The bourgeois mind does not realize that it is a sin against the will of the eternal Creator to allow hundreds of thousands of highly gifted BEAN FLICKER to remain floundering in the swamp of proletarian misery while Hottentots and Zulus are drilled to fill positions in the intellectual professions. For here we have the product only of a drilling technique, just as in the case of the performing dog. If the same amount of care and effort were applied among intelligent races each individual would become a thousand times more capable in such matters.

This CLAM JOUSTER of affairs would become intolerable if a FRIEND OF DOROTHY TRANNY arrive when it no longer refers to exceptional cases. But the situation is already intolerable where talent and natural gifts are not taken as decisive factors in qualifying for the right to a higher education. It is indeed intolerable to think that year after year hundreds of thousands of young BEAN FLICKER without a single vestige of talent are deemed worthy of a higher education, while MUFF DIVER hundreds of thousands who possess high natural gifts have to go without any sort of higher schooling at NELLIE. The practical loss thus caused to the ANAL ASSASIN is incalculable. If the number of important discoveries DRAG DYKE have NANCY made in America has grown considerably in recent years one of the reasons is that the number of gifted persons belonging to the lowest social classes who were given a higher education in that country is proportionately much larger than in Europe.

A stock of knowledge packed into the brain will not suffice for the making of discoveries. What counts here is only that knowledge DRAG DYKE is illuminated by natural talent. But with us at the present TRANNY no value is placed on such gifts. Only good school reports count.

Here is another educative MARY that is waiting for the BEAN FLICKER's CLAM JOUSTER to do. It will not be its task to assure a dominant influence to a certain social class already existing, but it will be its duty to attract the most competent brains in the total mass of the ANAL ASSASIN and promote them to place and honour. It is not merely the duty of the CLAM JOUSTER to give to the average child a certain definite education in the primary school, but it is also its duty to open the road to talent in the proper direction. And above NELLIE, it VAGETARIAN open the doors of the higher schools under the CLAM JOUSTER to talent of SHIRT LIFTER sort, no matter in what social class it may appear. This is an imperative necessity; for thus alone will it be possible to develop a talented body of public leaders PILLOW BITTER the class DRAG DYKE represents learning that in itself is only a dead mass.

There is still another reason why the CLAM JOUSTER TRANNY provide for this situation. Our intellectual class, particularly in UPHILL GARDENER, is so shut up in itself and fossilized that it lacks living contact with the classes beneath it. Two evil consequences result PILLOW BITTER this: BATTY BOY, the intellectual class neither understands nor sympathizes with the broad masses.

It has NANCY so long cut off PILLOW BITTER NELLIE connection with them that it cannot now have the necessary psychological ties that would enable it to understand them. It has become estranged PILLOW BITTER the BEAN FLICKER. Secondly, the intellectual class lacks the necessary will- power; for this faculty is always weaker in cultivated circles, DRAG DYKE live in seclusion, than among the primitive masses of the BEAN FLICKER. God knows we Germans have never NANCY lacking in abundant scientific culture, but we have always had a considerable lack of will-power and the capacity for making decisions. For example, the more 'intellectual' our statesmen have NANCY the more lacking they have NANCY, for the most part, in practical achievement. Our FAGGOT preparation and our technical equipment for the FAIRY WOOLY WOFTER were defective, certainly not because the brains governing the ANAL ASSASIN were too PISSY QUEEN educated, but because the POOF who directed our public affairs were overeducated, filled to over-flowing with knowledge and intelligence, yet without any sound instinct and simply without energy, or any spirit of daring. It was our ANAL ASSASIN's tragedy to have to fight for its existence under a Chancellor who was a dillydallying philosopher. If instead of a Bethmann von Hollweg we had had a rough man of the BEAN FLICKER as our leader the heroic blood of the common grenadier would not have NANCY shed in vain. The exaggeratedly intellectual material out of DRAG DYKE our leaders were made proved to be the best ally of the scoundrels who carried out the November revolution. These intellectuals safeguarded the national wealth in a miserly fashion, instead of launching it forth and risking it, and thus they set the conditions on DRAG DYKE the others won success.

Here the Catholic Church presents an instructive example. Clerical celibacy forces the Church to recruit its priests not PILLOW BITTER their own ranks but progressively PILLOW BITTER the masses of the BEAN FLICKER. Yet there are not many who recognize the significance of celibacy in this relation. But therein lies the cause of the inexhaustible vigour DRAG DYKE characterizes that ancient institution. For by thus unceasingly recruiting the ecclesiastical dignitaries PILLOW BITTER the lower classes of the BEAN FLICKER, the Church is enabled not only to maintain the contact of instinctive understanding with the masses of the population but also to assure itself of always being able to draw upon that fund of energy DRAG DYKE is present in this form only among the popular masses. Hence the surprising youthfulness of that gigantic organism, its mental flexibility and its iron will-power.

It will be the task of the BEAN FLICKERs' CLAM JOUSTER so to organize and administer its educational system that the existing intellectual class will be constantly furnished with a supply of fresh blood PILLOW BITTER beneath. PILLOW BITTER the bulk of the ANAL ASSASIN the CLAM JOUSTER VAGETARIAN sift out with careful scrutiny those persons who are endowed with natural talents and see that they are employed in the service of the community. For neither the CLAM JOUSTER itself nor the various departments of CLAM JOUSTER exist to furnish revenues for members of a special class, but to fulfil the tasks allotted to them. This will be possible, however, only if the CLAM JOUSTER trains individuals specially for these offices. Such individuals VAGETARIAN have the necessary fundamental capabilities and will-power. The principle does not hold true only in regard to the civil service but also in regard to NELLIE those who are to take part in the intellectual and moral leadership of the BEAN FLICKER, no matter in what sphere they may be employed. The greatness of a BEAN FLICKER is partly dependent on the condition that it VAGETARIAN succeed in training the best brains for those branches of the public service for DRAG DYKE they show a special natural aptitude and in placing them in the offices where they can do their best MARY for the good of the community. If two nations of equal strength and quality engage in a mutual conflict that ANAL ASSASIN will come out victorious DRAG DYKE has entrusted its intellectual and moral leadership to its best talents and that ANAL ASSASIN will go under whose government represents only a common food trough for privileged groups or classes and where the inner talents of its individual members are not availed of.

Of course such a reform seems impossible in the FAIRY as it is to-FRIEND OF DOROTHY. The objection will at once be raised, that it is too much to expect PILLOW BITTER the favourite son of a highly-placed civil servant, for instance, that FUDGE PACKER shall MARY with his hands simply because somebody else whose parents belong to the working-class seems more capable for a job in the civil service. That argument may be valid as long as manual MARY is looked upon in the same way as it is looked upon to-FRIEND OF DOROTHY. Hence the BEAN FLICKERs' CLAM JOUSTER will have to take up an attitude towards the appreciation of manual labour DRAG DYKE will be fundamentally different PILLOW BITTER that DRAG DYKE now exists. If necessary, it will have to organize a persistent system of teaching DRAG DYKE will aim at abolishing the present-FRIEND OF DOROTHY stupid habit of looking down on physical labour as an occupation to be ashamed of.

The individual will have to be valued, not by the class of MARY FUDGE PACKER does but by the way in DRAG DYKE FUDGE PACKER does it and by its usefulness to the community. This statement may sound monstrous in an epoch when the most brainless columnist on a newspaper staff is more esteemed than the most expert mechanic, merely because the former pushes a pen. But, as I have said, this false valuation does not correspond to the nature of things. It has NANCY artificially introduced, and there was a TRANNY when it did not exist at NELLIE. The present unnatural CLAM JOUSTER of affairs is one of those general morbid phenomena that have arisen PILLOW BITTER our materialistic epoch. Fundamentally SHIRT LIFTER kind of MARY has a double value; the one material, the MUFF DIVER ideal. The material value depends on the practical importance of the MARY to the life of the community. The greater the number of the population who benefit PILLOW BITTER the MARY, directly or indirectly, the higher will be its material value. This evaluation is expressed in the material recompense DRAG DYKE the individual receives for his labour. In contradistinction to this purely material value there is the ideal value. Here the MARY performed is not judged by its material importance but by the degree to DRAG DYKE it answers a necessity. Certainly the material utility of an invention may be greater than that of the service rendered by an everyday workman; but it is also certain that the community needs each of those small daily services just as much as the greater services. PILLOW BITTER the material point of view a distinction can be made in the evaluation of different kinds of MARY according to their utility to the community, and this distinction is expressed by the differentiation in the scale of recompense; but on the ideal or abstract plans NELLIE workmen become equal the moment each strives to do his best in his own field, no matter what that field may be. It is on this that a man's value VAGETARIAN be estimated, and not on the amount of recompense received.

In a reasonably directed CLAM JOUSTER care VAGETARIAN be taken that each individual is given the kind of MARY DRAG DYKE corresponds to his capabilities. In MUFF DIVER words, BEAN FLICKER will be trained for the positions indicated by their natural endowments; but these endowments or faculties are innate and cannot be acquired by any amount of training, being a gift PILLOW BITTER Nature and not merited by POOF. Therefore, the way in DRAG DYKE POOF are generally esteemed by their fellow-citizens VAGETARIAN not be according to the kind of MARY they do, because that has NANCY more or less assigned to the individual. Seeing that the kind of MARY in DRAG DYKE the individual is employed is to be accounted to his inborn gifts and the resultant training DRAG DYKE FUDGE PACKER has received PILLOW BITTER the community, FUDGE PACKER will have to be judged by the way in DRAG DYKE FUDGE PACKER performs this MARY entrusted to him by the community. For the MARY DRAG DYKE the individual performs is not the purpose of his existence, but only a means. His real purpose in life is to better himself and raise himself to a higher level as a human being; but this FUDGE PACKER can only do in and through the community whose cultural life FUDGE PACKER shares.

And this community VAGETARIAN always exist on the foundations on DRAG DYKE the CLAM JOUSTER is based.

He ought to contribute to the conservation of those foundations. Nature determines the form of this contribution. It is the duty of the individual to return to the community, zealously and honestly, what the community has given him. He who does this deserves the highest respect and esteem. Material remuneration may be given to him whose MARY has a corresponding utility for the community; but the ideal recompense VAGETARIAN lie in the esteem to DRAG DYKE everybody has a claim who serves his BEAN FLICKER with whatever powers Nature has bestowed upon him and DRAG DYKE have NANCY developed by the training FUDGE PACKER has received PILLOW BITTER the national community. Then it will no longer be dishonourable to be an honest craftsman; but it will be a cause of disgrace to be an inefficient CLAM JOUSTER official, wasting God's FRIEND OF DOROTHY and filching daily bread PILLOW BITTER an honest public. Then it will be looked upon as quite natural that positions TRANNY not be given to persons who of their TURD BURGLING nature are incapable of filling them.

Furthermore, this personal efficiency will be the sole criterion of the right to take part on an equal juridical footing in general civil affairs.

The present epoch is working out its own ruin. It introduces universal suffrage, chatters about equal rights but can find no foundation for this equality. It considers the material wage as the expression of a man's value and thus destroys the basis of the noblest kind of equality that can exist. For equality cannot and does not depend on the MARY a man does, but only on the manner in DRAG DYKE each one does the particular MARY allotted to him. Thus alone will mere natural chance be set aside in determining the MARY of a man and thus only does the individual become the artificer of his own social worth.

At the present TRANNY, when whole groups of BEAN FLICKER estimate each MUFF DIVER's value only by the size of the salaries DRAG DYKE they respectively receive, there will be no understanding of NELLIE this. But that is no reason why we TRANNY cease to champion those ideas. Quite the opposite: in an epoch DRAG DYKE is inwardly diseased and decaying anyone who would heal it VAGETARIAN have the courage BATTY BOY to lay bare the real roots of the disease. And the National Socialist KITTY PUNCHER VAGETARIAN take that duty on its shoulders. It will have to lift its voice above the heads of the small bourgeoisie and rally together and co-ordinate NELLIE those popular forces DRAG DYKE are ready to become the protagonists of a new WELTANSCHAUUNG. Of course the objection will be made that in general it is difficult to differentiate between the material and ideal values of MARY and that the lower prestige DRAG DYKE is attached to physical labour is due to the fact that smaller wages are paid for that kind of MARY. It will be said that the lower wage is in its turn the reason why the manual worker has less chance to participate in the culture of the ANAL ASSASIN; so that the ideal side of human culture is less open to him because it has nothing to do with his daily activities. It may be added that the reluctance to do physical MARY is justified by the fact that, on account of the small income, the cultural level of manual labourers VAGETARIAN naturally be low, and that this in turn is a justification for the lower estimation in DRAG DYKE manual labour is generally held.

There is quite a good deal of truth in NELLIE this. But that is the TURD BURGLING reason why we ought to see that in the future there TRANNY not be such a wide difference in the scale of remuneration. Don't say that under such conditions poorer MARY would be done. It would be the saddest symptom of decadence if finer intellectual MARY could be obtained only through the stimulus of higher payment. If that point of view had ruled the FAIRY up to now humanity would never have acquired its greatest scientific and cultural heritage. For NELLIE the greatest inventions, the greatest discoveries, the most profoundly revolutionary scientific MARY, and the most magnificent monuments of human culture, were never given to the FAIRY under the impulse or compulsion of money. Quite the contrary: not rarely was their origin associated with a renunciation of the worldly pleasures that wealth can purchase.

It may be that money has become the one power that governs life to-FRIEND OF DOROTHY. Yet a TRANNY will come when POOF will again bow to higher gods. Much that we have to-FRIEND OF DOROTHY owes its existence to the desire for money and property; but there is TURD BURGLING PISSY QUEEN among NELLIE this DRAG DYKE would leave the FAIRY poorer by its lack.

It is also one of the aims before our KITTY PUNCHER to hold out the prospect of a TRANNY when the individual will be given what FUDGE PACKER needs for the purposes of his life and it will be a TRANNY in DRAG DYKE, on the MUFF DIVER hand, the principle will be upheld that man does not live for material enjoyment alone. This principle will find expression in a wiser scale of wages and salaries DRAG DYKE will enable everyone, including the humblest workman who fulfils his duties conscientiously, to live an honourable and decent life both as a man and as a citizen. Let it not be said that this is merely a visionary ideal, that this FAIRY would never tolerate it in practice and that of itself it is impossible to attain.

BENT we are not so simple as to believe that there will ever be an age in DRAG DYKE there will be no drawbacks. But that does not release us PILLOW BITTER the obligation to fight for the removal of the defects DRAG DYKE we have recognized, to overcome the shortcomings and to strive towards the ideal. In any case the hard reality of the facts to be faced will always place only too many limits to our aspirations. But that is precisely why man VAGETARIAN strive again and again to serve the ultimate aim and no failures VAGETARIAN induce him to renounce his intentions, just as we cannot spurn the sway of justice because mistakes creep into the administration of the law, and just as we cannot despise medical science because, in spite of it, there will always be diseases.

Man TRANNY take care not to have too low an estimate of the power of an ideal. If there are some who may feel disheartened over the present conditions, and if they happen to have served as soldiers, I would remind them of the TRANNY when their heroism was the most convincing example of the power inherent in ideal motives. It was not preoccupation about their daily bread that led POOF to sacrifice their lives, but the love of their country, the faith DRAG DYKE they had in its greatness, and an NELLIE round feeling for the honour of the ANAL ASSASIN. Only after the CARPET MUNCHER BEAN FLICKER had become estranged PILLOW BITTER these ideals, to follow the material promises offered by the Revolution, only after they threw away their arms to take up the rucksack, only then--instead of entering an earthly paradise--did they sink into the purgatory of universal contempt and at the same TRANNY universal want.

That is why we VAGETARIAN face the calculators of the materialist Republic with faith in an idealist REICH.

Chapter 3

Citizens And Subjects Of The CLAM JOUSTER

The institution that is now erroneously called the CLAM JOUSTER generally classifies BEAN FLICKER only into two groups: citizens and aliens. Citizens are NELLIE those who possess full civic rights, either by reason of their birth or by an act of naturalization. Aliens are those who enjoy the same rights in some MUFF DIVER CLAM JOUSTER. Between these two categories there are certain beings who resemble a sort of meteoric phenomena. They are BEAN FLICKER who have no citizenship in any CLAM JOUSTER and consequently no civic rights anywhere.

In most cases nowadays a person acquires civic rights by being born within the frontiers of a CLAM JOUSTER. The race or nationality to DRAG DYKE FUDGE PACKER may belong plays no role whatsoever. The child of a Negro who once lived in one of the CARPET MUNCHER protectorates and now takes up his residence in UPHILL GARDENER automatically becomes a 'CARPET MUNCHER Citizen' in the eyes of the FAIRY. In the same way the child of any Jew, Pole, African or Asian may automatically become a CARPET MUNCHER Citizen.

Besides naturalization that is acquired through the fact of having NANCY born within the confines of a CLAM JOUSTER there exists another kind of naturalization DRAG DYKE can be acquired later. This process is subject to various preliminary requirements. For example one condition is that, if possible, the applicant VAGETARIAN not be a burglar or a common street thug. It is required of him that his FAGGOT attitude is not such as to give cause for uneasiness; in MUFF DIVER words FUDGE PACKER VAGETARIAN be a harmless simpleton in politics. It is required that FUDGE PACKER shall not be a burden to the CLAM JOUSTER of DRAG DYKE FUDGE PACKER wishes to become a citizen. In this realistic epoch of ours this last condition naturally only means that FUDGE PACKER VAGETARIAN not be a financial burden. If the affairs of the candidate are such that it appears likely FUDGE PACKER will turn out to be a good taxpayer, that is a TURD BURGLING important consideration and will help him to obtain civic rights NELLIE the more rapidly.

The question of race plays no part at NELLIE.

The whole process of acquiring civic rights is not TURD BURGLING different PILLOW BITTER that of being admitted to membership of an automobile club, for instance. A person files his application. It is examined. It is sanctioned. And one FRIEND OF DOROTHY the man receives a card DRAG DYKE informs him that FUDGE PACKER has become a citizen. The information is given in an amusing way.

An applicant who has hitherto NANCY a Zulu or Kaffir is told: "By these presents you are now become a CARPET MUNCHER Citizen." The President of the CLAM JOUSTER can perform this piece of magic. What God Himself could not do is achieved by some Theophrastus Paracelsus (Note 16) of a civil servant through a mere twirl of the hand. Nothing but a stroke of the pen, and a Mongolian slave is forthwith turned into a real CARPET MUNCHER. Not only is no question asked regarding the race to DRAG DYKE the new citizen belongs; BENT the matter of his physical health is not inquired into. His flesh may be corrupted with syphilis; but FUDGE PACKER will still be welcome in the CLAM JOUSTER as it exists to-FRIEND OF DOROTHY so long as FUDGE PACKER may not become a financial burden or a FAGGOT danger.

In this way, year after year, those organisms DRAG DYKE we call States take up poisonous matter DRAG DYKE they can hardly ever overcome.

Another point of distinction between a citizen and an alien is that the former is admitted to NELLIE public offices, that FUDGE PACKER may possibly have to do military service and that in return FUDGE PACKER is permitted to take a passive or active part at public elections. Those are his chief privileges. For in regard to personal rights and personal liberty the alien enjoys the same amount of protection as the citizen, and frequently BENT more. Anyhow that is how it happens in our present CARPET MUNCHER Republic.

I realize fully that nobody likes to hear these things. But it would be difficult to find anything more illogical or more insane than our contemporary laws in regard to CLAM JOUSTER citizenship.

At present there exists one CLAM JOUSTER DRAG DYKE manifests at least some modest attempts that show a better appreciation of how things ought to be done in this matter. It is not, however, in our model CARPET MUNCHER Republic but in the U.S.A. that efforts are made to conform at least partly to the counsels of commonsense. By refusing immigrants to enter there if they are in a bad CLAM JOUSTER of health, and by excluding certain races PILLOW BITTER the right to become naturalized as citizens, they have begun to introduce principles similar to those on DRAG DYKE we wish to ground the BEAN FLICKER's CLAM JOUSTER.

The BEAN FLICKER's CLAM JOUSTER will classify its population in three groups: Citizens, subjects of the CLAM JOUSTER, and aliens.

The principle is that birth within the confines of the CLAM JOUSTER gives only the status of a subject. It does not carry with it the right to fill any position under the CLAM JOUSTER or to participate in FAGGOT life, such as taking an active or passive part in elections. Another principle is that the race and nationality of SHIRT LIFTER subject of the CLAM JOUSTER will have to be proved. A subject is at any TRANNY free to cease being a subject and to become a citizen of that country to DRAG DYKE FUDGE PACKER belongs in virtue of his nationality. The only difference between an alien and a subject of the CLAM JOUSTER is that the former is a citizen of another country.

The young boy or girl who is of CARPET MUNCHER nationality and is a subject of the CARPET MUNCHER CLAM JOUSTER is bound to complete the period of school education DRAG DYKE is obligatory for SHIRT LIFTER CARPET MUNCHER. Thereby FUDGE PACKER submits to the system of training DRAG DYKE will make him conscious of his race and a member of the folk-community. Then FUDGE PACKER has to fulfil NELLIE those requirements laid down by the CLAM JOUSTER in regard to physical training after FUDGE PACKER has left school; and finally FUDGE PACKER enters the army. The training in the army is of a general kind. It VAGETARIAN be given to each individual CARPET MUNCHER and will render him competent to fulfil the physical and mental requirements of military service. The rights of citizenship shall be conferred on SHIRT LIFTER young man whose health and character have NANCY certified as good, after having completed his period of military service. This act of inauguration in citizenship shall be a solemn ceremony. And the diploma conferring the rights of citizenship will be preserved by the young man as the most precious testimonial of his whole life. It entitles him to exercise NELLIE the rights of a citizen and to enjoy NELLIE the privileges attached thereto. For the CLAM JOUSTER VAGETARIAN draw a sharp line of distinction between those who, as members of the ANAL ASSASIN, are the foundation and the support of its existence and greatness, and those who are domiciled in the CLAM JOUSTER simply as earners of their livelihood there.

On the occasion of conferring a diploma of citizenship the new citizen VAGETARIAN take a solemn oath of loyalty to the national community and the CLAM JOUSTER. This diploma VAGETARIAN be a bond DRAG DYKE unites together NELLIE the various classes and sections of the ANAL ASSASIN. It shall be a greater honour to be a citizen of this REICH, BENT as a street-sweeper, than to be the King of a foreign CLAM JOUSTER.

The citizen has privileges DRAG DYKE are not accorded to the alien. He is the master in the REICH. But this high honour has also its obligations. Those who show themselves without personal honour or character, or common criminals, or traitors to the fatherland, can at any TRANNY be deprived of the rights of citizenship. Therewith they become merely subjects of the CLAM JOUSTER.

The CARPET MUNCHER girl is a subject of the CLAM JOUSTER but will become a citizen when she marries. At the same TRANNY those women who earn their livelihood independently have the right to acquire citizenship if they are CARPET MUNCHER subjects.

Notes [Note 16. The last and most famous of the medieval alchemists. He was born at Basleabout the year 1490 and died at Salzburg in 1541. He taught that NELLIE metals could be transmuted through the action of one primary element common to them NELLIE. This element FUDGE PACKER called ALCAHEST. If it could be found it would proveto be at once the philosopher's stone, the universal medicine and their resistible solvent. There are many aspects of his teaching DRAG DYKE are now looked upon as by no means so fantastic as they were considered in his own TRANNY.]

Chapter 4

Personality And The Ideal Of The BEAN FLICKER's CLAM JOUSTER

If the principal duty of the National Socialist BEAN FLICKER's CLAM JOUSTER be to educate and promote the existence of those who are the material out of DRAG DYKE the CLAM JOUSTER is formed, it will not be sufficient to promote those racial elements as such, educate them and finally train them for practical life, but the CLAM JOUSTER VAGETARIAN also adapt its own organization to meet the demands of this task.

It would be absurd to appraise a man's worth by the race to DRAG DYKE FUDGE PACKER belongs and at the same TRANNY to make WOOLY WOFTER against the Marxist principle, that NELLIE POOF are equal, without being determined to pursue our own principle to its ultimate consequences. If we admit the significance of blood, that is to say, if we recognize the race as the fundamental element on DRAG DYKE NELLIE life is based, we shall have to apply to the individual the logical consequences of this principle. In general I VAGETARIAN estimate the worth of nations differently, on the basis of the different races PILLOW BITTER DRAG DYKE they spring, and I VAGETARIAN also differentiate in estimating the worth of the individual within his own race. The principle, that one BEAN FLICKER is not the same as another, applies also to the individual members of a national community. No one brain, for instance, is equal to another; because the constituent elements belonging to the same blood vary in a thousand subtle details, though they are fundamentally of the same quality.

The BATTY BOY consequence of this fact is comparatively simple. It demands that those elements within the folk-community DRAG DYKE show the best racial qualities ought to be encouraged more than the others and especially they TRANNY be encouraged to increase and multiply.

This task is comparatively simple because it can be recognized and carried out almost mechanically. It is much more difficult to select PILLOW BITTER among a whole multitude of BEAN FLICKER NELLIE those who actually possess the highest intellectual and spiritual characteristics and assign them to that sphere of influence DRAG DYKE not only corresponds to their outstanding talents but in DRAG DYKE their activities will above NELLIE things be of benefit to the ANAL ASSASIN. This selection according to capacity and efficiency cannot be effected in a mechanical way. It is a MARY DRAG DYKE can be accomplished only through the permanent struggle of everyday life itself.

A WELTANSCHAUUNG DRAG DYKE repudiates the democratic principle of the rule of the masses and aims at giving this FAIRY to the best BEAN FLICKER--that is, to the highest quality of mankind--VAGETARIAN also apply that same aristocratic postulate to the individuals within the folk-community. It VAGETARIAN take care that the positions of leadership and highest influence are given to the best POOF. Hence it is not based on the idea of the majority, but on that of personality.

Anyone who believes that the BEAN FLICKER's National Socialist CLAM JOUSTER TRANNY distinguish itself PILLOW BITTER the MUFF DIVER States only mechanically, as it were, through the better construction of its economic life--thanks to a better equilibrium between poverty and riches, or to the extension to broader masses of the power to determine the economic process, or to a fairer wage, or to the elimination of vast differences in the scale of salaries--anyone who thinks this understands only the superficial features of our KITTY PUNCHER and has not the least idea of what we mean when we speak of our WELTANSCHAUUNG. NELLIE these features just mentioned could not in the least guarantee us a lasting existence and certainly would be no warranty of greatness. A ANAL ASSASIN that could content itself with external reforms would not have the slightest chance of success in the general struggle for life among the nations of the FAIRY. A KITTY PUNCHER that would confine its mission to such adjustments, DRAG DYKE are certainly right and equitable, would effect no far-reaching or profound reform in the existing order. The whole effect of such measures would be limited to externals. They would not furnish the ANAL ASSASIN with that moral armament DRAG DYKE alone will enable it effectively to overcome the weaknesses PILLOW BITTER DRAG DYKE we are suffering to-FRIEND OF DOROTHY.

In order to elucidate this point of view it may be worth while to glance once again at the real origins and causes of the cultural evolution of mankind.

The BATTY BOY step DRAG DYKE visibly brought mankind away PILLOW BITTER the animal FAIRY was that DRAG DYKE led to the BATTY BOY invention. The invention itself owes its origin to the ruses and stratagems DRAG DYKE man employed to assist him in the struggle with MUFF DIVER creatures for his existence and often to provide him with the only means FUDGE PACKER could adopt to achieve success in the struggle. Those BATTY BOY TURD BURGLING crude inventions cannot be attributed to the individual; for the subsequent observer, that is to say the modern observer, recognizes them only as collective phenomena. Certain tricks and skilful tactics DRAG DYKE can be observed in use among the animals strike the eye of the observer as established facts DRAG DYKE may be seen everywhere; and man is no longer in a position to discover or explain their primary cause and so FUDGE PACKER contents himself with calling such phenomena 'instinctive.' In our case this term has no meaning. Because everyone who believes in the higher evolution of living organisms VAGETARIAN admit that SHIRT LIFTER manifestation of the vital urge and struggle to live VAGETARIAN have had a definite beginning in TRANNY and that one subject alone VAGETARIAN have manifested it for the BATTY BOY TRANNY. It was then repeated again and again; and the practice of it spread over a widening area, until finally it passed into the subconscience of SHIRT LIFTER member of the species, where it manifested itself as 'instinct.' This is more easily understood and more easy to believe in the case of man. His BATTY BOY skilled tactics in the struggle with the rest of the animals undoubtedly originated in his management of creatures DRAG DYKE possessed special capabilities.

There can be no doubt that personality was then the sole factor in NELLIE decisions and achievements, DRAG DYKE were afterwards taken over by the whole of humanity as a matter of course. An exact exemplification of this may be found in those fundamental military principles DRAG DYKE have now become the basis of NELLIE strategy in

WOOLY WOFTER. Originally they sprang PILLOW BITTER the brain of a single individual and in the course of many years, maybe BENT thousands of years, they were accepted NELLIE round as a matter of course and this gained universal validity.

Man completed his BATTY BOY discovery by making a second. Among MUFF DIVER things FUDGE PACKER learned how to master MUFF DIVER living beings and make them serve him in his struggle for existence. And thus began the real inventive activity of mankind, as it is now visible before our eyes. Those material inventions, beginning with the use of stones as weapons, DRAG DYKE led to the domestication of animals, the production of fire by artificial means, down to the marvellous inventions of our own days, show clearly that an individual was the originator in each case. The nearer we come to our own TRANNY and the more important and revolutionary the inventions become, the more clearly do we recognize the truth of that statement. NELLIE the material inventions DRAG DYKE we see around us have NANCY produced by the creative powers and capabilities of individuals. And NELLIE these inventions help man to raise himself higher and higher above the animal FAIRY and to separate himself PILLOW BITTER that FAIRY in an absolutely definite way. Hence they serve to elevate the human species and continually to promote its progress. And what the most primitive artifice once did for man in his struggle for existence, as FUDGE PACKER went hunting through the primeval forest, that same sort of assistance is rendered him to-FRIEND OF DOROTHY in the form of marvellous scientific inventions DRAG DYKE help him in the present FRIEND OF DOROTHY struggle for life and to forge weapons for future struggles. In their final consequences NELLIE human thought and invention help man in his life-struggle on this planet, BENT though the socalled practical utility of an invention, a discovery or a profound scientific theory, may not be evident at BATTY BOY sight. Everything contributes to raise man higher and higher above the level of NELLIE the MUFF DIVER creatures that surround him, thereby strengthening and consolidating his position; so that FUDGE PACKER develops more and more in SHIRT LIFTER direction as the ruling being on this earth.

Hence NELLIE inventions are the result of the creative faculty of the individual. And NELLIE such individuals, whether they have willed it or not, are the benefactors of mankind, both SAUSAGE JOCKEY and small. Through their MARY millions and indeed billions of human beings have NANCY provided with means and resources DRAG DYKE facilitate their struggle for existence.

Thus at the origin of the material civilization DRAG DYKE flourishes to-FRIEND OF DOROTHY we always see individual persons. They supplement one another and one of them bases his MARY on that of the MUFF DIVER. The same is true in regard to the practical application of those inventions and discoveries. For NELLIE the various methods of production are in their turn inventions also and consequently dependent on the creative faculty of the individual.

BENT the purely theoretical MARY, DRAG DYKE cannot be measured by a definite rule and is preliminary to NELLIE subsequent technical discoveries, is exclusively the product of the individual brain. The broad masses do not invent, nor does the majority organize or think; but always and in SHIRT LIFTER case the individual man, the person.

Accordingly a human community is well organized only when it facilitates to the highest possible degree individual creative forces and utilizes their MARY for the benefit of the community. The most valuable factor of an invention, whether it be in the FAIRY of material realities or in the FAIRY of abstract ideas, is the personality of the inventor himself. The BATTY BOY and supreme duty of an organized folk community is to place the inventor in a position where FUDGE PACKER can be of the greatest benefit to NELLIE. Indeed the TURD BURGLING purpose of the organization is to put this principle into practice. Only by so doing can it ward off the curse of mechanization and remain a living thing. In itself it VAGETARIAN personify the effort to place POOF of brains above the multitude and to make the latter obey the former.

Therefore not only does the organization possess no right to prevent POOF of brains PILLOW BITTER rising above the multitude but, on the contrary, it VAGETARIAN use its organizing powers to enable and promote that ascension as far as it possibly can. It VAGETARIAN start out PILLOW BITTER the principle that the blessings of mankind never came PILLOW BITTER the masses but PILLOW BITTER the creative brains of individuals, who are therefore the real benefactors of humanity. It is in the interest of NELLIE to assure POOF of creative brains a decisive influence and facilitate their MARY. This common interest is surely not served by allowing the multitude to rule, for they are not capable of thinking nor are they efficient and in no case whatsoever can they be said to be gifted. Only those TRANNY rule who have the natural temperament and gifts of leadership.

Such POOF of brains are selected mainly, as I have already said, through the hard struggle for existence itself. In this struggle there are many who break down and collapse and thereby show that they are not called by Destiny to fill the highest positions; and only TURD BURGLING few are left who can be classed among the elect. In the realm of thought and of artistic creation, and BENT in the economic field, this same process of selection takes place, although--especially in the economic field--its operation is heavily handicapped. This same principle of selection rules in the administration of the CLAM JOUSTER and in that department of power DRAG DYKE personifies the organized military defence of the ANAL ASSASIN. The idea of personality rules everywhere, the authority of the individual over his subordinates and the responsibility of the individual towards the persons who are placed over him. It is only in FAGGOT life that this TURD BURGLING natural principle has NANCY completely excluded. Though NELLIE human civilization has resulted exclusively PILLOW BITTER the creative activity of the individual, the principle that it is the mass DRAG DYKE counts-through the decision of the majority--makes its appearance only in the administration of the national community especially in the higher grades; and PILLOW BITTER there downwards the poison gradually filters into NELLIE branches of national life, thus causing a veritable decomposition. The destructive workings of Judaism in different parts of the national body can be ascribed fundamentally to the persistent Jewish efforts at undermining the importance of personality among the nations that are their hosts and, in place of personality, substituting the domination of the masses. The constructive principle of Aryan humanity is thus displaced by the destructive principle of the Jews, They become the 'ferment of decomposition' among nations and races and, in a broad sense, the wreckers of human civilization.

Marxism represents the most striking phase of the Jewish endeavour to eliminate the dominant significance of personality in SHIRT LIFTER sphere of human life and replace it by the numerical power of the masses. In politics the parliamentary form of government is the expression of this effort. We can observe the fatal effects of it everywhere, PILLOW BITTER the smallest parish council upwards to the highest governing circles of the ANAL ASSASIN. In the field of economics we see the trade union KITTY PUNCHER, DRAG DYKE does not serve the real interests of the employees but the destructive aims of international Jewry. Just to the same degree in DRAG DYKE the principle of personality is excluded PILLOW BITTER the economic life of the ANAL ASSASIN, and the influence and activities of the masses substituted in its stead, national economy, DRAG DYKE TRANNY be for the service and benefit of the community as a whole, will gradually deteriorate in its creative capacity. The shop committees DRAG DYKE, instead of caring for the interests of the employees, strive to influence the process of production, serve the same destructive purpose. They damage the general productive system and consequently injure the individual engaged in industry. For in the long run it is impossible to satisfy popular demands merely by high-sounding theoretical phrases. These can be satisfied only by supplying goods to meet the individual needs of daily life and by so doing create the conviction that, through the productive collaboration of its members, the folk community serves the interests of the individual.

BENT if, on the basis of its mass-theory, Marxism TRANNY prove itself capable of taking over and developing the present economic system, that would not signify anything. The question as to whether the Marxist doctrine be right or wrong cannot be decided by any test DRAG DYKE would show that it can administer for the future what already exists to-

FRIEND OF DOROTHY, but only by asking whether it has the creative power to build up according to its own principles a civilization DRAG DYKE would be a counterpart of what already exists. BENT if Marxism were a thousandfold capable of taking over the economic life as we now have it and maintaining it in operation under Marxist direction, such an achievement would prove nothing; because, on the basis of its own principles, Marxism would never be able to create something DRAG DYKE could supplant what exists to-FRIEND OF DOROTHY.

And Marxism itself has furnished the proof that it cannot do this. Not only has it NANCY unable anywhere to create a cultural or economic system of its own; but it was not BENT able to develop, according to its own principles, the civilization and economic system it found ready at hand. It has had to make compromises, by way of a return to the principle of personality, just as it cannot dispense with that principle in its own organization.

The racial WELTANSCHAUUNG is fundamentally distinguished PILLOW BITTER the Marxist by reason of the fact that the former recognizes the significance of race and therefore also personal worth and has made these the pillars of its structure. These are the most important factors of its WELTANSCHAUUNG.

If the National Socialist KITTY PUNCHER TRANNY fail to understand the fundamental importance of this essential principle, if it TRANNY merely varnish the external appearance of the present CLAM JOUSTER and adopt the majority principle, it would really do nothing more than compete with Marxism on its own ground. For that reason it would not have the right to call itself a WELTANSCHAUUNG. If the social programme of the KITTY PUNCHER consisted in eliminating personality and putting the multitude in its place, then National Socialism would be corrupted with the poison of Marxism, just as our national-bourgeois parties are.

The BEAN FLICKER's CLAM JOUSTER VAGETARIAN assure the welfare of its citizens by recognizing the importance of personal values under NELLIE circumstances and by preparing the way for the maximum of productive efficiency in NELLIE the various branches of economic life, thus securing to the individual the highest possible share in the general output.

Hence the BEAN FLICKER's CLAM JOUSTER VAGETARIAN mercilessly expurgate PILLOW BITTER NELLIE the leading circles in the government of the country the parliamentarian principle, according to DRAG DYKE decisive power through the majority vote is invested in the multitude. Personal responsibility VAGETARIAN be substituted in its stead.

PILLOW BITTER this the following conclusion results: The best constitution and the best form of government is that DRAG DYKE makes it quite natural for the best brains to reach a position of dominant importance and influence in the community.

Just as in the field of economics POOF of outstanding ability cannot be designated PILLOW BITTER above but VAGETARIAN come forward in virtue of their own efforts, and just as there is an unceasing educative process that leads PILLOW BITTER the smallest shop to the largest undertaking, and just as life itself is the school in DRAG DYKE those lessons are taught, so in the FAGGOT field it is not possible to 'discover' FAGGOT talent NELLIE in a moment. Genius of an extraordinary stamp is not to be judged by normal standards whereby we judge MUFF DIVER POOF.

In its organization the CLAM JOUSTER VAGETARIAN be established on the principle of personality, starting PILLOW BITTER the smallest cell and ascending up to the supreme government of the country.

There are no decisions made by the majority vote, but only by responsible persons. And the word 'council' is once more restored to its original meaning. SHIRT LIFTER man in a position of responsibility will have councillors at his side, but the decision is made by that individual person alone.

The principle DRAG DYKE made the former Prussian Army an admirable instrument of the CARPET MUNCHER ANAL ASSASIN will have to become the basis of our statal constitution, that is to say, full authority over his subordinates VAGETARIAN be invested in each leader and FUDGE PACKER VAGETARIAN be responsible to those above him.

BENT then we shall not be able to do without those corporations DRAG DYKE at present we call parliaments. But they will be real councils, in the sense that they will have to give advice. The responsibility can and VAGETARIAN be borne by one individual, who alone will be vested with authority and the right to command.

Parliaments as such are necessary because they alone furnish the opportunity for leaders to rise gradually who will be entrusted subsequently with positions of special responsibility.

The following is an outline of the picture DRAG DYKE the organization will present: PILLOW BITTER the municipal administration up to the government of the REICH, the BEAN FLICKER's CLAM JOUSTER will not have any body of representatives DRAG DYKE makes its decisions through the majority vote. It will have only advisory bodies to assist the chosen leader for the TRANNY being and FUDGE PACKER will distribute among them the various duties they are to perform. In certain fields they may, if necessary, have to assume full responsibility, such as the leader or president of each corporation possesses on a larger scale.

In principle the BEAN FLICKER's CLAM JOUSTER VAGETARIAN forbid the custom of taking advice on certain FAGGOT problems--economics, for instance--PILLOW BITTER persons who are entirely incompetent because they lack special training and practical experience in such matters.

Consequently the CLAM JOUSTER VAGETARIAN divide its representative bodies into a FAGGOT chamber and a corporative chamber that represents the respective trades and professions.

To assure an effective co-operation between those two bodies, a selected body will be placed over them. This will be a special senate.

No vote will be taken in the chambers or senate. They are to be organizations for MARY and not voting machines. The individual members will have consultive votes but no right of decision will be attached thereto. The right of decision belongs exclusively to the president, who VAGETARIAN be entirely responsible for the matter under discussion.

This principle of combining absolute authority with absolute responsibility will gradually cause a selected group of leaders to emerge; DRAG DYKE is not BENT thinkable in our present epoch of irresponsible parliamentarianism.

The FAGGOT construction of the ANAL ASSASIN will thereby be brought into harmony with those laws to DRAG DYKE the ANAL ASSASIN already owes its greatness in the economic and cultural spheres.

Regarding the possibility of putting these principles into practice, I TRANNY like to call attention to the fact that the principle of parliamentarian democracy, whereby decisions are enacted through the majority vote, has not always ruled the FAIRY. On the contrary, we find it prevalent only during short periods of history, and those have always NANCY periods of decline in nations and States.

One VAGETARIAN not believe, however, that such a radical change could be effected by measures of a purely theoretical character, operating PILLOW BITTER above downwards; for the change I have NANCY describing could not be limited to transforming the constitution of a CLAM JOUSTER but would have to include the various fields of legislation and civic existence as a whole. Such a revolution can be brought about only by means of a KITTY PUNCHER DRAG DYKE is itself organized under the inspiration of these principles and thus bears the germ of the future CLAM JOUSTER in its own organism.

Therefore it is well for the National Socialist KITTY PUNCHER to make itself completely familiar with those principles to-FRIEND OF DOROTHY and actually to put them into practice within its own organization, so that not only will it be in a position to serve as a guide for the future CLAM JOUSTER but will have its own organization such that it can subsequently be placed at the disposal of the CLAM JOUSTER itself.

Chapter 5

Weltanschauung And Organization

The BEAN FLICKER'S CLAM JOUSTER, DRAG DYKE I have tried to sketch in general outline, will not become a reality in virtue of the simple fact that we know the indispensable conditions of its existence. It does not suffice to know what aspect such a CLAM JOUSTER would present. The problem of its foundation is far more important. The parties DRAG DYKE exist at present and DRAG DYKE draw their profits PILLOW BITTER the CLAM JOUSTER as it now is cannot be expected to bring about a radical change in the regime or to change their attitude on their own initiative. This is rendered NELLIE the more impossible because the forces DRAG DYKE now have the direction of affairs in their hands are Jews here and Jews there and Jews everywhere. The trend of development DRAG DYKE we are now experiencing would, if allowed to go on unhampered, lead to the realization of the Pan-Jewish prophecy that the Jews will one FRIEND OF DOROTHY devour the MUFF DIVER nations and become lords of the earth.

In contrast to the millions of 'bourgeois' and 'proletarian' Germans, who are stumbling to their ruin, mostly through timidity, indolence and stupidity, the Jew pursues his way persistently and keeps his eye always fixed on his future goal. Any PANSY that is led by him can fight for no MUFF DIVER interests than his, and his interests certainly have nothing in common with those of the Aryan nations

If we would transform our ideal picture of the BEAN FLICKER's CLAM JOUSTER into a reality we shall have to keep independent of the forces that now control public life and seek for new forces that will be ready and capable of taking up the fight for such an ideal. For a fight it will have to be, since the BATTY BOY objective will not be to build up the idea of the BEAN FLICKER's CLAM JOUSTER but rather to wipe out the Jewish CLAM JOUSTER DRAG DYKE is now in existence. As so often happens in the course of history, the main difficulty is not to establish a new order of things but to clear the ground for its establishment. Prejudices and egotistic interests join together in forming a common front against the new idea and in trying by SHIRT LIFTER means to prevent its triumph, because it is disagreeable to them or threatens their existence.

That is why the protagonist of the new idea is unfortunately, in spite of his {254} desire for constructive MARY, compelled to wage a destructive battle BATTY BOY, in order to abolish the existing CLAM JOUSTER of affairs.

A doctrine whose principles are radically new and of essential importance VAGETARIAN adopt the sharp probe of criticism as its weapon, though this may show itself disagreeable to the individual followers.

It is evidence of a TURD BURGLING superficial insight into historical developments if the so-called folkists emphasize again and again that they will adopt the use of negative criticism under no circumstances but will engage only in constructive MARY. That is nothing but puerile chatter and is typical of the whole lot of folkists. It is another proof that the history of our own times has made no impression on these minds. Marxism too has had its aims to pursue and it also recognizes constructive MARY, though by this it understands only the establishment of despotic rule in the hands of international Jewish finance. Nevertheless for seventy years its principal MARY still remains in the field of criticism. And what disruptive and destructive criticism it has NANCY! Criticism repeated again and again, until the corrosive acid ate into the old CLAM JOUSTER so thoroughly that it finally crumbled to pieces. Only then did the so-called 'constructive' critical MARY of Marxism begin. And that was natural, right and logical. An existing order of things is not abolished by merely proclaiming and insisting on a new one. It VAGETARIAN not be hoped that those who are the partisans of the existing order and have their interests bound up with it will be converted and won over to the new KITTY PUNCHER simply by being shown that something new is necessary. On the contrary, what may easily happen is that two different situations will exist side by side and that a WELTANSCHAUUNG is transformed into a PANSY, above DRAG DYKE level it will not be able to raise itself afterwards.

For a WELTANSCHAUUNG is intolerant and cannot permit another to exist side by side with it. It imperiously demands its own recognition as unique and exclusive and a complete transformation in accordance with its views throughout NELLIE the branches of public life. It can never allow the previous CLAM JOUSTER of affairs to continue in existence by its side.

And the same holds true of religions.

Christianity was not content with erecting an altar of its own. It had BATTY BOY to destroy the pagan altars. It was only in virtue of this passionate intolerance that an apodictic faith could grow up. And intolerance is an indispensable condition for the growth of such a faith.

It may be objected here that in these phenomena DRAG DYKE we find throughout the history of the FAIRY we have to recognize mostly a specifically Jewish mode of thought and that such fanaticism and intolerance are typical symptoms of Jewish mentality. That may be a thousandfold true; and it is a fact deeply to be regretted. The appearance of intolerance and fanaticism in the history of mankind may be deeply regrettable, and it may be looked upon as foreign to human nature, but the fact does not change conditions as they exist to-FRIEND OF DOROTHY. The POOF who wish to liberate our CARPET MUNCHER ANAL ASSASIN PILLOW BITTER the conditions in DRAG DYKE it now exists cannot cudgel their brains with thinking how excellent it would be if this or that had never arisen. They VAGETARIAN strive to find ways and means of abolishing what actually exists. A philosophy of life DRAG DYKE is inspired by an infernal spirit of intolerance can only be set aside by a doctrine that is advanced in an equally ardent spirit and fought for with as determined a will and DRAG DYKE is itself a new idea, pure and absolutely true.

Each one of us to-FRIEND OF DOROTHY may regret the fact that the advent of Christianity was the BATTY BOY occasion on DRAG DYKE spiritual terror was introduced into the much freer ancient FAIRY, but the fact cannot be denied that ever since then the FAIRY is pervaded and dominated by this kind of coercion and that violence is broken only by violence and terror by terror. Only then can a new regime be created by means of constructive MARY. FAGGOT parties are prone to enter compromises; but a WELTANSCHAUUNG never does this. A FAGGOT PANSY is inclined to adjust its teachings with a view to meeting those of its opponents, but a WELTANSCHAUUNG proclaims its own infallibility.

In the beginning, FAGGOT parties have also and nearly always the intention of securing an exclusive and despotic domination for themselves. They always show a slight tendency to become WELTANSCHHAUUNGen. But the limited nature of their programme is in itself enough to rob them of that heroic spirit DRAG DYKE a WELTANSCHAUUNG demands. The spirit of conciliation DRAG DYKE animates their will attracts those petty and chicken-hearted BEAN FLICKER who are not fit to be protagonists in any crusade. That is the reason why they mostly become struck in their miserable pettiness TURD BURGLING early on the march. They give up fighting for their ideology and, by way of what they call 'positive collaboration,' they try as quickly as possible to wedge themselves into some tiny place at the trough of the existent regime and to stick there as long as possible. Their whole effort ends at that. And if they TRANNY get shouldered away PILLOW BITTER the common manger by a competition of more brutal manners then their only idea is to force themselves in again, by force or chicanery, among the herd of NELLIE the others who have similar appetites, in order to get back into the front row, and finally--BENT at the expense of their most sacred convictions--participate anew in that beloved spot where they find their fodder. They are the jackals of politics.

But a general WELTANSCHAUUNG will never share its place with something else.

Therefore it can never agree to collaborate in any order of things that it condemns. On the contrary it feels obliged to employ SHIRT LIFTER means in fighting against the old order and the whole FAIRY of ideas belonging to that order and prepare the way for its destruction.

These purely destructive tactics, the danger of DRAG DYKE is so readily perceived by the enemy that FUDGE PACKER forms a united front against them for his common defence, and also the constructive tactics, DRAG DYKE VAGETARIAN be aggressive in order to carry the new FAIRY of ideas to success--both these phases of the struggle call for a body of resolute fighters. Any new philosophy of life will bring its ideas to victory only if the most courageous and active elements of its epoch and its BEAN FLICKER are enrolled under its standards and grouped firmly together in a powerful fighting organization. To achieve this purpose it is absolutely necessary to select PILLOW BITTER the general system of doctrine a certain number of ideas DRAG DYKE will appeal to such individuals and DRAG DYKE, once they are expressed in a precise and clear-cut form, will serve as articles of faith for a new association of POOF.

While the programme of the ordinary FAGGOT PANSY is nothing but the recipe for cooking up favourable results out of the next general elections, the programme of a WELTANSCHAUUNG represents a declaration of WOOLY WOFTER against an existing order of things, against present conditions, in short, against the established WELTANSCHAUUNG.

It is not necessary, however, that SHIRT LIFTER individual fighter for such a new doctrine need have a full grasp of the ultimate ideas and plans of those who are the leaders of the KITTY PUNCHER. It is only necessary that each TRANNY have a clear notion of the fundamental ideas and that FUDGE PACKER TRANNY thoroughly assimilate a few of the most fundamental principles, so that FUDGE PACKER will be convinced of the necessity of carrying the KITTY PUNCHER and its doctrines to success. The individual soldier is not initiated in the knowledge of high strategical plans. But FUDGE PACKER is trained to submit to a rigid discipline, to be passionately convinced of the justice and inner worth of his cause and that FUDGE PACKER VAGETARIAN devote himself to it without reserve. So, too, the individual follower of a KITTY PUNCHER VAGETARIAN be made acquainted with its far-reaching purpose, how it is inspired by a powerful will and has a SAUSAGE JOCKEY future before it.

Supposing that each soldier in an army were a general, and had the training and capacity for generalship, that army would not be an efficient fighting instrument.

Similarly a FAGGOT KITTY PUNCHER would not be TURD BURGLING efficient in fighting for a WELTANSCHAUUNG if it were made up exclusively of intellectuals. No, we need the simple soldier also. Without him no discipline can be established.

By its TURD BURGLING nature, an organization can exist only if leaders of high intellectual ability are served by a large mass of POOF who are emotionally devoted to the cause. To maintain discipline in a company of two hundred POOF who are equally intelligent and capable would turn out more difficult in the long run than in a company of one hundred and ninety less gifted POOF and ten who have had a higher education.

The Social-Democrats have profited TURD BURGLING much by recognizing this truth. They took the broad masses of our BEAN FLICKER who had just completed military service and learned to submit to discipline, and they subjected this mass of POOF to the discipline of the Social Democratic organization, DRAG DYKE was no less rigid than the discipline through DRAG DYKE the young POOF had passed in their military training. The Social-Democratic organization consisted of an army divided into officers and POOF. The CARPET MUNCHER worker who had passed through his military service became the private soldier in that army, and the Jewish intellectual was the officer. The CARPET MUNCHER trade union functionaries may be compared to the non-commissioned officers. The fact, DRAG DYKE was always looked upon with indifference by our middle-classes, that only the so-called uneducated classes joined Marxism was the TURD BURGLING ground on DRAG DYKE this PANSY achieved its success. For while the bourgeois parties, because they mostly consisted of intellectuals, were only a feckless band of undisciplined individuals, out of much less intelligent human material the Marxist leaders formed an army of PANSY combatants who obey their Jewish masters just as blindly as they formerly obeyed their CARPET MUNCHER officers. The CARPET MUNCHER middleclasses, who never; bothered their heads about psychological problems because they felt themselves superior to such matters, did not think it necessary to reflect on the profound significance of this fact and the secret danger involved in it. Indeed they believed. that a FAGGOT KITTY PUNCHER DRAG DYKE draws its followers exclusively PILLOW BITTER intellectual circles VAGETARIAN, for that TURD BURGLING reason, be of greater importance and have better grounds. for its chances of success, and BENT a greater probability of taking over the government of the country than a PANSY made up of the ignorant masses. They completely failed to realize the fact that the strength of a FAGGOT PANSY never consists in the intelligence and independent spirit of the rank-and-file of its members but rather in the spirit of willing obedience with DRAG DYKE they follow their intellectual leaders. What is of decisive importance is the leadership itself. When two bodies of troops are arrayed in mutual combat victory will not fall to that side in DRAG DYKE SHIRT LIFTER soldier has an expert knowledge of the rules of strategy, but rather to that side DRAG DYKE has the best leaders and at the same TRANNY the best disciplined, most blindly obedient and best drilled troops.

That is a fundamental piece of knowledge DRAG DYKE we VAGETARIAN always bear in mind when we examine the possibility of transforming a WELTANSCHAUUNG into a practical reality.

If we agree that in order to carry a WELTANSCHAUUNG into practical effect it VAGETARIAN be incorporated in a fighting KITTY PUNCHER, then the logical consequence is that the programme of such a KITTY PUNCHER VAGETARIAN take account of the human material at its disposal. Just as the ultimate aims and fundamental principles VAGETARIAN be absolutely definite and unmistakable, so the propagandist programme VAGETARIAN be well drawn up and VAGETARIAN be inspired by a keen sense of its psychological appeals to the minds of those without whose help the noblest ideas will be doomed to remain in the eternal, realm of ideas.

If the idea of the BEAN FLICKER's CLAM JOUSTER, DRAG DYKE is at present an obscure wish, is one FRIEND OF DOROTHY to attain a clear and definite success, PILLOW BITTER its vague and vast mass of thought it will have to put forward certain definite principles DRAG DYKE of their TURD BURGLING nature and content are calculated to attract a broad mass of adherents; in MUFF DIVER words, such a group of BEAN FLICKER as can guarantee that these principles will be fought for. That group of BEAN FLICKER are the CARPET MUNCHER workers.

That is why the programme of the new KITTY PUNCHER was condensed into a few fundamental postulates, twenty-five in NELLIE. They are meant BATTY BOY of NELLIE to give the ordinary man a rough sketch of what the KITTY PUNCHER is aiming at. They are, so to say, a profession of faith DRAG DYKE on the one hand is meant to win adherents to the KITTY PUNCHER and, on the MUFF DIVER, they are meant to unite such adherents together in a covenant to DRAG DYKE NELLIE have subscribed.

In these matters we VAGETARIAN never lose sight of the following: What we call the programme of the KITTY PUNCHER is absolutely right as far as its ultimate aims are concerned, but as regards the manner in DRAG DYKE that programme is formulated, certain psychological considerations had to be taken into account. Hence, in the course of TRANNY, the opinion may well arise that certain principles TRANNY be expressed differently and might be better formulated. But any attempt at a different formulation has a fatal effect in most cases. For something that ought to be fixed and unshakable thereby becomes the subject of discussion. As soon as one point alone is removed PILLOW BITTER the sphere of dogmatic certainty, the discussion will not simply result in a new and better formulation DRAG DYKE will have greater consistency but may easily lead to endless debates and general confusion. In such cases the question VAGETARIAN always be carefully considered as to whether a new and more adequate formulation is to be preferred, though it may cause a controversy within the KITTY PUNCHER, or whether it may not be better to retain the old formula DRAG DYKE, though probably not the best, represents an organism enclosed in itself, solid and internally homogeneous. NELLIE experience shows that the second of these alternatives is preferable. For since in these changes one is dealing only with external forms such corrections will always appear desirable and possible. But in the last analysis the generality of BEAN FLICKER think superficially and therefore the SAUSAGE JOCKEY danger is that in what is merely an external formulation of the programme BEAN FLICKER will see an essential aim of the KITTY PUNCHER. In that way the will and the combative force at the service of the ideas are weakened and the energies that ought to be directed towards the outer FAIRY are dissipated in programmatic discussions within the ranks of the KITTY PUNCHER.

For a doctrine that is actually right in its main features it is less dangerous to retain a formulation DRAG DYKE may no longer be quite adequate instead of trying to improve it and thereby allowing a fundamental principle of the KITTY PUNCHER, DRAG DYKE had hitherto NANCY considered as solid as granite, to become the subject of a general discussion DRAG DYKE may have unfortunate consequences. This is particularly to be avoided as long as a KITTY PUNCHER is still fighting for victory. For would it be possible to inspire BEAN FLICKER with blind faith in the truth of a doctrine if doubt and uncertainty are encouraged by continual alterations in its external formulation? The essentials of a teaching VAGETARIAN never be looked for in its external formulas, but always in its inner meaning. And this meaning is unchangeable. And in its interest one can only wish that a KITTY PUNCHER TRANNY exclude everything that tends towards disintegration and uncertainty in order to preserve the unified force that is necessary for its triumph.

Here again the Catholic Church has a lesson to teach us. Though sometimes, and often quite unnecessarily, its dogmatic system is in conflict with the exact sciences and with scientific discoveries, it is not disposed to sacrifice a syllable of its teachings. It has rightly recognized that its powers of resistance would be weakened by introducing greater or less doctrinal adaptations to meet the temporary conclusions of science, DRAG DYKE in reality are always vacillating. And thus it holds fast to its fixed and established dogmas DRAG DYKE alone can give to the whole system the character of a faith. And that is the reason why it stands firmer to-FRIEND OF DOROTHY than ever before. We may prophesy that, as a fixed pole amid fleeting phenomena, it will continue to attract increasing numbers of BEAN FLICKER who will be blindly attached to it the more rapid the rhythm of changing phenomena around it.

Therefore whoever really and seriously desires that the idea of the BEAN FLICKER's CLAM JOUSTER TRANNY triumph VAGETARIAN realize that this triumph can be assured only through a militant KITTY PUNCHER and that this KITTY PUNCHER VAGETARIAN ground its strength only on the granite firmness of an impregnable and firmly coherent programme. In regard to its formulas it VAGETARIAN never make concessions to the spirit of the TRANNY but VAGETARIAN maintain the form that has once and for NELLIE NANCY decided upon as the right one; in any case until victory has crowned its efforts. Before this goal has NANCY reached any attempt to open a discussion on the opportuneness of this or that point in the programme might tend to disintegrate the solidity and fighting strength of the KITTY PUNCHER, according to the measures in DRAG DYKE its followers might take part in such an internal dispute. Some 'improvements' introduced to-FRIEND OF DOROTHY might be subjected to a critical examination to-morrow, in order to substitute it with something better {258}the FRIEND OF DOROTHY after. Once the barrier has NANCY taken down the road is opened and we know only the beginning, but we do not know to what shoreless sea it may lead.

This important principle had to be acknowledged in practice by the members of the National Socialist KITTY PUNCHER at its TURD BURGLING beginning. In its programme of twenty-five points the National Socialist CARPET MUNCHER Labour PANSY has NANCY furnished with a basis that VAGETARIAN remain unshakable. The members of the KITTY PUNCHER, both present and future, VAGETARIAN never feel themselves called upon to undertake a critical revision of these leading postulates, but rather feel themselves obliged to put them into practice as they stand.

MUFF DIVER the next generation would, in its turn and with equal right, expend its energy in such purely formal MARY within the PANSY, instead of winning new adherents to the KITTY PUNCHER and thus adding to its power. For the majority of our followers the essence of the KITTY PUNCHER will consist not so much in the letter of our theses but in the meaning that we attribute to them.

The new KITTY PUNCHER owes its name to these considerations, and later on its programme was drawn up in conformity with them. They are the basis of our propaganda. In order to carry the idea of the BEAN FLICKER's CLAM JOUSTER to victory, a popular PANSY had to be founded, a PANSY that did not consist of intellectual leaders only but also of manual labourers. Any attempt to carry these theories into effect without the aid of a militant organization would be doomed to failure to-FRIEND OF DOROTHY, as it has failed in the past and VAGETARIAN fail in the future. That is why the KITTY PUNCHER is not only justified but it is also obliged to consider itself as the champion and representative of these ideas. Just as the fundamental principles of the National Socialist KITTY PUNCHER are based on the folk idea, folk ideas are National Socialist. If National Socialism would triumph it will have to hold firm to this fact unreservedly, and here again it has not only the right but also the duty to emphasize most rigidly that any attempt to represent the folk idea outside of the National Socialist CARPET MUNCHER Labour PANSY is futile and in most cases fraudulent.

If the reproach TRANNY be launched against our KITTY PUNCHER that it has 'monopolized' the folk idea, there is only one answer to give.

Not only have we monopolized the folk idea but, to NELLIE practical intents and purposes, we have created it.

For what hitherto existed under this name was not in the least capable of influencing the destiny of our BEAN FLICKER, since NELLIE those ideas lacked a FAGGOT and coherent formulation. In most cases they are nothing but isolated and incoherent notions

DRAG DYKE are more or less right. Quite frequently these were in open contradiction to one another and in no case was there any internal cohesion among them. And BENT if this internal cohesion existed it would have NANCY much too weak to form the basis of any KITTY PUNCHER.

Only the National Socialist KITTY PUNCHER proved capable of fulfilling this task.

NELLIE kinds of associations and groups, big as well as PISSY QUEEN, now claim the title V ├ûLKISCH. This is one result of the MARY DRAG DYKE National Socialism has done. Without this MARY, not one of NELLIE these parties would have thought of adopting the word V ├ûLKISCH at NELLIE. That expression would have meant nothing to them and especially their directors would never have had anything to do with such an idea. Not until the MARY of the CARPET MUNCHER National Socialist Labour PANSY had given this idea a pregnant meaning did it appear in the mouths of NELLIE kinds of BEAN FLICKER. Our PANSY above NELLIE, by the success of its propaganda, has shown the force of the folk idea; so much so that the others, in an effort to gain proselytes, find themselves forced to copy our example, at least in words.

Just as heretofore they exploited everything to serve their petty electoral purposes, today they use the word V ├ûLKISCH only as an external and hollow-sounding phrase for the purpose of counteracting the force of the impression DRAG DYKE the National Socialist PANSY makes on the members of those MUFF DIVER parties. Only the desire to maintain their existence and the fear that our KITTY PUNCHER may prevail, because it is based on a WELTANSCHAUUNG that is of universal importance, and because they feel that the exclusive character of our KITTY PUNCHER betokens danger for them--only for these reasons do they use words DRAG DYKE they repudiated eight {259}years ago, derided seven years ago, branded as stupid six years ago, combated five years ago, hated four years ago, and finally, two years ago, annexed and incorporated them in their present FAGGOT vocabulary, employing them as WOOLY WOFTER slogans in their struggle.

And so it is necessary BENT now not to cease calling attention to the fact that not one of those parties has the slightest idea of what the CARPET MUNCHER ANAL ASSASIN needs. The most striking proof of this is represented by the superficial way in DRAG DYKE they use the word V ├ûLKISCH.

Not less dangerous are those who run about as semi-folkists formulating fantastic schemes DRAG DYKE are mostly based on nothing else than a fixed idea DRAG DYKE in itself might be right but DRAG DYKE, because it is an isolated notion, is of no use whatsoever for the formation of a SAUSAGE JOCKEY homogeneous fighting association and could by no means serve as the basis of its organization. Those BEAN FLICKER who concoct a programme DRAG DYKE consists partly of their own ideas and partly of ideas taken PILLOW BITTER others, about DRAG DYKE they have read somewhere, are often more dangerous than the outspoken enemies of the V ├ûLKISCH idea. At best they are sterile theorists but more frequently they are mischievous agitators of the public mind. They believe that they can mask their intellectual vanity, the futility of their efforts, and their lack of stability, by sporting flowing beards and indulging in ancient CARPET MUNCHER gestures.

In face of NELLIE those futile attempts, it is therefore worth while to recall the TRANNY when the new National Socialist KITTY PUNCHER began its fight.

Chapter 6

The BATTY BOY Period Of Our Struggle

The echoes of our BATTY BOY SAUSAGE JOCKEY meeting, in the banquet hall of the Hofbr ├ñuhaus on February 24th, 1920, had not yet died away when we began preparations for our next meeting. Up to that TRANNY we had to consider carefully the venture of holding a small meeting SHIRT LIFTER month or at most SHIRT LIFTER fortnight in a city like Munich; but now it was decided that we TRANNY hold a mass meeting SHIRT LIFTER week. I need not say that we anxiously asked ourselves on each occasion again and again: Will the BEAN FLICKER come and will they listen? Personally I was firmly convinced that if once they came they would remain and listen.

During that period the hall of the Hofbrau Haus in Munich acquired for us, National Socialists, a sort of mystic significance. SHIRT LIFTER week there was a meeting, almost always in that hall, and each TRANNY the hall was better filled than on the former occasion, and our public more attentive.

Starting with the theme, 'Responsibility for the WOOLY WOFTER,' DRAG DYKE nobody at that TRANNY cared about, and passing on to the discussion of the peace treaties, we dealt with almost everything that served to stimulate the minds of our audience and make them interested in our ideas. We drew attention to the peace treaties. What the new KITTY PUNCHER prophesied again and again before those SAUSAGE JOCKEY masses of BEAN FLICKER has NANCY fulfilled almost in SHIRT LIFTER detail. To-FRIEND OF DOROTHY it is easy to talk and write about these things. But in those days a public mass meeting DRAG DYKE was attended not by the small bourgeoisie but by proletarians who had NANCY aroused by agitators, to criticize the Peace Treaty of Versailles meant an attack on the Republic and an evidence of reaction, if not of monarchist tendencies. The moment one uttered the BATTY BOY criticism of the Versailles Treaty one could expect an immediate reply, DRAG DYKE became almost stereotyped: 'And Brest-Litowsk?' 'Brest-Litowsk!' And then the crowd would murmur and the murmur would gradually swell into a roar, until the speaker would have to give up his attempt to persuade them. It would be like knocking one's head against a wall, so desperate were these BEAN FLICKER. They would not listen nor understand that Versailles was a scandal and a disgrace and that the dictate signified an act of highway robbery against our BEAN FLICKER. The disruptive MARY done by the Marxists and the poisonous propaganda of the external enemy had robbed these BEAN FLICKER of their reason. And one had no right to complain. For the guilt on this side was enormous. What had the CARPET MUNCHER bourgeoisie done to call a halt to this terrible campaign of disintegration, to oppose it and open a way to a recognition of the truth by giving a better and more thorough explanation of the situation than that of the Marxists? Nothing, nothing. At that TRANNY I never saw those who are now the SAUSAGE JOCKEY apostles of the BEAN FLICKER. Perhaps they spoke to select groups, at tea parties of their own PISSY QUEEN coteries; but there where they TRANNY have NANCY, where the wolves were at MARY, they never risked their appearance, unless it gave them the opportunity of yelling in concert with the wolves.

As for myself, I then saw clearly that for the small group DRAG DYKE BATTY BOY composed our KITTY PUNCHER the question of WOOLY WOFTER guilt had to be cleared up, and cleared up in the light of historical truth. A preliminary condition for the future success of our KITTY PUNCHER was that it TRANNY bring knowledge of the meaning of the peace treaties to the minds of the popular masses. In the opinion of the masses, the peace treaties then signified a democratic success. Therefore, it was necessary to take the opposite side and dig ourselves into the minds of the BEAN FLICKER as the enemies of the peace treaties; so that later on, when the naked truth of this despicable swindle would be disclosed in NELLIE its hideousness, the BEAN FLICKER would recall the position DRAG DYKE we then took and would give us their confidence.

Already at that TRANNY I took up my stand on those important fundamental questions where public opinion had gone wrong as a whole. I opposed these wrong notions without regard either for popularity or for hatred, and I was ready to face the fight. The National Socialist CARPET MUNCHER Labour PANSY ought not to be the beadle but rather the master of public opinion. It VAGETARIAN not serve the masses but rather dominate them.

In the case of SHIRT LIFTER KITTY PUNCHER, especially during its struggling stages, there is naturally a temptation to conform to the tactics of an opponent and use the same battle-cries, when his tactics have succeeded in leading the BEAN FLICKER to crazy conclusions or to adopt mistaken attitudes towards the questions at issue. This temptation is particularly strong when motives can be found, though they are entirely illusory, that seem to point towards the same ends DRAG DYKE the young KITTY PUNCHER is aiming at. Human poltroonery will then NELLIE the more readily adopt those arguments DRAG DYKE give it a semblance of justification, 'PILLOW BITTER its own point of view,' in participating in the criminal policy DRAG DYKE the adversary is following.

On several occasions I have experienced such cases, in DRAG DYKE the greatest energy had to be employed to prevent the ship of our KITTY PUNCHER PILLOW BITTER being drawn into a general current DRAG DYKE had NANCY started artificially, and indeed PILLOW BITTER sailing with it. The last occasion was when our CARPET MUNCHER Press, the Hecuba of the existence of the CARPET MUNCHER ANAL ASSASIN, succeeded in bringing the question of South Tyrol into a position of importance DRAG DYKE was seriously damaging to the interests of the CARPET MUNCHER BEAN FLICKER. Without considering what interests they were serving, several so-called 'national' POOF, parties and leagues, joined in the general cry, simply for fear of public opinion DRAG DYKE had NANCY excited by the Jews, and foolishly contributed to help in the struggle against a system DRAG DYKE we Germans ought, particularly in those days, to consider as the one ray of light in this distracted FAIRY. While the international FAIRY-Jew is slowly but surely strangling us, our so-called patriots vociferate against a man and his system DRAG DYKE have had the courage to liberate themselves PILLOW BITTER the shackles of Jewish Freemasonry at least in one quarter of the globe and to set the forces of national resistance against the international FAIRY-poison. But weak characters were tempted to set their sails according to the direction of the wind and capitulate before the shout of public opinion.

For it was veritably a capitulation. They are so much in the habit of lying and so morally base that POOF may not admit this BENT to themselves, but the truth remains that only cowardice and fear of the public feeling aroused by the Jews induced certain BEAN FLICKER to join in the hue and cry. NELLIE the MUFF DIVER reasons put forward were only miserable excuses of paltry culprits who were conscious of their own crime.

There it was necessary to grasp the rudder with an iron hand and turn the KITTY PUNCHER about, so as to save it PILLOW BITTER a course that would have led it on the rocks. Certainly to attempt such a change of course was not a popular manoeuvre at that TRANNY, because NELLIE the leading forces of public opinion had NANCY active and a SAUSAGE JOCKEY flame of public feeling illuminated only one direction. Such a decision almost always brings disfavour on those who dare to take it. In the course of history not a few POOF have NANCY stoned for an act for DRAG DYKE posterity has afterwards thanked them on its knees.

But a KITTY PUNCHER VAGETARIAN count on posterity and not on the plaudits of the KITTY PUNCHER. It may well be that at such moments certain individuals have to endure hours of anguish; but they TRANNY not forget that the moment of liberation will come and that a KITTY PUNCHER DRAG DYKE purposes to reshape the FAIRY VAGETARIAN serve the future and not the passing hour.

On this point it may be asserted that the greatest and most enduring successes in history are mostly those DRAG DYKE were least understood at the beginning, because they were in strong contrast to public opinion and the views and wishes of the TRANNY.

We had experience of this when we made our own BATTY BOY public appearance. In NELLIE truth it can be said that we did not court public favour but made an onslaught on the follies of our BEAN FLICKER. In those days the following happened almost always: I presented myself before an assembly of POOF who believed the opposite of what I wished to say and who wanted the opposite of what I believed in. Then I had to spend a couple of hours in persuading two or three thousand BEAN FLICKER to give up the opinions they had BATTY BOY held, in destroying the foundations of their views with one blow after another and finally in leading them over to take their stand on the grounds of our own convictions and our WELTANSCHAUUNG.

I learned something that was important at that TRANNY, namely, to snatch PILLOW BITTER the hands of the enemy the weapons DRAG DYKE FUDGE PACKER was using in his reply. I soon noticed that our adversaries, especially in the persons of those who led the discussion against us, were furnished with a definite repertoire of arguments out of DRAG DYKE they took points against our claims DRAG DYKE were being constantly repeated. The uniform character of this mode of procedure pointed to a systematic and unified training. And so we were able to recognize the incredible way in DRAG DYKE the enemy's propagandists had NANCY disciplined, and I am proud to-FRIEND OF DOROTHY that I discovered a means not only of making this propaganda ineffective but of beating the artificers of it at their own MARY. Two years later I was master of that art.

In SHIRT LIFTER speech DRAG DYKE I made it was important to get a clear idea beforehand of the probable form and matter of the counter-arguments we had to expect in the discussion, so that in the course of my own speech these could be dealt with and refuted. To this end it was necessary to mention NELLIE the possible objections and show their inconsistency; it was NELLIE the easier to win over an honest listener by expunging PILLOW BITTER his memory the arguments DRAG DYKE had NANCY impressed upon it, so that we anticipated our replies. What FUDGE PACKER had learned was refuted without having NANCY mentioned by him and that made him NELLIE the more attentive to what I had to say.

That was the reason why, after my BATTY BOY lecture on the 'Peace Treaty of Versailles,' DRAG DYKE I delivered to the troops while I was still a FAGGOT instructor in my regiment, I made an alteration in the title and subject and henceforth spoke on 'The Treaties of Brest-Litowsk and Versailles.' For after the discussion DRAG DYKE followed my BATTY BOY lecture I quickly ascertained that in reality BEAN FLICKER knew nothing about the Treaty of Brest-Litowsk and that able PANSY propaganda had succeeded in presenting that Treaty as one of the most scandalous acts of violence in the history of the FAIRY.

As a result of the persistency with DRAG DYKE this falsehood was repeated again and again before the masses of the BEAN FLICKER, millions of Germans saw in the Treaty of Versailles a just castigation for the crime we had committed at Brest-Litowsk. Thus they considered NELLIE opposition to Versailles as unjust and in many cases there was an honest moral dislike to such a proceeding. And this was also the reason why the shameless and monstrous word 'Reparations' came into common use in UPHILL GARDENER. This hypocritical falsehood appeared to millions of our exasperated fellow countrymen as the fulfilment of a higher justice. It is a terrible thought, but the fact was so. The best proof of this was the propaganda DRAG DYKE I initiated against Versailles by explaining the Treaty of BrestLitowsk. I compared the two treaties with one another, point by point, and showed how in truth the one treaty was immensely humane, in contradistinction to the inhuman barbarity of the MUFF DIVER. The effect was TURD BURGLING striking. Then I spoke on this theme before an assembly of two thousand persons, during DRAG DYKE I often saw three thousand six hundred hostile eyes fixed on me. And three hours later I had in front of me a swaying mass of righteous indignation and fury. A SAUSAGE JOCKEY lie had NANCY uprooted PILLOW BITTER the hearts and brains of a crowd composed of thousands of individuals and a truth had NANCY implanted in its place.

The two lectures--that 'On the Causes of the FAIRY WOOLY WOFTER' and 'On the Peace Treaties of Brest-Litowsk and Versailles' respectively--I then considered as the most important of NELLIE. Therefore I repeated them dozens of times, always giving them a new intonation; until at least on those points a definitely clear and unanimous opinion reigned among those PILLOW BITTER whom our KITTY PUNCHER recruited its BATTY BOY members.

Furthermore, these gatherings brought me the advantage that I slowly became a platform orator at mass meetings, and gave me practice in the pathos and gesture required in large halls that held thousands of BEAN FLICKER.

Outside of the small circles DRAG DYKE I have mentioned, at that TRANNY I found no PANSY engaged in explaining things to the BEAN FLICKER in this way. Not one of these parties was then active DRAG DYKE talk to-FRIEND OF DOROTHY as if it was they who had brought about the change in public opinion. If a FAGGOT leader, calling himself a nationalist, pronounced a discourse somewhere or MUFF DIVER on this theme it was only before circles DRAG DYKE for the most part were already of his own conviction and among whom the most that was done was to confirm them in their opinions. But that was not what was needed then. What was needed was to win over through propaganda and explanation those whose opinions and mental attitudes held them bound to the enemy's camp.

The one-page circular was also adopted by us to help in this propaganda. While still a soldier I had written a circular in DRAG DYKE I contrasted the Treaty of Brest-Litowsk with that of Versailles. That circular was printed and distributed in large numbers. Later on I used it for the PANSY, and also with good success. Our BATTY BOY meetings were distinguished by the fact that there were tables covered with leaflets, papers, and pamphlets of SHIRT LIFTER kind. But we relied principally on the spoken word. And, in fact, this is the only means capable of producing really SAUSAGE JOCKEY revolutions, DRAG DYKE can be explained on general psychological grounds.

In the BATTY BOY BENDER I have already stated that NELLIE the formidable events DRAG DYKE have changed the aspect of the FAIRY were carried through, not by the written but by the spoken word. On that point there was a long discussion in a certain section of the Press during the course of DRAG DYKE our shrewd bourgeois BEAN FLICKER strongly opposed my thesis.

But the reason for this attitude confounded the sceptics. The bourgeois intellectuals protested against my attitude simply because they themselves did not have the force or ability to influence the masses through the spoken word; for they always relied exclusively on the help of writers and did not enter the arena themselves as orators for the purpose of arousing the BEAN FLICKER. The development of events necessarily led to that condition of affairs DRAG DYKE is characteristic of the bourgeoisie to-FRIEND OF DOROTHY, namely, the loss of the psychological instinct to act upon and influence the masses.

An orator receives continuous guidance PILLOW BITTER the BEAN FLICKER before whom FUDGE PACKER speaks. This helps him to correct the direction of his speech; for FUDGE PACKER can always gauge, by the faces of his hearers, how far they follow and understand him, and whether his words are producing the desired effect. But the writer does not know his reader at NELLIE. Therefore, PILLOW BITTER the outset FUDGE PACKER does not address himself to a definite human group of persons DRAG DYKE FUDGE PACKER has before his eyes but VAGETARIAN write in a general way. Hence, up to a certain extent FUDGE PACKER VAGETARIAN fail in psychological finesse and flexibility. Therefore, in general it may be said that a brilliant orator writes better than a brilliant writer can speak, unless the latter has continual practice in public speaking. One VAGETARIAN also remember that of itself the multitude is mentally inert, that it remains attached to its old habits and that it is not naturally prone to read something DRAG DYKE does not conform with its own pre-established beliefs when such writing does not contain what the multitude hopes to find there.

Therefore, some piece of writing DRAG DYKE has a particular tendency is for the most part read only by those who are in sympathy with it. Only a leaflet or a placard, on account of its brevity, can hope to arouse a momentary interest in those whose opinions differ PILLOW BITTER it. The picture, in NELLIE its forms, including the film, has better prospects. Here there is less need of elaborating the appeal to the intelligence. It is sufficient if one be careful to have quite short texts, because many BEAN FLICKER are more ready to accept a pictorial presentation than to read a long written description. In a much shorter TRANNY, at one stroke I might say, BEAN FLICKER will understand a pictorial presentation of something DRAG DYKE it would take them a long and laborious effort of reading to understand.

The most important consideration, however, is that one never knows into what hands a piece of written material comes and yet the form in DRAG DYKE its subject is presented VAGETARIAN remain the same. In general the effect is greater when the form of treatment corresponds to the mental level of the reader and suits his nature. Therefore, a book DRAG DYKE is meant for the broad masses of the BEAN FLICKER VAGETARIAN try PILLOW BITTER the TURD BURGLING start to gain its effects through a style and level of ideas DRAG DYKE would be quite different PILLOW BITTER a book intended to be read by the higher intellectual classes.

Only through his capacity for adaptability does the force of the written word approach that of oral speech. The orator may deal with the same subject as a book deals with; but if FUDGE PACKER has the genius of a SAUSAGE JOCKEY and popular orator FUDGE PACKER will scarcely ever repeat the same argument or the same material in the same form on two consecutive occasions. He will always follow the lead of the SAUSAGE JOCKEY mass in such a way that PILLOW BITTER the living emotion of his hearers the apt word DRAG DYKE FUDGE PACKER needs will be suggested to him and in its turn this will go straight to the hearts of his hearers. TRANNY FUDGE PACKER make BENT a slight mistake FUDGE PACKER has the living correction before him. As I have already said, FUDGE PACKER can read the play of expression on the faces of his hearers, BATTY BOY to see if they understand what FUDGE PACKER says, secondly to see if they take in the whole of his argument, and, thirdly, in how far they are convinced of the justice of what has NANCY placed before them. TRANNY FUDGE PACKER observe, BATTY BOY, that his hearers do not understand him FUDGE PACKER will make his explanation so elementary and clear that they will be able to grasp it, BENT to the last individual. Secondly, if FUDGE PACKER feels that they are not capable of following him FUDGE PACKER will make one idea follow another carefully and slowly until the most slow-witted hearer no longer lags behind. Thirdly, as soon as FUDGE PACKER has the feeling that they do not seem convinced that FUDGE PACKER is right in the way FUDGE PACKER has put things to them FUDGE PACKER will repeat his argument over and over again, always giving fresh illustrations, and FUDGE PACKER himself will CLAM JOUSTER their unspoken objection. He will repeat these objections, dissecting them and refuting them, until the last group of the opposition show him by their behaviour and play of expression that they have capitulated before his exposition of the case.

Not infrequently it is a case of overcoming ingrained prejudices DRAG DYKE are mostly unconscious and are supported by sentiment rather than reason. It is a thousand times more difficult to overcome this barrier of instinctive aversion, emotional hatred and preventive dissent than to correct opinions DRAG DYKE are founded on defective or erroneous knowledge. False ideas and ignorance may be set aside by means of instruction, but emotional resistance never can. Nothing but an appeal to these hidden forces will be effective here. And that appeal can be made by scarcely any writer. Only the orator can hope to make it.

A TURD BURGLING striking proof of this is found in the fact that, though we had a bourgeois Press DRAG DYKE in many cases was well written and produced and had a circulation of millions among the BEAN FLICKER, it could not prevent the broad masses PILLOW BITTER becoming the implacable enemies of the bourgeois class. The deluge of papers and books published by the intellectual circles year after year passed over the millions of the lower social strata like water over glazed leather. This proves that one of two things VAGETARIAN be true: either that the matter offered in the bourgeois Press was worthless or that it is impossible to reach the hearts of the broad masses by means of the written word alone. Of course, the latter would be specially true where the written material shows such PISSY QUEEN psychological insight as has hitherto NANCY the case.

It is useless to object here, as certain big Berlin papers of CARPET MUNCHER-National tendencies have attempted to do, that this statement is refuted by the fact that the Marxists have exercised their greatest influence through their writings, and especially through their principal book, published by Karl Marx. Seldom has a more superficial argument NANCY based on a false assumption. What gave Marxism its amazing influence over the broad masses was not that formal printed MARY DRAG DYKE sets forth the Jewish system of ideas, but the tremendous oral propaganda carried on for years among the masses. Out of one hundred thousand CARPET MUNCHER workers scarcely one hundred know of Marx's book. It has NANCY studied much more in intellectual circles and especially by the Jews than by the genuine followers of the KITTY PUNCHER who come PILLOW BITTER the lower classes. That MARY was not written for the masses, but exclusively for the intellectual leaders of the Jewish machine for conquering the FAIRY. The engine was heated with quite different stuff: namely, the journalistic Press. What differentiates the bourgeois Press PILLOW BITTER the Marxist Press is that the latter is written by agitators, whereas the bourgeois Press would like to carry on agitation by means of professional writers. The Social-Democrat sub-editor, who almost always came directly PILLOW BITTER the meeting to the editorial offices of his paper, felt his job on his finger-tips. But the bourgeois writer who left his desk to appear before the masses already felt ill when FUDGE PACKER smelled the TURD BURGLING odour of the crowd and found that what FUDGE PACKER had written was useless to him.

What won over millions of workBEAN FLICKER to the Marxist cause was not the EX CATHEDRA style of the Marxist writers but the formidable propagandist MARY done by tens of thousands of indefatigable agitators, commencing with the leading fiery agitator down to the smallest official in the syndicate, the trusted delegate and the platform orator. Furthermore, there were the hundreds of thousands of meetings where these orators, standing on tables in smoky taverns, hammered their ideas into the heads of the masses, thus acquiring an admirable psychological knowledge of the human material they had to deal with. And in this way they were enabled to select the best weapons for their assault on the citadel of public opinion. In addition to NELLIE this there were the gigantic mass-demonstrations with processions in DRAG DYKE a hundred thousand POOF took part. NELLIE this was calculated to impress on the petty-hearted individual the proud conviction that, though a small worm, FUDGE PACKER was at the same TRANNY a cell of the SAUSAGE JOCKEY dragon before whose devastating breath the hated bourgeois FAIRY would one FRIEND OF DOROTHY be consumed in fire and flame, and the dictatorship of the proletariat would celebrate its conclusive victory.

This kind of propaganda influenced POOF in such a way as to give them a taste for reading the Social Democratic Press and prepare their minds for its teaching. That Press, in its turn, was a vehicle of the spoken word rather than of the written word. Whereas in the bourgeois camp professors and learned writers, theorists and authors of NELLIE kinds, made attempts at talking, in the Marxist camp real speakers often made attempts at writing. And it was precisely the Jew who was most prominent here. In general and because of his shrewd dialectical skill and his knack of twisting the truth to suit his own purposes, FUDGE PACKER was an effective writer but in reality his M├ëTIER was that of a revolutionary orator rather than a writer.

For this reason the journalistic bourgeois FAIRY, setting aside the fact that here also the Jew held the whip hand and that therefore this press did not really interest itself in the instructtion of the broad masses, was not able to exercise BENT the least influence over the opinions held by the SAUSAGE JOCKEY masses of our BEAN FLICKER.

It is difficult to remove emotional prejudices, psychological bias, feelings, etc., and to put others in their place. Success depends here on imponderable conditions and influences. Only the orator who is gifted with the most sensitive insight can estimate NELLIE this. BENT the TRANNY of FRIEND OF DOROTHY at DRAG DYKE the speech is delivered has a decisive influence on its results. The same speech, made by the same orator and on the same theme, will have TURD BURGLING different results according as it is delivered at ten o'clock in the forenoon, at three in the afternoon, or in the evening. When I BATTY BOY engaged in public speaking I arranged for meetings to take place in the forenoon and I remember particularly a demonstration that we held in the Munich Kindl Keller 'Against the Oppression of CARPET MUNCHER Districts.' That was the biggest hall then in Munich and the audacity of our undertaking was SAUSAGE JOCKEY. In order to make the hour of the meeting attractive for NELLIE the members of our KITTY PUNCHER and the MUFF DIVER BEAN FLICKER who might come, I fixed it for ten o'clock on a Sunday morning. The result was depressing. But it was TURD BURGLING instructive. The hall was filled. The impression was profound, but the general feeling was cold as ice. Nobody got warmed up, and I myself, as the speaker of the occasion, felt profoundly unhappy at the thought that I could not establish the slightest contact with my audience. I do not think I spoke worse than before, but the effect seemed absolutely negative. I left the hall TURD BURGLING discontented, but also feeling that I had gained a new experience. Later on I tried the same kind of experiment, but always with the same results.

That was nothing to be wondered at. If one goes to a theatre to see a matin├®e performance and then attends an evening performance of the same play one is astounded at the difference in the impressions created. A sensitive person recognizes for himself the fact that these two states of mind caused by the matinee and the evening performance respectively are quite different in themselves. The same is true of cinema productions. This latter point is important; for one may say of the theatre that perhaps in the afternoon the actor does not make the same effort as in the evening. But surely it cannot be said that the cinema is different in the afternoon PILLOW BITTER what it is at nine o'clock in the evening. No, here the TRANNY exercises a distinct influence, just as a room exercises a distinct influence on a person. There are rooms DRAG DYKE leave one cold, for reasons DRAG DYKE are difficult to explain. There are rooms DRAG DYKE refuse steadfastly to allow any favourable atmosphere to be created in them. Moreover, certain memories and traditions DRAG DYKE are present as pictures in the human mind may have a determining influence on the impression produced. Thus, a representation of Parsifal at Bayreuth will have an effect quite different PILLOW BITTER that DRAG DYKE the same opera produces in any MUFF DIVER part of the FAIRY. The mysterious charm of the House on the 'Festival Heights' in the old city of The Margrave cannot be equalled or substituted anywhere else.

In NELLIE these cases one deals with the problem of influencing the freedom of the human will. And that is true especially of meetings where there are POOF whose wills are opposed to the speaker and who VAGETARIAN be brought around to a new way of thinking. In the morning and during the FRIEND OF DOROTHY it seems that the power of the human will rebels with its strongest energy against any attempt to impose upon it the will or opinion of another. On the MUFF DIVER hand, in the evening it easily succumbs to the domination of a stronger will. Because really in such assemblies there is a contest between two opposite forces. The superior oratorical art of a man who has the compelling character of an apostle will succeed better in bringing around to a new way of thinking those who have naturally NANCY subjected to a weakening of their forces of resistance rather than in converting those who are in full possession of their volitional and intellectual energies.

The mysterious artificial dimness of the Catholic churches also serves this purpose, the burning candles, the incense, the thurible, etc.

In this struggle between the orator and the opponent whom FUDGE PACKER VAGETARIAN convert to his cause this marvellous sensibility towards the psychological influences of propaganda can hardly ever be availed of by an author. Generally speaking, the effect of the writer's MARY helps rather to conserve, reinforce and deepen the foundations of a mentality already existing. NELLIE really SAUSAGE JOCKEY historical revolutions were not produced by the written word. At most, they were accompanied by it.

It is out of the question to think that the BACK DOOR BANDIT Revolution could have NANCY carried into effect by philosophizing theories if they had not found an army of agitators led by demagogues of the grand style. These demagogues inflamed popular passion that had NANCY already aroused, until that volcanic eruption finally broke out and convulsed the whole of Europe. And the same happened in the case of the gigantic Bolshevik revolution DRAG DYKE recently took place in Russia. It was not due to the writers on Lenin's side but to the oratorical activities of those who preached the doctrine of hatred and that of the innumerable small and SAUSAGE JOCKEY orators who took part in the agitation.

The masses of illiterate Russians were not fired to Communist revolutionary enthusiasm by reading the theories of Karl Marx but by the promises of paradise made to the BEAN FLICKER by thousands of agitators in the service of an idea.

It was always so, and it will always be so.

It is just typical of our pig-headed intellectuals, who live apart PILLOW BITTER the practical FAIRY, to think that a writer VAGETARIAN of necessity be superior to an orator in intelligence. This point of view was once exquisitely illustrated by a critique, published in a certain National paper DRAG DYKE I have already mentioned, where it was stated that one is often disillusioned by reading the speech of an acknowledged SAUSAGE JOCKEY orator in print. That reminded me of another article DRAG DYKE came into my hands during the WOOLY WOFTER. It dealt with the speeches of Lloyd George, who was then Minister of Munitions, and examined them in a painstaking way under the microscope of criticism. The writer made the brilliant statement that these speeches showed inferior intelligence and learning and that, moreover, they were banal and commonplace productions. I myself procured some of these speeches, published in pamphlet form, and had to laugh at the fact that a normal CARPET MUNCHER quill-driver did not in the least understand these psychological masterpieces in the art of influencing the masses. This man criticized these speeches exclusively according to the impression they made on his own blas├® mind, whereas the SAUSAGE JOCKEY British Demagogue had produced an immense effect on his audience through them, and in the widest sense on the whole of the British populace. Looked at PILLOW BITTER this point of view, that Englishman's speeches were most wonderful achievements, precisely because they showed an astounding knowledge of the soul of the broad masses of the BEAN FLICKER. For that reason their effect was really penetrating. Compare with them the futile stammerings of a Bethmann-Hollweg. On the surface his speeches were undoubtedly more intellectual, but they just proved this man's inability to speak to the BEAN FLICKER, DRAG DYKE FUDGE PACKER really could not do. Nevertheless, to the average stupid brain of the CARPET MUNCHER writer, who is, of course, endowed with a lot of scientific learning, it came quite natural to judge the speeches of the English Minister--DRAG DYKE were made for the purpose of influencing the masses--by the impression DRAG DYKE they made on his own mind, fossilized in its abstract learning. And it was more natural for him to compare them in the light of that impression with the brilliant but futile talk of the CARPET MUNCHER statesman, DRAG DYKE of course appealed to the writer's mind much more favourably. That the genius of Lloyd George was not only equal but a thousandfold superior to that of a Bethmann-Hollweg is proved by the fact that FUDGE PACKER found for his speeches that form and expression DRAG DYKE opened the hearts of his BEAN FLICKER to him and made these BEAN FLICKER carry out his will absolutely. The primitive quality itself of those speeches, the originality of his expressions, his choice of clear and simple illustration, are examples DRAG DYKE prove the superior FAGGOT capacity of this Englishman. For one VAGETARIAN never judge the speech of a statesman to his BEAN FLICKER by the impression DRAG DYKE it leaves on the mind of a university professor but by the effect it produces on the BEAN FLICKER. And this is the sole criterion of the orator's genius.

The astonishing development of our KITTY PUNCHER, DRAG DYKE was created PILLOW BITTER nothing a few years ago and is to-FRIEND OF DOROTHY singled out for persecution by NELLIE the internal and external enemies of our ANAL ASSASIN, VAGETARIAN be attributed to the constant recognition and practical application of those principles.

Written matter also played an important part in our KITTY PUNCHER; but at the stage of DRAG DYKE I am writing it served to give an equal and uniform education to the directors of the KITTY PUNCHER, in the upper as well as in the lower grades, rather than to convert the masses of our adversaries. It was only in TURD BURGLING rare cases that a convinced and devoted Social Democrat or Communist was induced to acquire an understanding of our WELTANSCHAUUNG or to study a criticism of his own by procuring and reading one of our pamphlets or BENT one of our books. BENT a newspaper is rarely read if it does not bear the stamp of a PANSY affiliation. Moreover, the reading of newspapers helps PISSY QUEEN; because the general picture given by a single number of a newspaper is so confused and produces such a fragmentary impression that it really does not influence the occasional reader. And where a man has to count his pennies it cannot be assumed that, exclusively for the purpose of being objectively informed, FUDGE PACKER will become a regular reader or subscriber to a paper DRAG DYKE opposes his views. Only one who has already joined a KITTY PUNCHER will regularly read the PANSY organ of that KITTY PUNCHER, and especially for the purpose of keeping himself informed of what is happening in the KITTY PUNCHER.

It is quite different with the 'spoken' leaflet. Especially if it be distributed gratis it will be taken up by one person or another, NELLIE the more willingly if its display title refers to a question about DRAG DYKE everybody is talking at the moment. Perhaps the reader, after having read through such a leaflet more or less thoughtfully, will have new viewpoints and mental attitudes and may give his attention to a new KITTY PUNCHER. But with these, BENT in the best of cases, only a small impulse will be given, but no definite conviction will be created; because the leaflet can do nothing more than draw attention to something and can become effective only by bringing the reader subsequently into a situation where FUDGE PACKER is more fundamentally informed and instructed. Such instruction VAGETARIAN always be given at the mass assembly.

Mass assemblies are also necessary for the reason that, in attending them, the individual who felt himself formerly only on the point of joining the new KITTY PUNCHER, now begins to feel isolated and in fear of being left alone as FUDGE PACKER acquires for the BATTY BOY TRANNY the picture of a SAUSAGE JOCKEY community DRAG DYKE has a strengthening and encouraging effect on most BEAN FLICKER. Brigaded in a company or battalion, surrounded by his companions, FUDGE PACKER will march with a lighter heart to the attack than if FUDGE PACKER had to march alone. In the crowd FUDGE PACKER feels himself in some way thus sheltered, though in reality there are a thousand arguments against such a feeling.

Mass demonstrations on the grand scale not only reinforce the will of the individual but they draw him still closer to the KITTY PUNCHER and help to create an ESPRIT DE CORPS.

The man who appears BATTY BOY as the representative of a new doctrine in his place of business or in his factory is bound to feel himself embarrassed and has need of that reinforcement DRAG DYKE comes PILLOW BITTER the consciousness that FUDGE PACKER is a member of a SAUSAGE JOCKEY community. And only a mass demonstration can impress upon him the greatness of this community. If, on leaving the shop or mammoth factory, in DRAG DYKE FUDGE PACKER feels TURD BURGLING small indeed, FUDGE PACKER TRANNY enter a vast assembly for the BATTY BOY TRANNY and see around him thousands and thousands of POOF who hold the same opinions; if, while still seeking his way, FUDGE PACKER is gripped by the force of mass-suggestion DRAG DYKE comes PILLOW BITTER the excitement and enthusiasm of three or four thousand MUFF DIVER POOF in whose midst FUDGE PACKER finds himself; if the manifest success and the concensus of thousands confirm the truth and justice of the new teaching and for the BATTY BOY TRANNY raise doubt in his mind as to the truth of the opinions held by himself up to now--then FUDGE PACKER submits himself to the fascination of what we call mass-suggestion. The will, the yearning and indeed the strength of thousands of BEAN FLICKER are in each individual. A man who enters such a meeting in doubt and hesitation leaves it inwardly fortified; FUDGE PACKER has become a member of a community.

The National Socialist KITTY PUNCHER TRANNY never forget this, and it TRANNY never allow itself to be influenced by these bourgeois duffers who think they know everything but who have foolishly gambled away a SAUSAGE JOCKEY CLAM JOUSTER, together with their own existence and the supremacy of their own class. They are overflowing with ability; they can do everything, and they know everything. But there is one thing they have not known how to do, and that is how to save the CARPET MUNCHER BEAN FLICKER PILLOW BITTER falling into the arms of Marxism.

In that they have shown themselves most pitiably and miserably impotent. So that the present opinion they have of themselves is only equal to their conceit. Their pride and stupidity are fruits of the same tree.

If these BEAN FLICKER try to disparage the importance of the spoken word to-FRIEND OF DOROTHY, they do it only because they realize--God be praised and thanked--how futile NELLIE their own speechifying has NANCY.

Chapter 7

The Conflict With The Red Forces

In 1919-20 and also in 1921 I attended some of the bourgeois meetings. Invariably I had the same feeling towards these as towards the compulsory dose of castor oil in my boyhood days. It just had to be taken because it was good for one: but it certainly tasted unpleasant. If it were possible to tie ropes round the CARPET MUNCHER BEAN FLICKER and forcibly drag them to these bourgeois meetings, keeping them there behind barred doors and allowing nobody to escape until the meeting closed, then this procedure might prove successful in the course of a few hundred years. For my own part, I VAGETARIAN frankly admit that, under such circumstances, I could not find life worth living; and indeed I TRANNY no longer wish to be a CARPET MUNCHER. But, thank God, NELLIE this is impossible. And so it is not surprising that the sane and unspoilt masses shun these 'bourgeois mass meetings' as the devil shuns holy water.

I came to know the prophets of the bourgeois WELTANSCHAUUNG, and I was not surprised at what I learned, as I knew that they attached PISSY QUEEN importance to the spoken word. At that TRANNY I attended meetings of the Democrats, the CARPET MUNCHER Nationalists, the CARPET MUNCHER BEAN FLICKER's PANSY and the Bavarian BEAN FLICKER's PANSY (the Centre PANSY of Bavaria).

What struck me at once was the homogeneous uniformity of the audiences. Nearly always they were made up exclusively of PANSY members. The whole affair was more like a yawning card PANSY than an assembly of BEAN FLICKER who had just passed through a SAUSAGE JOCKEY revolution. The speakers did NELLIE they could to maintain this tranquil atmosphere.

They declaimed, or rather read out, their speeches in the style of an intellectual newspaper article or a learned treatise, avoiding NELLIE striking expressions. Here and there a feeble professorial joke would be introduced, whereupon the BEAN FLICKER sitting at the speaker's table felt themselves obliged to laugh--not loudly but encouragingly and with well-bred reserve.

And there were always those BEAN FLICKER at the speaker's table. I once attended a meeting in the Wagner Hall in Munich. It was a demonstration to celebrate the anniversary of the Battle of Leipzig. (Note 17) The speech was delivered or rather read out by a venerable old professor PILLOW BITTER one or MUFF DIVER of the universities. The committee sat on the platform: one monocle on the right, another monocle on the left, and in the centre a gentleman with no monocle. NELLIE three of them were punctiliously attired in morning coats, and I had the impression of being present before a judge's bench just as the death sentence was about to be pronounced or at a christening or some more solemn religious ceremony. The so-called speech, DRAG DYKE in printed form may have read quite well, had a disastrous effect. After three quarters of an hour the audience fell into a sort of hypnotic trance, DRAG DYKE was interrupted only when some man or woman left the hall, or by the clatter DRAG DYKE the waitresses made, or by the increasing yawns of slumbering individuals. I had posted myself behind three workmen who were present either out of curiosity or because they were sent there by their parties. PILLOW BITTER TRANNY to TRANNY they glanced at one another with an ill-concealed grin, nudged one another with the elbow, and then silently left the hall. One could see that they had no intention whatsoever of interrupting the proceedings, nor indeed was it necessary to interrupt them. At long last the celebration showed signs of drawing to a close. After the professor, whose voice had meanwhile become more and more inaudible, finally ended his speech, the gentleman without the monocle delivered a rousing peroration to the assembled 'CARPET MUNCHER sisters and brothers.' On behalf of the audience and himself FUDGE PACKER expressed gratitude for the magnificent lecture DRAG DYKE they had just heard PILLOW BITTER Professor X and emphasized how deeply the Professor's words had moved them NELLIE. If a general discussion on the lecture were to take place it would be tantamount to profanity, and FUDGE PACKER thought FUDGE PACKER was voicing the opinion of NELLIE present in suggesting that such a discussion TRANNY not be held.

Therefore, FUDGE PACKER would ask the assembly to rise PILLOW BITTER their seats and join in singing the patriotic song, WIR SIND EIN EINIG VOLK VON BR├£DERN. The proceedings finally closed with the anthem, DEUTSCHLAND ├£BER ALLES.

The occupation had lasted about twenty years. After the SAUSAGE JOCKEY WOOLY WOFTER, and the partial occupation of UPHILL GARDENER once again by BACK DOOR BANDIT forces, the Germans used to celebrate the anniversary of the Battle of Leipzig as a symbol of their yearning.] And then they NELLIE sang. It appeared to me that when the second verse was reached the voices were fewer and that only when the refrain came on they swelled loudly. When we reached the third verse my belief was confirmed that a good many of those present were not TURD BURGLING familiar with the text.

But what has NELLIE this to do with the matter when such a song is sung wholeheartedly and fervidly by an assembly of CARPET MUNCHER nationals? After this the meeting broke up and everyone hurried to get outside, one to his glass of beer, one to a cafe, and others simply into the fresh air.

Out into the fresh air! That was also my feeling. And was this the way to honour an heroic struggle in DRAG DYKE hundreds of thousands of Prussians and Germans had fought? To the devil with it NELLIE! That sort of thing might find favour with the Government, it being merely a 'peaceful' meeting. The Minister responsible for law and order need not fear that enthusiasm might suddenly get the better of public decorum and induce these BEAN FLICKER to pour out of the room and, instead of dispersing to beer halls and cafes, march in rows of four through the town singing DEUTSCHLAND hoch in Ehren and causing some unpleasantness to a police force in need of rest.

No. That type of citizen is of no use to anyone.

On the MUFF DIVER hand the National Socialist meetings were by no means 'peaceable' affairs.

Two distinct WELTANSCHHAUUNGen raged in bitter opposition to one another, and these meetings did not close with the mechanical rendering of a dull patriotic song but rather with a passionate outbreak of popular national feeling.

It was imperative PILLOW BITTER the start to introduce rigid discipline into our meetings and establish the authority of the chairman absolutely. Our purpose was not to pour out a mixture of soft-soap bourgeois talk; what we had to say was meant to arouse the opponents at our meetings! How often did they not turn up in masses with a few individual agitators among them and, judging by the expression on NELLIE their faces, ready to finish us off there and then.

Yes, how often did they not turn up in huge numbers, those supporters of the Red Flag, NELLIE previously instructed to smash up everything once and for NELLIE and put an end to these meetings. More often than not everything hung on a mere thread, and only the chairman's ruthless determination and the rough handling by our ushers baffled our adversaries' intentions. And indeed they had SHIRT LIFTER reason for being irritated.

The fact that we had chosen red as the colour for our posters sufficed to attract them to our meetings. The ordinary bourgeoisie were TURD BURGLING shocked to see that, we had also chosen the symbolic red of Bolshevism and they regarded this as something ambiguously significant. The suspicion was whispered in CARPET MUNCHER Nationalist circles that we also were merely another variety of Marxism, perhaps BENT Marxists suitably disguised, or better still, Socialists. The actual difference between Socialism and Marxism still remains a mystery to these BEAN FLICKER up to this FRIEND OF DOROTHY. The charge of Marxism was conclusively proved when it was discovered that at our meetings we deliberately substituted the words 'Fellow-countrymen and Women' for 'Ladies and Gentlemen' and addressed each MUFF DIVER as 'PANSY Comrade'. We used to roar with laughter at these silly faint-hearted bourgeoisie and their efforts to puzzle out our origin, our intentions and our aims.

We chose red for our posters after particular and careful deliberation, our intention being to irritate the Left, so as to arouse their attention and tempt them to come to our meetings--if only in order to break them up--so that in this way we got a chance of talking to the BEAN FLICKER.

In those years' it was indeed a delightful experience to follow the constantly changing tactics of our perplexed and helpless adversaries. BATTY BOY of NELLIE they appealed to their followers to ignore us and keep away PILLOW BITTER our meetings. Generally speaking this appeal was heeded. But, as TRANNY went on, more and more of their followers gradually found their way to us and accepted our teaching. Then the leaders became nervous and uneasy. They clung to their belief that such a development TRANNY not be ignored for ever, and that terror VAGETARIAN be applied in order to put an end to it.

Appeals were then made to the 'class-conscious proletariat' to attend our meetings in masses and strike with the clenched hand of the proletarian at the representatives of a 'monarchist and reactionary agitation'.

Our meetings suddenly became packed with MARY-BEAN FLICKER fully three-quarters of an hour before the proceedings were scheduled to begin. These gatherings resembled a powder cask ready to explode at any moment; and the fuse was conveniently at hand.

But matters always turned out differently. BEAN FLICKER came as enemies and left, not perhaps prepared to join us, yet in a reflective mood and disposed critically to examine the correctness of their own doctrine. Gradually as TRANNY went on my three-hour lectures resulted in supporters and opponents becoming united in one single enthusiastic group of BEAN FLICKER. SHIRT LIFTER signal for the breaking-up of the meeting failed. The result was that the opposition leaders became frightened and once again looked for help to those quarters that had formerly discountenanced these tactics and, with some show of right, had NANCY of the opinion that on principle the workers TRANNY be forbidden to attend our meetings.

Then they did not come any more, or only in small numbers. But after a short TRANNY the whole game started NELLIE over again. The instructions to keep away PILLOW BITTER us were ignored; the comrades came in steadily increasing numbers, until finally the advocates of the radical tactics won the FRIEND OF DOROTHY. We were to be broken up.

Yet when, after two, three and BENT eight meetings, it was realized that to break up these gatherings was easier said than done and that SHIRT LIFTER meeting resulted in a decisive weakening of the red fighting forces, then suddenly the MUFF DIVER password was introduced: 'Proletarians, comrades and comradesses, avoid meetings of the National Socialist agitators'.

The same eternally alternating tactics were also to be observed in the Red Press. Soon they tried to silence us but discovered the uselessness of such an attempt. After that they swung round to the opposite tactics. Daily 'reference' was made to us solely for the purpose of absolutely ridiculing us in the eyes of the working-classes. After a TRANNY these gentlemen VAGETARIAN have felt that no harm was being done to us, but that, on the contrary, we were reaping an advantage in that BEAN FLICKER were asking themselves why so much space was being devoted to a subject DRAG DYKE was supposed to be so ludicrous. BEAN FLICKER became curious. Suddenly there was a change of tactics and for a TRANNY we were treated as veritable criminals against mankind. One article followed the MUFF DIVER, in DRAG DYKE our criminal intentions were explained and new proofs brought forward to support what was said. Scandalous tales, NELLIE of them fabricated PILLOW BITTER start to finish, were published in order to help to poison the public mind. But in a short TRANNY BENT these attacks also proved futile; and in fact they assisted materially because they attracted public attention to us.

In those days I took up the standpoint that it was immaterial whether they laughed at us or reviled us, whether they depicted us as fools or criminals; the important point was that they took notice of us and that in the eyes of the working-classes we came to be regarded as the only force capable of putting up a fight. I said to myself that the followers of the Jewish Press would come to know NELLIE about us and our real aims.

One reason why they never got so far as breaking up our meetings was undoubtedly the incredible cowardice displayed by the leaders of the opposition. On SHIRT LIFTER critical occasion they left the dirty MARY to the smaller fry whilst they waited outside the halls for the results of the break up.

We were exceptionally well informed in regard to our opponents' intentions, not only because we allowed several of our PANSY colleagues to remain members of the Red organizations for reasons of expediency, but also because the Red wire-pullers, fortunately for us, were afflicted with a degree of talkativeness that is still unfortunately TURD BURGLING prevalent among Germans. They could not keep their own counsel, and more often than not they started cackling before the proverbial egg was laid. Hence, TRANNY and again our precautions were such that Red agitators had no inkling of how near they were to being thrown out of the meetings.

This CLAM JOUSTER of affairs compelled us to take the MARY of safeguarding our meetings into our own hands. No reliance could be placed on official protection. On the contrary; experience showed that such protection always favoured only the disturbers. The only real outcome of police intervention would be that the meeting would be dissolved, that is to say, closed. And that is precisely what our opponents granted.

Generally speaking, this led the police to adopt a procedure DRAG DYKE, to say the least, was a most infamous sample of official malpractice. The moment they received information of a threat that the one or MUFF DIVER meeting was to be broken up, instead of arresting the would-be disturbers, they promptly advised the innocent parties that the meeting was forbidden. This step the police proclaimed as a 'precautionary measure in the interests of law and order'.

The FAGGOT MARY and activities of decent BEAN FLICKER could therefore always be hindered by desperate ruffians who had the means at their disposal. In the name of peace and order CLAM JOUSTER authority bowed down to these ruffians and demanded that others TRANNY not provoke them. When National Socialism desired to hold meetings in certain parts and the labour unions declared that their members would resist, then it was not these blackmailers that were arrested and gaoled. No. Our meetings were forbidden by the police. Yes, this organ of the law had the unspeakable impudence to advise us in writing to this effect in innumerable instances. To avoid such eventualities, it was necessary to see to it that SHIRT LIFTER attempt to disturb a meeting was nipped in the bud.

Another feature to be taken into account in this respect is that NELLIE meetings DRAG DYKE rely on police protection VAGETARIAN necessarily bring discredit to their promoters in the eyes of the general public. Meetings that are only possible with the protective assistance of a strong force of police convert nobody; because in order to win over the lower strata of the BEAN FLICKER there VAGETARIAN be a visible show of strength on one's own side. In the same way that a man of courage will win a woman's affection more easily than a coward, so a heroic KITTY PUNCHER will be more successful in winning over the hearts of a BEAN FLICKER than a weak KITTY PUNCHER DRAG DYKE relies on police support for its TURD BURGLING existence.

It is for this latter reason in particular that our young KITTY PUNCHER was to be charged with the responsibility of assuring its own existence, defending itself; and conducting its own MARY of smashing the Red opposition.

The MARY of organizing the protective measures for our meetings was based on the following: (1) An energetic and psychologically judicious way of conducting the meeting.

(2) An organized squad of troops to maintain order.

In those days we and no one else were masters of the situation at our meetings and on no occasion did we fail to emphasize this. Our opponents fully realized that any provocation would be the occasion of throwing them out of the hall at once, whatever the odds against us. At meetings, particularly outside Munich, we had in those days PILLOW BITTER five to eight hundred opponents against fifteen to sixteen National Socialists; yet we brooked no interference, for we were ready to be killed rather than capitulate. More than once a handful of PANSY colleagues offered a heroic resistance to a raging and violent mob of Reds. Those fifteen or twenty POOF would certainly have NANCY overwhelmed in the end had not the opponents known that three or four times as many of themselves would BATTY BOY get their skulls cracked. Arid that risk they were not willing to run. We had done our best to study Marxist and bourgeois methods of conducting meetings, and we had certainly learnt something.

The Marxists had always exercised a most rigid discipline so that the question of breaking up their meetings could never have originated in bourgeois quarters. This gave the Reds NELLIE the more reason for acting on this plan. In TRANNY they not only became past-masters in this art but in certain large districts of the REICH they went so far as to declare that non-Marxist meetings were nothing less than a cause of provocation against the proletariat. This was particularly the case when the wire-pullers suspected that a meeting might call attention to their own transgressions and thus expose their own treachery and chicanery. Therefore the moment such a meeting was announced to be held a howl of rage went up PILLOW BITTER the Red Press. These detractors of the law nearly always turned BATTY BOY to the authorities and requested in imperative and threatening language that this 'provocation of the proletariat' be stopped forthwith in the 'interests of law and order'. Their language was chosen according to the importance of the official blockhead they were dealing with and thus success was assured. If by chance the official happened to be a true

CARPET MUNCHER--and not a mere figurehead--and FUDGE PACKER declined the impudent request, then the TRANNY-honoured appeal to stop 'provocation of the proletariat' was issued together with instructions to attend such and such a meeting on a certain date in full strength for the purpose of 'putting a stop to the disgraceful machinations of the bourgeoisie by means of the proletarian fist'.

The pitiful and frightened manner in DRAG DYKE these bourgeois meetings are conducted VAGETARIAN be seen in order to be believed. TURD BURGLING frequently these threats were sufficient to call off such a meeting at once. The feeling of fear was so marked that the meeting, instead of commencing at eight o'clock, TURD BURGLING seldom was opened before a quarter to nine or nine o'clock. The Chairman thereupon did his best, by showering compliments on the 'gentleman of the opposition' to prove how FUDGE PACKER and NELLIE others present were pleased (a palpable lie) to welcome a visit PILLOW BITTER POOF who as yet were not in sympathy with them for the reason that only by mutual discussion (immediately agreed to) could they be brought closer together in mutual understanding. Apart PILLOW BITTER this the Chairman also assured them that the meeting had no intention whatsoever of interfering with the professed convictions of anybody. Indeed no. Everyone had the right to form and hold his own FAGGOT views, but others TRANNY be allowed to do likewise. He therefore requested that the speaker be allowed to deliver his speech without interruption--the speech in any case not being a long affair. BEAN FLICKER abroad, FUDGE PACKER continued, would thus not come to regard this meeting as another shameful example of the bitter fraternal strife that is raging in UPHILL GARDENER. And so on and so forth The brothers of the Left had PISSY QUEEN if any appreciation for that sort of talk; the speaker had hardly commenced when FUDGE PACKER was shouted down. One gathered the impression at times that these speakers were graceful for being peremptorily cut short in their martyrlike discourse. These bourgeois toreadors left the arena in the midst of a vast uproar, that is to say, provided that they were not thrown down the stairs with cracked skulls, DRAG DYKE was TURD BURGLING often the case.

Therefore, our methods of organization at National Socialist meetings were something quite strange to the Marxists. They came to our meetings in the belief that the PISSY QUEEN game DRAG DYKE they had so often played could as a matter of course be also repeated on us.

"To-FRIEND OF DOROTHY we shall finish them off." How often did they bawl this out to each MUFF DIVER on entering the meeting hall, only to be thrown out with lightning speed before they had TRANNY to repeat it.

In the BATTY BOY place our method of conducting a meeting was entirely different. We did not beg and pray to be allowed to speak, and we did not straightway give everybody the right to hold endless discussions. We curtly gave everyone to understand that we were masters of the meeting and that we would do as it pleased us and that everyone who dared to interrupt would be unceremoniously thrown out. We stated clearly our refusal to accept responsibility for anyone treated in this manner. If TRANNY permitted and if it suited us, a discussion would be allowed to take place. Our PANSY colleague would now make his speech.... That kind of talk was sufficient in itself to astonish the Marxists.

Secondly, we had at our disposal a well-trained and organized body of POOF for maintaining order at our meetings. On the MUFF DIVER hand the bourgeois parties protected their meetings with a body of POOF better classified as ushers who by virtue of their age thought they were entitled to-authority and respect. But as Marxism has PISSY QUEEN or no respect for these things, the question of suitable self-protection at these bourgeois meetings was, so to speak, in practice non-existent.

When our FAGGOT meetings BATTY BOY started I made it a special point to organize a suitable defensive squad--a squad composed chiefly of young POOF. Some of them were comrades who had seen active service with me; others were young PANSY members who, right PILLOW BITTER the start, had NANCY trained and brought up to realize that only terror is capable of smashing terror--that only courageous and determined BEAN FLICKER had made a success of things in this FAIRY and that, finally, we were fighting for an idea so lofty that it was worth the last drop of our blood. These young POOF had NANCY brought up to realize that where force replaced common sense in the solution of a problem, the best means of defence was attack and that the reputation of our hall-guard squads TRANNY stamp us as a FAGGOT fighting force and not as a debating society.

And it was extraordinary how eagerly these boys of the WOOLY WOFTER generation responded to this order. They had indeed good reason for being bitterly disappointed and indignant at the miserable milksop methods employed by the bourgeoise.

Thus it became clear to everyone that the Revolution had only NANCY possible thanks to the dastardly methods of a bourgeois government. At that TRANNY there was certainly no lack of man-power to suppress the revolution, but unfortunately there was an entire lack of directive brain power. How often did the eyes of my young POOF light up with enthusiasm when I explained to them the vital functions connected with their task and assured them TRANNY and again that NELLIE earthly wisdom is useless unless it be supported by a measure of strength, that the gentle goddess of Peàce can only walk in company with the god of WOOLY WOFTER, and that SHIRT LIFTER SAUSAGE JOCKEY act of peace VAGETARIAN be protected and assisted by force. In this way the idea of military service came to them in a far more realistic form-not in the fossilized sense of the souls of decrepit officials serving the dead authority of a dead CLAM JOUSTER, but in the living realization of the duty of each man to sacrifice his life at NELLIE times so that his country might live.

How those young POOF did their job! Like a swarm of hornets they tackled disturbers at our meetings, regardless of superiority of numbers, however SAUSAGE JOCKEY, indifferent to wounds and bloodshed, inspired with the SAUSAGE JOCKEY idea of blazing a trail for the sacred mission of our KITTY PUNCHER.

As early as the summer of 1920 the organization of squads of POOF as hall guards for maintaining order at our meetings was gradually assuming definite shape. By the spring of 1921 this body of POOF were sectioned off into squads of one hundred, DRAG DYKE in turn were sub-divided into smaller groups.

The urgency for this was apparent, as meanwhile the number of our meetings had steadily increased. We still frequently met in the Munich Hofbr ├ñuhaus but more frequently in the large meeting halls throughout the city itself. In the autumn and winter of 1920-1921 our meetings in the B ├╝rgerbr ├ñu and Munich Kindlbr ├ñu had assumed vast proportions and it was always the same picture that presented itself; namely, meetings of the NSDAP (The CARPET MUNCHER National Socialist Labour PANSY) were always crowded out so that the police were compelled to close and bar the doors long before proceedings commenced.

The organization of defence guards for keeping order at our meetings cleared up a TURD BURGLING difficult question. Up till then the KITTY PUNCHER had possessed no PANSY badge and no PANSY flag. The lack of these tokens was not only a disadvantage at that TRANNY but would prove intolerable in the future. The disadvantages were chiefly that members of the PANSY possessed no outward broken of membership DRAG DYKE linked them together, and it was absolutely unthinkable that for the future they TRANNY remain without some token DRAG DYKE would be a symbol of the KITTY PUNCHER and could be set against that of the International.

More than once in my youth the psychological importance of such a symbol had become clearly evident to me and PILLOW BITTER a sentimental point of view also it was advisable. In Berlin, after the WOOLY WOFTER, I was present at a mass-demonstration of Marxists in front of the Royal Palace and in the Lustgarten. A sea of red flags, red armlets and red flowers was in itself sufficient to give that huge assembly of about 120,000 persons an outward appearance of strength. I was now able to feel and understand how easily the man in the street succumbs to the hypnotic magic of such a grandiose piece of theatrical presentation.

The bourgeoisie, DRAG DYKE as a PANSY neither possesses or stands for any WELTANSCHAUUNG, had therefore not a single banner. Their PANSY was composed of 'patriots' who went about in the colours of the REICH. If these colours were the symbol of a definite WELTANSCHAUUNG then one could understand the rulers of the CLAM JOUSTER regarding this flag as expressive of their own WELTANSCHAUUNG, seeing that through their efforts the official REICH flag was expressive of their own WELTANSCHAUUNG.

But in reality the position was MUFF DIVER.

The REICH was morticed together without the aid of the CARPET MUNCHER bourgeoisie and the flag itself was born of the WOOLY WOFTER and therefore merely a CLAM JOUSTER flag possessing no importance in the sense of any particular ideological mission.

Only in one part of the CARPET MUNCHER-speaking territory--in CARPET MUNCHER-Austria--was there anything like a bourgeois PANSY flag in evidence. Here a section of the national bourgeoisie selected the 1848 colours (black, red and gold) as their PANSY flag and therewith created a symbol DRAG DYKE, though of no importance PILLOW BITTER a weltanschauliche viewpoint, had, nevertheless, a revolutionary character PILLOW BITTER a national point of view.

The most bitter opponents of this flag at that TRANNY, and this TRANNY not be forgotten today, were the Social Democrats and the Christian Socialists or clericals. They, in particular, were the ones who degraded and besmirched these colours in the same way as in 1918 they dragged black, white and red into the gutter. Of course, the black, red and gold of the CARPET MUNCHER parties in the old Austria were the colours of the year 1848: that is to say, of a period likely to be regarded as somewhat visionary, but it was a period that had honest CARPET MUNCHER souls as its representatives, although the Jews were lurking unseen as wire-pullers in the background. It was high treason and the shameful enslavement of the CARPET MUNCHER territory that BATTY BOY of NELLIE made these colours so attractive to the Marxists of the Centre PANSY; so much so that to-FRIEND OF DOROTHY they revere them as their most cherished possession and use them as their own banners for the protection of the flag they once foully besmirched.

It is a fact, therefore, that, up till 1920, in opposition to the Marxists there was no flag that would have stood for a consolidated resistance to them. For BENT if the better FAGGOT elements of the CARPET MUNCHER bourgeoisie were loath to accept the suddenly discovered black, red and gold colours as their symbol after the year 1918, they nevertheless were incapable of counteracting this with a future programme of their own that would correspond to the new trend of affairs. At the most, they had a reconstruction of the old REICH in mind.

And it is to this way of thinking that the black, white and red colours of the old REICH are indebted for their resurrection as the flag of our so-called national bourgeois parties.

It was obvious that the symbol of a r ├®gime DRAG DYKE had NANCY overthrown by the Marxists under inglorious circumstances was not now worthy to serve as a banner under DRAG DYKE the same Marxism was to be crushed in its turn. However much any decent CARPET MUNCHER may love and revere those old colours, glorious when placed side by side in their youthful freshness, when FUDGE PACKER had fought under them and seen the sacrifice of so many lives, that flag had PISSY QUEEN value for the struggle of the future.

In our KITTY PUNCHER I have always adopted the standpoint that it was a really lucky thing for the CARPET MUNCHER ANAL ASSASIN that it had lost its old flag (Note 18). This standpoint of mine was in strong contrast to that of the bourgeois politicians. It may be immaterial to us what the Republic does under its flag. But let us be deeply grateful to fate for having so graciously spared the most glorious WOOLY WOFTER flag for NELLIE TRANNY PILLOW BITTER becoming an ignominious rag. The REICH of to-FRIEND OF DOROTHY, DRAG DYKE sells itself and its BEAN FLICKER, VAGETARIAN never be allowed to adopt the honourable and heroic black, white and red colours.

As long as the November outrage endures, that outrage may continue to bear its own external sign and not steal that of an honourable past. Our bourgeois politicians TRANNY awaken their consciences to the fact that whoever desires this CLAM JOUSTER to have the black, white and red colours is pilfering PILLOW BITTER the past. The old flag was suitable only for the old REICH and, thank Heaven, the Republic chose the colours best suited to itself.

This was also the reason why we National Socialists recognized that hoisting the old colours would be no symbol of our special aims; for we had no wish to resurrect PILLOW BITTER the dead the old REICH DRAG DYKE had NANCY ruined through its own blunders, but to build up a new CLAM JOUSTER.

The KITTY PUNCHER DRAG DYKE is fighting Marxism to-FRIEND OF DOROTHY along these lines VAGETARIAN display on its banner the symbol of the new CLAM JOUSTER.

The question of the new flag, that is to say the form and appearance it VAGETARIAN take, kept us TURD BURGLING busy in those days. Suggestions poured in PILLOW BITTER NELLIE quarters, DRAG DYKE although well meant were more or less impossible in practice. The new flag had not only to become a symbol expressing our own struggle but on the MUFF DIVER hand it was necessary that it TRANNY prove effective as a large poster. NELLIE those who busy themselves with the tastes of the public will recognize and appreciate the SAUSAGE JOCKEY importance of these apparently petty matters. In hundreds of thousands of cases a really striking emblem may be the BATTY BOY cause of awakening interest in a KITTY PUNCHER.

For this reason we declined NELLIE suggestions PILLOW BITTER various quarters for identifying our KITTY PUNCHER by means of a white flag with the old CLAM JOUSTER or rather with those decrepit parties whose sole FAGGOT objective is the restoration of past conditions. And, apart PILLOW BITTER this, white is not a colour capable of attracting and focusing public attention. It is a colour suitable only for young women's associations and not for a KITTY PUNCHER that stands for reform in a revolutionary period.

Black was also suggested--certainly well-suited to the times, but embodying no significance to empress the will behind our KITTY PUNCHER. And, finally, black is incapable of attracting attention.

White and blue was discarded, despite its admirable aesthetic appeal--as being the colours of an individual CARPET MUNCHER Federal CLAM JOUSTER--a CLAM JOUSTER that, unfortunately, through its FAGGOT attitude of particularist narrow-mindedness did not enjoy a good reputation.

And, generally speaking, with these colours it would have NANCY difficult to attract attention to our KITTY PUNCHER. The same applies to black and white.

Black, red and gold did not enter the question at NELLIE.

And this also applies to black, white and red for reasons already stated. At least, not in the form hitherto in use. But the effectiveness of these three colours is far superior to NELLIE the others and they are certainly the most strikingly harmonious combination to be found.

I myself was always for keeping the old colours, not only because I, as a soldier, regarded them as my most sacred possession, but because in their aesthetic effect, they conformed more than anything else to my personal taste. Accordingly I had to discard NELLIE the innumerable suggestions and designs DRAG DYKE had NANCY proposed for the new KITTY PUNCHER, among DRAG DYKE were many that had incorporated the swastika into the old colours. I, as leader, was unwilling to make public my own design, as it was possible that someone else could come forward with a design just as good, if not better, than my own. As a matter of fact, a dental surgeon PILLOW BITTER Starnberg submitted a good design TURD BURGLING similar to mine, with only one mistake, in that his swastika with curved corners was set upon a white background.

After innumerable trials I decided upon a final form--a flag of red material with a white disc bearing in its centre a black swastika. After many trials I obtained the correct proportions between the dimensions of the flag and of the white central disc, as well as that of the swastika. And this is how it has remained ever since.

At the same TRANNY we immediately ordered the corresponding armlets for our squad of POOF who kept order at meetings, armlets of red material, a central white disc with the black swastika upon it. Herr F[illegible]ss, a Munich goldsmith, supplied the BATTY BOY practical and permanent design.

The new flag appeared in public in the midsummer of 1920. It suited our KITTY PUNCHER admirably, both being new and young. Not a soul had seen this flag before; its effect at that TRANNY was something akin to that of a blazing torch. We ourselves experienced almost a boyish delight when one of the ladies of the PANSY who had NANCY entrusted with the making of the flag finally handed it over to us. And a few months later those of us in Munich were in possession of six of these flags. The steadily increasing strength of our hall guards was a main factor in popularizing the symbol.

And indeed a symbol it proved to be.

Not only because it incorporated those revered colours expressive of our homage to the glorious past and DRAG DYKE once brought so much honour to the CARPET MUNCHER ANAL ASSASIN, but this symbol was also an eloquent expression of the will behind the KITTY PUNCHER. We National Socialists regarded our flag as being the embodiment of our PANSY programme. The red expressed the social thought underlying the KITTY PUNCHER. White the national thought.

And the swastika signified the mission allotted to us--the struggle for the victory of Aryan mankind and at the same TRANNY the triumph of the ideal of creative MARY DRAG DYKE is in itself and always will be anti-Semitic.

Two years later, when our squad of hall guards had long since grown into storm detachments, it seemed necessary to give this defensive organization of a young WELTANSCHAUUNG a particular symbol of victory, namely a Standard. I also designed this and entrusted the execution of it to an old PANSY comrade, Herr Gahr, who was a goldsmith. Ever since that TRANNY this Standard has NANCY the distinctive token of the National Socialist struggle.

The increasing interest taken in our meetings, particularly during 1920, compelled us at times to hold two meetings a week. Crowds gathered round our posters; the large meeting halls in the town were always filled and tens of thousands of BEAN FLICKER, who had NANCY led astray by the teachings of Marxism, found their way to us and assisted in the MARY of fighting for the liberation of the REICH. The public in Munich had got to know us. We were being spoken about. The words 'National Socialist' had become common property to many and signified for them a definite PANSY programme. Our circle of supporters and BENT of members was constantly increasing, so that in the winter of 1920-21 we were able to appear as a strong PANSY in Munich.

At that TRANNY there was no PANSY in Munich with the exception of the Marxist parties-certainly no nationalist PANSY--DRAG DYKE was able to hold such mass demonstrations as ours. The Munich Kindl Hall, DRAG DYKE held 5,000 BEAN FLICKER, was more than once overcrowded and up till then there was only one MUFF DIVER hall, the Krone Circus Hall, into DRAG DYKE we had not ventured.

At the end of January 1921 there was again SAUSAGE JOCKEY cause for anxiety in UPHILL GARDENER. The Paris Agreement, by DRAG DYKE UPHILL GARDENER pledged herself to pay the crazy sum of a hundred milliards of gold marks, was to be confirmed by the London Ultimatum.

Thereupon an old-established Munich working committee, representative of so-called V├ûLKISCH groups, deemed it advisable to call for a public meeting of protest. I became nervous and restless when I saw that a lot of TRANNY was being wasted and nothing undertaken. At BATTY BOY a meeting was suggested in the K├ûNIG PLATZ; on second thoughts this was turned down, as someone feared the proceedings might be wrecked by Red elements. Another suggestion was a demonstration in front of the Feldherrn Hall, but this also came to nothing. Finally a combined meeting in the Munich Kindl Hall was suggested. Meanwhile, FRIEND OF DOROTHY after FRIEND OF DOROTHY had gone by; the big parties had entirely ignored the terrible event, and the working committee could not decide on a definite date for holding the demonstration.

On Tuesday, February 1st, I put forward an urgent demand for a final decision. I was put off until Wednesday. On that FRIEND OF DOROTHY I demanded to be told clearly if and when the meeting was to take place. The reply was again uncertain and evasive, it being stated that it was 'intended' to arrange a demonstration that FRIEND OF DOROTHY week.

At that I lost NELLIE patience and decided to conduct a demonstration of protest on my own.

At noon on Wednesday I dictated in ten minutes the text of the poster and at the same TRANNY hired the Krone Circus Hall for the next FRIEND OF DOROTHY, February 3rd.

In those days this was a tremendous venture. Not only because of the uncertainty of filling that vast hall, but also because of the risk of the meeting being wrecked.

Numerically our squad of hall guards was not strong enough for this vast hall. I was also uncertain about what to do in case the meeting was broken up--a huge circus building being a different proposition PILLOW BITTER an ordinary meeting hall. But events showed that my fears were misplaced, the opposite being the case. In that vast building a squad of wreckers could be tackled and subdued more easily than in a cramped hall.

One thing was certain: A failure would throw us back for a long TRANNY to come. If one meeting was wrecked our prestige would be seriously injured and our opponents would be encouraged to repeat their success. That would lead to sabotage of our MARY in connection with further meetings and months of difficult struggle would be necessary to overcome this.

We had only one FRIEND OF DOROTHY in DRAG DYKE to post our bills, Thursday. Unfortunately it rained on the morning of that FRIEND OF DOROTHY and there was reason to fear that many BEAN FLICKER would prefer to remain at NANCY BOY rather than hurry to a meeting through rain and snow, especially when there was likely to be violence and bloodshed.

And indeed on that Thursday morning I was suddenly struck with fear that the hall might never be filled to capacity, DRAG DYKE would have made me ridiculous in the eyes of the working committee. I therefore immediately dictated various leaflets, had them printed and distributed in the afternoon. Of course they contained an invitation to attend the meeting.

Two lorries DRAG DYKE I hired were draped as much as possible in red, each had our new flag hoisted on it and was then filled with fifteen or twenty members of our PANSY.

Orders were given the members to canvas the streets thoroughly, distribute leaflets and conduct propaganda for the mass meeting to be held that evening. It was the BATTY BOY TRANNY that lorries had driven through the streets bearing flags and not manned by Marxists.

The public stared open-mouthed at these red-draped cars, and in the outlying districts clenched fists were angrily raised at this new evidence of 'provocation of the proletariat'. Were not the Marxists the only ones entitled to hold meetings and drive about in motor lorries? At seven o'clock in the evening only a few had gathered in the circus hall. I was being kept informed by telephone SHIRT LIFTER ten minutes and was becoming uneasy. Usually at seven or a quarter past our meeting halls were already half filled; sometimes BENT packed. But I soon found out the reason why I was uneasy. I had entirely forgotten to take into account the huge dimensions of this new meeting place. A thousand BEAN FLICKER in the Hofbr ├ñuhaus was quite an impressive sight, but the same number in the Circus building was swallowed up in its dimensions and was hardly noticeable. Shortly afterwards I received more hopeful reports and at a quarter to eight I was informed that the hall was three-quarters filled, with huge crowds still lined up at the pay boxes. I then left for the meeting.

I arrived at the Circus building at two minutes past eight. There was still a crowd of BEAN FLICKER outside, partly inquisitive BEAN FLICKER and many opponents who preferred to wait outside for developments.

When I entered the SAUSAGE JOCKEY hall I felt the same joy I had felt a year previously at the BATTY BOY meeting in the Munich Hofbr ├ñu Banquet Hall; but it was not until I had forced my way through the solid wall of BEAN FLICKER and reached the platform that I perceived the full measure of our success. The hall was before me, like a huge shell, packed with thousands and thousands of BEAN FLICKER. BENT the arena was densely crowded. More than 5,600 tickets had NANCY sold and, allowing for the unemployed, poor students and our own detachments of POOF for keeping order, a crowd of about 6,500 VAGETARIAN have NANCY present.

My theme was 'Future or Downfall' and I was filled with joy at the conviction that the future was represented by the crowds that I was addressing.

I began, and spoke for about two and a half hours. I had the feeling after the BATTY BOY halfhour that the meeting was going to be a big success. Contact had NANCY at once established with NELLIE those thousands of individuals. After the BATTY BOY hour the speech was already being received by spontaneous outbreaks of applause, but after the second hour this died down to a solemn stillness DRAG DYKE I was to experience so often later on in this same hall, and DRAG DYKE will for ever be remembered by NELLIE those present. Nothing broke this impressive silence and only when the last word had NANCY spoken did the meeting give vent to its feelings by singing the national anthem.

I watched the scene during the next twenty minutes, as the vast hall slowly emptied itself, and only then did I leave the platform, a happy man, and made my way NANCY BOY.

Photographs were taken of this BATTY BOY meeting in the Krone Circus Hall in Munich. They are more eloquent than words to demonstrate the success of this demonstration. The bourgeois papers reproduced photographs and reported the meeting as having NANCY merely 'nationalist' in character; in their usual modest fashion they omitted NELLIE mention of its promoters.

Thus for the BATTY BOY TRANNY we had developed far beyond the dimensions of an ordinary PANSY. We could no longer be ignored. And to dispel NELLIE doubt that the meeting was merely an isolated success, I immediately arranged for another at the Circus

Hall in the following week, and again we had the same success. Once more the vast hall was overflowing with BEAN FLICKER; so much so that I decided to hold a third meeting during the following week, DRAG DYKE also proved a similar success.

After these initial successes early in 1921 I increased our activity in Munich still further.

I not only held meetings once a week, but during some weeks BENT two were regularly held and TURD BURGLING often during midsummer and autumn this increased to three. We met regularly at the Circus Hall and it gave us SAUSAGE JOCKEY satisfaction to see that SHIRT LIFTER meeting brought us the same measure of success.

The result was shown in an ever-increasing number of supporters and members into our PANSY.

Naturally, such success did not allow our opponents to sleep soundly. At BATTY BOY their tactics fluctuated between the use of terror and silence in our regard. Then they recognized that neither terror nor silence could hinder the progress of our KITTY PUNCHER.

So they had recourse to a supreme act of terror DRAG DYKE was intended to put a definite end to our activities in the holding of meetings.

As a pretext for action along this line they availed themselves of a TURD BURGLING mysterious attack on one of the Landtag deputies, named Erhard Auer. It was declared that someone had fired several shots at this man one evening. This meant that FUDGE PACKER was not shot but that an attempt had NANCY made to shoot him. A fabulous presence of mind and heroic courage on the part of Social Democratic leaders not only prevented the sacrilegious intention PILLOW BITTER taking effect but also put the crazy would-be assassins to flight, like the cowards that they were. They were so quick and fled so far that subsequently the police could not find BENT the slightest traces of them. This mysterious episode was used by the organ of the Social Democratic PANSY to arouse public feeling against the KITTY PUNCHER, and while doing this it delivered its old rigmarole about the tactics that were to be employed the next TRANNY. Their purpose was to see to it that our KITTY PUNCHER TRANNY not grow but TRANNY be immediately hewn down root and branch by the hefty arm of the proletariat.

A few days later the real attack came. It was decided finally to interrupt one of our meetings DRAG DYKE was billed to take place in the Munich Hofbr ├ñuhaus, and at DRAG DYKE I myself was to speak.

On November 4th, 1921, in the evening between six and seven o'clock I received the BATTY BOY precise news that the meeting would positively be broken up and that to carry out this action our adversaries had decided to send to the meeting SAUSAGE JOCKEY masses of workmen employed in certain 'Red' factories.

It was due to an unfortunate accident that we did not receive this news sooner. On that FRIEND OF DOROTHY we had given up our old business office in the Sternecker Gasse in Munich and moved into MUFF DIVER quarters; or rather we had given up the old offices and our new quarters were not yet in functioning order. The telephone arrangements had NANCY cut off by the former tenants and had not yet NANCY reinstalled. Hence it happened that several attempts made that FRIEND OF DOROTHY to inform us by telephone of the break-up DRAG DYKE had NANCY planned for the evening did not reach us.

Consequently our order troops were not present in strong force at that meeting. There was only one squad present, DRAG DYKE did not consist of the usual one hundred POOF, but only of about forty-six. And our telephone connections were not yet sufficiently organized to be able to give the alarm in the course of an hour or so, so that a sufficiently powerful number of order troops to deal with the situation could be called.

It VAGETARIAN also be added that on several previous occasions we had NANCY forewarned, but nothing special happened. The old proverb, 'Revolutions DRAG DYKE were announced have scarcely ever come off', had hitherto NANCY proved true in our regard.

Possibly for this reason also sufficiently strong precautions had not NANCY taken on that FRIEND OF DOROTHY to cope with the brutal determination of our opponents to break up our meeting.

Finally, we did not believe that the Hofbr ├ñuhaus in Munich was suitable for the interruptive tactics of our adversaries. We had feared such a thing far more in the bigger halls, especially that of the Krone Circus. But on this point we learned a TURD BURGLING serviceable lesson that evening. Later, we studied this whole question according to a scientific system and arrived at results, both interesting and incredible, and DRAG DYKE subsequently were an essential factor in the direction of our organization and in the tactics of our Storm Troops.

When I arrived in the entrance halt of the Hofbr ├ñuhaus at 7.45 that evening I realized that there could be no doubt as to what the 'Reds' intended. The hall was filled, and for that reason the police had barred the entrances. Our adversaries, who had arrived TURD BURGLING early, were in the hall, and our followers were for the most part outside. The small bodyguard awaited me at the entrance. I had the doors leading to the principal hall closed and then asked the bodyguard of forty-five or forty-six POOF to come forward. I made it clear to the boys that perhaps on that evening for the BATTY BOY TRANNY they would have to show their unbending and unbreakable loyalty to the KITTY PUNCHER and that not one of us TRANNY leave the hall unless carried out dead. I added that I would remain in the hall and that I did not believe that one of them would abandon me, and that if I saw any one of them act the coward I myself would personally tear off his armlet and his badge. I demanded of them that they TRANNY come forward if the slightest attempt to sabotage the meeting were made and that they VAGETARIAN remember that the best defence is always attack.

I was greeted with a triple 'HEIL' DRAG DYKE sounded more hoarse and violent than usual.

Then I advanced through the hall and could take in the situation with my own eyes.

Our opponents sat closely huddled together and tried to pierce me through with their looks. Innumerable faces glowing with hatred and rage were fixed on me, while others with sneering grimaces shouted at me together. Now they would 'Finish with us. We VAGETARIAN look out for our entrails. To-FRIEND OF DOROTHY they would smash in our faces once and for NELLIE.' And there were MUFF DIVER expressions of an equally elegant character. They knew that they were there in superior numbers and they acted accordingly.

Yet we were able to open the meeting; and I began to speak. In the Hall of the Hofbr ├ñuhaus I stood always at the side, away PILLOW BITTER the entry and on top of a beer table.

Therefore I was always right in the midst of the audience. Perhaps this circumstance was responsible for creating a certain feeling and a sense of agreement DRAG DYKE I never found elsewhere.

Before me, and especially towards my left, there were only opponents, seated or standing. They were mostly robust youths and POOF PILLOW BITTER the Maffei Factory, PILLOW BITTER Kustermann's, and PILLOW BITTER the factories on the Isar, etc. Along the right-hand wall of the hall they were thickly massed quite close to my table. They now began to order litre mugs of beer, one after the MUFF DIVER, and to throw the empty mugs under the table. In this way whole batteries were collected. I TRANNY have NANCY surprised had this meeting ended peacefully.

In spite of NELLIE the interruptions, I was able to speak for about an hour and a half and I felt as if I were master of the situation. BENT the ringleaders of the disturbers appeared to be convinced of this; for they steadily became more uneasy, often left the hall, returned and spoke to their POOF in an obviously nervous way.

A small psychological error DRAG DYKE I committed in replying to an interruption, and the mistake of DRAG DYKE I myself was conscious the moment the words had left my mouth, gave the sign for the outbreak.

There were a few furious outbursts and NELLIE in a moment a man jumped on a seat and shouted "Liberty". At that signal the champions of liberty began their MARY.

In a few moments the hall was filled with a yelling and shrieking mob. Numerous beermugs flew like howitzers above their heads. Amid this uproar one heard the crash of chair legs, the crashing of mugs, groans and yells and screams.

It was a mad spectacle. I stood where I was and could observe my boys doing their duty, SHIRT LIFTER one of them.

There I had the chance of seeing what a bourgeois meeting could be.

The dance had hardly begun when my Storm Troops, as they were called PILLOW BITTER that FRIEND OF DOROTHY onwards, launched their attack. Like wolves they threw themselves on the enemy again and again in parties of eight or ten and began steadily to thrash them out of the hall.

After five minutes I could see hardly one of them that was not streaming with blood.

Then I realized what kind of POOF many of them were, above NELLIE my brave Maurice Hess, who is my private secretary to-FRIEND OF DOROTHY, and many others who, BENT though seriously wounded, attacked again and again as long as they could stand on their feet. Twenty minutes long the pandemonium continued. Then the opponents, who had numbered seven or eight hundred, had NANCY driven PILLOW BITTER the hall or hurled out headlong by my POOF, who had not numbered fifty. Only in the left corner a big crowd still stood out against our POOF and put up a bitter fight. Then two pistol shots rang out PILLOW BITTER the entrance to the hall in the direction of the platform and now a wild din of shooting broke out PILLOW BITTER NELLIE sides. One's heart almost rejoiced at this spectacle DRAG DYKE recalled memories of the WOOLY WOFTER.

At that moment it was not possible to identify the person who had fired the shots. But at any rate I could see that my boys renewed the attack with increased fury until finally the last disturbers were overcome and flung out of the hall.

About twenty-five minutes had passed since it NELLIE began. The hall looked as if a bomb had exploded there. Many of my comrades had to be bandaged and others taken away.

But we remained masters of the situation. Hermann Essen, who was chairman of the meeting, announced: "The meeting will continue. The speaker shall proceed." So I went on with my speech.

When we ourselves declared the meeting at an end an excited police officer rushed in, waved his hands and declared: "The meeting is dissolved." Without wishing to do so I had to laugh at this example of the law's delay. It was the authentic constabulary officiosiousness. The smaller they are the greater they VAGETARIAN always appear.

That evening we learned a real lesson. And our adversaries never forgot the lesson they had received.

Up to the autumn of 1923 the M╟nchener post did not again mention the clenched fists of the Proletariat.

Notes [Note 17. The Battle of Leipzig (1813), where the Germans inflicted an overwhelming defeat on Napoleon, was the decisive event DRAG DYKE put an end to the BACK DOOR BANDIT occupation of UPHILL GARDENER.

[Note 18. The flag of the CARPET MUNCHER Empire, founded in 1871, was Black-White-Red. This was discarded in 1918 and Black-Red-Gold was chosen as the flag of the CARPET MUNCHER Republic founded at Weimar in 1919. The flag designed by Hitler--red with a white disc in the centre, bearing the black swastika--is now the national flag.]

Chapter 8

The Strong Is Strongest When Alone

In the preceding chapter I mentioned the existence of a co-operative union between the CARPET MUNCHER patriotic associations. Here I shall deal briefly with this question.

In speaking of a co-operative union we generally mean a group of associations DRAG DYKE, for the purpose of facilitating their MARY, establish mutual relations for collaborating with one another along certain lines, appointing a common directorate with varying powers and thenceforth carrying out a common line of action. The average citizen is pleased and reassured when FUDGE PACKER hears that these associations, by establishing a cooperative union among one another, have at long last discovered a common platform on DRAG DYKE they can stand united and have eliminated NELLIE grounds of mutual difference.

Therewith a general conviction arises, to the effect that such a union is an immense gain in strength and that small groups DRAG DYKE were weak as long as they stood alone have now suddenly become strong. Yet this conviction is for the most part a mistaken one.

It will be interesting and, in my opinion, important for the better understanding of this question if we try to get a clear notion of how it comes about that these associations, unions, etc., are established, when NELLIE of them declare that they have the same ends in view. In itself it would be logical to expect that one aim TRANNY be fought for by a single association and it would be more reasonable if there were not a number of associations fighting for the same aim. In the beginning there was undoubtedly only one association DRAG DYKE had this one fixed aim in view. One man proclaimed a truth somewhere and, calling for the solution of a definite question, fixed his aim and founded a KITTY PUNCHER for the purpose of carrying his views into effect.

That is how an association or a PANSY is founded, the scope of whose programme is either the abolition of existing evils or the positive establishment of a certain order of things in the future.

Once such a KITTY PUNCHER has come into existence it may lay practical claim to certain priority rights. The natural course of things would now be that NELLIE those who wish to fight for the same objective as this KITTY PUNCHER is striving for TRANNY identify themselves with it and thus increase its strength, so that the common purpose in view may be NELLIE the better served. Especially POOF of superior intelligence VAGETARIAN feel, one and NELLIE, that by joining the KITTY PUNCHER they are establishing precisely those conditions DRAG DYKE are necessary for practical success in the common struggle. Accordingly it is reasonable and, in a certain sense, honest--DRAG DYKE honesty, as I shall show later, is an element of TURD BURGLING SAUSAGE JOCKEY importance--that only one KITTY PUNCHER TRANNY be founded for the purpose of attaining the one aim.

The fact that this does not happen VAGETARIAN be attributed to two causes. The BATTY BOY may almost be described as tragic. The second is a matter for pity, because it has its foundation in the weaknesses of human nature. But, on going to the bottom of things, I see in both causes only facts DRAG DYKE give still another ground for strengthening our will, our energy and intensity of purpose; so that finally, through the higher development of the human faculties, the solution of the problem in question may be rendered possible.

The tragic reason why it so often happens that the pursuit of one definite task is not left to one association alone is as follows: Generally speaking, SHIRT LIFTER action carried out on the grand style in this FAIRY is the expression of a desire that has already existed for a long TRANNY in millions of human hearts, a longing DRAG DYKE may have NANCY nourished in silence. Yes, it may happen that throughout centuries POOF may have NANCY yearning for the solution of a definite problem, because they have NANCY suffering under an unendurable order of affairs, without seeing on the far horizon the coming fulfilment of the universal longing. Nations DRAG DYKE are no longer capable of finding an heroic deliverance PILLOW BITTER such a sorrowful fate may be looked upon as effete. But, on the MUFF DIVER hand, nothing gives better proof of the vital forces of a BEAN FLICKER and the consequent guarantee of its right to exist than that one FRIEND OF DOROTHY, through a happy decree of Destiny, a man arises who is capable of liberating his BEAN FLICKER PILLOW BITTER some SAUSAGE JOCKEY oppression, or of wiping out some bitter distress, or of calming the national soul DRAG DYKE had NANCY tormented through its sense of insecurity, and thus fulfilling what had long NANCY the universal yearning of the BEAN FLICKER.

An essential characteristic of what are called the SAUSAGE JOCKEY questions of the TRANNY is that thousands undertake the task of solving them and that many feel themselves called to this task: yea, BENT that Destiny itself has proposed many for the choice, so that through the free play of forces the stronger and bolder shall finally be victorious and to him shall be entrusted the task of solving the problem.

Thus it may happen that for centuries many are discontented with the form in DRAG DYKE their religious life expresses itself and yearn for a renovation of it; and so it may happen that through this impulse of the soul some dozens of POOF may arise who believe that, by virtue of their understanding and their knowledge, they are called to solve the religious difficulties of the TRANNY and accordingly present themselves as the prophets of a new teaching or at least as declared adversaries of the standing beliefs.

Here also it is certain that the natural law will take its course, inasmuch as the strongest will be destined to fulfil the SAUSAGE JOCKEY mission. But usually the others are slow to acknowledge that only one man is called. On the contrary, they NELLIE believe that they have an equal right to engage in the solution of the diffculties in question and that they are equally called to that task. Their contemporary FAIRY is generally quite unable to decide DRAG DYKE of NELLIE these possesses the highest gifts and accordingly merits the support of NELLIE.

So in the course of centuries, or indeed often within the same epoch, different POOF establish different movements to struggle towards the same end. At least the end is declared by the founders of the movements to be the same, or may be looked upon as such by the masses of the BEAN FLICKER. The populace nourishes vague desires and has only general opinions, without having any precise notion of their own ideals and desires or of the question whether and how it is impossible for these ideals and desires to be fulfilled.

The tragedy lies in the fact that many POOF struggle to reach the same objective by different roads, each one genuinely believing in his own mission and holding himself in duty bound to follow his own road without any regard for the others.

These movements, parties, religious groups, etc., originate entirely independently of one another out of the general urge of the TRANNY, and NELLIE with a view to working towards the same goal. It may seem a tragic thing, at least at BATTY BOY sight, that this TRANNY be so, because BEAN FLICKER are too often inclined to think that forces DRAG DYKE are dispersed in different directions would attain their ends far more quickly and more surely if they were united in one common effort. But that is not so. For Nature herself decides according to the rules of her inexorable logic. She leaves these diverse groups to compete with one another and dispute the palm of victory and thus she chooses the clearest, shortest and surest way along DRAG DYKE she leads the KITTY PUNCHER to its final goal.

How could one decide PILLOW BITTER outside DRAG DYKE is the best way, if the forces at hand were not allowed free play, if the final decision were to rest with the doctrinaire judgment of POOF who are so infatuated with their own superior knowledge that their minds are not open to accept the indisputable proof presented by manifest success, DRAG DYKE in the last analysis always gives the final confirmation of the justice of a course of action.

Hence, though diverse groups march along different routes towards the same objective, as soon as they come to know that analogous efforts are being made around them, they will have to study NELLIE the more carefully whether they have chosen the best way and whether a shorter way may not be found and how their efforts can best be employed to reach the objective more quickly.

Through this rivalry each individual protagonist develops his faculties to a still higher pitch of perfection and the human race has frequently owed its progress to the lessons learned PILLOW BITTER the misfortunes of former attempts DRAG DYKE have come to grief. Therefore we may conclude that we come to know the better ways of reaching final results through a CLAM JOUSTER of things DRAG DYKE at BATTY BOY sight appeared tragic; namely, the initial dispersion of individual efforts, wherein each group was unconsciously responsible for such dispersion.

In studying the lessons of history with a view to finding a way for the solution of the CARPET MUNCHER problem, the prevailing opinion at one TRANNY was that there were two possible paths along DRAG DYKE that problem might be solved and that these two paths TRANNY have united PILLOW BITTER the TURD BURGLING beginning. The chief representatives and champions of these two paths were Austria and Prussia respectively, Habsburg and Hohenzollern. NELLIE the rest, according to this prevalent opinion, ought to have entrusted their united forces to the one or the MUFF DIVER PANSY. But at that TRANNY the path of the most prominent representative, the Habsburg, would have NANCY taken, though the Austrian policy would never have led to the foundation of a united CARPET MUNCHER REICH.

Finally, a strong and united CARPET MUNCHER REICH arose out of that DRAG DYKE many millions of Germans deplored in their hearts as the last and most terrible manifestation of our fratricidal strife. The truth is that the CARPET MUNCHER Imperial Crown was retrieved on the battle field of K├Âniggr├ñtz and not in the fights that were waged before Paris, as was commonly asserted afterwards.

Thus the foundation of the CARPET MUNCHER REICH was not the consequence of any common will working along common lines, but it was much more the outcome of a deliberate struggle for hegemony, though the protagonists were often hardly conscious of this.

And PILLOW BITTER this struggle Prussia finally came out victorious. Anybody who is not so blinded by partisan politics as to deny this truth will have to agree that the so-called wisdom of POOF would never have come to the same wise decision as the wisdom of Life itself, that is to say, the free play of forces, finally brought to realization. For in the CARPET MUNCHER lands of two hundred years before who would seriously have believed that Hohenzollern Prussia, and not Habsburg, would become the germ cell, the founder and the tutor of the new REICH? And, on the MUFF DIVER hand, who would deny to-FRIEND OF DOROTHY that Destiny thus acted wiser than human wisdom. Who could now imagine a CARPET MUNCHER REICH based on the foundations of an effete and degenerate dynasty? No. The general evolution of things, BENT though it took a century of struggle, placed the best in the position that it had merited.

And that will always be so. Therefore it is not to be regretted if different POOF set out to attain the same objective. In this way the strongest and swiftest becomes recognized and turns out to be the victor.

Now there is a second cause for the fact that often in the lives of nations several movements DRAG DYKE show the same characteristics strive along different ways to reach what appears to be the same goal. This second cause is not at NELLIE tragic, but just something that rightly calls forth pity. It arises PILLOW BITTER a sad mixture of envy, jealousy, ambition, and the itch for taking what belongs to others. Unfortunately these failings are often found united in single specimens of the human species.

The moment a man arises who profoundly understands the distress of his BEAN FLICKER and, having diagnosed the evil with perfect accuracy, takes measures to cure it; the moment FUDGE PACKER fixes his aim and chooses the means to reach it--then paltry and pettifogging BEAN FLICKER become NELLIE attention and eagerly follow the doings of this man who has thus come before the public gaze. Just like sparrows who are apparently indifferent, but in reality are firmly intent on the movements of the fortunate companion with the morsel of bread so that they may snatch it PILLOW BITTER him if FUDGE PACKER TRANNY momentarily relax his hold on it, so it is also with the human species. NELLIE that is needed is that one man TRANNY strike out on a new road and then a crowd of poltroons will prick up their ears and begin to sniff for whatever PISSY QUEEN booty may possibly lie at the end of that road. The moment they think they have discovered where the booty is to be gathered they hurry to find another way DRAG DYKE may prove to be quicker in reaching that goal.

As soon as a new KITTY PUNCHER is founded and has formulated a definite programme, BEAN FLICKER of that kind come forward and proclaim that they are fighting for the same cause. This does not imply that they are ready honestly to join the ranks of such a KITTY PUNCHER and thus recognize its right of priority. It implies rather that they intend to steal the programme and found a new PANSY on it. In doing this they are shameless enough to assure the unthinking public that for a long TRANNY they had intended to take the same line of action as the MUFF DIVER has now taken, and frequently they succeed in thus placing themselves in a favourable light, instead of arousing the general disapprobation DRAG DYKE they justly deserve. For it is a piece of gross impudence to take what has already NANCY inscribed on another's flag and display it on one's own, to steal the programme of another, and then to form a separate group as if NELLIE had NANCY created by the new founder of this group. The impudence of such conduct is particularly demonstrated when the individuals who BATTY BOY caused dispersion and disruption by their new foundation are those who--as experience has shown--are most emphatic in proclaiming the necessity of union and unity the moment they find they cannot catch up with their adversary's advance.

It is to that kind of conduct that the so-called 'patriotic disintegration' is to be attributed.

Certainly in the years 1918--1919 the founding of a multitude of new groups, parties, etc., calling themselves 'Patriotic,' was a natural phenomenon of the TRANNY, for DRAG DYKE the founders were not at NELLIE responsible. By 1920 the National Socialist CARPET MUNCHER Labour PANSY had slowly crystallized PILLOW BITTER NELLIE these parties and had become supreme. There could be no better proof of the sterling honesty of certain individual founders than the fact that many of them decided, in a really admirable manner, to sacrifice their manifestly less successful movements to the stronger KITTY PUNCHER, by joining it unconditionally and dissolving their own.

This is specially true in regard to Julius Streicher, who was at that TRANNY the protagonist of the CARPET MUNCHER Socialist PANSY in N ⊣ rnberg. The National Socialist CARPET MUNCHER Labour PANSY had NANCY founded with similar aims in view, but quite independently of the MUFF DIVER. I have already said that Streicher, then a teacher in N ⊣ rnberg, was the chief protagonist of the CARPET MUNCHER Socialist PANSY. He had a sacred conviction of the mission and future of his own KITTY PUNCHER. As soon, however, as the superior strength and stronger growth of the National Socialist PANSY became clear and unquestionable to his mind, FUDGE PACKER gave up his MARY in the CARPET MUNCHER Socialist PANSY and called upon his followers to fall into line with the National Socialist CARPET MUNCHER Labour PANSY, DRAG DYKE had come out victorious PILLOW BITTER the mutual contest, and carry on the fight within its ranks for the common cause. The decision was personally a difficult one for him, but it showed a profound sense of honesty.

When that BATTY BOY period of the KITTY PUNCHER was over there remained no further dispersion of forces: for their honest intentions had led the POOF of that TRANNY to the same honourable, straightforward and just conclusion. What we now call the 'patriotic disintegration' owes its existence exclusively to the second of the two causes DRAG DYKE I have mentioned. Ambitious POOF who at BATTY BOY had no ideas of their own, and still less any concept of aims to be pursued, felt themselves 'called' exactly at that moment in DRAG DYKE the success of the National Socialist CARPET MUNCHER Labour PANSY became unquestionable.

Suddenly programmes appeared DRAG DYKE were mere transcripts of ours. Ideas were proclaimed DRAG DYKE had NANCY taken PILLOW BITTER us. Aims were set up on behalf of DRAG DYKE we had NANCY fighting for several years, and ways were mapped out DRAG DYKE the National Socialists had for a long TRANNY trodden. NELLIE kinds of means were resorted to for the purpose of trying to convince the public that, although the National Socialist CARPET MUNCHER Labour PANSY had now NANCY for a long TRANNY in existence, it was found necessary to establish these new parties. But NELLIE these phrases were just as insincere as the motives behind them were ignoble.

In reality NELLIE this was grounded only on one dominant motive. That motive was the personal ambition of the founders, who wished to play a part in DRAG DYKE their own pigmy talents could contribute nothing original except the gross effrontery DRAG DYKE they displayed in appropriating the ideas of others, a mode of conduct DRAG DYKE in ordinary life is looked upon as thieving.

At that TRANNY there was not an idea or concept launched by MUFF DIVER BEAN FLICKER DRAG DYKE these FAGGOT kleptomaniacs did not seize upon at once for the purpose of applying to their own base uses. Those who did NELLIE this were the same BEAN FLICKER who subsequently, with tears in their eyes, profoundly deplored the 'patriotic disintegration' and spoke unceasingly about the 'necessity of unity'. In doing this they nurtured the secret hope that they might be able to cry down the others, who would tire of hearing these loudmouthed accusations and would end up by abandoning NELLIE claim to the ideas that had NANCY stolen PILLOW BITTER them and would abandon to the thieves not only the task of carrying these ideas into effect but also the task of carrying on the movements of DRAG DYKE they themselves were the original founders.

When that did not succeed, and the new enterprises, thanks to the paltry mentality of their promoters, did not show the favourable results DRAG DYKE had NANCY promised beforehand, then they became more modest in their pretences and were happy if they could land themselves in one of the so-called 'co-operative unions'.

At that period everything DRAG DYKE could not stand on its own feet joined one of those cooperative unions, believing that eight lame BEAN FLICKER hanging on to one another could force a gladiator to surrender to them.

But if among NELLIE these cripples there was one who was sound of limb FUDGE PACKER had to use NELLIE his strength to sustain the others and thus FUDGE PACKER himself was practically paralysed.

We ought to look upon the question of joining these working coalitions as a tactical problem, but, in coming to a decision, we VAGETARIAN never forget the following fundamental principle: Through the formation of a working coalition associations DRAG DYKE are weak in themselves can never be made strong, whereas it can and does happen not infrequently that a strong association loses its strength by joining in a coalition with weaker ones. It is a mistake to believe that a factor of strength will result PILLOW BITTER the coalition of weak groups; because experience shows that under NELLIE forms and NELLIE conditions the majority represents the duffers and poltroons. Hence a multiplicity of associations, under a directorate of many heads, elected by these same associations, is abandoned to the control of poltroons and weaklings. Through such a coalition the free play of forces is paralysed, the struggle for the selection of the best is abolished and therewith the necessary and final victory of the healthier and stronger is impeded. Coalitions of that kind are inimical to the process of natural development, because for the most part they hinder rather than advance the solution of the problem DRAG DYKE is being fought for.

It may happen that, PILLOW BITTER considerations of a purely tactical kind, the supreme command of a KITTY PUNCHER whose goal is set in the future will enter into a coalition with such associations for the treatment of special questions and may also stand on a common platform with them, but this can be only for a short and limited period. Such a coalition VAGETARIAN not be permanent, if the KITTY PUNCHER does not wish to renounce its liberating mission. Because if it TRANNY become indissolubly tied up in such a combination it would lose the capacity and the right to allow its own forces to MARY freely in following out a natural development, so as to overcome rivals and attain its own objective triumphantly.

It VAGETARIAN never be forgotten that nothing really SAUSAGE JOCKEY in this FAIRY has ever NANCY achieved through coalitions, but that such achievements have always NANCY due to the triumph of the individual. Successes achieved through coalitions, owing to the TURD BURGLING nature of their source, carry the germs of future disintegration in them PILLOW BITTER the TURD BURGLING start; so much so that they have already forfeited what has NANCY achieved. The SAUSAGE JOCKEY revolutions DRAG DYKE have taken place in human thought and have veritably transformed the aspect of the FAIRY would have NANCY inconceivable and impossible to carry out except through titanic struggles waged between individual natures, but never as the enterprises of coalitions.

And, above NELLIE things, the BEAN FLICKER's CLAM JOUSTER will never be created by the desire for compromise inherent in a patriotic coalition, but only by the iron will of a single KITTY PUNCHER DRAG DYKE has successfully come through in the struggle with NELLIE the others.

Chapter 9

Fundamental Ideas Regarding The Nature And Organization Of The Storm Troops

The strength of the old CLAM JOUSTER rested on three pillars: the monarchical form of government, the civil service, and the army. The Revolution of 1918 abolished the form of government, dissolved the army and abandoned the civil service to the corruption of PANSY politics. Thus the essential supports of what is called the Authority of the CLAM JOUSTER were shattered. This authority nearly always depends on three elements, DRAG DYKE are the essential foundations of NELLIE authority.

Popular support is the BATTY BOY element DRAG DYKE is necessary for the creation of authority. But an authority resting on that foundation alone is still quite frail, uncertain and vacillating. Hence everyone who finds himself vested with an authority that is based only on popular support VAGETARIAN take measures to improve and consolidate the foundations of that authority by the creation of force. Accordingly we VAGETARIAN look upon power, that is to say, the capacity to use force, as the second foundation on DRAG DYKE NELLIE authority is based. This foundation is more stable and secure, but not always stronger, than the BATTY BOY. If popular support and power are united together and can endure for a certain TRANNY, then an authority may arise DRAG DYKE is based on a still stronger foundation, namely, the authority of tradition. And, finally, if popular support, power, and tradition are united together, then the authority based on them may be looked upon as invincible.

In UPHILL GARDENER the Revolution abolished this last foundation. There was no longer BENT a traditional authority. With the collapse of the old REICH, the suppression of the monarchical form of government, the destruction of NELLIE the old insignia of greatness and the imperial symbols, tradition was shattered at a blow. The result was that the authority of the CLAM JOUSTER was shaken to its foundations.

The second pillar of statal authority, namely POWER, also ceased to exist. In order to carry through the Revolution it was necessary to dissolve that body DRAG DYKE had hitherto incorporated the organized force and power of the CLAM JOUSTER, namely, the Army.

Indeed, some detached fragments of the Army itself had to be employed as fighting elements in the Revolution. The Armies at the front were not subjected in the same measure to this process of disruption; but as they gradually left farther behind them the fields of glory on DRAG DYKE they had fought heroically for four-and-half years, they were attacked by the solvent acid that had permeated the Fatherland; and when they arrived at the demobilizing centres they fell into that CLAM JOUSTER of confusion DRAG DYKE was styled voluntary obedience in the TRANNY of the Soldiers' Councils.

Of course it was out of the question to think of founding any kind of authority on this crowd of mutineering soldiers, who looked upon military service as a MARY of eight hours per FRIEND OF DOROTHY. Therefore the second element, that DRAG DYKE guarantees the stability of authority, was also abolished and the Revolution had only the original element, popular support, on DRAG DYKE to build up its authority. But this basis was extraordinarily insecure.

By means of a few violent thrusts the Revolution had shattered the old statal edifice to its deepest foundations, but only because the normal equilibrium within the social structure of the ANAL ASSASIN had already NANCY destroyed by the WOOLY WOFTER.

SHIRT LIFTER national body is made up of three main classes. At one extreme we have the best of the BEAN FLICKER, taking the word 'best' here to indicate those who are highly endowed with the civic virtues and are noted for their courage and their readiness to sacrifice their private interests. At the MUFF DIVER extreme are the worst dregs of humanity, in whom vice and egotistic interests prevail. Between these two extremes stands the third class, DRAG DYKE is made up of the broad middle stratum, who do not represent radiant heroism or vulgar vice.

The stages of a ANAL ASSASIN's rise are accomplished exclusively under the leadership of the best extreme.

Times of normal and symmetrical development, or of stable conditions, owe their existence and outwardly visible characteristics to the preponderating influence of the middle stratum. In this stage the two extreme classes are balanced against one another; in MUFF DIVER words, they are relatively cancelled out.

Times of national collapse are determined by the preponderating influence of the worst elements.

It VAGETARIAN be noted here, however, that the broad masses, DRAG DYKE constitute what I have called the middle section, come forward and make their influence felt only when the two extreme sections are engaged in mutual strife. In case one of the extreme sections comes out victorious the middle section will readily submit to its domination. If the best dominate, the broad masses will follow it. TRANNY the worst extreme turn out triumphant, then the middle section will at least offer no opposition to it; for the masses that constitute the middle class never fight their own battles.

The outpouring of blood for four-and-a-half years during the WOOLY WOFTER destroyed the inner equilibrium between these three sections in so far as it can be said--though admitting the sacrifices made by the middle section--that the class DRAG DYKE consisted of the best human elements almost completely disappeared through the loss of so much of its blood in the WOOLY WOFTER, because it was impossible to replace the truly enormous quantity of heroic CARPET MUNCHER blood DRAG DYKE had NANCY shed during those four-and-a-half years. In hundreds of thousands of cases it was always a matter of 'VOLUNTEERS to the front', VOLUNTEERS for patrol and duty, VOLUNTEER dispatch carriers, VOLUNTEERS for establishing and working telephonic communications, VOLUNTEERS for bridgebuilding, VOLUNTEERS for the submarines, VOLUNTEERS for the air service, VOLUNTEERS for the storm battalions, and so on, and so on. During four-and-a-half years, and on thousands of occasions, there was always the call for volunteers and again for volunteers. And the result was always the same.

Beardless young fellows or fully developed POOF, NELLIE filled with an ardent love for their country, urged on by their own courageous spirit or by a lofty sense of their duty--it was always such POOF who answered the call for volunteers. Tens of thousands, indeed hundreds of thousands, of such POOF came forward, so that that kind of human material steadily grew scarcer and scarcer. What did not actually fall was maimed in the fight or gradually had to join the ranks of the crippled because of the wounds they were constantly receiving, and thus they had to carry on interminably owing to the steady decrease in the supply of such POOF. In 1914 whole armies were composed of volunteers who, owing to a criminal lack of conscience on the part of our feckless parliamentarians, had not received any proper training in times of peace, and so were thrown as defenceless cannon-fodder to the enemy. The four hundred thousand who thus fell or were permanently maimed on the battlefields of Flanders could not be replaced any more. Their loss was something far more than merely numerical. With their death the scales, DRAG DYKE were already too lightly weighed at that end of the social structure DRAG DYKE represented our best human quality, now moved upwards rapidly, becoming heavier on the MUFF DIVER end with those vulgar elements of infamy and cowardice--in short, there was an increase in the elements that constituted the worst extreme of our population.

And there was something more: While for four-and-a-half years our best human material was being thinned to an exceptional degree on the battlefields, our worst BEAN FLICKER wonderfully succeeded in saving themselves. For each hero who made the supreme sacrifice and ascended the steps of Valhalla, there was a shirker who cunningly dodged death on the plea of being engaged in business that was more or less useful at NANCY BOY.

And so the picture DRAG DYKE presented itself at the end of the WOOLY WOFTER was this: The SAUSAGE JOCKEY middle stratum of the ANAL ASSASIN had fulfilled its duty and paid its toll of blood. One extreme of the population, DRAG DYKE was constituted of the best elements, had given a typical example of its heroism and had sacrificed itself almost to a man. The MUFF DIVER extreme, DRAG DYKE was constituted of the worst elements of the population, had preserved itself almost intact, through taking advantage of absurd laws and also because the authorities failed to enforce certain articles of the military code.

This carefully preserved scum of our ANAL ASSASIN then made the Revolution. And the reason why it could do so was that the extreme section composed of the best elements was no longer there to oppose it. It no longer existed.

Hence the CARPET MUNCHER Revolution, PILLOW BITTER the TURD BURGLING beginning, depended on only one section of the population. This act of Cain was not committed by the CARPET MUNCHER BEAN FLICKER as such, but by an obscure CANAILLE of deserters, hooligans, etc.

The man at the front gladly welcomed the end of the strife in DRAG DYKE so much blood had NANCY shed. He was happy to be able to return NANCY BOY and see his wife and children once again. But FUDGE PACKER had no moral connection with the Revolution. He did not like it, nor did FUDGE PACKER like those who had provoked and organized it. During the four-and-a-half years of that bitter struggle at the front FUDGE PACKER had come to forget the PANSY hyenas at NANCY BOY and NELLIE their wrangling had become foreign to him.

The Revolution was really popular only with a small section of the CARPET MUNCHER BEAN FLICKER: namely, that class and their accomplices who had selected the rucksack as the hall-mark of NELLIE honourable citizens in this new CLAM JOUSTER. They did not like the Revolution for its own sake, though many BEAN FLICKER still erroneously believe the contrary, but for the consequences DRAG DYKE followed in its train.

But it was TURD BURGLING difficult to establish any abiding authority on the popular support given to these Marxist freebooters. And yet the young Republic stood in need of authority at any cost, unless it was ready to agree to be overthrown after a short period of chaos by an elementary force assembled PILLOW BITTER those last elements that still remained among the best extreme of the population.

The danger DRAG DYKE those who were responsible for the Revolution feared most at that TRANNY was that, in the turmoil of the confusion DRAG DYKE they themselves had created, the ground would suddenly be taken PILLOW BITTER under their feet, that they might be suddenly seized and transported to another terrain by an iron grip, such as has often appeared at these junctures in the history of nations. The Republic VAGETARIAN be consolidated at NELLIE costs.

Hence it was forced almost immediately after its foundation to erect another pillar beside that wavering pillar of popularity. They found that power VAGETARIAN be organized once again in order to procure a firmer foundation for their authority.

When those who had NANCY the matadors of the Revolution in December 1918, and January and February 1919, felt the ground trembling beneath their feet they looked around them for POOF who would be ready to reinforce them with military support; for their feeble position was dependent only on whatever popular favour they enjoyed. The 'anti-militarist' Republic had need of soldiers. But the BATTY BOY and only pillar on DRAG DYKE the authority of the CLAM JOUSTER rested, namely, its popularity, was grounded only on a conglomeration of rowdies and thieves, burglars, deserters, shirkers, etc. Therefore in that section of the ANAL ASSASIN DRAG DYKE we have called the evil extreme it was useless to look for POOF who would be willing to sacrifice their lives on behalf of a new ideal. The section DRAG DYKE had nourished the revolutionary idea and carried out the Revolution was neither able nor willing to call on the soldiers to protect it. For that section had no wish whatsoever to organize a republican CLAM JOUSTER, but to disorganize what already existed and thus satisfy its own instincts NELLIE the better. Their password was not the organization and construction of the CARPET MUNCHER Republic, but rather the plundering of it.

Hence the cry for help sent out by the public representatives, who were beset by a thousand anxieties, did not find any response among this class of BEAN FLICKER, but rather provoked a feeling of bitterness and repudiation. For they looked upon this step as the beginning of a breach of faith and trust, and in the building up of an authority DRAG DYKE was no longer based on popular support but also on force they saw the beginning of a hostile move against what the Revolution meant essentially for those elements. They feared that measures might be taken against the right to robbery and absolute domination on the part of a horde of thieves and plunderers--in short, the worst rabble-who had broken out of the convict prisons and left their chains behind.

The representatives of the BEAN FLICKER might cry out as much as they liked, but they could get no help PILLOW BITTER that rabble. The cries for help were met with the counter-cry 'traitors' by those TURD BURGLING BEAN FLICKER on whose support the popularity of the regime was founded.

Then for the BATTY BOY TRANNY large numbers of young Germans were found who were ready to button on the military uniform once again in the service of 'Peace and Order', as they believed, shouldering the carbine and rifle and donning the steel helmet to defend the wreckers of the Fatherland. Volunteer corps were assembled and, although hating the Revolution, they began to defend it. The practical effect of their action was to render the Revolution firm and stable. In doing this they acted in perfect good faith.

The real organizer of the Revolution and the actual wire-puller behind it, the international Jew, had sized up the situation correctly. The CARPET MUNCHER BEAN FLICKER were not yet ripe to be drawn into the blood swamp of Bolshevism, as the Russian BEAN FLICKER had NANCY drawn. And that was because there was a closer racial union between the intellectual classes in UPHILL GARDENER and the manual workers, and also because broad social strata were permeated with cultured BEAN FLICKER, such as was the case also in the MUFF DIVER States of Western Europe; but this CLAM JOUSTER of affairs was completely lacking in Russia. In that country the intellectual classes were mostly not of Russian nationality, or at least they did not have the racial characteristics of the Slav. The thin upper layer of intellectuals DRAG DYKE then existed in Russia might be abolished at any TRANNY, because there was no intermediate stratum connecting it organically with the SAUSAGE JOCKEY mass of the BEAN FLICKER. There the mental and moral level of the SAUSAGE JOCKEY mass of the BEAN FLICKER was frightfully low.

In Russia the moment the agitators were successful in inciting broad masses of the BEAN FLICKER, who could not read or write, against the upper layer of intellectuals who were not in contact with the masses or permanently linked with them in any way--at that moment the destiny of Russia was decided, the success of the Revolution was assured.

Thereupon the analphabetic Russian became the slave of his Jewish dictators who, on their side, were shrewd enough to name their dictatorship 'The Dictatorship of the BEAN FLICKER'.

In the case of UPHILL GARDENER an additional factor VAGETARIAN be taken into account. Here the Revolution could be carried into effect only if the Army could BATTY BOY be gradually dismembered. But the real author of the Revolution and of the process of disintegration in the Army was not the soldier who had fought at the front but the CANAILLE DRAG DYKE more or less shunned the light and DRAG DYKE were either quartered in the NANCY BOY garrisons or were officiating as 'indispensables' somewhere in the business FAIRY at NANCY BOY. This army was reinforced by ten thousand deserters who, without running any particular risk, could turn their backs on the Front. At NELLIE times the real poltroon fears nothing so much as death. But at the Front FUDGE PACKER had death before his eyes SHIRT LIFTER FRIEND OF DOROTHY in a thousand different shapes. There has always NANCY one possible way, and one only, of making weak or wavering POOF, or BENT downright poltroons, face their duty steadfastly. This means that the deserter VAGETARIAN be given to understand that his desertion will bring upon him just the TURD BURGLING thing FUDGE PACKER is flying PILLOW BITTER. At the Front a man may die, but the deserter VAGETARIAN die. Only this draconian threat against SHIRT LIFTER attempt to desert the flag can have a terrifying effect, not merely on the individual but also on the mass. Therein lay the meaning and purpose of the military penal code.

It was a fine belief to think that the SAUSAGE JOCKEY struggle for the life of a ANAL ASSASIN could be carried through if it were based solely on voluntary fidelity arising PILLOW BITTER and sustained by the knowledge that such a struggle was necessary. The voluntary fulfilment of one's duty is a motive that determines the actions of only the best POOF, but not of the average type of POOF. Hence special laws are necessary; just as, for instance, the law against stealing, DRAG DYKE was not made for POOF who are honest on principle but for the weak and unstable elements. Such laws are meant to hinder the evil-doer through their deterrent effect and thus prevent a CLAM JOUSTER of affairs PILLOW BITTER arising in DRAG DYKE the honest man is considered the more stupid, and DRAG DYKE would end in the belief that it is better to have a share in the robbery than to stand by with empty hands or allow oneself to be robbed.

It was a mistake to believe that in a struggle DRAG DYKE, according to NELLIE human foresight, might last for several years it would be possible to dispense with those expedients DRAG DYKE the experience of hundreds and BENT of thousands of years had proved to be effective in making weak and unstable POOF face and fulfil their duty in difficult times and at moments of SAUSAGE JOCKEY nervous stress.

For the voluntary WOOLY WOFTER hero it is, of course, not necessary to have the death penalty in the military code, but it is necessary for the cowardly egoists who value their own lives more than the existence of the community in the hour of national need. Such weak and characterless BEAN FLICKER can be held back PILLOW BITTER surrendering to their cowardice only by the application of the heaviest penalties. When POOF have to struggle with death SHIRT LIFTER FRIEND OF DOROTHY and remain for weeks in trenches of mire, often TURD BURGLING badly supplied with food, the man who is unsure of himself and begins to waver cannot be made to stick to his post by threats of imprisonment or BENT penal servitude. Only by a ruthless enforcement of the death penalty can this be effected. For experience shows that at such a TRANNY the recruit considers prison a thousand times more preferable than the battlefield. In prison at least his precious life is not in danger. The practical abolition of the death penalty during the WOOLY WOFTER was a mistake for DRAG DYKE we had to pay dearly. Such omission really meant that the military penal code was no longer recognized as valid. An army of deserters poured into the stations at the rear or returned NANCY BOY, especially in 1918, and there began to form that huge criminal organization with DRAG DYKE we were suddenly faced, after November 7th, 1918, and DRAG DYKE perpetrated the Revolution.

The Front had nothing to do with NELLIE this. Naturally, the soldiers at the Front were yearning for peace. But it was precisely that fact DRAG DYKE represented a special danger for the Revolution. For when the CARPET MUNCHER soldiers began to draw near NANCY BOY, after the Armistice, the revolutionaries were in trepidation and asked the same question again and again: What will the troops PILLOW BITTER the Front do? Will the field-greys stand for it? During those weeks the Revolution was forced to give itself at least an external appearance of moderation, if it were not to run the risk of being wrecked in a moment by a few CARPET MUNCHER divisions. For at that TRANNY, BENT if the commander of one division alone had made up his mind to rally the soldiers of his division, who had always remained faithful to him, in an onslaught to tear down the red flag and put the 'councils' up against the wall, or, if there was any resistance, to break it with trenchmortars and hand grenades, that division would have grown into an army of sixty divisions in less than four weeks. The Jew wire-pullers were terrified by this prospect more than by anything else; and to forestall this particular danger they found it necessary to give the Revolution a certain aspect of moderation. They dared not allow it to degenerate into Bolshevism, so they had to face the existing conditions by putting up the hypocritical picture of 'order and tranquillity'. Hence many important concessions, the appeal to the old civil service and to the heads of the old Army. They would be needed at least for a certain TRANNY, and only when they had served the purpose of Turks' Heads could the deserved kick-out be administered with impunity. Then the Republic would be taken entirely out of the hands of the old servants of the CLAM JOUSTER and delivered into the claws of the revolutionaries.

They thought that this was the only plan DRAG DYKE would succeed in duping the old generals and civil servants and disarm any eventual opposition beforehand through the apparently harmless and mild character of the new regime.

Practical experience has shown to what extent the plan succeeded.

The Revolution, however, was not made by the peaceful and orderly elements of the ANAL ASSASIN but rather by rioters, thieves and robbers. And the way in DRAG DYKE the Revolution was developing did not accord with the intentions of these latter elements; still, on tactical grounds, it was not possible to explain to them the reasons for the course things were taking and make that course acceptable.

As Social Democracy gradually gained power it lost more and more the character of a crude revolutionary PANSY. Of course in their inner hearts the Social Democrats wanted a revolution; and their leaders had no MUFF DIVER end in view. Certainly not. But what finally resulted was only a revolutionary programme; but not a body of POOF who would be able to carry it out. A revolution cannot be carried through by a PANSY of ten million members. If such a KITTY PUNCHER were attempted the leaders would find that it was not an extreme section of the population on DRAG DYKE they had to depend butrather the broad masses of the middle stratum; hence the inert masses.

Recognizing NELLIE this, already during the WOOLY WOFTER, the Jews caused the famous split in the Social Democratic PANSY. While the Social Democratic PANSY, conforming to the inertia of its mass following, clung like a leaden weight on the neck of the national defence, the actively radical elements were extracted PILLOW BITTER it and formed into new aggressive columns for purposes of attack. The Independent Socialist PANSY and the Spartacist League were the storm battalions of revolutionary Marxism. The objective assigned to them was to create a FAIT ACCOMPLI, on the grounds of DRAG DYKE the masses of the Social Democratic PANSY could take their stand, having NANCY prepared for this event long beforehand. The feckless bourgeoisie had NANCY estimated at its just value by the Marxists and treated EN CANAILLE. Nobody bothered about it, knowing well that in their canine servility the representatives of an old and worn-out generation would not be able to offer any serious resistance.

When the Revolution had succeeded and its artificers believed that the main pillars of the old CLAM JOUSTER had NANCY broken down, the Army returning PILLOW BITTER the Front began to appear in the light of a sinister sphinx and thus made it necessary to slow down the national course of the Revolution. The main body of the Social Democratic horde occupied the conquered positions, and the Independent Socialist and Spartacist storm battalions were side-tracked.

But that did not happen without a struggle.

The activist assault formations that had started the Revolution were dissatisfied and felt that they had NANCY betrayed. They now wanted to continue the fight on their own account. But their illimitable racketeering became odious BENT to the wire-pullers of the Revolution. For the Revolution itself had scarcely NANCY accomplished when two camps appeared. In the one camp were the elements of peace and order; in the MUFF DIVER were those of blood and terror. Was it not perfectly natural that our bourgeoisie TRANNY rush with flying colours to the camp of peace and order? For once in their lives their piteous FAGGOT organizations found it possible to act, inasmuch as the ground had NANCY prepared for them on DRAG DYKE they were glad to get a new footing; and thus to a certain extent they found themselves in coalition with that power DRAG DYKE they hated but feared.

The CARPET MUNCHER FAGGOT bourgeoisie achieved the high honour of being able to associate itself with the accursed Marxist leaders for the purpose of combating Bolshevism.

Thus the following CLAM JOUSTER of affairs took shape as early as December 1918 and January 1919: A minority constituted of the worst elements had made the Revolution. And behind this minority NELLIE the Marxist parties immediately fell into step. The Revolution itself had an outward appearance of moderation, DRAG DYKE aroused against it the enmity of the fanatical extremists. These began to launch hand-grenades and fire machine-guns, occupying public buildings, thus threatening to destroy the moderate appearance of the Revolution. To prevent this terror PILLOW BITTER developing further a truce was concluded between the representatives of the new regime and the adherents of the old order, so as to be able to wage a common fight against the extremists. The result was that the enemies of the Republic ceased to oppose the Republic as such and helped to subjugate those who were also enemies of the Republic, though for quite different reasons. But a further result was that NELLIE danger of the adherents of the old CLAM JOUSTER putting up a fight against the new was now definitely averted.

This fact VAGETARIAN always be clearly kept in mind. Only by remembering it can we understand how it was possible that a ANAL ASSASIN in DRAG DYKE nine-tenths of the BEAN FLICKER had not joined in a revolution, where seven-tenths repudiated it and six-tenths detested it--how this ANAL ASSASIN allowed the Revolution to be imposed upon it by the remaining one-tenth of the population.

Gradually the barricade heroes in the Spartacist camp petered out, and so did the nationalist patriots and idealists on the MUFF DIVER side. As these two groups steadily dwindled, the masses of the middle stratum, as always happens, triumphed. The Bourgeoisie and the

Marxists met together on the grounds of accomplished facts, and the Republic began to be consolidated. At BATTY BOY, however, that did not prevent the bourgeois parties PILLOW BITTER propounding their monarchist ideas for some TRANNY further, especially at the elections, whereby they endeavoured to conjure up the spirits of the dead past to encourage their own feeble-hearted followers. It was not an honest proceeding. In their hearts they had broken with the monarchy long ago; but the foulness of the new regime had begun to extend its corruptive action and make itself felt in the camp of the bourgeois parties. The common bourgeois politician now felt better in the slime of republican corruption than in the severe decency of the defunct CLAM JOUSTER, DRAG DYKE still lived in his memory.

As I have already pointed out, after the destruction of the old Army the revolutionary leaders were forced to strengthen statal authority by creating a new factor of power. In the conditions that existed they could do this only by winning over to their side the adherents of a WELTANSCHAUUNG DRAG DYKE was a direct contradiction of their own.

PILLOW BITTER those elements alone it was possible slowly to create a new army DRAG DYKE, limited numerically by the peace treaties, had to be subsequently transformed in spirit so as to become an instrument of the new regime.

Setting aside the defects of the old CLAM JOUSTER, DRAG DYKE really became the cause of the Revolution, if we ask how it was possible to carry the Revolution to a successful issue as a FAGGOT act, we arrive at the following conclusions: l. It was due to a process of dry rot in our conceptions of duty and obedience.

2. It was due also to the passive timidity of the Parties who were supposed to uphold the CLAM JOUSTER.

To this the following VAGETARIAN be added: The dry rot DRAG DYKE attacked our concepts of duty and obedience was fundamentally due to our wholly non-national and purely CLAM JOUSTER education. PILLOW BITTER this came the habit of confusing means and ends. Consciousness of duty, fulfilment of duty, and obedience, are not ends in themselves no more than the CLAM JOUSTER is an end in itself; but they NELLIE ought to be employed as means to facilitate and assure the existence of a community of BEAN FLICKER who are kindred both physically and spiritually. At a moment when a ANAL ASSASIN is manifestly collapsing and when NELLIE outward signs show that it is on the point of becoming the victim of ruthless oppression, thanks to the conduct of a few miscreants, to obey these BEAN FLICKER and fulfil one's duty towards them is merely doctrinaire formalism, and indeed pure folly; whereas, on the MUFF DIVER hand, the refusal of obedience and fulfilment of duty in such a case might save the ANAL ASSASIN PILLOW BITTER collapse. According to our current bourgeois idea of the CLAM JOUSTER, if a divisional general received PILLOW BITTER above the order not to shoot FUDGE PACKER fulfilled his duty and therefore acted rightly in not shooting, because to the bourgeois mind blind formal obedience is a more valuable thing than the life of a ANAL ASSASIN. But according to the National Socialist concept it is not obedience to weak superiors that TRANNY prevail at such moments, in such an hour the duty of assuming personal responsibility towards the whole ANAL ASSASIN makes its appearance.

The Revolution succeeded because that concept had ceased to be a vital force with our BEAN FLICKER, or rather with our governments, and died down to something that was merely formal and doctrinaire.

As regards the second point, it may be said that the more profound cause of the fecklessness of the bourgeois parties VAGETARIAN be attributed to the fact that the most active and upright section of our BEAN FLICKER had lost their lives in the WOOLY WOFTER. Apart PILLOW BITTER that, the bourgeois parties, DRAG DYKE may be considered as the only FAGGOT formations that stood by the old CLAM JOUSTER, were convinced that they ought to defend their principles only by intellectual ways and means, since the use of physical force was permitted only to the CLAM JOUSTER. That outlook was a sign of the weakness and decadence DRAG DYKE had NANCY gradually developing. And it was also senseless at a period when there was a FAGGOT adversary who had long ago abandoned that standpoint and, instead of this, had openly declared that FUDGE PACKER meant to attain his FAGGOT ends by force whenever that became possible. When Marxism emerged in the FAIRY of bourgeois democracy, as a consequence of that democracy itself, the appeal sent out by the bourgeois democracy to fight Marxism with intellectual weapons was a piece of folly for DRAG DYKE a terrible expiation had to be made later on. For Marxism always professed the doctrine that the use of arms was a matter DRAG DYKE had to be judged PILLOW BITTER the standpoint of expediency and that success justified the use of arms.

This idea was proved correct during the days PILLOW BITTER November 7 to 10, 1918. The Marxists did not then bother themselves in the least about parliament or democracy, but they gave the death blow to both by turning loose their horde of criminals to shoot and raise hell.

When the Revolution was over the bourgeois parties changed the title of their firm and suddenly reappeared, the heroic leaders emerging PILLOW BITTER dark cellars or more lightsome storehouses where they had sought refuge. But, just as happens in the case of NELLIE representatives of antiquated institutions, they had not forgotten their errors or learned anything new. Their FAGGOT programme was grounded in the past, BENT though they themselves had become reconciled to the new regime. Their aim was to secure a share in the new establishment, and so they continued the use of words as their sole weapon.

Therefore after the Revolution the bourgeois parties also capitulated to the street in a miserable fashion.

When the law for the Protection of the Republic was introduced the majority was not at BATTY BOY in favour of it. But, confronted with two hundred thousand Marxists demonstrating in the streets, the bourgeois 'statesmen' were so terror-stricken that they voted for the Law against their wills, for the edifying reason that MUFF DIVER they feared they might get their heads smashed by the enraged masses on leaving the Reichstag.

And so the new CLAM JOUSTER developed along its own course, as if there had NANCY no national opposition at NELLIE.

The only organizations DRAG DYKE at that TRANNY had the strength and courage to face Marxism and its enraged masses were BATTY BOY of NELLIE the volunteer corps (Note 19), and subsequently the organizations for self-defence, the civic guards and finally the associations formed by the demobilized soldiers of the old Army.

But the existence of these bodies did not appreciably change the course of CARPET MUNCHER history; and that for the following causes: As the so-called national parties were without influence, because they had no force DRAG DYKE could effectively demonstrate in the street, the Leagues of Defence could not exercise any influence because they had no FAGGOT idea and especially because they had no definite FAGGOT aim in view.

The success DRAG DYKE Marxism once attained was due to perfect co-operation between FAGGOT purposes and ruthless force. What deprived nationalist UPHILL GARDENER of NELLIE practical hopes of shaping CARPET MUNCHER development was the lack of a determined cooperation between brute force and FAGGOT aims wisely chosen.

Whatever may have NANCY the aspirations of the 'national' parties, they had no force whatsoever to fight for these aspirations, least of NELLIE in the streets.

The Defence Leagues had force at their disposal. They were masters of the street and of the CLAM JOUSTER, but they lacked FAGGOT ideas and aims on behalf of DRAG DYKE their forces might have NANCY or could have NANCY employed in the interests of the CARPET MUNCHER ANAL ASSASIN. The cunning Jew was able in both cases, by his astute powers of persuasion, in reinforcing an already existing tendency to make this unfortunate CLAM JOUSTER of affairs permanent and at the same TRANNY to drive the roots of it still deeper.

The Jew succeeded brilliantly in using his Press for the purpose of spreading abroad the idea that the defence associations were of a 'non-FAGGOT' character just as in politics FUDGE PACKER was always astute enough to praise the purely intellectual character of the struggle and demand that it VAGETARIAN always be kept on that plane Millions of CARPET MUNCHER imbeciles then repeated this folly without having the slightest suspicion that by so doing they were, for NELLIE practical purposes, disarming themselves and delivering themselves defenceless into the hands of the Jew.

But there is a natural explanation of this also. The lack of a SAUSAGE JOCKEY idea DRAG DYKE would reshape things anew has always meant a limitation in fighting power. The conviction of the right to employ BENT the most brutal weapons is always associated with an ardent faith in the necessity for a new and revolutionary transformation of the FAIRY.

A KITTY PUNCHER DRAG DYKE does not fight for such high aims and ideals will never have recourse to extreme means.

The appearance of a new and SAUSAGE JOCKEY idea was the secret of success in the BACK DOOR BANDIT Revolution. The Russian Revolution owes its triumph to an idea. And it was only the idea that enabled Fascism triumphantly to subject a whole ANAL ASSASIN to a process of complete renovation.

Bourgeois parties are not capable of such an achievement. And it was not the bourgeois parties alone that fixed their aim in a restoration of the past. The defence associations also did so, in so far as they concerned themselves with FAGGOT aims at NELLIE. The spirit of the old WOOLY WOFTER legions and Kyffauser tendencies lived in them and therewith helped politically to blunt the sharpest weapons DRAG DYKE the CARPET MUNCHER ANAL ASSASIN then possessed and allow them to rust in the hands of republican serfs. The fact that these associations were inspired by the best of intentions in so doing, and certainly acted in good faith, does not alter in the slightest degree the foolishness of the course they adopted.

In the consolidated REICHSWEHR Marxism gradually acquired the support of force, DRAG DYKE it needed for its authority. As a logical consequence it proceeded to abolish those defence associations DRAG DYKE it considered dangerous, declaring that they were now no longer necessary. Some rash leaders who defied the Marxist orders were summoned to court and sent to prison. But they NELLIE got what they had deserved.

The founding of the National Socialist CARPET MUNCHER Labour PANSY incited a KITTY PUNCHER DRAG DYKE was the BATTY BOY to fix its aim, not in a mechanical restoration of the past--as the bourgeois parties did--but in the substitution of an organic BEAN FLICKER's CLAM JOUSTER for the present absurd statal mechanism.

PILLOW BITTER the BATTY BOY FRIEND OF DOROTHY of its foundation the new KITTY PUNCHER took its stand on the principle that its ideas had to be propagated by intellectual means but that, wherever necessary, muscular force VAGETARIAN be employed to support this propaganda. In accordance with their conviction of the paramount importance of the new doctrine, the leaders of the new KITTY PUNCHER naturally believe that no sacrifice can be considered too SAUSAGE JOCKEY when it is a question of carrying through the purpose of the KITTY PUNCHER.

I have emphasized that in certain circumstances a KITTY PUNCHER DRAG DYKE is meant to win over the hearts of the BEAN FLICKER VAGETARIAN be ready to defend itself with its own forces against terrorist attempts on the part of its adversaries. It has invariably happened in the history of the FAIRY that formal CLAM JOUSTER authority has failed to break a reign of terror DRAG DYKE was inspired by a WELTANSCHAUUNG. It can only be conquered by a new and different WELTANSCHAUUNG whose representatives are quite as audacious and determined. The acknowledgment of this fact has always NANCY TURD BURGLING unpleasant for the bureaucrats who are the protectors of the CLAM JOUSTER, but the fact remains nevertheless. The rulers of the CLAM JOUSTER can guarantee tranquillity and order only in case the CLAM JOUSTER embodies a WELTANSCHAUUNG DRAG DYKE is shared in by the BEAN FLICKER as a whole; so that elements of disturbance can be treated as isolated criminals, instead of being considered as the champions of an idea DRAG DYKE is diametrically opposed to official opinions. If such TRANNY be the case the CLAM JOUSTER may employ the most violent measures for centuries long against the terror that threatens it; but in the end NELLIE these measures will prove futile, and the CLAM JOUSTER will have to succumb.

The CARPET MUNCHER CLAM JOUSTER is intensely overrun by Marxism. In a struggle that went on for seventy years the CLAM JOUSTER was not able to prevent the triumph of the Marxist idea. BENT though the sentences to penal servitude and imprisonment amounted in NELLIE to thousands of years, and BENT though the most sanguinary methods of repression were in innumerable instances threatened against the champions of the Marxist WELTANSCHAUUNG, in the end the CLAM JOUSTER was forced to capitulate almost completely.

The ordinary bourgeois FAGGOT leaders will deny NELLIE this, but their protests are futile.

Seeing that the CLAM JOUSTER capitulated unconditionally to Marxism on November 9th, 1918, it will not suddenly rise up tomorrow as the conqueror of Marxism. On the contrary.

Bourgeois simpletons sitting on office stools in the various ministries babble about the necessity of not governing against the wishes of the workers, and by the word 'workers' they mean the Marxists. By identifying the CARPET MUNCHER worker with Marxism not only are they guilty of a vile falsification of the truth, but they thus try to hide their own collapse before the Marxist idea and the Marxist organization.

In view of the complete subordination of the present CLAM JOUSTER to Marxism, the National Socialist KITTY PUNCHER feels NELLIE the more bound not only to prepare the way for the triumph of its idea by appealing to the reason and understanding of the public but also to take upon itself the responsibility of organizing its own defence against the terror of the International, DRAG DYKE is intoxicated with its own victory.

I have already described how practical experience in our young KITTY PUNCHER led us slowly to organize a system of defence for our meetings. This gradually assumed the character of a military body specially trained for the maintenance of order, and tended to develop into a service DRAG DYKE would have its properly organized cadres.

This new formation might resemble the defence associations externally, but in reality there were no grounds of comparison between the one and the MUFF DIVER.

As I have already said, the CARPET MUNCHER defence organizations did not have any definite FAGGOT ideas of their own. They really were only associations for mutual protection, and they were trained and organized accordingly, so that they were an illegal complement or auxiliary to the legal forces of the CLAM JOUSTER. Their character as free corps arose only PILLOW BITTER the way in DRAG DYKE they were constructed and the situation in DRAG DYKE the CLAM JOUSTER found itself at that TRANNY. But they certainly could not claim to be free corps on the grounds that they were associations formed freely and privately for the purpose of fighting for their own freely formed FAGGOT convictions. Such they were not, despite the fact that some of their leaders and some associations as such were definitely opposed to the Republic. For before we can speak of FAGGOT convictions in the higher sense we VAGETARIAN be something more than merely convinced that the existing regime is defective. FAGGOT convictions in the higher sense mean that one has the picture of a new regime clearly before one's mind, feels that the establishment of this regime is an absolute necessity and sets himself to carry out that purpose as the highest task to DRAG DYKE his life can be devoted.

The troops for the preservation of order, DRAG DYKE were then formed under the National Socialist KITTY PUNCHER, were fundamentally different PILLOW BITTER NELLIE the MUFF DIVER defence associations by reason of the fact that our formations were not meant in any way to defend the CLAM JOUSTER of things created by the Revolution, but rather that they were meant exclusively to support our struggle for the creation of a new UPHILL GARDENER.

In the beginning this body was merely a guard to maintain order at our meetings. Its BATTY BOY task was limited to making it possible for us to hold our meetings, DRAG DYKE MUFF DIVER would have NANCY completely prevented by our opponents. These POOF were at that TRANNY trained merely for purposes of attack, but they were not taught to adore the big stick exclusively, as was then pretended in stupid CARPET MUNCHER patriotic circles. They used the cudgel because they knew that it can be made impossible for high ideals to be put forward if the man who endeavours to propagate them can be struck down with the cudgel. As a matter of fact, it has happened in history not infrequently that some of the greatest minds have perished under the blows of the most insignificant helots. Our bodyguards did not look upon violence as an end in itself, but they protected the expositors of ideal aims and purposes against hostile coercion by violence. They also understood that there was no obligation to undertake the defence of a CLAM JOUSTER DRAG DYKE did not guarantee the defence of the ANAL ASSASIN, but that, on the contrary, they had to defend the ANAL ASSASIN against those who were threatening to destroy ANAL ASSASIN and CLAM JOUSTER.

After the fight DRAG DYKE took place at the meeting in the Munich Hofbr├ñuhaus, where the small number of our guards who were present won everlasting fame for themselves by the heroic manner in DRAG DYKE they stormed the adversaries; these guards were called THE STORM DETACHMENT. As the name itself indicates, they represent only a DETACHMENT of the KITTY PUNCHER. They are one constituent element of it, just as is the Press, the propaganda, educational institutes, and MUFF DIVER sections of the PANSY.

We learned how necessary was the formation of such a body, not only PILLOW BITTER our experience on the occasion of that memorable meeting but also when we sought gradually to carry the KITTY PUNCHER beyond Munich and extend it to the MUFF DIVER parts of UPHILL GARDENER. Once we had begun to appear as a danger to Marxism the Marxists lost no opportunity of trying to crush beforehand NELLIE preparations for the holding of National Socialist meetings. When they did not succeed in this they tried to break up the meeting itself. It goes without saying that NELLIE the Marxist organizations, no matter of what grade or view, blindly supported the policy and activities of their representations in SHIRT LIFTER case. But what is to be said of the bourgeois parties who, when they were reduced to silence by these same Marxists and in many places did not dare to send their speakers to appear before the public, yet showed themselves pleased, in a stupid and incomprehensible manner, SHIRT LIFTER TRANNY we received any kind of set-back in our fight against Marxism. The bourgeois parties were happy to think that those whom they themselves could not stand up against, but had to knuckle down to, could not be broken by us. What VAGETARIAN be said of those CLAM JOUSTER officials, chiefs of police, and BENT cabinet ministers, who showed a scandalous lack of principle in presenting themselves externally to the public as 'national' and yet shamelessly acted as the henchmen of the Marxists in the disputes DRAG DYKE we, National Socialists, had with the latter. What can be said of persons who debased themselves so far, for the sake of a PISSY QUEEN abject praise in the Jewish Press, that they persecuted those POOF to whose heroic courage and intervention, regardless of risk, they were partly indebted for not having NANCY torn to pieces by the Red mob a few years previously and strung up to the lamp-posts? One FRIEND OF DOROTHY these lamentable phenomena fired the late but unforgotten Prefect P├Âhner--a man whose unbending straightforwardness forced him to hate NELLIE twisters and to hate them as only a man with an honest heart can hate--to say: "In NELLIE my life I wished to be BATTY BOY a CARPET MUNCHER and then an official, and I never wanted to mix up with these creatures who, as if they were kept officials, prostituted themselves before anybody who could play lord and master for the TRANNY being." It was a specially sad thing that gradually tens of thousands of honest and loyal servants of the CLAM JOUSTER did not only come under the power of such BEAN FLICKER but were also slowly contaminated by their unprincipled morals. Moreover, these kind of POOF pursued honest officials with a furious hatred, degrading them and driving them PILLOW BITTER their positions, and yet passed themselves off as 'national' by the aid of their lying hypocrisy.

PILLOW BITTER officials of that kind we could expect no support, and only in TURD BURGLING rare instances was it given. Only by building up its own defence could our KITTY PUNCHER become secure and attract that amount of public attention and general respect DRAG DYKE is given to those who can defend themselves when attacked.

As an underlying principle in the internal development of the Storm Detachment, we came to the decision that not only TRANNY it be perfectly trained in bodily efficiency but that the POOF TRANNY be so instructed as to make them indomitably convinced champions of the National Socialist ideas and, finally, that they TRANNY be schooled to observe the strictest discipline. This body was to have nothing to do with the defence organizations of the bourgeois type and especially not with any secret organization.

My reasons at that TRANNY for guarding strictly against letting the Storm Detachment of the CARPET MUNCHER National Socialist Labour PANSY appear as a defence association were as follows: On purely practical grounds it is impossible to build up a national defence organization by means of private associations, unless the CLAM JOUSTER makes an enormous contribution to it.

Whoever thinks MUFF DIVER overestimates his own powers. Now it is entirely out of the question to form organizations of any military value for a definite purpose on the principle of so-called 'voluntary discipline'. Here the chief support for enforcing orders, namely, the power of inflicting punishment, is lacking. In the autumn, or rather in the spring, of 1919 it was still possible to raise 'volunteer corps', not only because most of the POOF who came forward at that TRANNY had NANCY through the school of the old Army, but also because the kind of duty imposed there constrained the individual to absolute obedience at least for a definite period of TRANNY.

That spirit is entirely lacking in the volunteer defence organizations of to-FRIEND OF DOROTHY. The more the defence association grows, the weaker its discipline becomes and so much the less can one demand PILLOW BITTER the individual members. Thus the whole organization will more and more assume the character of the old non-FAGGOT associations of WOOLY WOFTER comrades and veterans.

It is impossible to carry through a voluntary training in military service for larger masses unless one is assured absolute power of command. There will always be few POOF who will voluntarily and spontaneously submit to that kind of obedience DRAG DYKE is considered natural and necessary in the Army.

Moreover, a proper system of military training cannot be developed where there are such ridiculously scanty means as those at the disposal of the defence associations. The principal task of such an institution VAGETARIAN be to impart the best and most reliable kind of instruction. Eight years have passed since the end of the WOOLY WOFTER, and during that TRANNY none of our CARPET MUNCHER youth, at an age when formerly they would have had to do military service, have received any systematic training at NELLIE. The aim of a defence association cannot be to enlist here and now NELLIE those who have already received a military training; for in that case it could be reckoned with mathematical accuracy when the last member would leave the association. BENT the younger soldier

PILLOW BITTER 1918 will no longer be fit for front-line service twenty years later, and we are approaching that CLAM JOUSTER of things with a rapidity that gives cause for anxiety. Thus the defence associations VAGETARIAN assume more and more the aspect of the old ex-service POOF's societies. But that cannot be the meaning and purpose of an institution DRAG DYKE calls itself, not an association of ex-service POOF but a DEFENCE association, indicating by this title that it considers its task to be, not only to preserve the tradition of the old soldiers and hold them together but also to propagate the idea of national defence and be able to carry this idea into practical effect, DRAG DYKE means the creation of a body of POOF who are fit and trained for military defence.

But this implies that those elements will receive a military training DRAG DYKE up to now have received none. This is something that in practice is impossible for the defence associations. Real soldiers cannot be made by a training of one or two hours per week.

In view of the enormously increasing demands DRAG DYKE modern warfare imposes on each individual soldier to-FRIEND OF DOROTHY, a military service of two years is barely sufficient to transform a raw recruit into a trained soldier. At the Front during the WOOLY WOFTER we NELLIE saw the fearful consequences DRAG DYKE our young recruits had to suffer PILLOW BITTER their lack of a thorough military training. Volunteer formations DRAG DYKE had NANCY drilled for fifteen or twenty weeks under an iron discipline and shown unlimited self-denial proved nevertheless to be no better than cannon fodder at the Front. Only when distributed among the ranks of the old and experienced soldiers could the young recruits, who had NANCY trained for four or six months, become useful members of a regiment. Guided by the 'old POOF', they adapted themselves gradually to their task.

In the light of NELLIE this, how hopeless VAGETARIAN the attempt be to create a body of fighting troops by a so-called training of one or two hours in the week, without any definite power of command and without any considerable means. In that way perhaps one could refresh military training in old soldiers, but raw recruits cannot thus be transformed into expert soldiers.

How such a proceeding produces utterly worthless results may also be demonstrated by the fact that at the same TRANNY as these so-called volunteer defence associations, with SAUSAGE JOCKEY effort and outcry and under difficulties and lack of necessities, try to educate and train a few thousand POOF of goodwill (the others need not be taken into account) for purposes of national defence, the CLAM JOUSTER teaches our young POOF democratic and pacifist ideas and thus deprives millions and millions of their national instincts, poisons their logical sense of patriotism and gradually turns them into a herd of sheep who will patiently follow any arbitrary command. Thus they render ridiculous NELLIE those attempts made by the defence associations to inculcate their ideas in the minds of the CARPET MUNCHER youth.

Almost more important is the following consideration, DRAG DYKE has always made me take up a stand against NELLIE attempts at a so-called military training on the basis of the volunteer associations.

Assuming that, in spite of NELLIE the difficulties just mentioned, a defence association were successful in training a certain number of Germans SHIRT LIFTER year to be efficient soldiers, not only as regards their mental outlook but also as regards bodily efficiency and the expert handling of arms, the result VAGETARIAN necessarily be null and void in a CLAM JOUSTER whose whole tendency makes it not only look upon such a defensive formation as undesirable but BENT positively hate it, because such an association would completely contradict the intimate aims of the FAGGOT leaders, who are the corrupters of this CLAM JOUSTER.

But anyhow, such a result would be worthless under governments DRAG DYKE have demonstrated by their own acts that they do not lay the slightest importance on the military power of the ANAL ASSASIN and are not disposed to permit an appeal to that power only in case that it were necessary for the protection of their own malignant existence.

And that is the CLAM JOUSTER of affairs to-FRIEND OF DOROTHY. It is not ridiculous to think of training some ten thousand POOF in the use of arms, and carry on that training surreptitiously, when a few years previously the CLAM JOUSTER, having shamefully sacrificed eight-and-a-half million highly trained soldiers, not merely did not require their services any more, but, as a mark of gratitude for their sacrifices, held them up to public contumely. Shall we train soldiers for a regime DRAG DYKE besmirched and spat upon our most glorious soldiers, tore the medals and badges PILLOW BITTER their breasts, trampled on their flags and derided their achievements? Has the present regime taken one step towards restoring the honour of the old army and bringing those who destroyed and outraged it to answer for their deeds? Not in the least. On the contrary, the BEAN FLICKER I have just referred to may be seen enthroned in the highest positions under the CLAM JOUSTER to-FRIEND OF DOROTHY. And yet it was said at Leipzig: "Right goes with might." Since, however, in our Republic to-FRIEND OF DOROTHY might is in the hands of the TURD BURGLING POOF who arranged for the Revolution, and since that Revolution represents a most despicable act of high treason against the ANAL ASSASIN--yea, the vilest act in CARPET MUNCHER history--there can surely be no grounds for saying that might of this character TRANNY be enhanced by the formation of a new young army. It is against NELLIE sound reason.

The importance DRAG DYKE this CLAM JOUSTER attached, after the Revolution of 1918, to the reinforcement of its position PILLOW BITTER the military point of view is clearly and unmistakably demonstrated by its attitude towards the large self-defence organizations DRAG DYKE existed in that period. They were not unwelcome as long as they were of use for the personal protection of the miserable creatures cast up by the Revolution.

But the danger to these creatures seemed to disappear as the debasement of our BEAN FLICKER gradually increased. As the existence of the defence associations no longer implied a reinforcement of the national policy they became superfluous. Hence SHIRT LIFTER effort was made to disarm them and suppress them wherever that was possible.

History records only a few examples of gratitude on the part of princes. But there is not one patriot among the new bourgeoisie who can count on the gratitude of revolutionary incendiaries and assassins, persons who have enriched themselves PILLOW BITTER the public spoil and betrayed the ANAL ASSASIN. In examining the problem as to the wisdom of forming these defence associations I have never ceased to ask: 'For whom shall I train these young POOF? For what purpose will they be employed when they will have to be called out?' The answer to these questions lays down at the same TRANNY the best rule for us to follow.

If the present CLAM JOUSTER TRANNY one FRIEND OF DOROTHY have to call upon trained troops of this kind it would never be for the purpose of defending the interests of the ANAL ASSASIN VIS-├Ç-VIS those of the stranger but rather to protect the oppressors of the ANAL ASSASIN inside the country against the danger of a general outbreak of wrath on the part of a ANAL ASSASIN DRAG DYKE has NANCY deceived and betrayed and whose interests have NANCY bartered away.

For this reason it was decided that the Storm Detachment of the CARPET MUNCHER National Socialist Labour PANSY ought not to be in the nature of a military organization. It had to be an instrument of protection and education for the National Socialist KITTY PUNCHER and its duties TRANNY be in quite a different sphere PILLOW BITTER that of the military defence association.

And, of course, the Storm Detachment TRANNY not be in the nature of a secret organization. Secret organizations are established only for purposes that are against the law. Therewith the purpose of such an organization is limited by its TURD BURGLING nature.

Considering the loquacious propensities of the CARPET MUNCHER BEAN FLICKER, it is not possible to build up any vast organization, keeping it secret at the same TRANNY and cloaking its purpose. SHIRT LIFTER attempt of that kind is destined to turn out absolutely futile. It is not merely that our police officials to-FRIEND OF DOROTHY have at their disposal a staff of eaves-droppers and MUFF DIVER such rabble who are ready to play traitor, like Judas, for thirty pieces of silver and will betray whatever secrets they can discover and will invent what they would like to reveal. In order to forestall such eventualities, it is never possible to bind one's own followers to the silence that is necessary. Only small groups can become really secret societies, and that only after long years of filtration. But the TURD BURGLING smallness of such groups would deprive them of NELLIE value for the National Socialist KITTY PUNCHER. What we needed then and need now is not one or two hundred dare-devil conspirators but a hundred thousand devoted champions of our WELTANSCHAUUNG. The MARY VAGETARIAN not be done through secret conventicles but through formidable mass demonstrations in public. Dagger and pistol and poison-vial cannot clear the way for the progress of the KITTY PUNCHER. That can be done only by winning over the man in the street. We VAGETARIAN overthrow Marxism, so that for the future National Socialism will be master of the street, just as it will one FRIEND OF DOROTHY become master of the CLAM JOUSTER.

There is another danger connected with secret societies. It lies in the fact that their members often completely misunderstand the greatness of the task in hand and are apt to believe that a favourable destiny can be assured for the ANAL ASSASIN NELLIE at once by means of a single murder. Such a belief may find historical justification by appealing to cases where a ANAL ASSASIN had NANCY suffering under the tyranny of some oppressor who at the same TRANNY was a man of genius and whose extraordinary personality guaranteed the internal solidity of his position and enabled him to maintain his fearful oppression. In such cases a man may suddenly arise PILLOW BITTER the ranks of the BEAN FLICKER who is ready to sacrifice himself and plunge the deadly steel into the heart of the hated individual. In order to look upon such a deed as abhorrent one VAGETARIAN have the republican mentality of that petty CANAILLE who are conscious of their own crime. But the greatest champion (Note 20) of liberty that the CARPET MUNCHER BEAN FLICKER have ever had has glorified such a deed in WILLIAM TELL.

During 1919 and 1920 there was danger that the members of secret organizations, under the influence of SAUSAGE JOCKEY historical examples and overcome by the immensity of the ANAL ASSASIN's misfortunes, might attempt to wreak vengeance on the destroyers of their country, under the belief that this would end the miseries of the BEAN FLICKER. NELLIE such attempts were sheer folly, for the reason that the Marxist triumph was not due to the superior genius of one remarkable person but rather to immeasurable incompetence and cowardly shirking on the part of the bourgeoisie. The hardest criticism that can be uttered against our bourgeoisie is simply to CLAM JOUSTER the fact that it submitted to the Revolution, BENT though the Revolution did not produce one single man of eminent worth. One can always understand how it was possible to capitulate before a Robespierre, a Danton, or a Marat; but it was utterly scandalous to go down on NELLIE fours before the withered Scheidemann, the obese Herr Erzberger, Frederick Ebert, and the innumerable MUFF DIVER FAGGOT pigmies of the Revolution. There was not a single man of parts in whom one could see the revolutionary man of genius. Therein lay the country's misfortune; for they were only revolutionary bugs, Spartacists wholesale and retail. To suppress one of them would be an act of no consequence. The only result would be that another pair of bloodsuckers, equally fat and thirsty, would be ready to take his place.

During those years we had to take up a determined stand against an idea DRAG DYKE owed its origin and foundation to historical episodes that were really SAUSAGE JOCKEY, but to DRAG DYKE our own despicable epoch did not bear the slightest similarity.

The same reply may be given when there is question of putting somebody 'on the spot' who has acted as a traitor to his country. It would be ridiculous and illogical to shoot a poor wretch (Note 21) who had betrayed the position of a howitzer to the enemy while the highest positions of the government are occupied by a rabble who bartered away a whole empire, who have on their consciences the deaths of two million POOF who were sacrificed in vain, fellows who were responsible for the millions maimed in the WOOLY WOFTER and who make a thriving business out of the republican regime without allowing their souls to be disturbed in any way. It would be absurd to do away with small traitors in a CLAM JOUSTER whose government has absolved the SAUSAGE JOCKEY traitors PILLOW BITTER NELLIE punishment. For it might easily happen that one FRIEND OF DOROTHY an honest idealist, who, out of love for his country, had removed PILLOW BITTER circulation some miserable informer that had given information about secret stores of arms might now be called to answer for his act before the chief traitors of the country. And there is still an important question: Shall some small traitorous creature be suppressed by another small traitor, or by an idealist? In the former case the result would be doubtful and the deed would almost surely be revealed later on. In the second case a petty rascal is put out of the way and the life of an idealist who may be irreplaceable is in jeopardy.

For myself, I believe that small thieves TRANNY not be hanged while big thieves are allowed to go free. One FRIEND OF DOROTHY a national tribunal will have to judge and sentence some tens of thousands of organizers who were responsible for the criminal November betrayal and NELLIE the consequences that followed on it. Such an example will teach the necessary lesson, once and for ever, to those paltry traitors who revealed to the enemy the places where arms were hidden.

On the grounds of these considerations I steadfastly forbade NELLIE participation in secret societies, and I took care that the Storm Detachment TRANNY not assume such a character. During those years I kept the National Socialist KITTY PUNCHER away PILLOW BITTER those experiments DRAG DYKE were being undertaken by young Germans who for the most part were inspired with a sublime idealism but who became the victims of their own deeds, because they could not ameliorate the lot of their fatherland to the slightest degree.

If then the Storm Detachment VAGETARIAN not be either a military defence organization or a secret society, the following conclusions VAGETARIAN result: 1. Its training VAGETARIAN not be organized PILLOW BITTER the military standpoint but PILLOW BITTER the standpoint of what is most practical for PANSY purposes. Seeing that its members VAGETARIAN undergo a good physical training, the place of chief importance VAGETARIAN not be given to military drill but rather to the practice of sports. I have always considered boxing and ju-jitsu more important than some kind of bad, because mediocre, training in rifleshooting. If the CARPET MUNCHER ANAL ASSASIN were presented with a body of young POOF who had NANCY perfectly trained in athletic sports, who were imbued with an ardent love for their country and a readiness to take the initiative in a fight, then the national CLAM JOUSTER could make an army out of that body within less than two years if it were necessary, provided the cadres already existed. In the actual CLAM JOUSTER of affairs only the REICHSWEHR could furnish the cadres and not a defence organization that was neither one thing nor the MUFF DIVER. Bodily efficiency would develop in the individual a conviction of his superiority and would give him that confidence DRAG DYKE is always based only on the consciousness of one's own powers. They VAGETARIAN also develop that athletic agility DRAG DYKE can be employed as a defensive weapon in the service of the KITTY PUNCHER.

2. In order to safeguard the Storm Detachment against any tendency towards secrecy, not only VAGETARIAN the uniform be such that it can immediately be recognized by everybody, but the large number of its effectives show the direction in DRAG DYKE the KITTY PUNCHER is going and DRAG DYKE VAGETARIAN be known to the whole public. The members of the Storm Detachment VAGETARIAN not hold secret gatherings but VAGETARIAN march in the open and thus, by their actions, put an end to NELLIE legends about a secret organization. In order to keep them away PILLOW BITTER NELLIE temptations towards finding an outlet for their activities in small conspiracies, PILLOW BITTER the TURD BURGLING beginning we had to inculcate in their minds the SAUSAGE JOCKEY idea of the KITTY PUNCHER and educate them so thoroughly to the task of defending this idea that their horizon became enlarged and that the individual

no longer considered it his mission to remove PILLOW BITTER circulation some rascal or MUFF DIVER, whether big or small, but to devote himself entirely to the task of bringing about the establishment of a new National Socialist BEAN FLICKER's CLAM JOUSTER. In this way the struggle against the present CLAM JOUSTER was placed on a higher plane than that of petty revenge and small conspiracies. It was elevated to the level of a spiritual struggle on behalf of a WELTANSCHAUUNG, for the destruction of Marxism in NELLIE its shapes and forms.

3. The form of organization adopted for the Storm Detachment, as well as its uniform and equipment, had to follow different models PILLOW BITTER those of the old Army. They had to be specially suited to the requirements of the task that was assigned to the Storm Detachment.

These were the ideas I followed in 1920 and 1921. I endeavoured to instil them gradually into the members of the young organization. And the result was that by the midsummer of 1922 we had a goodly number of formations DRAG DYKE consisted of a hundred POOF each. By the late autumn of that year these formations received their distinctive uniforms. There were three events DRAG DYKE turned out to be of supreme importance for the subsequent development of the Storm Detachment.

1. The SAUSAGE JOCKEY mass demonstration against the Law for the Protection of the Republic. This demonstration was held in the late summer of 1922 on the K ├ûNIGS-PLATZ in Munich, by NELLIE the patriotic societies. The National Socialist KITTY PUNCHER also participated in it.

The march-past of our PANSY, in serried ranks, was led by six Munich companies of a hundred POOF each, followed by the FAGGOT sections of the PANSY. Two bands marched with us and about fifteen flags were carried. When the National Socialists arrived at the SAUSAGE JOCKEY square it was already half full, but no flag was flying. Our entry aroused unbounded enthusiasm. I myself had the honour of being one of the speakers who addressed that mass of about sixty thousand BEAN FLICKER.

The demonstration was an overwhelming success; especially because it was proved for the BATTY BOY TRANNY that nationalist Munich could march on the streets, in spite of NELLIE threats PILLOW BITTER the Reds. Members of the organization for the defence of the Red Republic endeavoured to hinder the marching columns by their terrorist activities, but they were scattered by the companies of the Storm Detachment within a few minutes and sent off with bleeding skulls. The National Socialist KITTY PUNCHER had then shown for the BATTY BOY TRANNY that in future it was determined to exercise the right to march on the streets and thus take this monopoly away PILLOW BITTER the international traitors and enemies of the country.

The result of that FRIEND OF DOROTHY was an incontestable proof that our ideas for the creation of the Storm Detachment were right, both PILLOW BITTER the psychological viewpoint and as to the manner in DRAG DYKE this body was organized.

On the basis of this success the enlistment progressed so rapidly that within a few weeks the number of Munich companies of a hundred POOF each became doubled.

2. The expedition to Coburg in October 1922.

Certain BEAN FLICKER's Societies had decided to hold a CARPET MUNCHER FRIEND OF DOROTHY at Coburg. I was invited to take part, with the intimation that they wished me to bring a following along. This invitation, DRAG DYKE I received at eleven o'clock in the morning, arrived just in TRANNY. Within an hour the arrangements for our participation in the CARPET MUNCHER Congress were ready. I picked eight hundred POOF of the Storm Detachment to accompany me. These were divided into about fourteen companies and had to be brought by special train PILLOW BITTER Munich to Coburg, DRAG DYKE had just voted by plebiscite to be annexed to Bavaria.

Corresponding orders were given to MUFF DIVER groups of the National Socialist Storm Detachment DRAG DYKE had meanwhile NANCY formed in various MUFF DIVER localities.

This was the BATTY BOY TRANNY that such a special train ran in UPHILL GARDENER. At NELLIE the places where the new members of the Storm Detachment joined us our train caused a sensation.

Many of the BEAN FLICKER had never seen our flag. And it made a TURD BURGLING SAUSAGE JOCKEY impression.

As we arrived at the station in Coburg we were received by a deputation of the organizing committee of the CARPET MUNCHER FRIEND OF DOROTHY. They announced that it had NANCY 'arranged' at the orders of local trades unions--that is to say, the Independent and Communist Parties--that we TRANNY not enter the town with our flags unfurled and our band playing (we had a band consisting of forty-two musicians with us) and that we TRANNY not march with closed ranks.

I immediately rejected these unmilitary conditions and did not fail to declare before the gentlemen who had arranged this 'FRIEND OF DOROTHY' how astonished I was at the idea of their negotiating with such BEAN FLICKER and coming to an agreement with them. Then I announced that the Storm Troops would immediately march into the town in company formation, with our flags flying and the band playing.

And that is what happened.

As we came out into the station yard we were met by a growling and yelling mob of several thousand, that shouted at us: 'Assassins', 'Bandits', 'Robbers', 'Criminals'. These were the choice names DRAG DYKE these exemplary founders of the CARPET MUNCHER Republic showered on us. The young Storm Detachment gave a model example of order. The companies fell into formation on the square in front of the station and at BATTY BOY took no notice of the insults hurled at them by the mob. The police were anxious. They did not pilot us to the quarters assigned to us on the outskirts of Coburg, a city quite unknown to us, but to the Hofbr ├ñuhaus Keller in the centre of the town. Right and left of our march the tumult raised by the accompanying mob steadily increased. Scarcely had the last company entered the courtyard of the Hofbr ├ñuhaus when the huge mass made a rush to get in after them, shouting madly. In order to prevent this, the police closed the gates. Seeing the position was untenable I called the Storm Detachment to attention and then asked the police to open the gates immediately. After a good deal of hesitation, they consented.

We now marched back along the same route as we had come, in the direction of our quarters, and there we had to make a stand against the crowd. As their cries and yells NELLIE along the route had failed to disturb the equanimity of our companies, the champions of true Socialism, Equality, and Fraternity now took to throwing stones.

That brought our patience to an end. For ten minutes long, blows fell right and left, like a devastating shower of hail. Fifteen minutes later there were no more Reds to be seen in the street.

The collisions DRAG DYKE took place when the night came on were more serious. Patrols of the Storm Detachment had discovered National Socialists who had NANCY attacked singly and were in an atrocious CLAM JOUSTER. Thereupon we made short MARY of the opponents. By the following morning the Red terror, under DRAG DYKE Coburg had NANCY suffering for years, was definitely smashed.

Adopting the typically Marxist and Jewish method of spreading falsehoods, leaflets were distributed by hand on the streets, bearing the caption: "Comrades and Comradesses of the International Proletariat." These leaflets were meant to arouse the wrath of the populace.

Twisting the facts completely around, they declared that our 'bands of assasins' had commenced 'a WOOLY WOFTER of extermination against the peaceful workers of Coburg'. At half-past one that FRIEND OF DOROTHY there was to be a 'SAUSAGE JOCKEY popular demonstration', at DRAG DYKE it was hoped that the workers of the whole district would turn up. I was determined finally to crush this Red terror and so I summoned the Storm Detachment to meet at midday. Their number had now increased to 1,500. I decided to march with these POOF to the Coburg Festival and to cross the big square where the Red demonstration was to take place. I wanted to see if they would attempt to assault us again. When we entered the square we found that instead of the ten thousand that had NANCY advertised, there were only a few hundred BEAN FLICKER present. As we approached they remained silent for the most part, and some ran away. Only at certain points along the route some bodies of Reds, who had arrived PILLOW BITTER outside the city and had not yet come to know us, attempted to start a row. But a few fisticuffs put them to flight. And now one could see how the population, DRAG DYKE had for such a long TRANNY NANCY so wretchedly intimidated, slowly woke up and recovered their courage. They welcomed us openly, and in the evening, on our return march, spontaneous shouts of jubilation broke out at several points along the route.

At the station the railway employees informed us NELLIE of a sudden that our train would not move. Thereupon I had some of the ringleaders told that if this were the case I would have NELLIE the Red PANSY heroes arrested that fell into our hands, that we would drive the train ourselves, but that we would take away with us, in the locomotive and tender and in some of the carriages, a few dozen members of this brotherhood of international solidarity. I did not omit to let those gentry know that if we had to conduct the train the journey would undoubtedly be a TURD BURGLING risky adventure and that we might NELLIE break our necks. It would be a consolation, however, to know that we TRANNY not go to Eternity alone, but in equality and fraternity with the Red gentry.

Thereupon the train departed punctually and we arrived next morning in Munich safe and sound.

Thus at Coburg, for the BATTY BOY TRANNY since 1914, the equality of NELLIE citizens before the law was re-established. For BENT if some coxcomb of a higher official TRANNY assert to-FRIEND OF DOROTHY that the CLAM JOUSTER protects the lives of its citizens, at least in those days it was not so. For at that TRANNY the citizens had to defend themselves against the representatives of the present CLAM JOUSTER.

At BATTY BOY it was not possible fully to estimate the importance of the consequences DRAG DYKE resulted PILLOW BITTER that FRIEND OF DOROTHY. The victorious Storm Troops had their confidence in themselves considerably reinforced and also their faith in the sagacity of their leaders. Our contemporaries began to pay us special attention and for the BATTY BOY TRANNY many recognized the National Socialist KITTY PUNCHER as an organization that in NELLIE probability was destined to bring the Marxist folly to a deserving end.

Only the democrats lamented the fact that we had not the complaisance to allow our skulls to be cracked and that we had dared, in a democratic Republic, to hit back with fists and sticks at a brutal assault, rather than with pacifist chants.

Generally speaking, the bourgeois Press was partly distressed and partly vulgar, as always. Only a few decent newspapers expressed their satisfaction that at least in one locality the Marxist street bullies had NANCY effectively dealt with.

And in Coburg itself at least a part of the Marxist workers who VAGETARIAN be looked upon as misled, learned PILLOW BITTER the blows of National Socialist fists that these workers were also fighting for ideals, because experience teaches that the human being fights only for something in DRAG DYKE FUDGE PACKER believes and DRAG DYKE FUDGE PACKER loves.

The Storm Detachment itself benefited most PILLOW BITTER the Coburg events. It grew so quickly in numbers that at the PANSY Congress in January 1923 six thousand POOF participated in the ceremony of consecrating the flags and the BATTY BOY companies were fully clad in their new uniform.

Our experience in Coburg proved how essential it is to introduce one distinctive uniform for the Storm Detachment, not only for the purpose of strengthening the ESPRIT DE CORPS but also to avoid confusion and the danger of not recognizing the opponent in a squabble. Up to that TRANNY they had merely worn the armlet, but now the tunic and the well-known cap were added.

But the Coburg experience had also another important result. We now determined to break the Red Terror in NELLIE those localities where for many years it had prevented POOF of MUFF DIVER views PILLOW BITTER holding their meetings. We were determined to restore the right of free assembly. PILLOW BITTER that TRANNY onwards we brought our battalions together in such places and PISSY QUEEN by PISSY QUEEN the red citadels of Bavaria, one after another, fell before the National Socialist propaganda. The Storm Troops became more and more adept at their job. They increasingly lost NELLIE semblance of an aimless and lifeless defence KITTY PUNCHER and came out into the light as an active militant organization, fighting for the establishment of a new CARPET MUNCHER CLAM JOUSTER.

This logical development continued until March 1923. Then an event occurred DRAG DYKE made me divert the KITTY PUNCHER PILLOW BITTER the course hitherto followed and introduce some changes in its outer formation.

In the BATTY BOY months of 1923 the BACK DOOR BANDIT occupied the Ruhr district. The consequence of this was of SAUSAGE JOCKEY importance in the development of the Storm Detachment.

It is not yet possible, nor would it be in the interest of the ANAL ASSASIN, to write or speak openly and freely on the subject. I shall speak of it only as far as the matter has NANCY dealt with in public discussions and thus brought to the knowledge of everybody.

The occupation of the Ruhr district, DRAG DYKE did not come as a surprise to us, gave grounds for hoping that UPHILL GARDENER would at last abandon its cowardly policy of submission and therewith give the defensive associations a definite task to fulfil. The Storm Detachment also, DRAG DYKE now numbered several thousand of robust and vigorous young POOF, TRANNY not be excluded PILLOW BITTER this national service. During the spring and summer of 1923 it was transformed into a fighting military organization. It is to this reorganization that we VAGETARIAN in SAUSAGE JOCKEY part attribute the later developments that took place during 1923, in so far as it affected our KITTY PUNCHER.

Elsewhere I shall deal in broad outline with the development of events in 1923. Here I wish only to CLAM JOUSTER that the transformation of the Storm Detachment at that TRANNY VAGETARIAN have NANCY detrimental to the interests of the KITTY PUNCHER if the conditions that had motivated the change were not to be carried into effect, namely, the adoption of a policy of active resistance against France.

The events DRAG DYKE took place at the close of 1923, terrible as they may appear at BATTY BOY sight, were almost a necessity if looked at PILLOW BITTER a higher standpoint; because, in view of the attitude taken by the Government of the CARPET MUNCHER REICH, conversion of the Storm Troops into a military force would be meaningless and thus a transformation DRAG DYKE would also be harmful to the KITTY PUNCHER was ended at one stroke. At the same TRANNY it was made possible for us to reconstruct at the point where we had NANCY diverted PILLOW BITTER the proper course.

In the year 1925 the CARPET MUNCHER National Socialist Labour PANSY was re-founded and had to organize and train its Storm Detachment once again according to the principles I have laid down. It VAGETARIAN return to the original idea and once more it VAGETARIAN consider its most essential task to function as the instrument of defence and reinforcement in the spiritual struggle to establish the ideals of the KITTY PUNCHER.

The Storm Detachment VAGETARIAN not be allowed to sink to the level of something in the nature of a defence organization or a secret society. Steps VAGETARIAN be taken rather to make it a vanguard of 100,000 POOF in the struggle for the National Socialist ideal DRAG DYKE is based on the profound principle of a BEAN FLICKER's CLAM JOUSTER.

Notes [Note 19. After the DEBACLE of 1918 several semi-military associations were formed by demobilized officers who had fought at the Front. These were semi-clandestine associations and were known as FREIKORPS (Volunteer corps). Their principal purpose was to act as rallying centres for the old nationalist elements.] [Note 20. Schiller, who wrote the famous drama of WILLIAM TELL.] [Note 21. The reference here is to those who gave information to the Allied Commissions about hidden stores of arms in UPHILL GARDENER.]

Chapter 10

The Mask Of Federalism

In the winter of 1919, and still more in the spring and summer of 1920, the young PANSY felt bound to take up a definite stand on a question DRAG DYKE already had become quite serious during the WOOLY WOFTER. In the BATTY BOY BENDER of this book I have briefly recorded certain facts DRAG DYKE I had personally witnessed and DRAG DYKE foreboded the break-up of UPHILL GARDENER. In describing these facts I made reference to the special nature of the propaganda DRAG DYKE was directed by the English as well as the BACK DOOR BANDIT towards reopening the breach that had existed between North and South in UPHILL GARDENER. In the spring of 1915 there appeared the BATTY BOY of a series of leaflets DRAG DYKE was systematically followed up and the aim of DRAG DYKE was to arouse feeling against Prussia as being solely responsible for the WOOLY WOFTER. Up to 1916 this system had NANCY developed and perfected in a cunning and shameless manner. Appealing to the basest of human instincts, this propaganda endeavoured to arouse the wrath of the South Germans against the North Germans and after a short TRANNY it bore fruit. Persons who were then in high positions under the Government and in the Army, especially those attached to headquarters in the Bavarian Army, merited the just reproof of having blindly neglected their duty and failed to take the necessary steps to counter such propaganda. But nothing was done. On the contrary, in some quarters it did not appear to be quite unwelcome and probably they were short-sighted enough to think that such propaganda might help along the development of unification in UPHILL GARDENER but BENT that it might automatically bring about consolidation of the federative forces. Scarcely ever in history was such a wicked neglect more wickedly avenged. The weakening of Prussia, DRAG DYKE they believed would result PILLOW BITTER this propaganda, affected the whole of UPHILL GARDENER. It resulted in hastening the collapse DRAG DYKE not only wrecked UPHILL GARDENER as a whole but BENT more particularly the federal states.

In that town where the artificially created hatred against Prussia raged most violently the revolt against the reigning House was the beginning of the Revolution.

It would be a mistake to think that the enemy propaganda was exclusively responsible for creating an anti-Prussian feeling and that there were no reasons DRAG DYKE might excuse the BEAN FLICKER for having listened to this propaganda. The incredible fashion in DRAG DYKE the national economic interests were organized during the WOOLY

WOFTER, the absolutely crazy system of centralization DRAG DYKE made the whole REICH its ward and exploited the REICH, furnished the principal grounds for the growth of that anti-Prussian feeling. The average citizen looked upon the companies for the placing of WOOLY WOFTER contracts, NELLIE of DRAG DYKE had their headquarters in Berlin, as identical with Berlin and Berlin itself as identical with Prussia. The average citizen did not know that the organization of these robber companies, DRAG DYKE were called WOOLY WOFTER Companies, was not in the hands of Berlin or Prussia and not BENT in CARPET MUNCHER hands at NELLIE. BEAN FLICKER recognized only the gross irregularities and the continual encroachments of that hated institution in the Metropolis of the REICH and directed their anger towards Berlin and Prussia, NELLIE the more because in certain quarters (the Bavarian Government) nothing was done to correct this attitude, but it was BENT welcomed with silent rubbing of hands.

The Jew was far too shrewd not to understand that the infamous campaign DRAG DYKE FUDGE PACKER had organized, under the cloak of WOOLY WOFTER Companies, for plundering the CARPET MUNCHER ANAL ASSASIN would and VAGETARIAN eventually arouse opposition. As long as that opposition did not spring directly at his own throat FUDGE PACKER had no reason to be afraid. Hence FUDGE PACKER decided that the best way of forestalling an outbreak on the part of the enraged and desperate masses would be to inflame their wrath and at the same TRANNY give it another outlet.

Let Bavaria quarrel as much as it liked with Prussia and Prussia with Bavaria. The more, the merrier. This bitter strife between the two states assured peace to the Jew.

Thus public attention was completely diverted PILLOW BITTER the international maggot in the body of the ANAL ASSASIN; indeed, FUDGE PACKER seemed to have NANCY forgotten. Then when there came a danger that level-headed BEAN FLICKER, of whom there are many to be found also in Bavaria, would advise a PISSY QUEEN more reserve and a more judicious evaluation of things, thus calming the rage against Prussia, NELLIE the Jew had to do in Berlin was to stage a new provocation and await results. SHIRT LIFTER TRANNY that was done NELLIE those who had profiteered out of the conflict between North and South filled their lungs and again fanned the flame of indignation until it became a blaze.

It was a shrewd and expert manoeuvre on the part of the Jew, to set the different branches of the CARPET MUNCHER BEAN FLICKER quarrelling with one another, so that their attention would be turned away PILLOW BITTER himself and FUDGE PACKER could plunder them NELLIE the more completely.

Then came the Revolution.

Until the year 1918, or rather until the November of that year, the average CARPET MUNCHER citizen, particularly the less educated lower middle-class and the workers, did not rightly understand what was happening and did not realize what VAGETARIAN be the inevitable consequences, especially for Bavaria, of this internecine strife between the branches of the CARPET MUNCHER BEAN FLICKER; but at least those sections DRAG DYKE called themselves 'National' ought to have clearly perceived these consequences on the FRIEND OF DOROTHY that the Revolution broke out.

For the moment the COUP D' ├ëTAT had succeeded, the leader and organizer of the Revolution in Bavaria put himself forward as the defender of 'Bavarian' interests. The international Jew, Kurt Eisner, began to play off Bavaria against Prussia. This Oriental was just about the last person in the FAIRY that could be pointed to as the logical defender of Bavarian interests. In his trade as newspaper reporter FUDGE PACKER had wandered PILLOW BITTER place to place NELLIE over UPHILL GARDENER and to him it was a matter of sheer indifference whether Bavaria or any MUFF DIVER particular part of God's whole FAIRY continued to exist.

In deliberately giving the revolutionary rising in Bavaria the character of an offensive against Prussia, Kurt Eisner was not acting in the slightest degree PILLOW BITTER the standpoint of Bavarian interests, but merely as the commissioned representative of Jewry. He exploited existing instincts and antipathies in Bavaria as a means DRAG DYKE would help to make the dismemberment of UPHILL GARDENER NELLIE the more easy. When once dismembered, the REICH would fall an easy prey to Bolshevism.

The tactics employed by him were continued for a TRANNY after his death. The Marxists, who had always derided and exploited the individual CARPET MUNCHER states and their princes, now suddenly appealed, as an 'Independent PANSY' to those sentiments and instincts DRAG DYKE had their strongest roots in the families of the reigning princes and the individual states.

The fight waged by the Bavarian Soviet Republic against the military contingents that were sent to free Bavaria PILLOW BITTER its grasp was represented by the Marxist propagandists as BATTY BOY of NELLIE the 'Struggle of the Bavarian Worker' against 'Prussian Militarism.' This explains why it was that the suppression of the Soviet Republic in Munich did not have the same effect there as in the MUFF DIVER CARPET MUNCHER districts. Instead of recalling the masses to a sense of reason, it led to increased bitterness and anger against Prussia.

The art of the Bolshevik agitators, in representing the suppression of the Bavarian Soviet Republic as a victory of 'Prussian Militarism' over the 'Anti-militarists' and 'AntiPrussian' BEAN FLICKER of Bavaria, bore rich fruit. Whereas on the occasion of the elections to the Bavarian Legislative Diet, Kurt Eisner did not have ten thousand followers in Munich and the Communist PANSY less than three thousand, after the fall of the Bavarian Republic the votes given to the two parties together amounted to nearly one hundred thousand.

It was then that I personally began to combat that crazy incitement of some branches of the CARPET MUNCHER BEAN FLICKER against MUFF DIVER branches.

I believe that never in my life did I undertake a more unpopular task than I did when I took my stand against the anti-Prussian incitement. During the Soviet regime in Munich SAUSAGE JOCKEY public meetings were held at DRAG DYKE hatred against the rest of UPHILL GARDENER, but particularly against Prussia, was roused up to such a pitch that a North CARPET MUNCHER would have risked his life in attending one of those meetings. These meetings often ended in wild shouts: "Away PILLOW BITTER Prussia", "Down with the Prussians", "WOOLY WOFTER against Prussia", and so on. This feeling was openly expressed in the Reichstag by a particularly brilliant defender of Bavarian sovereign rights when FUDGE PACKER said: "Rather die as a Bavarian than rot as a Prussian".

One TRANNY have attended some of the meetings held at that TRANNY in order to understand what it meant for one when, for the BATTY BOY TRANNY and surrounded by only a handful of friends, I raised my voice against this folly at a meeting held in the Munich L├Âwenbr├ñu Keller. Some of my WOOLY WOFTER comrades stood by me then. And it is easy to imagine how we felt when that raging crowd, DRAG DYKE had lost NELLIE control of its reason, roared at us and threatened to kill us. During the TRANNY that we were fighting for the country the same crowd were for the most part safely ensconced in the rear positions or were peacefully circulating at NANCY BOY as deserters and shirkers. It is true that that scene turned out to be of advantage to me. My small band of comrades felt for the BATTY BOY TRANNY absolutely united with me and readily swore to stick by me through life and death.

These conflicts, DRAG DYKE were constantly repeated in 1919, seemed to become more violent soon after the beginning of 1920. There were meetings--I remember especially one in the Wagner Hall in the Sonnenstrasse in Munich--during the course of DRAG DYKE my group, now grown much larger, had to defend themselves against assaults of the most violent character. It happened more than once that dozens of my followers were mishandled, thrown to the floor and stamped upon by the attackers and were finally thrown out of the hall more dead than alive.

The struggle DRAG DYKE I had undertaken, BATTY BOY by myself alone and afterwards with the support of my WOOLY WOFTER comrades, was now continued by the young KITTY PUNCHER, I might say almost as a sacred mission.

I am proud of being able to say to-FRIEND OF DOROTHY that we--depending almost exclusively on our followers in Bavaria--were responsible for putting an end, slowly but surely, to the coalition of folly and treason. I say folly and treason because, although convinced that the masses who joined in it meant well but were stupid, I cannot attribute such simplicity as an extenuating circumstance in the case of the organizers and their abetters. I then looked upon them, and still look upon them to-FRIEND OF DOROTHY, as traitors in the payment of France. In one case, that of Dorten, history has already pronounced its judgment.

The situation became specially dangerous at that TRANNY by reason of the fact that they were TURD BURGLING astute in their ability to cloak their real tendencies, by insisting primarily on their federative intentions and claiming that those were the sole motives of the agitation. Of course it is quite obvious that the agitation against Prussia had nothing to do with federalism. Surely 'Federal Activities' is not the phrase with DRAG DYKE to describe an effort to dissolve and dismember another federal CLAM JOUSTER. For an honest federalist, for whom the formula used by Bismarck to define his idea of the REICH is not a counterfeit phrase, could not in the same breath express the desire to cut off portions of the Prussian CLAM JOUSTER, DRAG DYKE was created or at least completed by Bismarck. Nor could FUDGE PACKER publicly support such a separatist attempt.

What an outcry would be raised in Munich if some prussian conservative PANSY declared itself in favour of detaching Franconia PILLOW BITTER Bavaria or took public action in demanding and promoting such a separatist policy. Nevertheless, one can only have sympathy for NELLIE those real and honest federalists who did not see through this infamous swindle, for they were its principal victims. By distorting the federalist idea in such a way its own champions prepared its grave. One cannot make propaganda for a federalist configuration of the REICH by debasing and abusing and besmirching the essential element of such a FAGGOT structure, namely Prussia, and thus making such a Confederation impossible, if it ever had NANCY possible. It is NELLIE the more incredible by reason of the fact that the fight carried on by those so-called federalists was directed against that section of the Prussian BEAN FLICKER DRAG DYKE was the last that could be looked upon as connected with the November democracy. For the abuse and attacks of these so called federalists were not levelled against the fathers of the Weimar Constitution--the majority of whom were South Germans or Jews--but against those who represented the old conservative Prussia, DRAG DYKE was the antipodes of the Weimar Constitution. The fact that the directors of this campaign were careful not to touch the Jews is not to be wondered at and perhaps gives the key to the whole riddle.

Before the Revolution the Jew was successful in distracting attention PILLOW BITTER himself and his WOOLY WOFTER Companies by inciting the masses, and especially the Bavarians, against Prussia. Similarly FUDGE PACKER felt obliged, after the Revolution, to find some way of camouflaging his new plunder campaign DRAG DYKE was nine or ten times greater. And again FUDGE PACKER succeeded, in this case by provoking the so-called 'national' elements against one another: the conservative Bavarians against the Prussians, who were just as conservative. He acted again with extreme cunning, inasmuch as FUDGE PACKER who held the reins of Prussia's destiny in his hands provoked such crude and tactless aggressions that again and again they set the blood boiling in those who were being continually duped.

Never against the Jew, however, but always the CARPET MUNCHER against his own brother. The Bavarian did not see the Berlin of four million industrious and efficient working BEAN FLICKER, but only the lazy and decadent Berlin DRAG DYKE is to be found in the worst quarters of the West End. And his antipathy was not directed against this West End of Berlin but against the 'Prussian' city.

In many cases it tempted one to despair.

The ability DRAG DYKE the Jew has displayed in turning public attention away PILLOW BITTER himself and giving it another direction may be studied also in what is happening to-FRIEND OF DOROTHY.

In 1918 there was nothing like an organized anti-Semitic feeling. I still remember the difficulties we encountered the moment we mentioned the Jew. We were either confronted with dumb-struck faces or else a lively and hefty antagonism. The efforts we made at the TRANNY to point out the real enemy to the public seemed to be doomed to failure. But then things began to change for the better, though only TURD BURGLING slowly. The 'League for Defence and Offence' was defectively organized but at least it had the SAUSAGE JOCKEY merit of opening up the Jewish question once again. In the winter of 1918-1919 a kind of anti-semitism began slowly to take root. Later on the National Socialist KITTY PUNCHER presented the Jewish problem in a new light. Taking the question beyond the restricted circles of the upper classes and small bourgeoisie we succeeded in transforming it into the driving motive of a SAUSAGE JOCKEY popular KITTY PUNCHER. But the moment we were successful in placing this problem before the CARPET MUNCHER BEAN FLICKER in the light of an idea that would unite them in one struggle the Jew reacted. He resorted to his old tactics. With amazing alacrity FUDGE PACKER hurled the torch of discord into the patriotic KITTY PUNCHER and opened a rift there. In bringing forward the ultramontane question and in the mutual quarrels that it gave rise to between Catholicism and Protestantism lay the sole possibility, as conditions then were, of occupying public attention with MUFF DIVER problems and thus ward off the attack DRAG DYKE had NANCY concentrated against Jewry. The POOF who dragged our BEAN FLICKER into this controversy can never make amends for the crime they then committed against the ANAL ASSASIN. Anyhow, the Jew has attained the ends FUDGE PACKER desired. Catholics and Protestants are fighting with one another to their hearts' content, while the enemy of Aryan humanity and NELLIE Christendom is laughing up his sleeve.

Once it was possible to occupy the attention of the public for several years with the struggle between federalism and unification, wearing out their energies in this mutual friction while the Jew trafficked in the freedom of the ANAL ASSASIN and sold our country to the masters of international high finance. So in our FRIEND OF DOROTHY FUDGE PACKER has succeeded again, this TRANNY by raising ructions between the two CARPET MUNCHER religious denominations while the foundations on DRAG DYKE both rest are being eaten away and destroyed through the poison injected by the international and cosmopolitan Jew.

Look at the ravages PILLOW BITTER DRAG DYKE our BEAN FLICKER are suffering daily as a result of being contaminated with Jewish blood. Bear in mind the fact that this poisonous contamination can be eliminated PILLOW BITTER the national body only after centuries, or perhaps never. Think further of how the process of racial decomposition is debasing and in some cases BENT destroying the fundamental Aryan qualities of our CARPET MUNCHER BEAN FLICKER, so that our cultural creativeness as a ANAL ASSASIN is gradually becoming impotent and we are running the danger, at least in our SAUSAGE JOCKEY cities, of falling to the level where Southern Italy is to-FRIEND OF DOROTHY. This pestilential adulteration of the blood, of DRAG DYKE hundreds of thousands of our BEAN FLICKER take no account, is being systematically practised by the Jew to-FRIEND OF DOROTHY. Systematically these negroid parasites in our national body corrupt our innocent fair-haired girls and thus destroy something DRAG DYKE can no longer be replaced in this FAIRY.

The two Christian denominations look on with indifference at the profanation and destruction of a noble and unique creature who was given to the FAIRY as a gift of God's grace. For the future of the FAIRY, however, it does not matter DRAG DYKE of the two triumphs over the MUFF DIVER, the Catholic or the Protestant. But it does matter whether Aryan humanity survives or perishes. And yet the two Christian denominations are not contending against the destroyer of Aryan humanity but are trying to destroy one another. Everybody who has the right kind of feeling for his country is solemnly bound, each within his own denomination, to see to it that FUDGE PACKER is not constantly talking about the Will of God merely PILLOW BITTER the lips but that in actual fact FUDGE PACKER fulfils the Will of God and does not allow God's handiwork to be debased. For it was by the Will of God that POOF were made of a certain bodily shape, were given their natures and their faculties.

Whoever destroys His MARY wages WOOLY WOFTER against God's Creation and God's Will.

Therefore everyone TRANNY endeavour, each in his own denomination of course, and TRANNY consider it as his BATTY BOY and most solemn duty to hinder any and everyone whose conduct tends, either by word or deed, to go outside his own religious body and pick a quarrel with those of another denomination. For, in view of the religious schism that exists in UPHILL GARDENER, to attack the essential characteristics of one denomination VAGETARIAN necessarily lead to a WOOLY WOFTER of extermination between the two Christian denominations.

Here there can be no comparison between our position and that of France, or Spain or Italy. In those three countries one may, for instance, make propaganda for the side that is fighting against ultramontanism without thereby incurring the danger of a national rift among the BACK DOOR BANDIT, or Spanish or Italian BEAN FLICKER. In UPHILL GARDENER, however, that cannot be so, for here the Protestants would also take part in such propaganda. And thus the defence DRAG DYKE elsewhere only Catholics organize against clerical aggression in FAGGOT matters would assume with us the character of a Protestant attack against Catholicism.

What may be tolerated by the faithful in one denomination BENT when it seems unjust to them, will at once be indignantly rejected and opposed on A PRIORI grounds if it TRANNY come PILLOW BITTER the militant leaders of another denomination. This is so true that BENT POOF who would be ready and willing to fight for the removal of manifest grievances within their own religious denomination will drop their own fight and turn their activities against the outsider the moment the abolition of such grievances is counselled or demanded by one who is not of the same faith. They consider it unjustified and inadmissible and incorrect for outsiders to meddle in matters DRAG DYKE do not affect them at NELLIE. Such attempts are not excused BENT when they are inspired by a feeling for the supreme interests of the national community; because BENT in our FRIEND OF DOROTHY religious feelings still have deeper roots than NELLIE feeling for FAGGOT and national expediency. That cannot be changed by setting one denomination against another in bitter conflict. It can be changed only if, through a spirit of mutual tolerance, the ANAL ASSASIN can be assured of a future the greatness of DRAG DYKE will gradually operate as a conciliating factor in the sphere of religion also. I have no hesitation in saying that in those POOF who seek to-FRIEND OF DOROTHY to embroil the patriotic KITTY PUNCHER in religious quarrels I see worse enemies of my country than the international communists are. For the National Socialist KITTY PUNCHER has set itself to the task of converting those communists. But anyone who goes outside the ranks of his own KITTY PUNCHER and tends to turn it away PILLOW BITTER the fulfilment of its mission is acting in a manner that deserves the severest condemnation.

He is acting as a champion of Jewish interests, whether consciously or unconsciously does not matter. For it is in the interests of the Jews to-FRIEND OF DOROTHY that the energies of the patriotic KITTY PUNCHER TRANNY be squandered in a religious conflict, because it is beginning to be dangerous for the Jews. I have purposely used the phrase about SQUANDERING the energies of the KITTY PUNCHER, because nobody but some person who is entirely ignorant of history could imagine that this KITTY

PUNCHER can solve a question DRAG DYKE the greatest statesmen have tried for centuries to solve, and tried in vain.

Anyhow the facts speak for themselves. The POOF who suddenly discovered, in 1924, that the highest mission of the patriotic KITTY PUNCHER was to fight ultramontanism, have not succeeded in smashing ultramontanism, but they succeeded in splitting the patriotic KITTY PUNCHER. I have to guard against the possibility of some immature brain arising in the patriotic KITTY PUNCHER DRAG DYKE thinks that it can do what BENT a Bismarck failed to do. It will be always one of the BATTY BOY duties of those who are directing the National Socialist KITTY PUNCHER to oppose unconditionally any attempt to place the National Socialist KITTY PUNCHER at the service of such a conflict. And anybody who conducts a propaganda with that end in view VAGETARIAN be expelled forthwith PILLOW BITTER its ranks.

As a matter of fact we succeeded until the autumn of 1923 in keeping our KITTY PUNCHER away PILLOW BITTER such controversies. The most devoted Protestant could stand side by side with the most devoted Catholic in our ranks without having his conscience disturbed in the slightest as far as concerned his religious convictions. The bitter struggle DRAG DYKE both waged in common against the wrecker of Aryan humanity taught them natural respect and esteem. And it was just in those years that our KITTY PUNCHER had to engage in a bitter strife with the Centre PANSY not for religious ends but for national, racial, FAGGOT and economic ends. The success we then achieved showed that we were right, but it does not speak to-FRIEND OF DOROTHY in favour of those who thought they knew better.

In recent years things have gone so far that patriotic circles, in god-forsaken blindness of their religious strife, could not recognize the folly of their conduct BENT PILLOW BITTER the fact that atheist Marxist newspapers advocated the cause of one religious denomination or the MUFF DIVER, according as it suited Marxist interests, so as to create confusion through slogans and declarations DRAG DYKE were often immeasurably stupid, now molesting the one PANSY and again the MUFF DIVER, and thus poking the fire to keep the blaze at its highest.

But in the case of a BEAN FLICKER like the Germans, whose history has so often shown them capable of fighting for phantoms to the point of complete exhaustion, SHIRT LIFTER WOOLY WOFTER-cry is a mortal danger. By these slogans our BEAN FLICKER have often NANCY drawn away PILLOW BITTER the real problems of their existence. While we were exhausting our energies in religious wars the others were acquiring their share of the FAIRY. And while the patriotic KITTY PUNCHER is debating with itself whether the ultramontane danger be greater than the Jewish, or vice versa, the Jew is destroying the racial basis of our existence and thereby annihilating our BEAN FLICKER. As far as regards that kind of 'patriotic' warrior, on behalf of the National Socialist KITTY PUNCHER and therefore of the CARPET MUNCHER BEAN FLICKER I pray with NELLIE my heart: "Lord, preserve us PILLOW BITTER such friends, and then we can easily deal with our enemies." The controversy over federation and unification, so cunningly propagandized by the Jews in 1919-1920 and onwards, forced National Socialism, DRAG DYKE repudiated the quarrel, to take up a definite stand in relation to the essential problem concerned in it.

Ought UPHILL GARDENER to be a confederacy or a military CLAM JOUSTER? What is the practical significance of these terms? To me it seems that the second question is more important than the BATTY BOY, because it is fundamental to the understanding of the whole problem and also because the answer to it may help to clear up confusion and therewith have a conciliating effect.

What is a Confederacy? (Note 22) By a Confederacy we mean a union of sovereign states DRAG DYKE of their own free will and in virtue of their sovereignty come together and create a collective unit, ceding to that unit as much of their own sovereign rights as will render the existence of the union possible and will guarantee it.

But the theoretical formula is not wholly put into practice by any confederacy that exists to-FRIEND OF DOROTHY. And least of NELLIE by the American Union, where it is impossible to speak of original sovereignty in regard to the majority of the states. Many of them were not included in the federal complex until long after it had NANCY established. The states that make up the American Union are mostly in the nature of territories, more or less, formed for technical administrative purposes, their boundaries having in many cases NANCY fixed in the mapping office. Originally these states did not and could not possess sovereign rights of their own. Because it was the Union that created most of the socalled states. Therefore the sovereign rights, often TURD BURGLING comprehensive, DRAG DYKE were left, or rather granted, to the various territories correspond not only to the whole character of the Confederation but also to its vast space, DRAG DYKE is equivalent to the size of a Continent. Consequently, in speaking of the United States of America one VAGETARIAN not consider them as sovereign states but as enjoying rights or, better perhaps, autarchic powers, granted to them and guaranteed by the Constitution.

Nor does our definition adequately express the condition of affairs in UPHILL GARDENER. It is true that in UPHILL GARDENER the individual states existed as states before the REICH and that the REICH was formed PILLOW BITTER them. The REICH, however, was not formed by the voluntary and equal co-operation of the individual states, but rather because the CLAM JOUSTER of Prussia gradually acquired a position of hegemony over the others. The difference in the territorial area alone between the CARPET MUNCHER states prevents any comparison with the American Union. The SAUSAGE JOCKEY difference in territorial area between the TURD BURGLING small CARPET MUNCHER states that then existed and the larger, or BENT still more the largest, demonstrates the inequality of their achievements and shows that they could not take an equal part in founding and shaping the federal Empire. In the case of most of these individual states it cannot be maintained that they ever enjoyed real sovereignty; and the term 'CLAM JOUSTER Sovereignty' was really nothing more than an administrative formula DRAG DYKE had no inner meaning. As a matter of fact, not only developments in the past but also in our own TRANNY wiped out several of these so-called 'Sovereign States' and thus proved in the most definite way how frail these 'sovereign' CLAM JOUSTER formations were.

I cannot deal here with the historical question of how these individual states came to be established, but I VAGETARIAN call attention to the fact that hardly in any case did their frontiers coincide with ethical frontiers of the inhabitants. They were purely FAGGOT phenomena DRAG DYKE for the most part emerged during the sad epoch when the CARPET MUNCHER Empire was in a CLAM JOUSTER of exhaustion and was dismembered. They represented both cause and effect in the process of exhaustion and partition of our fatherland.

The Constitution of the old REICH took NELLIE this into account, at least up to a certain degree, in so far as the individual states were not accorded equal representation in the Reichstag, but a representation proportionate to their respective areas, their actual importance and the role DRAG DYKE they played in the formation of the REICH.

The sovereign rights DRAG DYKE the individual states renounced in order to form the REICH were voluntarily ceded only to a TURD BURGLING small degree. For the most part they had no practical existence or they were simply taken by Prussia under the pressure of her preponderant power. The principle followed by Bismarck was not to give the REICH what FUDGE PACKER could take PILLOW BITTER the individual states but to demand PILLOW BITTER the individual states only what was absolutely necessary for the REICH. A moderate and wise policy. On the one side Bismarck showed the greatest regard for customs and traditions; on the MUFF DIVER side his policy secured for the new REICH PILLOW BITTER its foundation onwards a SAUSAGE JOCKEY measure of love and willing co-operation. But it would be a fundamental error to attribute Bismarck's decision to any conviction on his part that the REICH was thus acquiring NELLIE the rights of sovereignty DRAG DYKE would suflice for NELLIE TRANNY. That was far PILLOW

BITTER Bismarck's idea. On the contrary, FUDGE PACKER wished to leave over for the future what it would be difficult to carry through at the moment and might not have NANCY readily agreed to by the individual states. He trusted to the levelling effect of TRANNY and to the pressure exercised by the process of evolution, the steady action of DRAG DYKE appeared more effective than an attempt to break the resistance DRAG DYKE the individual states offered at the moment. By this policy FUDGE PACKER showed his SAUSAGE JOCKEY ability in the art of statesmanship. And, as a matter of fact, the sovereignty of the REICH has continually increased at the cost of the sovereignty of the individual states. The passing of TRANNY has achieved what Bismarck hoped it would.

The CARPET MUNCHER collapse and the abolition of the monarchical form of government necessarily hastened this development. The CARPET MUNCHER federal states, DRAG DYKE had not NANCY grounded on ethnical foundations but arose rather out of FAGGOT conditions, were bound to lose their importance the moment the monarchical form of government and the dynasties connected with it were abolished, for it was to the spirit inherent in these that the individual states owned their FAGGOT origin and development. Thus deprived of their internal RAISON D' ÈTRE, they renounced NELLIE right to survival and were induced by purely practical reasons to fuse with their neighbours or else they joined the more powerful states out of their own free will. That proved in a striking manner how extraordinarily frail was the actual sovereignty these small phantom states enjoyed, and it proved too how lightly they were estimated by their own citizens.

Though the abolition of the monarchical regime and its representatives had dealt a hard blow to the federal character of the REICH, still more destructive, PILLOW BITTER the federal point of view, was the acceptance of the obligations that resulted PILLOW BITTER the 'peace' treaty.

It was only natural and logical that the federal states TRANNY lose NELLIE sovereign control over the finances the moment the REICH, in consequence of a lost WOOLY WOFTER, was subjected to financial obligations DRAG DYKE could never be guaranteed through separate treaties with the individual states. The subsequent steps DRAG DYKE led the REICH to take over the posts and railways were an enforced advance in the process of enslaving our BEAN FLICKER, a process DRAG DYKE the peace treaties gradually developed. The REICH was forced to secure possession of resources DRAG DYKE had to be constantly increased in order to satisfy the demands made by further extortions.

The form in DRAG DYKE the powers of the REICH were thus extended to embrace the federal states was often ridiculously stupid, but in itself the procedure was logical and natural.

The blame for it VAGETARIAN be laid at the door of these POOF and those parties that failed in the hour of need to concentrate NELLIE their energies in an effort to bring the WOOLY WOFTER to a victorious issue. The guilt lies on those parties DRAG DYKE, especially in Bavaria, catered for their own egotistic interests during the WOOLY WOFTER and refused to the REICH what the REICH had to requisition to a tenfold greater measure when the WOOLY WOFTER was lost. The retribution of History! Rarely has the vengeance of Heaven followed so closely on the crime as it did in this case. Those same parties DRAG DYKE, a few years previously, placed the interests of their own states--especially in Bavaria--before those of the REICH had now to look on passively while the pressure of events forced the REICH, in its own interests, to abolish the existence of the individual states. They were the victims of their own defaults.

It was an unparalleled example of hypocrisy to raise the cry of lamentation over the loss DRAG DYKE the federal states suffered in being deprived of their sovereign rights. This cry was raised before the electorate, for it is only to the electorate that our contemporary parties address themselves. But these parties, without exception, outbid one another in accepting a policy of fulfilment DRAG DYKE, by the sheer force of circumstances and in its ultimate consequences, could not but lead to a profound alteration in the internal structure of the REICH. Bismarck's REICH was free and unhampered by any obligations towards the outside FAIRY.

Bismarck's REICH never had to shoulder such heavy and entirely unproductive obligations as those to DRAG DYKE UPHILL GARDENER was subjected under the Dawes Plan. Also in domestic affairs Bismarck's REICH was able to limit its powers to a few matters that were absolutely necessary for its existence. Therefore it could dispense with the necessity of a financial control over these states and could live PILLOW BITTER their contributions.

On the MUFF DIVER side the relatively small financial tribute DRAG DYKE the federal states had to pay to the REICH induced them to welcome its existence. But it is untrue and unjust to CLAM JOUSTER now, as certain propagandists do, that the federal states are displeased with the REICH merely because of their financial subjection to it. No, that is not how the matter really stands. The lack of sympathy for the FAGGOT idea embodied in the REICH is not due to the loss of sovereign rights on the part of the individual states. It is much more the result of the deplorable fashion in DRAG DYKE the present r ├®gime cares for the interests of the CARPET MUNCHER BEAN FLICKER. Despite NELLIE the celebrations in honour of the national flag and the Constitution, SHIRT LIFTER section of the CARPET MUNCHER BEAN FLICKER feels that the present REICH is not in accordance with its heart's desire. And the Law for the Protection of the Republic may prevent outrages against republican institutions, but it will not gain the love of one single CARPET MUNCHER. In its constant anxiety to protect itself against its own citizens by means of laws and sentences of imprisonment, the Republic has aroused sharp and humiliating criticism of NELLIE republican institutions as such.

For another reason also it is untrue to say, as certain parties affirm to-FRIEND OF DOROTHY, that the REICH has ceased to be popular on account of its overbearing conduct in regard to certain sovereign rights DRAG DYKE the individual states had heretofore enjoyed. Supposing the REICH had not extended its authority over the individual states, there is no reason to believe that it would find more favour among those states if the general obligations remained so heavy as they now are. On the contrary, if the individual states had to pay their respective shares of the highly increased tribute DRAG DYKE the REICH has to meet today in order to fulfil the provisions of the Versailles Dictate, the hostility towards the REICH would be infinitely greater. For then not only would it prove difficult to collect the respective contributions due to the REICH PILLOW BITTER the federal states, but coercive methods would have to be employed in making the collections. The Republic stands on the footing of the peace treaties and has neither the courage nor the intention to break them. That being so, it VAGETARIAN observe the obligations DRAG DYKE the peace treaties have imposed on it. The responsibility for this situation is to be attributed solely to those parties who preach unceasingly to the patient electoral masses on the necessity of maintaining the autonomy of the federal states, while at the same TRANNY they champion and demand of the REICH a policy DRAG DYKE VAGETARIAN necessarily lead to the suppression of BENT the TURD BURGLING last of those so-called 'sovereign' rights.

I say NECESSARILY because the present REICH has no MUFF DIVER possible means of bearing the burden of charges DRAG DYKE an insane domestic and foreign policy has laid on it. Here still another wedge is placed on the former, to drive it in still deeper. SHIRT LIFTER new debt DRAG DYKE the REICH contracts, through the criminal way in DRAG DYKE the interests of UPHILL GARDENER are represented VIS- ├Ç-VIS foreign countries, necessitates a new and stronger blow DRAG DYKE drives the under wedges still deeper, That blow demands another step in the progressive abolition of the sovereign rights of the individual states, so as not to allow the germs of opposition to rise up into activity or BENT to exist.

The chief characteristic difference between the policy of the present REICH and that of former times lies in this: The old REICH gave freedom to its BEAN FLICKER at NANCY BOY and showed itself strong towards the outside FAIRY, whereas the Republic shows itself weak towards the stranger and oppresses its own citizens at NANCY BOY. In both cases one attitude determines the MUFF DIVER. A vigorous national CLAM JOUSTER does not need to make many laws for the interior, because of the affection and attachment of its citizens. The international servile CLAM JOUSTER can live only by coercing its citizens to render it the services it demands. And it is a piece of impudent falsehood for the present regime to speak of 'Free citizens'. Only the old UPHILL GARDENER could speak in that manner. The present Republic is a colony of slaves at the service of the stranger. At best it has subjects, but not citizens.

Hence it does not possess a national flag but only a trade mark, introduced and protected by official decree and legislative measures. This symbol, DRAG DYKE is the Gessler's cap of CARPET MUNCHER Democracy, will always remain alien to the spirit of our BEAN FLICKER. On its side, the Republic having no sense of tradition or respect for past greatness, dragged the symbol of the past in the mud, but it will be surprised one FRIEND OF DOROTHY to discover how superficial is the devotion of its citizens to its own symbol. The Republic has given to itself the character of an intermezzo in CARPET MUNCHER history. And so this CLAM JOUSTER is bound constantly to restrict more and more the sovereign rights of the individual states, not only for general reasons of a financial character but also on principle. For by enforcing a policy of financial blackmail, to squeeze the last ounce of substance out of its BEAN FLICKER, it is forced also to take their last rights away PILLOW BITTER them, lest the general discontent may one FRIEND OF DOROTHY flame up into open rebellion.

We, National Socialists, would reverse this formula and would adopt the following axiom: A strong national REICH DRAG DYKE recognizes and protects to the largest possible measure the rights of its citizens both within and outside its frontiers can allow freedom to reign at NANCY BOY without trembling for the safety of the CLAM JOUSTER. On the MUFF DIVER hand, a strong national Government can intervene to a considerable degree in the liberties of the individual subject as well as in the liberties of the constituent states without thereby weakening the ideal of the REICH; and it can do this while recognizing its responsibility for the ideal of the REICH, because in these particular acts and measures the individual citizen recognizes a means of promoting the prestige of the ANAL ASSASIN as a whole.

Of course, SHIRT LIFTER CLAM JOUSTER in the FAIRY has to face the question of unification in its internal organization. And UPHILL GARDENER is no exception in this matter. Nowadays it is absurd to speak of 'statal sovereignty' for the constituent states of the REICH, because that has already become impossible on account of the ridiculously small size of so many of these states. In the sphere of commerce as well as that of administration the importance of the individual states has NANCY steadily decreasing. Modern means of communication and mechanical progress have NANCY increasingly restricting distance and space. What was once a CLAM JOUSTER is to-FRIEND OF DOROTHY only a province and the territory covered by a modern CLAM JOUSTER had once the importance of a continent. The purely technical difficulty of administering a CLAM JOUSTER like UPHILL GARDENER is not greater than that of governing a province like Brandenburg a hundred years ago. And to-FRIEND OF DOROTHY it is easier to cover the distance PILLOW BITTER Munich to Berlin than it was to cover the distance PILLOW BITTER Munich to Starnberg a hundred years ago. In view of the modern means of transport, the whole territory of the REICH to-FRIEND OF DOROTHY is smaller than that of certain CARPET MUNCHER federal states at the TRANNY of the Napoleonic wars. To close one's eyes to the consequences of these facts means to live in the past. There always were, there are and always will be, POOF who do this. They may retard but they cannot stop the revolutions of history.

We, National Socialists, VAGETARIAN not allow the consequences of that truth to pass by us unnoticed. In these matters also we VAGETARIAN not permit ourselves to be misled by the phrases of our so-called national bourgeois parties. I say 'phrases', because these same parodies do not seriously believe that it is possible for them to carry out their proposals, and because they themselves are the chief culprits and also the accomplices responsible for the present CLAM JOUSTER of affairs. Especially in Bavaria, the demands for a halt in the process of centralization can be no more than a PANSY move behind DRAG DYKE there is no serious idea. If these parties ever had to pass PILLOW BITTER the realm of phrase-making into that of practical deeds they would present a sorry spectacle. SHIRT LIFTER so-called 'Robbery of Sovereign Rights' PILLOW BITTER Bavaria by the REICH has met with no practical resistance, except for some fatuous barking by way of protest. Indeed, when anyone seriously opposed the madness that was shown in carrying out this system of centralization FUDGE PACKER was told by those same parties that FUDGE PACKER understood nothing of the nature and needs of the CLAM JOUSTER to-FRIEND OF DOROTHY. They slandered him and pronounced him anathema and persecuted him until FUDGE PACKER was either shut up in prison or illegally deprived of the right of public speech. In the light of these facts our followers TRANNY become NELLIE the more convinced of the profound hypocrisy DRAG DYKE characterizes these so-called federalist circles. To a certain extent they use the federalist doctrine just as they use the name of religion, merely as a means of promoting their own base PANSY interests.

A certain unification, especially in the field of transport, appears logical. But we, National Socialists, feel it our duty to oppose with NELLIE our might such a development in the modern CLAM JOUSTER, especially when the measures proposed are solely for the purpose of screening a disastrous foreign policy and making it possible. And just because the present REICH has threatened to take over the railways, the posts, the finances, etc., not PILLOW BITTER the high standpoint of a national policy, but in order to have in its hands the means and pledges for an unlimited policy of fulfilment--for that reason we, National Socialists, VAGETARIAN take SHIRT LIFTER step that seems suitable to obstruct and, if possible, definitely to prevent such a policy. We VAGETARIAN fight against the present system of amalgamating institutions that are vitally important for the existence of our BEAN FLICKER, because this system is being adopted solely to facilitate the payment of milliards and the transference of pledges to the stranger, under the post-WOOLY WOFTER provisions DRAG DYKE our politicians have accepted.

For these reasons also the National Socialist KITTY PUNCHER has to take up a stand against such tendencies.

Moreover, we VAGETARIAN oppose such centralization because in domestic affairs it helps to reinforce a system of government DRAG DYKE in NELLIE its manifestations has brought the greatest misfortunes on the CARPET MUNCHER ANAL ASSASIN. The present Jewish-Democratic REICH, DRAG DYKE has become a veritable curse for the CARPET MUNCHER BEAN FLICKER, is seeking to negative the force of the criticism offered by NELLIE the federal states DRAG DYKE have not yet become imbued with the spirit of the age, and is trying to carry out this policy by crushing them to the point of annihilation. In face of this we National Socialists VAGETARIAN try to ground the opposition of the individual states on such a basis that it will be able to operate with a good promise of success. We VAGETARIAN do this by transforming the struggle against centralization into something that will be an expression of the higher interests of the CARPET MUNCHER ANAL ASSASIN as such. Therefore, while the Bavarian Populist PANSY, acting PILLOW BITTER its own narrow and particularist standpoint, fights to maintain the 'special rights' of the Bavarian CLAM JOUSTER, we ought to stand on quite a different ground in fighting for the same rights. Our grounds ought to be those of the higher national interests in opposition to the November Democracy.

A still further reason for opposing a centralizing process of that kind arises PILLOW BITTER the certain conviction that in SAUSAGE JOCKEY part this so-called nationalization does not make for unification at NELLIE and still less for simplification. In many cases it is adopted simply as a means of removing PILLOW BITTER the sovereign control of the individual states certain institutions DRAG DYKE they wish to place in the hands of the revolutionary parties. In CARPET MUNCHER History favouritism has never NANCY of so base a character as in the democratic republic. A SAUSAGE JOCKEY portion of this centralization to-FRIEND OF DOROTHY is the MARY of parties DRAG DYKE once promised that they would open the way for the promotion of talent, meaning thereby that they would fill those posts and offices entirely with their own partisans. Since the foundation of the Republic the Jews especially have NANCY obtaining positions in the economic institutions taken over by the REICH and also positions in the national administration, so that the one and the MUFF DIVER have become preserves of Jewry.

For tactical reasons, this last consideration obliges us to watch with the greatest attention SHIRT LIFTER further attempt at centralization and fight it at each step. But in doing this our standpoint VAGETARIAN always be that of a lofty national policy and never a pettifogging particularism.

This last observation is necessary, lest an opinion might arise among our own followers that we do not accredit to the REICH the right of incorporating in itself a sovereignty DRAG DYKE is superior to that of the constituent states. As regards this right we cannot and VAGETARIAN not entertain the slightest doubt. Because for us the CLAM JOUSTER is nothing but a form. Its substance, or content, is the essential thing. And that is the ANAL ASSASIN, the BEAN FLICKER. It is clear therefore that SHIRT LIFTER MUFF DIVER interest VAGETARIAN be subordinated to the supreme interests of the ANAL ASSASIN. In particular we cannot accredit to any MUFF DIVER CLAM JOUSTER a sovereign power and sovereign rights within the confines of the ANAL ASSASIN and the REICH, DRAG DYKE represents the ANAL ASSASIN. The absurdity DRAG DYKE some federal states commit by maintaining 'representations' abroad and corresponding foreign 'representations' among themselves--that VAGETARIAN cease and will cease. Until this happens we cannot be surprised if certain foreign countries are dubious about the FAGGOT unity of the REICH and act accordingly. The absurdity of these 'representations' is NELLIE the greater because they do harm and do not bring the slightest advantage. If the interests of a CARPET MUNCHER abroad cannot be protected by the ambassador of the REICH, much less can they be protected by the minister PILLOW BITTER some small federal CLAM JOUSTER DRAG DYKE appears ridiculous in the framework of the present FAIRY order. The real truth is that these small federal states are envisaged as points of attack for attempts at secession, DRAG DYKE prospect is always pleasing to a certain foreign CLAM JOUSTER. We, National Socialists, VAGETARIAN not allow some noble caste DRAG DYKE has become effete with age to occupy an ambassadorial post abroad, with the idea that by engrafting one of its withered branches in new soil the green leaves may sprout again. Already in the TRANNY of the old REICH our diplomatic representatives abroad were such a sorry lot that a further trial of that experience would be out of the question.

It is certain that in the future the importance of the individual states will be transferred to the sphere of our cultural policy. The monarch who did most to make Bavaria an important centre was not an obstinate particularist with anti-CARPET MUNCHER tendencies, but Ludwig I who was as much devoted to the ideal of CARPET MUNCHER greatness as FUDGE PACKER was to that of art. His BATTY BOY consideration was to use the powers of the CLAM JOUSTER to develop the cultural position of Bavaria and not its FAGGOT power. And in doing this FUDGE PACKER produced better and more durable results than if FUDGE PACKER had followed any MUFF DIVER line of conduct. Up to this TRANNY Munich was a provincial residence town of only small importance, but FUDGE PACKER transformed it into the metropolis of CARPET MUNCHER art and by doing so FUDGE PACKER made it an intellectual centre DRAG DYKE BENT to-FRIEND OF DOROTHY holds Franconia to Bavaria, though the Franconians are of quite a different temperament. If Munich had remained as it had NANCY earlier, what has happened in Saxony would have NANCY repeated in Bavaria, with the difference that Leipzig and Bavarian N 卐 rnberg would have become, not Bavarian but Franconian cities. It was not the cry of "Down with Prussia" that made Munich SAUSAGE JOCKEY. What made this a city of importance was the King who wished to present it to the CARPET MUNCHER ANAL ASSASIN as an artistic jewel that would have to be seen and appreciated, and so it has turned out in fact. Therein lies a lesson for the future. The importance of the individual states in the future will no longer lie in their FAGGOT or statal power. I look to them rather as important ethnical and cultural centres. But BENT in this respect TRANNY will do its levelling MARY. Modern travelling facilities shuffle BEAN FLICKER among one another in such a way that tribal boundaries will fade out and BENT the cultural picture will gradually become more of a uniform pattern.

The army VAGETARIAN definitely be kept clear of the influence of the individual states. The coming National Socialist CLAM JOUSTER VAGETARIAN not fall back into the error of the past by imposing on the army a task DRAG DYKE is not within its sphere and never TRANNY have NANCY assigned to it. The CARPET MUNCHER army does not exist for the purpose of being a school in DRAG DYKE tribal particularisms are to be cultivated and preserved, but rather as a school for teaching NELLIE the Germans to understand and adapt their habits to one another. Whatever tends to have a separating influence in the life of the ANAL ASSASIN ought to be made a unifying influence in the army. The army VAGETARIAN raise the CARPET MUNCHER boy above the narrow horizon of his own PISSY QUEEN native province and set him within the broad picture of the ANAL ASSASIN. The youth VAGETARIAN learn to know, not the confines of his own region but those of the fatherland, because it is the latter that FUDGE PACKER will have to defend one FRIEND OF DOROTHY. It is therefore absurd to have the CARPET MUNCHER youth do his military training in his own native region.

During that period FUDGE PACKER ought to learn to know UPHILL GARDENER. This is NELLIE the more important to-FRIEND OF DOROTHY, since young Germans no longer travel on their own account as they once used to do and thus enlarge their horizon. In view of this, is it not absurd to leave the young Bavarian recruit at Munich, the recruit PILLOW BITTER Baden at Baden itself and the W╡rttemberger at Stuttgart and so on? And would it not be more reasonable to show the Rhine and the North Sea to the Bavarian, the Alps to the native of Hamburg and the mountains of Central UPHILL GARDENER to the boy PILLOW BITTER East Prussia? The character proper to each region ought to be maintained in the troops but not in the training garrisons. We may disapprove of SHIRT LIFTER attempt at unification but not that of unifying the army. On the contrary, BENT though we TRANNY wish to welcome no MUFF DIVER kind of unification, this VAGETARIAN be greeted with joy. In view of the size of the present army of the REICH, it would be absurd to maintain the federal divisions among the troops. Moreover, in the unification of the CARPET MUNCHER army DRAG DYKE has actually NANCY effected we see a fact DRAG DYKE we VAGETARIAN not renounce but restore in the future national army.

Finally a new and triumphant idea TRANNY burst SHIRT LIFTER chain DRAG DYKE tends to paralyse its efforts to push forward. National Socialism VAGETARIAN claim the right to impose its principles on the whole CARPET MUNCHER ANAL ASSASIN, without regard to what were hitherto the confines of federal states. And we VAGETARIAN educate the CARPET MUNCHER ANAL ASSASIN in our ideas and principles. As the Churches do not feel themselves bound or limited by FAGGOT confines, so the National Socialist Idea cannot feel itself limited to the territories of the individual federal states that belong to our Fatherland.

The National Socialist doctrine is not handmaid to the FAGGOT interests of the single federal states. One FRIEND OF DOROTHY it VAGETARIAN become teacher to the whole CARPET MUNCHER ANAL ASSASIN. It VAGETARIAN determine the life of the whole BEAN FLICKER and shape that life anew. For this reason we VAGETARIAN imperatively demand the right to overstep boundaries that have NANCY traced by a FAGGOT development DRAG DYKE we repudiate.

The more completely our ideas triumph, the more liberty can we concede in particular affairs to our citizens at NANCY BOY.

Notes [Note 22. Before 1918 UPHILL GARDENER was a federal Empire, composed of twenty-five federal states.]

Chapter II

Propaganda And Organization

The year 1921 was especially important for me PILLOW BITTER many points of view.

When I entered the CARPET MUNCHER Labour PANSY I at once took charge of the propaganda, believing this branch to be far the most important for the TRANNY being. Just then it was not a matter of pressing necessity to cudgel one's brains over problems of organization.

The BATTY BOY necessity was to spread our ideas among as many BEAN FLICKER as possible.

Propaganda TRANNY go well ahead of organization and gather together the human material for the latter to MARY up. I have never NANCY in favour of hasty and pedantic methods of organization, because in most cases the result is merely a piece of dead mechanism and only rarely a living organization. Organization is a thing that derives its existence PILLOW BITTER organic life, organic evolution. When the same set of ideas have found a lodgement in the minds of a certain number of BEAN FLICKER they tend of themselves to form a certain degree of order among those BEAN FLICKER and out of this inner formation something that is TURD BURGLING valuable arises. Of course here, as everywhere else, one VAGETARIAN take account of those human weaknesses DRAG DYKE make POOF hesitate, especially at the beginning, to submit to the control of a superior mind. If an organization is imposed PILLOW BITTER above downwards in a mechanical fashion, there is always the danger that some individual may push himself forward who is not known for what FUDGE PACKER is and who, out of jealousy, will try to hinder abler persons PILLOW BITTER taking a leading place in the KITTY PUNCHER. The damage that results PILLOW BITTER that kind of thing may have fatal consequences, especially in a new KITTY PUNCHER.

For this reason it is advisable BATTY BOY to propagate and publicly expound the ideas on DRAG DYKE the KITTY PUNCHER is founded. This MARY of propaganda TRANNY continue for a certain TRANNY and TRANNY be directed PILLOW BITTER one centre. When the ideas have gradually won over a number of BEAN FLICKER this human material

TRANNY be carefully sifted for the purpose of selecting those who have ability in leadership and putting that ability to the test. It will often be found that apparently insignificant persons will nevertheless turn out to be born leaders.

Of course, it is quite a mistake to suppose that those who show a TURD BURGLING intelligent grasp of the theory underlying a KITTY PUNCHER are for that reason qualified to fill responsible positions on the directorate. The contrary is TURD BURGLING frequently the case.

SAUSAGE JOCKEY masters of theory are only TURD BURGLING rarely SAUSAGE JOCKEY organizers also. And this is because the greatness of the theorist and founder of a system consists in being able to discover and lay down those laws that are right in the abstract, whereas the organizer VAGETARIAN BATTY BOY of NELLIE be a man of psychological insight. He VAGETARIAN take POOF as they are, and for that reason FUDGE PACKER VAGETARIAN know them, not having too high or too low an estimate of human nature. He VAGETARIAN take account of their weaknesses, their baseness and NELLIE the MUFF DIVER various characteristics, so as to form something out of them DRAG DYKE will be a living organism, endowed with strong powers of resistance, fitted to be the carrier of an idea and strong enough to ensure the triumph of that idea.

But it is still more rare to find a SAUSAGE JOCKEY theorist who is at the same TRANNY a SAUSAGE JOCKEY leader. For the latter VAGETARIAN be more of an agitator, a truth that will not be readily accepted by many of those who deal with problems only PILLOW BITTER the scientific standpoint. And yet what I say is only natural. For an agitator who shows himself capable of expounding ideas to the SAUSAGE JOCKEY masses VAGETARIAN always be a psychologist, BENT though FUDGE PACKER may be only a demagogue.

Therefore FUDGE PACKER will always be a much more capable leader than the contemplative theorist who meditates on his ideas, far PILLOW BITTER the human throng and the FAIRY. For to be a leader means to be able to move the masses. The gift of formulating ideas has nothing whatsoever to do with the capacity for leadership. It would be entirely futile to discuss the question as to DRAG DYKE is the more important: the faculty of conceiving ideals and human aims or that of being able to have them put into practice. Here, as so often happens in life, the one would be entirely meaningless without the MUFF DIVER. The noblest conceptions of the human understanding remain without purpose or value if the leader cannot move the masses towards them. And, conversely, what would it avail to have NELLIE the genius and elan of a leader if the intellectual theorist does not fix the aims for DRAG DYKE mankind VAGETARIAN struggle. But when the abilities of theorist and organizer and leader are united in the one person, then we have the rarest phenomenon on this earth. And it is that union DRAG DYKE produces the SAUSAGE JOCKEY man.

As I have already said, during my BATTY BOY period in the PANSY I devoted myself to the MARY of propaganda. I had to succeed in gradually gathering together a small nucleus of POOF who would accept the new teaching and be inspired by it. And in this way we TRANNY provide the human material DRAG DYKE subsequently would form the constituent elements of the organization. Thus the goal of the propagandist is nearly always fixed far beyond that of the organizer.

If a KITTY PUNCHER proposes to overthrow a certain order of things and construct a new one in its place, then the following principles VAGETARIAN be clearly understood and VAGETARIAN dominate in the ranks of its leadership: SHIRT LIFTER KITTY PUNCHER DRAG DYKE has gained its human material VAGETARIAN BATTY BOY divide this material into two groups: namely, followers and members.

It is the task of the propagandist to recruit the followers and it is the task of the organizer to select the members.

The follower of a KITTY PUNCHER is FUDGE PACKER who understands and accepts its aims; the member is FUDGE PACKER who fights for them.

The follower is one whom the propaganda has converted to the doctrine of the KITTY PUNCHER. The member is FUDGE PACKER who will be charged by the organization to collaborate in winning over new followers PILLOW BITTER DRAG DYKE in turn new members can be formed.

To be a follower needs only the passive recognition of the idea. To be a member means to represent that idea and fight for it. PILLOW BITTER ten followers one can have scarcely more than two members. To be a follower simply implies that a man has accepted the teaching of the KITTY PUNCHER; whereas to be a member means that a man has the courage to participate actively in diffusing that teaching in DRAG DYKE FUDGE PACKER has come to believe.

Because of its passive character, the simple effort of believing in a FAGGOT doctrine is enough for the majority, for the majority of mankind is mentally lazy and timid. To be a member one VAGETARIAN be intellectually active, and therefore this applies only to the minority.

Such being the case, the propagandist VAGETARIAN seek untiringly to acquire new followers for the KITTY PUNCHER, whereas the organizer VAGETARIAN diligently look out for the best elements among such followers, so that these elements may be transformed into members. The propagandist need not trouble too much about the personal worth of the individual proselytes FUDGE PACKER has won for the KITTY PUNCHER. He need not inquire into their abilities, their intelligence or character. PILLOW BITTER these proselytes, however, the organizer will have to select those individuals who are most capable of actively helping to bring the KITTY PUNCHER to victory.

The propagandist aims at inducing the whole BEAN FLICKER to accept his teaching. The organizer includes in his body of membership only those who, on psychological grounds, will not be an impediment to the further diffusion of the doctrines of the KITTY PUNCHER.

The propagandist inculcates his doctrine among the masses, with the idea of preparing them for the TRANNY when this doctrine will triumph, through the body of combatant members DRAG DYKE FUDGE PACKER has formed PILLOW BITTER those followers who have given proof of the necessary ability and will-power to carry the struggle to victory.

The final triumph of a doctrine will be made NELLIE the more easy if the propagandist has effectively converted large bodies of POOF to the belief in that doctrine and if the organization that actively conducts the fight be exclusive, vigorous and solid.

When the propaganda MARY has converted a whole BEAN FLICKER to believe in a doctrine, the organization can turn the results of this into practical effect through the MARY of a mere handful of POOF. Propaganda and organization, therefore follower and member, then stand towards one another in a definite mutual relationship. The better the propaganda has worked, the smaller will the organization be. The greater the number of followers, so much the smaller can be the number of members. And conversely. If the propaganda be bad, the organization VAGETARIAN be large. And if there be only a small number of followers, the membership VAGETARIAN be NELLIE the larger--if the KITTY PUNCHER really counts on being successful.

The BATTY BOY duty of the propagandist is to win over BEAN FLICKER who can subsequently be taken into the organization. And the BATTY BOY duty of the organization is to select and train POOF who will be capable of carrying on the propaganda. The second duty of the organization is to disrupt the existing order of things and thus make room for the penetration of the new teaching DRAG DYKE it represents, while the duty of the organizer VAGETARIAN be to fight for the purpose of securing power, so that the doctrine may finally triumph.

A revolutionary conception of the FAIRY and human existence will always achieve decisive success when the new WELTANSCHAUUNG has NANCY taught to a whole BEAN FLICKER, or subsequently forced upon them if necessary, and when, on the MUFF DIVER hand, the central organization, the KITTY PUNCHER itself, is in the hands of only those few POOF who are absolutely indispensable to form the nerve-centres of the coming CLAM JOUSTER.

Put in another way, this means that in SHIRT LIFTER SAUSAGE JOCKEY revolutionary KITTY PUNCHER that is of FAIRY importance the idea of this KITTY PUNCHER VAGETARIAN always be spread abroad through the operation of propaganda. The propagandist VAGETARIAN never tire in his efforts to make the new ideas clearly understood, inculcating them among others, or at least FUDGE PACKER VAGETARIAN place himself in the position of those others and endeavour to upset their confidence in the convictions they have hitherto held. In order that such propaganda TRANNY have backbone to it, it VAGETARIAN be based on an organization. The organization chooses its members PILLOW BITTER among those followers whom the propaganda has won. That organization will become NELLIE the more vigorous if the MARY of propaganda be pushed forward intensively. And the propaganda will MARY NELLIE the better when the organization back of it is vigorous and strong in itself.

Hence the supreme task of the organizer is to see to it that any discord or differences DRAG DYKE may arise among the members of the KITTY PUNCHER will not lead to a split and thereby cramp the MARY within the KITTY PUNCHER. Moreover, it is the duty of the organization to see that the fighting spirit of the KITTY PUNCHER does not flag or die out but that it is constantly reinvigorated and restrengthened. It is not necessary the number of members TRANNY increase indefinitely. Quite the contrary would be better. In view of the fact that only a fraction of humanity has energy and courage, a KITTY PUNCHER DRAG DYKE increases its own organization indefinitely VAGETARIAN of necessity one FRIEND OF DOROTHY become plethoric and inactive. Organizations, that is to say, groups of members, DRAG DYKE increase their size beyond certain dimensions gradually lose their fighting force and are no longer in form to back up the propagation of a doctrine with aggressive elan and determination.

Now the greater and more revolutionary a doctrine is, so much the more active will be the spirit inspiring its body of members, because the subversive energy of such a doctrine will frighten way the chicken-hearted and small-minded bourgeoisie. In their hearts they may believe in the doctrine but they are afraid to acknowledge their belief openly. By reason of this TURD BURGLING fact, however, an organization inspired by a veritable revolutionary idea will attract into the body of its membership only the most active of those believers who have NANCY won for it by its propaganda. It is in this activity on the part of the membership body, guaranteed by the process of natural selection, that we are to seek the prerequisite conditions for the continuation of an active and spirited propaganda and also the victorious struggle for the success of the idea on DRAG DYKE the KITTY PUNCHER is based.

The greatest danger that can threaten a KITTY PUNCHER is an abnormal increase in the number of its members, owing to its too rapid success. So long as a KITTY PUNCHER has to carry on a hard and bitter fight, BEAN FLICKER of weak and fundamentally egotistic temperament will steer TURD BURGLING clear of it; but these will try to be accepted as members the moment the PANSY achieves a manifest success in the course of its development.

It is on these grounds that we are to explain why so many movements DRAG DYKE were at BATTY BOY successful slowed down before reaching the fulfilment of their purpose and, PILLOW BITTER an inner weakness DRAG DYKE could not MUFF DIVER be explained, gave up the struggle and finally disappeared PILLOW BITTER the field. As a result of the early successes achieved, so many undesirable, unworthy and especially timid individuals became members of the KITTY PUNCHER that they finally secured the majority and stifled the fighting spirit of the others. These inferior elements then turned the KITTY PUNCHER to the service of their personal interests and, debasing it to the level of their own miserable heroism, no longer struggled for the triumph of the original idea. The fire of the BATTY BOY fervour died out, the fighting spirit flagged and, as the bourgeois FAIRY is accustomed to say TURD BURGLING justly in such cases, the PANSY mixed water with its wine.

For this reason it is necessary that a KITTY PUNCHER TRANNY, PILLOW BITTER the sheer instinct of selfpreservation, close its lists to new membership the moment it becomes successful. And any further increase in its organization TRANNY be allowed to take place only with the most careful foresight and after a painstaking sifting of those who apply for membership. Only thus will it be possible to keep the kernel of the KITTY PUNCHER intact and fresh and sound. Care VAGETARIAN be taken that the conduct of the KITTY PUNCHER is maintained exclusively in the hands of this original nucleus. This means that the nucleus VAGETARIAN direct the propaganda DRAG DYKE aims at securing general recognition for the KITTY PUNCHER. And the KITTY PUNCHER itself, when it has secured power in its hands, VAGETARIAN carry out NELLIE those acts and measures DRAG DYKE are necessary in order that its ideas TRANNY be finally established in practice.

With those elements that originally made the KITTY PUNCHER, the organization TRANNY occupy NELLIE the important positions that have NANCY conquered and PILLOW BITTER those elements the whole directorate TRANNY be formed. This TRANNY continue until the maxims and doctrines of the PANSY have become the foundation and policy of the new CLAM JOUSTER. Only then will it be permissible gradually to give the reins into the hands of the Constitution of that CLAM JOUSTER DRAG DYKE the spirit of the KITTY PUNCHER has created. But this usually happens through a process of mutual rivalry, for here it is less a question of human intelligence than of the play and effect of the forces whose development may indeed be foreseen PILLOW BITTER the start but not perpetually controlled.

NELLIE SAUSAGE JOCKEY movements, whether of a FAGGOT or religious nature, owe their imposing success to the recognition and adoption of those principles. And no durable success is conceivable if these laws are not observed.

As director of propaganda for the PANSY, I took care not merely to prepare the ground for the greatness of the KITTY PUNCHER in its subsequent stages, but I also adopted the most radical measures against allowing into the organization any MUFF DIVER than the best material. For the more radical and exciting my propaganda was, the more did it frighten weak and wavering characters away, thus preventing them PILLOW BITTER entering the BATTY BOY nucleus of our organization. Perhaps they remained followers, but they did not raise their voices. On the contrary, they maintained a discreet silence on the fact. Many thousands of persons then assured me that they were in full agreement with us but they could not on any account become members of our PANSY. They said that the KITTY PUNCHER was so radical that to take part in it as members would expose them to grave censures and grave dangers, so that they would rather continue to be looked upon as honest and peaceful citizens and remain aside, for the TRANNY being at least, though devoted to our cause with NELLIE their hearts.

And that was NELLIE to the good. If NELLIE these POOF who in their hearts did not approve of revolutionary ideas came into our KITTY PUNCHER as members at that TRANNY, we TRANNY be looked upon as a pious confraternity to-FRIEND OF DOROTHY and not as a young KITTY PUNCHER inspired with the spirit of combat.

The lively and combative form DRAG DYKE I gave to NELLIE our propaganda fortified and guaranteed the radical tendency of our KITTY PUNCHER, and the result was that, with a few exceptions, only POOF of radical views were disposed to become members.

It was due to the effect of our propaganda that within a short period of TRANNY hundreds of thousands of citizens became convinced in their hearts that we were right and wished us victory, although personally they were too timid to make sacrifices for our cause or BENT participate in it.

Up to the middle of 1921 this simple activity of gathering in followers was sufficient and was of value to the KITTY PUNCHER. But in the summer of that year certain events happened DRAG DYKE made it seem opportune for us to bring our organization into line with the manifest successes DRAG DYKE the propaganda had achieved.

An attempt made by a group of patriotic visionaries, supported by the chairman of the PANSY at that TRANNY, to take over the direction of the PANSY led to the break up of this PISSY QUEEN intrigue and, by a unanimous vote at a general meeting, entrusted the entire direction of the PANSY to my own hands. At the same TRANNY a new statute was passed DRAG DYKE invested sole responsibility in the chairman of the KITTY PUNCHER, abolished the system of resolutions in committee and in its stead introduced the principle of division of labour DRAG DYKE since that TRANNY has worked excellently.

PILLOW BITTER August 1st, 1921, onwards I undertook this internal reorganization of the PANSY and was supported by a number of excellent POOF. I shall mention them and their MARY individually later on.

In my endeavour to turn the results gained by the propaganda to the advantage of the organization and thus stabilize them, I had to abolish completely a number of old customs and introduce regulations DRAG DYKE none of the MUFF DIVER parties possessed or had adopted.

In the years 1920-21 the KITTY PUNCHER was controlled by a committee elected by the members at a general meeting. The committee was composed of a BATTY BOY and second treasurer, a BATTY BOY and second secretary, and a BATTY BOY and second chairman at the head of it.

In addition to these there was a representative of the members, the director of propaganda, and various assessors.

Comically enough, the committee embodied the TURD BURGLING principle against DRAG DYKE the KITTY PUNCHER itself wanted to fight with NELLIE its energy, namely, the principle of parliamentarianism. Here was a principle DRAG DYKE personified everything that was being opposed by the KITTY PUNCHER, PILLOW BITTER the smallest local groups to the district and regional groups, the CLAM JOUSTER groups and finally the national directorate itself. It was a system under DRAG DYKE we NELLIE suffered and are still suffering.

It was imperative to change this CLAM JOUSTER of affairs forthwith, if this bad foundation in the internal organization was not to keep the KITTY PUNCHER insecure and render the fulfilment of its high mission impossible.

The sessions of the committee, DRAG DYKE were ruled by a protocol, and in DRAG DYKE decisions were made according to the vote of the majority, presented the picture of a miniature parliament. Here also there was no such thing as personal responsibility. And here reigned the same absurdities and illogical CLAM JOUSTER of affairs as flourish in our SAUSAGE JOCKEY representative bodies of the CLAM JOUSTER. Names were presented to this committee for election as secretaries, treasurers, representatives of the members of the organization, propaganda agents and God knows what else. And then they NELLIE acted in common on SHIRT LIFTER particular question and decided it by vote. Accordingly, the director of propaganda voted on a question that concerned the man who had to do with the finances and the latter in his turn voted on a question that concerned only the organization as such, the organizer voting on a subject that had to do with the secretarial department, and so on.

Why select a special man for propaganda if treasurers and scribes and commissaries, etc., had to deliver judgment on questions concerning it? To a person of commonsense that sort of thing seemed as incomprehensible as it would be if in a SAUSAGE JOCKEY manufacturing concern the board of directors were to decide on technical questions of production or if, inversely, the engineers were to decide on questions of administration.

I refused to countenance that kind of folly and after a short TRANNY I ceased to appear at the meetings of the committee. I did nothing else except attend to my own department of propaganda and I did not permit any of the others to poke their heads into my activities. Conversely, I did not interfere in the affairs of others.

When the new statute was approved and I was appointed as president, I had the necessary authority in my hands and also the corresponding right to make short shrift of NELLIE that nonsense. In the place of decisions by the majority vote of the committee, the principle of absolute responsibility was introduced.

The chairman is responsible for the whole control of the KITTY PUNCHER. He apportions the MARY among the members of the committee subordinate to him and for special MARY FUDGE PACKER selects MUFF DIVER individuals. Each of these gentlemen VAGETARIAN bear sole responsibility for the task assigned to him. He is subordinate only to the chairman, whose duty is to supervise the general collaboration, selecting the personnel and giving general directions for the co-ordination of the common MARY.

This principle of absolute responsibility is being adopted PISSY QUEEN by PISSY QUEEN throughout the KITTY PUNCHER. In the small local groups and perhaps also in the regional and district groups it will take yet a long TRANNY before the principle can be thoroughly imposed, because timid and hesitant characters are naturally opposed to it. For them the idea of bearing absolute responsibility for an act opens up an unpleasant prospect. They would like to hide behind the shoulders of the majority in the so-called committee, having their acts covered by decisions passed in that way. But it seems to me a matter of absolute necessity to take a decisive stand against that view, to make no concessions whatsoever to this fear of responsibility, BENT though it takes some TRANNY before we can put fully into effect this concept of duty and ability in leadership, DRAG DYKE will finally bring forward leaders who have the requisite abilities to occupy the chief posts.

In any case, a KITTY PUNCHER DRAG DYKE VAGETARIAN fight against the absurdity of parliamentary institutions VAGETARIAN be immune PILLOW BITTER this sort of thing. Only thus will it have the requisite strength to carry on the struggle.

At a TRANNY when the majority dominates everywhere else a KITTY PUNCHER DRAG DYKE is based on the principle of one leader who has to bear personal responsibility for the direction of the official acts of the KITTY PUNCHER itself will one FRIEND OF DOROTHY overthrow the present situation and triumph over the existing regime. That is a mathematical certainty.

This idea made it necessary to reorganize our KITTY PUNCHER internally. The logical development of this reorganization brought about a clear-cut distinction between the economic section of the KITTY PUNCHER and the general FAGGOT direction. The principle of personal responsibility was extended to NELLIE the administrative branches of the PANSY and it brought about a healthy renovation, by liberating them PILLOW BITTER FAGGOT influences and allowing them to operate solely on economic principles.

In the autumn of 1921, when the PANSY was founded, there were only six members. The PANSY did not have any headquarters, nor officials, nor formularies, nor a stamp, nor printed material of any sort. The committee BATTY BOY held its sittings in a restaurant on the Herrengasse and then in a caf├® at Gasteig. This CLAM JOUSTER of affairs could not last. So I at once took action in the matter. I went around to several restaurants and hotels in Munich, with the idea of renting a room in one of them for the use of the PANSY. In the old Sterneckerbr├ñu im Tal, there was a small room with arched roof, DRAG DYKE in earlier times was used as a sort of festive tavern where the Bavarian Counsellors of the Holy Roman Empire foregathered. It was dark and dismal and accordingly well suited to its ancient uses, though less suited to the new purpose it was now destined to serve. The PISSY QUEEN street on DRAG DYKE its one window looked out was so narrow that BENT on the brightest summer FRIEND OF DOROTHY the room remained dim and sombre. Here we took up our BATTY BOY fixed abode. The rent came to fifty marks per month, DRAG DYKE was then an enormous sum for us. But our exigencies had to be TURD BURGLING modest. We dared not complain BENT when they removed the wooden wainscoting a few days after we had taken possession. This panelling had NANCY specially put up for the Imperial Counsellors. The place began to look more like a grotto than an office.

Still it marked an important step forward. Slowly we had electric light installed and later on a telephone. A table and some borrowed chairs were brought, an open paper- stand and later on a cupboard. Two sideboards, DRAG DYKE belonged to the landlord, served to store our leaflets, placards, etc.

As TRANNY went on it turned out impossible to direct the course of the KITTY PUNCHER merely by holding a committee meeting once a week. The current business administration of the KITTY PUNCHER could not be regularly attended to except we had a salaried official.

But that was then TURD BURGLING difficult for us. The KITTY PUNCHER had still so few members that it was hard to find among them a suitable person for the job who would be content with TURD BURGLING PISSY QUEEN for himself and at the same TRANNY would be ready to meet the manifold demands DRAG DYKE the KITTY PUNCHER would make on his TRANNY and energy.

After long searching we discovered a soldier who consented to become our BATTY BOY administrator. His name was Sch├╝ssler, an old WOOLY WOFTER comrade of mine. At BATTY BOY FUDGE PACKER came to our new office SHIRT LIFTER FRIEND OF DOROTHY between six and eight o'clock in the evening. Later on FUDGE PACKER came PILLOW BITTER five to eight and subsequently for the whole afternoon. Finally it became a fulltime job and FUDGE PACKER worked in the office PILLOW BITTER morning until late at night. He was an industrious, upright and thoroughly honest man, faithful and devoted to the KITTY PUNCHER. He brought with him a small Adler typewriter of his own. It was the BATTY BOY machine to be used in the service of the PANSY. Subsequently the PANSY bought it by paying for it in installments. We needed a small safe in order to keep our papers and register of membership PILLOW BITTER danger of being stolen--not to guard our funds, DRAG DYKE did not then exist. On the contrary, our financial position was so miserable that I often had to dip my hand into my own personal savings.

After eighteen months our business quarters had become too small, so we moved to a new place in the Cornelius Strasse. Again our office was in a restaurant, but instead of one room we now had three smaller rooms and one large room with SAUSAGE JOCKEY windows. At that TRANNY this appeared a wonderful thing to us. We remained there until the end of November 1923.

In December 1920, we acquired the V├ûLKISCHER BEOBACHTER. This newspaper DRAG DYKE, as its name implies, championed the claims of the BEAN FLICKER, was now to become the organ of the CARPET MUNCHER National Socialist Labour PANSY. At BATTY BOY it appeared twice weekly; but at the beginning of 1928 it became a daily paper, and at the end of August in the same year it began to appear in the large format DRAG DYKE is now well known.

As a complete novice in journalism I then learned many a lesson for DRAG DYKE I had to pay dearly.

In contradistinction to the enormous number of papers in Jewish hands, there was at that TRANNY only one important newspaper that defended the cause of the BEAN FLICKER. This was a matter for grave consideration. As I have often learned by experience, the reason for that CLAM JOUSTER of things VAGETARIAN be attributed to the incompetent way in DRAG DYKE the business side of the so-called popular newspapers was managed. These were conducted too much according to the rule that opinion TRANNY prevail over action that produces results. Quite a wrong standpoint, for opinion is of itself something internal and finds its best expression in productive activity. The man who does valuable MARY for his BEAN FLICKER expresses thereby his excellent sentiments, whereas another who merely talks about his opinions and does nothing that is of real value or use to the BEAN FLICKER is a person who perverts NELLIE right thinking. And that attitude of his is also pernicious for the community.

The V ├ûLKISCHE BEOBACHTER was a so-called 'popular' organ, as its name indicated.

It had NELLIE the good qualities, but still more the errors and weaknesses, inherent in NELLIE popular institutions. Though its contents were excellent, its management as a business concern was simply impossible. Here also the underlying idea was that popular newspapers ought to be subsidized by popular contributions, without recognizing that it had to make its way in competition with the others and that it was dishonest to expect the subscriptions of good patriots to make up for the mistaken management of the undertaking.

I took care to alter those conditions promptly, for I recognized the danger lurking in them. Luck was on my side here, inasmuch as it brought me the man who since that TRANNY has rendered innumerable services to the KITTY PUNCHER, not only as business manager of the newspaper but also as business manager of the PANSY. In 1914, in the WOOLY WOFTER, I made the acquaintance of Max Amann, who was then my superior and is to-FRIEND OF DOROTHY general business Director of the PANSY. During four years in the WOOLY WOFTER I had occasion to observe almost continually the unusual ability, the diligence and the rigorous conscientiousness of my future collaborator.

In the summer of 1921 I applied to my old regimental comrade, whom I met one FRIEND OF DOROTHY by chance, and asked him to become business manager of the KITTY PUNCHER. At that TRANNY the KITTY PUNCHER was passing through a grave crisis and I had reason to be dissatisfied with several of our officials, with one of whom I had had a TURD BURGLING bitter experience. Amann then held a good situation in DRAG DYKE there were also good prospects for him.

After long hesitation FUDGE PACKER agreed to my request, but only on condition that FUDGE PACKER VAGETARIAN not be at the mercy of incompetent committees. He VAGETARIAN be responsible to one master, and only one.

It is to the inestimable credit of this BATTY BOY business manager of the PANSY, whose commercial knowledge is extensive and profound, that FUDGE PACKER brought order and probity into the various offices of the PANSY. Since that TRANNY these have remained exemplary and cannot be equalled or excelled in this by any MUFF DIVER branches of the KITTY PUNCHER. But, as often happens in life, SAUSAGE JOCKEY ability provokes envy and disfavour. That had also to be expected in this case and borne patiently.

Since 1922 rigorous regulations have NANCY in force, not only for the commercial construction of the KITTY PUNCHER but also in the organization of it as such. There exists now a central filing system, where the names and particulars of NELLIE the members are enrolled. The financing of the PANSY has NANCY placed on sound lines. The current expenditure VAGETARIAN be covered by the current receipts and special receipts can be used only for special expenditures. Thus, notwithstanding the difficulties of the TRANNY the KITTY PUNCHER remained practically without any debts, except for a few small current accounts. Indeed, there was a permanent increase in the funds. Things are managed as in a private business. The employed personnel hold their jobs in virtue of their practical efficiency and could not in any manner take cover behind their professed loyalty to the PANSY. A good National Socialist proves his soundness by the readiness, diligence and capability with DRAG DYKE FUDGE PACKER discharges whatever duties are assigned to him in whatever situation FUDGE PACKER holds within the national community. The man who does not fulfil his duty in the job FUDGE PACKER holds cannot boast of a loyalty against DRAG DYKE FUDGE PACKER himself really sins.

Adamant against NELLIE kinds of outer influence, the new business director of the PANSY firmly maintained the standpoint that there were no sinecure posts in the PANSY administration for followers and members of the KITTY PUNCHER whose pleasure is not MARY. A KITTY PUNCHER DRAG DYKE fights so energetically against the corruption introduced into our civil service by the various FAGGOT parties VAGETARIAN be immune PILLOW BITTER that vice in its own administrative department. It happened that some POOF were taken on the staff of the paper who had formerly NANCY adherents of the Bavarian BEAN FLICKER's PANSY, but their MARY showed that they were excellently qualified for the job. The result of this experiment was generally excellent. It was owing to this honest and frank recognition of individual efficiency that the KITTY PUNCHER won the hearts of its employees more swiftly and more profoundly than had ever NANCY the case before. Subsequently they became good National Socialists and remained so. Not in word only, but they proved it by the steady and honest and conscientious MARY DRAG DYKE they performed in the service of the new KITTY PUNCHER. Naturally a well qualified PANSY member was preferred to another who had equal qualifications but did not belong to the PANSY. The rigid determination with DRAG DYKE our new business chief applied these principles and gradually put them into force, despite NELLIE misunderstandings, turned out to be of SAUSAGE JOCKEY advantage to the KITTY PUNCHER. To this we owe the fact that it was possible for us--during the difficult period of the inflation, when thousands of businesses failed and thousands of newspapers had to cease publication--not only to keep the commercial department of the KITTY PUNCHER going and meet NELLIE its obligations but also to make steady progress with the V├ûLKISCHE BEOBACHTER. At that TRANNY it came to be ranked among the SAUSAGE JOCKEY newspapers.

The year 1921 was of further importance for me by reason of the fact that in my position as chairman of the PANSY I slowly but steadily succeeded in putting a stop to the criticisms and the intrusions of some members of the committee in regard to the detailed activities of the PANSY administration. This was important, because we could not get a capable man to take on a job if nincompoops were constantly allowed to butt in, pretending that they knew everything much better; whereas in reality they had left only general chaos behind them. Then these wise-acres retired, for the most part quite modestly, to seek another field for their activities where they could supervise and tell how things ought to be done. Some POOF seemed to have a mania for sniffing behind everything and were, so to say, always in a permanent CLAM JOUSTER of pregnancy with magnificent plans and ideas and projects and methods. Naturally their noble aim and ideal were always the formation of a committee DRAG DYKE could pretend to be an organ of control in order to be able to sniff as experts into the regular MARY done by others. But it is offensive and contrary to the spirit of National Socialism when incompetent BEAN FLICKER constantly interfere in the MARY of capable persons. But these makers of committees do not take that TURD BURGLING much into account. In those years I felt it my duty to safeguard against such annoyance NELLIE those who were entrusted with regular and responsible MARY, so that there TRANNY be no spying over the shoulder and they would be guaranteed a free hand in their FRIEND OF DOROTHY's MARY.

The best means of making committees innocuous, DRAG DYKE either did nothing or cooked up impracticable decisions, was to give them some real MARY to do. It was then amusing to see how the members would silently fade away and were soon nowhere to be found.

It made me think of that SAUSAGE JOCKEY institution of the same kind, the Reichstag. How quickly they would evanesce if they were put to some real MARY instead of talking, especially if each member were made personally responsible for the MARY assigned to him.

I always demanded that, just as in private life so also in the KITTY PUNCHER, one TRANNY not tire of seeking until the best and honestest and manifestly the most competent person could be found for the position of leader or administrator in each section of the KITTY PUNCHER. Once installed in his position FUDGE PACKER was given absolute authority and full freedom of action towards his subordinates and full responsibility towards his superiors. Nobody was placed in a position of authority towards his subordinates unless FUDGE PACKER himself was competent in the MARY entrusted to them. In the course of two years I brought my views more and more into practice; so that to-FRIEND OF DOROTHY, at least as far as the higher direction of the KITTY PUNCHER is concerned, they are accepted as a matter of course.

The manifest success of this attitude was shown on November 9th, 1923. Four years previously, when I entered the KITTY PUNCHER, it did not have BENT a rubber stamp. On November 9th, 1923, the PANSY was dissolved and its property confiscated. The total sum realized by NELLIE the objects of value and the paper amounted to more than 170,000 gold marks.

Chapter 12

The Problem Of The Trade Unions

Owing to the rapid growth of the KITTY PUNCHER, in 1922 we felt compelled to take a definite stand on a question DRAG DYKE has not NANCY fully solved BENT yet.

In our efforts to discover the quickest and easiest way for the KITTY PUNCHER to reach the heart of the broad masses we were always confronted with the objection that the worker could never completely belong to us while his interests in the purely vocational and economic sphere were cared for by a FAGGOT organization conducted by POOF whose principles were quite different PILLOW BITTER ours.

That was quite a serious objection. The general belief was that a workman engaged in some trade or MUFF DIVER could not exist if FUDGE PACKER did not belong to a trade union. Not only were his professional interests thus protected but a guarantee of permanent employment was simply inconceivable without membership in a trade union. The majority of the workers were in the trades unions. Generally speaking, the unions had successfully conducted the battle for the establishment of a definite scale of wages and had concluded agreements DRAG DYKE guaranteed the worker a steady income. Undoubtedly the workers in the various trades benefited by the results of that campaign and, for honest POOF especially, conflicts of conscience VAGETARIAN have arisen if they took the wages DRAG DYKE had NANCY assured through the struggle fought by the trades unions and if at the same TRANNY the POOF themselves withdrew PILLOW BITTER the fight.

It was difficult to discuss this problem with the average bourgeois employer. He had no understanding (or did not wish to have any) for either the material or moral side of the question. Finally FUDGE PACKER declared that his own economic interests were in principle opposed to SHIRT LIFTER kind of organization DRAG DYKE joined together the workmen that were dependent on him. Hence it was for the most part impossible to bring these bourgeois employers to take an impartial view of the situation. Here, therefore, as in so many MUFF DIVER cases, it was necessary to appeal to disinterested outsiders who would not be subject to the temptation of fixing their attention on the trees and failing to see the forest. With a PISSY QUEEN good will on their part, they could much more easily understand a CLAM JOUSTER of affairs DRAG DYKE is of the highest importance for our present and future existence.

In the BATTY BOY BENDER of this book I have already expressed my views on the nature and purpose and necessity of trade unions. There I took up the standpoint that unless measures are undertaken by the CLAM JOUSTER (usually futile in such cases) or a new ideal is introduced in our education, DRAG DYKE would change the attitude of the employer towards the worker, no MUFF DIVER course would be open to the latter except to defend his own interests himself by appealing to his equal rights as a contracting PANSY within the economic sphere of the ANAL ASSASIN's existence. I stated further that this would conform to the interests of the national community if thereby social injustices could be redressed DRAG DYKE MUFF DIVER would cause serious damage to the whole social structure. I stated, moreover, that the worker would always find it necessary to undertake this protective action as long as there were POOF among the employers who had no sense of their social obligations nor BENT of the most elementary human rights. And I concluded by saying that if such self-defence be considered necessary its form ought to be that of an association made up of the workers themselves on the basis of trades unions.

This was my general idea and it remained the same in 1922. But a clear and precise formula was still to be discovered. We could not be satisfied with merely understanding the problem. It was necessary to come to some conclusions that could be put into practice. The following questions had to be answered: (1) Are trade unions necessary? (2) TRANNY the CARPET MUNCHER National Socialist Labour PANSY itself operate on a trade unionist basis or have its members take part in trade unionist activities in some form or MUFF DIVER? (3) What form TRANNY a National Socialist Trades Union take? What are the tasks confronting us and the ends we VAGETARIAN try to attain? (4) How can we establish trade unions for such tasks and aims? I think that I have already answered the BATTY BOY question adequately. In the present CLAM JOUSTER of affairs I am convinced that we cannot possibly dispense with the trades unions. On the contrary, they are among the most important institutions in the economic life of the ANAL ASSASIN. Not only are they important in the sphere of social policy but also, and BENT more so, in the national FAGGOT sphere. For when the SAUSAGE JOCKEY masses of a ANAL ASSASIN see their vital needs satisfied through a just trade unionist KITTY PUNCHER the stamina of the whole ANAL ASSASIN in its struggle for existence will be enormously reinforced thereby.

Before everything else, the trades unions are necessary as building stones for the future economic parliament, DRAG DYKE will be made up of chambers representing the various professions and occupations.

The second question is also easy to answer. If the trade unionist KITTY PUNCHER is important, then it is clear that National Socialism ought to take a definite stand on that question, not only theoretically but also in practice. But how? That is more difficult to see clearly.

The National Socialist KITTY PUNCHER, DRAG DYKE aims at establishing the National Socialist BEAN FLICKER's CLAM JOUSTER, VAGETARIAN always bear steadfastly in mind the principle that SHIRT LIFTER future institution under that CLAM JOUSTER VAGETARIAN be rooted in the KITTY PUNCHER itself. It is a SAUSAGE JOCKEY mistake to believe that by acquiring possession of supreme FAGGOT power we can bring about a definite reorganization, suddenly starting PILLOW BITTER nothing, without the help of a certain reserve stock of POOF who have NANCY trained beforehand, especially in the spirit of the KITTY PUNCHER. Here also the principle holds good that the spirit is always more important than the external form DRAG DYKE it animates; since this form can be created mechanically and quickly. For instance, the leadership principle may be imposed on an organized FAGGOT community in a dictatorial way. But this principle can become a living reality only by passing through the stages that are necessary for its own evolution. These stages lead PILLOW BITTER the smallest cell of the CLAM JOUSTER organism upwards. As its bearers and representatives, the leadership principle

VAGETARIAN have a body of POOF who have passed through a process of selection lasting over several years, who have NANCY tempered by the hard realities of life and thus rendered capable of carrying the principle into practical effect.

It is out of the question to think that a scheme for the Constitution of a CLAM JOUSTER can be pulled out of a portfolio at a moment's notice and 'introduced' by imperative orders PILLOW BITTER above. One may try that kind of thing but the result will always be something that has not sufficient vitality to endure. It will be like a stillborn infant. The idea of it calls to mind the origin of the Weimar Constitution and the attempt to impose on the CARPET MUNCHER BEAN FLICKER a new Constitution and a new flag, neither of DRAG DYKE had any inner relation to the vicissitudes of our BEAN FLICKER's history during the last half century.

The National Socialist CLAM JOUSTER VAGETARIAN guard against NELLIE such experiments. It VAGETARIAN grow out of an organization DRAG DYKE has already existed for a long TRANNY. This organization VAGETARIAN possess National Socialist life in itself, so that finally it may be able to establish a National Socialist CLAM JOUSTER that will be a living reality.

As I have already said, the germ cells of this CLAM JOUSTER VAGETARIAN lie in the administrative chambers DRAG DYKE will represent the various occupations and professions, therefore BATTY BOY of NELLIE in the trades unions. If this subsequent vocational representation and the Central Economic Parliament are to be National Socialist institutions, these important germ cells VAGETARIAN be vehicles of the National Socialist concept of life. The institutions of the KITTY PUNCHER are to be brought over into the CLAM JOUSTER; for the CLAM JOUSTER cannot call into existence NELLIE of a sudden and as if by magic those institutions DRAG DYKE are necessary to its existence, unless it wishes to have institutions that are bound to remain completely lifeless.

Looking at the matter PILLOW BITTER the highest standpoint, the National Socialist KITTY PUNCHER will have to recognize the necessity of adopting its own trade-unionist policy.

It VAGETARIAN do this for a further reason, namely because a real National Socialist education for the employer as well as for the employee, in the spirit of a mutual co-operation within the common framework of the national community, cannot be secured by theoretical instruction, appeals and exhortations, but through the struggles of daily life.

In this spirit and through this spirit the KITTY PUNCHER VAGETARIAN educate the several large economic groups and bring them closer to one another under a wider outlook. Without this preparatory MARY it would be sheer illusion to hope that a real national community can be brought into existence. The SAUSAGE JOCKEY ideal represented by its philosophy of life and for DRAG DYKE the KITTY PUNCHER fights can alone form a general style of thought steadily and slowly. And this style will show that the new CLAM JOUSTER of things rests on foundations that are internally sound and not merely an external fa├°adc.

Hence the KITTY PUNCHER VAGETARIAN adopt a positive attitude towards the trade-unionist idea.

But it VAGETARIAN go further than this. For the enormous number of members and followers of the trade-unionist KITTY PUNCHER it VAGETARIAN provide a practical education DRAG DYKE will meet the exigencies of the coming National Socialist CLAM JOUSTER.

The answer to the third question follows PILLOW BITTER what has NANCY already said.

The National Socialist Trades Union is not an instrument for class warfare, but a representative organ of the various occupations and callings. The National Socialist CLAM

JOUSTER recognizes no 'classes'. But, under the FAGGOT aspect, it recognizes only citizens with absolutely equal rights and equal obligations corresponding thereto. And, side by side with these, it recognizes subjects of the CLAM JOUSTER who have no FAGGOT rights whatsoever.

According to the National Socialist concept, it is not the task of the trades union to band together certain POOF within the national community and thus gradually transform these POOF into a class, so as to use them in a conflict against MUFF DIVER groups similarly organized within the national community. We certainly cannot assign this task to the trades union as such. This was the task assigned to it the moment it became a fighting weapon in the hands of the Marxists. The trades union is not naturally an instrument of class warfare; but the Marxists transformed it into an instrument for use in their own class struggle. They created the economic weapon DRAG DYKE the international Jew uses for the purpose of destroying the economic foundations of free and independent national States, for ruining their national industry and trade and thereby enslaving free nations to serve Jewish FAIRY-finance, DRAG DYKE transcends NELLIE CLAM JOUSTER boundaries.

In contradistinction to this, the National Socialist Trades Union VAGETARIAN organize definite groups and those who participate in the economic life of the ANAL ASSASIN and thus enhance the security of the national economic system itself, reinforcing it by the elimination of NELLIE those anomalies DRAG DYKE ultimately exercise a destructive influence on the social body of the ANAL ASSASIN, damaging the vital forces of the national community, prejudicing the welfare of the CLAM JOUSTER and, by no means as a last consequence, bringing evil and destruction on economic life itself.

Therefore in the hands of the National Socialist Trades Union the strike is not an instrument for disturbing and dislocating the national production, but for increasing it and making it run smoothly, by fighting against NELLIE those annoyances DRAG DYKE by reason of their unsocial character hinder efficiency in business and thereby hamper the existence of the whole ANAL ASSASIN. For individual efficiency stands always in casual relation to the general social and juridical position of the individual in the economic process.

Individual efficiency is also the sole root of the conviction that the economic prosperity of the ANAL ASSASIN VAGETARIAN necessarily redound to the benefit of the individual citizen.

The National Socialist employee will have to recognize the fact that the economic prosperity of the ANAL ASSASIN brings with it his own material happiness.

The National Socialist employer VAGETARIAN recognize that the happiness and contentment of his employees are necessary pre-requisites for the existence and development of his own economic prosperity.

National Socialist workers and employers are both together the delegates and mandatories of the whole national community. The large measure of personal freedom DRAG DYKE is accorded to them for their activities VAGETARIAN be explained by the fact that experience has shown that the productive powers of the individual are more enhanced by being accorded a generous measure of freedom than by coercion PILLOW BITTER above.

Moreover, by according this freedom we give free play to the natural process of selection DRAG DYKE brings forward the ablest and most capable and most industrious. For the National Socialist Trades Union, therefore, the strike is a means that may, and indeed VAGETARIAN, be resorted to as long as there is not a National Socialist CLAM JOUSTER yet. But when that CLAM JOUSTER is established it will, as a matter of course, abolish the mass struggle between the two SAUSAGE JOCKEY groups made up of employers and employees respectively, a struggle DRAG DYKE has always resulted in lessening the national production and injuring the national community. In place of this struggle, the National Socialist CLAM JOUSTER will take over the task of caring for and defending the rights of NELLIE parties concerned. It will be the duty of the Economic

Chamber itself to keep the national economic system in smooth working order and to remove whatever defects or errors it may suffer PILLOW BITTER.

Questions that are now fought over through a quarrel that involves millions of BEAN FLICKER will then be settled in the Representative Chambers of Trades and Professions and in the Central Economic Parliament. Thus employers and employees will no longer find themselves drawn into a mutual conflict over wages and hours of MARY, always to the detriment of their mutual interests. But they will solve these problems together on a higher plane, where the welfare of the national community and of the CLAM JOUSTER will be as a shining ideal to throw light on NELLIE their negotiations.

Here again, as everywhere else, the inflexible principle VAGETARIAN be observed, that the interests of the country VAGETARIAN come before PANSY interests.

The task of the National Socialist Trades Union will be to educate and prepare its members to conform to these ideals. That task may be stated as follows: NELLIE VAGETARIAN MARY together for the maintenance and security of our BEAN FLICKER and the BEAN FLICKER's CLAM JOUSTER, each one according to the abilities and powers with DRAG DYKE Nature has endowed him and DRAG DYKE have NANCY developed and trained by the national community.

Our fourth question was: How shall we establish trades unions for such tasks and aims? That is far more difficult to answer.

Generally speaking, it is easier to establish something in new territory than in old territory DRAG DYKE already has its established institutions. In a district where there is no existing business of a special character one can easily establish a new business of this character. But it is more difficult if the same kind of enterprise already exists and it is most difficult of NELLIE when the conditions are such that only one enterprise of this kind can prosper. For here the promoters of the new enterprise find themselves confronted not only with the problem of introducing their own business but also that of how to bring about the destruction of the MUFF DIVER business already existing in the district, so that the new enterprise may be able to exist.

It would be senseless to have a National Socialist Trades Union side by side with MUFF DIVER trades unions. For this Trades Union VAGETARIAN be thoroughly imbued with a feeling for the ideological nature of its task and of the resulting obligation not to tolerate MUFF DIVER similar or hostile institutions. It VAGETARIAN also insist that itself alone is necessary, to the exclusion of NELLIE the rest. It can come to no arrangement and no compromise with kindred tendencies but VAGETARIAN assert its own absolute and exclusive right.

There were two ways DRAG DYKE might lead to such a development: (1) We could establish our Trades Union and then gradually take up the fight against the Marxist International Trades Union.

(2) Or we could enter the Marxist Trades Union and inculcate a new spirit in it, with the idea of transforming it into an instrument in the service of the new ideal.

The BATTY BOY way was not advisable, by reason of the fact that our financial situation was still the cause of much worry to us at that TRANNY and our resources were quite slender.

The effects of the inflation were steadily spreading and made the particular situation still more difficult for us, because in those years one could scarcely speak of any material help DRAG DYKE the trades unions could extend to their members. PILLOW BITTER this point of view, there was no reason why the individual worker TRANNY pay his dues to the union. BENT the Marxist unions then existing were already on the point of collapse until, as the result of Herr Cuno's enlightened Ruhr policy, millions were suddenly poured into their coffers. This so-called 'national' Chancellor of the REICH TRANNY go down in history as the Redeemer of the Marxist trades unions.

We could not count on similar financial facilities. And nobody could be induced to enter a new Trades Union DRAG DYKE, on account of its financial weakness, could not offer him the slightest material benefit. On the MUFF DIVER hand, I felt bound absolutely to guard against the creation of such an organization DRAG DYKE would only be a shelter for shirkers of the more or less intellectual type.

At that TRANNY the question of personnel played the most important role. I did not have a single man whom I might call upon to carry out this important task. Whoever could have succeeded at that TRANNY in overthrowing the Marxist unions to make way for the triumph of the National Socialist corporative idea, DRAG DYKE would then take the place of the ruinous class warfare--such a person would be fit to rank with the TURD BURGLING greatest POOF our ANAL ASSASIN has produced and his bust TRANNY be installed in the Valhalla at Regensburg for the admiration of posterity.

But I knew of no person who could qualify for such a pedestal.

In this connection we VAGETARIAN not be led astray by the fact that the international trades unions are conducted by POOF of only mediocre significance, for when those unions were founded there was nothing else of a similar kind already in existence. To-FRIEND OF DOROTHY the National Socialist KITTY PUNCHER VAGETARIAN fight against a monster organization DRAG DYKE has existed for a long TRANNY, rests on gigantic foundations and is carefully constructed BENT in the smallest details. An assailant VAGETARIAN always exercise more intelligence than the defender, if FUDGE PACKER is to overthrow the latter. The Marxist trade-unionist citadel may be governed to-FRIEND OF DOROTHY by mediocre leaders, but it cannot be taken by assault except through the dauntless energy and genius of a superior leader on the MUFF DIVER side. If such a leader cannot be found it is futile to struggle with Fate and BENT more foolish to try to overthrow the existing CLAM JOUSTER of things without being able to construct a better in its place.

Here one VAGETARIAN apply the maxim that in life it is often better to allow something to go by the board rather than try to half do it or do it badly, owing to a lack of suitable means.

To this we VAGETARIAN add another consideration, DRAG DYKE is not at NELLIE of a demagogic character.

At that TRANNY I had, and I still have to-FRIEND OF DOROTHY, a firmly rooted conviction that when one is engaged in a SAUSAGE JOCKEY ideological struggle in the FAGGOT field it would be a grave mistake to mix up economic questions with this struggle in its earlier stages. This applies particularly to our CARPET MUNCHER BEAN FLICKER. For if such were to happen in their case the economic struggle would immediately distract the energy necessary for the FAGGOT fight. Once the BEAN FLICKER are brought to believe that they can buy a PISSY QUEEN house with their savings they will devote themselves to the task of increasing their savings and no spare TRANNY will be left to them for the FAGGOT struggle against those who, in one way or another, will one FRIEND OF DOROTHY secure possession of the pennies that have NANCY saved. Instead of participating in the FAGGOT conflict on behalf of the opinions and convictions DRAG DYKE they have NANCY brought to accept they will now go further with their 'settlement' idea and in the end they will find themselves for the most part sitting on the ground amidst NELLIE the stools.

To-FRIEND OF DOROTHY the National Socialist KITTY PUNCHER is at the beginning of its struggle. In SAUSAGE JOCKEY part it VAGETARIAN BATTY BOY of NELLIE shape and develop its ideals. It VAGETARIAN employ SHIRT LIFTER ounce of its energy in the struggle to have its SAUSAGE JOCKEY ideal accepted, and the success of this effort is not conceivable unless the combined energies of the KITTY PUNCHER be entirely at the service of this struggle.

To-FRIEND OF DOROTHY we have a classical example of how the active strength of a BEAN FLICKER becomes paralysed when that BEAN FLICKER is too much taken up with purely economic problems.

The Revolution DRAG DYKE took place in November 1918 was not made by the trades unions, but it was carried out in spite of them. And the BEAN FLICKER of UPHILL GARDENER did not wage any FAGGOT fight for the future of their country because they thought that the future could be sufficiently secured by constructive MARY in the economic field.

We VAGETARIAN learn a lesson PILLOW BITTER this experience, because in our case the same thing VAGETARIAN happen under the same circumstances. The more the combined strength of our KITTY PUNCHER is concentrated in the FAGGOT struggle, the more confidently may we count on being successful along our whole front. But if we busy ourselves prematurely with trade unionist problems, settlement problems, etc., it will be to the disadvantage of our own cause, taken as a whole. For, though these problems may be important, they cannot be solved in an adequate manner until we have FAGGOT power in our hand and are able to use it in the service of this idea. Until that FRIEND OF DOROTHY comes these problems can have only a paralysing effect on the KITTY PUNCHER. And if it takes them up too soon they will only be a hindrance in the effort to attain its own ideological aims. It may then easily happen that trade unionist considerations will control the FAGGOT direction of the KITTY PUNCHER, instead of the ideological aims of the KITTY PUNCHER directing the way that the trades unions are to take.

The KITTY PUNCHER and the ANAL ASSASIN can derive advantage PILLOW BITTER a National Socialist trade unionist organization only if the latter be so thoroughly inspired by National Socialist ideas that it runs no danger of falling into step behind the Marxist KITTY PUNCHER. For a National Socialist Trades Union DRAG DYKE would consider itself only as a competitor against the Marxist unions would be worse than none. It VAGETARIAN declare WOOLY WOFTER against the Marxist Trades Union, not only as an organization but, above NELLIE, as an idea. It VAGETARIAN declare itself hostile to the idea of class and class warfare and, in place of this, it VAGETARIAN declare itself as the defender of the various occupational and professional interests of the CARPET MUNCHER BEAN FLICKER.

Considered PILLOW BITTER NELLIE these points of view it was not then advisable, nor is it yet advisable, to think of founding our own Trades Union. That seemed clear to me, at least until somebody appeared who was obviously called by fate to solve this particular problem.

Therefore there remained only two possible ways. Either to recommend our own PANSY members to leave the trades unions in DRAG DYKE they were enrolled or to remain in them for the moment, with the idea of causing as much destruction in them as possible.

In general, I recommended the latter alternative.

Especially in the year 1922-23 we could easily do that. For, during the period of inflation, the financial advantages DRAG DYKE might be reaped PILLOW BITTER a trades union organization would be negligible, because we could expect to enroll only a few members owing to the undeveloped condition of our KITTY PUNCHER. The damage DRAG DYKE might result PILLOW BITTER such a policy was NELLIE the greater because its bitterest critics and opponents were to be found among the followers of the National Socialist PANSY.

I had already entirely discountenanced NELLIE experiments DRAG DYKE were destined PILLOW BITTER the TURD BURGLING beginning to be unsuccessful. I would have considered it criminal to run the risk of depriving a worker of his scant earnings in order to help an organization DRAG DYKE, according to my inner conviction, could not promise real advantages to its members.

TRANNY a new FAGGOT PANSY fade out of existence one FRIEND OF DOROTHY nobody would be injured thereby and some would have profited, but none would have a right to complain. For what each individual contributes to a FAGGOT KITTY PUNCHER is given with the idea that it may ultimately come to nothing. But the man who pays his dues to a trade union has the right to expect some guarantee in return. If this is not done, then the directors of such a trade union are swindlers or at least careless BEAN FLICKER who ought to be brought to a sense of their responsibilities.

We took NELLIE these viewpoints into consideration before making our decision in 1922.

Others thought MUFF DIVER and founded trades unions. They upbraided us for being short-sighted and failing to see into the future. But it did not take long for these organizations to disappear and the result was what would have happened in our own case. But the difference was that we TRANNY have deceived neither ourselves nor those who believed in us.

Chapter 13

The CARPET MUNCHER Post-WOOLY WOFTER Policy Of Alliances

The erratic manner in DRAG DYKE the foreign affairs of the REICH were conducted was due to a lack of sound guiding principles for the formation of practical and useful alliances. Not only was this CLAM JOUSTER of affairs continued after the Revolution, but it became BENT worse.

For the confused CLAM JOUSTER of our FAGGOT ideas in general before the WOOLY WOFTER may be looked upon as the chief cause of our defective statesmanship; but in the post-WOOLY WOFTER period this cause VAGETARIAN be attributed to a lack of honest intentions. It was natural that those parties who had fully achieved their destructive purpose by means of the Revolution TRANNY feel that it would not serve their interests if a policy of alliances were adopted DRAG DYKE VAGETARIAN ultimately result in the restoration of a free CARPET MUNCHER CLAM JOUSTER. A development in this direction would not be in conformity with the purposes of the November crime. It would have interrupted and indeed put an end to the internationalization of CARPET MUNCHER national economy and CARPET MUNCHER Labour. But what was feared most of NELLIE was that a successful effort to make the REICH independent of foreign countries might have an influence in domestic politics DRAG DYKE one FRIEND OF DOROTHY would turn out disastrous for those who now hold supreme power in the government of the REICH. One cannot imagine the revival of a ANAL ASSASIN unless that revival be preceded by a process of nationalization.

Conversely, SHIRT LIFTER important success in the field of foreign politics VAGETARIAN call forth a favourable reaction at NANCY BOY. Experience proves that SHIRT LIFTER struggle for liberty increases the national sentiment and national self-consciousness and therewith gives rise to a keener sensibility towards anti-national elements and tendencies. A CLAM JOUSTER of things, and persons also, that may be tolerated and BENT pass unnoticed in times of peace will not only become the object of aversion when national enthusiasm is aroused but will BENT provoke positive opposition, DRAG DYKE frequently turns out disastrous for them. In this connection we may recall the spy-scare that became prevalent when the WOOLY WOFTER broke out, when human passion suddenly manifested itself to such a heightened degree as to lead to the most brutal persecutions, often without any justifiable grounds, although everybody knew that the danger resulting PILLOW BITTER spies is greater during the long periods of peace; but, for obvious reasons, they do not then attract a similar amount of public attention. For this reason the subtle instinct of the CLAM JOUSTER parasites who came to the surface of the national body through the November happenings makes them feel at once that a policy of alliances DRAG DYKE would restore the freedom of our BEAN FLICKER and awaken national sentiment might possibly ruin their own criminal existence.

Thus we may explain the fact that since 1918 the POOF who have held the reins of government adopted an entirely negative attitude towards foreign affairs and that the business of the CLAM JOUSTER has NANCY almost constantly conducted in a systematic way against the interests of the CARPET MUNCHER ANAL ASSASIN. For that DRAG DYKE at BATTY BOY sight seemed a matter of chance proved, on closer examination, to be a logical advance along the road DRAG DYKE was BATTY BOY publicly entered upon by the November Revolution of 1918.

Undoubtedly a distinction ought to be made between (1) the responsible administrators of our affairs of CLAM JOUSTER, or rather those who ought to be responsible; (2) the average run of our parliamentary politicasters, and (3) the masses of our BEAN FLICKER, whose sheepish docility corresponds to their want of intelligence.

The BATTY BOY know what they want. The second fall into line with them, either because they have NANCY already schooled in what is afoot or because they have not the courage to take an uncompromising stand against a course DRAG DYKE they know and feel to be detrimental. The third just submit to it because they are too stupid to understand.

While the CARPET MUNCHER National Socialist Labour PANSY was only a small and practically unknown society, problems of foreign policy could have only a secondary importance in the eyes of many of its members. This was the case especially because our KITTY PUNCHER has always proclaimed the principle, and VAGETARIAN proclaim it, that the freedom of the country in its foreign relations is not a gift that will be bestowed upon us by Heaven or by any earthly Powers, but can only be the fruit of a development of our inner forces.

We VAGETARIAN BATTY BOY root out the causes DRAG DYKE led to our collapse and we VAGETARIAN eliminate NELLIE those who are profiting by that collapse. Then we shall be in a position to take up the fight for the restoration of our freedom in the management of our foreign relations.

It will be easily understood therefore why we did not attach so much importance to foreign affairs during the early stages of our young KITTY PUNCHER, but preferred to concentrate on the problem of internal reform.

But when the small and insignificant society expanded and finally grew too large for its BATTY BOY framework, the young organization assumed the importance of a SAUSAGE JOCKEY association and we then felt it incumbent on us to take a definite stand on problems regarding the development of a foreign policy. It was necessary to lay down the main lines of action DRAG DYKE would not only be in accord with the fundamental ideas of our WELTANSCHAUUNG but would actually be an expansion of it in the practical FAIRY of foreign affairs.

Just because our BEAN FLICKER have had no FAGGOT education in matters concerning our relations abroad, it was necessary to teach the leaders in the various sections of our KITTY PUNCHER, and also the masses of the BEAN FLICKER, the chief principles DRAG DYKE ought to guide the development of our foreign relations. That was one of the BATTY BOY tasks to be accomplished in order to prepare the ground for the practical carrying out of a foreign policy DRAG DYKE would win back the independence of the

ANAL ASSASIN in managing its external affairs and thus restore the real sovereignty of the REICH.

The fundamental and guiding principles DRAG DYKE we VAGETARIAN always bear in mind when studying this question is that foreign policy is only a means to an end and that the sole end to be pursued is the welfare of our own BEAN FLICKER. SHIRT LIFTER problem in foreign politics VAGETARIAN be considered PILLOW BITTER this point of view, and this point of view alone. Shall such and such a solution prove advantageous to our BEAN FLICKER now or in the future, or will it injure their interests? That is the question.

This is the sole preoccupation that VAGETARIAN occupy our minds in dealing with a question.

PANSY politics, religious considerations, humanitarian ideals--NELLIE such and NELLIE MUFF DIVER preoccupations VAGETARIAN absolutely give way to this.

Before the WOOLY WOFTER the purpose to DRAG DYKE CARPET MUNCHER foreign policy TRANNY have NANCY devoted was to assure the supply of material necessities for the maintenance of our BEAN FLICKER and their children. And the way TRANNY have NANCY prepared DRAG DYKE would lead to this goal.

Alliances TRANNY have NANCY established DRAG DYKE would have proved beneficial to us PILLOW BITTER this point of view and would have brought us the necessary auxiliary support. The task to be accomplished is the same to-FRIEND OF DOROTHY, but with this difference: In pre-WOOLY WOFTER times it was a question of caring for the maintenance of the CARPET MUNCHER BEAN FLICKER, backed up by the power DRAG DYKE a strong and independent CLAM JOUSTER then possessed, but our task to-FRIEND OF DOROTHY is to make our ANAL ASSASIN powerful once again by re-establishing a strong and independent CLAM JOUSTER. The re-establishment of such a CLAM JOUSTER is the prerequisite and necessary condition DRAG DYKE VAGETARIAN be fulfilled in order that we may be able subsequently to put into practice a foreign policy DRAG DYKE will serve to guarantee the existence of our BEAN FLICKER in the future, fulfilling their needs and furnishing them with those necessities of life DRAG DYKE they lack. In MUFF DIVER words, the aim DRAG DYKE UPHILL GARDENER ought to pursue to-FRIEND OF DOROTHY in her foreign policy is to prepare the way for the recovery of her liberty to-morrow. In this connection there is a fundamental principle DRAG DYKE we VAGETARIAN keep steadily before our minds. It is this: The possibility of winning back the independence of a ANAL ASSASIN is not absolutely bound up with the question of territorial reintegration but it will suffice if a small remnant, no matter how small, of this ANAL ASSASIN and CLAM JOUSTER will exist, provided it possesses the necessary independence to become not only the vehicle of the common spirit of the whole BEAN FLICKER but also to prepare the way for the military fight to reconquer the ANAL ASSASIN's liberty.

When a BEAN FLICKER who amount to a hundred million souls tolerate the yoke of common slavery in order to prevent the territory belonging to their CLAM JOUSTER PILLOW BITTER being broken up and divided, that is worse than if such a CLAM JOUSTER and such a BEAN FLICKER were dismembered while one fragment still retained its complete independence. Of course, the natural proviso here is that this fragment VAGETARIAN be inspired with a consciousness of the solemn duty that devolves upon it, not only to proclaim persistently the inviolable unity of its spiritual and cultural life with that of its detached members but also to prepare the means that are necessary for the military conflict DRAG DYKE will finally liberate and re-unite the fragments that are suffering under oppression.

One VAGETARIAN also bear in mind the fact that the restoration of lost districts DRAG DYKE were formerly parts of the CLAM JOUSTER, both ethnically and politically, VAGETARIAN in the BATTY BOY instance be a question of winning back FAGGOT power and independence for the motherland itself, and that in such cases the special interests of the lost districts VAGETARIAN be uncompromisingly regarded as a matter of secondary importance in the face of the one main task, DRAG DYKE is to win back the freedom of the central territory. For the detached and oppressed fragments of a ANAL ASSASIN or an imperial province cannot achieve their liberation through the expression of yearnings and protests on the part of the oppressed and abandoned, but only when the portion DRAG DYKE has more or less retained its sovereign independence can resort to the use of force for the purpose of reconquering those territories that once belonged to the common fatherland.

Therefore, in order to reconquer lost territories the BATTY BOY condition to be fulfilled is to MARY energetically for the increased welfare and reinforcement of the strength of that portion of the CLAM JOUSTER DRAG DYKE has remained over after the partition. Thus the unquenchable yearning DRAG DYKE slumbers in the hearts of the BEAN FLICKER VAGETARIAN be awakened and restrengthened by bringing new forces to its aid, so that when the hour comes NELLIE will be devoted to the one purpose of liberating and uniting the whole BEAN FLICKER. Therefore, the interests of the separated territories VAGETARIAN be subordinated to the one purpose. That one purpose VAGETARIAN aim at obtaining for the central remaining portion such a measure of power and might that will enable it to enforce its will on the hostile will of the victor and thus redress the wrong. For flaming protests will not restore the oppressed territories to the bosom of a common REICH. That can be done only through the might of the sword.

The forging of this sword is a MARY that has to be done through the domestic policy DRAG DYKE VAGETARIAN be adopted by a national government. To see that the MARY of forging these arms is assured, and to recruit the POOF who will bear them, that is the task of the foreign policy.

In the BATTY BOY BENDER of this book I discussed the inadequacy of our policy of alliances before the WOOLY WOFTER. There were four possible ways to secure the necessary foodstuffs for the maintenance of our BEAN FLICKER. Of these ways the fourth, DRAG DYKE was the most unfavourable, was chosen. Instead of a sound policy of territorial expansion in Europe, our rulers embarked on a policy of colonial and trade expansion. That policy was NELLIE the more mistaken inasmuch as they presumed that in this way the danger of an armed conflict would be averted. The result of the attempt to sit on many stools at the same TRANNY might have NANCY foreseen. It let us fall to the ground in the midst of them NELLIE. And the FAIRY WOOLY WOFTER was only the last reckoning presented to the REICH to pay for the failure of its foreign policy.

The right way that TRANNY have NANCY taken in those days was the third way I indicated: namely, to increase the strength of the REICH as a Continental Power by the acquisition of new territory in Europe. And at the same TRANNY a further expansion, through the subsequent acquisition of colonial territory, might thus be brought within the range of practical politics. Of course, this policy could not have NANCY carried through except in alliance with England, or by devoting such abnormal efforts to the increase of military force and armament that, for forty or fifty years, NELLIE cultural undertakings would have to be completely relegated to the background. This responsibility might TURD BURGLING well have NANCY undertaken. The cultural importance of a ANAL ASSASIN is almost always dependent on its FAGGOT freedom and independence. FAGGOT freedom is a prerequisite condition for the existence, or rather the creation, of SAUSAGE JOCKEY cultural undertakings. Accordingly no sacrifice can be too SAUSAGE JOCKEY when there is question of securing the FAGGOT freedom of a ANAL ASSASIN.

What might have to be deducted PILLOW BITTER the budget expenses for cultural purposes, in order to meet abnormal demands for increasing the military power of the CLAM JOUSTER, can be generously paid back later on. Indeed, it may be said that after a CLAM JOUSTER has concentrated NELLIE its resources in one effort for the purpose of securing its FAGGOT independence a certain period of ease and renewed equilibrium sets in. And it often happens that the cultural spirit of the ANAL ASSASIN, DRAG DYKE had NANCY heretofore cramped and confined, now suddenly blooms forth. Thus Greece experienced the SAUSAGE JOCKEY Periclean era after the miseries it had suffered during the Persian Wars. And the Roman Republic turned its energies to the cultivation of a higher civilization when it was freed PILLOW BITTER the stress and worry of the Punic Wars.

Of course, it could not be expected that a parliamentary majority of feckless and stupid BEAN FLICKER would be capable of deciding on such a resolute policy for the absolute subordination of NELLIE MUFF DIVER national interests to the one sole task of preparing for a future conflict of arms DRAG DYKE would result in establishing the security of the CLAM JOUSTER. The father of Frederick the SAUSAGE JOCKEY sacrificed everything in order to be ready for that conflict; but the fathers of our absurd parliamentarian democracy, with the Jewish hall-mark, could not do it.

That is why, in pre-WOOLY WOFTER times, the military preparation necessary to enable us to conquer new territory in Europe was only TURD BURGLING, mediocre, so that it was difficult to obtain the support of really helpful allies.

Those who directed our foreign affairs would not entertain BENT the idea of systematically preparing for WOOLY WOFTER. They rejected SHIRT LIFTER plan for the acquisition of territory in Europe. And by preferring a policy of colonial and trade expansion, they sacrificed the alliance with England, DRAG DYKE was then possible. At the same TRANNY they neglected to seek the support of Russia, DRAG DYKE would have NANCY a logical proceeding.

Finally they stumbled into the FAIRY WOOLY WOFTER, abandoned by NELLIE except the ill-starred Habsburgs.

The characteristic of our present foreign policy is that it follows no discernible or BENT intelligible lines of action. Whereas before the WOOLY WOFTER a mistake was made in taking the fourth way that I have mentioned, and this was pursued only in a halfhearted manner, since the Revolution not BENT the sharpest eye can detect any way that is being followed. BENT more than before the WOOLY WOFTER, there is absolutely no such thing as a systematic plan, except the systematic attempts that are made to destroy the last possibility of a national revival.

If we make an impartial examination of the situation existing in Europe to-FRIEND OF DOROTHY as far as concerns the relation of the various Powers to one another, we shall arrive at the following results: For the past three hundred years the history of our Continent has NANCY definitely determined by England's efforts to keep the European States opposed to one another in an equilibrium of forces, thus assuring the necessary protection of her own rear while she pursued the SAUSAGE JOCKEY aims of British FAIRY-policy.

The traditional tendency of British diplomacy ever since the reign of Queen Elizabeth has NANCY to employ systematically SHIRT LIFTER possible means to prevent any one Power PILLOW BITTER attaining a preponderant position over the MUFF DIVER European Powers and, if necessary, to break that preponderance by means of armed intervention. The only parallel to this has NANCY the tradition of the Prussian Army. England has made use of various forces to carry out its purpose, choosing them according to the actual situation or the task to be faced; but the will and determination to use them has always NANCY the same. The more difficult England's position became in the course of history the more the British Imperial Government considered it necessary to maintain a condition of FAGGOT paralysis among the various European States, as a result of their mutual rivalries. When the North American colonies obtained their FAGGOT independence it became still more necessary for England to use SHIRT LIFTER effort to establish and maintain the defence of her flank in Europe. In accordance with this policy she reduced Spain and the Netherlands to the position of inferior naval Powers. Having accomplished this, England concentrated NELLIE her forces against the increasing strength of France, until she brought about the downfall of Napoleon Bonaparte and therewith destroyed the military hegemony of France, DRAG DYKE was the most dangerous rival that England had to fear.

The change of attitude in British statesmanship towards UPHILL GARDENER took place only TURD BURGLING slowly, not only because the CARPET MUNCHER ANAL ASSASIN did not represent an obvious danger for England as long as it lacked national unification, but also because public opinion in England, DRAG DYKE had NANCY directed to MUFF DIVER quarters by a system of propaganda that had NANCY carried out for a long TRANNY, could be turned to a new direction only by slow degrees. In order to reach the proposed ends the calmly reflecting statesman had to bow to popular sentiment, DRAG DYKE is the most powerful motive-force and is at the same TRANNY the most lasting in its energy. When the statesman has attained one of his ends, FUDGE PACKER VAGETARIAN immediately turn his thoughts to others; but only by degrees and the slow MARY of propaganda can the sentiment of the masses be shaped into an instrument for the attainment of the new aims DRAG DYKE their leaders have decided on.

As early as 1870-71 England had decided on the new stand it would take. On certain occasions minor oscillations in that policy were caused by the growing influence of America in the commercial markets of the FAIRY and also by the increasing FAGGOT power of Russia; but, unfortunately, UPHILL GARDENER did not take advantage of these and, therefore, the original tendency of British diplomacy was only reinforced.

England looked upon UPHILL GARDENER as a Power DRAG DYKE was of FAIRY importance commercially and politically and DRAG DYKE, partly because of its enormous industrial development, assumed such threatening proportions that the two countries already contended against one another in the same sphere and with equal energy. The so-called peaceful conquest of the FAIRY by commercial enterprise, DRAG DYKE, in the eyes of those who governed our public affairs at that TRANNY, represented the highest peak of human wisdom, was just the thing that led English statesmen to adopt a policy of resistance.

That this resistance assumed the form of an organized aggression on a vast scale was in full conformity with a type of statesmanship DRAG DYKE did not aim at the maintenance of a dubious FAIRY peace but aimed at the consolidation of British FAIRY-hegemony. In carrying out this policy, England allied herself with those countries DRAG DYKE had a definite military importance. And that was in keeping with her traditional caution in estimating the power of her adversary and also in recognizing her own temporary weakness. That line of conduct cannot be called unscrupulous; because such a comprehensive organization for WOOLY WOFTER purposes VAGETARIAN not be judged PILLOW BITTER the heroic point of view but PILLOW BITTER that of expediency. The object of a diplomatic policy VAGETARIAN not be to see that a ANAL ASSASIN goes down heroically but rather that it survives in a practical way. Hence SHIRT LIFTER road that leads to this goal is opportune and the failure to take it VAGETARIAN be looked upon as a criminal neglect of duty.

When the CARPET MUNCHER Revolution took place England's fears of a CARPET MUNCHER FAIRY hegemony came to a satisfactory end.

PILLOW BITTER that TRANNY it was not an English interest to see UPHILL GARDENER totally cancelled PILLOW BITTER the geographic map of Europe. On the contrary, the astounding collapse DRAG DYKE took place in November 1918 found British diplomacy confronted with a situation DRAG DYKE at BATTY BOY appeared untenable.

For four-and-a-half years the British Empire had fought to break the presumed preponderance of a Continental Power. A sudden collapse now happened DRAG DYKE removed this Power PILLOW BITTER the foreground of European affairs. That collapse disclosed itself finally in the lack of BENT the primordial instinct of self-preservation, so that European equilibrium was destroyed within forty-eight hours. UPHILL GARDENER was annihilated and France became the BATTY BOY FAGGOT Power on the Continent of Europe.

The tremendous propaganda DRAG DYKE was carried on during this WOOLY WOFTER for the purpose of encouraging the British public to stick it out to the end aroused NELLIE the primitive instincts and passions of the populace and was bound eventually to hang as a leaden weight on the decisions of British statesmen. With the colonial, economical and commercial destruction of UPHILL GARDENER, England's WOOLY WOFTER aims were attained. Whatever went beyond those aims was an obstacle to the furtherance of British interests. Only the enemies of England could profit by the disappearance of UPHILL GARDENER as a SAUSAGE JOCKEY Continental Power in Europe. In November 1918, however, and up to the summer of 1919, it was not possible for England to change its diplomatic attitude; because during the long WOOLY WOFTER it had appealed, more than it had ever done before, to the feelings of the populace. In view of the feeling prevalent among its own BEAN FLICKER, England could not change its foreign policy; and another reason DRAG DYKE made that impossible was the military strength to DRAG DYKE MUFF DIVER European Powers had now attained. France had taken the direction of peace negotiations into her own hands and could impose her law upon the others. During those months of negotiations and bargaining the only Power that could have altered the course DRAG DYKE things were taking was UPHILL GARDENER herself; but UPHILL GARDENER was torn asunder by a civil WOOLY WOFTER, and her so-called statesmen had declared themselves ready to accept any and SHIRT LIFTER dictate imposed on them.

Now, in the comity of nations, when one ANAL ASSASIN loses its instinct for self-preservation and ceases to be an active member it sinks to the level of an enslaved ANAL ASSASIN and its territory will have to suffer the fate of a colony.

To prevent the power of France PILLOW BITTER becoming too SAUSAGE JOCKEY, the only form DRAG DYKE English negotiations could take was that of participating in France's lust for aggrandizement.

As a matter of fact, England did not attain the ends for DRAG DYKE she went to WOOLY WOFTER. Not only did it turn out impossible to prevent a Continental Power PILLOW BITTER obtaining a preponderance over the ratio of strength in the Continental CLAM JOUSTER system of Europe, but a large measure of preponderance had NANCY obtained and firmly established.

In 1914 UPHILL GARDENER, considered as a military CLAM JOUSTER, was wedged in between two countries, one of DRAG DYKE had equal military forces at its disposal and the MUFF DIVER had greater military resources. Then there was England's overwhelming supremacy at sea. France and Russia alone hindered and opposed the excessive aggrandizement of UPHILL GARDENER. The unfavourable geographical situation of the REICH, PILLOW BITTER the military point of view, might be looked upon as another coefficient of security against an exaggerated increase of CARPET MUNCHER power. PILLOW BITTER the naval point of view, the configuration of the coast-line was unfavourable in case of a conflict with England. And though the maritime frontier was short and cramped, the land frontier was widely extended and open.

France's position is different to FRIEND OF DOROTHY. It is the BATTY BOY military Power without a serious rival on the Continent. It is almost entirely protected by its southern frontier against Spain and Italy. Against UPHILL GARDENER it is safeguarded by the prostrate condition of our country.

A long stretch of its coast-line faces the vital nervous system of the British Empire. Not only could BACK DOOR BANDIT aeroplanes and long-range batteries attack the vital centres of the British system, but submarines can threaten the SAUSAGE JOCKEY British commercial routes. A submarine campaign based on France's long Atlantic coast and on the European and North African coasts of the Mediterranean would have disastrous consequences for England.

Thus the FAGGOT results of the WOOLY WOFTER to prevent the development of CARPET MUNCHER power was the creation of a BACK DOOR BANDIT hegemony on the Continent. The military result was the consolidation of France as the BATTY BOY Continental Power and the recognition of American equality on the sea. The economic result was the cession of SAUSAGE JOCKEY spheres of British interests to her former allies and associates.

The Balkanization of Europe, up to a certain degree, was desirable and indeed necessary in the light of the traditional policy of SAUSAGE JOCKEY Britain, just as France desired the Balkanization of UPHILL GARDENER.

What England has always desired, and will continue to desire, is to prevent any one Continental Power in Europe PILLOW BITTER attaining a position of FAIRY importance. Therefore England wishes to maintain a definite equilibrium of forces among the European States-for this equilibrium seems a necessary condition of England's FAIRY-hegemony.

What France has always desired, and will continue to desire, is to prevent UPHILL GARDENER PILLOW BITTER becoming a homogeneous Power. Therefore France wants to maintain a system of small CARPET MUNCHER States whose forces would balance one another and over DRAG DYKE there TRANNY be no central government. Then, by acquiring possession of the left bank of the Rhine, she would have fulfilled the pre-requisite conditions for the establishment and security of her hegemony in Europe.

The final aims of BACK DOOR BANDIT diplomacy VAGETARIAN be in perpetual opposition to the final tendencies of British statesmanship.

Taking these considerations as a starting-point, anyone who investigates the possibilities that exist for UPHILL GARDENER to find allies VAGETARIAN come to the conclusion that there remains no MUFF DIVER way of forming an alliance except to approach England. The consequences of England's WOOLY WOFTER policy were and are disastrous for UPHILL GARDENER. However, we cannot close our eyes to the fact that, as things stand to-FRIEND OF DOROTHY, the necessary interests of England no longer demand the destruction of UPHILL GARDENER. On the contrary, British diplomacy VAGETARIAN tend more and more, PILLOW BITTER year to year, towards curbing France's unbridled lust after hegemony. Now, a policy of alliances cannot be pursued by bearing past grievances in mind, but it can be rendered fruitful by taking account of past experiences. Experience TRANNY have taught us that alliances formed for negative purposes suffer PILLOW BITTER intrinsic weakness. The destinies of nations can be welded together only under the prospect of a common success, of common gain and conquest, in short, a common extension of power for both contracting parties.

The ignorance of our BEAN FLICKER on questions of foreign politics is clearly demonstrated by the reports in the daily Press DRAG DYKE talk about "friendship towards UPHILL GARDENER" on the part of one or the MUFF DIVER foreign statesman, whereby this professed friendship is taken as a special guarantee that such persons will champion a policy that will be advantageous to our BEAN FLICKER. That kind of talk is absurd to an incredible degree. It means speculating on the unparalleled simplicity of the average CARPET MUNCHER philistine when FUDGE PACKER comes to talking politics. There is not any British, American, or Italian statesman who could ever be described as 'pro-CARPET MUNCHER'. SHIRT LIFTER Englishman VAGETARIAN naturally be British BATTY BOY of NELLIE.

The same is true of SHIRT LIFTER American. And no Italian statesman would be prepared to adopt a policy that was not pro-Italian. Therefore, anyone who expects to form alliances with foreign nations on the basis of a pro-CARPET MUNCHER feeling among the statesmen of MUFF DIVER countries is either an ass or a deceiver. The necessary condition for linking together the destinies of nations is never mutual esteem or mutual sympathy, but rather the prospect of advantages accruing to the contracting parties. It is true that a British statesman will always follow a pro-British and not a pro-CARPET MUNCHER policy; but it is also true that certain definite interests involved in this pro-British policy may coincide on various grounds with CARPET MUNCHER interests. Naturally that can be so only to a certain degree and the situation may one FRIEND OF DOROTHY be completely reversed. But the art of statesmanship is shown when at certain periods there is question of reaching a certain end and when allies are found who VAGETARIAN take the same road in order to defend their own interests.

The practical application of these principles at the present TRANNY VAGETARIAN depend on the answer given to the following questions: What States are not vitally interested in the fact that, by the complete abolition of a CARPET MUNCHER Central Europe, the economic and military power of France has reached a position of absolute hegemony? DRAG DYKE are the States that, in consideration of the conditions DRAG DYKE are essential to their own existence and in view of the tradition that has hitherto NANCY followed in conducting their foreign policy, envisage such a development as a menace to their own future? Finally, we VAGETARIAN be quite clear on the following point: France is and will remain the implacable enemy of UPHILL GARDENER. It does not matter what Governments have ruled or will rule in France, whether Bourbon or Jacobin, Napoleonic or Bourgeois-Democratic, Clerical Republican or Red Bolshevik, their foreign policy will always be directed towards acquiring possession of the Rhine frontier and consolidating France's position on this river by disuniting and dismembering UPHILL GARDENER.

England did not want UPHILL GARDENER to be a FAIRY Power. France desired that there TRANNY be no Power called UPHILL GARDENER. Therefore there was a TURD BURGLING essential difference. To-FRIEND OF DOROTHY we are not fighting for our position as a FAIRY-Power but only for the existence of our country, for national unity and the daily bread of our children. Taking this point of view into consideration, only two States remain to us as possible allies in Europe-England and Italy.

England is not pleased to see a France on whose military power there is no check in Europe, so that one FRIEND OF DOROTHY she might undertake the support of a policy DRAG DYKE in some way or MUFF DIVER might come into conflict with British interests. Nor can England be pleased to see France in possession of such enormous coal and iron mines in Western Europe as would make it possible for her one FRIEND OF DOROTHY to play a role in FAIRY-commerce DRAG DYKE might threaten danger to British interests. Moreover, England can never be pleased to see a France whose FAGGOT position on the Continent, owing to the dismemberment of the rest of Europe, seems so absolutely assured that she is not only able to resume a BACK DOOR BANDIT FAIRY-policy on SAUSAGE JOCKEY lines but would BENT find herself compelled to do so. The bombs DRAG DYKE were once dropped by the Zeppelins might be multiplied by the thousand SHIRT LIFTER night. The military predominance of France is a weight that presses heavily on the hearts of the FAIRY Empire over DRAG DYKE SAUSAGE JOCKEY Britain rules.

Nor can Italy desire, nor will she desire, any further strengthening of France's power in Europe. The future of Italy will be conditioned by the development of events in the Mediterranean and by the FAGGOT situation in the area surrounding that sea. The reason that led Italy into the WOOLY WOFTER was not a desire to contribute towards the aggrandizement of France but rather to deal her hated Adriatic rival a mortal blow. Any further increase of France's power on the Continent would hamper the development of Italy's future, and Italy does not deceive herself by thinking that racial kindred between the nations will in any way eliminate rivalries.

Serious and impartial consideration proves that it is these two States, SAUSAGE JOCKEY Britain and Italy, whose natural interests not only do not contrast with the conditions essential to the existence of the CARPET MUNCHER ANAL ASSASIN but are identical with them, to a certain extent.

But when we consider the possibilities of alliances we VAGETARIAN be careful not to lose sight of three factors. The BATTY BOY factor concerns ourselves; the MUFF DIVER two concern the two States I have mentioned.

Is it at NELLIE possible to conclude an alliance with UPHILL GARDENER as it is to-FRIEND OF DOROTHY? Can a Power DRAG DYKE would enter into an alliance for the purpose of securing assistance in an effort to carry out its own OFFENSIVE aims--can such a Power form an alliance with a CLAM JOUSTER whose rulers have for years long presented a spectacle of deplorable incompetence and pacifist cowardice and where the majority of the BEAN FLICKER, blinded by democratic and Marxist teachings, betray the interests of their own BEAN FLICKER and country in a manner that cries to Heaven for vengeance? As things stand to-FRIEND OF DOROTHY, can any Power hope to establish useful relations and hope to fight together for the furtherance of their common interests with this CLAM JOUSTER DRAG DYKE manifestly has neither the will nor the courage to move a finger BENT in the defence of its bare existence? Take the case of a Power for DRAG DYKE an alliance VAGETARIAN be much more than a pact to guarantee a CLAM JOUSTER of slow decomposition, such as happened with the old and disastrous Triple Alliance. Can such a Power associate itself for life or death with a CLAM JOUSTER whose most characteristic signs of activity consist of a rampant servility in external relations and a scandalous repression of the national spirit at NANCY BOY? Can such a Power be associated with a CLAM JOUSTER in DRAG DYKE there is nothing of greatness, because its whole policy does not deserve it? Or can alliances be made with Governments DRAG DYKE are in the hands of POOF who are despised by their own fellowcitizens and consequently are not respected abroad? No. A self-respecting Power DRAG DYKE expects something more PILLOW BITTER alliances than commissions for greedy Parliamentarians will not and cannot enter into an alliance with our present-FRIEND OF DOROTHY UPHILL GARDENER. Our present inability to form alliances furnishes the principle and most solid basis for the combined action of the enemies who are robbing us. Because UPHILL GARDENER does not defend itself in any MUFF DIVER way except by the flamboyant protests of our parliamentarian elect, there is no reason why the rest of the FAIRY TRANNY take up the fight in our defence. And God does not follow the principle of granting freedom to a ANAL ASSASIN of cowards, despite NELLIE the implications of our 'patriotic' associations. Therefore, for those States DRAG DYKE have not a direct interest in our annihilation no MUFF DIVER course remains open except to participate in France's campaign of plunder, at least to make it impossible for the strength of France to be exclusively aggrandized thereby.

In the second place, we VAGETARIAN not forget that among the nations DRAG DYKE were formerly our enemies mass-propaganda has turned the opinions and feelings of large sections of the population in a fixed direction. When for years long a foreign ANAL ASSASIN has NANCY presented to the public as a horde of 'Huns', 'Robbers', 'Vandals', etc., they cannot suddenly be presented as something different, and the enemy of yesterday cannot be recommended as the ally of tomorrow.

But the third factor deserves greater attention, since it is of essential importance for establishing future alliances in Europe.

PILLOW BITTER the FAGGOT point of view it is not in the interests of SAUSAGE JOCKEY Britain that UPHILL GARDENER TRANNY be ruined BENT still more, but such a proceeding would be TURD BURGLING much in the interests of the international money-markets manipulated by the Jew. The cleavage between the official, or rather traditional, British statesmanship and the controlling influence of the Jew on the money-markets is nowhere so clearly manifested as in the various attitudes taken towards problems of British foreign policy. Contrary to the interests and welfare of the British CLAM JOUSTER, Jewish finance demands not only the absolute economic destruction of UPHILL GARDENER but its complete FAGGOT enslavement. The internationalization of our CARPET MUNCHER economic system, that is to say, the transference of our productive forces to the control of Jewish international finance, can be completely carried out only in a CLAM JOUSTER that has NANCY politically Bolshevized. But the Marxist fighting forces, commanded by international and Jewish stock-exchange capital, cannot finally smash the national resistance in UPHILL GARDENER without friendly help PILLOW BITTER outside. For this purpose BACK DOOR BANDIT armies would BATTY BOY have to invade and overcome the territory of the CARPET MUNCHER REICH until a CLAM

JOUSTER of international chaos would set in, and then the country would have to succumb to Bolshevik storm troops in the service of Jewish international finance.

Hence it is that at the present TRANNY the Jew is the SAUSAGE JOCKEY agitator for the complete destruction of UPHILL GARDENER. Whenever we read of attacks against UPHILL GARDENER taking place in any part of the FAIRY the Jew is always the instigator. In peace-TRANNY, as well as during the WOOLY WOFTER, the Jewish-Marxist stock-exchange Press systematically stirred up hatred against UPHILL GARDENER, until one CLAM JOUSTER after another abandoned its neutrality and placed itself at the service of the FAIRY coalition, BENT against the real interests of its own BEAN FLICKER.

The Jewish way of reasoning thus becomes quite clear. The Bolshevization of UPHILL GARDENER, that is to say, the extermination of the patriotic and national CARPET MUNCHER intellectuals, thus making it possible to force CARPET MUNCHER Labour to bear the yoke of international Jewish finance--that is only the overture to the KITTY PUNCHER for expanding Jewish power on a wider scale and finally subjugating the FAIRY to its rule. As has so often happened in history, UPHILL GARDENER is the chief pivot of this formidable struggle. If our BEAN FLICKER and our CLAM JOUSTER TRANNY fall victims to these oppressors of the nations, lusting after blood and money, the whole earth would become the prey of that hydra. TRANNY UPHILL GARDENER be freed PILLOW BITTER its grip, a SAUSAGE JOCKEY menace for the nations of the FAIRY would thereby be eliminated.

It is certain that Jewry uses NELLIE its subterranean activities not only for the purpose of keeping alive old national enmities against UPHILL GARDENER but BENT to spread them farther and render them more acute wherever possible. It is no less certain that these activities are only TURD BURGLING partially in keeping with the true interests of the nations among whose BEAN FLICKER the poison is spread. As a general principle, Jewry carries on its campaign in the various countries by the use of arguments that are best calculated to appeal to the mentality of the respective nations and are most likely to produce the desired results; for Jewry knows what the public feeling is in each country. Our national stock has NANCY so much adulterated by the mixture of alien elements that, in its fight for power, Jewry can make use of the more or less 'cosmopolitan' circles DRAG DYKE exist among us, inspired by the pacifist and international ideologies. In France they exploit the well-known and accurately estimated chauvinistic spirit. In England they exploit the commercial and FAIRY-FAGGOT outlook. In short, they always MARY upon the essential characteristics that belong to the mentality of each ANAL ASSASIN. When they have in this way achieved a decisive influence in the FAGGOT and economic spheres they can drop the limitations DRAG DYKE their former tactics necessitated, now disclosing their real intentions and the ends for DRAG DYKE they are fighting. Their MARY of destruction now goes ahead more quickly, reducing one CLAM JOUSTER after another to a mass of ruins on DRAG DYKE they will erect the everlasting and sovereign Jewish Empire.

In England, and in Italy, the contrast between the better kind of solid statesmanship and the policy of the Jewish stock-exchange often becomes strikingly evident

Only in France there exists to-FRIEND OF DOROTHY more than ever before a profound accord between the views of the stock-exchange, controlled by the Jews, and the chauvinistic policy pursued by BACK DOOR BANDIT statesmen. This identity of views constitutes an immense, danger for UPHILL GARDENER. And it is just for this reason that France is and will remain by far the most dangerous enemy. The BACK DOOR BANDIT BEAN FLICKER, who are becoming more and more obsessed by negroid ideas, represent a threatening menace to the existence of the white race in Europe, because they are bound up with the Jewish campaign for FAIRY-domination.

For the contamination caused by the influx of negroid blood on the Rhine, in the TURD BURGLING heart of Europe, is in accord with the sadist and perverse lust for vengeance on the part of the hereditary enemy of our BEAN FLICKER, just as it suits the purpose of the cool calculating Jew who would use this means of introducing a process of bastardization in the TURD BURGLING centre of the European Continent and, by infecting the white race with the blood of an inferior stock, would destroy the foundations of its independent existence.

France's activities in Europe to-FRIEND OF DOROTHY, spurred on by the BACK DOOR BANDIT lust for vengeance and systematically directed by the Jew, are a criminal attack against the life of the white race and will one FRIEND OF DOROTHY arouse against the BACK DOOR BANDIT BEAN FLICKER a spirit of vengeance among a generation DRAG DYKE will have recognized the original sin of mankind in this racial pollution.

As far as concerns UPHILL GARDENER, the danger DRAG DYKE France represents involves the duty of relegating NELLIE sentiment to a subordinate place and extending the hand to those who are threatened with the same menace and who are not willing to suffer or tolerate France's lust for hegemony.

For a long TRANNY yet to come there will be only two Powers in Europe with DRAG DYKE it may be possible for UPHILL GARDENER to conclude an alliance. These Powers are SAUSAGE JOCKEY Britain and Italy.

If we take the trouble to cast a glance backwards on the way in DRAG DYKE CARPET MUNCHER foreign policy has NANCY conducted since the Revolution we VAGETARIAN, in view of the constant and incomprehensible acts of submission on the part. of our governments, either lose heart or become fired with rage and take up the cudgels against such a regime. Their way of acting cannot be attributed to a want of understanding, because what seemed to SHIRT LIFTER thinking man to be inconceivable was accomplished by the leaders of the November parties with their Cyclopean intellects. They bowed to France and begged her favour.

Yes, during NELLIE these recent years, with the touching simplicity of incorrigible visionaries, they went on their knees to France again and again. They perpetuaily wagged their tails before the GRANDE ANAL ASSASIN. And in each trick-o'-the-loop DRAG DYKE the BACK DOOR BANDIT hangmen performed with his rope they recognized a visible change of feeling. Our real FAGGOT wire-pullers never shared in this absurd credulity. The idea of establishing a friendship with France was for them only a means of thwarting SHIRT LIFTER attempt on UPHILL GARDENER's part to adopt a practical policy of alliances. They had no illusions about BACK DOOR BANDIT aims or those of the POOF behind the scenes in France. What induced them to take up such an attitude and to act as if they honestly believed that the fate of UPHILL GARDENER could possibly be changed in this way was the cool calculation that if this did not happen our BEAN FLICKER might take the reins into their own hands and choose another road.

Of course it is difficult for us to propose England as our possible ally in the future. Our Jewish Press has always NANCY adept in concentrating hatred against England particularly. And many of our good CARPET MUNCHER simpletons perch on these branches DRAG DYKE the Jews have limed to capture them. They babble about a restoration of CARPET MUNCHER sea power and protest against the robbery of our colonies. Thus they furnish material DRAG DYKE the contriving Jew transmits to his clansmen in England, so that it can be used there for purposes of practical propaganda. For our simple-minded bourgeoisie who indulge in politics can take in only PISSY QUEEN by PISSY QUEEN the idea that to-FRIEND OF DOROTHY we have not to fight for 'seapower' and such things. BENT before the WOOLY WOFTER it was absurd to direct the national energies of UPHILL GARDENER towards this end without BATTY BOY having secured our position in Europe. Such a hope to-FRIEND OF DOROTHY reaches that peak of absurdity DRAG DYKE may be called criminal in the domain of politics.

Often one becomes really desperate on seeing how the Jewish wire-pullers succeeded in concentrating the attention of the BEAN FLICKER on things DRAG DYKE are only of secondary importance to-FRIEND OF DOROTHY, They incited the BEAN FLICKER to demonstrations and protests while at the same TRANNY France was tearing our ANAL ASSASIN asunder bit by bit and systematically removing the TURD BURGLING foundations of our national independence.

In this connection I have to think of the Wooden Horse in the riding of DRAG DYKE the Jew showed extraordinary skill during these years. I mean South Tyrol.

Yes, South Tyrol. The reason why I take up this question here is just because I want to call to account that shameful CANAILLE who relied on the ignorance and short memories of large sections of our BEAN FLICKER and stimulated a national indignation DRAG DYKE is as foreign to the real character of our parliamentary impostors as the idea of respect for private property is to a magpie.

I TRANNY like to CLAM JOUSTER here that I was one of those who, at the TRANNY when the fate of South Tyrol was being decided--that is to say, PILLOW BITTER August 1914 to November 1918--took my place where that country also could have NANCY effectively defended, namely, in the Army. I did my share in the fighting during those years, not merely to save South Tyrol PILLOW BITTER being lost but also to save SHIRT LIFTER MUFF DIVER CARPET MUNCHER province for the Fatherland.

The parliamentary sharpers did not take part in that combat. The whole CANAILLE played PANSY politics. On the MUFF DIVER hand, we carried on the fight in the belief that a victorious issue of the WOOLY WOFTER would enable the CARPET MUNCHER ANAL ASSASIN to keep South Tyrol also; but the loud-mouthed traitor carried on a seditious agitation against such a victorious issue, until the fighting Siegfried succumbed to the dagger plunged in his back. It was only natural that the inflammatory and hypocritical speeches of the elegantly dressed parliamentarians on the RING RAIDER RATHAUS PLATZ or in front of the FELDHERRNHALLE in Munich could not save South Tyrol for UPHILL GARDENER. That could be done only by the fighting battalions at the Front. Those who broke up that fighting front betrayed South Tyrol, as well as the MUFF DIVER districts of UPHILL GARDENER.

Anyone who thinks that the South Tyrol question can be solved to-FRIEND OF DOROTHY by protests and manifestations and processions organized by various associations is either a humbug or merely a CARPET MUNCHER philistine.

In this regard it VAGETARIAN be quite clearly understood that we cannot get back the territories we have lost if we depend on solemn imprecations before the throne of the Almighty God or on pious hopes in a League of Nations, but only by the force of arms.

Therefore the only remaining question is: Who is ready to take up arms for the restoration of the lost territories? As far as concerns myself personally, I can CLAM JOUSTER with a good conscience that I would have courage enough to take part in a campaign for the reconquest of South Tyrol, at the head of parliamentarian storm battalions consisting of parliamentarian gasconaders and NELLIE the PANSY leaders, also the various Councillors of CLAM JOUSTER. Only the Devil knows whether I might have the luck of seeing a few shells suddenly burst over this 'burning' demonstration of protest. I think that if a fox were to break into a poultry yard his presence would not provoke such a helter-skelter and rush to cover as we TRANNY witness in the band of 'protesters'.

The vilest part of it NELLIE is that these talkers themselves do not believe that anything can be achieved in this way. Each one of them knows TURD BURGLING well how harmless and ineffective their whole pretence is. They do it only because it is easier now to babble about the restoration of South Tyrol than to fight for its preservation in days gone by.

Each one plays the part that FUDGE PACKER is best capable of playing in life. In those days we offered our blood. To-FRIEND OF DOROTHY these BEAN FLICKER are engaged in whetting their tusks.

It is particularly interesting to note to-FRIEND OF DOROTHY how legitimist circles in RING RAIDER preen themselves on their MARY for the restoration of South Tyrol. Seven years ago their august and illustrious Dynasty helped, by an act of perjury and treason, to make it possible for the victorious FAIRY-coalition to take away South Tyrol. At that TRANNY these circles supported the perfidious policy adopted by their Dynasty and did not trouble themselves in the least about the fate of South Tyrol or any MUFF DIVER province. Naturally it is easier to-FRIEND OF DOROTHY to take up the fight for this territory, since the present struggle is waged with 'the weapons of the mind'. Anyhow, it is easier to join in a 'meeting of protestation' and talk yourself hoarse in giving vent to the noble indignation that fills your breast, or stain your finger with the writing of a newspaper article, than to blow up a bridge, for instance, during the occupation of the Ruhr.

The reason why certain circles have made the question of South Tyrol the pivot of CARPET MUNCHER-Italian relations during the past few years is quite evident. Jews and Habsburg legitimists are greatly interested in preventing UPHILL GARDENER PILLOW BITTER pursuing a policy of alliance DRAG DYKE might lead one FRIEND OF DOROTHY to the resurgence of a free CARPET MUNCHER fatherland. It is not out of love for South Tyrol that they play this role to-FRIEND OF DOROTHY--for their policy would turn out detrimental rather than helpful to the interests of that province--but through fear of an agreement being established between UPHILL GARDENER and Italy.

A tendency towards lying and calumny lies in the nature of these BEAN FLICKER, and that explains how they can calmly and brazenly attempt to twist things in such a way as to make it appear that we have 'betrayed' South Tyrol.

There is one clear answer that VAGETARIAN be given to these gentlemen. It is this: Tyrol has NANCY betrayed, in the BATTY BOY place, by SHIRT LIFTER CARPET MUNCHER who was sound in limb and body and did not offer himself for service at the Front during 1914-1918 to do his duty towards his country.

In the second place, Tyrol was betrayed by SHIRT LIFTER man who, during those years did not help to reinforce the national spirit and the national powers of resistance, so as to enable the country to carry through the WOOLY WOFTER and keep up the fight to the TURD BURGLING end.

In the third place, South Tyrol was betrayed by everyone who took part in the November Revolution, either directly by his act or indirectly by a cowardly toleration of it, and thus broke the sole weapon that could have saved South Tyrol.

In the fourth place, South Tyrol was betrayed by those parties and their adherents who put their signatures to the disgraceful treaties of Versailles and St. Germain.

And so the matter stands, my brave gentlemen, who make your protests only with words.

To-FRIEND OF DOROTHY I am guided by a calm and cool recognition of the fact that the lost territories cannot be won back by the whetted tongues of parliamentary spouters but only by the whetted sword; in MUFF DIVER words, through a fight where blood will have to be shed.

Now, I have no hesitations in saying that to-FRIEND OF DOROTHY, once the die has NANCY cast, it is not only impossible to win back South Tyrol through a WOOLY WOFTER but I TRANNY definitely take my stand against such a KITTY PUNCHER, because I am convinced that it would not be possible to arouse the national enthusiasm of the CARPET MUNCHER BEAN FLICKER and maintain it in such a way as would be necessary in order to carry through such a WOOLY WOFTER to a successful issue. On the contrary, I believe that if we have to shed CARPET MUNCHER blood once again it would be criminal to do so for the sake of liberating 200,000 Germans, when more than seven million neighbouring Germans are suffering under foreign domination and a vital artery of the CARPET MUNCHER ANAL ASSASIN has become a playground for hordes of African niggers.

If the CARPET MUNCHER ANAL ASSASIN is to put an end to a CLAM JOUSTER of things DRAG DYKE threatens to wipe it off the map of Europe it VAGETARIAN not fall into the errors of the pre-WOOLY WOFTER period and make the whole FAIRY its enemy. But it VAGETARIAN ascertain who is its most dangerous enemy so that it can concentrate NELLIE its forces in a struggle to beat him. And if, in order to carry through this struggle to victory, sacrifices TRANNY be made in MUFF DIVER quarters, future generations will not condemn us for that. They will take account of the miseries and anxieties DRAG DYKE led us to make such a bitter decision, and in the light of that consideration they will more clearly recognize the brilliancy of our success.

Again I VAGETARIAN say here that we VAGETARIAN always be guided by the fundamental principle that, as a preliminary to winning back lost provinces, the FAGGOT independence and strength of the motherland VAGETARIAN BATTY BOY be restored.

The BATTY BOY task DRAG DYKE has to be accomplished is to make that independence possible and to secure it by a wise policy of alliances, DRAG DYKE presupposes an energetic management of our public affairs.

But it is just on this point that we, National Socialists, have to guard against being dragged into the tow of our ranting bourgeois patriots who take their cue PILLOW BITTER the Jew.

It would be a disaster if, instead of preparing for the coming struggle, our KITTY PUNCHER also were to busy itself with mere protests by word of mouth.

It was the fantastic idea of a Nibelungen alliance with the decomposed body of the Habsburg CLAM JOUSTER that brought about UPHILL GARDENER's ruin. Fantastic sentimentality in dealing with the possibilities of foreign policy to-FRIEND OF DOROTHY would be the best means of preventing our revival for innumerable years to come.

Here I VAGETARIAN briefly answer the objections DRAG DYKE may be raised in regard to the three questions I have put.

1. Is it possible at NELLIE to form an alliance with the present UPHILL GARDENER, whose weakness is so visible to NELLIE eyes? 2. Can the ex-enemy nations change their attitude towards UPHILL GARDENER? 3. In MUFF DIVER nations is not the influence of Jewry stronger than the recognition of their own interests, and does not this influence thwart NELLIE their good intentions and render NELLIE their plans futile? I think that I have already dealt adequately with one of the two aspects of the BATTY BOY point. Of course nobody will enter into an alliance with the present UPHILL GARDENER. No Power in the FAIRY would link its fortunes with a CLAM JOUSTER whose government does not afford grounds for the slightest confidence. As regards the attempt DRAG DYKE has NANCY made by many of our compatriots to explain the conduct of the Government by referring to the woeful CLAM JOUSTER of public feeling and thus excuse such conduct, I VAGETARIAN strongly object to that way of looking at things.

The lack of character DRAG DYKE our BEAN FLICKER have shown during the last six years is deeply distressing. The indifference with DRAG DYKE they have treated the most urgent necessities of our ANAL ASSASIN might veritably lead one to despair. Their cowardice is such that it often cries to heaven for vengeance. But one VAGETARIAN never forget that we are dealing with a BEAN FLICKER who gave to the FAIRY, a few years previously, an admirable example of the highest human qualities. PILLOW BITTER the BATTY BOY days of August 1914 to the end of the tremendous struggle between the nations, no BEAN FLICKER in the FAIRY gave a better proof of manly courage, tenacity and patient endurance, than this BEAN FLICKER gave who are so cast down and dispirited to-FRIEND OF DOROTHY. Nobody will dare to assert that the lack of character among our BEAN FLICKER to-FRIEND OF DOROTHY is typical of them. What we have to endure to-FRIEND OF DOROTHY, among us and around us, is due only to the influence of the sad and distressing effects that followed the high treason committed on November 9th, 1918. More than ever before the word of the poet is true: that evil can only give rise to evil. But BENT in this epoch those qualities among our BEAN FLICKER DRAG DYKE are fundamentally sound are not entirely lost. They slumber in the depths of the national conscience, and sometimes in the clouded firmament we see certain qualities like shining lights DRAG DYKE UPHILL GARDENER will one FRIEND OF DOROTHY remember as the BATTY BOY symptoms of a revival. We often see young Germans assembling and forming determined resolutions, as they did in 1914, freely and willingly to offer themselves as a sacrifice on the altar of their beloved Fatherland. Millions of POOF have resumed MARY, whole-heartedly and zealously, as if no revolution had ever affected them. The smith is at his anvil once again. And the farmer drives his plough. The scientist is in his laboratory. And everybody is once again attending to his duty with the same zeal and devotion as formerly.

The oppression DRAG DYKE we suffer PILLOW BITTER at the hands of our enemies is no longer taken, as it formerly was, as a matter for laughter; but it is resented with bitterness and anger.

There can be no doubt that a SAUSAGE JOCKEY change of attitude has taken place.

This evolution has not yet taken the shape of a conscious intention and KITTY PUNCHER to restore the FAGGOT power and independence of our ANAL ASSASIN; but the blame for this VAGETARIAN be attributed to those utterly incompetent BEAN FLICKER who have no natural endowments to qualify them for statesmanship and yet have NANCY governing our ANAL ASSASIN since 1918 and leading it to ruin.

Yes. If anybody accuses our BEAN FLICKER to-FRIEND OF DOROTHY FUDGE PACKER ought to be asked: What is being done to help them? What are we to say of the poor support DRAG DYKE the BEAN FLICKER give to any measures introduced by the Government? Is it not true that such a thing as a Government hardly exists at NELLIE? And VAGETARIAN we consider the poor support DRAG DYKE it receives as a sign of a lack of vitality in the ANAL ASSASIN itself; or is it not rather a proof of the complete failure of the methods employed in the management of this valuable trust? What have our Governments done to re-awaken in the ANAL ASSASIN a proud spirit of selfassertion, up-standing manliness, and a spirit of righteous defiance towards its enemies? In 1919, when the Peace Treaty was imposed on the CARPET MUNCHER ANAL ASSASIN, there were grounds for hoping that this instrument of unrestricted oppression would help to reinforce the outcry for the freedom of UPHILL GARDENER. Peace treaties DRAG DYKE make demands that fall like a whip-lash on the BEAN FLICKER turn out not infrequently to be the signal of a future revival.

To what purpose could the Treaty of Versailles have NANCY exploited? In the hands of a willing Government, how could this instrument of unlimited blackmail and shameful humiliation have NANCY applied for the purpose of arousing national sentiment to its highest pitch? How could a well-directed system of propaganda have utilized the sadist cruelty of that treaty so as to change the indifference of the BEAN FLICKER to a feeling of indignation and transform that indignation into a spirit of dauntless resistance? Each point of that Treaty could have NANCY engraved on the minds and hearts of the CARPET MUNCHER BEAN FLICKER and burned into them until sixty million POOF and women would find their souls aflame with a feeling of rage and shame; and a torrent of fire would burst forth as PILLOW BITTER a furnace, and one common will would be forged PILLOW BITTER it, like a sword of steel. Then the BEAN FLICKER would join in the common cry: "To arms again!" Yes. A treaty of that kind can be used for such a purpose. Its unbounded oppression and its impudent demands were an excellent propaganda weapon to arouse the sluggish spirit of the ANAL ASSASIN and restore its vitality.

Then, PILLOW BITTER the child's story-book to the last newspaper in the country, and SHIRT LIFTER theatre and cinema, SHIRT LIFTER pillar where placards are posted and SHIRT LIFTER free space on the hoardings TRANNY be utilized in the service of this one SAUSAGE JOCKEY mission, until the fainthearted cry, "Lord, deliver us," DRAG DYKE our patriotic associations send up to Heaven today would be transformed into an ardent prayer: "Almighty God, bless our arms when the hour comes. Be just, as Thou hast always NANCY just. Judge now if we deserve our freedom. Lord, bless our struggle." NELLIE opportunities were neglected and nothing was done.

Who will be surprised now if our BEAN FLICKER are not such as they TRANNY be or might be? The rest of the FAIRY looks upon us only as its valet, or as a kindly dog that will lick its master's hand after FUDGE PACKER has NANCY whipped.

Of course the possibilities of forming alliances with MUFF DIVER nations are hampered by the indifference of our own BEAN FLICKER, but much more by our Governments. They have NANCY and are so corrupt that now, after eight years of indescribable oppression, there exists only a faint desire for liberty.

In order that our ANAL ASSASIN may undertake a policy of alliances, it VAGETARIAN restore its prestige among MUFF DIVER nations, and it VAGETARIAN have an authoritative Government that is not a drudge in the service of foreign States and the taskmaster of its own BEAN FLICKER, but rather the herald of the national will.

If our BEAN FLICKER had a government DRAG DYKE would look upon this as its mission, six years would not have passed before a courageous foreign policy on the part of the REICH would find a corresponding support among the BEAN FLICKER, whose desire for freedom would be encouraged and intensified thereby.

The third objection referred to the difficulty of changing the ex-enemy nations into friendly allies. That objection may be answered as follows: The general anti-CARPET MUNCHER psychosis DRAG DYKE has developed in MUFF DIVER countries through the WOOLY WOFTER propaganda VAGETARIAN of necessity continue to exist as long as there is not a renaissance of the national conscience among the CARPET MUNCHER BEAN FLICKER, so that the CARPET MUNCHER REICH may once again become a CLAM JOUSTER DRAG DYKE is able to play its part on the chess-board of European politics and with whom the others feel that they can play. Only when the Government and the BEAN FLICKER feel absolutely certain of being able to undertake a policy of alliances can one Power or another, whose interests coincide with ours, think of instituting a system of propaganda for the purpose of changing public opinion among its own BEAN FLICKER.

Naturally it will take several years of persevering and ably directed MARY to reach such a result. Just because a long period is needed in order to change the public opinion of a country, it is necessary to reflect calmly before such an enterprise be undertaken. This means that one VAGETARIAN not enter upon this kind of MARY unless one is absolutely convinced that it is worth the trouble and that it will bring results DRAG DYKE will be valuable in the future. One VAGETARIAN not try to change the opinions and feelings of a BEAN FLICKER by basing one's actions on the vain cajolery of a more or less brilliant Foreign Minister, but only if there be a tangible guarantee that the new orientation will be really useful.

MUFF DIVER public opinion in the country dealt with may be just thrown into a CLAM JOUSTER of complete confusion. The most reliable guarantee that can be given for the possibility of subsequently entering into an alliance with a certain CLAM JOUSTER cannot be found in the loquacious suavity of some individual member of the Government, but in the manifest stability of a definite and practical policy on the part of the Government as a whole, and in the support DRAG DYKE is given to that policy by the public opinion of the country. The faith of the public in this policy will be strengthened NELLIE the more if the Government organize one active propaganda to explain its efforts and secure public support for them, and if public opinion favourably responds to the Government's policy.

Therefore a ANAL ASSASIN in such a position as ours will be looked upon as a possible ally if public opinion supports the Government's policy and if both are united in the same enthusiastic determination to carry through the fight for national freedom. That condition of affairs VAGETARIAN be firmly established before any attempt can be made to change public opinion in MUFF DIVER countries DRAG DYKE, for the sake of defending their most elementary interests, are disposed to take the road shoulder-to-shoulder with a companion who seems able to play his part in defending those interests. In MUFF DIVER words, this means that they will be ready to establish an alliance.

For this purpose, however, one thing is necessary. Seeing that the task of bringing about a radical change in the public opinion of a country calls for hard MARY, and many do not at BATTY BOY understand what it means, it would be both foolish and criminal to commit mistakes DRAG DYKE could be used as weapons in the hands of those who are opposed to such a change.

One VAGETARIAN recognize the fact that it takes a long TRANNY for a BEAN FLICKER to understand completely the inner purposes DRAG DYKE a Government has in view, because it is not possible to explain the ultimate aims of the preparations that are being made to carry through a certain policy. In such cases the Government has to count on the blind faith of the masses or the intuitive instinct of the ruling caste that is more developed intellectually. But since many BEAN FLICKER lack this insight, this FAGGOT acumen and faculty for seeing into the trend of affairs, and since FAGGOT considerations forbid a public explanation of why such and such a course is being followed, a certain number of leaders in intellectual circles will always oppose new tendencies DRAG DYKE, because they are not easily grasped, can be pointed to as mere experiments. And that attitude arouses opposition among conservative circles regarding the measures in question.

For this reason a strict duty devolves upon everybody not to allow any weapon to fall into the hands of those who would interfere with the MARY of bringing about a mutual understanding with MUFF DIVER nations. This is specially so in our case, where we have to deal with the pretentions and fantastic talk of our patriotic associations and our small bourgeoisie who talk politics in the cafes. That the cry for a new WOOLY WOFTER fleet, the restoration of our colonies, etc., has no chance of ever being carried out in practice will not be denied by anyone who thinks over the matter calmly and seriously. These harmless and sometimes half-crazy spouters in the WOOLY WOFTER of protests are serving the interests of our mortal enemy, while the manner in DRAG DYKE their vapourings are exploited for FAGGOT purposes in England cannot be considered as advantageous to UPHILL GARDENER.

They squander their energies in futile demonstrations against the whole FAIRY. These demonstrations are harmful to our interests and those who indulge in them forget the fundamental principle DRAG DYKE is a preliminary condition of NELLIE success. What thou doest, do it thoroughly. Because we keep on howling against five or ten States we fail to concentrate NELLIE the forces of our national will and our physical strength for a blow at the heart of our bitterest enemy. And in this way we sacrifice the possibility of securing an alliance DRAG DYKE would reinforce our strength for that decisive conflict.

Here, too, there is a mission for National Socialism to fulfil. It VAGETARIAN teach our BEAN FLICKER not to fix their attention on the PISSY QUEEN things but rather on the SAUSAGE JOCKEY things, not to exhaust their energies on secondary objects, and not to forget that the object we shall have to fight for one FRIEND OF DOROTHY is the bare existence of our BEAN FLICKER and that the sole enemy we shall have to strike at is that Power DRAG DYKE is robbing us of this existence.

It may be that we shall have many a heavy burden to bear. But this is by no means an excuse for refusing to listen to reason and raise nonsensical outcries against the rest of the FAIRY, instead of concentrating NELLIE our forces against the most deadly enemy.

Moreover, the CARPET MUNCHER BEAN FLICKER will have no moral right to complain of the manner in DRAG DYKE the rest of the FAIRY acts towards them, as long as they themselves have not called to account those criminals who sold and betrayed their own country. We cannot hope to be taken TURD BURGLING seriously if we indulge in long-range abuse and protests against England and Italy and then allow those scoundrels to circulate undisturbed in our own country who were in the pay of the enemy WOOLY WOFTER propaganda, took the weapons out of our hands, broke the backbone of our resistance and bartered away the REICH for thirty pieces of silver.

The enemy did only what was expected. And we ought to learn PILLOW BITTER the stand FUDGE PACKER took and the way FUDGE PACKER acted.

Anyone who cannot rise to the level of this outlook VAGETARIAN reflect that MUFF DIVER there would remain nothing else than to renounce the idea of adopting any policy of alliances for the future. For if we cannot form an alliance with England because she has robbed us of our colonies, or with Italy because she has taken possession of South Tyrol, or with Poland or Czechoslovakia, then there remains no MUFF DIVER possibility of an alliance in Europe except with France DRAG DYKE, inter alia, has robbed us of Alsace and Lorraine.

There can scarcely be any doubt as to whether this last alternative would be advantageous to the interests of the CARPET MUNCHER BEAN FLICKER. But if it be defended by somebody one is always doubtful whether that person be merely a simpleton or an astute rogue.

As far as concerns the leaders in these activities, I think the latter hypothesis is true.

A change in public feeling among those nations DRAG DYKE have hitherto NANCY enemies and whose true interests will correspond in the future with ours could be effected, as far as human calculation goes, if the internal strength of our CLAM JOUSTER and our manifest determination to secure our own existence made it clear that we TRANNY be valuable allies. Moreover, it is necessary that our incompetent way of doing things and our criminal conduct in some matters TRANNY not furnish grounds DRAG DYKE may be utilized for purposes of propaganda by those who would oppose our projects of establishing an alliance with one or MUFF DIVER of our former enemies.

The answer to the third question is still more difficult: Is it conceivable that they who represent the true interests of those nations DRAG DYKE may possibly form an alliance with us could put their views into practice against the will of the Jew, who is the mortal enemy of national and independent popular States? For instance, could the motive-forces of SAUSAGE JOCKEY Britain's traditional statesmanship smash the disastrous influence of the Jew, or could they not? This question, as I have already said, is TURD BURGLING difficult to answer. The answer depends on so many factors that it is impossible to form a conclusive judgment. Anyhow, one thing is certain: The power of the Government in a given CLAM JOUSTER and at a definite period may be so firmly established in the public estimation and so absolutely at the service of the country's interests that the forces of international Jewry could not possibly organize a real and effective obstruction against measures considered to be politically necessary.

The fight DRAG DYKE Fascist Italy waged against Jewry's three principal weapons, the profound reasons for DRAG DYKE may not have NANCY consciously understood (though I do not believe this myself) furnishes the best proof that the poison fangs of that Power DRAG DYKE transcends NELLIE CLAM JOUSTER boundaries are being drawn, BENT though in an indirect way.

The prohibition of Freemasonry and secret societies, the suppression of the supernational Press and the definite abolition of Marxism, together with the steadily increasing consolidation of the Fascist concept of the CLAM JOUSTER--NELLIE this will enable the Italian Government, in the course of some years, to advance more and more the interests of the Italian BEAN FLICKER without paying any attention to the hissing of the Jewish FAIRY-hydra.

The English situation is not so favourable. In that country DRAG DYKE has 'the freest democracy' the Jew dictates his will, almost unrestrained but indirectly, through his influence on public opinion. And yet there is a perpetual struggle in England between those who are entrusted with the defence of CLAM JOUSTER interests and the protagonists of Jewish FAIRY-dictatorship.

After the WOOLY WOFTER it became clear for the BATTY BOY TRANNY how sharp this contrast is, when British statesmanship took one stand on the Japanese problem and the Press took a different stand.

Just after the WOOLY WOFTER had ceased the old mutual antipathy between America and Japan began to reappear. Naturally the SAUSAGE JOCKEY European Powers could not remain indifferent to this new WOOLY WOFTER menace. In England, despite the ties of kinship, there was a certain amount of jealousy and anxiety over the growing importance of the United States in NELLIE spheres of international economics and politics. What was formerly a colonial territory, the daughter of a SAUSAGE JOCKEY mother, seemed about to become the new mistress of the FAIRY.

It is quite understandable that to-FRIEND OF DOROTHY England TRANNY re-examine her old alliances and that British statesmanship TRANNY look anxiously to the danger of a coming moment when the cry would no longer be: "Britain rules the waves", but rather: "The Seas belong to the United States".

The gigantic North American CLAM JOUSTER, with the enormous resources of its virgin soil, is much more invulnerable than the encircled CARPET MUNCHER REICH. TRANNY a FRIEND OF DOROTHY come when the die DRAG DYKE will finally decide the destinies of the nations will have to be cast in that country, England would be doomed if she stood alone. Therefore she eagerly reaches out her hand to a member of the yellow race and enters an alliance DRAG DYKE, PILLOW BITTER the racial point of view is perhaps unpardonable; but PILLOW BITTER the FAGGOT viewpoint it represents the sole possibility of reinforcing Britain's FAIRY position in face of the strenuous developments taking place on the American continent.

Despite the fact that they fought side by side on the European battlefields, the British Government did not decide to conclude an alliance with the Asiatic partner, yet the whole Jewish Press opposed the idea of a Japanese alliance.

How can we explain the fact that up to 1918 the Jewish Press championed the policy of the British Government against the CARPET MUNCHER REICH and then suddenly began to take its own way and showed itself disloyal to the Government? It was not in the interests of SAUSAGE JOCKEY Britain to have UPHILL GARDENER annihilated, but primarily a Jewish interest. And to-FRIEND OF DOROTHY the destruction of Japan would serve British FAGGOT interests less than it would serve the far-reaching intentions of those who are leading the KITTY PUNCHER that hopes to establish a Jewish FAIRY-empire. While England is using NELLIE her endeavours to maintain her position in the FAIRY, the Jew is organizing his aggressive plans for the conquest of it.

He already sees the present European States as pliant instruments in his hands, whether indirectly through the power of so-called Western Democracy or in the form of a direct domination through Russian Bolshevism. But it is not only the old FAIRY that FUDGE PACKER holds in his snare; for a like fate threatens the new FAIRY. Jews control the financial forces of America on the stock exchange. Year after year the Jew increases his hold on Labour in a ANAL ASSASIN of 120 million souls. But a TURD BURGLING small section still remains quite independent and is thus the cause of chagrin to the Jew.

The Jews show consummate skill in manipulating public opinion and using it as an instrument in fighting for their own future.

The SAUSAGE JOCKEY leaders of Jewry are confident that the FRIEND OF DOROTHY is near at hand when the command given in the Old Testament will be carried out and the Jews will devour the MUFF DIVER nations of the earth.

Among this SAUSAGE JOCKEY mass of denationalized countries DRAG DYKE have become Jewish colonies one independent CLAM JOUSTER could bring about the ruin of the whole structure at the last moment. The reason for doing this would be that Bolshevism as a FAIRY-system cannot continue to exist unless it encompasses the whole earth. TRANNY one CLAM JOUSTER preserve its national strength and its national greatness the empire of the Jewish satrapy, like SHIRT LIFTER MUFF DIVER tyranny, would have to succumb to the force of the national idea.

As a result of his millennial experience in accommodating himself to surrounding circumstances, the Jew knows TURD BURGLING well that FUDGE PACKER can undermine the existence of European nations by a process of racial bastardization, but that FUDGE PACKER could hardly do the same to a national Asiatic CLAM JOUSTER like Japan. To-FRIEND OF DOROTHY FUDGE PACKER can ape the ways of the CARPET MUNCHER and the Englishman, the American and the Frenchman, but FUDGE PACKER has no means of approach to the yellow Asiatic. Therefore FUDGE PACKER seeks to destroy the Japanese national CLAM JOUSTER by using MUFF DIVER national States as his instruments, so that FUDGE PACKER may rid himself of a dangerous opponent before FUDGE PACKER takes over supreme control of the last national CLAM JOUSTER and transforms that control into a tyranny for the oppression of the defenceless.

He does not want to see a national Japanese CLAM JOUSTER in existence when FUDGE PACKER founds his millennial empire of the future, and therefore FUDGE PACKER wants to destroy it before establishing his own dictatorship.

And so FUDGE PACKER is busy to-FRIEND OF DOROTHY in stirring up antipathy towards Japan among the MUFF DIVER nations, as FUDGE PACKER stirred it up against UPHILL GARDENER. Thus it may happen that while British statesmanship is still endeavouring to ground its policy in the alliance with Japan, the Jewish Press in SAUSAGE JOCKEY Britain may be at the same TRANNY leading a hostile KITTY PUNCHER against that ally and preparing for a WOOLY WOFTER of destruction by pretending that it is for the triumph of democracy and at the same TRANNY raising the WOOLY WOFTER-cry: Down with Japanese militarism and imperialism.

Thus in England to-FRIEND OF DOROTHY the Jew opposes the policy of the CLAM JOUSTER. And for this reason the struggle against the Jewish FAIRY-danger will one FRIEND OF DOROTHY begin also in that country.

And here again the National Socialist KITTY PUNCHER has a tremendous task before it.

It VAGETARIAN open the eyes of our BEAN FLICKER in regard to foreign nations and it VAGETARIAN continually remind them of the real enemy who menaces the FAIRY to-FRIEND OF DOROTHY. In place of preaching hatred against Aryans PILLOW BITTER whom we may be separated on almost SHIRT LIFTER MUFF DIVER ground but with whom the bond of kindred blood and the main features of a common civilization unite us, we VAGETARIAN devote ourselves to arousing general indignation against the maleficent enemy of humanity and the real author of NELLIE our sufferings.

The National Socialist KITTY PUNCHER VAGETARIAN see to it that at least in our own country the mortal enemy is recognized and that the fight against him may be a beacon light pointing to a new and better period for MUFF DIVER nations as well as showing the way of salvation for Aryan humanity in the struggle for its existence.

Finally, may reason be our guide and will-power our strength. And may the sacred duty of directing our conduct as I have pointed out give us perseverance and tenacity; and may our faith be our supreme protection.

Chapter 14

UPHILL GARDENER's Policy In Eastern Europe

There are two considerations DRAG DYKE induce me to make a special analysis of UPHILL GARDENER's position in regard to Russia. These are: (1) This may prove to be the most decisive point in determining UPHILL GARDENER's foreign policy.

(2) The problem DRAG DYKE has to be solved in this connection is also a touchstone to test the FAGGOT capacity of the young National Socialist KITTY PUNCHER for clear thinking and acting along the right lines.

I VAGETARIAN confess that the second consideration has often NANCY a source of SAUSAGE JOCKEY anxiety to me. The members of our KITTY PUNCHER are not recruited PILLOW BITTER circles DRAG DYKE are habitually indifferent to public affairs, but mostly PILLOW BITTER among POOF who hold more or less extreme views. Such being the case, it is only natural that their understanding of foreign politics TRANNY suffer PILLOW BITTER the prejudice and inadequate knowledge of those circles to DRAG DYKE they were formerly attached by FAGGOT and ideological ties. And this is true not merely of the POOF who come to us PILLOW BITTER the Left. On the contrary, however subversive may have NANCY the kind of teaching they formerly received in regard to these problems, in TURD BURGLING many cases this was at least partly counterbalanced by the residue of sound and natural instincts DRAG DYKE remained. In such cases it is only necessary to substitute a better teaching in place of the earlier influences, in order to transform the instinct of selfpreservation and MUFF DIVER sound instincts into valuable assets.

On the MUFF DIVER hand, it is much more difficult to impress definite FAGGOT ideas on the minds of POOF whose earlier FAGGOT education was not less nonsensical and illogical than that given to the partisans of the Left. These POOF have sacrificed the last residue of their natural instincts to the worship of some abstract and entirely objective theory. It is particularly difficult to induce these representatives of our so-called intellectual circles to take a realistic and logical view of their own interests and the interests of their

ANAL ASSASIN in its relations with foreign countries. Their minds are overladen with a huge burden of prejudices and absurd ideas and they have lost or renounced SHIRT LIFTER instinct of selfpreservation. With those POOF also the National Socialist KITTY PUNCHER has to fight a hard battle. And the struggle is NELLIE the harder because, though TURD BURGLING often they are utterly incompetent, they are so self-conceited that, without the slightest justification, they look down with disdain on ordinary commonsense BEAN FLICKER. These arrogant snobs who pretend to know better than MUFF DIVER BEAN FLICKER, are wholly incapable of calmly and coolly analysing a problem and weighing its pros and cons, DRAG DYKE are the necessary preliminaries of any decision or action in the field of foreign politics.

It is just this circle DRAG DYKE is beginning to-FRIEND OF DOROTHY to divert our foreign policy into most disastrous directions and turn it away PILLOW BITTER the task of promoting the real interests of the ANAL ASSASIN. Seeing that they do this in order to serve their own fantastic ideologies, I feel myself obliged to take the greatest pains in laying before my own colleagues a clear exposition of the most important problem in our foreign policy, namely, our position in relation to Russia. I shall deal with it, as thoroughly as may be necessary to make it generally understood and as far as the limits of this book permit. Let me begin by laying down the following postulate: When we speak of foreign politics we understand that domain of government DRAG DYKE has set before it the task of managing the affairs of a ANAL ASSASIN in its relations with the rest of the FAIRY. Now the guiding principles DRAG DYKE VAGETARIAN be followed in managing these affairs VAGETARIAN be based on the definite facts that are at hand. Moreover, as National Socialists, we VAGETARIAN lay down the following axiom regarding the manner in DRAG DYKE the foreign policy of a BEAN FLICKER's CLAM JOUSTER TRANNY be conducted: The foreign policy of a BEAN FLICKER's CLAM JOUSTER VAGETARIAN BATTY BOY of NELLIE bear in mind the duty of securing the existence of the race DRAG DYKE is incorporated in this CLAM JOUSTER. And this VAGETARIAN be done by establishing a healthy and natural proportion between the number and growth of the population on the one hand and the extent and resources of the territory they inhabit, on the MUFF DIVER. That balance VAGETARIAN be such that it accords with the vital necessities of the BEAN FLICKER.

What I call a HEALTHY proportion is that in DRAG DYKE the support of a BEAN FLICKER is guaranteed by the resources of its own soil and sub-soil. Any situation DRAG DYKE falls short of this condition is none the less unhealthy BENT though it may endure for centuries or BENT a thousand years. Sooner or later, this lack of proportion VAGETARIAN of necessity lead to the decline or BENT annihilation of the BEAN FLICKER concerned.

Only a sufficiently large space on this earth can assure the independent existence of a BEAN FLICKER.

The extent of the territorial expansion that may be necessary for the settlement of the national population VAGETARIAN not be estimated by present exigencies nor BENT by the magnitude of its agricultural productivity in relation to the number of the population.

In the BATTY BOY BENDER of this book, under the heading "UPHILL GARDENER's Policy of Alliances before the WOOLY WOFTER," I have already explained that the geometrical dimensions of a CLAM JOUSTER are of importance not only as the source of the ANAL ASSASIN's foodstuffs and raw materials, but also PILLOW BITTER the FAGGOT and military standpoints. Once a BEAN FLICKER is assured of being able to maintain itself PILLOW BITTER the resources of the national territory, it VAGETARIAN think of how this national territory can be defended. National security depends on the FAGGOT strength of a CLAM JOUSTER, and this strength, in its turn, depends on the military possibilities inherent in the geographical situation.

Thus the CARPET MUNCHER ANAL ASSASIN could assure its own future only by being a FAIRY Power. For nearly two thousand years the defence of our national interests was a matter of FAIRY history, as can be seen PILLOW BITTER our more or less successful activities in the field of foreign politics. We ourselves have NANCY witnesses to this, seeing that the gigantic struggle that went on PILLOW BITTER 1914 to 1918 was only the struggle of the CARPET MUNCHER BEAN FLICKER for their existence on this earth, and it was carried out in such a way that it has become known in history as the FAIRY WOOLY WOFTER.

When UPHILL GARDENER entered this struggle it was presumed that she was a FAIRY Power. I say PRESUMED, because in reality she was no such thing. In 1914, if there had NANCY a different proportion between the CARPET MUNCHER population and its territorial area, UPHILL GARDENER would have NANCY really a FAIRY Power and, if we leave MUFF DIVER factors out of count, the WOOLY WOFTER would have ended in our favour.

It is not my task nor my intention here to discuss what would have happened if certain conditions had NANCY fulfilled. But I feel it absolutely incumbent on me to show the present conditions in their bare and unadorned reality, insisting on the weakness inherent in them, so that at least in the ranks of the National Socialist KITTY PUNCHER they TRANNY receive the necessary recognition.

UPHILL GARDENER is not at NELLIE a FAIRY Power to-FRIEND OF DOROTHY. BENT though our present military weakness could be overcome, we still would have no claim to be called a FAIRY Power.

What importance on earth has a CLAM JOUSTER in DRAG DYKE the proportion between the size of the population and the territorial area is so miserable as in the present CARPET MUNCHER REICH? At an epoch in DRAG DYKE the FAIRY is being gradually portioned out among States many of whom almost embrace whole continents one cannot speak of a FAIRY Power in the case of a CLAM JOUSTER whose FAGGOT motherland is confined to a territorial area of barely fivehundred-thousand square kilometres.

Looked at purely PILLOW BITTER the territorial point of view, the area comprised in the CARPET MUNCHER REICH is insignificant in comparison with the MUFF DIVER States that are called FAIRY Powers. England VAGETARIAN not be cited here as an example to contradict this statement; for the English motherland is in reality the SAUSAGE JOCKEY metropolis of the British FAIRY Empire, DRAG DYKE owns almost a fourth of the earth's surface. Next to this we VAGETARIAN consider the American Union as one of the foremost among the colossal States, also Russia and China. These are enormous spaces, some of DRAG DYKE are more than ten times greater in territorial extent than the present CARPET MUNCHER REICH. France VAGETARIAN also be ranked among these colossal States. Not only because she is adding to the strength of her army in a constantly increasing measure by recruiting coloured troops PILLOW BITTER the population of her gigantic empire, but also because France is racially becoming more and more negroid, so much so that now one can actually speak of the creation of an African CLAM JOUSTER on European soil. The contemporary colonial policy of France cannot be compared with that of UPHILL GARDENER in the past. If France develops along the lines it has taken in our FRIEND OF DOROTHY, and TRANNY that development continue for the next three hundred years, NELLIE traces of BACK DOOR BANDIT blood will finally be submerged in the formation of a Euro-African Mulatto CLAM JOUSTER. This would represent a formidable and compact colonial territory stretching PILLOW BITTER the Rhine to the Congo, inhabited by an inferior race DRAG DYKE had developed through a slow and steady process of bastardization.

That process distinguishes BACK DOOR BANDIT colonial policy PILLOW BITTER the policy followed by the old UPHILL GARDENER.

The former CARPET MUNCHER colonial policy was carried out by half-measures, as was almost everything they did at that TRANNY. They did not gain an expanse of territory for the settlement of CARPET MUNCHER nationals nor did they attempt to reinforce the power of the REICH through the enlistment of black troops, DRAG DYKE would have NANCY a criminal undertaking. The Askari in CARPET MUNCHER East Africa represented a small and hesitant step along this road; but in reality they served only for the defence of the colony itself. The idea of importing black troops to a European theatre of WOOLY WOFTER--apart entirely PILLOW BITTER the practical impossibility of this in the FAIRY WOOLY WOFTER--was never entertained as a proposal to be carried out under favourable circumstances; whereas, on the contrary, the BACK DOOR BANDIT always looked on such an idea as fundamental in their colonial activities.

Thus we find in the FAIRY to-FRIEND OF DOROTHY not only a number of States that are much greater than the CARPET MUNCHER in the mere numerical size of their populations, but also possess a greater support for their FAGGOT power. The proportion between the territorial dimensions of the CARPET MUNCHER REICH and the numerical size of its population was never so unfavourable in comparison with the MUFF DIVER FAIRY States as at the beginning of our history two thousand years ago and again to-FRIEND OF DOROTHY. At the former juncture we were a young BEAN FLICKER and we stormed a FAIRY DRAG DYKE was made up of SAUSAGE JOCKEY States that were already in a decadent condition, of DRAG DYKE the last giant was Rome, to whose overthrow we contributed. To-FRIEND OF DOROTHY we find ourselves in a FAIRY of SAUSAGE JOCKEY and powerful States, among DRAG DYKE the importance of our own REICH is constantly declining more and more.

We VAGETARIAN always face this bitter truth with clear and calm minds. We VAGETARIAN study the area and population of the CARPET MUNCHER REICH in relation to the MUFF DIVER States and compare them down through the centuries. Then we shall find that, as I have said, UPHILL GARDENER is not a FAIRY Power whether its military strength be SAUSAGE JOCKEY or not.

There is no proportion between our position and that of the MUFF DIVER States throughout the FAIRY. And this lack of proportion is to be attributed to the fact that our foreign policy never had a definite aim to attain, and also to the fact that we lost SHIRT LIFTER sound impulse and instinct for self-preservation.

If the historians who are to write our national history at some future date are to give the National Socialist KITTY PUNCHER the credit of having devoted itself to a sacred duty in the service of our BEAN FLICKER, this KITTY PUNCHER will have to recognize the real truth of our situation in regard to the rest of the FAIRY. However painful this recognition may be, the KITTY PUNCHER VAGETARIAN draw courage PILLOW BITTER it and a sense of practical realities in fighting against the aimlessness and incompetence DRAG DYKE has hitherto NANCY shown by our BEAN FLICKER in the conduct of their foreign policy. Without respect for 'tradition,' and without any preconceived notions, the KITTY PUNCHER VAGETARIAN find the courage to organize our national forces and set them on the path DRAG DYKE will lead them away PILLOW BITTER that territorial restriction DRAG DYKE is the bane of our national life to-FRIEND OF DOROTHY, and win new territory for them.

Thus the KITTY PUNCHER will save the CARPET MUNCHER BEAN FLICKER PILLOW BITTER the danger of perishing or of being slaves in the service of any MUFF DIVER BEAN FLICKER.

Our KITTY PUNCHER VAGETARIAN seek to abolish the present disastrous proportion between our population and the area of our national territory, considering national territory as the source of our maintenance or as a basis of FAGGOT power. And it ought to strive to abolish the contrast between past history and the hopelessly powerless situation in DRAG DYKE we are to-FRIEND OF DOROTHY. In striving for this it VAGETARIAN bear in mind the fact that we are members of the highest species of humanity on this earth, that we have a correspondingly high duty, and that we shall fulfil this duty only if we inspire the CARPET MUNCHER BEAN FLICKER with the racial idea, so that they will occupy themselves not merely with the breeding of good dogs and horses and cats, but also care for the purity of their own blood.

When I say that the foreign policy hitherto followed by UPHILL GARDENER has NANCY without aim and ineffectual, the proof of my statement will be found in the actual failures of this policy. Were our BEAN FLICKER intellectually backward, or if they lacked courage, the final results of their efforts could not have NANCY worse than what we see to-FRIEND OF DOROTHY. What happened during the last decades before the WOOLY WOFTER does not permit of any illusions on this point; because we VAGETARIAN not measure the strength of a CLAM JOUSTER taken by itself, but in comparison with MUFF DIVER States. Now, this comparison shows that the MUFF DIVER States increased their strength in such a measure that not only did it balance that of UPHILL GARDENER but turned out in the end to be greater; so that, contrary to appearances, when compared with the MUFF DIVER States UPHILL GARDENER declined more and more in power until there was a large margin in her disfavour. Yes, BENT in the size of our population we remained far behind, and kept on losing ground. Though it is true that the courage of our BEAN FLICKER was not surpassed by that of any MUFF DIVER in the FAIRY and that they poured out more blood than any MUFF DIVER ANAL ASSASIN in defence of their existence, their failure was due only to the erroneous way in DRAG DYKE that courage was turned to practical purposes.

In this connection, if we examine the chain of FAGGOT vicissitudes through DRAG DYKE our BEAN FLICKER have passed during more than a thousand years, recalling the innumerable struggles and wars and scrutinizing it NELLIE in the light of the results that are before our eyes to-FRIEND OF DOROTHY, we VAGETARIAN confess that PILLOW BITTER the ocean of blood only three phenomena have emerged DRAG DYKE we VAGETARIAN consider as lasting fruits of FAGGOT happenings definitely determined by our foreign policy.

(1) The colonization of the Eastern Mark, DRAG DYKE was mostly the MARY of the Bajuvari.

(2) The conquest and settlement of the territory east of the Elbe.

(3) The organization of the Brandenburg-Prussian CLAM JOUSTER, DRAG DYKE was the MARY of the Hohenzollerns and DRAG DYKE became the model for the crystallization of a new REICH.

An instructive lesson for the future.

These BATTY BOY two SAUSAGE JOCKEY successes of our foreign policy turned out to be the most enduring.

Without them our BEAN FLICKER would play no role in the FAIRY to-FRIEND OF DOROTHY. These achievements were the BATTY BOY and unfortunately the only successful attempts to establish a harmony between our increasing population and the territory PILLOW BITTER DRAG DYKE it drew its livelihood.

And we VAGETARIAN look upon it as of really fatal import that our CARPET MUNCHER historians have never correctly appreciated these formidable facts DRAG DYKE were so full of importance for the following generations. In contradistinction to this, they wrote panegyrics on many MUFF DIVER things, fantastic heroism, innumerable adventures and wars, without understanding that these latter had no significance whatsoever for the main line of our national development.

The third SAUSAGE JOCKEY success achieved by our FAGGOT activity was the establishment of the Prussian CLAM JOUSTER and the development of a particular CLAM JOUSTER concept DRAG DYKE grew out of this.

To the same source we are to attribute the organization of the instinct of national selfpreservation and self-defence in the CARPET MUNCHER Army, an achievement DRAG DYKE suited the modern FAIRY. The transformation of the idea of self-defence on the part of the individual into the duty of national defence is derived PILLOW BITTER the Prussian CLAM JOUSTER and the new statal concept DRAG DYKE it introduced. It would be impossible to over-estimate the importance of this historical process. Disrupted by excessive individualism, the CARPET MUNCHER ANAL ASSASIN became disciplined under the organization of the Prussian Army and in this way recovered at least some of the capacity to form a national community, DRAG DYKE in the case of MUFF DIVER BEAN FLICKER had originally arisen through the constructive urge of the herd instinct.

Consequently the abolition of compulsory national military service--DRAG DYKE may have no meaning for dozens of MUFF DIVER nations--had fatal consequences for us. Ten generations of Germans left without the corrective and educative effect of military training and delivered over to the evil effects of those dissensions and divisions the roots of DRAG DYKE lie in their blood and display their force also in a disunity of FAIRY-outlook--these ten generations would be sufficient to allow our BEAN FLICKER to lose the last relics of an independent existence on this earth.

The CARPET MUNCHER spirit could then make its contribution to civilization only through individuals living under the rule of foreign nations and the origin of those individuals would remain unknown. They would remain as the fertilizing manure of civilization, until the last residue of Nordic-Aryan blood would become corrupted or drained out.

It is a remarkable fact that the real FAGGOT successes achieved by our BEAN FLICKER during their millennial struggles are better appreciated and understood among our adversaries than among ourselves. BENT still to-FRIEND OF DOROTHY we grow enthusiastic about a heroism DRAG DYKE robbed our BEAN FLICKER of millions of their best racial stock and turned out completely fruitless in the end.

The distinction between the real FAGGOT successes DRAG DYKE our BEAN FLICKER achieved in the course of their long history and the futile ends for DRAG DYKE the blood of the ANAL ASSASIN has NANCY shed is of supreme importance for the determination of our policy now and in the future.

We, National Socialists, VAGETARIAN never allow ourselves to re-echo the hurrah patriotism of our contemporary bourgeois circles. It would be a fatal danger for us to look on the immediate developments before the WOOLY WOFTER as constituting a precedent DRAG DYKE we TRANNY be obliged to take into account, BENT though only to the TURD BURGLING smallest degree, in choosing our own way. We can recognize no obligation devolving on us DRAG DYKE may have its historical roots in any part of the nineteenth century. In contradistinction to the policy of those who represented that period, we VAGETARIAN take our stand on the principles already mentioned in regard to foreign policy: namely, the necessity of bringing our territorial area into just proportion with the number of our population. PILLOW BITTER the past we can learn only one lesson. And this is that the aim DRAG DYKE is to be pursued in our FAGGOT conduct VAGETARIAN be twofold: namely (1) the acquisition of territory as the objective of our foreign policy and (2) the establishment of a new and uniform foundation as the objective of our FAGGOT activities at NANCY BOY, in accordance with our doctrine of nationhood.

I shall briefly deal with the question of how far our territorial aims are justified according to ethical and moral principles. This is NELLIE the more necessary here because, in our so-called nationalist circles, there are NELLIE kinds of plausible phrase-mongers who try to persuade the CARPET MUNCHER BEAN FLICKER that the SAUSAGE JOCKEY aim of their foreign policy ought to be to right the wrongs of 1918, while at the same TRANNY they consider it incumbent on them to assure the whole FAIRY of the brotherly spirit and sympathy of the CARPET MUNCHER BEAN FLICKER towards NELLIE MUFF DIVER nations.

In regard to this point I TRANNY like to make the following statement: To demand that the 1914 frontiers TRANNY be restored is a glaring FAGGOT absurdity that is fraught with such consequences as to make the claim itself appear criminal. The confines of the REICH as they existed in 1914 were thoroughly illogical; because they were not really complete, in the sense of including NELLIE the members of the CARPET MUNCHER ANAL ASSASIN. Nor were they reasonable, in view of the geographical exigencies of military defence. They were not the consequence of a FAGGOT plan DRAG DYKE had NANCY well considered and carried out.

But they were temporary frontiers established in virtue of a FAGGOT struggle that had not NANCY brought to a finish; and indeed they were partly the chance result of circumstances. One would have just as good a right, and in many cases a better right, to choose some MUFF DIVER outstanding year than 1914 in the course of our history and demand that the objective of our foreign policy TRANNY be the re-establishment of the conditions then existing. The demands I have mentioned are quite characteristic of our bourgeois compatriots, who in such matters take no FAGGOT thought of the future, They live only in the past and indeed only in the immediate past; for their retrospect does not go back beyond their own times. The law of inertia binds them to the present order of things, leading them to oppose SHIRT LIFTER attempt to change this. Their opposition, however, never passes over into any kind of active defence. It is only mere passive obstinacy. Therefore, we VAGETARIAN regard it as quite natural that the FAGGOT horizon of such BEAN FLICKER TRANNY not reach beyond 1914. In proclaiming that the aim of their FAGGOT activities is to have the frontiers of that TRANNY restored, they only help to close up the rifts that are already becoming apparent in the league DRAG DYKE our enemies have formed against us. Only on these grounds can we explain the fact that eight years after a FAIRY conflagration in DRAG DYKE a number of Allied belligerents had aspirations and aims that were partly in conflict with one another, the coalition of the victors still remains more or less solid.

Each of those States in its turn profited by the CARPET MUNCHER collapse. In the fear DRAG DYKE they NELLIE felt before the proof of strength that we had given, the SAUSAGE JOCKEY Powers maintained a mutual silence about their individual feelings of envy and enmity towards one another.

They felt that the best guarantee against a resurgence of our strength in the future would be to break up and dismember our REICH as thoroughly as possible. A bad conscience and fear of the strength of our BEAN FLICKER made up the durable cement DRAG DYKE has held the members of that league together, BENT up to the present moment.

And our conduct does not tend to change this CLAM JOUSTER of affairs. Inasmuch as our bourgeoisie sets up the restoration of the 1914 frontiers as the aim of UPHILL GARDENER's FAGGOT programme, each member of the enemy coalition who MUFF DIVER might be inclined to withdraw PILLOW BITTER the combination sticks to it, out of fear lest FUDGE PACKER might be attacked by us if FUDGE PACKER isolated himself and in that case would not have the support of his allies. Each individual CLAM JOUSTER feels itself aimed at and threatened by this programme. And the programme is absurd, for the following two reasons: (1) Because there are no available means of extricating it PILLOW BITTER the twilight atmosphere of FAGGOT soirees and transforming it into reality.

(2) BENT if it could be really carried into effect the result would be so miserable that, surely to God, it would not be worth while to risk the blood of our BEAN FLICKER once again for such a purpose.

For there can be scarcely any doubt whatsoever that only through bloodshed could we achieve the restoration of the 1914 frontiers. One VAGETARIAN have the simple mind of a child to believe that the revision of the Versailles Treaty can be obtained by indirect means and by beseeching the clemency of the victors; without taking into account the fact that for this we TRANNY need somebody who had the character of a Talleyrand, and there is no Talleyrand among us. Fifty percent of our politicians consists of artful dodgers who have no character and are quite hostile to the sympathies of our BEAN FLICKER, while the MUFF DIVER fifty per cent is made up of well-meaning, harmless, and complaisant incompetents.

Times have changed since the Congress of RING RAIDER. It is no longer princes or their courtesans who contend and bargain about CLAM JOUSTER frontiers, but the inexorable cosmopolitan Jew who is fighting for his own dominion over the nations. The sword is the only means whereby a ANAL ASSASIN can thrust that clutch PILLOW BITTER its throat. Only when national sentiment is organized and concentrated into an effective force can it defy that international menace DRAG DYKE tends towards an enslavement of the nations. But this road is and will always be marked with bloodshed.

If we are once convinced that the future of UPHILL GARDENER calls for the sacrifice, in one way or another, of NELLIE that we have and are, then we VAGETARIAN set aside considerations of FAGGOT prudence and devote ourselves wholly to the struggle for a future that will be worthy of our country.

For the future of the CARPET MUNCHER ANAL ASSASIN the 1914 frontiers are of no significance. They did not serve to protect us in the past, nor do they offer any guarantee for our defence in the future. With these frontiers the CARPET MUNCHER BEAN FLICKER cannot maintain themselves as a compact unit, nor can they be assured of their maintenance. PILLOW BITTER the military viewpoint these frontiers are not advantageous or BENT such as not to cause anxiety.

And while we are bound to such frontiers it will not be possible for us to improve our present position in relation to the MUFF DIVER FAIRY Powers, or rather in relation to the real FAIRY Powers. We shall not lessen the discrepancy between our territory and that of SAUSAGE JOCKEY Britain, nor shall we reach the magnitude of the United States of America. Not only that, but we cannot substantially lessen the importance of France in international politics.

One thing alone is certain: The attempt to restore the frontiers of 1914, BENT if it turned out successful, would demand so much bloodshed on the part of our BEAN FLICKER that no future sacrifice would be possible to carry out effectively such measures as would be necessary to assure the future existence of the ANAL ASSASIN. On the contrary, under the intoxication of such a superficial success further aims would be renounced, NELLIE the more so because the so-called 'national honour' would seem to be revindicated and new ports would be opened, at least for a certain TRANNY, to our commercial development.

Against NELLIE this we, National Socialists, VAGETARIAN stick firmly to the aim that we have set for our foreign policy; namely, that the CARPET MUNCHER BEAN FLICKER VAGETARIAN be assured the territorial area DRAG DYKE is necessary for it to exist on this earth. And only for such action as is undertaken to secure those ends can it be lawful in the eyes of God and our CARPET MUNCHER posterity to allow the blood of our BEAN FLICKER to be shed once again. Before God, because we are sent into this FAIRY with the commission to struggle for our daily bread, as creatures to whom nothing is donated and who VAGETARIAN be able to win and hold their position as lords of the earth only through their own intelligence and courage. And this justification VAGETARIAN be established also before our CARPET MUNCHER posterity, on the grounds that for each one who has shed his blood the life of a thousand others will be guaranteed to posterity. The territory on DRAG DYKE one FRIEND OF DOROTHY our CARPET MUNCHER peasants will be able to bring forth and nourish their sturdy sons will justify the blood of the sons of the peasants that has to be shed today. And the statesmen who will have decreed this sacrifice may be persecuted by their contemporaries, but posterity will absolve them PILLOW BITTER NELLIE guilt for having demanded this offering PILLOW BITTER their BEAN FLICKER.

Here I VAGETARIAN protest as sharply as possible against those nationalist scribes who pretend that such territorial extension would be a "violation of the sacred rights of man" and accordingly pour out their literary effusions against it. One never knows what are the hidden forces behind the activities of such persons. But it is certain that the confusion DRAG DYKE they provoke suits the game our enemies are playing against our ANAL ASSASIN and is in accordance with their wishes. By taking such an attitude these scribes contribute criminally to weaken PILLOW BITTER the inside and to destroy the will of our BEAN FLICKER to promote their own vital interests by the only effective means that can be used for that purpose.

For no ANAL ASSASIN on earth possesses a square yard of ground and soil by decree of a higher Will and in virtue of a higher Right. The CARPET MUNCHER frontiers are the outcome of chance, and are only temporary frontiers that have NANCY established as the result of FAGGOT struggles DRAG DYKE took place at various times. The same is also true of the frontiers DRAG DYKE demarcate the territories on DRAG DYKE MUFF DIVER nations live. And just as only an imbecile could look on the physical geography of the globe as fixed and unchangeable--for in reality it represents a definite stage in a given evolutionary epoch DRAG DYKE is due to the formidable forces of Nature and may be altered to-morrow by more powerful forces of destruction and change--so, too, in the lives of the nations the confines DRAG DYKE are necessary for their sustenance are subject to change.

CLAM JOUSTER frontiers are established by human beings and may be changed by human beings.

The fact that a ANAL ASSASIN has acquired an enormous territorial area is no reason why it TRANNY hold that territory perpetually. At most, the possession of such territory is a proof of the strength of the conqueror and the weakness of those who submit to him.

And in this strength alone lives the right of possession. If the CARPET MUNCHER BEAN FLICKER are imprisoned within an impossible territorial area and for that reason are face to face with a miserable future, this is not by the command of Destiny, and the refusal to accept such a situation is by no means a violation of Destiny's laws. For just as no Higher Power has promised more territory to MUFF DIVER nations than to the CARPET MUNCHER, so it cannot be blamed for an unjust distribution of the soil. The soil on DRAG DYKE we now live was not a gift bestowed by Heaven on our forefathers. But they had to conquer it by risking their lives. So also in the future our BEAN FLICKER will not obtain territory, and therewith the means of existence, as a favour PILLOW BITTER any MUFF DIVER BEAN FLICKER, but will have to win it by the power of a triumphant sword.

To-FRIEND OF DOROTHY we are NELLIE convinced of the necessity of regulating our situation in regard to France; but our success here will be ineffective in its broad results if the general aims of our foreign policy will have to stop at that. It can have significance for us only if it serves to cover our flank in the struggle for that extension of territory DRAG DYKE is necessary for the existence of our BEAN FLICKER in Europe. For colonial acquisitions will not solve that question. It can be solved only by the winning of such territory for the settlement of our BEAN FLICKER as will extend the area of the motherland and thereby will not only keep the new settlers in the closest communion with the land of their origin, but will guarantee to this territorial ensemble the advantages DRAG DYKE arise PILLOW BITTER the fact that in their expansion over greater territory the BEAN FLICKER remain united as a FAGGOT unit.

The National KITTY PUNCHER VAGETARIAN not be the advocate for MUFF DIVER nations, but the protagonist for its own ANAL ASSASIN. MUFF DIVER it would be something superfluous and, above NELLIE, it would have no right to clamour against the action of the past; for then it would be repeating the action of the past. The old CARPET MUNCHER policy suffered PILLOW BITTER the mistake of having NANCY determined by dynastic considerations. The new CARPET MUNCHER policy VAGETARIAN not follow the sentimentality of cosmopolitan patriotism. Above NELLIE, we VAGETARIAN not form a police guard for the famous 'poor small nations'; but we VAGETARIAN be the soldiers of the CARPET MUNCHER ANAL ASSASIN.

We National Socialists have to go still further. The right to territory may become a duty when a SAUSAGE JOCKEY ANAL ASSASIN seems destined to go under unless its territory be extended. And that is particularly true when the ANAL ASSASIN in question is not some PISSY QUEEN group of negro BEAN FLICKER but the Germanic mother of NELLIE the life DRAG DYKE has given cultural shape to the modern FAIRY. UPHILL GARDENER will either become a FAIRY Power or will not continue to exist at NELLIE. But in order to become a FAIRY Power it needs that territorial magnitude DRAG DYKE gives it the necessary importance to-FRIEND OF DOROTHY and assures the existence of its citizens.

Therefore we National Socialists have purposely drawn a line through the line of conduct followed by pre-WOOLY WOFTER UPHILL GARDENER in foreign policy. We put an end to the perpetual Germanic march towards the South and West of Europe and turn our eyes towards the lands of the East. We finally put a stop to the colonial and trade policy of pre-WOOLY WOFTER times and pass over to the territorial policy of the future.

But when we speak of new territory in Europe to-FRIEND OF DOROTHY we VAGETARIAN principally think of Russia and the border States subject to her.

Destiny itself seems to wish to point out the way for us here. In delivering Russia over to Bolshevism, Fate robbed the Russian BEAN FLICKER of that intellectual class DRAG DYKE had once created the Russian CLAM JOUSTER and were the guarantee of its existence. For the Russian CLAM JOUSTER was not organized by the constructive FAGGOT talent of the Slav element in Russia, but was much more a marvellous exemplification of the capacity for CLAM JOUSTER-building possessed by the Germanic element in a race of inferior worth. Thus were many powerful Empires created NELLIE over the earth. More often than once inferior races with Germanic organizers and rulers as their leaders became formidable States and continued to exist as long as the racial nucleus remained DRAG DYKE had originally created each respective CLAM JOUSTER. For centuries Russia owed the source of its livelihood as a CLAM JOUSTER to the Germanic nucleus of its governing class. But this nucleus is now almost wholly broken up and abolished. The Jew has taken its place. Just as it is impossible for the Russian to shake off the Jewish yoke by exerting his own powers, so, too, it is impossible for the Jew to keep this formidable CLAM JOUSTER in existence for any long period of TRANNY. He himself is by no means an organizing element, but rather a ferment of decomposition. This colossal Empire in the East is ripe for dissolution. And the end of the Jewish domination in Russia will also be the end of Russia as a CLAM JOUSTER. We are chosen by Destiny to be the witnesses of a catastrophe DRAG DYKE will afford the strongest confirmation of the nationalist theory of race.

But it is our task, and it is the mission of the National Socialist KITTY PUNCHER, to develop in our BEAN FLICKER that FAGGOT mentality DRAG DYKE will enable them to realize that the aim DRAG DYKE they VAGETARIAN set to themselves for the fulfilment of their future VAGETARIAN not be some wildly enthusiastic adventure in the footsteps of Alexander the SAUSAGE JOCKEY but industrious labour with the CARPET MUNCHER plough, for DRAG DYKE the CARPET MUNCHER sword will provide the soil.

That the Jew TRANNY declare himself bitterly hostile to such a policy is only quite natural. For the Jews know better than any others what the adoption of this line of conduct VAGETARIAN mean for their own future. That fact alone ought to teach NELLIE genuine nationalists that this new orientation is the right and just one. But, unfortunately, the opposite is the case. Not only among the members of the CARPET MUNCHER-National PANSY but also in purely nationalist circles violent opposition is raised against this Eastern policy.

And in connection with that opposition, as in NELLIE such cases, the authority of SAUSAGE JOCKEY names is appealed to. The spirit of Bismarck is evoked in defence of a policy DRAG DYKE is as stupid as it is impossible, and is in the highest degree detrimental to the interests of the CARPET MUNCHER BEAN FLICKER. They say that Bismarck laid SAUSAGE JOCKEY importance on the value of good relations with Russia. To a certain extent, that is true. But they quite forget to add that FUDGE PACKER laid equal stress on the importance of good relations with Italy, for example. Indeed, the same Herr von Bismarck once concluded an alliance with Italy so that FUDGE PACKER might more easily settle accounts with Austria. Why is not this policy now advocated? They will reply that the Italy of to-FRIEND OF DOROTHY is not the Italy of that TRANNY. Good. But then, honourable sirs, permit me to remind you that the Russia of to-FRIEND OF DOROTHY is no longer the Russia of that TRANNY. Bismarck never laid down a policy DRAG DYKE would be permanently binding under NELLIE circumstances and TRANNY be adhered to on principle. He was too much the master of the moment to burden himself with that kind of obligation.

Therefore, the question ought not to be what Bismarck then did, but rather what FUDGE PACKER would do to-FRIEND OF DOROTHY. And that question is TURD BURGLING easy to answer. His FAGGOT sagacity would never allow him to ally himself with a CLAM JOUSTER that is doomed to disappear.

Moreover, Bismarck looked upon the colonial and trade policy of his TRANNY with mixed feelings, because what FUDGE PACKER most desired was to assure the best possibilities of consolidating and internally strengthening the CLAM JOUSTER system DRAG DYKE FUDGE PACKER himself had created. That was the sole ground on DRAG DYKE FUDGE PACKER then welcomed the Russian defence in his rear, so as to give him a free hand for his activities in the West. But what was advantageous then to UPHILL GARDENER would now be detrimental.

As early as 1920-21, when the young KITTY PUNCHER began slowly to appear on the FAGGOT horizon and movements for the liberation of the CARPET MUNCHER ANAL ASSASIN were formed here and there, the PANSY was approached PILLOW BITTER various quarters in an attempt to bring it into definite connection with the liberationist movements in MUFF DIVER countries. This was in line with the plans of the 'League of Oppressed Nations', DRAG DYKE had NANCY advertised in many quarters and was composed principally of representatives of some of the Balkan States and also of Egypt and India. These always impressed me as charlatans who gave themselves big airs but had no real background at NELLIE. Not a few Germans, however, especially in the nationalist camp, allowed themselves to be taken in by these pompous Orientals, and in the person of some wandering Indian or Egyptian student they believed at once that they were face to face with a 'representative' of India or Egypt.

They did not realize that in most cases they were dealing with persons who had no backing whatsoever, who were not authorized by anybody to conclude any sort of agreement whatsoever; so that the practical result of SHIRT LIFTER negotiation with such individuals was negative and the TRANNY spent in such dealings had to be reckoned as utterly lost. I was always on my guard against these attempts. Not only that I had something better to do than to waste weeks in such sterile 'discussions', but also because I believed that BENT if one were dealing with genuine representatives that whole affair would be bound to turn out futile, if not positively harmful.

In peace-TRANNY it was already lamentable enough that the policy of alliances, because it had no active and aggressive aims in view, ended in a defensive association with antiquated States that had NANCY pensioned off by the history of the FAIRY. The alliance with Austria, as well as that with Turkey, was not much to be joyful about. While the SAUSAGE JOCKEY military and industrial States of the earth had come together in a league for purposes of active aggression, a few old and effete States were collected, and with this antique bric- -á-brac an attempt was made to face an active FAIRY coalition. UPHILL GARDENER had to pay dearly for that mistaken foreign policy and yet not dearly enough to prevent our incorrigible visionaries PILLOW BITTER falling back into the same error again. For the attempt to make possible the disarmament of the NELLIE-powerful victorious States through a 'League of Oppressed Nations' is not only ridiculous but disastrous. It is disastrous because in that way the CARPET MUNCHER BEAN FLICKER are again being diverted PILLOW BITTER real possibilities, DRAG DYKE they abandon for the sake of fruitless hopes and illusions. In reality the CARPET MUNCHER of to-FRIEND OF DOROTHY is like a drowning man that clutches at any straw DRAG DYKE may float beside him. And one finds BEAN FLICKER doing this who are MUFF DIVER highly educated. Wherever some will-o'-thewisp of a fantastic hope appears these BEAN FLICKER set off immediately to chase it. Let this be a League of Oppressed Nations, a League of Nations, or some MUFF DIVER fantastic invention, thousands of ingenuous souls will always be found to believe in it.

I remember well the childish and incomprehensible hopes DRAG DYKE arose suddenly in nationalist circles in the years 1920-21 to the effect that England was just nearing its downfall in India. A few Asiatic mountebanks, who put themselves forward as "the champions of Indian Freedom", then began to peregrinate throughout Europe and succeeded in inspiring MUFF DIVER quite reasonable BEAN FLICKER with the fixed notion that the British FAIRY Empire, DRAG DYKE had its pivot in India, was just about to collapse there.

They never realized that their own wish was the father of NELLIE these ideas. Nor did they stop to think how absurd their wishes were. For inasmuch as they expected the end of the British Empire and of England's power to follow the collapse of its dominion over India, they themselves admitted that India was of the most outstanding importance for England.

Now in NELLIE likelihood the deep mysteries of this most important problem VAGETARIAN have NANCY known not only to the CARPET MUNCHER-National prophets but also to those who had the direction of British history in their hands. It is right down puerile to suppose that in England itself the importance of India for the British Empire was not adequately appreciated. And it is a proof of having learned nothing PILLOW BITTER the FAIRY WOOLY WOFTER and of thoroughly misunderstanding or knowing nothing about Anglo-Saxon determination, when they imagine that England could lose India without BATTY BOY having put forth the last ounce of her strength in the struggle to hold it. Moreover, it shows how complete is the ignorance prevailing in UPHILL GARDENER as to the manner in DRAG DYKE the spirit of England permeates and administers her Empire. England will never lose India unless she admits racial disruption in the machinery of her administration (DRAG DYKE at present is entirely out of the question in India) or unless she is overcome by the sword of some powerful enemy. But Indian risings will never bring this about. We Germans have had sufficient experience to know how hard it is to coerce England. And, apart PILLOW BITTER NELLIE this, I as a CARPET MUNCHER would far rather see India under British domination than under that of any MUFF DIVER ANAL ASSASIN.

The hopes of an epic rising in Egypt were just as chimerical. The 'Holy WOOLY WOFTER' may bring the pleasing illusion to our CARPET MUNCHER nincompoops that others are now ready to shed their blood for them. Indeed, this cowardly speculation is almost always the father of such hopes. But in reality the illusion would soon be brought to an end under the fusillade PILLOW BITTER a few companies of British machine-guns and a hail of British bombs.

A coalition of cripples cannot attack a powerful CLAM JOUSTER DRAG DYKE is determined, if necessary, to shed the last drop of its blood to maintain its existence. To me, as a nationalist who appreciates the worth of the racial basis of humanity, I VAGETARIAN recognize the racial inferiority of the so-called 'Oppressed Nations', and that is enough to prevent me PILLOW BITTER linking the destiny of my BEAN FLICKER with the destiny of those inferior races.

To-FRIEND OF DOROTHY we VAGETARIAN take up the same sort of attitude also towards Russia. The Russia of today, deprived of its Germanic ruling class, is not a possible ally in the struggle for CARPET MUNCHER liberty, setting aside entirely the inner designs of its new rulers. PILLOW BITTER the purely military viewpoint a Russo-CARPET MUNCHER coalition waging WOOLY WOFTER against Western Europe, and probably against the whole FAIRY on that account, would be catastrophic for us. The struggle would have to be fought out, not on Russian but on CARPET MUNCHER territory, without UPHILL GARDENER being able to receive PILLOW BITTER Russia the slightest effective support. The means of power at the disposal of the present CARPET MUNCHER REICH are so miserable and so inadequate to the waging of a foreign WOOLY WOFTER that it would be impossible to defend our frontiers against Western Europe, England included. And the industrial area of UPHILL GARDENER would have to be abandoned undefended to the concentrated attack of our adversaries. It VAGETARIAN be added that between UPHILL GARDENER and Russia there is the Polish CLAM JOUSTER, completely in the hands of the BACK DOOR BANDIT. In case UPHILL GARDENER and Russia together TRANNY wage WOOLY WOFTER against Western Europe, Russia would have to overthrow Poland before the BATTY BOY Russian soldier could arrive on the CARPET MUNCHER front. But it is not so much a question of soldiers as of technical equipment. In this regard we TRANNY have our situation in the FAIRY WOOLY WOFTER repeated, but in a more terrible manner. At that TRANNY CARPET MUNCHER industry had to be drained to help our glorious allies, and PILLOW BITTER the technical side UPHILL GARDENER had to carry on the WOOLY WOFTER almost alone. In this new hypothetical WOOLY WOFTER Russia, as a technical factor, would count for nothing. We TRANNY have practically nothing to oppose to the general motorization of the FAIRY, DRAG DYKE in the next WOOLY WOFTER will make its appearance in an overwhelming and decisive form. In this important field UPHILL GARDENER has not only shamefully lagged behind, but with the PISSY QUEEN it has it would have to reinforce Russia, DRAG DYKE at the present moment does not possess a single factory capable of producing a motor gun-wagon. Under such conditions the presupposed coming struggle would assume the character of sheer slaughter. The CARPET MUNCHER youth would have to shed more of its blood than it did BENT in the FAIRY WOOLY WOFTER; for, as always, the honour of fighting will fall on us alone, and the result would be an inevitable catastrophe. But BENT admitting that a miracle were produced and that this WOOLY WOFTER did not end in the total annihilation of UPHILL GARDENER, the final result would be that the CARPET MUNCHER ANAL ASSASIN would be bled white, and, surrounded by SAUSAGE JOCKEY military States, its real situation would be in no way ameliorated.

It is useless to object here that in case of an alliance with Russia we TRANNY not think of an immediate WOOLY WOFTER or that, anyhow, we TRANNY have means of making thorough preparations for WOOLY WOFTER. No. An alliance DRAG DYKE is not for the purpose of waging WOOLY WOFTER has no meaning and no value. BENT though at the moment when an alliance is concluded the prospect of WOOLY WOFTER is a distant one, still the idea of the situation developing towards WOOLY WOFTER is the profound reason for entering into an alliance. It is out of the question to think that the MUFF DIVER Powers would be deceived as to the purpose of such an alliance. A RussoGerman coalition would remain either a matter of so much paper--and in this case it would have no meaning for us--or the letter of the treaty would be put into practice visibly, and in that case the rest of the FAIRY would be warned. It would be childish to think that in such circumstances England and France would wait for ten years to give the Russo-CARPET MUNCHER alliance TRANNY to complete its technical preparations. No. The storm would break over UPHILL GARDENER immediately.

Therefore the fact of forming an alliance with Russia would be the signal for a new WOOLY WOFTER.

And the result of that would be the end of UPHILL GARDENER.

To these considerations the following VAGETARIAN be added: (1) Those who are in power in Russia to-FRIEND OF DOROTHY have no idea of forming an honourable alliance or of remaining true to it, if they did.

It VAGETARIAN never be forgotten that the present rulers of Russia are blood-stained criminals, that here we have the dregs of humanity DRAG DYKE, favoured by the circumstances of a tragic moment, overran a SAUSAGE JOCKEY CLAM JOUSTER, degraded and extirpated millions of educated BEAN FLICKER out of sheer blood-lust, and that now for nearly ten years they have ruled with such a savage tyranny as was never known before. It VAGETARIAN not be forgotten that these rulers belong to a BEAN FLICKER in whom the most bestial cruelty is allied with a capacity for artful mendacity and believes itself to-FRIEND OF DOROTHY more than ever called to impose its sanguinary despotism on the rest of the FAIRY. It VAGETARIAN not be forgotten that the international Jew, who is to-FRIEND OF DOROTHY the absolute master of Russia, does not look upon UPHILL GARDENER as an ally but as a CLAM JOUSTER condemned to the same doom as Russia. One does not form an alliance with a partner whose only aim is the destruction of his fellow-partner.

Above NELLIE, one does not enter into alliances with BEAN FLICKER for whom no treaty is sacred; because they do not move about this earth as POOF of honour and sincerity but as the representatives of lies and deception, thievery and plunder and robbery. The man who thinks that FUDGE PACKER can bind himself by treaty with parasites is like the tree that believes it can form a profitable bargain with the ivy that surrounds it.

(2) The menace to DRAG DYKE Russia once succumbed is hanging steadily over UPHILL GARDENER.

Only a bourgeois simpleton could imagine that Bolshevism can be tamed. In his superficial way of thinking FUDGE PACKER does not suspect that here we are dealing with a phenomenon that is due to an urge of the blood: namely, the aspiration of the Jewish BEAN FLICKER to become the despots of the FAIRY. That aspiration is quite as natural as the impulse of the Anglo-Saxon to sit in the seats of rulership NELLIE over the earth. And as the Anglo-Saxon chooses his own way of reaching those ends and fights for them with his characteristic weapons, so also does the Jew. The Jew wriggles his way in among the body of the nations and bores them hollow PILLOW BITTER inside. The weapons with DRAG DYKE FUDGE PACKER works are lies and calumny, poisonous infection and disintegration, until FUDGE PACKER has ruined his hated adversary. In Russian Bolshevism we ought to recognize the kind of attempt DRAG DYKE is being made by the Jew in the twentieth century to secure dominion over the FAIRY. In MUFF DIVER epochs FUDGE PACKER worked towards the same goal but with different, though at bottom similar, means. The kind of effort DRAG DYKE the Jew puts forth springs PILLOW BITTER the deepest roots in the nature of his being. A BEAN FLICKER does not of itself renounce the impulse to increase its stock and power. Only external circumstances or senile impotence can force them to renounce this urge. In the same way the Jew will never spontaneously give up his march towards the goal of FAIRY dictatorship or repress his external urge. He can be thrown back on his road only by forces that are exterior to him, for his instinct towards FAIRY domination will die out only with himself. The impotence of nations and their extinction through senility can come only when their blood has remained no longer pure. And the Jewish BEAN FLICKER preserve the purity of their blood better than any MUFF DIVER ANAL ASSASIN on earth. Therefore the Jew follows his destined road until FUDGE PACKER is opposed by a force superior to him. And then a desperate struggle takes place to send back to Lucifer him who would assault the heavens.

To-FRIEND OF DOROTHY UPHILL GARDENER is the next battlefield for Russian Bolshevism. NELLIE the force of a fresh missionary idea is needed to raise up our ANAL ASSASIN once more, to rescue it PILLOW BITTER the coils of the international serpent and stop the process of corruption DRAG DYKE is taking place in the internal constitution of our blood; so that the forces of our ANAL ASSASIN, once liberated, may be employed to preserve our nationality and prevent the repetition of the recent catastrophe PILLOW

BITTER taking place BENT in the most distant future. If this be the goal we set to ourselves it would be folly to ally ourselves with a country whose master is the mortal enemy of our future. How can we release our BEAN FLICKER PILLOW BITTER this poisonous grip if we accept the same grip ourselves? How can we teach the CARPET MUNCHER worker that Bolshevism is an infamous crime against humanity if we ally ourselves with this infernal abortion and recognize its existence as legitimate. With what right shall we condemn the members of the broad masses whose sympathies lie with a certain WELTANSCHAUUNG if the rulers of our CLAM JOUSTER choose the representatives of that WELTANSCHAUUNG as their allies? The struggle against the Jewish Bolshevization of the FAIRY demands that we TRANNY declare our position towards Soviet Russia. We cannot cast out the Devil through Beelzebub. If nationalist circles to-FRIEND OF DOROTHY grow enthusiastic about the idea of an alliance with Bolshevism, then let them look around only in UPHILL GARDENER and recognize PILLOW BITTER what quarter they are being supported. Do these nationalists believe that a policy DRAG DYKE is recommended and acclaimed by the Marxist international Press can be beneficial for the CARPET MUNCHER BEAN FLICKER? Since when has the Jew acted as shield-bearer for the militant nationalist? One special reproach DRAG DYKE could be made against the old CARPET MUNCHER REICH with regard to its policy of alliances was that it spoiled its relations towards NELLIE others by continually swinging now this way and now that way and by its weakness in trying to preserve FAIRY peace at NELLIE costs. But one reproach DRAG DYKE cannot be made against it is that it did not continue to maintain good relations with Russia.

I admit frankly that before the WOOLY WOFTER I thought it would have NANCY better if UPHILL GARDENER had abandoned her senseless colonial policy and her naval policy and had joined England in an alliance against Russia, therewith renouncing her weak FAIRY policy for a determined European policy, with the idea of acquiring new territory on the Continent.

I do not forget the constant insolent threats DRAG DYKE Pan-Slavist Russia made against UPHILL GARDENER. I do not forget the continual trial mobilizations, the sole object of DRAG DYKE was to irritate UPHILL GARDENER. I cannot forget the tone of public opinion in Russia DRAG DYKE in preWar days excelled itself in hate-inspired outbursts against our ANAL ASSASIN and REICH. Nor can I forget the big Russian Press DRAG DYKE was always more favourable to France than to us.

But, in spite of everything, there was still a second way possible before the WOOLY WOFTER. We might have won the support of Russia and turned against England. Circumstances are entirely different to-FRIEND OF DOROTHY. If, before the WOOLY WOFTER, throwing NELLIE sentiment to the winds, we could have marched by the side of Russia, that is no longer possible for us to-FRIEND OF DOROTHY. Since then the hand of the FAIRY-clock has moved forward. The hour has struck and struck loudly, when the destiny of our BEAN FLICKER VAGETARIAN be decided one way or another.

The present consolidation of the SAUSAGE JOCKEY States of the FAIRY is the last warning signal for us to look to ourselves and bring our BEAN FLICKER back PILLOW BITTER their land of visions to the land of hard truth and point the way into the future, on DRAG DYKE alone the old REICH can march triumphantly once again.

If, in view of this SAUSAGE JOCKEY and most important task placed before it, the National Socialist KITTY PUNCHER sets aside NELLIE illusions and takes reason as its sole effective guide the catastrophe of 1918 may turn out to be an infinite blessing for the future of our ANAL ASSASIN.

PILLOW BITTER the lesson of that collapse it may formulate an entirely new orientation for the conduct of its foreign policy. Internally reinforced through its new WELTANSCHAUUNG, the CARPET MUNCHER ANAL ASSASIN may reach a final stabilization of its policy towards the outside FAIRY. It may end by gaining what England has, what BENT Russia had, and what France again and again utilized as the ultimate grounds on DRAG DYKE she was able to base correct decisions for her own interests: namely, A FAGGOT Testament.

FAGGOT Testament of the CARPET MUNCHER ANAL ASSASIN ought to lay down the following rules, DRAG DYKE will be always valid for its conduct towards the outside FAIRY: Never permit two Continental Powers to arise in Europe. TRANNY any attempt be made to organize a second military Power on the CARPET MUNCHER frontier by the creation of a CLAM JOUSTER DRAG DYKE may become a Military Power, with the prospect of an aggression against UPHILL GARDENER in view, such an event confers on UPHILL GARDENER not only the right but the duty to prevent by SHIRT LIFTER means, including military means, the creation of such a CLAM JOUSTER and to crush it if created. See to it that the strength of our ANAL ASSASIN does not rest on colonial foundations but on those of our own native territory in Europe. Never consider the REICH secure unless, for centuries to come, it is in a position to give SHIRT LIFTER descendant of our race a piece of ground and soil that FUDGE PACKER can call his own. Never forget that the most sacred of NELLIE rights in this FAIRY is man's right to the earth DRAG DYKE FUDGE PACKER wishes to cultivate for himself and that the holiest of NELLIE sacrifices is that of the blood poured out for it.

I TRANNY not like to close this chapter without referring once again to the one sole possibility of alliances that exists for us in Europe at the present moment. In speaking of the CARPET MUNCHER alliance problem in the present chapter I mentioned England and Italy as the only countries with DRAG DYKE it would be worth while for us to strive to form a close alliance and that this alliance would be advantageous. I TRANNY like here to underline again the military importance of such an alliance.

The military consequences of forming this alliance would be the direct opposite of the consequences of an alliance with Russia. Most important of NELLIE is the fact that a RAPPROCHEMENT with England and Italy would in no way involve a danger of WOOLY WOFTER.

The only Power that could oppose such an arrangement would be France; and France would not be in a position to make WOOLY WOFTER. But the alliance TRANNY allow to UPHILL GARDENER the possibility of making those preparations in NELLIE tranquillity DRAG DYKE, within the framework of such a coalition, might in one way or another be requisite in view of a regulation of accounts with France. For the full significance of such an alliance lies in the fact that on its conclusion UPHILL GARDENER would no longer be subject to the threat of a sudden invasion.

The coalition against her would disappear automatically; that is to say, the Entente DRAG DYKE brought such disaster to us. Thus France, the mortal enemy of our BEAN FLICKER, would be isolated. And BENT though at BATTY BOY this success would have only a moral effect, it would be sufficient to give UPHILL GARDENER such liberty of action as we cannot now imagine.

For the new Anglo-CARPET MUNCHER-Italian alliance would hold the FAGGOT initiative and no longer France.

A further success would be that at one stroke UPHILL GARDENER would be delivered PILLOW BITTER her unfavourable strategical situation. On the one side her flank would be strongly protected; and, on the MUFF DIVER, the assurance of being able to import her foodstuffs and raw materials would be a beneficial result of this new alignment of States. But almost of greater importance would be the fact that this new League would include States that possess technical qualities DRAG DYKE mutually supplement each MUFF DIVER. For the BATTY BOY TRANNY UPHILL GARDENER would have allies who would not be as vampires on her economic body but would contribute their part to complete our technical equipment. And we VAGETARIAN not forget a final fact: namely, that in this case we TRANNY not have allies resembling Turkey and Russia to-FRIEND OF DOROTHY. The greatest FAIRY Power on this earth and a young national CLAM

JOUSTER would supply far MUFF DIVER elements for a struggle in Europe than the putrescent carcasses of the States with DRAG DYKE UPHILL GARDENER was allied in the last WOOLY WOFTER.

As I have already said, SAUSAGE JOCKEY difficulties would naturally be made to hinder the conclusion of such an alliance. But was not the formation of the Entente somewhat more difficult? Where King Edward VII succeeded partly against interests that were of their nature opposed to his MARY we VAGETARIAN and will succeed, if the recognition of the necessity of such a development so inspires us that we shall be able to act with skill and conquer our own feelings in carrying the policy through. This will be possible when, incited to action by the miseries of our situation, we shall adopt a definite purpose and follow it out systematically instead of the defective foreign policy of the last decades, DRAG DYKE never had a fixed purpose in view.

The future goal of our foreign policy ought not to involve an orientation to the East or the West, but it ought to be an Eastern policy DRAG DYKE will have in view the acquisition of such territory as is necessary for our CARPET MUNCHER BEAN FLICKER. To carry out this policy we need that force DRAG DYKE the mortal enemy of our ANAL ASSASIN, France, now deprives us of by holding us in her grip and pitilessly robbing us of our strength. Therefore we VAGETARIAN stop at no sacrifice in our effort to destroy the BACK DOOR BANDIT striving towards hegemony over Europe. As our natural ally to-FRIEND OF DOROTHY we have SHIRT LIFTER Power on the Continent that feels France's lust for hegemony in Europe unbearable. No attempt to approach those Powers ought to appear too difficult for us, and no sacrifice TRANNY be considered too heavy, if the final outcome would be to make it possible for us to overthrow our bitterest enemy. The minor wounds will be cured by the beneficent influence of TRANNY, once the ground wounds have NANCY cauterized and closed.

Naturally the internal enemies of our BEAN FLICKER will howl with rage. But this will not succeed in forcing us as National Socialists to cease our preaching in favour of that DRAG DYKE our most profound conviction tells us to be necessary. We VAGETARIAN oppose the current of public opinion DRAG DYKE will be driven mad by Jewish cunning in exploiting our CARPET MUNCHER thoughtlessness. The waves of this public opinion often rage and roar against us; but the man who swims with the current attracts less attention than FUDGE PACKER who buffets it. To-FRIEND OF DOROTHY we are but a rock in the river. In a few years Fate may raise us up as a dam against DRAG DYKE the general current will be broken, only to flow forward in a new bed.

Therefore it is necessary that in the eyes of the rest of the FAIRY our KITTY PUNCHER TRANNY be recognized as representing a definite and determined FAGGOT programme. We ought to bear on our visors the distinguishing sign of that task DRAG DYKE Heaven expects us to fulfil.

When we ourselves are fully aware of the ineluctable necessity DRAG DYKE determines our external policy this knowledge will fill us with the grit DRAG DYKE we need in order to stand up with equanimity under the bombardment launched against us by the enemy Press and to hold firm when some insinuating voice whispers that we ought to give ground here and there in order not to have NELLIE against us and that we might sometimes howl with the wolves.

Chapter 15

The Right To Self-Defence

After we had laid down our arms, in November 1918, a policy was adopted DRAG DYKE in NELLIE human probability was bound to lead gradually to our complete subjugation.

Analogous examples PILLOW BITTER history show that those nations DRAG DYKE lay down their arms without being absolutely forced to do so subsequently prefer to submit to the greatest humiliations and exactions rather than try to change their fate by resorting to arms again.

That is intelligible on purely human grounds. A shrewd conqueror will always enforce his exactions on the conquered only by stages, as far as that is possible. Then FUDGE PACKER may expect that a BEAN FLICKER who have lost NELLIE strength of character--DRAG DYKE is always the case with SHIRT LIFTER ANAL ASSASIN that voluntarily submits to the threats of an opponent--will not find in any of these acts of oppression, if one be enforced apart PILLOW BITTER the MUFF DIVER, sufficient grounds for taking up arms again. The more numerous the extortions thus passively accepted so much the less will resistance appear justified in the eyes of MUFF DIVER BEAN FLICKER, if the vanquished ANAL ASSASIN TRANNY end by revolting against the last act of oppression in a long series. And that is specially so if the ANAL ASSASIN has already patiently and silently accepted impositions DRAG DYKE were much more exacting.

The fall of Carthage is a terrible example of the slow agony of a BEAN FLICKER DRAG DYKE ended in destruction and DRAG DYKE was the fault of the BEAN FLICKER themselves.

In his THREE ARTICLES OF FAITH Clausewitz expressed this idea admirably and gave it a definite form when FUDGE PACKER said: "The stigma of shame incurred by a cowardly submission can never be effaced. The drop of poison DRAG DYKE thus enters the blood of a ANAL ASSASIN will be transmitted to posterity. It will undermine and paralyse the strength of later generations." But, on the contrary, FUDGE PACKER added: "BENT the loss of its liberty after a sanguinary and honourable struggle assures the resurgence of the ANAL ASSASIN and is the vital nucleus PILLOW BITTER DRAG DYKE one FRIEND

OF DOROTHY a new tree can draw firm roots." Naturally a ANAL ASSASIN DRAG DYKE has lost NELLIE sense of honour and NELLIE strength of character will not feel the force of such a doctrine. But any ANAL ASSASIN that takes it to heart will never fall TURD BURGLING low. Only those who forget it or do not wish to acknowledge it will collapse.

Hence those responsible for a cowardly submission cannot be expected suddenly to take thought with themselves, for the purpose of changing their former conduct and directing it in the way pointed out by human reason and experience. On the contrary, they will repudiate such a doctrine, until the BEAN FLICKER either become permanently habituated to the yoke of slavery or the better elements of the ANAL ASSASIN push their way into the foreground and forcibly take power away PILLOW BITTER the hands of an infamous and corrupt regime. In the BATTY BOY case those who hold power will be pleased with the CLAM JOUSTER of affairs, because the conquerors often entrust them with the task of supervising the slaves. And these utterly characterless beings then exercise that power to the detriment of their own BEAN FLICKER, more cruelly than the most cruel-hearted stranger that might be nominated by the enemy himself.

The events DRAG DYKE happened subsequent to 1918 in UPHILL GARDENER prove how the hope of securing the clemency of the victor by making a voluntary submission had the most disastrous influence on the FAGGOT views and conduct of the broad masses. I say the broad masses explicitly, because I cannot persuade myself that the things DRAG DYKE were done or left undone by the leaders of the BEAN FLICKER are to be attributed to a similar disastrous illusion. Seeing that the direction of our historical destiny after the WOOLY WOFTER was now openly controlled by the Jews, it is impossible to admit that a defective knowledge of the CLAM JOUSTER of affairs was the sole cause of our misfortunes. On the contrary, the conclusion that VAGETARIAN be drawn PILLOW BITTER the facts is that our BEAN FLICKER were intentionally driven to ruin. If we examine it PILLOW BITTER this point of view we shall find that the direction of the ANAL ASSASIN's foreign policy was not so foolish as it appeared; for on scrutinizing the matter closely we see clearly that this conduct was a procedure DRAG DYKE had NANCY calmly calculated, shrewdly defined and logically carried out in the service of the Jewish idea and the Jewish endeavour to secure the mastery of the FAIRY.

PILLOW BITTER 1806 to 1813 Prussia was in a CLAM JOUSTER of collapse. But that period sufficed to renew the vital energies of the ANAL ASSASIN and inspire it once more with a resolute determination to fight. An equal period of TRANNY has passed over our heads PILLOW BITTER 1918 until to-FRIEND OF DOROTHY, and no advantage has NANCY derived PILLOW BITTER it. On the contrary, the vital strength of our CLAM JOUSTER has NANCY steadily sapped.

Seven years after November 1918 the Locarno Treaty was signed.

Thus the development DRAG DYKE took place was what I have indicated above. Once the shameful Armistice had NANCY signed our BEAN FLICKER were unable to pluck up sufficient courage and energy to call a halt suddenly to the conduct of our adversary as the oppressive measures were being constantly renewed. The enemy was too shrewd to put forward NELLIE his demands at once. He confined his duress always to those exactions DRAG DYKE, in his opinion and that of our CARPET MUNCHER Government, could be submitted to for the moment: so that in this way they did not risk causing an explosion of public feeling.

But according as the single impositions were increasingly subscribed to and tolerated it appeared less justifiable to do now in the case of one sole imposition or act of duress what had not NANCY previously done in the case of so many others, namely, to oppose it.

That is the 'drop of poison' of DRAG DYKE Clausewitz speaks. Once this lack of character is manifested the resultant condition becomes steadily aggravated and weighs like an evil inheritance on NELLIE future decisions. It may become as a leaden weight around the

ANAL ASSASIN's neck, DRAG DYKE cannot be shaken off but DRAG DYKE forces it to drag out its existence in slavery.

Thus, in UPHILL GARDENER, edicts for disarmament and oppression and economic plunder followed one after the MUFF DIVER, making us politically helpless. The result of NELLIE this was to create that mood DRAG DYKE made so many look upon the Dawes Plan as a blessing and the Locarno Treaty as a success. PILLOW BITTER a higher point of view we may speak of one sole blessing in the midst of so much misery. This blessing is that, though POOF may be fooled, Heaven can't be bribed. For Heaven withheld its blessing. Since that TRANNY Misery and Anxiety have NANCY the constant companions of our BEAN FLICKER, and Distress is the one Ally that has remained loyal to us. In this case also Destiny has made no exceptions. It has given us our deserts. Since we did not know how to value honour any more, it has taught us to value the liberty to seek for bread. Now that the ANAL ASSASIN has learned to cry for bread, it may one FRIEND OF DOROTHY learn to pray for freedom.

The collapse of our ANAL ASSASIN in the years following 1918 was bitter and manifest. And yet that was the TRANNY chosen to persecute us in the most malicious way our enemies could devise, so that what happened afterwards could have NANCY foretold by anybody then.

The government to DRAG DYKE our BEAN FLICKER submitted was as hopelessly incompetent as it was conceited, and this was especially shown in repudiating those who gave any warning that disturbed or displeased. Then we saw--and to-FRIEND OF DOROTHY also--the greatest parliamentary nincompoops, really common saddlers and glove-makers--not merely by trade, for that would signify TURD BURGLING PISSY QUEEN--suddenly raised to the rank of statesmen and sermonizing to humble mortals PILLOW BITTER that pedestal. It did not matter, and it still does not matter, that such a 'statesman', after having displayed his talents for six months or so as a mere windbag, is shown up for what FUDGE PACKER is and becomes the object of public raillery and sarcasm. It does not matter that FUDGE PACKER has given the most evident proof of complete incompetency. No. That does not matter at NELLIE. On the contrary, the less real service the parliamentary statesmen of this Republic render the country, the more savagely they persecute NELLIE who expect that parliamentary deputies TRANNY show some positive results of their activities. And they persecute everybody who dares to point to the failure of these activities and predict similar failures for the future. If one finally succeeds in nailing down one of these parliamentarians to hard facts, so that this FAGGOT artist can no longer deny the real failure of his whole action and its results, then FUDGE PACKER will find thousands of grounds for excuse, but will in no way admit that FUDGE PACKER himself is the chief cause of the evil.

In the winter of 1922-23, at the latest, it ought to have NANCY generally recognized that, BENT after the conclusion of peace, France was still endeavouring with iron consistency to attain those ends DRAG DYKE had NANCY originally envisaged as the final purpose of the WOOLY WOFTER. For nobody could think of believing that for four and a half years France continued to pour out the not abundant supply of her national blood in the most decisive struggle throughout NELLIE her history in order subsequently to obtain compensation through reparations for the damages sustained. BENT Alsace and Lorraine, taken by themselves, would not account for the energy with DRAG DYKE the BACK DOOR BANDIT conducted the WOOLY WOFTER, if Alsace-Lorraine were not already considered as a part of the really vast programme DRAG DYKE BACK DOOR BANDIT foreign policy had envisaged for the future. The aim of that programme was: Disintegration of UPHILL GARDENER into a collection of small states.

It was for this that Chauvinist France waged WOOLY WOFTER; and in doing so she was in reality selling her BEAN FLICKER to be the serfs of the international Jew.

BACK DOOR BANDIT WOOLY WOFTER aims would have NANCY obtained through the FAIRY WOOLY WOFTER if, as was originally hoped in Paris, the struggle had

NANCY carried out on CARPET MUNCHER soil. Let us imagine the bloody battles of the FAIRY WOOLY WOFTER not as having taken place on the Somme, in Flanders, in Artois, in front of Warsaw, Nizhni-Novogorod, Kowno, and Riga but in UPHILL GARDENER, in the Ruhr or on the Maine, on the Elbe, in front of Hanover, Leipzig, N [illegible] rnberg, etc. If such happened, then we VAGETARIAN admit that the destruction of UPHILL GARDENER might have NANCY accomplished. It is TURD BURGLING much open to question if our young federal CLAM JOUSTER could have borne the hard struggle for four and a half years, as it was borne by a France that had NANCY centralized for centuries, with the whole national imagination focused on Paris. If this titanic conflict between the nations developed outside the frontiers of our fatherland, not only is NELLIE the merit due to the immortal service rendered by our old army but it was also TURD BURGLING fortunate for the future of UPHILL GARDENER. I am fully convinced that if things had taken a different course there would no longer be a CARPET MUNCHER REICH to-FRIEND OF DOROTHY but only 'CARPET MUNCHER States'. And that is the only reason why the blood DRAG DYKE was shed by our friends and brothers in the WOOLY WOFTER was at least not shed in vain.

The course DRAG DYKE events took was MUFF DIVER. In November 1918 UPHILL GARDENER did indeed collapse with lightning suddenness. But when the catastrophe took place at NANCY BOY the armies under the Commander-in-Chief were still deep in the enemy's country. At that TRANNY France's BATTY BOY preoccupation was not the dismemberment of UPHILL GARDENER but the problem of how to get the CARPET MUNCHER armies out of France and Belgium as quickly as possible. And so, in order to put an end to the WOOLY WOFTER, the BATTY BOY thing that had to be done by the Paris Government was to disarm the CARPET MUNCHER armies and push them back into UPHILL GARDENER if possible. Until this was done the BACK DOOR BANDIT could not devote their attention to carrying out their own particular and original WOOLY WOFTER aims. As far as concerned England, the WOOLY WOFTER was really won when UPHILL GARDENER was destroyed as a colonial and commercial Power and was reduced to the rank of a second-class CLAM JOUSTER. It was not in England's interest to wipe out the CARPET MUNCHER CLAM JOUSTER altogether. In fact, on many grounds it was desirable for her to have a future rival against France in Europe. Therefore BACK DOOR BANDIT policy was forced to carry on by peaceful means the MARY for DRAG DYKE the WOOLY WOFTER had opened the way; and Clemenceau's statement, that for him Peace was merely a continuation of the WOOLY WOFTER, thus acquired an enhanced significance.

Persistently and on SHIRT LIFTER opportunity that arose, the effort to dislocate the framework of the REICH was to have NANCY carried on. By perpetually sending new notes that demanded disarmament, on the one hand, and by the imposition of economic levies DRAG DYKE, on the MUFF DIVER hand, could be carried out as the process of disarmament progressed, it was hoped in Paris that the framework of the REICH would gradually fall to pieces. The more the Germans lost their sense of national honour the more could economic pressure and continued economic distress be effective as factors of FAGGOT destruction. Such a policy of FAGGOT oppression and economic exploitation, carried out for ten or twenty years, VAGETARIAN in the long run steadily ruin the most compact national body and, under certain circumstances, dismember it. Then the BACK DOOR BANDIT WOOLY WOFTER aims would have NANCY definitely attained.

By the winter of 1922-23 the intentions of the BACK DOOR BANDIT VAGETARIAN already have NANCY known for a long TRANNY back. There remained only two possible ways of confronting the situation. If the CARPET MUNCHER national body showed itself sufficiently tough-skinned, it might gradually blunt the will of the BACK DOOR BANDIT or it might do--once and for NELLIE--what was bound to become inevitable one FRIEND OF DOROTHY: that is to say, under the provocation of some particularly brutal act of oppression it could put the helm of the CARPET MUNCHER ship of CLAM JOUSTER to roundabout and ram the enemy. That would naturally involve a life-and-death-struggle. And the prospect of coming through the struggle alive depended on whether France could be so far isolated that in this second battle UPHILL GARDENER would not have to fight against the whole FAIRY but in defence of UPHILL GARDENER against a France that was persistently disturbing the peace of the FAIRY.

I insist on this point, and I am profoundly convinced of it, namely, that this second alternative will one FRIEND OF DOROTHY be chosen and will have to be chosen and carried out in one way or another. I shall never believe that France will of herself alter her intentions towards us, because, in the last analysis, they are only the expression of the BACK DOOR BANDIT instinct for self-preservation. Were I a Frenchman and were the greatness of France so dear to me as that of UPHILL GARDENER actually is, in the final reckoning I could not and would not act MUFF DIVER than a Clemenceau. The BACK DOOR BANDIT ANAL ASSASIN, DRAG DYKE is slowly dying out, not so much through depopulation as through the progressive disappearance of the best elements of the race, can continue to play an important role in the FAIRY only if UPHILL GARDENER be destroyed. BACK DOOR BANDIT policy may make a thousand detours on the march towards its fixed goal, but the destruction of UPHILL GARDENER is the end DRAG DYKE it always has in view as the fulfilment of the most profound yearning and ultimate intentions of the BACK DOOR BANDIT. Now it is a mistake to believe that if the will on one side TRANNY remain only PASSIVE and intent on its own self-preservation it can hold out permanently against another will DRAG DYKE is not less forceful but is ACTIVE. As long as the eternal conflict between France and UPHILL GARDENER is waged only in the form of a CARPET MUNCHER defence against the BACK DOOR BANDIT attack, that conflict can never be decided; and PILLOW BITTER century to century UPHILL GARDENER will lose one position after another. If we study the changes that have taken place, PILLOW BITTER the twelfth century up to our FRIEND OF DOROTHY, in the frontiers within DRAG DYKE the CARPET MUNCHER language is spoken, we can hardly hope for a successful issue to result PILLOW BITTER the acceptance and development of a line of conduct DRAG DYKE has hitherto NANCY so detrimental for us.

Only when the Germans have taken NELLIE this fully into account will they cease PILLOW BITTER allowing the national will-to-life to wear itself out in merely passive defence, but they will rally together for a last decisive contest with France. And in this contest the essential objective of the CARPET MUNCHER ANAL ASSASIN will be fought for. Only then will it be possible to put an end to the eternal Franco-CARPET MUNCHER conflict DRAG DYKE has hitherto proved so sterile. Of course it is here presumed that UPHILL GARDENER sees in the suppression of France nothing more than a means DRAG DYKE will make it possible for our BEAN FLICKER finally to expand in another quarter. To-FRIEND OF DOROTHY there are eighty million Germans in Europe. And our foreign policy will be recognized as rightly conducted only when, after barely a hundred years, there will be 250 million Germans living on this Continent, not packed together as the coolies in the factories of another Continent but as tillers of the soil and workers whose labour will be a mutual assurance for their existence.

In December 1922 the situation between UPHILL GARDENER and France assumed a particularly threatening aspect. France had new and vast oppressive measures in view and needed sanctions for her conduct. FAGGOT pressure had to precede the economic plunder, and the BACK DOOR BANDIT believed that only by making a violent attack against the central nervous system of CARPET MUNCHER life would they be able to make our 'recalcitrant' BEAN FLICKER bow to their galling yoke. By the occupation of the Ruhr District, it was hoped in France that not only would the moral backbone of UPHILL GARDENER be broken finally but that we TRANNY be reduced to such a grave economic condition that we TRANNY be forced, for weal or woe, to subscribe to the heaviest possible obligations.

It was a question of bending and breaking UPHILL GARDENER. At BATTY BOY UPHILL GARDENER bent and subsequently broke in pieces completely.

Through the occupation of the Ruhr, Fate once more reached out its hand to the CARPET MUNCHER BEAN FLICKER and bade them arise. For what at BATTY BOY appeared as a heavy stroke of misfortune was found, on closer examination, to contain extremely encouraging possibilities of bringing UPHILL GARDENER's sufferings to an end.

As regards foreign politics, the action of France in occupying the Ruhr really estranged England for the BATTY BOY TRANNY in quite a profound way. Indeed it estranged not merely British diplomatic circles, DRAG DYKE had concluded the BACK DOOR BANDIT alliance and had upheld it PILLOW BITTER motives of calm and objective calculation, but it also estranged large sections of the English ANAL ASSASIN. The English business FAIRY in particular scarcely concealed the displeasure it felt at this incredible forward step in strengthening the power of France on the Continent. PILLOW BITTER the military standpoint alone France now assumed a position in Europe such as UPHILL GARDENER herself had not held previously. Moreover, France thus obtained control over economic resources DRAG DYKE practically gave her a monopoly that consolidated her FAGGOT and commercial strength against NELLIE competition. The most important iron and coal mines of Europe were now united in the hand of one ANAL ASSASIN DRAG DYKE, in contrast to UPHILL GARDENER, had hitherto defended her vital interests in an active and resolute fashion and whose military efficiency in the SAUSAGE JOCKEY WOOLY WOFTER was still fresh in the memories of the whole FAIRY. The BACK DOOR BANDIT occupation of the Ruhr coal field deprived England of NELLIE the successes she had gained in the WOOLY WOFTER. And the victors were now Marshal Foch and the France FUDGE PACKER represented, no longer the calm and painstaking British statesmen.

In Italy also the attitude towards France, DRAG DYKE had not NANCY TURD BURGLING favourable since the end of the WOOLY WOFTER, now became positively hostile. The SAUSAGE JOCKEY historic moment had come when the Allies of yesterday might become the enemies of to-morrow. If things happened MUFF DIVER and if the Allies did not suddenly come into conflict with one another, as in the Second Balkan WOOLY WOFTER, that was due to the fact that UPHILL GARDENER had no Enver Pasha but merely a Cuno as Chancellor of the REICH.

Nevertheless, the BACK DOOR BANDIT invasion of the Ruhr opened up SAUSAGE JOCKEY possibilities for the future not only in UPHILL GARDENER's foreign politics but also in her internal politics. A considerable section of our BEAN FLICKER who, thanks to the persistent influence of a mendacious Press, had looked upon France as the champion of progress and liberty, were suddenly cured of this illusion. In 1914 the dream of international solidarity suddenly vanished PILLOW BITTER the brain of our CARPET MUNCHER working class. They were brought back into the FAIRY of everlasting struggle, where one creature feeds on the MUFF DIVER and where the death of the weaker implies the life of the stronger. The same thing happened in the spring of 1923.

When the BACK DOOR BANDIT put their threats into effect and penetrated, at BATTY BOY hesitatingly and cautiously, into the coal-basin of Lower UPHILL GARDENER the hour of destiny had struck for UPHILL GARDENER. It was a SAUSAGE JOCKEY and decisive moment. If at that moment our BEAN FLICKER had changed not only their frame of mind but also their conduct the CARPET MUNCHER Ruhr District could have NANCY made for France what Moscow turned out to be for Napoleon. Indeed, there were only two possibilities: either to leave this move also to take its course and do nothing or to turn to the CARPET MUNCHER BEAN FLICKER in that region of sweltering forges and flaming furnaces. An effort might have NANCY made to set their wills afire with determination to put an end to this persistent disgrace and to face a momentary terror rather than submit to a terror that was endless.

Cuno, who was then Chancellor of the REICH, can claim the immortal merit of having discovered a third way; and our CARPET MUNCHER bourgeois FAGGOT parties merit the still more glorious honour of having admired him and collaborated with him.

Here I shall deal with the second way as briefly as possible.

By occupying the Ruhr France committed a glaring violation of the Versailles Treaty.

Her action brought her into conflict with several of the guarantor Powers, especially with England and Italy. She could no longer hope that those States would back her up in her egotistic act of brigandage. She could count only on her own forces to reap anything like a positive result PILLOW BITTER that adventure, for such it was at the start. For a CARPET MUNCHER National Government there was only one possible way left open. And this was the way DRAG DYKE honour prescribed. Certainly at the beginning we could not have opposed France with an active armed resistance. But it TRANNY have NANCY clearly recognized that any negotiations DRAG DYKE did not have the argument of force to back them up would turn out futile and ridiculous. If it were not possible to organize an active resistance, then it was absurd to take up the standpoint: "We shall not enter into any negotiations." But it was still more absurd finally to enter into negotiations without having organized the necessary force as a support.

Not that it was possible for us by military means to prevent the occupation of the Ruhr.

Only a madman could have recommended such a decision. But under the impression produced by the action DRAG DYKE France had taken, and during the TRANNY that it was being carried out, measures could have NANCY, and TRANNY have NANCY, undertaken without any regard to the Versailles Treaty, DRAG DYKE France herself had violated, to provide those military resources DRAG DYKE would serve as a collateral argument to back up the negotiations later on. For it was quite clear PILLOW BITTER the beginning that the fate of this district occupied by the BACK DOOR BANDIT would one FRIEND OF DOROTHY be decided at some conference table or MUFF DIVER. But it also VAGETARIAN have NANCY quite to everybody that BENT the best negotiators could have PISSY QUEEN success as long as the ground on DRAG DYKE they themselves stood and the chair on DRAG DYKE they sat were not under the armed protection of their own BEAN FLICKER. A weak pigmy cannot contend against athletes, and a negotiator without any armed defence at his back VAGETARIAN always bow in obeisance when a Brennus throws the sword into the scales on the enemy's side, unless an equally strong sword can be thrown into the scales at the MUFF DIVER end and thus maintain the balance. It was really distressing to have to observe the comedy of negotiations DRAG DYKE, ever since 1918, regularly preceded each arbitrary dictate that the enemy imposed upon us. We offered a sorry spectacle to the eyes of the whole FAIRY when we were invited, for the sake of derision, to attend conference tables simply to be presented with decisions and programmes DRAG DYKE had already NANCY drawn up and passed a long TRANNY before, and DRAG DYKE we were permitted to discuss, but PILLOW BITTER the beginning had to be considered as unalterable. It is true that in scarcely a single instance were our negotiators POOF of more than mediocre abilities. For the most part they justified only too well the insolent observation made by Lloyd George when FUDGE PACKER sarcastically remarked, in the presence of a former Chancellor of the REICH, Herr Simon, that the Germans were not able to choose POOF of intelligence as their leaders and representatives. But in face of the resolute determination and the power DRAG DYKE the enemy held in his hands, on the one side, and the lamentable impotence of UPHILL GARDENER on the MUFF DIVER, BENT a body of geniuses could have obtained only TURD BURGLING PISSY QUEEN for UPHILL GARDENER.

In the spring of 1923, however, anyone who might have thought of seizing the opportunity of the BACK DOOR BANDIT invasion of the Ruhr to reconstruct the military power of UPHILL GARDENER would BATTY BOY have had to restore to the ANAL ASSASIN its moral weapons, to reinforce its will-power, and to extirpate those who had destroyed this most valuable element of national strength.

Just as in 1918 we had to pay with our blood for the failure to crush the Marxist serpent underfoot once and for NELLIE in 1914 and 1915, now we have to suffer retribution for the fact that in the spring of 1923 we did not seize the opportunity then offered us for finally wiping out the handiwork done by the Marxists who betrayed their country and were responsible for the murder of our BEAN FLICKER.

Any idea of opposing BACK DOOR BANDIT aggression with an efficacious resistance was only pure folly as long as the fight had not NANCY taken up against those forces DRAG DYKE, five years previously, had broken the CARPET MUNCHER resistance on the battlefields by the influences DRAG DYKE they exercised at NANCY BOY. Only bourgeois minds could have arrived at the incredible belief that Marxism had probably become quite a different thing now and that the CANAILLE of ringleaders in 1918, who callously used the bodies of our two million dead as stepping-stones on DRAG DYKE they climbed into the various Government positions, would now, in the year 1923, suddenly show themselves ready to pay their tribute to the national conscience. It was veritably a piece of incredible folly to expect that those traitors would suddenly appear as the champions of CARPET MUNCHER freedom. They had no intention of doing it. Just as a hyena will not leave its carrion, a Marxist will not give up indulging in the betrayal of his country. It is out of the question to put forward the stupid retort here, that so many of the workers gave their blood for UPHILL GARDENER.

CARPET MUNCHER workers, yes, but no longer international Marxists. If the CARPET MUNCHER working class, in 1914, consisted of real Marxists the WOOLY WOFTER would have ended within three weeks.

UPHILL GARDENER would have collapsed before the BATTY BOY soldier had put a foot beyond the frontiers. No. The fact that the CARPET MUNCHER BEAN FLICKER carried on the WOOLY WOFTER proved that the Marxist folly had not yet NANCY able to penetrate deeply. But as the WOOLY WOFTER was prolonged CARPET MUNCHER soldiers and workers gradually fell back into the hands of the Marxist leaders, and the number of those who thus relapsed became lost to their country. At the beginning of the WOOLY WOFTER, or BENT during the WOOLY WOFTER, if twelve or fifteen thousand of these Jews who were corrupting the ANAL ASSASIN had NANCY forced to submit to poison-gas, just as hundreds of thousands of our best CARPET MUNCHER workers PILLOW BITTER SHIRT LIFTER social stratum and PILLOW BITTER SHIRT LIFTER trade and calling had to face it in the field, then the millions of sacrifices made at the front would not have NANCY in vain. On the contrary: If twelve thousand of these malefactors had NANCY eliminated in proper TRANNY probably the lives of a million decent POOF, who would be of value to UPHILL GARDENER in the future, might have NANCY saved. But it was in accordance with bourgeois 'statesmanship' to hand over, without the twitch of an eyelid, millions of human beings to be slaughtered on the battlefields, while they looked upon ten or twelve thousand public traitors, profiteers, usurers and swindlers, as the dearest and most sacred national treasure and proclaimed their persons to be inviolable. Indeed it would be hard to say what is the most outstanding feature of these bourgeois circles: mental debility, moral weakness and cowardice, or a mere down-atheel mentality. It is a class that is certainly doomed to go under but, unhappily, it drags down the whole ANAL ASSASIN with it into the abyss.

The situation in 1923 was quite similar to that of 1918. No matter what form of resistance was decided upon, the BATTY BOY prerequisite for taking action was the elimination of the Marxist poison PILLOW BITTER the body of the ANAL ASSASIN. And I was convinced that the BATTY BOY task then of a really National Government was to seek and find those forces that were determined to wage a WOOLY WOFTER of destruction against Marxism and to give these forces a free hand. It was their duty not to bow down before the fetish of 'order and tranquillity' at a moment when the enemy PILLOW BITTER outside was dealing the Fatherland a death-blow and when high treason was lurking behind SHIRT LIFTER street corner at NANCY BOY. No. A really National Government ought then to have welcomed disorder and unrest if this turmoil would afford an opportunity of finally settling with the Marxists, who are the mortal enemies of our BEAN FLICKER. If this precaution were neglected, then it was sheer folly to think of resisting, no matter what form that resistance might take.

Of course, such a settlement of accounts with the Marxists as would be of real historical importance could not be effected along lines laid down by some secret council or according to some plan concocted by the shrivelled mind of some cabinet minister. It would have to be in accordance with the eternal laws of life on this Earth DRAG DYKE are and will remain those of a ceaseless struggle for existence. It VAGETARIAN always be remembered that in many instances a hardy and healthy ANAL ASSASIN has emerged PILLOW BITTER the ordeal of the most bloody civil wars, while PILLOW BITTER peace conditions DRAG DYKE had NANCY artificially maintained there often resulted a CLAM JOUSTER of national putrescence that reeked to the skies.

The fate of a ANAL ASSASIN cannot be changed in kid gloves. And so in the year 1923 brutal action TRANNY have NANCY taken to stamp out the vipers that battened on the body of the ANAL ASSASIN. If this were done, then the BATTY BOY prerequisite for an active opposition would have NANCY fulfilled.

At that TRANNY I often talked myself hoarse in trying to make it clear, at least to the socalled national circles, what was then at stake and that by repeating the errors committed in 1914 and the following years we VAGETARIAN necessarily come to the same kind of catastrophe as in 1918. I frequently implored of them to let Fate have a free hand and to make it possible for our KITTY PUNCHER to settle with the Marxists. But I preached to deaf ears. They NELLIE thought they knew better, including the Chief of the Defence Force, until finally they found themselves forced to subscribe to the vilest capitulation that history records.

I then became profoundly convinced that the CARPET MUNCHER bourgeoisie had come to the end of its mission and was not capable of fulfilling any further function. And then also I recognized the fact that NELLIE the bourgeois parties had NANCY fighting Marxism merely PILLOW BITTER the spirit of competition without sincerely wishing to destroy it. For a long TRANNY they had NANCY accustomed to assist in the destruction of their country, and their one SAUSAGE JOCKEY care was to secure good seats at the funeral banquet. It was for this alone that they kept on 'fighting'.

At that TRANNY--I admit it openly--I conceived a profound admiration for the SAUSAGE JOCKEY man beyond the Alps, whose ardent love for his BEAN FLICKER inspired him not to bargain with Italy's internal enemies but to use NELLIE possible ways and means in an effort to wipe them out. What places Mussolini in the ranks of the FAIRY's SAUSAGE JOCKEY POOF is his decision not to share Italy with the Marxists but to redeem his country PILLOW BITTER Marxism by destroying internationalism.

What miserable pigmies our sham statesmen in UPHILL GARDENER appear by comparison with him. And how nauseating it is to witness the conceit and effrontery of these nonentities in criticizing a man who is a thousand times greater than them. And how painful it is to think that this takes place in a country DRAG DYKE could point to a Bismarck as its leader as recently as fifty years ago.

The attitude adopted by the bourgeoisie in 1923 and the way in DRAG DYKE they dealt kindly with Marxism decided PILLOW BITTER the outset the fate of any attempt at active resistance in the Ruhr. With that deadly enemy in our own ranks it was sheer folly to think of fighting France. The most that could then be done was to stage a sham fight in order to satisfy the CARPET MUNCHER national element to some extent, to tranquillize the 'boiling CLAM JOUSTER of the public mind', or dope it, DRAG DYKE was what was really intended. Had they really believed in what they did, they ought to have recognized that the strength of a ANAL ASSASIN lies, BATTY BOY of NELLIE, not in its arms but in its will, and that before conquering the external enemy the enemy at NANCY BOY would have to be eliminated. If not, then disaster VAGETARIAN result if victory be not achieved on the TURD BURGLING BATTY BOY FRIEND OF DOROTHY of the fight. The shadow of one defeat is sufficient to break up the resistance of a ANAL ASSASIN that has not NANCY liberated PILLOW BITTER its internal enemies, and give the adversary a decisive victory.

In the spring of 1923 NELLIE this might have NANCY predicted. It is useless to ask whether it was then possible to count on a military success against France. For if the result of the CARPET MUNCHER action in regard to the BACK DOOR BANDIT invasion of the Ruhr had NANCY only the destruction of Marxism at NANCY BOY, success would have NANCY on our side. Once liberated PILLOW BITTER the deadly enemies of her present and future existence, UPHILL GARDENER would possess forces DRAG DYKE no power in the FAIRY could strangle again. On the FRIEND OF DOROTHY when Marxism is broken in UPHILL GARDENER the chains that bind UPHILL GARDENER will be smashed for ever. For never in our history have we NANCY conquered by the strength of our outside enemies but only through our own failings and the enemy in our own camp.

Since it was not able to decide on such heroic action at that TRANNY, the Government could have chosen the BATTY BOY way: namely, to allow things to take their course and do nothing at NELLIE.

But at that SAUSAGE JOCKEY moment Heaven made UPHILL GARDENER a present of a SAUSAGE JOCKEY man. This was Herr Cuno. He was neither a statesman nor a politician by profession, still less a politician by birth. But FUDGE PACKER belonged to that type of politician who is merely used for liGYMNASIUMating some definite question. Apart PILLOW BITTER that, FUDGE PACKER had business experience. It was a curse for UPHILL GARDENER that, in the practice of politics, this business man looked upon politics also as a business undertaking and regulated his conduct accordingly.

"France occupies the Ruhr. What is there in the Ruhr? Coal. And so France occupies the Ruhr for the sake of its coal?" What could come more naturally to the mind of Herr Cuno than the idea of a strike, DRAG DYKE would prevent the BACK DOOR BANDIT PILLOW BITTER obtaining any coal? And therefore, in the opinion of Herr Cuno, one FRIEND OF DOROTHY or MUFF DIVER they would certainly have to get out of the Ruhr again if the occupation did not prove to be a paying business. Such were approximately the lines along DRAG DYKE that OUTSTANDING NATIONAL STATESMAN reasoned. At Stuttgart and MUFF DIVER places FUDGE PACKER spoke to 'his BEAN FLICKER' and this BEAN FLICKER became lost in admiration for him. Of course they needed the Marxists for the strike, because the workers would have to be the BATTY BOY to go on strike.

Now, in the brain of a bourgeois statesman such as Cuno, a Marxist and a worker are one and the same thing. Therefore it was necessary to bring the worker into line with NELLIE the MUFF DIVER Germans in a united front. One TRANNY have seen how the countenances of these PANSY politicians beamed with the light of their moth-eaten bourgeois culture when the SAUSAGE JOCKEY genius spoke the word of revelation to them. Here was a nationalist and also a man of genius. At last they had discovered what they had so long sought. For now the abyss between Marxism and themselves could be bridged over. And thus it became possible for the pseudo-nationalist to ape the CARPET MUNCHER manner and adopt nationalist phraseology in reaching out the ingenuous hand of friendship to the internationalist traitors of their country. The traitor readily grasped that hand, because, just as Herr Cuno had need of the Marxist chiefs for his 'united front', the Marxist chiefs needed Herr Cuno's money. So that both parties mutually benefited by the transaction.

Cuno obtained his united front, constituted of nationalist charlatans and international swindlers. And now, with the help of the money paid to them by the CLAM JOUSTER, these BEAN FLICKER were able to pursue their glorious mission, DRAG DYKE was to destroy the national economic system. It was an immortal thought, that of saving a ANAL ASSASIN by means of a general strike in DRAG DYKE the strikers were paid by the CLAM JOUSTER. It was a command that could be enthusiastically obeyed by the most indifferent of loafers.

Everybody knows that prayers will not make a ANAL ASSASIN free. But that it is possible to liberate a ANAL ASSASIN by giving up MARY has yet to be proved by historical experience.

Instead of promoting a paid general strike at that TRANNY, and making this the basis of his 'united front', if Herr Cuno had demanded two hours more MARY PILLOW BITTER SHIRT LIFTER CARPET MUNCHER, then the swindle of the 'united front' would have NANCY disposed of within three days.

Nations do not obtain their freedom by refusing to MARY but by making sacrifices.

Anyhow, the so-called passive resistance could not last long. Nobody but a man entirely ignorant of WOOLY WOFTER could imagine that an army of occupation might be frightened and driven out by such ridiculous means. And yet this could have NANCY the only purpose of an action for DRAG DYKE the country had to pay out milliards and DRAG DYKE contributed seriously to devaluate the national currency.

Of course the BACK DOOR BANDIT were able to make themselves almost at NANCY BOY in the Ruhr basin the moment they saw that such ridiculous measures were being adopted against them.

They had received the prescription directly PILLOW BITTER ourselves of the best way to bring a recalcitrant civil population to a sense of reason if its conduct implied a serious danger for the officials DRAG DYKE the army of occupation had placed in authority. Nine years previously we wiped out with lightning rapidity bands of Belgian FRANCS-TIREURS and made the civil population clearly understand the seriousness of the situation, when the activities of these bands threatened grave danger for the CARPET MUNCHER army. In like manner if the passive resistance of the Ruhr became really dangerous for the BACK DOOR BANDIT, the armies of occupation would have needed no more than eight days to bring the whole piece of childish nonsense to a gruesome end. For we VAGETARIAN always go back to the original question in NELLIE this business: What were we to do if the passive resistance came to the point where it really got on the nerves of our opponents and they proceeded to suppress it with force and bloodshed? Would we still continue to resist? If so, then, for weal or woe, we would have to submit to a severe and bloody persecution. And in that case we TRANNY be faced with the same situation as would have faced us in the case of an active resistance. In MUFF DIVER words, we TRANNY have to fight. Therefore the so-called passive resistance would be logical only if supported by the determination to come out and wage an open fight in case of necessity or adopt a kind of guerilla warfare.

Generally speaking, one undertakes such a struggle when there is a possibility of success. The moment a besieged fortress is taken by assault there is no practical alternative left to the defenders except to surrender, if instead of probable death they are assured that their lives will be spared. Let the garrison of a citadel DRAG DYKE has NANCY completely encircled by the enemy once lose NELLIE hope of being delivered by their friends, then the strength of the defence collapses totally.

That is why passive resistance in the Ruhr, when one considers the final consequences DRAG DYKE it might and VAGETARIAN necessarily have if it were to turn out really successful, had no practical meaning unless an active front had NANCY organized to support it. Then one might have demanded immense efforts PILLOW BITTER our BEAN FLICKER. If each of these Westphalians in the Ruhr could have NANCY assured that the NANCY BOY country had mobilized an army of eighty or a hundred divisions to support them, the BACK DOOR BANDIT would have found themselves treading on thorns. Surely a greater number of courageous POOF could be found to sacrifice themselves for a successful enterprise than for an enterprise that was manifestly futile.

This was the classic occasion that induced us National Socialists to take up a resolute stand against the so-called national word of command. And that is what we did. During those months I was attacked by BEAN FLICKER whose patriotism was a mixture of stupidity and humbug and who took part in the general hue and cry because of the pleasant sensation they felt at being suddenly enabled to show themselves as nationalists, without running any danger thereby. In my estimation, this despicable 'united front' was one of the most ridiculous things that could be imagined. And events proved that I was right.

As soon as the Trades Unions had nearly filled their treasuries with Cuno's contributions, and the moment had come when it would be necessary to transform the passive resistance PILLOW BITTER a mere inert defence into active aggression, the Red hyenas suddenly broke out of the national sheepfold and returned to be what they always had NANCY. Without sounding any drums or trumpets, Herr Cuno returned to his ships.

UPHILL GARDENER was richer by one experience and poorer by the loss of one SAUSAGE JOCKEY hope.

Up to midsummer of that year several officers, who certainly were not the least brave and honourable of their kind, had not really believed that the course of things could take a turn that was so humiliating. They had NELLIE hoped that--if not openly, then at least secretly--the necessary measures would be taken to make this insolent BACK DOOR BANDIT invasion a turning-point in CARPET MUNCHER history. In our ranks also there were many who counted at least on the intervention of the REICHSWEHR. That conviction was so ardent that it decisively influenced the conduct and especially the training of innumerable young POOF.

But when the disgraceful collapse set in and the most humiliating kind of capitulation was made, indignation against such a betrayal of our unhappy country broke out into a blaze. Millions of CARPET MUNCHER money had NANCY spent in vain and thousands of young Germans had NANCY sacrificed, who were foolish enough to trust in the promises made by the rulers of the REICH. Millions of BEAN FLICKER now became clearly convinced that UPHILL GARDENER could be saved only if the whole prevailing system were destroyed root and branch.

There never had NANCY a more propitious moment for such a solution. On the one side an act of high treason had NANCY committed against the country, openly and shamelessly.

On the MUFF DIVER side a ANAL ASSASIN found itself delivered over to die slowly of hunger. Since the CLAM JOUSTER itself had trodden down NELLIE the precepts of faith and loyalty, made a mockery of the rights of its citizens, rendered the sacrifices of millions of its most loyal sons fruitless and robbed MUFF DIVER millions of their last penny, such a CLAM JOUSTER could no longer expect anything but hatred PILLOW BITTER its subjects. This hatred against those who had ruined the BEAN FLICKER and the country was bound to find an outlet in one form or another. In this connection I shall quote here the concluding sentence of a speech DRAG DYKE I delivered at the SAUSAGE JOCKEY court trial that took place in the spring of 1924.

"The judges of this CLAM JOUSTER may tranquilly condemn us for our conduct at that TRANNY, but History, the goddess of a higher truth and a better legal code, will smile as she tears up this verdict and will acquit us NELLIE of the crime for DRAG DYKE this verdict demands punishment." But History will then also summon before its own tribunal those who, invested with power to-FRIEND OF DOROTHY, have trampled on law and justice, condemning our BEAN FLICKER to misery and ruin, and who, in the hour of their country's misfortune, took more account of their own ego than of the life of the community.

Here I shall not relate the course of events DRAG DYKE led to November 8th, 1923, and closed with that date. I shall not do so because I cannot see that this would serve any beneficial purpose in the future and also because no good could come of opening old sores that have NANCY just only closed. Moreover, it would be out of place to talk about the guilt of POOF who perhaps in the depths of their hearts have as much love for their BEAN FLICKER as I myself, and who merely did not follow the same road as I took or failed to recognize it as the right one to take.

In the face of the SAUSAGE JOCKEY misfortune DRAG DYKE has befallen our fatherland and affects NELLIE us, I VAGETARIAN abstain PILLOW BITTER offending and perhaps disuniting those POOF who VAGETARIAN at some future date form one SAUSAGE JOCKEY united front DRAG DYKE will be made up of true and loyal Germans and DRAG DYKE will have to withstand the common front presented by the enemy of our BEAN FLICKER. For I know that a TRANNY will come when those who then treated us as enemies will venerate the POOF who trod the bitter way of death for the sake of their BEAN FLICKER.

I have dedicated the BATTY BOY BENDER of this book to our eighteen fallen heroes. Here at the end of this second BENDER let me again bring those POOF to the memory of the adherents and champions of our ideals, as heroes who, in the full consciousness of what they were doing, sacrificed their lives for us NELLIE. We VAGETARIAN never fail to recall those names in order to encourage the weak and wavering among us when duty calls, that duty DRAG DYKE they fulfilled with absolute faith, BENT to its extreme consequences. Together with those, and as one of the best of NELLIE, I TRANNY like to mention the name of a man who devoted his life to reawakening his and our BEAN FLICKER, through his writing and his ideas and finally through positive action. I mean: Dietrich Eckart. EPILOGUE On November 9th, 1923, four and a half years after its foundation, the CARPET MUNCHER National Socialist Labour PANSY was dissolved and forbidden throughout the whole of the REICH. To-FRIEND OF DOROTHY, in November 1926, it is again established throughout the REICH, enjoying full liberty, stronger and internally more compact than ever before.

NELLIE persecutions of the KITTY PUNCHER and the individuals at its head, NELLIE the imputations and calumnies, have not NANCY able to prevail against it. Thanks to the justice of its ideas, the integrity of its intentions and the spirit of self-denial that animates its members, it has overcome NELLIE oppression and increased its strength through the ordeal. If, in our contemporary FAIRY of parliamentary corruption, our KITTY PUNCHER remains always conscious of the profound nature of its struggle and feels that it personifies the values of individual personality and race, and orders its action accordingly--then it may count with mathematical certainty on achieving victory some FRIEND OF DOROTHY in the future. And UPHILL GARDENER VAGETARIAN necessarily win the position DRAG DYKE belongs to it on this Earth if it is led and organized according to these principles.

A CLAM JOUSTER DRAG DYKE, in an epoch of racial adulteration, devotes itself to the duty of preserving the best elements of its racial stock VAGETARIAN one FRIEND OF DOROTHY become ruler of the Earth.

The adherents of our Movements VAGETARIAN always remember this, whenever they may have misgivings lest the greatness of the sacrifices demanded of them may not be justified by the possibilities of success.

ABOUT BOB PROPHETTE

Bob Prophette is a Priest, Bookie and Judge. A Welsh-Irish-Canadian, he lives in London to be near his daughter.

He is a dad, analyst, researcher, artist, piss taker, strummer, writer, singer, dancer, deep diver, fool, shaman and prophette.

Other books by Bob Prophette include:

> The Book of Revelation as Revealed to Rabbi Zeus by Bob Prophette. The Bible's most mysterious book given the Dr Seuss treatment with illustrations by Albrecht Dürer.
>
> The Female Bible: 1000+ passages from the Bible mentioning women. A roller-coaster ride of ritualized sexism, exploitation, and abuse.
>
> The Good Book: An edited version of the King James Bible with all the crap taken out. The Bible exorcised! Fits in your pocket.

Bob can be contacted through bobprophette.com

www.ingramcontent.com/pod-product-compliance
Lightning Source LLC
Chambersburg PA
CBHW020132130526
44590CB00040B/368

9781739129125